Unions and Economic Crisis: Britain, West Germany and Sweden

PETER GOUREVITCH, *University of California at San Diego*

ANDREW MARTIN, *Massachusetts Institute of Technology*

GEORGE ROSS, *Brandeis University*

CHRISTOPHER ALLEN, *Center for European Studies, Harvard University*

STEPHEN BORNSTEIN, *McGill University*

ANDREI MARKOVITS, *Boston University*

London
GEORGE ALLEN & UNWIN
Boston   Sydney

George Allen & Unwin (Publishers) Ltd,
40 Museum Street, London WC1A 1LU, UK

George Allen & Unwin (Publishers) Ltd,
Park Lane, Hemel Hempstead, Herts HP2 4TE, UK

Allen & Unwin, Inc.,
9 Winchester Terrace, Winchester, Mass. 01890, USA

George Allen & Unwin Australia Pty Ltd,
8 Napier Street, North Sydney, NSW 2060, Australia

First published in 1984.

British Library Cataloguing in Publication Data

Unions and economic crisis: Britain, West Germany and Sweden.
1. Trade-unions—Great Britain—1945-
2. Trade-unions—Germany (West)—1945-
3. Trade-unions—Sweden—1945-
4. Great Britain—Economic conditions—1945-
5. Germany (West)—Economic conditions—1945-
6. Sweden—Economic conditions—1945-
I. Ross, George
331.88'0941   HC254
ISBN 0-04-331094-X

Library of Congress Cataloging in Publication Data

Main entry under title:
    Unions and economic crisis.
"Second volume of the Harvard Center for European Studies Project on European Trade Union Responses to Economic Crisis"—P.
Includes bibliographical references and index.
1. Trade-unions—Great Britain—Political activity. 2. Great Britain—Economic policy—1945-   . 3. Trade-unions—Germany (West)—Political activity. 4. Germany (West)—Economic policy. 5. Trade-unions—Sweden—Political activity. 6. Sweden—Economic policy. I. Ross, George, 1940-   . II. Harvard University, Center for European Studies.
HD6667.U54 1984   331.88'094   83-25784
ISBN 0-04-331094-X

Set in 10 on 11 point Times by Fotographics (Bedford) Ltd
and printed in Great Britain by Mackays of Chatham.

To the Harvard Center for European Studies, with Gratitude

Unions and Economic Crisis: Britain, West Germany and Sweden is the second volume of the Harvard Center for European Studies Project on European Trade Union Responses to Economic Crisis conducted by Peter Gourevitch, Peter Lange, Andrew Martin, George Ross, Christopher Allen, Stephen Bornstein, Andrei Markovits and Maurizio Vannicelli.

Volume One, Unions, Change and Crisis: French and Italian Union Strategy and the Political Economy, 1945–80, by Peter M. Lange, George Ross and Maurizio Vannicelli, was published by George Allen & Unwin in 1982.

Contents

Acknowledgements

Unions and Economic Crisis: Britain, West Germany and Sweden is the second of two volumes reporting and analyzing European trade union responses to contemporary economic crisis. The study on which both volumes are based emerged initially from long talks among colleagues in 1976–7, prodded by Peter Gourevitch, at the Harvard University Center for European Studies. An initial paper drafted by Andrew Martin, George Ross, Peter Gourevitch and Peter Lange was then subjected to the probing and far-sighted criticisms of participants in the Research Planning Group on Comparative Labor Studies, financed by the Council on European Studies. A final research proposal was funded by the Ford Foundation (where Mr Peter Ruof was of great help), enabling members of the project group – expanded from the original four to include Christopher Allen, Stephen Bornstein, Andrei Markovits and Maurizio Vannicelli – to carry out field research in 1978–9. During the periods of research design, field investigation and subsequent analysis of results the group met often at Harvard CES, where most of the final writing was done.

Unions and Economic Crisis is dedicated to the Harvard Center for European Studies. For more than a decade Harvard CES has been a major crossroads for students of European societies, a place where dignity, civility, a great rigor and intellectual energy and extraordinary tolerance across disciplinary, political and cultural lines have coexisted. In one way or another all of the researchers in this trade union project have been uniquely helped by their association with the Center. The kind of openness and vitality which they have known at Harvard CES is rare anywhere. The dedication is presented in the fervent hope that, at a moment when the value of cross-national research is being doubted in some quarters, the Center's past decade of great success will serve as the foundation-stone of an even more brilliant and vital future. Three people in particular have made CES happen. To Stanley Hoffmann, Guido Goldman and Abby Collins we therefore express our special gratitude. To those many scholars for whom Harvard CES has been a stopping-place on important intellectual voyages, and whose presence has enriched our work, we also give thanks. Abby Collins, in addition to her general responsibility for providing our project with a wondrous environment, has seen us through thick and thin with intelligence, authority and grace. Markovits, the senior author of the West German chapter, and Allen would like to thank Volker Bahl, Angelika Bahl-Benker, Hartmut Kuechle, Gerhard Leminsky, Heinz Markmann and Werner Vitt. Martin is deeply indebted to the many persons in Sweden who provided invaluable help, although he refers to none of them by name in order to preserve the anonymity of those who requested it. Bornstein and Gourevitch thank Norma Percy, Martin Upshaw, Peter Hall, David Lee, William Callaghan and the most gracious librarians of the TUC.

Introduction

This is a study of European trade union response to the economic crisis that engulfed the advanced industrial countries in the mid-1970s. This crisis, the most serious since the interwar Great Depression, confronted unions, along with most other economic actors, with new risks and, perhaps, new opportunities. How the unions understood the crisis and reacted to it was bound to be important not only for its impact on the unions themselves, but also for the structure of relationships existing between unions and other major social groups. That the reactions of governments and business should be important was evidently taken for granted; that union responses mattered as well seemed more easily overlooked. It was precisely our recollection of the significance of union responses to the crisis that began in 1929 that prevented us from overlooking it.

How unions understood the Great Depression and the extent to which the policies they urged to cope with it were implemented had a great deal to do with the subsequent unfolding of events. British unions broke with balanced budget orthodoxy and called for expansionist, proto-Keynesian policies. They failed to convince their Labour Party allies who were then governing the country, however. German unions proposed similar policies but likewise failed to convince their Social Democratic allies. In both cases the results were setbacks for the unions and their members, severe in Britain and disastrous in Germany. In Britain the Labour government's insistence on orthodoxy precipitated the split that brought its fall, and a continuation by its successor of policies imposing the immense burden of unemployment on the workers. Still, British democracy proved sufficiently robust to survive. In Germany, by contrast, economic orthodoxy played a key role in undermining the coalition on which the preservation of Germany's fragile democracy depended, opening the way for Hitler's seizure of power. In France Popular Front efforts to expand the economy, prompted by unions, were thwarted by a rapid reversion to orthodoxy, although not before uncertainty and confusion about economic policy had strained the French social fabric in ways that contributed to the capitulation of 1940 and the Vichy regime. Only in Sweden did the unions and their Social Democratic allies agree on unorthodox expansionist budget policies, which in turn laid the political basis for the development of Sweden's welfare state under continuous Social Democratic rule.

Of course, the economic crisis beginning in the mid-1970s was not the same as the Great Depression. No complete collapse of economic activity occurred. Yet the postwar pattern of growth was drastically and, perhaps, irreparably disrupted. Inflation reached peak rates even as unemployment rose toward the highest postwar levels. Having been ever-more completely integrated into the international economy, national economies found it increasingly difficult to remain competitive in the face of the changed international structure of production. This, together with the collapse of the postwar monetary system, amplified the effects of the oil shock, making equilibrium in many of the countries' foreign transactions an ever-more-elusive goal. Thus, after an unprecedented period in which nearly everything seemed to work, policy-makers faced an economic environment in which all options were increasingly bad ones.

With the breakdown of growth, the possibility of meeting the terms for what we shall refer to as the 'postwar settlements' was called into question. While these terms varied from country to country, they provided essentially for the preservation of a predominantly capitalist economy in exchange for continued full employment and expansion of the welfare state. Whether the settlements were the outcome of explicit negotiations as in Britain, or the implicit result of the perceived balance of social power, as in Sweden and France, they were sustainable as long as growth continued. The Great Depression tore asunder one socioeconomic world and, ultimately, led to the establishment of another. In the confusion, conflict and pain of all this unions both suffered a great deal and played important roles. Similarly, the crisis of the 1970s challenged and threatened to tear apart the socioeconomic world of the postwar settlements. Only this time the unions, endowed by these settlements with substantially more power and centrality than they had possessed in the 1930s, were less likely to suffer such widespread defeat in struggles with other actors over alternative responses to crisis.

Accordingly, our expectation was that unions would develop new analyses and strategies of their own to counterpose those of the other actors, and that they would be much more influential in shaping national responses to crisis than in the 1930s. It seemed to us that crisis-induced social renegotiations, whatever their final shape might turn out to be, would not be simple linear translations of the schemes of official policy-makers and economists. Whatever happened, it would be the product of complicated social conflict involving all the major collective actors in advanced industrial societies. In this conflict the specific coalitions which developed between different social and political actors would be central – who allied with whom for what reasons would be a deciding factor. In this process of new coalition-building for social renegotiation precipitated by crisis unions' analyses of the situation and union strategies to cope with it were likely to be very important. What the unions thought was happening in the economy, what programs they decided to advocate and how they decided to deploy their resources to realize these programs would make certain patterns of collaboration possible between unions and political actors, for example, while excluding others. Economic policy proposals which the unions came to endorse would, by virtue of such endorsement, become more plausible.

Our initial intuition about the importance of unions in the modern crisis situation plus our memory of how they had been important in the past led us, therefore, to want to know more about European union responses to the changing economic circumstances of the 1970s. In the past union perceptions of the economic world had been essential in the constitution of union actions. How, and for what reasons, did the unions come to perceive and understand the crisis of the 1970s? What kinds of agendas and programs did the unions derive from such theories and maps of the new situations, and why these? What types of general strategies did the unions devise to mobilize their own resources and to influence other actors? What features in the unions' environments most influenced such union analytical, programmatic and strategic reflection? Did economic change directly cause union reevaluations? Or did such change lead to reevaluation through the prisms of politics, union organizational considerations and ideology?

From the outset we were firm believers in the comparative method. We knew enough about European unions to be aware of the quite striking differences which existed from one nation's labor movement to the next. We, therefore, wanted to research a sufficiently broad range of European cases to make possible generalizations about trends of response to crisis which were common across all union movements, while also facilitating the classification of different types of responses which might turn up in one or several of the cases. Our ultimate task, of course, was to arrive at an explanation for such similarities and differences.

Given the complexity of union movements, the wide range of different national situations which we wished to sample, the relatively long period (1970–80) in which we were interested and limitations on our own resources – personal and financial – we obviously had to make a choice between what was possible to research and what lay beyond our scope. Our first decision was to focus on the economic thought, programs and strategies of unions. We were aware of the problematic implications of such a decision – we were looking primarily at what unions *said*, which was not exactly the same thing as what they were doing. We, thus, assumed that what unions said had something to do with what they did, not necessarily a safe assumption. We did our best to control this problem, however. We chose to study not only formal union economic thought (that is, unions' 'high theories' about the dynamics of the economic environment), but also unions' desired policy programs and general strategies. Both of the latter were, of course, still in the realm of union thought and declaration, but they were both behaviorally oriented. Thus, any major contradictions between union high theory and practical orientations toward behavior would be likely to turn up in our research, even though we were to remain within the realm of thought more generally. Secondly, the period of union response to economic change in which we were interested was quite long. In reviewing such a long period any major contradictions between union thought and behavior were bound to manifest themselves clearly.

We also decided to focus primarily on the economic thought, programs and strategies of trade union peak associations – the coordinating national confederal organizations in each country (only *one* in countries with unified movements, several in those with pluralistic movements). This choice simplified our task greatly. We could zero-in on confederal statements, documents, publications on union economic perspectives, programs and strategies, and interview top-level officials, researchers and experts. At the same time we could deemphasize what happened at subcentral organizational levels (federations, branches, locals) and thorny questions of measuring actual rank-and-file behavior. This focus, of course, created greater or lesser problems for our national researchers, depending upon the degree to which theoretical and strategic matters were centralized or decentralized in their countries. We tried to build-in some control for this problem as well. In each national case we gathered data not only for peak associations, but also for union organizations in certain industrial areas which we thought were likely to be particularly sensitive to the crisis (iron and steel, autos, construction and municipal workers). While this data did not figure greatly in our final papers, it was useful in informing our works-in-progress where, in a specific national case, confederal-level data was not predictive of the concerns of particular unions.

Anyone experienced in social science research will understand why we made such strategic choices. A project which set out to understand European trade union responses to the crisis of the 1970s by documenting union thought at peak and other organizational levels plus developing some effective measures for deciding the influence of such thought on organizational and rank-and-file behavior, not to speak of the behavior of other actors in European political economies, would have called for methodological sophistication of an extraordinarily ingenious kind plus financial resources which were far, far beyond our reach. We had to deal with such problems, as do many researchers, by simplifying. We assumed that union thought and intention had some significant relationship to union behavior, that unions were 'conscious actors'. Moreover, we knew that one could never test the specific behavioral implications of union thought and intention without knowing, first of all, what these thoughts and intentions were. So we proceeded to try to find out what they were, with the confidence that we were looking at an important component of trade union practice and that our work might be of use subsequently to others with the much larger resources needed to look at the broader range of union practices.

In thinking about our general problem – accounting for the whys and wherefores of European trade union choices in response to contemporary economic crisis – we also were motivated by a sense of intellectual malaise. The 'conventional wisdom' about unions and workers, which we have labeled 'liberal optimism', was, we believed, profoundly economistic and historicist in its basic orientations. These biases, we felt, rendered 'liberal optimism' quite problematic for understanding and predicting union behavior. 'Liberal optimism' asserted an underlying logic in industrialism which led, over time, to a growing similarity in institutions in different societies. Advancing industrialism brought with it quite precise functional demands which had to be satisfied by all advanced industrial societies in more or less similar ways, regardless of national particularities. While, of course, such a convergence thesis was true in the most general of ways – if one stands far enough away from any social phenomena, they do tend, ultimately, to resemble one another – the 'liberal optimists' were more specific in their projections. Unions, in particular, were likely to move toward increasing 'subsystemic' autonomy, in which their major focus increasingly fell on issues specific to the 'industrial relations system' – relationships between themselves and employers around a limited number of questions. Moreover, with the development of a 'web of rules' and consensus upon it within this industrial relations system, unions would become both more moderate and more 'functionally specific'. In particular, trade union politicization would decline. Behind such predictions lay a huge, almost teleological, assumption. In contrast to Marxian thought, which posited that 'capitalism' was a social order fraught with such contradictions that it would ultimately be transcended, through class conflict, to 'socialism', 'liberal optimist' theory saw major social conflict around industrialism confined to the long transition period between 'traditional' and 'industrial' societies. This transition might be painful, and it usually created utopian expectations among those most affected by such pain, but once completed successfully, it would give way to an industrial society in which the division of labor and industrial rationality would be generally acceptable to all.

We were troubled by this conventional wisdom, both for epistemological and empirical reasons. In many of the studies of industrial relations this logic of advancing industrialism, once posited by analysts, seemed to become the *subject* of historical evolution. In contrast unions (along with all other significant actors) were relegated to the status of *objects* of this subject, whose task it was to register and react to exogenous change. In other words, the intervention of real actors did not make history occur, rather something labeled industrialism marched forward, obliging actors to adapt. Industrialism tended to become the first cause of human behavior in an almost metaphysical way. Our sense, very different, was that major organizational actors – like unions were 'conscious subjects', armed with systems of perceptions, values and goals, which attempted through complex patterns of resource generation and exchanges with other actors to shape their environments. To the extent that there was any 'logic of industrialism' it did not exist *a priori*. Rather, it emerged from the interaction of such conscious organizational subjects.

Such philosophical reservations were only one part of our malaise. From what we knew, almost from the outset, about the union movements which we were studying, we were certain that most of the specific hypotheses/ predictions of the 'liberal optimists' didn't work. In recent years European unions had not gravitated towards the moderation, depoliticization, 'functional specificity' and 'subsystemic autonomy' which the liberal optimists had anticipated. Rather, from the late 1960s onwards at least, there had been a striking increase in union militancy which, far from being confined within earlier-established 'limits' on union demands, had focussed on a number of radical new issues. In addition, this new militancy was everywhere connected to increased union involvement in politics both in terms of new union concern about state policies and commitment to partisan political programs and activities. Furthermore, not only did the specific predictions about union behavior not work, the more general assumption of convergence across national boundaries due to a general logic of industrialism did not pan out either. Union movements did change their outlooks, goals and behavior as industrial economies developed, of course. But such change seemed to lead as much toward divergence between different national movements as toward convergence.

If 'liberal optimist' conventional wisdom was not useful as a theoretical guide, then where were we left? Marxist perspectives had attractiveness, to the degree that they were somewhat less sanguine about the automatic propensities of industrial societies to produce moderation and consensus and much more sensitive to the profundity of cleavages between different major groups in capitalist industrial orders. Despite these assets, Marxist accounts also tended to suffer from many of the central conceptual problems which we found in 'liberal optimism'. In Marxian views there also was an historical logic exogenous to central social actors which propelled them forward inexorably as historical objects. This 'logic of capital accumulation', in its externality to major collective actors, seemed to us quite as metaphysical and economistic as the 'logic of industrialism'. Moreover, the historicism of most Marxist accounts – inevitable movement toward bigger and better class conflict – seemed quite as unreliable a guide to empirical events as did the 'liberal optimists'' belief in the inevitability of consensus. Finally, most such Marxist writing was quite as replete with 'epicyclic' explanations for deviations from expected trajectories as was 'liberal optimist' work.

We were on our own, or so it seemed, with our instincts. These were twofold from the beginning. First, we felt that explanations of trade union behavior rooted in general theories of economic development were unlikely to be effective for explaining European union responses to the crisis of the 1970s. The crisis obliged all of the national union movements we were studying to devise responses, to be sure. But the crisis, in itself, did not necessarily lead to any set of specific union responses which we were likely to find in all national cases. Rather, we were strongly inclined to think that the nature of each national union movement's response, even where the indices of crisis were relatively similar to those elsewhere, was more likely to be forged out of the particular structures of the economy, labor market and political system which it faced in its own country. In other words, if circumstances of crisis obliged unions to adapt, the ways in which they chose to do so could not be explained directly by any 'functional demands' derivable from crisis itself. Our second instinct told us that, since we regarded unions as 'conscious actors' in their specific national environments, the nature of their responses to changing environmental circumstances would depend, in important ways, on their 'consciousness'. At any given point in time a union movement had to be seen as possessing an identity (which included distinctive ways of mapping the world, values and goals) which would serve as a prism for integrating stimuli from outside and as a constraint on the range of likely responses to them. In turn, this identity had to be seen as constituted developmentally out of the union's past exchanges with class structure, other actors and economic realities. When placed together, these two instincts led us very far away from conventional wisdoms. We were far from denying the existence of powerful constraints placed on unions by economic development. But if one took the vantage-point of a union making choices at any given moment, it did seem that how unions as actors responded to such constraints depended quite as much upon their identities as organizations – their 'consciousness' – and upon the national nature of the fields of action which they faced as upon the nature of these constraints themselves. Furthermore, viewed in the light of process, the very constraints of the economy faced by a union at time T^2 were, to a certain extent, the products of intergroup action and conflict in which the union had participated at time T^1.

These instincts, plus our concern for tapping the widest possible range of trade union responses to crisis, were the initial premises for the choice of national union movements to research. To begin with, we wanted to find cases where the structures of the unions' political environment varied significantly. Basically this meant seeking out national situations in which the nature of union ties to the state, policy processes and political parties were different. Another political-related variation of whose importance we were well aware was the presence or absence of trade union organizational pluralism. We were also concerned with large variations in the structuring of labor markets, such as the degree of institutionalization (in Kerr's 'web of rules' sense) of the industrial relations system, the strength/weakness of unions themselves (often connected to institutionalization) and the centralization/decentralization of union organization. Finally, we were concerned with finding cases where the incidence of economic crisis itself varied.

Since we were interested in European national cases, and since there was only a limited number of such cases available, it was obviously not possible for us to develop a sample sophisticated enough to test national trade union responses to crisis against variations in all of these different environmental factors. Thus, we were obliged to proceed in a more rough-and-ready way, choosing national cases both because some or all of these variations existed and because the specific countries were important and/or interesting economically. The UK, West Germany and Sweden were all cases in which ties between unions and social democratic political parties were of central importance. Even if the exact nature of these ties varied substantially from case to case, their existence meant that the unions in question had all had experience with allied political parties holding governmental power. In consequence, each of the unions had had to develop some perspectives on behaving 'responsibly' in order to help the party-ally gain and keep power. In other ways, however, the three 'social democratic' cases were very different. While in all three cases there existed a high degree of labor market institutionalization (although of different kinds in each case), in West Germany and Sweden union movements were highly centralized, while in the UK the TUC, the British peak association, was relatively weak in its control over events. Finally, the incidence in each country of the crisis of the 1970s was very different. The UK was hurt dramatically very early on, while West Germany proved very resilient until very late. Sweden, a very small economy long used to the volatility of international markets, was hurt by crisis, to be sure, but managed to postpone major economic drama by specific national policy choices again until very late.

The French and Italian cases were very different from these three Northern European ones in which social democratic partisan affiliations were central to unions. In both France and Italy the most important union organizations had strong ties to communist parties. From this a number of other differences flowed. Since communist parties had been excluded from political power since the immediate postwar years, much of organized labor in France and Italy had little or no experience in situations where trade union support for the economic policies of an allied party in power was called for. Instead the experience of at least CP-affiliated segments of French and Italian labor had been one of exclusion – sometimes brutal exclusion – and opposition in relationship to the state and to state power. Another significant difference came with this CP-union affiliation – trade union pluralism. Strong communist labor presence in both countries implied the fragmentation of organized labor along lines of partisan political cleavage, resulting in an often bitterly divided union movement in which several different confederations existed. There were also specific labor market correlates to such political phenomena. In both countries individual union confederations tended to be strongly centralized, while all unions tended to be weak, especially when compared with the 'social democratic' cases, at shopfloor and firm level. In addition, industrial relations systems in both countries were relatively underinstitutionalized. If France and Italy resembled one another more than they resembled our other three chosen cases, they also differed. The communist parties in each country had different traditions, faced very different coalitional settings and had quite different strategies for achieving their goals, facts which influenced the union movements in important ways. The French and Italian states were structured differently and performed differently – the first highly centralized and effective, the second decentralized and ineffective. Finally, economic crisis hit the two countries in different ways. France was touched severely, but nowhere near as severely as Italy.

It did not take us long, once we had begun our research, to uncover a serious problem. Our major task was to discover, analyze, explain and compare the responses of five different national union movements to the economic crisis of the 1970s. With much of the material in hand, however, we discovered that it was impossible to discuss European trade union responses to the crisis of the 1970s while restricting our purview to the events of the 1970s themselves. In effect, what we found almost universally was that our union movements responded to crisis through systems of perceptions, values and goals which had been formulated substantially *before* the crisis occurred, often in the later 1960s. In other words, rather than dramatically changing their frameworks of analysis because of crisis, the unions reacted to crisis on the basis of frameworks which had been developed prior to crisis and in other circumstances. We were forced to recognize, then, that the historical development of our unions *prior to the crisis* was quite as important to their response in crisis as, say, the economic shape of the crisis itself. In each case, then, we found ourselves drawn back from the 1970s toward earlier union behavior in search of full explanations for union action in the 1970s. For this reason, and because we soon realized that the literature in English on the modern history of most of our movements was scanty at best, we expanded our scope.

In all of our national cases there seemed to have been roughly parallel developments. Union response to crisis in the 1970s was formulated from within union ideas and strategies which had been worked out in the later 1960s. These ideas and strategies, in turn, had been devised in response to major changes in the basic parameters of postwar social settlements which had occurred at that time. We were, therefore, also thrown back to an examination of these settlements, which everywhere had emerged to blunt the thrust of postwar reformism, and the unions' place within them. Our explanatory tasks were, therefore, considerably enlarged – we had to become historians as much as social scientists interested in the present. And our national case studies were lengthened.

As our work progressed we also realized that we would gain most from undertaking three different, if interrelated, comparative analyses, instead of the one with which we began. Our initial sense that the nature of union–politics relationships was the most important variable in explaining different union responses to crisis turned out to be accurate. This gave us two subtypes of union response, the 'social democratic' and the 'communist presence–union pluralist'. Yet, it was also true that substantial differences *within* these subtypes were also significant. We decided, therefore, to proceed analytically on three different levels. We would compare the communist-presence–union-pluralist cases, France and Italy, with one another. Then we would compare the three social democratic cases – the UK, West Germany and Sweden – together. Finally, in order to discern response trends general to *all* union movements, in order to reconsider the utility of the social democrat/communist-presence dichotomy, and in order to isolate and discuss responses which were purely individual to national cases, we had to undertake a full five-case comparison.

It was the logic of these three separate comparisons which structured our study into its present two-volume form. Volume One of *Unions, Change and Crisis* (Peter Lange, George Ross, Maurizio Vannicelli, London, George Allen and Unwin, 1982) included separate national case studies of France and Italy, plus a third chapter which developed a more general analytical approach to comparative union studies based on the French and Italian materials. Volume Two contains three additional national chapters (the UK, West Germany and Sweden) on the social democratic union cases, plus a conclusion which reviews these cases comparatively and then raises a number of the general issues which our five-country study raises for the future of unions in West European political economies.

The union movements of the UK, West Germany and Sweden are 'similar cases', collectively different from the 'similar cases' of Volume One, France and Italy. In each country the peak blue-collar union organization, the TUC in Britain, the DGB in West Germany and LO in Sweden, has a longstanding, well-developed tie to a social democratic party which is the dominant party on the left. Partly for this reason the TUC, DGB and LO are the only major confederal blue-collar associations in their societies; ideologically based trade union pluralism, at least among unions representing industrial workers, does not exist. The social democratic parties to which the unions have traditional links have, moreover, all been at some time a majority party in power, or when out of power, a plausible candidate for returning to power at some proximate future date.

Unions need certain policies from government which can be translated into tangible payoffs for their members and supporters. Such policies-become-payoffs help ensure the unions' own survival as representatives of their bases. Linkage with a plausible government party gives the union reasonable certainty that all, or most, of these desirable policies can be delivered, if not immediately, then in the near future. In exchange for these policies and payoffs the union is likely to be called upon to produce electoral support for the party from its supporters and, should it be necessary, to accept certain duties of restraint to keep the party-ally in power or in the running to come to power. Once in office, the social democratic party faces the complex task of governing and assumes managerial responsibility for the success or failure of a sophisticated and delicate capitalist economy. Inevitably the demands of governance and economic management place constraints on the party's ability to supply the policies which the union desires. The union, in turn, derives benefits from having its social democratic ally in power, even if these benefits are not always as great as the union might hope for in the abstract. Thus, other things being equal, the union will conceive a strong interest in having the party succeed at such governing and managerial tasks. It will, as a result, try to limit behavior, on its own or its constitutents' parts, which might compromise this success.

The patterns of exchange between social democratic unions and parties are historic, not simply analytical. In the post World War II period, which each national case study reviews, each union–party exchange relationship tended to solidify into a succession of definite 'deals'. In very general terms the essential components of such deals can be specified. The unions wanted full employment and prosperity for their membership, plus a just system of social services. Once the brief period of political renegotiation after the war was over (Sweden excepted, since the Swedish renegotiation began before the war), the major instrumentality for achieving such ends advocated by the unions throughout much of the postwar period was Keynesian demand management deployed in the context of a mixed-economy welfare state. In exchange the unions provided political support – finances, votes, militant energies – for the party. In general party–union relationships were conceived strategically. The union was willing to act in its own sphere so as to aid and abet the party in its economic management tasks. The party, in turn, acted to provide the union with the programs which it needs to maintain its support. As this exchange developed in time, however, the union tended to come to share the general managerial responsibilities of its party-ally not only in action, but also in the ways by which the union actually conceived of the structures of economic life. Thus, our social democratic unions, by virtue of their ongoing relationships with governing or plausible opposition parties, developed 'cooperative' approaches to economic life, as opposed to the 'oppositional' postures which characterized the French and Italian unions we reviewed in Volume One.

These union–party 'deals' were rarely as straightforward as such a brief description implies, however. No matter how 'cooperative' a union may have wanted to be with its party-ally, union–party relationships were not the only exchange networks which the union had to maintain. It had to preserve satisfactory ties with its support-base as well. Nothing guaranteed that a particular 'deal' between union and party would optimize union support at the base, however. Indeed, these two sets of exchange relationships often pulled the union in strategically contradictory directions. A union may have wanted to 'cooperate' with its party-ally both in the political and market spheres but have been unable to do so, because its rank-and-file judged the particular form of cooperation in question not to be sufficiently beneficial in labor market terms. For these reasons, and for others, the union sometimes found it necessary to hold the party's program 'hostage' for different policies than those which the party desired. The opposite type of 'hostage' situation was also frequent, in which the party in power retreated from policy promises made to the union. This 'hostage dilemma' usually justified by the party in terms of the exigencies of realistic economic management, forced the union either to comply, often at considerable risk to its own abilities to maintain rank-and-file support, or to take risks of union action which might cause substantial political trouble, up to and including loss of power, for the party-ally.

Social democratic union–party deals, then, even when both sides approached them with cooperative goodwill, were likely to prove unstable. Indeed, as the national chapters which follow demonstrate, this was very clearly the case in all three countries. Unions and parties in each case developed sets of expectations about their relationships. The relationships themselves stabilized for only brief moments, however. Movements from earlier to later 'deals' happened when such expectations ceased to be useful guides to action in the face of new circumstances and contradictions. In fact, the unions which we will examine evolved from deal to new deal after 1945 until they had developed to the positions which they ultimately used to understand and confront economic crisis in the 1970s. In the process, however, some major changes in union ideas and strategy did occur. During the postwar boom the unions came to accept a free market economy coordinated by Keynesian techniques and oriented toward private profit accompanied by a reasonably comprehensive welfare state system. By the time that unions had reflected upon the new economic circumstances of the 1970s, however, most of them had come to be mistrustful of the efficacy and justice of the free market as economic allocator and were quite skeptical of the utility of Keynesian techniques, on their own, without major new policy initiatives. To the degree to which such changes occurred the unions tended to push their party-allies to move beyond the policy packages and equilibria which had become habitual during the postwar boom. Such generalizations, however, do not do justice to the variety of situations which came to exist in the UK, West Germany and Sweden. It is time, then, to turn to our national case study chapters.

1 Unions in a Declining Economy: The Case of the British TUC

Stephen Bornstein and Peter Gourevitch

Part 1

Introduction

The troubles of the British economy did not, as is well known, begin in 1974. As early as the 1950s British economic growth lagged behind that of its European neighbors: while the British standard of living did rise substantially in the 1950s, there was no talk of the 'economic miracle' such as characterized the development of other European economies in this period. Similarly, during the 1960s and early 1970s the British economy was plagued by high inflation and slow growth that prompted serious discussions of 'the British disease' or 'the decline of Britain'. None the less, in Britain as elsewhere, 1974 marks a turning-point, a widespread new consciousness that the era of the easy politics of welfare state Keynesianism had come to an end.

For the British trade union movement the decade of the 1970s has witnessed dramatic shifts in thought and action. In the years just prior to the 1973–4 crisis the unions had, in response to the problems of the domestic economy and the pressures of domestic politics, rethought their economic analysis and strategy. In a series of conferences and reports during the early 1970s the TUC adopted a set of proposals that involved transcending 'market Keynesianism' by significantly expanding the activities of the state and the unions in the areas of economic planning and the provision of investment funds. In a break with the moderate leadership of its political ally, the Labour Party, the union movement's peak organization, the Trades Union Congress (TUC) shifted markedly leftward in its economic program. Then the international economic crisis hit in 1973–4 and, at about the same moment, Labour was returned to office following the general election of February 1974. In these doubly new circumstances (acute economic difficulties and a new, friendly government) the TUC did not press its criticisms of the market economy or its demands for structural reform very hard. Rather, it retreated to a familiar posture of curtailing demands in order to help keep Labour in power in spite of the government's adoption of a strict austerity program for managing the economic crisis. In place of structural radicalism the unions demanded reforms of industrial relations law and the expansion of union power in the workplace, while accepting considerable wage restraint and sharp reductions in social spending by the state. In the winter of 1978–9, however, this arrangement came unstuck. Wage militancy and a wave of strikes undermined the standing of the Labour government and the Conservatives under Margaret Thatcher returned to power intent on reducing the power of the unions; while moderates within the Labour Party broke away to form a new party, the Social Democrats.

The TUC's policy shifts during this tumultuous period obviously require explanation. We shall seek to understand them by setting them within the context of the development of the British union movement's thought and action in the postwar period. The TUC's approach to the institutions of the postwar political economy was, we shall argue, based on a theoretical and strategic package that took form in the years from 1945 to the early 1950s. The unions, despite their occasional rhetorical flourishes about societal transformation and foreign policy, sought – much like their American counterparts – to realize a narrow set of goals: to maximize the incomes and security of their members. They sought to do this by tapping two basic sources of potential benefits, namely, the labor market and the state.

For the unions composing the TUC, action in the labor market represented the central function of genuine trade unions. One of the lessons the TUC drew from the Great Depression was that unions had to rely primarily on their own collective bargaining resources, rather than counting on the goodwill of politicians, even Labour politicians. To use their labor market power to best effect the unions had to guard their autonomy in the area of collective bargaining as zealously as possible. Attempts by the state to impose legal restraints on bargaining were, therefore, to be strenuously resisted, as was any attempt to alter the legal and institutional framework within which such bargaining took place. The essential instability of the market economy required, however, that unions also work in the political arena to pressure the state to maintain sufficient demand in the economy to keep employment levels high, to provide a guaranteed and equitable distribution of income and economic opportunity, and to ensure employment security. Beyond this funda-mental Keynesian position neither the TUC nor its major unions paid much attention to macroeconomic issues. It was the task of business and government to look after the global operation of the economy; the unions' business was to look after the material interests of their members. In order to influence the actions of the state in favor of their members British unions deployed not only the standard weapons of pressure-group politics, but also their special structural relationship with the Labour Party. The Conservatives had been responsible for the disastrous policies of the Depression era. Despite their apparent acceptance of the welfare state and of Keynesianism in the postwar period, the unions still considered them, therefore, less reliable than Labour, with which the unions enjoyed not only historical links, but strong financial and organizational ties as well.

Built into this package of objectives and means was a series of internal contradictions that made it very difficult for the unions to achieve their aims. The tendency of Britain's economy to inflationary spirals and balance of payments difficulties made the unions' considerable market power into a two-edged sword: if the unions were too successful in the market, they risked compromising the capacity of the economy to generate real wage increases; and their labor market visibility, moreover, meant that they were vulnerable to attacks for creating such problems, whatever their actual degree of success. Similarly, the unions' political weapon could cut in two directions. If they succeeded in getting their Labour allies into power, they risked finding themselves with less freedom of maneuver in the labor market than they might enjoy under the Tories. Labour governments were much readier to resort to incomes policies than were the Conservatives. Moreover, they were given to demanding industrial quiescence as the unions' contribution to the electoral survival of their governments. The unions, thus, risked becoming the hostages of their own political allies.

These contradictions were difficult to manage. In theory, however, British unions could control them as long as the British economy could limit its international vulnerability and deliver a modicum of real growth. Once, however, Britain's international position and its domestic economic growth became a problem – as they had by the mid-1960s – the unions were forced to reexamine their strategic package. It was this reexamination that led them to their new program of the early 1970s. This program, labeled the Social Contract, constituted the TUC's initial attempt, in alliance with the Labour Party, to navigate the difficult waters of the international economic crisis. And it was this program which was partially abandoned in the mid-1970s in the puzzling manner we have described.

This chapter will analyze the TUC's response to the crisis as the latest in a series of its attempts to rethink, in minor and ultimately unsuccessful ways, the strategic and analytical package it first put together in the early postwar period. To this end we shall begin by describing, in Part 2, the way in which that package took shape in the years of 'postwar settlement'. Next, in Part 3, we shall discuss the TUC's efforts to adjust this strategic package in the light of the obvious troubles of the British economy in the 1960s and early 1970s. Finally, in Part 4, we shall turn to the period of the crisis itself, to examine the paradoxical manner in which the TUC attempted to use its newly changed strategic package to wrestle with a drastically altered economic environment.

Part 2

Union Strategy and the Postwar Settlement

Union designs for Postwar Britain

In Britain, as elsewhere, the pattern of social and economic relations which was to prevail during the boom years of the 1950s and 1960s was set in the early years of the postwar period. This pattern, Britain's 'postwar settlement', involved a number of quite extensive changes from the framework of economic policy, social services, public expenditure, state intervention and class relations that had operated in the interwar years. Because of events both during and immediately following World War II, British unions were called upon to play an important role in working such changes, both on their own and as central participants in the Labour Party. The unions inevitably brought their own organizational and political past to the tasks of defining this role.[1] In general, they were haunted by an overpowering collective memory, that of the catastrophe lived by British workers during the Great Depression. If there was one central motivating idea behind their postwar actions, it was to rebuild postwar Britain in ways which would ensure that nothing like the events of the Great Depression could recur. In terms of their own organization the unions were determined to pursue this idea by using the immediate postwar period to enhance and, if possible, firmly institutionalize their capacities to achieve material goals in the labor market – primarily to win wage gains and promote job security for their members. This organizational concern had certain political implications as well, since maximal union autonomy and power in the labor market would give the unions greater leverage over the Labour Party (to prevent the kinds of events which had occurred in 1931) and substantial new power to resist any Conservative turn toward the labor-repressive economic strategies which, in the unions' eyes, had caused so much misery in the 1930s. The unions had more directly political objectives as well. One basic concern, of course, was to bring the Labour Party to power and to keep it there not only because of the historic ties between unions and the Labour Party, but also because the Conservatives had been primarily responsible for the hated policies of the 1930s.[2] Beyond this, however, more specific goals had to be achieved. First of all, structural reforms in the economy were needed, for reasons of equity, to be sure, but more importantly, to give the state more control over economic processes. Secondly, the conceptual framework within which state economic policies were defined had to be reformulated such that resort to Depression-type programs for confronting economic difficulties at the expense of workers through massive unemployment and a Draconian compression of working-class living standards would become unthinkable in the postwar world.

Postwar Reformism

World War II laid the foundations for the transformation of the British political economy which occurred in the immediate postwar period. During the war Britain operated under a very different set of procedures from those of the prewar period.[3] Leading members of the Labour Party held crucial posts in an all-party National Government. The social welfare system was considerably expanded. State control of the economy, previously limited to minor forms of intervention primarily in agriculture, became detailed and extensive. The trade unions, alongside representatives of the peak organizations of business, began to play a vastly expanded role in the making of economic and social policy.[4] As the victory of the Allies appeared increasingly likely in 1943–4 political and social actors in Britain began to turn at least part of their attention toward the future. The National Government established a Ministry of Reconstruction and a Reconstruction Joint Advisory Council, and it commissioned reports from various sources on aspects of postwar policy including the celebrated report on the social services by Sir William Beveridge.[5] At the war's end British society faced a crucial set of choices for the shape of future economic and social development. How much of the war-effort innovations in policy content and processes would be carried over into the new era? How different would postwar Britain be from the class-ridden society of the interwar years? Would the innovations in social policy, economic management and class relations of the war prove to be merely a temporary arrangement, the beginning of a vast transformation of British capitalism, or simply the outside limit of acceptable change?

The trade unions, both individually and through the Trades Union Congress, entered forcefully into this debate from the very beginning. As early as the fall of 1943 the TUC's Annual Congress debated a set of resolutions from member-unions on the issue of postwar reconstruction and charged the movement's highest executive body with preparing a report on the subject.[6] At the following year's Congress the report was presented by the General Council under the title of 'Interim report on postwar reconstruction'. It was adopted by the delegates and distilled into a special motion declaring the TUC's official views on the shape of Britain in the coming era.[7] The thrust of this motion was that British unions had no intention of allowing the end of hostilities to inaugurate a return to the liberal policies and practices of interwar Britain.[8] Rather, the TUC desired to see the wartime experiments serve as a stepping-stone toward a major transformation of economic policies and structures: a program of industrial nationalizations; vastly more state intervention in the economy; economic planning; the establishment of a broad network of social services; and a greatly increased union role in the policy process at all levels of society.

For the TUC, the interwar economy had been an unstable and inequitable system, failing to provide adequate levels of income or security for workers. Two fundamental types of reform were required to remedy these defects. First, a broad system of welfare services ought to be established more or less along the lines suggested by Sir William

Beveridge's famous wartime report. Such a welfare system would make Britain's overall distribution of income somewhat less unjust and reduce the insecurity that had plagued workers and their families.

In addition, a series of reforms were needed to ensure that the British economy operated at the level of full employment. What was required was the establishment of 'public control' over crucial levers of the economic system.[9] The most drastic form of public control advanced by the TUC was nationalization or, as the TUC preferred to say, 'public ownership'. Selected industries of 'vital importance to the life and well-being of the nation' were to be purchased at a 'fair' rate of compensation and turned into public corporations directly responsible to an appropriate Cabinet minister. [10] The TUC proposed nationalizing fuel and power (essentially coalmining and electricity generating), transport (railways and road haulage), and iron and steel.[11]

The vast majority of firms remaining in private hands were also to be subjected to a considerable degree of public control. Through legislation and administrative regulation the state was to prohibit forms of economic activity deemed to be 'essentially anti-social'.[12] Moreover, in each industry there was to be established a series of 'industrial boards', consisting of representatives of the unions and of management associations as well as independent members. The aim of such boards, operating within each industry at both an industrial and a regional level, would be to guarantee the 'general planning of the industry', to regulate output and prices, and to direct efforts at rationalization and reorganization. A Consumer Council, with participation by the unions and by the Cooperative movement, would also be established to regulate prices and scrutinize product quality.[13]

In addition, if the instability of investment and the inadequate and fluctuating demand for labor that had plagued interwar Britain were to be transcended, the global operation of the economy would have to be subjected to public control. The TUC, therefore, advocated the retention and, where necessary, the reinforcement of those wartime controls which would allow the state to influence the overall level of economic activity in the postwar period, while suggesting that controls over private consumption and the allocation of labor be eased as supply problems receded.[14] More generally, monetary and fiscal policy was to be used to maintain a level of demand that was 'adequate but not excessive'. Tax levels and government spending should be adjusted so as to guarantee full employment without making any concessions to demands for a balanced budget.[15] The government was to maintain a 'shelf' of public works projects which could be begun whenever the economy needed to be stimulated. Fiscal policy was to be used to promote full employment not only by stimulating global demand, but also by redistributing income into the hands of those most likely to spend it on consumption.[16]

This commitment by the state to maintain full employment would not, according to the TUC, necessarily entail an endemic inflationary spiral. The danger of postwar inflation, the TUC insisted, was greatly exaggerated. Once the initial period of postwar shortages had passed, the real problem was likely to be a recurrence of the recessionary conditions of the 1920s. Moreover, in a statement apparently conceding that the combination of full employment and free collective bargaining might contain a built-in inflationary tendency the TUC assured Sir William Beveridge that if a government committed to full employment acted sincerely to control the private sector, it would find the unions 'not . . . unwilling' to 'give suitable guarantees about moderation in wage settlements and reasonable assurances that such guarantees would be generally observed'. Compulsory arbitration or mandatory incomes policies, however, were entirely out of the question.[17]

Keynesian demand management, aided and abetted by an enlarged public sector and greater state regulatory power, was not all that the TUC had in mind by 'public control'. According to the General Council, the British economy suffered not only from cyclical instability requiring state manipulation of fiscal and monetary aggregates, but also from insufficient industrial investment and a general lack of public participation in decision-making. To deal with these issues the establishment of a system of economic planning was necessary. The adaptation of British industry to the postwar international environment would require considerably more funds for investment in manufacturing and a more stable supply of such funds than had been available in the interwar period. Citing the findings of the Macmillan Committee of 1930 concerning the failure of the banking system to provide adequate financing for industry, and noting also the growing autonomy of large corporations from external money markets, the TUC rejected the conventional solution to Britain's investment problems – closer links between the banks and industry – and advocated instead a system of public control involving 'a comprehensive planning of all large-scale investment, public and private, according to certain national and social priorities'.[18] Such a planning system would require a number of important institutional reforms. The state would have to bring the banking system under its control in order to ensure, among other objectives, that interest rates were set sufficiently low to facilitate industrial investment. The Bank of England would have to be turned into 'an agency of the Government' with its governor appointed by the government.[19] The joint stock banks would also have to be subject to a variety of controls the object of which would be to secure governmental control over lending practices, interest rates and movements of capital in and out of the country.[20] In addition, the government would have to undertake to formulate an annual 'manpower budget', a novel instrument whereby the level of employment entailed for the coming year by the investment intentions of private industry and the likely levels of private consumption would be forecast and public expenditure planned 'on a sufficient scale to employ all available labor'.[21] Finally, and most audaciously of all, the TUC proposed the creation of a National Investment Board. This Board would consist of three departments: a Surveying Department to prepare the manpower budget on the basis of public statistics and investment plans to be required from all firms; a Planning Department to 'exercise guidance' over all long-term investment, controlling levels of public and private investment, directing investment on a geographical basis 'to avoid structural unemployment', proposing and supervising 'special schemes for industrial reorganization' and having access to a 'licensing system' for private investment should 'advisory powers' prove inadequate; and a Lending Department to provide funds where necessary either by raising loan capital or by tapping public funds from a variety of sources.[22]

In this scheme for attaining security and full employment through public control workers and the unions were to play a greatly expanded role. In the proposed nationalized sector the TUC did not, as a number of left critics have pointed out, demand any drastic democratization of authority structures for the new public corporations: these would be hierarchically structured with a Board of Governors at the top, workers at the bottom, and managers, supervisors and foremen in between. The workers were, however, to be given a 'voice in the determination of . . . policy' through the establishment of 'consultative machinery' at all levels of the company.[23] Moreover, an unspecified number of representatives of the workers should be made full members of the Governing Board of each public corporation. In private industry workers designated by the unions would sit on Industrial Boards responsible for planning at industry level and would also acquire some control over production at the workshop level through works councils and Joint Production Committees, bodies that had become widespread during the war and that the TUC now wanted preserved and endowed with additional authority.[24]

Unions were to occupy an important role in the policy process at the national level, too, through their representation in a new body called a National Industrial Council. The TUC had been calling for such a council to be formed since 1932, arguing that it was desirable to establish 'some such machinery representative of all parties to industry and economic life'.[25] How this body would be composed and what its exact powers would be were not specified in the various TUC documents of the period.

Thus, the TUC had ambitious plans for macroeconomic change in the postwar world, as well as additional plans for the introduction of workers and unions into decision-making processes from the firm level upwards, to which we will presently turn. Relationships between the state and the private sector had to be drastically recast through 'public control'. And the basic objectives of state economic policy had to be reformulated so that full employment and an equitable distribution of income became essential goals. British unions had yet another central priority, which merits strong underlining at this point. The private sector of the economy was to be encapsulated in a new state-centred web of constraints and regulations, and the state was to be endowed with new overarching economic policy goals. In all this, however, the unions themselves were to retain, hopefully in enhanced form, their own complete autonomy. Thus, while union officials were to become involved in a variety of consultative and administrative bodies in private and public industry, they were to avoid in any way compromising the freedom of action of their organizations. Once appointed to such posts, they were to resign all their union positions and to serve in a purely private capacity.[26] In no case would the unions allow themselves to accept any share of responsibility for managerial decisions. Nor would the unions tolerate any interference by the state in the industrial relations system as part of its new venture into economic intervention. The traditionally 'voluntarist' character of British industrial relations – the abstention of the state from interfering in the collective bargaining process – was to be preserved intact. Similarly, no legislative restructuring would be permitted of the unions themselves, of their complex and extremely decentralized structures, of their tendency to frequent jurisdictional disputes or of the various sorts of 'custom and practice' through which they sought to control the labor process.[27]

It should not be concluded that the TUC and its constituents believed that their labor market practices and organizational structures were beyond reform. Indeed, there was a certain amount of TUC reflection on the desirability of some change in such realms. We have already noted that the General Council was willing to grant that a degree of union wage moderation might be necessary in a full-employment economy. It also sensed that full employment might necessitate relaxing union 'demarcation practices' to allow greater labor mobility.[28] Moreover, in 1944, the TUC broached, very timidly, the problem of the extreme decentralization of British unionism and the concomitant weakness, in terms of capacity for mobilization and financial resources, of the TUC itself. Perhaps some changes were in order here as well.[29] Likewise, the TUC's membership-base was unduly concentrated, for historic reasons, among blue-collar operatives and weak among women, office workers and in other white-collar occupational groups. This narrowness of coverage was likely to limit trade union effectiveness in the postwar world, particularly in the new public corporations.[30] Some changes in trade union recruitment practices and patterns would be needed, too. Zealously protecting trade union labor market autonomy and the existing system of collective bargaining did not, then, necessarily imply complacency. What is essential to note about the TUC's reflections on the labor movement's inadequacies is, however, that such inadequacies were seen as matters for the labor movement itself to rectify without interference or prodding from outside.

The basic outlines of the TUC's immediate postwar strategic package should by now be clear. The state would acquire vast new powers to coordinate the British economy. The state was to assume as its central economic policy goal the promotion of full employment. The private sector should henceforth be obliged to function within the imperatives of this 'public control' and its actions shaped so as to contribute to the achievement of full employment. An important network of welfare state measures should be enacted as suggested in the Beveridge report – to promote an equitable distribution of income and economic opportunity between different classes and different categories of the population. Unions and workers should acquire significant new roles in economic decision-making processes from the level of the firm upwards. Some form of economic planning was desirable. To produce all of this British unions relied heavily on the Labour Party not only because of the traditional ties between unions and Labour, but also because the Conservatives had been responsible for the disasters of the 1930s. Reliance on Labour and the state was anything but complete, however. While Labour was the chosen political vehicle for trade union reformist goals, the TUC and its constituents simultaneously nursed a deep skepticism that Labour and the state would be able to prevent reversion to the dreaded circumstances of earlier British liberal capitalism. For this reason, and for internal trade union organizational reasons as well, the TUC concluded that whatever else ought to be changed, the collective bargaining system and, more importantly, the autonomy of the unions to pursue their goals in the labor market ought to be preserved.

The package was, moreover, in no way explicitly 'socialist'. Indeed, the TUC's studious avoidance of socialist terminology ('public ownership' rather than 'nationalization', 'public control' rather than 'socialism') indicated both the power of Fabian ideas and considerable internal union resistance to more radical approaches. Despite occasional rhetorical flourishes, the purpose of the proposed reforms was to prevent a return to the 1930s, not to transcend capitalism. The goals were greater social equity and full employment. Basically the TUC wanted what was later to be labeled Keynesianism. The broad structural reforms which it proposed were not ends in themselves, but means to achieve these Keynesian goals. The only seemingly paradoxical element in its package was its zealous insistence that, even if Keynesian goals could only be achieved by some mixture of detailed and comprehensive state supervision of production and distribution, trade union freedom of action in the labor market was to remain unrestrained and unregulated.[31]

The Postwar Settlement

The postwar reformist goals of the TUC were only partially attained. The Labour government of 1945–51, beleaguered by economic problems and by international difficulties, had essentially exhausted its zeal for change by 1948. By that point, however, it had created the broad network of social services to protect the British people from 'cradle to grave' against the more extreme ravages of economic life which came to be labeled the 'welfare state'. It had also brought roughly 20 percent of the country's productive capacity under public ownership, although it had tended to specialize in nationalizing public utilities and unprofitable industrial firms, leaving profitable areas of the private sector untouched.[32] Labour in power had also committed itself to the active management of British economic activity to maintain full employment. High levels of domestic demand were promoted by manipulating government spending, interest rates (the Bank of England had been brought under government control) and tax levels in accordance with Keynesian precepts. Despite this considerable record of accomplishment, however, Labour fell far short of full implementation of the TUC's expressed desires. Unions did not obtain the new voice in economic decision-making advocated in TUC programs. Management prerogatives in the private sector remained what they had been in the prewar period. In nationalized industries very few worker-directors were appointed, despite the early enthusiasm of the Labour government for the idea.[33] In national economic policy-making unions were, indeed, allowed to continue their wartime role as major consultants on important issues: whereas in 1939 TUC representatives sat on only twelve government bodies, by 1947 they were on sixty.[34] But the perpetuation of this role was contingent on ties between the TUC and the Labour Party, and thus on the presence of Labour in government. No official 'corporatist' institutions were established to assure regular union access to national policy-making processes.[35] The creation of 'public control' fell far short of TUC desiderata as well. Control over the accumulation process remained essentially in private hands. Leftover wartime controls were, for the most part, abolished in Harold Wilson's 1948 'bonfire of controls', and they were not replaced by any system of economic planning worthy of the name. By 1950 references to planning and even notions of medium-term economic forecasting had disappeared from the official *Economic Survey* and from the minds of Labour politicians.[36]

Even before the Conservatives returned to power in 1951, then, major structural change had come to an end in Britain. The 'postwar settlement' which resulted involved a 'mixed economy' in which the bulk of industry, key investment decisions and economic power remained in private hands. State economic intervention was strictly confined to the aggregate level. The investment strategies of private industry were not subjected to any planning, even of an indicative variety, once Labour abandoned its rather weak planning attempts in the late 1940s. State policy did play an important role in shaping the framework within which the private sector's search for profit was carried on, however. The welfare system did cushion the British population against the effects of the business cycle, even if the level of benefits was set relatively low. More importantly, the state absorbed a considerable portion of gross domestic product for a variety of purposes (welfare, economic management, defense), thus acquiring considerable leverage for demand management (fully 40 percent of GDP passed through state hands throughout the 1940s and 1950s).[37] Finally, the state's commitment to managing demand in order to promote full employment was sustained.

How did the institutions and patterns of action crystallized in the British postwar settlement actually function? Quite well, or so it seemed to actors at the time. Once it had overcome the serious shortages and bottlenecks of the immediate reconstruction years, the domestic British economy appeared to make an impressive shift into a sustained period of growth and prosperity. From the war's end into the mid-1960s the British economy underwent a period of growth in output, productivity and national income unprecedented in the nation's history. For the overall period 1870–1964, for example, real per capita income in Britain rose by only 1·2 percent per annum, whereas in the years 1950–64 the growth rate was in the order of 2·2 percent annually.[38] The only troublesome feature evident during these years was a comparatively high level of price inflation (4 percent per year during 1946–58).[39] In all this the management of the economy was governed by a consensus on fundamental policy goals among policy-makers in both major parties, the civil service and business elites. In addition to full employment, accepted goals included the preservation of the pound's international role as a reserve currency, the maintenance of its exchange rate at high and stable levels, the protection of Britain's role as a major international finance center, of a large military budget and of great-power pretensions in colonial and diplomatic realms. The only dissent from this consensus in elite circles involved an old complaint that the interests of financial capital were being placed ahead of those of industrial capital.[40]

The Unions in the Postwar Political Economy

Despite the discrepancies between the TUC's postwar reform goals and the actual structures of the postwar settlement, the union movement was, for the most part, quite pleased with the 'mixed economy' created by Labour in 1945–51. Only a small number of 'left-wing' unionists demurred, disappointed at Labour's lack of enthusiasm for economic planning and for further extensions of 'public control'. The unions' satisfaction with the new arrangements was such that even when the 1951 election brought Labour's tenure of power to an end, the TUC declared itself willing to deal in good faith with any government that would respect the basic terms of the postwar settlement – mixed-economy, welfare state, full employment and free collective bargaining. When, as it transpired, the Conservatives did accept the general framework established by postwar changes, British unions turned a decisive corner. In effect, their immediate postwar reformism had one essential goal, as we have noted, the installation of a system of state economic policy which would, through demand management, achieve continuing high levels of employment. The TUC's central postwar concerns were preventing a return to the 1930s, while maintaining complete trade union autonomy in the labor market. The elaborate program of structural changes envisaged by the TUC in the immediate postwar months was primarily a means to these ends. When experience demonstrated that Keynesian demand management could produce relative prosperity and security of employment without requiring extensive structural change, TUC reformism rapidly receded. Basically the TUC wanted Keynesianism and free collective bargaining. And this is what the British postwar settlement provided.

With Keynesianism institutionalized and postwar economic prospects seemingly bright, the British unions settled down to do what they had always considered their most important task at hand, promoting the interests of their membership in the labor market through unfettered collective bargaining. In effect, little or nothing in the British industrial relations system changed as a result of Britain's postwar economic reorientation. Industrial relations were regarded as an area that the state should leave to determination by collective bargaining along the lines of the 'voluntarism' or 'collective laissez-faire' which had traditionally prevailed in Britain.[41] Areas of industrial relations which many other nations submitted to state regulation and legislation – such as minimum wages, maximum hours for male adults, vocational training, and standards of occupational health and safety – were left in postwar Britain, as previously, to negotiations between unions and managers. Bargaining took place, as it had in the prewar period, at a variety of levels in a profoundly decentralized manner. The general peak organizations of labor and business rarely engaged in anything that could be called collective bargaining. The TUC and the three organizations representing various segments of capital – the Federation of British Industries, the British Employers' Confederation and the National Association of British Manufacturers – met occasionally in various tripartite committees organized by the state.[42] Conditions of employment, however, and other matters pertaining to production were negotiated lower down. In many industries bargaining took place between the various unions involved in the sector and the employers' association of the industry. Such bargaining determined only a general framework of wages and employment conditions. Actual wages, differentials, hours, conditions, and so on, were set in negotiations at regional, local, company and even workshop levels. None of the agreements reached at any level carried any legally binding status and could be abrogated at any time by any of the signatories. The result was a system of essentially continuous bargaining of a very informal sort taking place at the local and plant levels, loosely connected to a somewhat more periodic and formalized system of regional and industry bargaining. At all levels collective bargaining was further complicated by the peculiarly British pattern of multiple unionism, resulting from early industrialization and the consolidation of union structures in the period prior to the spread of mass-production techniques. In most plants and industries workers were members not of a single or even of a few unions, but of a large number of unions constituted partly along craft lines but partly according to a complicated array of criteria.[43] This decentralized and complex pattern of industrial relations made for organizations of both business and labor that were quite loosely organized. On the business side there was no unified corporate body before 1965 when the CBI was formed by a merger of the three existing bodies. The three business groups were, furthermore, organizationally weak relative to their component organizations and even the strongest industrial associations wielded little power over their individual members. On the union side a similar condition of decentralization prevailed. The TUC commanded very few resources in terms of finances and staff compared to its affiliated unions, and possessed no real authority over them. The TUC possessed, in fact, no independent existence but was, officially speaking, simply the tool of its affiliates. Decisions of the TUC were not effectively binding on individual unions.[44] Similarly, within each of the TUC's several hundred component unions, the national leadership faced a welter of regional and local organizations each active in bargaining in its own right and enjoying considerable autonomy within the union.[45]

Following patterns set under the 1945–51 Labour governments (the TUC had urged wage restraint before 1948, and then accepted a strict incomes policy in 1948–50 in an attempt to aid the government to cope with the extreme economic difficulties of the immediate postwar years) British unions used their labor market freedom in quite moderate ways into the mid-1950s. Under the Tories up until about 1955 the TUC General Council continued to portray the economy as vulnerable and to justify wage moderation as necessary to its international competitiveness. Even after 1953 when the end of the Korean War and the elimination of the last of the direct controls left over from World War II made it no longer possible to portray the nation's resources as strained by the temporary burdens of rearmament and reconstruction, the General Council continued to describe the economy as endangered by a chronic trade imbalance caused by the inefficiency of British export industries, insufficient levels of industrial investment and excessively high export prices. What was needed was an effort 'at almost any cost' to increase exports by restraining wages and profits in order to keep down prices and channel resources into industrial investment.[46] The General Council clearly attached overriding importance in this period to the maintenance of full employment and was afraid that excessive wage militancy could provoke the Tories into abandoning their full-employment commitment and sacrificing jobs to the balance of payments.[47] Wage restraint was justified by the TUC as a reasonable response to make to the Labour government's request for a union contribution to a 'collective effort' to rescue the economy from a serious balance of payments crisis that developed in the winter of 1947–8. The crisis – the TUC agreed with the official explanation – was the result of the residual effect of the war effort on the nation's resources: the inflationary spiral was caused by the persistent shortages of important commodities and the payments crisis resulted from the country's inability to reconstruct and modernize its productive apparatus rapidly enough to cover its imports to dollar countries with exports as well as from the severe depletion during the war of the country's foreign reserves and assets.[48] In response to this situation the government was correct to choose to devalue the pound and to secure voluntary wage restraint as a way of shifting resources toward exports rather than resorting – as had prewar governments – to deflation and unemployment.[49] Wage restraint was acceptable because it was not being used in isolation, but was rather part of a package of controls including monitoring of prices and profits, and because it was to be 'voluntary', leaving the collective bargaining function of the unions free from legal controls. Moreover, incomes policy could contribute to the long-run recovery of the British economy only if it were combined with a national push, in which the unions would assist, to increase industrial productivity by industrial modernization, increased overtime and the extension of piecework payment systems.[50] In addition to this economic reasoning and increasingly as the 1951 elections approached and the rank-and-file became steadily more disenchanted with wage restraint the TUC leadership invoked the traditional ties of loyalty linking the unions to the Labour Party.[51]

Union labor market moderation stemming from cooperative union attitudes about the vulnerability of the British economy in the postwar period abated somewhat after 1955, however. The problem was that Britain's vulnerability persisted, albeit in more complex forms. Throughout the 1950s and into the 1960s Britain ran a consistent international deficit on trade in manufactured goods: British exports of manufactures failed to expand in volume with the expansion in world trade, while British imports rose steadily.[52] Even the successful performance of the financial and insurance sector in exporting 'invisibles' was never sufficient in this period to close the country's overall trade gap entirely, and the considerable rate of capital investment overseas also contributed to an overall imbalance of considerable dimensions in the country's external long-range account.[53] From time to time the country's trade gap would turn into a major deficit of crisis proportions as occurred in 1947, 1949, 1951, 1955 and again in 1957, crises which were generally accompanied by serious runs on the pound sterling.

As such crises recurred, successive Tory governments developed policy responses that impinged on the domestic economy in ways which posed considerable difficulties for unions. This pattern of policy, involving erratic if generally purposeful demand management, became known as 'stop–go'. In order to secure economic growth and maintain employment governments would 'go' by pursuing expansionary fiscal and monetary policies, especially when elections were in the offing. This 'go' phase would, however, run up against the balance of payments constraint as expansion fueled inflation, declining exports, rising imports and pressure on the pound by the foreign holders of sterling balances. The response chosen repeatedly by the Conservatives in the 1950s and early 1960s (used also by Labour in 1948) was to apply the brakes to the domestic economy in order to save the pound and the balance of payments. Fiscal and monetary levels would be adjusted downwards, with the hope of slowing down the economy and easing the pressure in the labor market (without raising unemployment above tolerable levels). The British economy thus went through cycles of expansion and contraction in which domestic growth was regularly subordinated as an objective of policy-making to the requirements of Britain's international economic activities. The 'stop' phases obviously impinged on the working class by raising unemployment, reducing investment and putting pressure on capitalists not to raise wages. Governments also attempted to exert direct pressure on wage levels through a series of incomes policies, setting ceilings on annual wage settlements. Although both management and labor, as well as most of the dominant industrial relations experts, emphasized the need for a 'free' collective bargaining process, incomes policies of one sort or another were promoted frequently during the period under consideration. Labour turned to a strict incomes policy in 1948–50. Under the Tories incomes policies were applied somewhat half-heartedly in 1956–7 and with considerably greater ardor in 1961–4.[54]

The Emergence of Doubts

In response to recurrent 'stop–go' policies after 1956, and for a period of five years or so thereafter, TUC willingness to make labor market allowances for British international vulnerability was considerably attenuated. Just when the balance of payments crises of 1955 and 1957, together with Tory 'stop–go' policies, was beginning to generate a certain alarm among economists and business elites, the TUC abandoned its resistance to rank-and-file wage militancy. In the realm of economic reflection, too, the TUC shifted its ground. Earlier, largely because of situational postwar factors attendant upon the difficulties of restarting the British economy and the strains surrounding the Korean War, trade union cooperation in the labor market to help the nation through temporary troubled times had seemed advisable. After the mid-1950s, however, the extent of Britain's economic problem, although not denied, was downplayed by the TUC. Neither inflation nor balance of payments difficulties was seen as serious enough to warrant letting unemployment rise as high as the Tories were willing to allow. Moreover, both sets of difficulties owed more to Tory deflationary policies than they did to deeper structural questions. Although the TUC General Council admitted that there did exist a danger of 'overheating', it saw the solution to Britain's difficulties as lying not in deflation and certainly not in wage restraint, but rather in expansionary demand management.[55] Clearly, once the Tories decided to let unemployment rise as they did in 1956, the TUC had lost its incentive to counsel wage moderation and began to adjust its descriptions of the British economic problem accordingly.

At about the same moment in time, however, analysts of all kinds – economists, journalists and politicians in both parties – had begun to speculate that more profound structural problems might indeed lie beneath the pattern of recurrent international payments crises, stop–go economic policies and erratic growth rates. The unending debate about the 'British disease' which continues to the present was, in fact, beginning.[56] The prosperity of the postwar period began to look more problematic than it had earlier. Britain's postwar growth record was, to be sure, impressive when compared to earlier British figures but decidedly less so when set next to similar figures for Britain's major competitors. While Britain had been enjoying a sedate economic recovery and expansion, the economies of Germany, Italy, France and Japan had been experiencing a 'boom' of extraordinary dimensions. In 1950–64, while the British national income grew at an annual rate of 2·6 percent, the economies of the USA, France, Italy and West Germany were expanding at rates of 3·5, 4·9, 5·6 and 7·1 percent, respectively. [57] British productivity also grew at a rate much lower than that of other major industrial nations. During 1950–60, for example, output per man grew by only 1·9 percent a year, while in the USA the figure was 2·1 percent, in France 4·0 percent, in Italy 4·1 percent and in West Germany 5·3 percent.[58] Although a number of factors (including the defensive shopfloor control over changes in work organization and technology exercised by groups of organized, skilled workers) obviously contributed to Britain's relatively slow growth during this period, one important factor was clear: Britain's unusually low rate of industrial investment. In 1950–62 the rate of investment in fixed capital by industry was, as a percentage of GNP, lower in Britain than in any other major industrial country except the USA. As a result, the ratio of capital stock to persons employed in Britain, which was low in Britain to begin with, remained so.[59] British capitalists were clearly being very cautious during this period about investing in domestic industry, whereas the rate of capital flows for investment overseas was extremely high.[60] Somewhere in the structural realities lying beneath these statistics could be found the reasons for Britain's international vulnerability.

By the early 1960s voices would be heard attributing the country's economic difficulties to the structure of the postwar settlement and urging major changes in its provisions. Economists such as A. W. Phillips and F. W. Paish[61] offered econometric data to support their contentions that the country's high inflation rate was the result of an excessive level of employment and suggested that a step be taken away from the 1944 commitment to full employment in order to restore British competitiveness and growth. Others focussed their attacks on the industrial relations component to the postwar settlement and on the unions. Industrial relations experts such as Ben Roberts and Alan Flanders, sociologists such as Michael Shanks and political groups such as the Inns of Court Conservative and Unionist Society, all agreed that full employment and Britain's system of decentralized collective bargaining gave the unions excessive power to bid up wages and to block changes in production methods thus retarding growth and discouraging investment.[62] If Britain were to attain faster growth, a major overhaul of her industrial relations system and a considerable reduction of union power were required. Such theoretical reflection was echoed, and powerfully amplified, in the day-to-day rhetoric of Conservative politicians and much of the British press. British unions, given their vocal commitment to unfettered freedom of action in the labor market, and in particular, given their open refusal in the late 1950s to accept more alarmist interpretations of the 'British disease', became choice targets in the search for its causes by conservative elements in British society.

There was more than a degree of irony in all of this. The bargaining power of organized British workers had always been comparatively high because of a variety of factors: the decentralized character of British collective bargaining; the inability of British management (because of a lack of technical expertise) or its unwillingness (because of access to 'soft' product markets in the empire) to challenge the veto power exercised by groups of skilled workers; the high density of union membership; and the exceptional organizational presence of the unions in the workplace. During the postwar settlement this bargaining power was augmented by two developments. The first was the relative tightness of labor markets that resulted from policies of full employment. The second was the wave of unionization that in wartime and the immediate postwar era brought the unions by 1948 to a peak of some 9·4 million members or 45·2 percent of the laborforce, a density that was the highest of any labor movement in the major capitalist nations.[63] Union coverage was not, to be sure, evenly distributed throughout the laborforce. Certain types of workers were especially well organized; in such industries as coalmining, cotton textiles, railroads, other forms of transport and national government agencies the unionization rate was over 70 percent, while other industries (such as the distributive trades, fishing, and the finance and insurance sector) lacking long traditions of union activity had especially lower scores.[64] Men were much better organized than women, only 25·7 percent of female workers being union members as compared to 52·9 percent of male workers.[65] Similarly, white-collar workers throughout this period proved much less susceptible to union influence than manual workers.[66] In general, however, unionization was widespread throughout the laborforce and the union movement with its 9 million workers constituted a force to be reckoned with in most sectors throughout the economy. This newly enhanced bargaining power was, we must note, a power exercised not so much by the national category unions as by local union officials and by shop stewards on the shopfloor, who were often not formally connected to the unions at all. Neither the TUC nor the category unions could count on being able to mobilize such industrial power on their own initiative or for their own purposes, be they economic or political.

The irony lay in the fact that this bargaining power, although highly visible and regularly amplified in the British media, was, in fact, employed in rather restrained fashion during the postwar settlement years. Strikes occurred at what by comparative standards was only a medium level of frequency and intensity. Industrial conflict was endemic but not severe, highly diffuse and with a tendency toward an increasing decentralization beginning in the mid-1950s. Workers' demands were generally moderate in both extent and nature, being largely confined to traditional issues of salaries and working conditions.[67] The outcome was regular increases in nominal wages punctuated by periods of containment under the incomes policies that operated in 1948–50, 1956–7 and 1961–3. During 1948–63 gross weekly earnings rose by a total of 26·07 percent. Real earnings, however, rose only 22 percent, and indeed by only 7·23 percent if the effect of increased taxation is taken into account.[68] While they were able to secure long-term gains in nominal and real wages, the unions were less successful in using collective bargaining to increase the size of the wage share of national income during the 1945–64 period. After having jumped from 61·9 percent of national income in 1939 to 68·8 percent in 1944 and again to 72·2 percent in 1945, the share of wages grew only very slowly to 73·0 percent in 1959.[69]

What had begun to happen by the late 1950s was that British unions were becoming increasingly mired in one of the central internal contradictions of their postwar strategic package. The TUC had eagerly accepted the British postwar settlement's twin offerings, Keynesianism and welfare benefits in state economic policies, plus unfettered trade union autonomy in the labor market. Unfortunately for the TUC and British unions, effective Keynesianism and free collective bargaining could coexist only within a successful British economy, capable of producing structurally sound and regular economic growth. Despite a spate of somewhat misleading prosperity, however, the British economy was not structurally sound. Given Britain's international openness, relatively low levels of growth of a kind which in themselves led to international vulnerability created a situation in which the free collective bargaining which was British unionism's most cherished possession led to wage drift and inflation. Wage drift and inflation, in turn, led to increased international vulnerability. Conservative 'stop–go' programs in the 1950s and early 1960s were the policy responses to this. Despite the fact that the comparative structural unsoundness of the British economy was the underlying cause of difficulty, in the shorter run it was not at all implausible for politicians, analysts and the media to blame trade union selfishness in the labor market for the economy's endemic problems, even if the unions were, according to most indices, behaving with considerable moderation. The TUC was caught with limited options. It could attempt to rein in its troops in the labor market and induce them to restrain themselves further, even if this would be a very difficult task given the decentralization of power in the movement. It could begin to develop new reformist economic analyses and strategies directed toward making British economic structures more dynamic so that the combination of governmental Keynesianism and trade union labor market autonomy would become more workable. And it could try to bring the Labour Party back to power in the hope that a Labour government might be more effective economically than the Tories and less prone to scapegoating the unions for British economic problems in its rhetoric and policy orientations.

In the wake of the 1959 general election, the third consecutive polling won by the Tories, the TUC turned toward a posture which combined all three of these options. Persisting economic difficulties in the early 1960s made a return of Labour to power quite conceivable. The TUC, therefore, devoted a great deal of effort to making this return possible, banking on the hope that Tory economic policies and anti-unionism might bring an important number of working-class voters who had strayed into the Tory electoral camp back home. At the same time public criticism of the union movement grew so intense that the TUC General Council (under pressure as well from the large general unions complaining of stagnating, in some cases even declining, memberships) agreed to launch a study of union organizational structures, to be carried out along lines similar to those of an earlier study in 1943. After investigating a series of major issues – the feasibility of industrial unionism, the desirability of union mergers and the problem of demarcation disputes – all of which pointed toward the need for greater union centralization, the Council concluded that no drastic restructuring of the union movement was practicable. None the less, a series of recommendations for minor changes in individual unions and at workplace level was made.[70] Here the important thing was not the result of the study – the TUC clearly shied away from advocating any major changes – but the fact that the TUC was willing to recognize publicly that all was not as it might be in the house of organized labor.

Finally, by the early 1960s the context of economic discourse between Britain's major political parties had changed in ways which obliged the TUC to rethink its own economic perspectives. Both major parties had come to share certain general concerns about the state of the national economy which involved definite steps away from Keynesian optimism. Neither party went so far as to propose any major alterations in the terms of the postwar settlement. Both were content to suggest minor revisions and along remarkably similar lines. In both cases what was proposed was a combination of concerted indicative planning to accelerate economic growth and modernization, and a voluntary incomes policy to reduce inflation and protect the balance of payments in order to eliminate the need for the 'stop–go' cycle. In the case of the Conservatives the new program – the establishment of the tripartite National Economic Development Council (Neddy) to plan the national economy, industry-level development councils ('little Neddies') to help modernize individual sectors and the proposal of a variety of tradeoffs to the unions in return for participating in the planning venture and agreeing to discuss voluntary wage restraint – involved a fundamental shift in orientation away from the party's previous liberal orthodoxy.[71] For Labour, on the other hand, its version of indicative planning ('the National Plan') amounted to a return to the ideas of 1945, newly decked out in the technocratic language of Harold Wilson's 'white-hot heat of the scientific revolution', while its proposal to the TUC in 1963 of a party–union agreement on economic strategy involved an attempt to use the 'special relation' with the unions as a stepping-stone to power after a decade in opposition.

In this new context the TUC retreated from its late 1950s view that the basis of British economic difficulties was Tory and that which it had held in the earlier 1950s when it had recognized that real structural problems underlay British problems. In the new perspective the British economy was, indeed, in serious trouble: industrial inefficiency, insufficient investment and excessive foreign commitments had combined to produce a pattern of slow growth ('sluggishness') that had been aggravated by the short-sighted stop–go policies of Tory governments. Wage restraint could help ease the burden on the balance of payments and reduce inflation but only in conjunction with a serious program of economic planning to regenerate British industry.[72]

The Conservative initiative provoked considerable debate within the TUC leadership. Many members of the General Council were skeptical about the Tories' intentions and eager to reaffirm the unions' traditional insistence on the need for a Labour government. The prevailing position, however, was that advocated by General Secretary George Woodcock, who was eager to demonstrate the TUC's willingness to work with any government toward the national interest. Thus, the General Council agreed to participate in the activities of the NEDC, while letting it be understood that genuine economic planning of the sort required if the TUC were to accept voluntary wage restraint was conceivable only under a future Labour government.[73]

The Postwar Package Revised, Challenged and Reconsidered

The Strategy as of 1964

As the 1964 elections approached, the TUC attempted to refurbish its postwar strategic package in several ways to take into account the problems that had plagued its efforts in the previous period: inflation and stop–go, slow growth, and the rising chorus of anti-union voices in the media and the political arena. The revisions of the strategy were not, as we shall see, sufficient to eliminate the contradictions built into the TUC's situation; indeed, these contradictions became even more severe.

During the period prior to and immediately following the 1964 election the TUC adapted its economic strategy in a number of ways. With the prospect of a friendly party in power, the unions could place greater emphasis on the political side of their strategy. The state would be called on to intervene in the economy in order to restructure it in such a way as to eliminate the phenomenon of stop–go with its deleterious effects on employment levels and working-class welfare. The state under a Labour government would use the instruments of tripartite economic planning created by the Tories in a newly aggressive manner to modernize Britain's manufacturing base by the application of a 'National Plan' for rapid growth.[74] The latest advances of the 'scientific and technical revolution' would be applied to make British industry once again internationally competitive and the unions would cooperate fully with this venture in industrial policy, although neither they nor Harold Wilson's Labour Party appeared to have any clear idea of what was to be involved in such an operation.[75] The unions were convinced, however, that their cooperation in the National Plan would bring them a number of benefits: a greatly expanded access to the corridors of power, increased national prestige and, as a result, an influx of new members. The state, meanwhile, would also be called upon to support working-class incomes by increasing the levels of transfer payments and by improving public services in general.[76]

While the revised strategy placed a new emphasis on the state, action in the labor market remained, as before, the primary method by which the unions hoped to defend the interests of their members. The unions would continue to insist on rejecting any statutory incomes policy in order to retain their ultimate autonomy in collective bargaining and on preserving their freedom from legislative attempts to alter the industrial relations system or the structures of the unions themselves. However, the unions now prepared to make a number of concessions. In order to cooperate with the efforts of the state to eliminate the stop–go syndrome the unions declared themselves willing to accept an incomes policy, provided it was non-statutory, supervised by the unions themselves and linked to a system of price controls. In early 1965 this commitment by the unions was converted into a reality by the signing of a 'Joint declaration of intent on prices and incomes' by the TUC, the CBI and the Minister of Economic Affairs, George Brown.[77] The TUC's leaders also agreed to accept the creation of a Royal Commission to examine the whole issue of industrial relations and union structures, their hope being that the existence of the commission would defuse some of the worst anti-union sentiment, especially within the Labour Party itself and perhaps even facilitate a certain centralization of authority within the TUC at the expense of the shop stewards' movement.[78]

Just as the Donovan Commission, as it came to be called, would reduce the pressure of public opinion on the unions, so it was hoped that the combination of mild wage restraint and industrial planning and modernization would go a long way toward eliminating the balance of payments constraint on British economic growth and allow the unions, after a certain delay, to resume wielding their bargaining power in the market.

The Strategy Fails

For such a strategy to work as far as TUC leaders were concerned, it was necessary, above all, that economic growth continue at a reasonable pace so that the degree of wage restraint required would not exceed their limited capacity to discipline their troops and so that the struggle for income shares and the resulting inflation would not become so severe as to bring the unions to the foreground of public attention – as chief villains in the drama of British economic difficulties. In fact, precisely the opposite occurred. The principal difficulty was that the economy, and in particular the balance of payments, proved much more intractable than Harold Wilson and the TUC had anticipated. The unprecedentedly large payments deficit that the Labour government inherited from the Tories did not vanish, but grew rapidly into the most severe exchange crisis in recent British history, as foreign holders of sterling displayed little faith in the pound or in the viability of the new government's economic programs.[79]

Having rejected out of hand any resort to devaluation to stave off the growing crisis and having eschewed the more drastic and untried route of restrictions on imports, controls on movements of capital and direct state intervention to modernize industrial plant, the government was left with only one approach – fiscal and monetary deflation accompanied by increasingly rigorous pressure on incomes.[80] It was this policy choice – however reluctantly made – that quashed any hopes that the TUC's strategy might prove successful. The deflationary path chosen by Wilson, Callaghan and Brown was utterly incompatible with the 5 percent growth target and the investment schemes that were central to the National Plan. Indeed, the very first dose of deflation administered in July 1965, involving as it did the postponement of a large number of public and private investment projects, set the National Plan (officially announced just two months later) off its tracks from the very start.[81] But what really vitiated the unions' strategy was the implication of the government's crisis-management approach for wages. By choosing deflation instead of devaluation the government obliged itself to restrict the growth of incomes much more severely than it or the unions had originally thought necessary. In July 1966 the Cabinet moved to reduce the acceptable limit for wage increases from the original 5 percent accepted by the TUC in February to zero.[82] Neither this wage freeze nor the stringent limits on bargaining that succeeded it were at all to the liking of the unions. Left-wing union leaders such as Frank Cousins, who had only reluctantly accepted even a voluntary incomes policy, found the new statutory approach entirely unacceptable and offered the government no assistance in its application. For the more moderate TUC leaders, however, the situation was extremely complicated. On the one hand, they felt a strong impulsion to help the government through a difficult situation: they agreed that the crisis was serious and accepted the need for wage restraint as part of the solution. Even the July 1966 wage freeze with its statutory penalties and concomitant deflation was endorsed by a large majority of the General Council after they had failed to persuade the government to adopt less severe measures.[83] On the other hand, TUC moderates were aware that blocked wages, especially when accompanied by rising unemployment, would after a brief period of grace begin to generate disaffection among their own shop stewards and members. The fragmented character of the union movement and the decentralization of bargaining activities meant that their militancy would be extremely difficult for the TUC leadership to control. Thus, as the rank-and-file in many unions became increasingly militant in 1967-8, and as inflation remained high, TUC moderates found themselves assailed from two directions for developments over which they had relatively little control. The government and the media blamed them for the persistence of wage drift and the rising strike rates, while local union officials and militants criticized them for supporting the government's incomes policies. The only response available to the General Council was to press the government for more favorable demand management and less stringent restrictions on wages, while attempting to discourage unofficial strikes. At the same time, they had to avoid completely demobilizing the plant-level activism and organizational life that, they knew, constituted the ultimate basis of their own influence within the Labor movement and within the political economy as a whole.

The ensuing three-year-long controversy within the TUC and between the TUC and the Labour government over economic policy not only undermined the unions' attempt to remain out of the public limelight, but also weakened their faith in the utility of the Labour Party as an element in union strategy. The party's decision to abandon its incomes policy in 1968 did not, moreover, bring about any reconciliation between the two wings of the movement. For what replaced statutory incomes policy in the Wilson government's plan for keeping union wage push within manageable limits was an attempt to undermine union market power by means of a legislative restructuring of the industrial relations system.

Many Labour ministers had hoped that the Donovan Commission

would recommend changes in the industrial relations laws which would help reduce the incidence of 'unofficial' strikes and give the central union leaderships greater control over the activities on the shopfloor of the local work groups.[84] In fact, when it finally issued its report in June 1968, the Commission agreed with much of the conventional wisdom about excess shopfloor power as the cause of wage drift and low productivity growth, but it avoided recommending any legislative intervention. The majority of the Commission's members agreed that such corrective measures as were appropriate should reflect the 'voluntaristic' character of British industrial relations.[85] Spurred by the rising tide of rank-and-file militancy developing in 1968 and eager to find a new means of damping union power now that its incomes policy had proved untenable the government, none the less, decided to proceed with legislative intervention. In 1969 the government introduced a White Paper, entitled, *In Place of Strife*.[86] The Bill proposed – alongside a number of concessions to the unions on organizing rights – several important restrictions on union activity. A Commission on Industrial Relations would be established as suggested by Donovan to adjudicate recognition disputes and grievances with the aim of heading off strikes. Unions would be required to register with the CIR in order to qualify for various privileges. The government would, furthermore, be empowered to intervene as it saw fit to resolve strikes in three ways: by imposing settlements in union recognition disputes which the CIR had been unable to resolve; by imposing an American-style 'conciliation pause' of twenty-eight days in 'unconstitutional strikes'; and by calling for strike ballots in any strike deemed to be contrary to the public interest. Union members or officials violating these new procedures would be subject to fines deductible, if necessary, from their wages.[87]

The TUC, as we have noted, had initially hoped that the Donovan Commission might serve as a vehicle for rationalizing the union movement's admittedly archaic and anarchic structures and for increasing the TUC's own influence over local militants and officials. Once the Commission had reported, the TUC hierarchy undertook a wide campaign to popularize its findings within the unions and to organize the implementation of some of its less controversial recommendations.[88] When, however, the government opted for the legislative approach to industrial relations reform, the TUC, after some hesitation, mobilized its considerable lobbying resources in the Cabinet and the Parliamentary Labour Party to secure the defeat of the White Paper.[89]

The TUC Reconsiders

The TUC's difficulties under the Wilson government in terms of incomes policy, deflationary demand management and, above all, industrial relations legislation appear to have prompted them to begin reexamining their strategy and economic analysis. The extremely conflictual nature of union–party relations under the Wilson government and, in particular, what was seen as the betrayal on industrial relations legislation by a Prime Minister with Bevanite credentials and a minister long-affiliated with the left of the party seem to have raised the specter of Ramsay MacDonald for many union leaders and to have persuaded them to reconsider the efficacy of the Labour Party connection as a weapon in the TUC's arsenal.

The struggle against *In Place of Strife* seems to have marked a decisive shift in the way TUC leaders conceived their relationship with the Labour government and their role within the decision-making bodies of the party as well. Prior to the late 1960s, the unions seem to have been content to play a generally passive role within the party's apparatus – Conference, National Executive Committee and special committees – contenting themselves with supporting the moderate party leadership against the extravagances of the Bevanite (later 'Tribune') left wing and confining their active interventions to issues traditionally acknowledged as union prerogatives.[90] It was only when the unions feared that positions would be taken that could reduce the value of the party as a vehicle for the defense of workers' rights that they intervened forcefully in party activities. Such, of course, was what had occurred in the 1950s when the Gaitskellites had sought to drop the commitment to 'common ownership' in clause IV of the party program. The protracted battles over incomes policy and especially over industrial relations legislation appear to have convinced the TUC's leaders – some of the recently elected left-wingers such as Jack Jones of the TGWU and Hugh Scanlon of the Engineers needed little convincing – that the 'political wing' would not, when in office, necessarily and consistently support the interests of the 'industrial wing' unless the unions insisted on playing a permanently active role in the decision-making bodies of the party.[91]

The TUC's irritation with the government over its economic policies and its industrial relations legislation did not only express itself in a newly aggressive approach by the unions to party politics. A further result, and one that is of great interest to those studying the evolution of TUC economic thinking, was a marked reorientation of both the form and content of TUC economic analysis and strategy.

The change in *form* was quite straightforward. Prior to 1968, the TUC published relatively few documents on matters of economic policy. Each year's report by the General Council to Congress would contain a chapter on 'Economic organization' that would include a description of the General Council's dealings with the government along with reprints of or extracts from the various (generally quite brief) statements issued during the year by the General Council in anticipation of, or reaction to, the government's actions. The TUC's recommendations to the Chancellor of the Exchequer concerning the annual budget generally consisted of a few pages and dealt not with broad issues of economic policy and development, but with the details of tax proposals and demand management. Only occasionally would the General Council produce longer economic documents such as the 1944 Interim Report on Reconstruction, the 1950 Report on Public Ownership or the 'Appendix' to the 1959 report, *The Economic Situation*. In the mid-1960s there was an intensification of TUC publishing activity: in 1965 and again in 1967 reports were issued containing the proceedings of so-called Conferences of Executives convened to approve the General Council's positions on the government's latest incomes policy initiatives.[92] The year 1968, however, marks a significant departure. In January the TUC issued the first of what was to become an annual publication: an *Economic Review* in which the General Council (its economic staff in actual fact) presented its views on the state of the economy, its comments on past government policies and its recommendations for the upcoming budget as well as for longer-term economic and social policy. The document ran to ninety-two pages (this would be a typical length over the next decade) and constituted the first public effort by the TUC at elaborate, sustained economic analysis.[93]

This change in the form of the TUC's economic thinking was accompanied by changes in *content* as well, changes which occurred in two distinct stages. The first shift is discernible in the *Economic Review* for 1968 through 1970 and marks off the union's economic analysis and strategy in these years from those of the preceding period. There was, to begin with, a greater interest than before in the problem of Britain's long-term economic decline and a greater awareness of the character of the stop–go cycle which had plagued the country's attempts at rapid expansion and modernization.[94] A 'vicious cycle' of 'low productivity, low growth and balance of payments difficulties' was described by the TUC and attributed to the tendency for any period of extended expansion of disposable income to draw in a disproportionate amount of manufactured imports.[95] No elaborate explanation of the phenomenon was offered in any *Economic Review* during this period, but a number of findings by the National Economic Development Office were noted that constituted departures from previous TUC positions. Excessive rises in wages were still, as in the mid-1960s, regarded as a cause of Britain's trading problems, and the use of income policies (voluntary and TUC-supervised rather than statutory, of course) was still recommended.[96] For the first time, however, the TUC pointed to factors other than costs – product quality, technical performance, marketing, and the 'structure and scale of industry' as important explanations of Britain's poor trading performance in manufactured goods.[97] In keeping with its efforts to respond voluntarily to some of the Donovan recommendations, and thus head off legislative reform of industrial relations, the General Council admitted, as it had in its submissions to the Commission, that union practices and structures played a part in contributing to the problem of British manufacturing but they also alluded – for the first time to our knowledge – to the defects of British management, to what they suggestively labeled a 'management gap'.[98] In equally elliptical fashion the *Economic Review* for 1968 and 1969 noted in passing the harmful predominance of banking over industry in the economy but without fleshing out the details of the claim or its economic consequences.[99] At this point, and in fact until as late as 1975, the TUC did not attempt any detailed explanation of the real causes of the British 'vicious cycle'.

More interesting than the TUC's economic diagnosis were its policy recommendations. For it is here that the *Economic Review* for 1968 through 1970 marked a distinct (if, as we shall see, comparatively limited) departure from the 1950s and 1960s. The principal departures were the TUC's new attention to the problem of investment and its interest in extending the planning mechanism and the involvement of the unions into the investment activities of the largest UK firms.

Proceeding from the contention that something was wrong with the structure of British manufacturing, as well as from its finding that regional inequalities had grown worse during the 1960s, the *Economic Review* for 1968 and 1969 suggested that British investment, while adequate in global quantity, might be inappropriate in 'direction' or 'orientation'.[100] As a remedy, the TUC suggested, very tentatively, that Britain's very largest companies be required to communicate their investment plans on a three-to-five-year basis to the economic planning authorities and to include manpower projections in these reports. In addition, the 1968 Report suggested the possibility of special corporate investment funds (their source and function remained unspecified), containing an 'element of public and workers' rights'.[101] There was nothing especially audacious about most of these proposals. The formulation was hypothetical and timid and the content often not very innovative. The notion of including manpower estimates in company planning reports was no more than a pale version of the 'manpower planning' advocated by the TUC back in the 1940s. The planning envisaged by the *Economic Review* of 1968 through 1970 remained, moreover, of a purely indicative kind. Nor was there any demand for a departure from the predominantly private ownership pattern of the mixed economy. The state was to give increased aid for modernization to private industry, rather than (as the TUC had advocated as late as 1950, and the trade union and Labour Party left had always demanded) extending public ownership and control.[102] What was novel, however, and what would be built upon in coming years, was the notion that government aid to industry and government incentives to employment and investment should be 'selective' in their applications and contingent upon a company's willingness to participate in the planning operation.[103]

Thus far, the TUC had reexamined only partially its postwar strategic package as revised in the early 1960s. It was the experience of the Heath government that induced them to move further in this rethinking. The essential lesson of the Heath years, for TUC leaders, was that a Labour government, no matter how misguided or even perfidious, was clearly preferable to a government led by Tories. Not only did the Heath government, like its Labour predecessor, blame the woes of the feeble British economy on the unions, and attempt to impose its costs on them by means of a statutory incomes policy even more restrictive and punitive than George Brown's; it also sought to restructure the industrial relations system by legislation (the Industrial Relations Act of 1971) much more severe and more threatening for union market autonomy than Barbara Castle's proposals.[104] Worse still, it delighted in jettisoning some of the basic foundations of the postwar settlement on which the security and incomes of workers had long depended, scaling down the provision of services by the welfare state, and explicitly abandoning the state's commitment to full employment and support both for the nationalized industries and for ailing private firms as well.[105]

From all this the unions drew an obvious conclusion. They should do everything they could to secure the return of Labour to power: the lukewarm electoral effort made by the union 'machine' in 1970 was not to be repeated. On the other hand, no future Labour government should ever be given the free hand in policy-making that the unions had granted to the two Wilson governments of the 1960s. Under a future Labour government the unions would have to maintain the greatest possible freedom of action in the use of their own industrial and organizational resources. In addition, the Labour Party would have to commit itself to repeal all Conservative legislation restricting wage bargaining and undermining union market power. The party must further pledge itself not to institute any restrictive industrial relations legislation of its own and promise, moreover, to pass legislation augmenting union power on the shopfloor. Such a commitment was relatively easy to secure from the Labour Party. The 1970 defeat had initiated a process of strategic and ideological rethinking within party circles and, in particular, within the National Executive Committee and the Labour Party's Research Department.[106] Here the influence of left-wing union leaders such as Hugh Scanlon and Jack Jones coincided with that of a group of left-wing party militants and intellectuals to secure acceptance of the view that Labour had lost the election and wasted the opportunities of the Wilson years because it had come into conflict with its natural allies, the unions, allies who, moreover, were increasingly displaying their indispensable role as the only organized force willing and able to stand up to the Tory assault on the welfare state. It was on the basis of this growing consensus that a Liaison Committee linking the TUC and the NEC was formed, and the agreements were hammered out – beginning with a set of party pledges on industrial relations legislation – that led to the establishment of the 'Social Contract', a program for a future Labour government endorsed by both the party and the unions and first consecrated in February 1973, in a document, entitled, *Economic Policy and the Cost of Living*.[107]

From the point of view of many trade union leaders, it was not enough to secure a Labour Party commitment on labor market legislation. It was also necessary to ensure that no future Labour government would, when faced with economic difficulties, choose a deflationary strategy based on incomes policy and budget cuts, thus sacrificing the unions and their members to the requirements of economic and political crisis management. TUC leaders, therefore, wanted to have built into the party platform and the Social Contract, commitments for increased welfare spending and tax reforms and, above all, a repudiation of statutory incomes policy. Both the Liaison Committee's 1973 document and subsequent formulations of the Social Contract contained elaborate promises to avoid legislative incomes policies and to use state expenditure and fiscal policies to restore full employment and generate a 'large scale redistribution of income and wealth'.[108] According to the 1973 agreement, inflation was to be prevented by a 'wide-ranging and permanent system of price controls', while the various reforms proposed in the document would generate a 'strong feeling of mutual confidence' between unions and government, altering the 'whole climate of collective bargaining' in such a way as to moderate wage demands without any need for formal incomes policy.

Some TUC leaders also wanted another set of policy commitments built into the Social Contract – a set of programs for the restructuring of British industry through state interaction and union participation in the planning and implementation of investment decisions. The TUC *Economic Review* for 1972 and 1973 contained demands for a considerable expansion of economic planning and direct economic action by the state. The capital market had, the TUC suggested, proved itself an inappropriate mechanism for the allocation of investment and would have to be supplemented by deliberate state planning and allocation to control the 'composition' of Britain's growth with an eye to a more even regional distribution of industry and a faster overall rate of growth.[109] What was required was a new Public Investment Agency both to channel public funds into private industry (in return for equity or loan capital in the firm concerned) and to create new public enterprises, especially in poor regions.[110]

On these points, the TUC was drawing on the findings of a series of policy groups established within the Labour Party in the wake of the 1970 defeat. Under the aegis of the Home Committee of the party's left-dominated National Executive Committee, two subcommittees (one on industrial policy and the other on the public sector) worked through the early years of Conservative rule to refurbish Labour's economic and social programs and to shift them substantially leftward.[111] The TUC and the left of the party now agreed that public ownership should be extended by the nationalization of industries such as shipbuilding, aircraft construction and pharmaceuticals which has survived only by 'continuous subvention from the public sector'.[112] Moreover, the investment behavior of the country's largest firms would have to be brought under state supervision through as-yet-unspecified planning mechanisms. Public investment should be greatly increased and used both as a countercyclical mover and to alleviate regional disparities.

The role of the unions in economic decision-making would, simultaneously, be vastly expanded. The unions would participate in the planning venture at all levels. In the individual firm 'industrial democracy' would be established, giving union delegates not only access to more information on company intentions and activities, but also seats on corporate boards.[113]

Where could the resources for this new investment both public and private come from, and how would rapid growth be possible without a severe aggravation of Britain's already-high inflation? There was considerable disagreement within the TUC on this issue. Moderate unions – such as the General and Municipal Workers and the National Union of Railwaymen – and the majority of the General Council saw, as in 1964, the need for wage restraint by means of a voluntary incomes policy in order to divert necessary resources from consumption to investment and export. The cooperation of the unions in such an incomes policy as well as in the industrial relocations and work reorganization required to modernize Britain's industrial sector could, according to this majority position, be secured once the hated Industrial Relations Act had been repealed by the incoming Labour government.[114] On the other hand, the left unions – the

Transport and General Workers, the Engineers (AUEW), and the white-collar workers of ASTMS and TASS – denied that an incomes policy was necessary or desirable and argued, rather, that reflationary government policies could generate sufficient resources not only for rising real wages, but also for the required surge of investment.[115]

The Social Contract between Labour's Shadow Cabinet and the TUC thus came to include party commitments not only on demand management, welfare spending and industrial relations legislation, but also on economic planning and industrial policy. It was the latter that constituted the most striking innovation in TUC strategy, though, of course, the very *idea* of a contract binding Labour in advance represented a considerable novelty as well. The status of the planning and intervention schemes within the overall Social Contract package was, however, not very high. Although the party's left-dominated National Executive Committee endorsed the nationalization and intervention schemes, many of the moderates who would control the key posts in a future government – James Callaghan, Denis Healey, Harold Lever and Anthony Crosland – regarded these proposals with suspicion as unrealistic products of Tony Benn's ideological enthusiasm liable to alienate voters and frighten investors. Many TUC moderates were inclined to agree with this assessment. Those who endorsed the NEB planning and intervention proposals did so, we suggest, for essentially tactical reasons, seeing in them a handy form of political cement for solidifying a pro-union coalition within the party, since it was the partisans of these proposals on the left wing who were traditionally the strongest opponents of a statutory incomes policy and the firmest defenders of union rights.[116]

Even among those union leaders, moreover, who were strongly committed to the planning and nationalization aspect of the Social Contract, few were prepared to assign it very high priority on their list of demands for tradeoffs by a future Labour government. Industrial relations legislation came first for almost everyone at the TUC. The restoration of full employment and of workers' living standards came next, particularly since these appeared to be increasingly endangered by the poor performance of the economy under the Tories. While other industrial nations were enjoying a period of impressive if inflationary expansion, the British economy was confronting yet another round of trade deficits, inflation and currency instability accompanied by unprecedented levels of unemployment.[117] These developments prompted a growing concern in the TUC's *Economic Review* for 1972 and 1973 about the state of the British economy.

The nation's long-run relative decline was seen by the TUC's economists as the result of a failure of the structure of British industry to adjust to the changing patterns of world demand. Britain's slow growth, aggravated by deflationary policies, was seen as the cause of an unprecedented level of unemployment of almost 1,000,000 coexisting, moreover, with a persistently high inflation rate, a combination of symptoms whose novelty was duly noted by the TUC.[118] It was as a remedy for these failures that the *Economic Review* called for structural reforms involving planning and state intervention. Yet many of the TUC leaders and the Labour Party officials most favorable to these schemes continued to see them less as urgent measures of *economic* policy required to begin the badly needed modernization of British industry than as steps in a long-range *political* strategy designed to push Britain along the path toward socialism by resuming the reformist endeavor abandoned in the late 1940s.

The TUC's program in 1973–4 and the Social Contract documents in which it was embodied constituted a notable, if limited, departure from its previous strategic package. To the traditional combination of union organizational and market autonomy plus welfare state spending plus Keynesian demand management was added a new element – a demand for increased state and union control over microeconomic decision-making. This new package represented an attempt by the TUC and its party allies to develop a strategy that would prevent the next Labour government from being as disappointing an experience for the unions as the last. The coalminers' strike and the decision of Prime Minister Heath to call an election on the issue of union power gave the Labour Party and the unions the opportunity to try out their new strategy with, as we shall see, less than entirely satisfying results.

Part 4

The Crisis Years

The TUC's program of 1972–3, and the Social Contract which incorporated it, constituted an attempt by the union leadership to transcend some of the contradictions of earlier TUC strategic packages and, in particular, to prevent a recurrence of the kind of party–union battles that had plagued the first and second Wilson governments. Expansionary demand management aimed at reducing unemployment and measures to increase union power on the shopfloor had to be rendered compatible with manageable inflation, a stable balance of payments and, therefore, with the electoral viability of the government. This would be accomplished by a combination of voluntary wage restraint on the unions' part and an extension of state investment in industry to promote faster growth by increasing the country's exports of manufactured goods. The national economy could then be made competitive and the traditional stop–go cycle could be eliminated without recourse to statutory incomes policy, or to legislative interference with the industrial relations system, or with the traditional structures and practices of the union movement.

In order for the new strategy to have a chance of working inflationary pressure from sources other than wages had to remain within reasonable limits; and the underlying rate of growth of world demand had to be sufficient so that the growth of British export sales could provide the resources necessary for at least moderate wage increases and profits. The TUC's *Economic Review* for 1972, 1973 and 1974 assumed a steady expansion of world trade and a substantial rate of domestic growth – 6·2 percent in the 1973 *Economic Review* and 3·5 percent as late as in 1974.[119] It was precisely such price stability and growth that were rendered unattainable by the international economic crisis that followed upon the energy squeeze of 1973–4.

The international crisis hit Britain very hard. Inflation which had already been very high, comparatively speaking, in the fall of 1973 (9·3 percent), skyrocketed to reach an annual rate of 27 percent by mid-1976. For the entire period 1974–80, the average annual rate of inflation was 16 percent. Investment rates dropped off very sharply after peaking in 1974. During 1975–6 gross fixed investment in plant and machinery actually declined and it was not until 1978 that the 1974 level was regained. Output statistics were equally alarming: GDP fell during 1974 and 1975 and grew only very slowly in 1976 and 1977 before returning to a respectable level in 1978, thus giving an average annual growth rate of –1·1 percent for 1973–5 and only 2·3 percent for 1975–8.[120] The unemployment figures also make depressing reading and give an idea of the extremely difficult environment within which the unions had to operate during this period. After remaining steady during most of 1974, the number of unemployed began to rise. By April 1975 800,000 or 3·4 percent of the laborforce were out of work; by September the figure was 1,000,000. Thereafter, the numbers increased steadily until sticking at 1·4 million or 5·8 percent of the laborforce in the summer of 1977.[121] As the domestic economy deteriorated the country's international position became increasingly difficult. The balance of payments problems that had plagued the Labour government of the 1960s returned with a vengeance. In 1974, 1975, 1976 and 1979 the British current account registered enormous deficits of £7·8 billion, £3·4 billion, £1·5 billion and £1·8 billion, respectively. Sterling, accordingly, was subjected to heavy pressure on international exchanges. In the winter of 1975–6 the pound dropped so precipitously that only a major intervention by the IMF saved it from total collapse.[122]

Clearly, a recession of such proportions rendered completely unattainable the economic preconditions of the TUC–Labour Party strategy. It was difficult to see how inflation rates above 20 percent could be effectively controlled by voluntary wage restraint, especially when applied by a highly decentralized union movement within a fragmented bargaining system. Similarly, the collapse of world trade made nonsense of any export-led growth strategy. Without a minimal rate of growth, moreover, the conflict over income shares between workers facing escalating prices and capitalists suffering from squeezed profits was bound to make the unions, their bargaining strength and their industrial practices into highly visible issues in precisely the ways that the Social Contract strategy had been designed to avoid. And the combination of rising unemployment and declining tax revenues was bound to exacerbate the state's financial problems, tightening the financial margins available for expensive social and industrial reform and further politicizing the whole issue of state spending and demand management.

For the unions in Britain as elsewhere, the economic crisis presented a very difficult set of problems. The TUC found itself trying to operate a strategic package whose economic, and as a result political, preconditions had vanished. The rest of this section will trace the TUC's efforts – ultimately unsuccessful – to come to grips with this dilemma.

The Initial Phase

For the first year or so of the crisis the pressure on the unions to reconsider their strategy was not especially severe. Having emerged victorious from their prolonged and bitter confrontation with the Tories the unions were bound to enjoy the early moments of Labour rule, regardless of economic conditions. The challenge to the unions was also slow to materialize because of the manner in which the economic crisis unfolded in Britain. While most economic indicators in 1974 began rapidly to register a situation of emergency, the variables most pertinent to the unions – employment and investment – were relatively slow to turn downwards. It was not until the first quarter of 1975 that investment levels began to drop off, while the number of unemployed – already quite high in 1972–3 – did not rise substantially during 1974.[123] In addition, despite the generally unfavorable economic conditions of this period, the unions found themselves in an unusually comfortable bargaining situation. There was, to begin with, no formal incomes policy in effect beyond the vague agreement in the Social Contract that wage moderation was desirable. Union negotiators at all levels were thus free, after several years of strict Conservative norms, to exercise their considerable bargaining power on the wage front. In addition, workers were able to benefit from steady and automatic wage increases because of the 'threshold' provisions left over from the Conservatives. The result was a powerful upward surge of income levels during 1974: weekly wage rates rose by 20 percent from October 1973 to October 1974 and real personal disposable income by 2·5 percent.

Not only were the unions succeeding in using their own bargaining power to secure substantial material gains for their members in the labor market, they were also making major advances in the political arena as well, as the new Labour Cabinet began to make good many of the promises of social and economic reforms contained in the original Social Contract.[124] A number of measures introduced in Chancellor Denis Healey's first budget in March 1974 were direct enactments of Social Contract commitments and brought considerable benefits to workers and their families: old-age pensions were increased substantially; food subsidies were increased; a freeze was imposed on rents; and the structure of the income tax was altered to provide higher allowances at the lower end of the scale and higher rates at the highest brackets. In addition, a number of laws were enacted which significantly augmented the rights of workers and unions in the labor market. The Trade Union and Labour Relations Act of July 1974 repealed the Conservatives' Industrial Relations Act and augmented somewhat the rights of unions in matters of picketing and the closed shop.[125] A Health and Safety at Work Act tightened up standards and enforcement procedures and provided for the creation of health and safety committees and workers' safety delegates.[126] Finally, the the Employment Protection Act, passed in March 1975, established a conciliation board called the Advisory Conciliation and Arbitration Service (ACAS) and provided substantial increases in union rights in a number of domains: recognition disputes, disclosure of company information, appeals against 'unfair dismissal', maternity leave and paid time-off for workers enrolled in trade union training courses.[127]

At the same time, the feeling of optimism within union circles generated by these labor market successes and legislative victories was reinforced not only by a steady influx of new members (see Table 1.1) mentioned above, but also by the new prominence of union officials in the policy-making process and in public affairs generally. As was usual under Labour governments, the unions found themselves much more welcome in the offices of Cabinet ministers and civil servants than under the Tories. This time, moreover, the central role played by the unions in defeating Heath and the importance of the Social Contract in the election campaign, and in subsequent government policy-making, gave the unions especially privileged access, at least during this early period.[128]

Accordingly, in this early stage of the crisis, the TUC's economic thinking and strategy remained very close to the positions it had worked out during the period of Labour opposition. The TUC's economic documents of 1974 and the first part of 1975 were, to begin with, extremely cautious in the way they described the economic situation. The *Economic Review* of both 1974 and 1975 avoided using the term 'crisis', preferring instead to speak of 'the recession' or 'the economic slowdown'. Although the 1975 *Economic Review* was considerably more pessimistic about economic conditions and prospects, all of the TUC's pronouncements prior to the spring of 1975 displayed a peculiarly serene tone when compared to later documents. The 1974 *Economic Review*, for example, expected the overall growth rate of the economy to attain 3·5 percent and even in 1975 the TUC called for a 2·9 percent rate of growth.[129]

The recession was seen not as a novel development in the evolution of domestic or international capitalism, but rather as a standard – if especially severe – cyclical downturn whose origins could be traced to the oil cutbacks and price hikes of 1973–4, and whose severity could be attributed to the simultaneity of its incidence in all the major Western economies.[130] Following the analysis of British economic weaknesses that it had developed in the late 1960s and early 1970s, the TUC perceived the recession as having two dimensions. While the immediate origins of the recession were to be found in international economic circumstances, its impact on Britain had to be understood in the light of the long-term structural weaknesses of the British domestic economy.[131] The principal symptoms of the recession in Britain were seen by the TUC's economists to be inflation, balance of payments difficulties and unemployment, with the relative emphasis during this period varying essentially in rhythm with the movement of the economic indicators. Thus in 1974 the TUC's main concern was Britain's growing balance of payments deficit as well as the rate of inflation.[132] By the time of the 1975 *Economic Review* unemployment had begun to loom somewhat larger among the TUC's preoccupations and the coexistence of unprecedentedly high inflation and rising unemployment had begun to puzzle the organization's economic policy-makers.[133] That the TUC should in this period have chosen to place a very heavy emphasis on the balance of payments dimension of the crisis may have been misguided from the point of view of finding immediate policy responses to the oil crisis but made perfect sense in terms of the union movement's accumulated experience with Britain's postwar 'stop–go' and the importance attributed in the 1950s and 1960s by most economists to the 'balance of payments constraint' as the key to the 'stop–go' syndrome.[134]

In describing the reasons for Britain's economic difficulties the TUC analyses of 1974–5 relied on lines of argument developed in TUC and Labour Party documents of the previous period and reinforced by the findings of subsequent research projects by such bodies as NEDC and OECD. Britain's trading problem – a high and growing level of import penetration and a poor and declining export record – was the result of the poor 'industrial performance' of the manufacturing sector. British plants were – when compared to their European and Japanese counterparts – often too small for optimum productivity and they tended to contain old machines and outmoded technology.[135] The principal reason for these structural defects was 'chronic underinvestment': rates of investment in British manufacturing were substantially below those of other industrial economies. British industrialists were investing abroad at a very high rate, while the financial sector was investing not in industry, but in property and services. British industrial investment was, moreover, deficient not only in quantity, but in 'quality' as well. In the words of the 1974 *Economic Review*, 'This extra output produced by investment in the U.K. is less than other industrial countries', the main reason being apparently the absence of sufficient investment planning.[136]

On the basis of this diagnosis of the economic situation as merely a cyclical downturn within an unchanged set of structures the TUC put forward a set of policy proposals that differed remarkably little from those they had advocated in the closing years of the Heath government and many of which had become incorporated into the agreements of the Social Contract. Beginning with the economy's immediate difficulties, inflation was to be curbed by a combination of measures: prices were to be held in check by strict price controls along with increased food subsidies and rent controls; and wages were, as agreed in the February 1973 Liaison Committee declaration, to be controlled by the voluntary restraint of union members operating within an unregulated system of free collective bargaining. A formal incomes policy was neither necessary nor desirable: the restraint on unit costs that was required, according to the TUC, if British goods were to be internationally competitive could be secured if union negotiators took into consideration legislative tradeoffs being provided by the new government and the difficult economic situation.[137] The TUC, while resisting increasing pressure from the government to accept a formal incomes policy, urged its officials and activists to moderate their wage demands. They were asked to aim only at keeping living standards at present levels, to include the growing 'social wage' in their calculations of workers' incomes and to emphasize non-wage issues such as health and safety, sick leave, pensions and industrial democracy rather than wage demands.[138] The country's current account deficit, meanwhile, should be reduced not by deflationary demand management – this would merely exacerbate the effects of the recession – but by 'selective and temporary' import controls, special arrangements with raw-materials producers for recycling and for long-term pricing, and the use of 30 percent of the expected annual growth in national income to repay the outstanding deficit.[139]

A first step in protecting the balance of payments and improving the overall prospects of the economy would be to leave the European Economic Community (EEC). Although there were some pro-marketeers in the TUC leadership, the prevailing opinion favored a negative vote in the upcoming referendum. While some moderate unions disapproved only of the new terms of membership that had been negotiated, others such as the TGWU and ASTMS condemned the EEC more broadly as an agent of American and West German economic domination and felt that the British economy could develop effectively only if it stayed outside such a body.[140]

As for the economy's longer-term 'structural' problems, the remedies advocated in the TUC's *Economic Review* for 1972 and 1973 and embodied in the Social Contract were still considered applicable and sufficient. A substantial programme of investment in industry was advocated along with a system of economic planning directed by NEDC and with a large role for the state, through the auspices of the National Enterprise Board.[141] Resources for this investment push were to be derived partly from the expected economic growth, and partly by using voluntary wage restraint to divert resources from consumption to investment.[142] The overall level of demand in the economy would, meanwhile, be kept from flagging by an expansion of government expenditures on education and social services, while import controls would keep the reflation from sucking in excessive imports.[143]

What the TUC was proposing, then, was the pre-1974 package of reflationary Keynesianism and expanded welfare provision along with a number of measures for increased state intervention in matters of planning and investment. The latter proposals – which, as we have seen, constituted the principal innovation in Social Contract strategy – seem to have been assigned relatively low priority by most TUC leaders during this period. The *Economic Review* did, indeed, devote a certain amount of space to questions of planning and industrial intervention[144] in the early part of the crisis; but when negotiating with party and Cabinet leaders concerning the enactment of the Social Contract, the TUC leadership seems to have placed the highest priority not on these matters, but on welfare spending, demand management and, above all, labor market reform, including repeal of the Industrial Relations Act and its replacement by an Employment Protection Act that would widen the freedom of action of shopfloor union organizers.[145] Thus, so long as the government delivered on most of its promises in the latter areas – which as we have seen it did handsomely for the first eighteen months or so of its tenure – the TUC leadership, and most of the major unions as well, were satisfied to allow the industrial policy component of the Social Contract to be neglected, delayed, or watered down. Thus, the TUC seems to have protested very little when the investment intervention schemes of the 1973 Liaison Committee discussions were progressively weakened in the February 1974 Labour Party manifesto and, again, in the White Paper on industrial policy that appeared in August. The reduction of the National Enterprise Board's (NEB) overall budget, the elimination of the new agency's power to acquire shares in firms that were unwilling to sell and the reduction of the proposed planning agreements from a compulsory scheme to a purely voluntary one evoked little more than *pro forma* protest from the TUC as did the removal of Tony Benn from his position as Secretary of State for Industry – the department responsible for industrial policy and planning – and his replacement by the moderate Eric Varley.[146]

The Crisis Deepens

So long, apparently, as economic and political pressures did not become too severe, the TUC would stand by its original strategy and would continue to give very low priority within that strategy to matters of industrial policy. Once, however, the recession started to deepen and the existence of a crisis of unprecedented severity had become indisputable, the TUC would begin to change its tune somewhat. By the early spring of 1975 a rapid deterioration of Britain's economy had set in. Investment levels and intentions dropped off sharply beginning in early 1975 and the growth of output sagged badly. The inflation rate climbed to levels previously confined to the Third World and unemployment began, as we have already seen, to rise rapidly. As unemployment increased and the demand for welfare services expanded while tax revenues shrank, the government's financial deficit ballooned to unprecedented levels. The most commonly used indicator of the budgetary situation – the 'public sector borrowing requirement' (PSBR) reached £7·6 billion in 1974–5 and by 1975–6 it had climbed to an all-time high of £10·5 billion.[147] As the domestic economy deteriorated, the country's international position also became increasingly threatened. Although the balance of payments deficit was narrowed significantly in both 1975 and 1976, the pound suffered a drastic decline. During the course of 1975 the pound lost 8·2 percent of its 'effective exchange rate', falling some 4 percent in one six-week period in the spring. During one particularly bad trading day a run on the pound cut its value by a full 1·3 percent.[148] During 1976 the run on the pound brought its value to record lows and induced a state of near-panic not only in British financial and ministerial circles, but in the international banking world as well. During that year the pound lost nearly 10 percent of its Smithsonian value. From $2·40 in March of 1975, sterling shrank to $2 in March, to $1·70 in June and to an all-time low of $1·55 on 25 October.[149]

As the crisis intensified the tone of public discourse in Britain rapidly returned to the level of hysteria that had prevailed during the miners' strike and the three-day week in the winter of 1973. In Parliament and in the media phrases like the 'English disease', the 'condition of England' and even the 'decline of Britain as an industrial civilization' became common fare. Economists, along with Britain's special breed of semi-academic economic journalists, worked out new theories or dug up old ones to describe and account for the country's economic difficulties. Politicians and pundits produced their own analyses, with one of the shrillest contributions coming from the group of radical monetarists who had recently taken over control of the Conservative Party.[150]

Amid the welter of diagnoses, prognoses and prescriptions there were three points of general agreement. First, the current stagnation, hyper-inflation, balance of payments difficulties and currency crises were not simply short-term cyclical phenomena, but reflected rather a profound deterioration of Britain's long-term economic prospects. Secondly, the key to the country's external financial difficulties was its rate of inflation. Thirdly, the principal culprits in the inflationary spiral were wages and government spending and the unions who were blamed for both.[151]

It was in the context of the severe deterioration of the country's international economic position and of this mood of hysteria and anti-union sentiment that the government shifted its crisis management approach decisively in the direction of a strict austerity program. The government's approach consisted of two elements both of which involved imposing important sacrifices on workers and unions: incomes policy, and cutbacks in government spending. Quite early in its term the Labour government, and Chancellor Healey in particular, became convinced that the voluntary wage restraint of the original Social Contract was totally inadequate and that a formal and strict incomes policy was required. At the TUC's Annual Congress in September 1974 James Callaghan, then Foreign Secretary, made a vigorous plea for TUC acceptance of a real incomes policy. The choice, he told the delegates, was between effective wage restraint and massive unemployment.[152] By the summer of 1975 the government abandoned the original Social Contract's approach and resorted to a conventional incomes policy with a firm £6-per-week ceiling on all salary increases for the coming year. In its White Paper announcing the new approach the government declared its intention to bring inflation rapidly into single digits. Otherwise, they insisted, the country would be 'engulfed in a general economic catastrophe of incalculable proportions'.[153]

Incomes policy, which had been the 'unmentionable' of the original Social Contract, now became its central motif. When the first instalment of the policy ran out in August 1976, a second version of the policy dubbed 'Stage II' set an even lower ceiling for the following twelve months than had Stage I; instead of a £6 limit that had amounted to about a 10 percent increase, only 5 percent was to be allowed, with a ceiling of £4 per week.

The other component of the austerity package was a shift toward fiscal and monetary conservatism so decisive that many observers claimed to see in Labour's budgets an abandonment of Keynesianism in favor of the newly fashionable monetarist approach advocated by the IMF, the British Treasury, the financial press and the Tory leadership. The original Social Contract had featured strong commitments by Labour to use expansionary spending and generous tax policies to restore full employment and engineer a 'large-scale redistribution of income and wealth'.[154] Denis Healey's first budget, in March 1974, had taken a number of steps in the direction of income redistribution, although its general intention had been mildly deflationary.[155] By the time of the November 1974 budget the Chancellor had clearly come to regard inflation as the primary problem to be combatted, even at the cost of higher unemployment. What little *largesse* the budget contained was aimed not at workers, but at private capital.[156] The April 1975 budget contained no handouts at all. Its primary aim was to combat inflation and stabilize the balance of payments deficit by contracting the money supply and cutting back government spending. Healey's principal objective, he declared, was to reduce the growing 'public sector borrowing requirement'. This was to be achieved by increasing income taxes, duties and sales taxes and by examining ways to reduce future government expenditures. That unemployment could be expected to rise by about 0·5 percent by the end of the year as a direct result was, according to Healey, unfortunate but unavoidable.[157]

How did the unions react to these threatening economic and political conditions? The TUC began by taking seriously the apocalyptic picture of Britain's economic condition painted by the government and the media.

What was occurring was not, as previously claimed, merely a typical if extreme cyclical recession, but rather a major crisis of unprecedented proportions and novel character.[158] The combination of hyperinflation, a yawning balance of payments deficit, a runaway state deficit and a shrinking pound was extremely dangerous from the union movement's perspective not only economically, but politically as well. It was undermining the viability of the government and threatening to bring the dreaded Thatcher–Joseph Tories to power in their stead.[159] As a result, the TUC under the persuasive influence of Jack Jones of the TGWU and David Lea, head of the TUC Economic Department, accepted the government's claim that the strategy of the original Social Contract was no longer viable. A brief dose of fiscal and monetary restraint was needed to bring the budgetary deficit under control, to combat inflation and to transfer resources from services into manufacturing and exports.[160] The obviously ineffective wage-restraint provision of the original Social Contract would have to be replaced by a strict and effective incomes policy. In order to avoid sacrificing all of their economical and political goals Jones and Lea told their colleagues on the Economic Committee, the General Council and, finally, the movement's broad leadership at the TUC in September 1975 that the unions would have to put aside some of their market autonomy. By agreeing, at Jones's urging, to endorse the incomes policy that the government was prepared in any case to impose on them the unions were making the best of a bad situation. They succeeded, first of all, in keeping the incomes policy officially as a 'voluntary one' in which the unions retained a portion of their previous freedom of action. As organizations, the unions were not legally bound by the policy and could, in principle, withdraw their endorsement when they chose. Moreover, individual unions and their officials would not be liable to legal sanctions if they bargained for wage increases beyond the policy's norm because sanctions would be applied only to management.[161] In addition, by participating in the formulation of the policy Jones and his fellow-members of the Economic Committee managed to shape it in a way that they hoped would benefit the union movement as a whole. Instead of the typical percentage norm, Stage I of Labour's incomes policy set a flat sum of £6 as its ceiling, thus allowing the lowest-paid workers (one of the primary targets of current recruitment efforts by such unions as the TGWU, NUPE and the GMWU) to improve their relative positions within the working class.[162]

These were not the only tradeoffs that the TUC sought from the government in return for accepting its incomes policy. While the Chancellor, the IMF and the financial press were preoccupied with the inflation/balance of payments side of the crisis, the TUC was now becoming increasingly alarmed by its employment dimension. The immediate impact of the crisis on the level of unemployment was, the TUC's *Economic Review* for 1976 and 1977 pointed out, quite devastating. The total number of unemployed was higher than at any time in the postwar period and was still rising.[163] Decisive government action was required to alleviate the effects of this situation: an 'industrial strategy' involving the extension of subsidies to prevent or defer plant closures and the establishment of new subsidies for firms that created jobs in hard-hit regions; a considerable increase in the funds available for manpower training and retraining; a reduction of working time; and an improvement of welfare payment rates.[164] The generalized spending cuts of the April 1975 budget could, therefore, not become a permanent feature of Labour policy, even if they were understandable as an emergency measure.[165]

Even more alarming from the TUC's perspective was the medium-term unemployment consequences of the crisis. The international recession had accentuated and accelerated what the TUC now described as the 'secular decline' of Britain's manufacturing sector. The TUC's economic documents of this period dwelt at some length on the phenomenon that British economists would soon dub 'deindustrialization' – the long-term shrinkage of manufacturing as a component of national output, investment and employment; a secular growth in the penetration of imports into British markets for manufactured and semi-manufactured goods; a concomitant decline of the UK's share of world trade in manufactured goods; and a steady haemorrhage of funds for industrial investment out of the country.[166] In order to reverse this alarming process the TUC began to emphasize a set of programs to which it had previously paid relatively little attention. In its economic policy documents, and in its dealings with the Labour Party and the government, the TUC began to seek the application of controls on imports. First mentioned by the TUC in its 1973 *Economic Review*, import controls reappear as a priority in 1975 and with greater emphasis and detail in 1976. Unlike many left-wing economists and political groups, however, and despite the urgings of a number of large left-leaning unions such as NUPE and ASTMS, the TUC resisted the idea of across-the-board restrictions and advocated rather what it called 'temporary and selective' controls designed to protect the most vulnerable sectors, while minimizing the risk of international retaliation. In addition, the TUC began to think more seriously about industrial policy. As we have seen, planning and industrial policy do not appear to have been very high on the list of priorities of much of the TUC leadership at the time of the signing of the original Social Contract and during the first phase of the crisis. Indeed, many TUC moderates appear to have found the Tony Benn–Stuart Holland approach to industrial policy – emphasizing as it did centralized state intervention, new nationalizations and a *dirigiste* and aggressive NEB – rather unattractive. The new approach embodied in the 1975 Industry Act, with its decentralized consultative bodies (the Sectoral Working Parties), its smaller role for the NEB and central planning, and its increased emphasis on collective bargaining was much more to their liking and TUC policy statements began to support this program vigorously.[167]

On the basis of these calculations and preoccupations, then, the TUC leadership agreed to accept and to help enforce a strict incomes policy in order to fight inflation and free resources for transfer from consumption into manufacturing investment. The unions would agree to this sacrifice of labor market autonomy and material gains on the condition, first, that the policy remain (as we have seen) a 'voluntary' one, and secondly, that the government pledge itself to fight unemployment both through measures for immediate relief and through the implementation of long-range structural policies in consultation with the unions.

The Contradictions of the Social Contract Strategy

As a short-term expedient the renegotiation of the Social Contract in the form of an austerity package was useful both for the Labour Party and for the unions. For the government it brought partial relief from the inflationary spiral and support for unpopular policies, while for the unions it brought the continued prestige of association in policy-making as well as the gratitude of the low-paid for the flat-rate increases – prestige and gratitude that were converted into organizational strength as members flowed into the unions to continue the steady expansion that had begun in the late 1960s.[168] As the economic crisis dragged on, however, and the policy of austerity was stretched by the government from an emergency package into a fixture of labour rule, the costs for the unions rapidly began to outweigh the benefits.

In essence what happened was that the government attempted to extend its incomes policy over and over again, while failing to deliver to the unions the kinds of tradeoffs on demand management, unemployment relief, industrial democracy, or structural modernization that might have eased their task of selling and enforcing the increasingly unpopular wage-restraint program. As Stage II – a 5 percent limit with a £4-a-week ceiling and a twelve-month rule restricting each union to one increase a year – was about to expire, the government ignored TUC warnings and asked for union endorsement of a third stage, involving the same twelve-month rule and a 10 percent limit. One year later Prime Minister Callaghan added a fourth stage, this time with an astonishingly rigid 5 per cent norm and called on the General Council and Congress to support his efforts to reduce inflation in preparation for the upcoming general elections.[169] These government demands placed the TUC General Council in an extremely difficult position. Wage restraint had become unpopular among much of the rank-and-file membership as well as among the lower echelons of union activists. Rank-and-file resentment had accumulated as workers saw their standard of living undermined by the wage-restraint provisions of the Social Contract. Although money wages continued to grow slowly (at an annual rate of 9·4 percent in 1975–8 as compared to 27·7 percent for 1973–5), real wages actually fell (by an annual average rate of –13 percent for 1975–8). In terms of post-tax income British workers, particularly for those with families, found themselves taking substantial cuts in their standard of living.[170] Discontent was especially likely to develop among groups of workers with strong bargaining positions and well-developed union organizations such as skilled metalworkers, miners and railway workers, and among recently unionized categories like civil servants, white-collar and scientific workers, and local government manual employees, who had, prior to the establishment of the incomes policy, been making important wage gains through free collective bargaining. In addition, the prolongation of the incomes policy provoked growing discontent among skilled workers and aggravated interunion rivalries because of its distorting impact on conventional wage differentials among various segments of the laborforce.[171]

The extension of incomes policies also increased the restiveness not only of ordinary union members, but also of shop stewards and local officials in many unions, thus setting them into conflict with their own regional and national leaders as well as with the TUC. Some of these local activists followed the lead of the Communist Party or the various Trotskyist groups in opposing wage restraint on political grounds.[172] Even the moderates, however, felt that the prolongation of centrally determined incomes policy was depriving them of their principal *raison d'être* and – along with rising levels of unemployment – undermining their capacity to attract new members into their organizations, thus threatening not only their own self-esteem and influence within their unions, but also their power *vis-à-vis* management.

As these resentments festered at the plant and local levels rebellions against nationally established bargaining orders became increasingly frequent.[173] Moreover, the policy-making meetings of a growing number of important unions passed resolutions against any further wage restraint. The most significant opposition involved NUPE, ASTMS and the 'big batallions' of the AUEW and the TGWU.[174] Even those unions, such as the NUR and GMWU, that continued to support incomes policy in principle grew steadily less confident of their ability to discipline their restless local organizations. What made the position of moderate union leaders especially difficult was that they were able to show their members very few tradeoffs from government in return for the acceptance of incomes policy. True, the rate of inflation had come down considerably, the balance of payments had been stabilized and the pound rescued from collapse but unemployment – which preoccupied local union activists directly – was at record postwar levels and still rising. The government had made good very few of its promises so far as combating unemployment was concerned either in terms of expansionary demand management or in terms of the industrial restructuring that the TUC increasingly came, as we have seen, to regard as necessary for long-term employment prospects in the UK.[175]

The unions had conceived the April 1975 budget as an exceptional dose of deflation to be followed, now that an incomes policy had been established, by measures aimed at creating jobs and encouraging expanded demand. Under heavy pressure from Treasury officials, the City of London and the foreign holders of large sterling deposits, and the IMF, the Cabinet clearly decided that the inflation/sterling/balance of payments complex of problems was more pressing than the unemployment/industrial decline side of the crisis.[176] To cure inflation, according to this view, the government had not only to control wages, but also to restrain its own spending. The monetarist doctrine that Keynesian-style deficit spending was the principal cause of inflation came to be accepted by what had previously been the most Keynesian of parties. By 1976 James Callaghan, who had replaced Wilson as Prime Minister, and Denis Healey were sounding like convinced monetarists:

> We used to think [Callaghan told the Labour Party's 1976 Conference] that you could just spend your way out of a recession and increase employment by cutting taxes and boosting government spending. I tell you in all candor that that option no longer exists and that insofar as it ever did exist, it worked by injecting inflation into the economy. And each time that happened the average level of unemployment has risen. Higher inflation, followed by higher unemployment. That is the history of the past twenty years.[177]

Public spending was regarded as harmful not only because it was inflationary, but also because it was held to hamper industrial development. Monetarists and other neo-liberal economists had long argued that the expansion of the public sector discouraged private investment and initiative. Beginning in 1974 a number of less conservative economists, and in particular Robert Bacon and Walter Eltis of Oxford, developed a statistically decorated case that was generally taken to imply that the growth of public expenditure and public sector borrowing requirement restricted private manufacturing by 'crowding' private investors out of capital markets.[178] Callaghan and Healey came increasingly to accept the claim that Britain's public sector borrowing was excessive (though comparative statistics indicate this not to be the case) and that this excessive deficit was contributing significantly to the long-term problems of British manufacturing. In his 1976 budget speech Chancellor Healey actually used the Bacon–Eltis terminology: 'I am', he told the Commons, 'concerned to ensure that industry's requirements for finance are not crowded out by other demands, notably by those of the public sector.'[179]

As a result of this mode of economic thinking, the deflationary approach of the April 1975 budget turned out to be merely the first in a series of restrictive budgets that deliberately sacrificed jobs in order to combat inflation through tax increases, cuts in government spending, restriction of the money supply, the imposition of rigid 'cash limits' to prevent government departments and local authorities from raising their expenditures on wages and public services in line with inflation, and the reduction of subsidies to nationalized industries. The most Draconian set of measures came in December 1976 as the government's *quid pro quo* for a standby arrangement granted by the IMF. Public expenditure plans were slashed by £1 billion for 1977–8 and a further £1·5 billion for 1978–9 and £500-million-worth of shares in British Petroleum were offered for sale.[180] Alternatives to this strategy suggested by the TUC, the Tribune Group of Labour MPs and a variety of academic economists – most frequently devaluation followed by reflation behind a protective wall of import controls – were rejected out of hand by Healey. Import controls might provoke retaliation, he insisted, and touch off a tariff war reminiscent of the 1930s. Any substantial reflation, Healey told the TUC, would have to await the return of price stability, the reequilibration of the pound and a significant reduction in the trade deficit.[181]

At subsequent budgets the TUC's pleas for reflation presented to the Chancellor in the *Economic Review* and in person were rejected in favor of renewed fiscal and monetary caution. The impact of this conservative approach on public expenditure was considerable. A government pledged to a massive expansion of public services ended up actually reducing both total spending in real terms and the share of GDP spent by the state on goods and services.[182] Even the editorialists of *The Economist* found the 24 percent decline recorded in real investment (as distinct from overall expenditure) by the state to represent 'false economies'.[183]

Not only did the government fail to deliver to the TUC substantial short-term policy tradeoffs to counter rising unemployment, it also proved very hesitant with regard to the medium-term measures for industrial modernization that the TUC leaders had, as noted, begun to take increasingly seriously in the period following 1975. By mid-1975 the government had already gone a long way toward emasculating the original Tony Benn–Stuart Holland Liaison Committee program for industrial restructuring through state intervention and planning. The budget and scope of the National Enterprise Board had been whittled down to a size less threatening to business interests and Labour Party moderates. 'Planning agreements' had been reduced from compulsory contracts designed to coordinate the activities of the 'commanding heights' of the economy to the status of voluntary arrangements for the communication of information between large firms and the government. And the vision of a central plan had been jettisoned in favor of a series of sectoral indicative plans, baptized 'the industrial strategy'. Now, under the cautious stewardship of Benn's successor, Eric Varley, planning agreements became a bit of Labour folklore: only one was ever signed and that was with the bankrupt British division of Chrysler. As for the 'industrial strategy', despite a considerable investment of resources and manpower by the unions and much public relations fanfare by the government, very little materialized from the forty or so tripartite sectoral bodies that were set up, except for a number of reports on export performance and import-penetration targets.[184]

With real wages falling and unemployment rising, and with the government providing very few tradeoffs for working-class sacrifice, the TUC was increasingly hardpressed to keep its revised Social Contract strategy intact. As shopfloor resentment of wage restraint spread, more and more affiliated unions dropped their support of incomes policy and became advocates of a return to 'free collective bargaining'. By the summer of 1977 the list of unions opposed to an endorsement of Stage III had become impressive and when the TGWU's annual conference defied its own secretary-general, Jack Jones, and repudiated wage restraint, the outcome was settled. The TUC's 1977 Congress withdrew its endorsement of the government's incomes policy. Congress passed a resolution instructing the General Council to 'reject the theory that wage rises are a major contributing factor towards inflation' and another demanding what was called 'an orderly return to free collective bargaining'.[185] As a result of these resolutions, the TUC's official policy was to accept a continuation of the 'twelve-month rule' which limited unions to one wage increase a year but not to support the government's 10 percent ceiling. In 1978 the TUC's position became even more difficult. As rank-and-file unrest increased and more and more affiliated unions took up positions against the government's austerity policies the Prime Minister, as we have seen, declared his intention to hold wage increases to a mere 5 percent and called on the General Council and Congress to support his efforts in order to secure a Labour victory in the upcoming elections.[186] As in the previous year, wage restraint was decisively defeated by Congress, leaving the General Council with a set of resolutions asserting both the TUC's desire to see a Labour government returned and a categorical rejection of 'any form of restrictive Government incomes policy'.[187]

Nor did opposition within the ranks of the TUC confine itself to the single issue of incomes policy. The budgetary aspect of the austerity program generated substantial opposition from left-led unions and from public sector unions, in particular, whose organizational prospects and wage levels were directly threatened by the Chancellor's public expenditure cuts, by the imposition of 'cash limits' and hiring freezes in the civil service and local authorities, and by schemes for the reorganization of the National Health Service.[188] It was the failure of the TUC to challenge effectively either the monetarist underpinnings or the practical consequences of the April 1975 budget that led the public sector unions and, in particular, the National Union of Public Employees (NUPE) to initiate a campaign against government policy and the TUC's complicity in it, beginning with the publication of NUPE's pamphlet *Inflation: Attack or Retreat?* and leading to the creation of an interunion umbrella group, entitled the National Steering Committee against the Cuts, to organize meetings, demonstrations and lobbying efforts.[189]

As this movement against the cuts developed it expanded in two directions. On the one hand, it developed links with the non-union left both inside the Labour Party and outside it to the Communist Party and the various Trotskyist groups as well as to academic circles such as the Cambridge Economic Policy Group, the principal professional advocates of a protectionist strategy for British economic recovery.[190] On the other hand, the opposition to the cuts linked up inside the TUC with groups opposed to wage restraint. The outcome of this complicated process was the emergence within the TUC of the so-called 'alternative economic strategy', a set of proposals for a 'socialist' approach to the economic crisis whose supporters formed at first a vocal minority at TUC meetings and, by the fall of 1977, an absolute majority. This program derived from a variety of not entirely compatible sources: the left of the Labour Party (Tony Benn, Stuart Holland, the Tribune group), the Communist Party and its various publications, especially *Labour Monthly* and the *Morning Star*, and the Cambridge Economic Policy Group. It was circulated within the TUC in a variety of forms and documents including NUPE's pamphlet *Time to Change Course: An Economic Review* (1976) and *Fight Back* (1977), and ASTMS publications including *The Crisis in British Planning* (1975) and the *Quarterly Economic Review* which began appearing in 1975.[191] As formulated by NUPE and ASTMS the 'alternative economic strategy' now involved both a more *Marxisant* analysis of the crisis and of the British economic problem than that embodied in TUC documents and a more radical set of proposals for remedies. The crisis was the product, according to NUPE, of 'the inability of capitalism to plan rationally' and its development, as far as Britain's outmoded and uncompetitive industrial system was concerned, had been aggravated rather than impeded by Labour's policies of wage restraint, deflation and reliance on the private sector to generate the capital for industrial investment.[192] Britain's headlong decline could only be reversed by a fundamental shift of approach. Strict price controls, a wealth tax and cuts in defence spending should replace incomes policy, fiscal conservatism and general austerity. Workers should be shielded from the impact of unemployment by an expansion of transfer payments and a reduction of the working week to 35 hours, as well as by a general reflationary approach to be facilitated by the imposition of broad controls to prevent excessive imports from being sucked in.[193] This system of import controls was seen as necessary also to protect the other principal aspect of the 'alternative economic strategy' – a broad program of industrial modernization based on state funding and state ownership via a vastly expanded National Enterprise Board and a national planning system under NEB auspices articulated with compulsory planning agreements at firm level supervised by union representatives on corporate boards. The crisis, according to this vision, should be used as an occasion for a drastic restructuring of British industry along the lines originally proposed by the Labour left in 1973 and involving 'a radical, interventionist industrial policy'.[194]

At the 1975 Trades Union Congress, resolutions incorporating these proposals were introduced by NUPE, ASTMS and the AUEW (Engineering Section), with the support of several other organizations, but the resulting 'composite motion' was defeated in favor of a more moderate resolution sponsored by the TGWU, NALGO and the GMWU.[195] As early as September 1976 the combination of resentment over wage restraint and opposition to budgetary austerity enabled the proponents of this 'alternative strategy' to have a number of their ideas incorporated into the resolutions on economic policy passed by the TUC. Composite Motion 8, entitled, 'Unemployment, imports and industrial policy,' called for a 'socialist economic and industrial strategy' involving, among other things, an increase in funding of the National Enterprise Board, an extension of public ownership in the financial and other sectors as well as selective control of imports. Similarly, Composite 10 on 'Public expenditure' rejected any further cuts, pledged the TUC General Council's support for any union resisting such cuts and urged 'selective action on imports, exchange controls and supervision of the investment activities of pension funds and insurance companies'.[196]

By the 1977 Congress the partisans of the alternative strategy had gained control of the floor and succeeded in passing a variety of motions declaring the TUC's support for most of their basic positions. Motion 86, presented by the TASS section of the AUEW, specifically mentioned 'an alternative economic strategy' and listed ten planks, including municipalization of rented housing; increased public expenditure on basic services; 'substantial' increases in public ownership along with 'public supervision' of the investment policies of major private firms; 'substantial cuts' in defence spending; the creation of a National Planning Centre; and the establishment of 'effective controls to direct internal investment and prevent damaging capital outflows'. Other motions rejected any further wage restraint, called for the use of North Sea oil and gas revenues as part of a 'reflationary economic strategy' to be managed through an expansion of the NEB's regional development activities and a broad program of employment subsidies, especially in the public sector.[197]

As a result, the TUC leadership found itself caught between a series of conflicting pressures in 1977–8. The government was pressing for support of its incomes policy and warning of dire political and economic consequences if such support failed to materialize. Government leaders, painfully conscious of the Conservatives' growing lead in the opinion polls, were furious at the unions for refusing to support government anti-inflation policies. They were not, however, eager to devote much of their limited resources to job-creation schemes or to risk losing control over price levels by adopting a more expansionary approach to demand management. Within the unions, moderate pro-government leaders were having increasing difficulties in restraining the growing wage militancy of shop stewards and local organizers over whom they had, in any case, relatively little control, given the extremely decentralized structure of the TUC and its affiliated unions and of the collective bargaining process. The leaders of the General Council also found themselves in an awkward position *vis-à-vis* their allies in the government, since the resolutions of Congress committed them to supporting a new set of economic policies many of which they and their economic advisors regarded as economically unsound and politically unwise.[198]

Through the fall of 1978 the General Council managed to keep these contradictory pressures from exploding. On the wages front it urged moderation on its affiliates and leniency on the government, while attempting to ignore or downplay the importance of the growing number of wage settlements in major firms or industrial branches that exceeded the official 5 percent norm.[199] In November the TUC's Economic Committee negotiated with members of the Cabinet a joint statement on inflation and economic policy that pledged 'responsible' collective bargaining as a prerequisite for bringing inflation into single figures. This reassertion of the 'special relationship' between unions and Labour would, it was hoped, not only bring local union bargainers into line prior to impending general elections, but also persuade voters that now, as in 1973–4, only a Labour government could maintain close enough cooperation with the unions to manage the economy effectively. The General Council of the TUC, however, split down the middle at its meeting of 15 November and the joint statement did not pass.[200]

While attempting to bridge the gap between itself and the government on the wage front, the General Council attempted to do the same on other issues of economic policy as well. The *Economic Review* for 1978 and 1979 adopted most of the positions of the resolutions on the 'alternative economic strategy' but it formulated many of them in more cautious terms. On the question of import controls, for example, the 1978 and 1979 document spoke of 'temporary and selective' controls rather than the general protectionism advocated by sponsors of the alternative strategy.[201] Similarly, the TUC's economic policy-makers chose to emphasize a number of issues which did not put the organization into direct confrontation with the government. Thus, beginning in 1977 and increasingly in 1978 and thereafter, the TUC's economic texts emphasized the 35-hour working week as the key to a program of job creation.[202] And from 1979 on the TUC began to devote considerable attention to silicon-chip technology and its implications in the medium term for unemployment in both the industrial and service sectors.[203] At the same time, the General Council pressed the government – in its publications, in the Liaison Committee and in private meetings – to fulfill its part of the Social Contract bargain. The TUC leadership called for more expansionary demand management, more unemployment relief and more resources for the 'industrial strategy'.[204]

The Strategy Collapses

In the fall and winter of 1978–9 this delicate balancing-act collapsed as a vast wave of strikes destroyed Callaghan's incomes policy, divided the union movement against itself, set the unions and the government at each other's throats and paved the way for a decisive Tory victory in the elections of May 1979. The strike wave began with a series of conflicts in the private sector most notably at the Ford Motor Co. and at British Oxygen. The success of these two groups of workers in breaking the 5 percent limit and in persuading management to defy the official sanctions unleashed an explosion of wage militancy pent up by over three years of incomes policy. Demands for increases far beyond the 5 percent limit (with some as high as 40 percent) spread through parts of the private manufacturing sector, the transport industry, engineering, mining and large segments of the public sector, especially health workers and local government employees. For much of the winter road and rail transportation were interrupted, government offices were intermittently closed and hospitals, schools, garbage pickups, road maintenance and other public services were interrupted.[205]

What turned this powerful strike wave into a spectacular, and for the labor movement disastrous, political confrontation was partly the unusual severity of the winter, which amplified the inconvenience caused by the interruption of government and transport services, partly the hysteria fomented by the press and especially the reactionary London tabloids and partly the government's stubborn insistence on holding the line on its 5 percent norm and treating the strikes – especially those in the public sector – as a struggle to the death between itself and its erstwhile allies in the unions.[206]

With the struggle posed in these terms, the TUC found itself brought face to face with the irreconcilable contradictions of its strategy and of its position in Britain's political economy. Three years of exemplary wage restraint involving cuts in real wages and requiring the marshaling of vast organizational resources for its enforcement had not sufficed to restore stability and growth to the country's feeble economy. Indeed, the recent period of international and domestic recession had seen an acceleration of

Britain's comparative industrial decline and an aggravation of the structural defects of the country's outmoded productive apparatus.[207] The unions, by keeping their industrial weapon sheathed for three years, had not brought themselves significant gains in terms of real wages. Now, moreover, that the weapon had begun to be brandished once again it seemed to inflict more damage on the unions and on their relations with their governmental allies than on business. Nor did the TUC's *political* weapon appear any more effective. The unions were confronted with a choice between a Labour government determined to squeeze wages and to treat union market activism as treason and a Conservative alternative much more unpalatable than before.

The TUC's response to this renewed assertion of its endemic strategic dilemma involved, once again, an attempt to make the best of a bad situation – a response that left the contradictions unresolved. During the summer of 1978 TUC leaders had attempted to persuade Callaghan to drop his 5 percent policy and to call a general election as early as possible.[208] Once the Prime Minister had set himself on a collision-course with rank-and-file militancy, the TUC Economic Committee attempted, as we have seen, to moderate local wage demands, while negotiating a compromise with the government involving a loosening of wage settlement norms in return for the issuing by the TUC of 'guidelines' for bargainers urging 'responsibility' and 'moderation'.

In February, at the height of the strikes, an agreement along these lines was accepted by the General Council and the government and signed with much fanfare under the unofficial title of 'the Concordat'.[209] In the document the TUC endorsed the government's target of bringing inflation down to 5 percent within three years and pledged to 'ask' its affiliates to 'have regard' for this objective as well as for the government's other economic and social goals when negotiating wage settlements. The government and the TUC also promised to pursue discussions on new price controls, coordination of wage bargaining by means of an 'annual assessment' of national economic needs and capacities, and means for avoiding strikes in the essential public services. As an annex to the agreement the TUC issued a text of 'Advice and Guidance to Affiliated Unions' on collective bargaining procedures, on appropriate behavior during strikes and the correct application of closed-shop rules. This attempt to patch up union–party relations, to restore the public image of the unions after months of unpopular strikes and to present a brave front in view of the imminent elections, did not impress much of the press or enough of the voters to prevent the Conservatives led by Margaret Thatcher from sweeping into office with a forty-three-seat majority – and what they interpreted to be a mandate to impose a new discipline on the overbearing and irresponsible union movement.[210]

The TUC and the Tories

In a certain sense the defeat of the Callaghan government simplified the strategic tasks of the TUC's leaders. No longer caught between loyalty to a friendly government and the requirements for organizational maintenance imposed by the economic demands of rank-and-file militants, they are now free to devote all their energies to mobilizing opposition to an unabashedly anti-union government. On the other hand, the unions now find themselves in a more serious economic situation than ever before. After a brief and very partial recovery in 1978, the British economy has tumbled into a severe recessionary spiral that has accentuated the country's accumulated structural weaknesses.

Under the impact of the international recession and the stringent monetarist policies of successive Thatcherite budgets the British economy has virtually ceased growing. From the beginning of 1980 through the first half of 1981 real growth of GDP was negative and since then growth rates, while positive, have been too low to erase previous losses, thus leaving total output at the beginning of 1982 at 5 percent below the rate of mid-1979.[211] Industrial production has experienced the same contraction and is now 14 percent below the 1979 level. Investment figures have been equally discouraging: the UK has had the lowest rate of gross fixed capital accumulation in the OECD.[212] From the perspective of the unions, the most troublesome aspect of Britain's current economic decline is, of course, the impact of slow growth and industrial deterioration on levels of employment. Official unemployment figures have grown steadily under the Tories and have now reached 3·3 million or some 14 percent of the laborforce.[213] Levels of unemployment in much of the country's old industrial heartland are far above the national average.[214] The unions now face not only escalating unemployment, but also two additional threats. They have been unable to prevent significant declines in the growth of real wages.[215] Simultaneously, they have found the level of unionization to be declining for the first time since 1972.[216]

Along with this rapidly deteriorating economic situation, the TUC faces a government determined to let the latest bout of Britain's economic disease run its course and to impose the costs of its cure on workers through rising unemployment, reduced social services and drastic cuts in public sector investment and employment.[217] Not only is the Thatcher government set on a course of economic and social policy detrimental to workers, but it has also taken up where the Heath government left off in seeking to curb union power. The government's attack on the union movement is embodied in two pieces of legislation – the Employment Acts of 1980 and 1982. Taken together, they involve a set of important changes; both union leaders and unions as organizations are to be legally and financially responsible for damages suffered by employers as a result of industrial action deemed to be illegal; the scope of what constitutes such illegality is to be considerably broadened to include such traditional union practices as large-scale picketing, 'secondary' boycotts (that is, sympathy strikes or strikes against suppliers of the original firm being struck) and strikes deemed to be 'political' rather than purely industrial in motivation such as strikes in protest against government policies. The institution of the closed shop is to be challenged by requiring regular postal ballots requiring large majorities (80–85 percent) of the workers in a unit and by making unions responsible for financially compensating workers who lose their jobs because of closed-shop agreements. Also the ability of owners to dismiss striking workers and union organizers is considerably increased.[218] Despite substantial efforts at mobilizing support against the Bills, the TUC has been unable to prevent the government from proceeding with them, although it is not yet clear how long the 1982 Bill will take to be passed or how these provisions will actually be enforced by the courts.[219]

The TUC is, thus, confronted with an unprecedentedly difficult situation and it faces its immediate task of defending its members and itself with a severely depleted strategic arsenal. With unemployment at unprecedented levels and bankruptcies occurring at rates unheard of since the 1930s, the unions' economic weapon, their capacity to mobilize in the industrial arena in order to defend their members' jobs and wages, has lost much of its efficacy. The past three years have witnessed a considerable decline in strike activity, the failure of nearly every major national strike movement that has been undertaken, and disappointing turnouts for most of the TUC's efforts at mass demonstrations and protests.[220] The unions' capacity to act in the political arena has suffered an even more severe setback. The Conservatives enjoy considerable freedom of action not only because of their large parliamentary majority, but also because of widespread anti-union sentiment among public opinion.[221] Moreover, the TUC's traditional political strategy has lost its coherence because of recent developments in the Labour Party. In the wake of the 1979 defeat the internal conflict between moderates and radicals that had always been a feature of Labour politics erupted into full-scale warfare. The party's left wing, led by Tony Benn, sought to capture control of policy-making by increasing the influence of rank-and-file activists over the selection of the leadership, the designation of election candidates and the writing of the party platform, while diminishing the power and autonomy of the parliamentary party and especially of the parliamentary leadership. Partly as a result of the left's successes and partly for other reasons, a number of Labour moderates, led by such former Cabinet ministers as Shirley Williams, William Rogers, Roy Jenkins and David Owen, made good their threat to leave the party and create a new one. The emergence of the Social Democratic Party as a serious electoral force (in alliance with the Liberals they have been scoring very well in by-elections and in opinion polls) poses a fundamental threat to the TUC's conventional approach to political action. The next election will probably be, for the first time since the 1920s, a serious three-way fight whose outcome in terms of parliamentary seats and in terms of the political composition of the government will be exceedingly unpredictable. Of the four conceivable results – a one-party Labour government, a one-party Conservative government, a Labour–Social Democrat–Liberal coalition, or a Conservative–Social Democrat–Liberal coalition – only the first is one that the unions can look forward to, but it appears to be the least likely of the four. Two of the other possibilities – the two coalition governments – involve a high degree of uncertainty for the TUC, since their approaches to economic policy, social issues and industrial relations are at present very hard to foresee. Thus, the unions' time-honored approach to politics during periods of Conservative rule –mobilizing funds, activists and voters in support of Labour's upcoming campaign while seeking to shape the policies of a future Labour government through their influence within the National Executive Committee, the Liaison Committee and the Annual Conference – has lost much of its logic, although it is precisely this approach that the moderate unions have continued to pursue through 'Trade Unions for a Labour Victory', a political lobby created in the winter of 1979.

The unions, thus, face a novel challenge in the political arena just as they confront an increasingly difficult situation in the labor market. At the same time, the TUC's task of formulating a coherent economic stategy has become increasingly arduous. The package of policies that the TUC advocated in the 1977–9 period – investment-led recovery, economic planning to 'pick the winners' in various economic sectors and funnel state and private investment to them, 'industrial democracy' to increase union involvement in investment decisions and reduced work time to spread available work more evenly – has proved inappropriate to current political and economic conditions. Investment in productive industry has been extremely scarce as private capitalists have preferred to invest overseas or in real estate and services at home and the Thatcherites have divested the state of a significant role in industrial production and investment. Planning, even the truncated sectoral consultations of Labour's 'industrial strategy', has been unpopular with Tory policy-makers, who prefer to let investment decisions be determined by market forces, and the task of 'picking the winners' has become increasingly difficult in the current international climate. Industrial democracy, similarly, has been very far from the minds of the Thatcher government, who seek to reduce rather than augment the influence of the unions in the economy. Nor does job-sharing as advocated by the TUC in its Campaign for Reduced Working Time have much appeal to capitalists whose profit margins are squeezed to levels that discourage such innovation.

With their more positive schemes thus excluded, the unions have fallen back on an economic policy package that strongly resembles their program of 1977–9. This package contains three principal components. The first is a defensive battle to protect jobs in firms and industries threatened by layoffs, closures and bankruptcies. This defense of 'lame ducks' in such industries as steel, automobiles, textiles and engineering is not always justifiable on long-term economic grounds but is hard to avoid, especially in the absence of investment and new jobs in growth sectors and particularly for unions in regions such as the north and north-east of England, the Midlands, Wales and Scotland, where unemployment rates far exceed national averages. The second element of the TUC approach has been to devote considerable energy to criticizing government policies and calling for a shift to a more expansionary approach to state management of the economy with regard to interest rates, monetary policy, public expenditure and state borrowing. The TUC critique has been voiced not only in the organization's *Economic Review* and in the resolutions of its annual congresses, but also in various pamphlets, broadsheets and newspapers published under the auspices of the TUC Campaign for Economic and Social Advance, whose slogan is 'No return to the thirties'.[222] Thirdly, as in the early 1970s, the TUC has undertaken, both on its own and within the TUC–Labour Party Liaison Committee, to plan the economic programs of a future Labour government, despite the fact that such an eventuality appears increasingly remote. What is striking about the content of these reflections is how little they contain that is really new.

The central proposals of the TUC's medium-term economic program have changed rather little since 1978. The most noteworthy change in the TUC economic program does not involve any change in content, but rather an alteration of format and style. The TUC has, since 1981, markedly transformed its *Economic Review* with the clear aim of reaching a broader audience: the two most recent issues are shorter, less technical and more 'popular' in expository approach featuring numerous colored bar graphs and other simple graphics, together with the avoidance of abstruse economic terminology and a generally more 'commercial' presentation.

Aside from this change in format and apparently in intended audience, however, the TUC's economic programs have remained basically the same. The principal proposals have remained constant since the late 1970s. The TUC's *Economic Review* and its other economic publications continue to advocate a package of reforms, including an investment-led recovery based principally on public sector investment; a planning system involving both a central plan and decentralized institutions for individual industries and regions; 'industrial democracy to augment workers' and unions' input into economic decision-making'; selective import controls and effective exchange controls to protect the balance of payments and reduce the outflow of investment funds (the whole scheme now being referred to as the 'management of trade'); and work-sharing, especially through the reduction of the working week to 35 hours as a remedy for unemployment. What differences can be detected are often merely changes of emphasis: recent documents have placed greater weight on economic planning as the key to an effective recovery and on industrial democracy as a means for increasing social justice as well as economic efficiency.

Other changes are matters of refinements of previous positions, rather than new ideas: this is true, for example, of the introduction into the 1982 *Economic Review*'s section on import controls of specific recommendations for individual industries based on the work of various Sector Working Parties.[223] In two cases, however, there are interesting shifts but ones whose implications for TUC action are not yet clear. The first is the TUC's admission that industrial investment, given the character of new technologies, is not liable to create many new jobs and that, therefore, the emphasis of the investment program will have to be in services and especially public services. Another is the notion, mentioned very briefly in the 1982 *Economic Review*, of an annual National Economic Assessment.[224]

More striking than these changes, however, is the absence thus far of any serious reconsideration by the TUC of the experiences and failures of the 1974–9 period and, in particular, of the problem of inflation and wage restraint. The documents of the TUC have very little to say on the question of how the organization's highly expansionary economic program for a future Labour government can avoid running into the same inflationary difficulties and incomes policy confrontation as before. The 1981 *Economic Review* is almost completely silent on this issue, while the 1982 edition simply presents econometric data, claiming that its 'program for recovery' will generate only some 1·5 percent of added inflation.[225] Similarly, the TUC–Labour Party Liaison Committee's pamphlet *Economic Issues Facing the Next Labour Government* avoids discussing incomes policy just as had the original Social Contract text of 1973.[226] According to the new version of the union–party agreement, inflation is to be combatted by strict controls on prices, while wages are to be kept within limits 'compatible with our economic and social objectives' by the creation of consensus ('an agreed policy to control inflation') through increased union participation in policy-making and the annual practice of a national economic assessment involving such questions as the shares of national income going to the various factors of production.[227]

Part 5

Conclusion

In the period since World War II the British union movement has faced a very demanding challenge. Like its counterparts elsewhere in Europe, it has had to operate within a political economy whose basic structures were beyond its control. Like them, too, it has sought to attain a complex array of objectives: immediate economic objectives (maximizing material gains for its members); organizational objectives (maximizing the number of its members, its ability to influence their behavior, its internal coherence and efficacy, and its own freedom of action in the market arena); political objectives (bringing to, and maintaining in, office political parties sympathetic to its cause); and policy objectives (securing from friendly governments economic and social legislation consistent with its reformist perspectives, while preventing conservative governments from moving too far along other paths). Unlike most of its counterparts, however, the British union movement has been forced to seek these objectives in the context of a domestic economy that, long before the onset of the international economic crisis of the 1970s, was consistently weak and uncompetitive.

The poor performance of the British economy complicated the strategic tasks of the TUC and its leaders considerably by making each of their objectives harder to attain and by generating or reinforcing contradictions among these various objectives. Clearly, slow growth and tight industrial profit margins made it difficult for union negotiators to satisfy the economic demands of their members without generating either significant distributional conflict with capital or rising inflation. In either case union bargainers tended to find themselves in what has been called 'the pay paradox': they were able to secure the short-run material interests of their members only at the cost of endangering the long-run health of the national economy or, at least, of being accused of doing so and therefore exposing their organizations to hostile publicity and even legislation. The unions thus found their own short-run objectives coming into potential conflict with both their organizational goals and their policy objectives. The recurrence of inflation in the British economy posed similar problems for union leaders. The incomes policies that governments regularly employed to combat inflation confronted British union leaders with difficult choices. Accepting wage restraint involved sacrificing their members' immediate material objectives in the name of national economic well-being, improved union–government relations and possibly improved policy tradeoffs. However, participation in incomes policies exposed the unions to important organizational risks: conflict among various groups of union members and various affiliated unions resulting from the impact of incomes policies on traditional wage differentials, and conflict at various levels within the TUC between union leaders and the rank-and-file. Similarly, slow growth, a weak currency and balance of payments difficulties confronted union leaders with an unpleasant choice between their economic objectives and their social policy goals. Well before the 'fiscal crisis of the state' became fashionable as a concept and widespread as a problem, the difficulties of macroeconomic management in Britain put pressure on governments to reduce expenditures and borrowing and to pose for unions a choice between the 'market wage' and the 'social wage'.

Not only did the TUC's leaders have to operate, throughout much of the postwar period, in a weak and declining economy, but they had to do so using a set of union structures not well suited at all to such a situation. The postwar British union movement was characterized by a distinctive combination of strengths and weaknesses. From a comparative perspective, British unions were among the stronger national movements in terms of the size of their memberships and their overall coverage of the laborforce: with almost 8 million members (44·1 percent of the laborforce) in 1950 and over 10 million members (47·9 percent of the laborforce) in 1972, the TUC ranked among the large and more inclusive union movements in Europe. Moreover, within the manufacturing sector, unionization rates were considerably higher: for 1974, 73·3 percent among manual workers in manufacturing; 96·2 percent in coalmining; and 69·4 percent among all employees in metals and engineering.[228] The real locus of British union strength was in the workplace where, operating through networks of shop stewards, the widespread institution of the closed shop, a highly decentralized system of collective bargaining and long-established patterns of 'custom and practice' arrangements, the unions exercised an unusual degree of influence over wage levels, work practices and hiring procedures. The weaknesses of British unions were directly related to these strengths. The overall influence of the unions even at the level of individual firms but especially at the level of industrial branches and of the economy as a whole was reduced by the fragmented and competitive basis on which the unions were constituted: unions organized on a variety of different formulae from traditional craft to modern industrial often competed for the same workers, and their bargaining practices tended to assume a highly sectional, economistic and competitive orientation. Similarly, the mirror-image of the unions' organizational power at the shopfloor was their relative weakness at the peak levels. Most of the major unions affiliated to the TUC enjoyed not only limited resources in terms of finances, facilities and staff, but also limited leverage over their own regional and local organizations and activists. At the very top the TUC itself suffered from precisely the same difficulties *vis-à-vis* its affiliates: its resources for doing research, making policy and implementing its recommendations were surprisingly small and its ability to enforce its decisions on recalcitrant unions very limited.[229]

Taken together, this combination of power and impotence produced a union movement much better suited to good economic times than to bad. In a declining economy where inflation was a major issue and the right-wing press eager to pin the blame on 'union power', the British union movement's organizational characteristics gave it high visibility but limited capacity for coordinated strategic action. The shopfloor bargaining practices and competitive sectionalism of local unions fit very well into the portrait of 'overmighty subjects' painted by Conservative politicians and publicists but the weakness of the economy, as a whole, made the unions very reluctant to allow governments, even friendly ones, to tinker with industrial relations or union structures in ways that would reduce the only sure form of unions' power – their autonomy in the labor market as embodied in so-called 'free collective bargaining'. Moreover, even when the TUC was willing to restrain the market power of the workers in order to contribute to government efforts to fight inflation or strengthen the currency, its capacity to deliver was limited by the fact that it did not itself engage in any collective bargaining and its influence over the levels of the union movement that did the bargaining was limited to persuasion.

As the narrative of this chapter has demonstrated in detail, the problems posed for the TUC by the interaction of a declining national economy and its own distinctive structures stood out in particularly bold relief when its political ally, the Labour Party, was in power. Relations between union and party were always better during periods of Conservative rule: when it was Labour's turn to manage the brittle national economy, the party and the TUC had great and increasing difficulty doing each other anything but harm. The proneness of the economy to crisis made it difficult for Labour governments to provide their union allies with consistent policy rewards for their electoral support. Similarly, the organizational structure of the unions and their sensitivity concerning their market autonomy made the TUC an unreliable partner for Labour governments in difficult economic straits.

The TUC's actions and analyses during the 1974–9 period appear to us to make most sense when seen as the continuation and elaboration of a pattern of union–Labour government relations going back to the immediate postwar years. First, in the 1940s under Clement Attlee and, again, more severely in the 1960s under Harold Wilson, TUC leaders found themselves hostages to their own political allies who invoked national economic emergencies to curtail promised reform ventures, to impose wage restraint and, in the case of the Wilson government, to introduce legislation curtailing union power in the labor market. In both cases the TUC's strategy was to cooperate with the government until the organizational costs became unbearable, and then to succumb to rank-and-file pressures while attempting to preserve the 'party connection' and the Labour incumbency by diplomatic maneuvers. And in both cases this set of choices proved harmful to the unions: wage restraint cut into workers' real incomes, while the TUC's ultimately unsuccessful attempts to cooperate with the government's economic programs undermined internal cohesion so long as they were successful, and union–party relations as well as the electoral performance of the party, once they began to break down.

After its second experience of the disruptive effects of Labour incumbency, the TUC, as we have seen, undertook some strategic and organizational innovations in preparation for the following change of government. The TUC expanded its facilities for economic research and began to publish an annual *Economic Review* containing not only its immediate budgetary proposals, but also reflections on the longer-range problems of the economy. The organization also moved forward cautiously to rationalize its own structures by encouraging mergers of small craft unions with larger industrial bodies. Above all, the 'Social Contract' was worked out with the leadership of the Parliamentary Labour Party in order to secure the party's pledge to avoid repeating the errors of the past.

Unfortunately, the intensification of Britain's economic woes under the impact of the international crisis made these strategic preparations largely ineffective. Once again, an economic emergency brought the TUC's various goals into conflict with one another, undermined the unity of the union movement and generated intense conflict between the government and the TUC, culminating in the disastrous events of the winter and spring of 1978–9. No more than in the 1940s or the 1960s were TUC leaders able to overcome the cross-pressures imposed on them by the vulnerability of the economy, their own internal politics and their special but fratricidal relationship with the Labour Party.

Since the 1979 election the TUC's strategic problems have changed substantially but become no less serious. The unions face a challenge to their economic objectives unprecedented since the 1930s as the Thatcher government's rigid monetarist policies have shifted the burden of the crisis onto the working class. At the same time, the TUC's traditional response during periods of Conservative rule – to wait and plan for the return of Labour in the following elections – has become much less appropriate now that the rise of the Social Democratic Party and the exacerbation of the internal splits within what remains of the Labour Party have made a Labour victory somewhat improbable. The TUC's reaction has been to continue in the traditional manner with planning for a future Labour government, while devoting considerable energy to defending their own organizational interests against Conservative legislative assaults, and at the same time using their considerable influence within the structures of the Labour Party to maximize the electoral chances of their traditional ally. Different unions, to be sure, have envisaged the latter part of the strategy quite differently: some have supported the party's left wing in its attempts to democratize the party's operation and to radicalize its programs; while others, acting separately or under the umbrella of Trade Unions for a Labour Victory, have supported efforts to shore up the parliamentary leadership against grassroots insurgency, to keep the party's program from diverging too much from established positions and to promote reconciliation between the rival factions. The TUC's economic analysis and strategy, the principal focus of this chapter, has not thus far undergone any major revision that might indicate that TUC leaders have seen their strategic situation to have changed substantially. The TUC has continued to formulate elaborate programs for economic reform whose implementation clearly requires a Labour government. It remains to be seen whether, as the next general election approaches, the TUC and its component organizations will begin to adjust their economic thinking to accommodate the other, more probable, political outcomes.

Statistical Tables

Table 1.1   *TUC Membership, 1945–81*

Year	Members	%age change	Union density (%)
1945	6,575,654	—	38·6
1946	6,671,120	+1·45	n.a.
1947	7,540,397	+13	n.a.
1948	7,791,470	+3·32	45·2
1949	7,937,091	+1·87	44·8
1950	7,883,355	−0·07	44·1
1951	7,827,945	−0·07	45·0
1952	8,020,079	+2·45	45·1
1953	8,088,450	+0·85	44·6
1954	8,093,837	+0·07	44·2
1955	8,106,958	+0·16	44·5
1956	8,263,741	+1·93	44·1
1957	8,304,709	+0·50	44·0
1958	8,337,325	+0·39	43·2
1959	8,176,252	−1·93	42·9
1960	8,128,251	−0·59	43·1
1961	8,229,393	+1·24	42·9
1962	8,312,875	+1·01	42·7
1963	8,315,332	+0·03	42·7
1964	8,325,790	+0·13	43·1
1965	8,771,012	+5·35	43·2
1966	8,886,522	+1·32	42·6
1967	8,787,282	−1·12	42·8
1968	8,725,604	−0·70	43·1
1969	8,875,381	+1·72	44·4
1970	9,402,170	+5·94	47·7
1971	10,002,204	+6·38	47·9
1972	9,894,881	−1·07	49·4
1973	10,001,419	+1·08	49·2
1974	10,002,224	+0·01	50·4
1975	10,363,724	+3·61	51·7
1976	11,036,326	+6·49	51·8
1977	11,515,920	+4·25	52·9
1978	11,865,390	+3·03	n.a.
1979	12,128,078	+2·21	n.a.
1980	12,172,508	+0·37	n.a.
1981	11,601,413	−4·70	n.a.

Sources: TUC, *Annual Report, 1980*, p. 656; *Statistical Statement, 1981*, p. 12. Density figures are from R. Price and G. Bain, 'Union growth revisited: 1948–1974 in perspective', *British Journal of Industrial Relations*, vol. XIV, no. 3 (November 1976), p. 340, as corrected and supplemented by the authors. The membership figures are for unions affiliated with the TUC only, while the density figures represent the proportion of the entire laborforce belonging to any union whether affiliated to the TUC or not.

Table 1.2 *Principal Unions Affiliated to the TUC*

Abbreviation	Name	Membership (1981)
APEX	Association of Professional, Executive, Clerical and Computer Staffs	140,292
ASLEF	Associated Society of Locomotive Engineers and Firemen	27,000
ASTMS	Association of Scientific, Technical and Managerial Staffs	491,000
AUEW	Amalgamated Union of Engineering Workers	1,180,220
COHSE	Confederation of Health Service Employees	216,482
CPSA	Civil and Public Services' Association	216,415
EETPU	Electrical, Electronic, Tele-communications and Plumbing Union	405,000
GMWU	General and Municipal Workers' Union	915,654
ISTC	Iron and Steel Trades Confederation	100,175
NALGO	National and Local Government Officers' Association	782,343
NATSOPA	National Association of Operative Printers, Graphical and Media Personnel	54,487
NGA	National Graphical Association	116,438
NUM	National Union of Mineworkers	256,962
NUPE	National Union of Public Employees	699,156
NUR	National Union of Railwaymen	170,000
NUT	National Union of Teachers	232,397
TASS	Technical, Administrative and Supervisory Section (of AUEW)	
TGWU	Transport and General Workers' Union	1,886,971
UCATT	Union of Construction, Allied Trades and Technicians	312,000
UCW	Union of Communications Workers	202,293
USDAW	Union of Shop, Distributive and Allied Workers	450,287

Source: TUC, *Statistical Statement, 1981.*

Table 1.3   *British Economic Performance, 1961–82*

Year	Growth of real GDP at market prices (percentage change from preceding year)	Consumer prices (percentage change from preceding year)	Current balance (millions)	Unemployed (as percentage of total laborforce)
1961	3·3	3·4	6	1·52
1962	1·0	4·2	122	2·03
1963	3·9	2·0	124	2·2
1964	5·2	3·3	−382	1·6
1965	2·3	4·8	−84	2·3
1966	2·0	3·9	363	2·2
1967	2·6	2·5	−738	3·3
1968	4·1	4·7	−584	3·3
1969	1·5	5·4	1,207	3·0
1970	2·2	6·4	1,972	3·1
1971	2·7	9·4	2,747	4·0
1972	2·2	7·1	617	4·2
1973	7·5	9·2	−2,548	3·2
1974	−1·0	16·0	−7,832	3·1
1975	−0·7	24·2	−3,367	4·7
1976	3·6	16·5	−1,572	6·1
1977	1·3	15·8	−38	6·5
1978	3·7	8·3	1,953	6·4
1979	1·6	13·4	−1,807	5·7
1980	−2·0	18·0	6,660	7·3
1981	−2·0	11·9	11,527	11·4
1982	0·75	7·9	n.a.	12·9

Sources: OECD, *Economic Outlook*, no. 32 (December 1982); OECD, *Economic Survey: United Kingdom*, 1961–5.

Notes

The authors wish to thank George Ross for his important editorial contribution.

1 For the history of trade unionism in Britain, see H. Pelling, *A Short History of British Trade Unionism*, 3rd edn (London: Penguin, 1976); R. Currie, *Industrial Politics* (Oxford: Oxford University Press, 1979); and J. Lovell and B. C. Roberts, *A Short History of the TUC* (London: Macmillan, 1968).

2 See R. Skidelsky, *Politicians and the Slump* (London: Macmillan, 1967); and C. L. Mowat, *Britain between the Wars* (Chicago: University of Chicago Press, 1955).

3 See P. Addison, *The Road to 1945* (London: Quartet Books, 1977); and A. Martin, 'Is democratic control of capitalist economies possible?' in L. Lindberg, R. Alford, C. Crouch and C. Offe (eds), *Stress and Contradiction in Contemporary Capitalism* (Lexington, Mass.: Heath, 1977), pp. 13–55, esp. pp. 25–7.

4 See C. Crouch, 'The changing role of the state in industrial relations', in C. Crouch and A. Pizzorno, *The Resurgence of Class Conflict in Europe* (New York: Holmes & Meier, 1978), Vol. 1, pp. 203–4; and L. Minkin, 'Radicalism and reconstruction: the British experience, 1944–7', paper submitted to the Fourth International Colloquium of the Montreal Interuniversity Centre for European Studies, 25–27 March 1981.

5 The report was entitled, *Social Insurance and Allied Services*, Cmd 6404 (London: HMSO, 1942). For analyses of the report and its context, see D. Fraser, *The Evolution of the British Welfare State* (London: Macmillan, 1973), ch. 9; and H. Heclo, *Modern Social Politics in Britain and Sweden* (New Haven, Conn.: Yale University Press, 1974), pp. 141–7.

6 Trades Union Congress, *Report of the 75th Annual Congress, 1943* (London: TUC, 1943), pp. 371–2. This report will henceforth be cited simply as TUC, *Annual Report, 1943* and a similar notation will be used for the annual reports of other years as well.

7 TUC, 'Interim report on postwar reconstruction', in TUC, *Annual Report, 1944*, pp. 393–417. Other important sources for the TUC's views on postwar economic and social reconstruction are: 'Answer to Sir William Beveridge's questionnaire', ibid., pp. 418–22; 'Statement on finance and investment policy', ibid., pp. 422–36; and 'Statement on fiscal policy', TUC, *Annual Report, 1945*, appendix C, pp. 527–42.

8 TUC, 'Interim report', op. cit., p. 393.

9 ibid., p. 397.

10 ibid., pp. 400–1.

11 ibid., p. 399.

12 ibid., p. 402.

13 ibid., pp. 406–8.

14 TUC, 'Statement on finance and investment policy', pp. 424–5.

15 ibid., pp. 433–4. The TUC report distinguished between 'current' government spending, which it felt should be financed out of current revenues, and spending on 'capital assets', for which it regarded borrowing as justifiable.

16 'Statement on fiscal policy', op. cit., p. 3.

17 'Reply to Sir William Beveridge's questionnaire', op. cit., pp. 420–1.

18 'Statement on finance and investment policy', op. cit., p. 423.

19 ibid., pp. 425–6. It is worth noting the TUC's extreme caution on this issue: no reference is made to 'nationalisation' of the Bank, and even the goal of turning it into a 'public agency' is presented as a long-term objective to be attempted only 'ultimately'. In the short run the TUC urged that the Bank's governor be appointed by the government.

20 ibid., pp. 426, 428.

21 ibid., pp. 430–2.

22   ibid.
23   TUC, 'Interim report on postwar reconstruction', op. cit., pp. 410–3.
24   ibid.
25   ibid., p. 409.
26   ibid., pp. 410–11.
27   For the TUC's rejection of increased state intervention into industrial relations, see 'Reply to Sir William Beveridge's questionnaire', op. cit., pp. 420–1.
28   ibid., pp. 418–9.
29   TUC, 'Interim report on trade union structure and closer unity', appendix A in TUC, *Annual Report, 1944*, op. cit.
30   ibid.
31   Samuel Beer noted this insistence and attributed to it much of the blame for the failure of Labour's postwar effort at planning. See S. Beer, *Modern British Politics* (London: Faber, 1965), pp. 200–8.
32   ibid., ch. 7. See also A. A. Rogow, *The Labour Government and British Industry, 1945–51* (Oxford: Blackwell, 1955), chs 3 and 8; and D. Coates, *The Labour Party and the Struggle for Socialism* (Cambridge: Cambridge University Press, 1975), ch. 3.
33   Rogow, op. cit., pp. 105–7.
34   L. Panitch, *Social Democracy and Industrial Militancy* (Cambridge: Cambridge University Press, 1976), p. 268, n. 1.
35   C. Crouch, 'The changing role of the state in industrial relations', op. cit., pp. 204–5.
36   See Beer, op. cit., pp. 188–216; J. Leruez, *Economic Planning and Politics in Britain* (London: Martin Robertson, 1975), ch. 2; and A. Shonfield, *Modern Capitalism* (Oxford: Oxford University Press, 1969), chs 6 and 8.
37   R. E. Caves (ed.), *Britain's Economic Prospects* (London: Allen & Unwin, 1968), pp. 30, 33–4.
38   D. H. Aldcroft and P. Fearon, *Economic Growth in Twentieth-Century Britain* (London: Macmillan, 1969), pp. x–xi. The standard work on long-term British economic development is W. A. Cole and P. Deane, *British Economic Growth, 1688–1959* (Cambridge: Cambridge University Press, 1969). See also E. F. Denison, 'Economic growth', in Caves, *et al.*, op. cit., ch. 6.
39   M. Stewart, *Politics and Economic Policy since 1964: The Jekyll and Hyde Years* (London: Pergamon, 1978), p. 6.
40   See S. Blank, 'Britain: the politics of foreign economic policy, the domestic economy and the problem of pluralistic stagnation', in P. J. Katzenstein (ed.), *Between Power and Plenty: Foreign Economic Policies of Advanced Industrial States* (Madison, Wisconsin: University of Wisconsin Press, 1978), pp. 89–106. See also F. Longstreth, 'The city, industry and the state', in C. Crouch (ed.), *State and Economy in Contemporary Capitalism* (London: Croom Helm, 1979), pp. 157–90.
41   For discussions of the traditional British system of industrial relations, see the following: H. Clegg, *The System of Industrial Relations in Great Britain* (Oxford: Blackwell, 1979), chs 1, 2, 6, 7 and 9; C. Crouch, *Class Conflict and the Industrial Relations Crisis* (London: Heinemann, 1977), ch. 3; A. Flanders, 'The tradition of voluntarism', *British Journal of Industrial Relations*, vol. VIII, no. 4 (November 1974), pp. 358–61; and R. Lewis, 'The historical development of labour law', *British Journal of Industrial Relations*, vol. XIV, no. 1 (March 1976), pp. 1–17.
42   For a study of British business organizations and their relations with the state, see. S. Blank, *Government and Industry in Britain: The Federation of British Industries in Politics, 1945–1965* (Farnborough: Saxon House, 1973).
43   See Clegg, op. cit., ch. 2.
44   On organized business, see Blank, op. cit.; and W. Grant and D. Marsh, *The Confederation of British Industry* (London: Hodder & Stoughton, 1977). On the internal politics of the union movement, see Minkin, op. cit.; and Clegg, op. cit., ch. 2. In theory the TUC's General Council possessed a number of sanctions that could be used against uncooperative member-unions, but it rarely chose to employ them except against small organizations.
45   For a highly critical view of British union structure and internal politics, see

L. Ulman, 'Collective bargaining and industrial efficiency', in Caves, *et al.*, op. cit., ch. 8.

46 TUC, *Annual Report, 1954*, pp. 291–301; the quotation is from p. 298, para. 37. The principal documentary sources for TUC economic thought during this period are the regular chapters on 'Economic policy and organisation' in the TUC's *Annual Report*. The best secondary source on TUC economic analysis and action during these years is Panitch, op. cit.

47 TUC, *Annual Report, 1954*, p. 295, para. 24.

48 *Trade Unions and Wages Policy: Report of the Special Conference of Trade Union Executive Committees, London, 12 January 1950* (London: TUC, 1950). See also Panitch, op. cit., chs 1–2.

49 TUC, *Trade Unions and Wages Policy*, op. cit., p. 50: 'The General Council consider they should once again stress the gravity of the present economic situation, and emphasise the fact that devaluation has been adopted as an alternative to deflation. The dangerous inflationary tendencies which devaluation inevitably intensifies must be counteracted by vigorous restraints upon all increases of wages, salaries and dividends.'

50 ibid., p. 43.

51 Panitch, op. cit., ch. 1, provides a well-documented account of TUC debates for this period. A number of unions opposed the incomes policy completely or endorsed it only halfheartedly at the 12 January 1950 conference. Among the former were the miners, the Civil Service Union and the Engineering and shipbuilding draftsmen, while the latter group included the hospital workers of COHSE and the railway drivers of ASLEF.

52 Caves, *et al.*, op. cit., p. 161, provides data on the British balance of payments for 1955–61.

53 On the notion of 'available' exports, see ibid., p. 193, and for overseas investment data, see p. 173.

54 The details can be found in Panitch, op. cit., ch. 2; and in D. C. Smith, 'Incomes policy', in Caves, *et al.*, op. cit., ch. 3.

55 TUC, *Annual Report, 1959*, pp. 485–511. The Conservative government is accused by the TUC of deliberately abandoning the 'Beveridge doctrine' of full employment in an attempt to curb an inflationary problem whose seriousness is, according to the TUC, largely exaggerated (p. 495). The government is urged to regard unemployment as the real problem and to 'operate positive expansionary policies' to encourage investment (p. 511).

56 Tom Nairn provides a provocative review of the literature on England's crisis in 'The future of Britain's crisis', *New Left Review*, no. 113–14 (January–April 1979), pp. 43–70. Some of the early contributions to the debate were Arthur Koestler (ed.), *Suicide of a Nation* (London: Secker & Warburg, 1963); Michael Shanks, *The Stagnant Society* (Harmondsworth: Penguin, 1961); and a series of Penguin books on various British institutions, each entitled, *What's Wrong with . . .?*

57 Caves *et al.*, op. cit., p. 232.

58 J. Knapp and K. Lomax, 'Britain's growth performance: the enigma of the 1950s', in Aldcroft and Fearon, op. cit., ch. 6, p. 104.

59 Britain had the lowest ratio of capital to persons employed of any industrial economy with the exception of the Italian. See Denison in Caves, *et al.*, op. cit., p. 272.

60 See ibid., pp. 272–3; and political and economic planning, *Growth in the British Economy* (London: Allen & Unwin, 1960), pp. 126–7, 174–81.

61 F. W. Paish, *Studies in an Inflationary Economy* (London: Macmillan, 1962); and A. W. Phillips, 'The relationship between unemployment and the rate of money wage changes in the United Kingdom, 1861–1957', *Economica*, n.s., vol. XXV, no. 100 (November 1958), pp. 283–99.

62 B. C. Roberts, *Trade Unions in a Free Society* (London: Institute for Economic Affairs, 1959); A. Flanders, *The Fawley Productivity Agreements* (London: Faber, 1964); M. Shanks, *The Stagnant Society* (Harmondsworth: Penguin, 1961); and *A Giant's Strength* (London: Inns of Court Conservative and Unionist Society, 1958).

63   R. Price and G. S. Bain, 'Union growth revisited: 1948–1974 in perspective', *British Journal of Industrial Relations*, vol. XIV, no. 3 (November 1976), pp. 339–40.

64   ibid., pp. 342–3.

65   ibid., p. 349.

66   ibid.

67   C. Crouch, 'The intensification of industrial conflict in the United Kingdom', in C. Crouch and A. Pizzorno, *The Resurgence of Class Conflict in Europe*, op. cit., Vol. 1, pp. 207 ff.

68   R. Tarling and F. Wilkinson, 'The social contract: post-war incomes policies and their inflationary impact', *Cambridge Journal of Economics*, vol. I, no. 4 (March 1977), pp. 395–414, esp. p. 403.

69   ibid.

70   Pressure for some reorganization first emerged at the 1958 Trades Union Congress and resulted after a considerable amount of delay in an inquiry being undertaken by the Finance and General Purposes Committee during 1962–3. The inquiry produced little more than a report to the General Council, declaring that the establishment of industrial unions in place of the existing complex structures would be 'impracticable and undesirable' and recommending amalgamation of unions by a process of 'discussion and agreement'. A series of meetings of unions organizing similar workers was held under General Council auspices during 1964–6 but the results, as reported in TUC documents, were rather meager: TUC, *Annual Report, 1959*, p. 118; *Annual Report, 1960*, p. 119; *Annual Report, 1963*, pp. 122–3; *Annual Report, 1964*, pp. 108–10; *Annual Report, 1965*, pp. 118–20; and *Annual Report, 1966*, pp. 118–22.

71   See Beer, op. cit., ch. 9; and N. Harris, *Competition and the Corporate Society* (Cambridge: Cambridge University Press, pp. 235–46; and Leruez, op. cit., pp. 81–96.

72   TUC, 'Economic planning and development', appendix A of *Annual Report, 1963*, pp. 480–95.

73   ibid., p. 494: 'Any agreement, within the framework of economic planning, on a wages strategy which involved unions in modifying their own bargaining objectives could only be reached within the context of a more general agreement on national economic and social priorities.' For Woodcock's concerns regarding relations with the Conservatives, see Minkin, 'The party connection', op. cit.

74   See Stewart, op. cit., chs 2–3; and R. Opie, 'Economic planning and growth', in W. Beckerman (ed.), *The Labour Government's Economic Record, 1964–1970* (London: Duckworth, 1972), pp. 157–77.

75   Stewart, op. cit., chs 2–3, contain a good account of the hopes and failures of this period. See also Beckerman, chs 1, 4 and 5; and B. Lapping, *The Labour Government, 1964–1970* (Harmondsworth: Penguin, 1970).

76   The debates within the union movement during this period are admirably presented in Panitch, op. cit., pp. 52–76.

77   C. Crouch, *The Politics of Industrial Relations* (London: Fontana, 1979), pp. 51–3; and Panitch, op. cit., pp. 68 ff.

78   For the origins and history of the Donovan Commission, see Crouch, 'The intensification of industrial conflict in the United Kingdom', op. cit., pp. 244–5; Crouch, *The Politics of Industrial Relations*, op. cit., ch. 2; and M. Moran, *The Politics of Industrial Relations* (London: Macmillan, 1977), ch. 3.

79   Beckerman, op. cit., pp. 11–74; Stewart, op. cit., ch. 4; and W. Blackaby, 'Narrative, 1960–74', in Blackaby, *British Economic Policy, 1960–74*, op. cit., pp. 28–42.

80   Beckerman, op. cit., pp. 24–5; and Stewart, op. cit., pp. 79–83.

81   Panitch, op. cit., pp. 115–16; Opie, op. cit., pp. 170–4; and Stewart, op. cit., pp. 53–4.

82   Panitch, op. cit., ch. 4, analyzes this period in detail. See also Tarling and Wilkinson, op. cit., pp. 588–9, for a helpful tabular presentation of all the incomes periods of the postwar period.

83   Panitch, op. cit., ch. 4.

84   C. Crouch, *Class Conflict and the Industrial Relations Crisis* (London: Humanities Press, 1977), pp. 143–59.

85   Great Britain, *Royal Commission on Trade Unions and Employers' Associations, 1965–1968*, Cmnd 3623 (London: HMSO, June 1968), pp. 46–7, 137–8, 183, 203.

86   For the background to the White Paper and the contents and vicissitudes of the Bill, see

Jenkins, *The Battle of Downing Street* (London: Charles Knight, 1970); and Crouch, *Class Conflict and the Industrial Relations Crisis*, op. cit., chs 9 and 13.

87 See Crouch, *The Politics of Industrial Relations*, op. cit., pp. 70–3.

88 The TUC's position is presented in a pamphlet, entitled, *Action on Donovan: Interim Statement by the TUC General Council in Response to the Report of the Royal Commission on Trade Unions and Employers' Associations* (London: TUC, 1968). The TUC's testimony to the Commission, which reveals a great deal about its self-image and strategy, can be found in *Trade Unionism: The Evidence of the Trades Union Congress to the Royal Commission on Trade Unions and Employers' Associations* (London: TUC, 1967).

89 Jenkins, op. cit., presents the liveliest account of this confrontation.

90 The best treatments of the political role played by the unions are by L. Minkin. See his 'The party connection: divergence and convergence in the British Labour movement', *Government and Opposition*, vol. XIII, no. 4 (Autumn 1978), pp. 458–84, and *The Labour Party Conference* (London: Allen Lane, 1978). See also M. Harrison, *Trade Unions and the Labour Party since 1945* (London: Allen & Unwin, 1960); and I. Richter, *Political Purpose in Trade Unions* (London: Allen & Unwin, 1973).

91 Minkin, 'The party connection', op. cit., pp. 471–2.

92 TUC, *Productivity, Prices and Incomes: Report of a Conference of Executive Committees of Affiliated Organisations Held on 30th April 1965* (London: TUC, 1965), and *Incomes Policy: Report of a Conference of Executive Committees of Affiliated Organisations Held on 2nd March 1967* (London: TUC, 1967).

93 Initially the document was submitted for approval to a 'conference of executive committees' of TUC affiliates held in February. After 1969, however, the *Economic Review* was simply circulated to affiliated unions and published in late February or early March of each year.

94 *TUC Economic Review, 1968*, pp. 7, 10.

95 ibid., p. 37.

96 The position of the TUC and of its affiliated unions on the issue of incomes policies oscillated rapidly during the late 1960s, as Leo Panitch has documented (op. cit., pp. 149–63). The Conference of Executives held in February 1968 approved the *Economic Review* with its cautious endorsement of incomes policy, although for many unions this approval was very reluctant and the overall margin of victory for the *Review* was very narrow. By the time of the following TUC Congress in September 1968 the government had introduced a statutory program of wage restraint which the unions rejected by a considerable margin as a violation of the principle of 'free collective bargaining' (whereas 'voluntary', TUC-administered incomes policies were not regarded as such). By the time of the 1969 *Economic Review*, however, the General Council was again advocating incomes policy (voluntary, to be sure) as a substitute for the legal and organizational changes entailed by *In Place of Strife* (*TUC Economic Review, 1969*, pp. 32–46).

97 *TUC Economic Review, 1968*, p. 38.

98 ibid.

99 *TUC Economic Review, 1969*, p. 10.

100 *TUC Economic Review, 1968*, pp. 10–13; and *TUC Economic Review, 1969*, p. 53.

101 *TUC Economic Review, 1968*, pp. 10, 91.

102 At a rhetorical level the TUC remained committed to extending public ownership, its 1964 Congress having called for 'an extension of public ownership based on popular control in which trade unions participate on a democratic basis at all levels': Resolution on 'Economic planning and wages', TUC, *Annual Report, 1964*, p. 561.

103 *TUC Economic Review, 1968*, pp. 8, 14–15.

104 For the provisions of the Act, see Moran, op. cit., ch. 6; and R. Dorfman, *Government versus Trade Unions in British Politics since 1968* (London: Macmillan, 1979), pp. 50–8.

105 On the economic policies of the Heath government, see Stewart, op. cit., ch. 5; and Blackaby, op. cit., pp. 52–76, 117–24.

106 This process of rethinking has been described in R. Taylor, *Labour and the Social Contract*, Fabian Tract 458 (London: Fabian Society, 1978), and in M. Hatfield, *The House that Left Built* (London: Gollanz, 1978), ch. 5.

107 London: TUC–Labour Party Liaison Committee, February 1973. The document is reprinted in TUC, *Annual Report, 1973*, pp. 312–15.

108   Incomes policy is dealt with only tangentially in the 1973 document. Paragraph 5 acknowledges the need to control inflation: trade unionists are said to be aware that 'what matters is real wages, not paper ones'. But wage push is treated as a secondary factor in the inflationary process: 'wages and salaries are very far indeed from being the only factor affecting prices.' Moreover, British wage levels are said to be not excessive by comparative standards and their recent rates of increase are said to be 'below the average for industrial countries'. Price controls receive detailed attention in the document (para. 7) but wage controls are never specifically mentioned.

109   *TUC Economic Review, 1972*, pp. 20–1.

110   The TUC appears to have first mentioned this 'agency' (which would become the National Enterprise Board) in the *Economic Review*, 1972, p. 21. Its 1971 *Review* had been silent on this point, speaking only of the need for some 'new public enterprises' p. 49).

111   See Hatfield, op. cit., chs 2–3.

112   *TUC Economic Review, 1972*, p. 25.

113   *Economic Policy and the Cost of Living*, op. cit., para. 17. The notion of 'industrial democracy' had been gaining currency within the British labor movement since the mid-1960s, partly as a result of the propaganda efforts of the Nottingham-based Institute for Workers' Control in which a number of prominent TUC leaders such as Hugh Scanlon and Jack Jones were involved. See, for example, K. Coates and T. Topham, *Catching Up with the Times: How far the TUC Got the Message about Workers' Control* (Nottingham: Institute for Workers' Control, 1973). Under the influence of Jack Jones, leader of the TGWU, the idea was first adopted by various TUC affiliates and then by the TUC itself when the 1973 Congress adopted the General Council's *Interim Report on Industrial Democracy* (see TUC, *Annual Report, 1974*, pp. 240, 292–6).

114   This is the position developed in the document, *Economic Policy and Collective Bargaining in 1973* (London: TUC, 1973), esp. pp. 40–4.

115   The best sources for these debates on incomes policy are the TUC's *Annual Report* for 1972–4, and the *Report of Proceedings of the Special Trades Union Congress Held to Discuss Economic Policy and Collective Bargaining in 1973* (these debates are included in the published version of the report).

116   This hypothesis is based on interviews conducted by the authors during the winter, spring and summer of 1979 with a variety of union officials, TUC staff members, academics and journalists.

117   See Stewart, op. cit., pp. 131–4; and Blackaby, op. cit., pp. 58–74.

118   *TUC Economic Review, 1972*, pp. 15, 21; and *Economic Policy and Collective Bargaining in 1973*, pp. 5, 9, 12–13.

119   *TUC Economic Review, 1972*, p. 15; *Economic Policy and Collective Bargaining in 1973*, pp. 26–7; and *TUC Economic Review, 1974*, pp. 23–4.

120   J. D. Sachs, 'Wages, profits and macroeconomic adjustment: a comparative study', *Brookings Papers on Economic Activity, 1979*, No. 2, pp. 269–319 at p. 56, table 12; and UK Central Statistical Office, *Economic Trends*, No. 308 (London: CSO, June 1979), pp. 42–3.

121   UK Central Statistical Office, *Economic Trends*, op. cit., p. 36.

122   See Table 1.3 and the fascinating account by S. Fay and H. Young, *The Day the £ Almost Died* (London: Sunday Times Reprint, June 1978).

123   UK Central Statistical Office, *Economic Trends*, op. cit., p. 36.

124   See Taylor, op. cit., pp. 3–6; and Dorfman, op. cit., ch. 6.

125   See Crouch, *Politics of Industrial Relations*, op. cit., pp. 106–18; and Taylor, op. cit., p. 4.

126   Health and Safety at Work Act 1974. See also: *The Public General Acts and General Synod Meetings, 1974* (London: HMSO, 1975), pt I, ch. 37, pp. 643–759.

127   Employment Protection Act, 1975, pt III, ch. 71, pp. 2105-312. For the TUC's assessment of the legislation, see TUC's *Annual Report, 1975*, pp. 90–104. See also D. Coates, *Labour in Power?* (London and New York: Longman, 1980), pp. 57–8.

128   TUC leaders placed considerable emphasis on this aspect of the Social Contract, especially during the early years of the Labour government. See, for example, Norman Willis, 'Statement for the General Council', in *The Social Contract, 1976–77: Report of the Special Trades Union Congress 1976*, op. cit., pp. 17, 20.

129 *TUC Economic Review, 1974*, p. 22; and *TUC Economic Review, 1975*, p. 72.

130 See, for example, *TUC Economic Review, 1975*, pp. 7–9.

131 ibid., p. 13.

132 'The rate of inflation and the balance of payments deficit have both reached record levels. Action to moderate the rate of inflation and improve the UK's overseas trade and payments position must be paramount in the Chancellor's mind': *TUC Economic Review, 1974*, p. 5.

133 *TUC Economic Review, 1975*, pp. 9–10.

134 See Stewart, op. cit., ch. 1, for a review of some of this literature. See also A. Graham and W. Beckerman, 'Introduction: economic performance and the foreign balance', in Beckerman, op. cit., pp. 11–28; and R. N. Cooper, 'The balance of payments', in Caves, *et al.*, op. cit., pp. 147–97.

135 The 1974 *Economic Review* deals with these matters quite cursorily (pp. 34–5), whereas the 1975 *Review* devotes an entire chapter (pp. 14–25) to the weaknesses of Britain's economic structures.

136 *TUC Economic Review, 1974*, pp. 35–6.

137 The official document specifying the terms of the Social Contract *(Economic Policy and the Cost of Living)* avoided, as we have seen, any specific discussion of incomes policies but insisted that a 'wide-ranging agreement between unions and government' would produce a 'strong feeling of mutual confidence required for controlling inflation'. The TUC's opposition to formal wage restraint was reiterated in various texts during 1974 and early 1975, for example, *Collective Bargaining and the Social Contract* (London: TUC, June 1974), in which the TUC's General Council reasserted its opposition to formal wage guidelines and its faith in the capacity of moderation and good faith by union bargainers to restrain inflation (paras 26 and 33). See also *TUC Economic Review, 1975*, ch. 5.

138 *Collective Bargaining and the Social Contract*, paras 26–33; and *TUC Economic Review, 1975*, ch. 5, esp. para. 174 on the 'social wage' and paras 198–208 on the 'extension of collective bargaining to non-wage issues'.

139 On import controls, see *TUC Economic Review, 1974*, which calls for 'the temporary imposition of import controls for manufactured and some semi-manufactured goods' by means of a system of quotas and deposits by importers. These controls are seen as merely a 'holding operation' to give British industry time to improve its competitiveness (p. 22). See also *TUC Economic Review, 1975*, where 'temporary and selective import controls' are to be combined with a 'Buy British' campaign (p. 17).

140 The TUC position on the EEC is best expressed in *Renegotiation and the Referendum: The TUC View* (London: TUC, April 1975), where a clear 'no' stand is taken on the ground that the terms of entry negotiated by the Heath government had not been altered sufficiently in the renegotiation to be 'fair and beneficial to Britain'. For debates among the various unions on the referendum question, see TUC, *Annual Report, 1975*, pp. 181–2, 486–7, 491–2. See also L. Murray, 'Speech to the French Chamber of Commerce in Great Britain, London, Savoy Hotel, 7 March 1975' (transcript in TUC files).

141 For the TUC's position on the NEB and on the other provisions of the Industry Act of 1975, see *TUC Economic Review, 1975*, pp. 27–30.

142 *TUC Economic Review, 1974*, p. 24.

143 For the role of public expenditure in sustaining demand, see *TUC Economic Review, 1975*, pp. 10, 73–7.

144 The TUC *Economic Review* of 1974 glanced very rapidly (pp. 35–9) over the area of industrial policy and the 1975 issue devoted only a few pages (pp. 26–30) to these questions.

145 A telling indicator of the priorities of TUC moderates during this period can be found in the remarks of Assistant General Secretary Norman Willis to the Special Trades Union Congress held in July 1976 to evaluate the second phase of the government's incomes policy. In his 'Statement for the General Council' Willis stated that 'if this Government had done nothing more than to repeal the Industrial Relations Act it would have deserved a hearing from the trade union movement, for that Act was not only poisoning the whole system of peaceful industrial relations in this country, it was a symbol of confrontationist politics which was a dead end for our country': *The Social Contract 1976–77: Report of the Special Trades Union Congress, 1976*, op. cit., p. 18.

146 See *Annual Report, 1975*, p. 351; and *Annual Report, 1976*, pp. 305, 316–20.

147   OECD, *Economic Surveys, UK, 1980*, p. 39.
148   *OECD Economic Surveys, 1979*, p. 60. For long-term patterns in the value of sterling, see OECD, *Main Economic Indicators: Historical Statistics, 1960–1979*, p. 614. For details of developments during 1975–76, see Fay and Young, op. cit., esp. pp. 6–7.
149   Stewart, op. cit., p. 211; and Fay and Young, op. cit., p. 1.
150   K. Joseph, *Solving the Union Problem is the Key to Britain's Recovery: A Talk Given to the Bow Group, 5 February 1979* (London: Centre for Policy Studies, 1979); S. Brittan, *Second Thoughts on Full Employment* (London: Barry Rose, 1975); and *Why Britain Needs a Social Market Economy* (London: Centre for Policy Studies, 1975).
151   Useful overviews of this literature can be found in H. Phelps Brown, 'What is the British predicament?', *Three Banks Review*, no. 116 (December 1977); and S. Blank, 'Britain's economic problem: lies and damn lies', in I. Kramnick (ed.), *Is Britain Dying? Perspectives on the Current Crisis* (Ithaca and London: Cornell University Press, 1979), pp. 66–88.
152   TUC, *Annual Report, 1974*, pp. 395–8, esp. p. 397.
153   *The Attack on Inflation*, Cmnd 6151 (London: HMSO, July 1975), p. 12.
154   TUC–Labour Party Liaison Committee, *Economic Policy and the Cost of Living*, para. 11.
155   *The Times*, 2 April 1974.
156   See *The Times*, 13 November 1974, pp. 1, 4–7 and, especially, the 'Business Editorial', 'A budget to keep business afloat', p. 23.
157   *The Times*, 16 April 1975.
158   TUC, *The Development of the Social Contract* (London: TUC, 1975), pp. 14–15; N. Willis, 'Statement for the General Council', in *The Social Contract, 1976–77: Report of the Special Trades Union Congress, 16 June 1976* (London: TUC, 1976), pp. 16–22; and *TUC Economic Review, 1976*, pp. 15–16, 20–1.
159   The threat of a return of the Conservatives and the appeal to the traditional loyalty to the Labour Party were arguments used by numerous speakers during TUC debates on economic policy in general, and incomes policy in particular, during this period. See, for example, the speech by Tom Jackson, leader of the Union of Postal Workers, in *The Social Contract, 1976–77*, op. cit., p. 45, or David Basnett of the General and Municipal Workers' Union, ibid., p. 41, or Jack Jones, ibid., p. 37.
160   ibid., pp. 12–16.
161   For a discussion of the terms of the policy, see *The Attack on Inflation*, op. cit., pp. 4–5; and TUC, *The Development of the Social Contract*, op. cit., pp. 15-16.
162   See Jones's explanation in TUC, *Annual Report, 1975*, p. 460.
163   *TUC Economic Review, 1976*, pp. 17–20; and *Economic Review, 1977*, p. 11.
164   *TUC Economic Review, 1976*, ch. 3; 1977, pp. 39–48, 52–60, 87–9.
165   *TUC Economic Review, 1976*, pp. 77–82.
166   *TUC Economic Review, 1975*, pp. 33–5; and *TUC Economic Review, 1976*, pp. 15–16, 52.
167   Whereas questions of industrial policy had been given very little space in the *Economic Review* of 1974 and 1975, beginning in 1976 they began to receive more attention. The 1976 issue contained a full eighteen-page chapter on 'Industrial strategy' along with an annex containing a 'Checklist for trade union representatives in industrial strategy talks'. The 1977 *Economic Review* similarly devoted an entire chapter (twenty-seven pages) to 'The industrial strategy'. The new emphasis on strategies to combat unemployment in the TUC's approach to negotiating with the government can be seen in the report of the General Council to the 1976 Special Congress on the second phase of incomes policy (*The Social Contract, 1976–77*, op. cit., pp. 11–13), and in the heavy emphasis on employment policies and industrial strategy in the Liaison Committee's document *The Next Three Years and the Problem of Priorities* (London: TUC, 28 July 1976), pp. 6–7.
168   Bain and Price, op. cit.; G. S. Bain and R. Price, *Profiles of Union Growth: A Comparative Statistical Portrait of Eight Countries* (Oxford: Blackwell, 1980), p. 38, table 2.1. See also J. Hughes, 'British trade union development in the crisis of the 1970s', unpublished ms.
169   For Callaghan's speech, see TUC, *Annual Report, 1978*, pp. 517–23, esp. p. 521.
170   *Hansard*, 4 April 1979, quoted in R. Taylor, 'Contracted troubles', *Observer*, 22 April 1979.

171 For the complex issue of the impact of incomes policy on wage differentials, see A. J. H. Dean, 'Incomes policies and differentials', *National Institute Economic Review*, no. 85 (August 1978), pp. 40–8.

172 For the Communist Party's position on incomes policy, see B. Ramelson, *Social Contract: Cure-All or Con-Trick?* (London: CPGB, 1975), and *Bury the Social Contract: The Case for an Alternative Policy* (London: CPGB, 1977). Trotskyist positions can best be followed in such party periodicals as the *Militant* and *Revolutionary Communist*. For the opposition to the social contract by the so-called 'broad left' (an informal grouping running from the left of the Labour Party through the various organizations of the far left), see London CSE Group, 'Crisis, the labour movement and the alternative economic strategy', *Capital and Class*, no. 8 (Summer 1979), pp. 68–94.

173 See C. Hitchens, 'Strange death of a social contract', *New Statesman*, 26 January 1979; R. Taylor, *The Fifth Estate*, op. cit., ch. 4; and *Labour Research*, December 1978, January 1979.

174 For NUPE's consistent and vigorous opposition to wage restraint, see *Public Employee*, May 1975; *Economic Outlook*, July 1976; *Inflation: Attack or Retreat* (London: NUPE, 1975); and *Time to Change Course* (London: NUPE, 1976). The positions of ASTMS can be followed in the union's newspaper, *ASTMS Journal* (esp. July–August 1975 issue), and its *Quarterly Economic Review* (esp. first issue, I-1, of January 1976). For ASTMS's general economic analysis and strategy, see *The Crisis in British Economic Planning* (London: ASTMS, 1976), and *Unemployment: Emergency Edition of Economic Review* (September 1976). The AUEW's oscillations on incomes policy can be followed in the resolutions of its National Conferences and National Committees *(Report of the Proceedings . . .)* as well as in the *AUEW Journal*. For the TGWU, see *TGWU Record*, especially the report on the debates at the critical 1977 Biennial Delegates Conference in the issue of August 1977. See also annual *TGWU, Report and Balance Sheet*, 1977.

175 For summaries of the course of government policy in this period, see Taylor, *Labour and the Social Contract*, pp. 3–13; and D. Coates, *Labour in Power?* (London: Longman), chs 1–3.

176 In a speech to the Commons on 1 July 1975 Chancellor Callaghan expressed unambiguously the government's priorities in economic policy: 'A sharp reduction in the rate of inflation is an over-riding priority for millions of our fellow citizens, particularly the housewives and pensioners. It is also a pre-condition for the reduction of unemployment and the increase in investment which the Government, the TUC and the CBI all want to see' (quoted in *The Attack on Inflation*), Cmnd 6151 (London: HMSO, July 1975), p. 1. See also Fay and Young, op. cit.

177 Labour Party, Annual Conference, 1976, p. 188.

178 R. Bacon and W. Eltis, *Britain's Economic Problem: Too Few Producers* (London: Macmillan, 1976). See the brief but incisive critique in Stewart, op. cit., pp. 224–7.

179 See *The Times*, 13 April 1976.

180 For the terms of the IMF agreement, see Fay and Young, op. cit., pp. 36–46; Coates, *Labour in Power?*, op. cit., pp. 38–43; and D. Healey, *Letter of Intent*, 15 December 1976 (copy in TUC files).

181 TUC *Annual Report, 1977*, pp. 219–20, 224, 226–7.

182 N. Bosanquet and P. Townsend, *Labour and Inequality, a Fabian Study of Labour in Power, 1974–1979* (London: Heinemann, 1980), p. 31.

183 *The Economist*, 21 April 1979.

184 The morphology of the government's industrial strategy and planning efforts can be followed in Coates, *Labour in Power?*, op. cit., ch. 3. The TUC's view of government performance in these areas can be found in *TUC Economic Review, 1977*, ch. 3, and *1979*, ch. 4. See also S. Hall, 'Planning disagreements', in S. Hall (ed.), *Beyond Capitalist Planning* (Oxford: Blackwell, 1978), pp. 137–64.

185 TUC, *Annual Report, 1977*, pp. 582, 589.

186 TUC, *Annual Report, 1978*, pp. 520–2.

187 ibid., p. 678.

188 Early manifestations of this growing opposition can be seen as early as the 1976 TUC in a series of critical resolutions moved by the National Union of Teachers, the AUEW and NALGO respectively. See TUC, *Annual Report, 1976*, pp. 636–7, 646–7, 638–9,

639–40. The NALGO motion, for example (pp. 639–40), noted that reductions in public expenditures not only undermined the quality of public services thus 'placing the burden of the economic crisis on those least able to bear it', but also were inappropriate in a period of voluntary wage restraint when the 'social wage' was becoming increasingly important to all wage-earners.

189   For a description of the campaign and a bibliography of primary and secondary materials, see R. Fryer, 'British trade unions and the cuts', *Capital and Class*, no. 8 (Summer 1979), pp. 94–110.

190   Based in Cambridge University's Department of Applied Economics, the Cambridge Economic Policy Group has its own computerized model of the British economy and its own journal, the *Cambridge Economic Policy Review.* For a succinct summary of the model and its implications for British trade policy, see F. Cripps and W. Godley, 'Control of imports as a means to full employment and the expansion of world trade: the UK's case', *Cambridge Journal of Economics*, vol. II, no. 3 (September 1978), pp. 327–34.

191   A more recent formulation of the Alternative Economic Strategy has been published by a group of economists affiliated with the Conference of Socialist Economists under the title of *The Alternative Economic Strategy: A Labour Movement Response to the Economic Crisis* (London: CSE, 1980). For a critique of this plan from the left, see A. Glynn and J. Harrison, *The British Economic Disaster* (London: Pluto, 1980), pp. 147–63.

192   NUPE, *Time to Change Course: An Economic Review* (London: NUPE, March 1976), p. 15. NUPE first made public its disapproval of the government's economic strategy in *Inflation: Attack or Retreat?* (London: NUPE, August 1975). See also *Fight Back* (London: NUPE, June 1977), in which the NUPE executive made its case against cuts in public expenditures, and *North Sea Oil and Economic Strategy: An Executive Council Discussion Document* (London: NUPE, April 1978). NUPE's version of the 'alternative economic strategy' is presented in *Time to Change Course*, op. cit., pp. 16–17.

193   The debate on import controls has been a fundamental issue on the British left since the mid-1970s. The TUC's *Economic Review* has always been very cautious in endorsements of such controls, insisting that they be only 'temporary' and 'selective', while several of the more left-leaning unions such as NUPE, ASTMS and the AUEW have called for 'across-the-board' protection along lines endorsed by the Tribune Group of the Labour Party, the Conference of Socialist Economists, the Cambridge Economic Policy Group and the British Communist Party. The debate among left economists can be followed in A. Glynn, *Capitalist Crisis* (London: Militant, n.d.); and V. Cable, *Import Controls: The Case Against*, Fabian Research series, No. 335 (London: Fabian Society, 1977); and *Cambridge Economic Policy Review*, no. 2 (March 1976), chs 1 and 4. See also the exchange among three prominent Labour-oriented economists – Wynn Godley, Alex Cairncross and Wilfred Beckerman – in *The Times*, 1 November, 4 November and 16 November 1976. For the position of Denis Healey, Chancellor of the Exchequer in the Callaghan government, see his speech to the 1976 Annual Conference of the Labour Party (p. 319), where he argues that general controls would provoke international retaliation and that selective controls would simply not work.

194   NUPE, *Time to Change Course*, op. cit., p. 2.

195   See TUC, *Annual Report, 1975*, pp. 590 and 592–3 for the defeated 'Composite 9', and for the original motions on which it was based; for the successful 'Composite 8', see pp. 570–1.

196   TUC, *Annual Report, 1976*, pp. 638–40.

197   TUC, *Annual Report, 1977*, Motion 86, pp. 582–3; Composite 7, p. 589; and pp. 590, 591, 588, 589, 582–3.

198   Based on numerous interviews conducted by the authors with TUC leaders and with staff members of the TUC's Economic Department.

199   A brief but useful account of these developments can be found in D. Coates, *Labour in Power?*, op. cit., pp. 77–82. The best places to follow industrial developments for this period are in the regular accounts in *Labour Research*. Coverage of industrial relations by both the *Guardian* and *Financial Times* was good and the weekly columns by Robert Taylor in the *Observer* are extremely useful.

200   Hitchens, 'Strange death . . .', op. cit., and Coates, *Labour in Power?*, op. cit., pp. 78–9. For the TUC's version of these events, see TUC, *Annual Report, 1979*, pp. 270 ff.

201 *TUC Economic Review*, 1979, p. 35. The 1976 *Economic Review* contains the first TUC endorsement of even this mild form of protectionism (p. 54). Previously the TUC had not felt that the problems of the British economy or the character of international trading arrangements justified interfering with free trade. The 1976 *Review* endorsed 'import penetration ceilings', which it hoped would be set by the various Sector Working Parties, while the 1977 edition introduced the term 'direct and selective' action.

202 It was only in 1977 that the idea of work-sharing and in particular the 35-hour week became the TUC's primary solutions to the problem of unemployment. No mention of the 35-hour scheme is made in the 1975 or 1976 *Economic Review* but the idea figures prominently in the 1977 issue (pp. 60–1) and in that of 1978 (pp. 11–17), where it appears as part of a series of work-sharing proposals including reduction of overtime work, early retirement and increased vacations. Beginning in 1981 the TUC devoted much of its propaganda efforts to publicizing the European Trade Union Confederation (ETUC) 'Campaign for Reduced Working Time' in a series of broadsheets, entitled, 'ETUC campaign for reduced working time: TUC progress report', and in pamphlets such as *Unemployment and Working Time: TUC Consultative Document* (London: TUC, February 1981).

203 For the TUC's analysis of the microchip challenge, see *Employment and Technology* (London: TUC, September 1979); *TUC Economic Review*, 1979, ch. 1, 'Industry, technological change and employment'; and TUC Education, *New Technology Case Studies* (London: TUC, August 1980).

204 In 1977 the TUC began to expend considerable organizational resources on the sectoral activities of the industrial strategy known as the 'sector working parties'. TUC efforts included: a conference in October 1977 eventuating in a report, entitled, *The Trade Union Role in Industrial Policy* (London: TUC, 1977); the regular publication of enthusiastic analyses of the program in the *Economic Review* along with 'industrial strategy checklists' for the use of union members of the working parties and of plant-level planning bodies; a series of decentralized conferences held during 1978–9 (see TUC, 'Industrial strategy – action at company and plant level: TUC programme'); and the publication of a series of broadsheets during the same period, entitled, *TUC Industrial Strategy Spotlight*, each focussing on one industrial sector and coordinated with a conference of union activists involved in that sector's planning activities.

205 The developments of the winter can best be followed in the daily accounts of the *Guardian* and *Financial Times* (*The Times* was itself on strike for this entire period.) The weekly analyses in the *New Statesman* are also quite helpful.

206 Hitchens, 'Strange death of a social contract', op. cit., and Coates, *Labour in Power?*, op. cit., pp. 79–82.

207 See Blackaby, *De-Industrialisation*, op. cit., esp. C. J. F. Brown and T. D. Sheriff, 'De-industrialisation: a background paper', pp. 233–62. For the TUC's analysis, see *TUC Economic Review*, 1980, pp. 34–42.

208 Hitchens, op. cit.; Coates, *Labour in Power?*, op. cit., pp. 77–8; and author's interviews with union leaders and with a former member of the Prime Minister's staff.

209 The official title of the document was *The Economy, the Government and Trade Union Responsibilities: Joint Statement by the TUC and the Government* (see TUC, *Annual Report, 1979*, pp. 392–7).

210 See *Guardian*, 5 May 1979; *Financial Times*, 5 May 1979; and *The Economist*, 12 May 1979. The Conservatives gained 56 seats for a total of 339 on a popular vote of 43·9 percent, while Labour lost 40 seats for a total of 268 on a popular vote of 36·9 percent. For Thatcher's intentions with regard to the unions, see, for example, 'Thatcher sees "union threat to end British democracy" ', *Financial Times*, 26 April 1979, or 'Hard-line Thatcher promises to deal with "the wreckers"', *Guardian*, 25 April 1979.

211 *OECD Economic Outlook*, No. 31 (July 1982), p. 96.

212 ibid., p. 144.

213 *Guardian*, 21 September 1982.

214 UK Central Statistical Office, *Monthly Digest of Statistics*, No. 438 (London: CSO, June 1982), pp. 30–1.

215 *TUC Economic Review*, 1982, p. 11.

216 See Table 1.1.

217 See 'Economic policy in the UK', *Cambridge Economic Policy Review*, vol. VII, no. 1 (April 1981), pp. 1–6.

218 *Labour Research*, May 1982 and January 1982; TUC, *Commentary on the Employment Bill* (London: TUC, 1980); TUC, *Bargain or Battleground: The Choice in Industrial Relations* (London: TUC, 1979); TUC, *TUC Handbook on the Employment Act, 1980* (London: TUC, 1980); and TUC, *Industrial Relations Legislation: The Employment Act, 1980 and Employment Bill, 1982: Report by the General Council* (London: TUC, 1982).

219 It appears that the government has decided to leave its assault on the unions for its second term in office on the assumption that a renewed, and perhaps enlarged, mandate will facilitate the task.

220 Some of the most prominent failures have been the steel strike of the spring of 1980 (*Observer*, 6 April 1980), the rail strike of the summer of 1982 (*Guardian*, 28 June–8 July 1982) and the miners' strike of the winter of 1983 (*Manchester Guardian Weekly*, 13 March, 20 March and 27 March 1983).

221 In a Gallup Poll taken in August 1979, for example, 42 percent of those interviewed thought unions were 'a bad thing' and over half thought that the unions were the 'main cause' of Britain's economic problems.

222 See, for example, TUC, *The Threat to Industry and the Welfare State* (London: TUC, 1980); and TUC, *The Cuts: 400,000 Jobs at Risk* (London: TUC, 1980).

223 *TUC Economic Review*, 1982, p. 36.

224 ibid., p. 44.

225 ibid., p. 15.

226 TUC–Labour Party Liaison Committee, *Economic Issues Facing the Next Labour Government* (London: TUC Publications, 1981).

227 ibid., pp. 12–13.

228 Price and Bain, op. cit., p. 342.

229 The best treatment of the resources of the British union movement is R. Taylor, *The Fifth Estate: Britain's Unions in the Modern World*, rev. edn (London and Sydney: Pan, 1980), ch. 2.

2 Trade Unions and the Economic Crisis: The West German Case

Andrei S. Markovits
Christopher S. Allen

Part 1

Introduction

West German society has proved singularly resilient in the face of the changing world economy of the 1970s. At the heart of this resilience is, of course, the success of the German economy. German economic strength, however, does not account for everything. The socioeconomic arrangements struck between major social groups and the state in the postwar years – the German postwar settlement – have withstood the tests of time and change perhaps better than anywhere else in Europe. The orientations of German unions have been central to the solidity of this postwar settlement. Unions have been conflictual participants in German economic life since the war but their conflict perspectives, thus far, have remained confined within a broader consensual framework shared with other actors about basic social goals. Thus, while there have been changes in German trade union objectives in the postwar period, these changes have always taken place within a larger context of agreement about the legitimacy of basic German institutions. If West German society has proved singularly resilient in modern times, then the unions contributed significantly to this through their own acceptance of German economic structures and processes.

The German postwar settlement legitimated a liberal political economy within which private sector capital and the free flow of market forces were allocated pride of place. Beginning in the early 1950s consensus was built around what was labeled the 'social market economy', which placed primary stress on private sector expansion and profitability as the cutting-edge of economic life. The German welfare state was not conceptualized as a system for transferring wealth away from the private sector, but as a 'trickle-down' series of mechanisms for disseminating the fruits of private sector success after their accumulation. State planning and other forms of state interference with market forces were explicitly omitted from the postwar German developmental model. Controversy over the equity and effectiveness of this economy was not absent in the German postwar settlement, of course. But such controversy was confined to disagreement over the relative role which the state ought to play in shaping the extramarket environment within which this free market/private sector economic motor should operate. Although the Germans rarely used the term 'Keynesianism', conflict centered around how much, and what kind of, Keynesianism was appropriate. To what degree demand management should stimulate or restrict popular consumption was an important question, as was the nature and extent of desirable state policies to remedy the growing pains of the economy – to counteract regional difficulties arising from shifting patterns of activity.

German unions came to accept the legitimacy of the postwar German political economy for a number of reasons. The combination in the 1950s of the Cold War, which eradicated German labor radicalism, and postwar boom, which brought substantial payoffs to labor, was of essential importance. Continuing steady economic growth in the 1960s and early 1970s helped as well. In addition, the postwar settlement encapsulated German unions in a network of institutional obligations which deepened their commitment to existing economic arrangements. *Mitbestimmung* – codetermination in a narrow sense but also viewed by the unions as participation in a more general context – made organized labor a junior partner, at firm level, in important economic decisions, even if private capital maintained predominance in such decision-making. The Federal Republic's industrial relations system, an unusually dense web of legal rules and regulations, created complex patterns of reciprocal rights and obligations for labor. Collective bargaining was highly developed and codified, and its legal structures established important limits on the unions' resorting to strikes (contracts were legally sanctioned, thus strikes could only occur during moments of contract renegotiation). The centralized structure of German unions, built in the postwar period out of a deliberate desire to avoid the costly union pluralism of the Weimar period, plus the dues checkoff system, gave union federations both the power and the financial resources to control rank-and-file behavior. On the shopfloor elected works councils (*Betriebsräte*) acquired significant control over important local matters. Because of the close relationship of such councils with unions (members of councils were elected as individuals, but councils became *de facto* union bodies in the majority of cases), and because of an impressively detailed body of labor legislation, the already existing ties to the economic system were further reinforced.

Union participation in the general consensus about the shape of Germany's postwar economy has been enthusiastic. Within this consensus, however, unions have been the major proponents of more expansive state demand management. They have also consistently asked for more vigorous policies to compensate for pockets of hardship created in the course of economic development. More generally, if unions have accepted the legitimacy of Germany's postwar economic model and recognized the need for union cooperation to enhance its effectiveness, they have also been concerned to maximize the share of economic results going to labor and to minimize the dislocation and discomfort suffered by labor in the economy's expansion. The unions have sought to increase their institutional power to effect such policy goals as well – most notably by informal but quite profound support for the Social Democratic Party (Sozialdemokratische Partei Deutschlands – SPD) and by attempts to broaden the scope of *Mitbestimmung*. Thus, the history of German union participation in the political economy has been of consensus, but it has not been one of passivity.

If we are correct in asserting that German trade unions have consistently accepted their economic surroundings since the postwar period of broad social negotiations which established these surroundings, then we should not expect to find any dramatic reevaluations of union economic thought and strategy in response to changing economic circumstances. If German unions have instead participated in controversy within consensus about economic arrangements, we should look rather for changes in union positions in such controversy, plus changes in union strategy and tactics to implement such positions in response to economic change. Our central questions, therefore, will be the following. How have German unions reformulated their economic thought and policy objectives at different points in German postwar development? When, and according to what criteria, have they chosen the precise strategic avenues to achieve such objectives? In other words, we are hypothesizing that German unions will review both their economic objectives and the specific arenas within which they choose to pursue these objectives in the context of changes in their economic environment.

This chapter will address these questions in accordance with a rough periodization of historical change in the postwar German political economy. Part 2 examines the construction of the German postwar settlement itself and its meaning for German unions, from the blunting of postwar reformism through the years of *Wirtschaftswunder* to the first major recession of the 1960s. Part 3 analyzes the period between the late 1960s and the advent of crisis in 1973–4 during which German unions reacted both to economic and political changes. Part 4 reviews German trade union responses to the changed economic circumstances of the mid-1970s, the crisis period itself.

Part 2

The Unions during Reconstruction and Wirtschaftswunder, 1945–66

The German Postwar Settlement

The German postwar settlement crystallized in the early 1950s as the product of the confrontation between demands for reform by the workers' movement and pressures for moderation from conservative forces in German society. Five concerns were central to the unions' overall project. It was important to restructure the union movement along non-partisan and industrial lines so as to avoid the ideological divisions and industrial competition that had plagued them during the Weimar period. Next a transformation of the relations between labor and capital was needed to provide workers with full participation in economic decision-making at all levels of society. Thirdly, the unions foresaw an expanded role for the state – including the centrality of planning – in managing the economy so as to guarantee full employment. Fourthly, the unions desired the creation of an extensive system of welfare services by the state. Finally, they wanted the socialization of key industries.

Conservative forces in German society, although originally discredited and in disarray immediately after World War II, managed in the context of the Cold War to reassert their control and to impose on the workers' movement a settlement for the postwar economy that fell considerably short of the unions' vision. The unions succeeded in reorganizing themselves as they had originally planned. The state did expand its role to include the creation of a broad welfare package. However, it did not assume any new planning responsibility for intervening in market mechanisms. In terms of participatory democracy the unions' hopes were only partially fulfilled, and the socialization of key industries did not take place. Thus, while continuing to assert their original project, the unions resigned themselves by the mid-1950s to working within the structures of the German postwar settlement. At the same time, they saw their role as attempting to secure the largest possible gains for their membership within this framework.

UNION PROJECT FOR A RECONSTRUCTED GERMANY

In 1945, as one of the few institutions untainted by National Socialism, the unions found themselves in a strong position to influence the process of reconstruction. Capitalism and the old order were completely discredited due to their complicity with the Third Reich. Thus, for instance, even the Christian Democratic Union (Christliche Demokratische Union – CDU), the newly formed clerical-conservative party, pleaded in its founding statement, the Ahlener Program, for the socialization of key industries, a renunciation of the old economic order and some form of economic democracy.[1] Indeed, many industrialists voluntarily offered important decision-making and control positions to the unions.[2]

The unions codified their vision of a new social order at the founding Congress of their confederation (the Deutsche Gewerkschaftsbund – DGB), which met on 12–14 October 1949, in Munich. Concerned with securing a progressive future for German society[3] the DGB founding Congress – uniting sixteen constituent unions and comprising some 85 percent of the organized German working class[4] – saw as one of its major tasks the fundamental restructuring of the unions along completely new lines. Avoiding the mistakes of the Weimar period – during which divisions between competing, politically oriented union confederations had perilously weakened labor – was the major aim of this restructuring.

Thus, from the very beginning the postwar union movement was unitary – that is, encompassing all organized workers regardless of party affiliation – representing a nominally supraparty labor movement. Furthermore, again countering the Weimar experience, the unions alleviated interunion competition at the workplace and among workers of differing skills by decreeing that only one union could exist in one industry and, above all, in one plant. These two organizational innovations, the *Einheitsgewerk-schaft* (unitary union movement) and *Industriegewerkschaft* (unions organized along industrial lines), have remained the most uncontested foundations of the postwar German union structure. Attacks upon these concepts in subsequent years in the form of creating splits along political lines have been met with unmitigated opposition from all quarters of the union leadership and of the rank-and-file.[5]

Beyond the organizational question the DGB's postwar vision focussed upon most aspects of German public life, including state–society relations, collectivity vs individualism, the role of the 'New German' and the moral implications of the Nazi past for the beginnings of a new German society. The confederation was centrally concerned, however, with constructing a more just economic order. To 'alleviate social injustice and economic deprivation and to provide work and meaningful existence to every person seeking a job'[6] the following four points summarized the core of this concern:

I   An economic policy which secures with complete dignity the full employment of every person willing to work, the most aim-oriented development of all economic forces of production and the securing of economically important needs.

II   Codetermination (*Mitbestimmung*) on the part of organized workers in all personal, economic and social questions related to the shaping and conducting of all economic affairs.

III   The process of moving toward a socialization of key industries, especially in mining, iron and steel, large chemical firms, the energy-producing companies, the important transportation network and the banking industry.

IV   Social justice via the appropriate participation of all working people in the fruits of national economic life and the granting of an adequate livelihood for those incapacitated by age, handicaps or sickness.[7]

Although their salience faded with the passage of time, these remained the official guiding principles of the unions' economic policy until the Düsseldorf program of 1963. The economic and political reforms expressed in the original Munich program of 1949 were not entirely new: they drew upon certain aspects of the unions' prewar thinking and in particular the idea of *Wirtschaftsdemokratie* (economic democracy), which constituted essentially a 'third way' between the inequities of capitalism on the one hand, and the inefficiencies of a totally centralized planned economy[8] on the other. Democratization in this framework, by necessity, always implied the active participation of workers in the production process. Only through the complete democratization of economic life could capitalism's *Profitlogik* (profit logic) be defeated by a more equitable and more socially oriented system. This democratizing process, never fully implemented during Weimar, was to involve the institutionalization of an all-encompassing framework of *Mitbestimmung* (codetermination).

If we accept union statements at the time, there seems little doubt that the unions felt *Mitbestimmung* to be the most important axis of this postwar program for a 'fundamental new order'. Unions foresaw the installation of *Mitbestimmung* at all levels of society, from shopfloor, firm and industrial levels, through chambers of commerce and industry, up to the public institutions which would give macroeconomic direction to the economy such as federal and state economic councils.[9] Moreover, *Mitbestimmung* was important in the unions' eyes not only in principle, but because it was seen as the chosen strategic vehicle for implementing the other parts of the unions' package of postwar goals – full employment, production for social needs, socialization of key industries and social justice. It was no accident, then, that the frustration of union hopes for *Mitbestimmung* was the key process in blunting the unions' postwar reformist thrust.

The process of cutting down *Mitbestimmung* to manageable size by its opponents – occupying allied forces, capital and the first CDU-led government of the Federal Republic after 1949 – began almost immediately after the DGB announced its objectives at its 1949 Congress. The DGB, backed by the SPD, proposed an ambitious codetermination scheme in 1950. It was to involve parity union representation and the installation of a labor director on the boards of all firms larger than 300 employees and/or with equity of more than DM3,000,000. Beyond this, the scheme also suggested legislation to create codetermination on a society ('suprafirm') level – full parity institutions for the guidance of industry, commerce and even agriculture, plus parity union participation in organisms to oversee regional and sectoral development. This ambitious program foundered, however, in the face of changing circumstances which were rapidly reconstituting the power of German capital. Pressing economic needs progressively overrode moral questions about the guilt of capital during the war. Germany's pivotal position in Cold War geopolitics, in particular, in American plans for the consolidation of an Atlantic anti-Soviet bloc, worked in the same direction. The CDU-led government and German industrialists began to emerge as a reliable bulwark against the perceived threat from the East, and their alliance was legitimated domestically by developments in the eastern portion of the country. The Allies, still in control of basic natural resource industries, opposed *Mitbestimmung* on national security grounds. The industrialists, in turn, argued that the predominance of Allied power in Germany made *Mitbestimmung* unfeasible, while simultaneously opposing it as a limitation on their property rights which would impede their capacity to make important economic decisions (a view for which they found support in the Basic Law, the Federal Republic's constitution). The CDU repeated these same arguments.

The furthest point of advance for the DGB's *Mitbestimmung* offensive was codified in the *Montanmitbestimmung* law for the coal and steel industry of 1951. Codetermination in coal and steel had been established *de facto* in 1947 due to a favorable balance of power for unions in these industrial sectors. The Rhine–Ruhr coal and steel barons were in a particularly weak position in the immediate postwar period because of their record of collaboration with the Nazis. In a move to reestablish their credibility, and to counter various expropriation schemes being discussed by the Allies, coal and steel interests made voluntary efforts to include workers in industrial decision-making after the war.[10] The geographical situation of coal and steel in the British zone of occupation undoubtedly facilitated codetermination as well, given the British Labour government's willingness to sanction social democratic measures of worker participation. This *de facto* arrangement was targeted for attack by the opponents of *Mitbestimmung* in the early years of the Federal Republic, however. Only massive union mobilization in its favor, SPD support and the likelihood of conflict involved in dismantling an already existing institution prompted the CDU to allow the legislative codification of *Montanmitbestimmung* in 1951.

The law itself – viewed by the unions as a major victory and as one of the major pillars of West German democracy – did embody the kind of codetermination which the DGB desired to extend throughout German society.[11] Labor and capital were granted parity on boards of directors and unions were allowed to place outside directors (that is, from union headquarters or from other companies) on these boards, while labor representatives on such boards were overwhelmingly (90 percent) union members. The law also provided for union nomination of a labor director –responsible for personnel relations, workplace safety, employee grievances, implementing collective agreements, on-the-job training and employee housing problems – on the day-to-day management board of each firm. Finally, the law provided for a neutral member of the board of directors – appointed by both labor and capital – to cast the tie-breaking vote on deadlocked issues.

Impressive as it was, *Montanmitbestimmung* in coal and steel was as far as the unions were able to go in promoting societal codetermination.

Although worker participation of this kind remained confined to these two industries, it retained considerable symbolic value beyond its immediate instrumental impact. Codetermination at the workplace level or in other major German institutions central to the shaping of macroeconomic policies was not established. The unions regarded the coal and steel success as but a first step toward broader participatory democracy in society and the economy. The resurgence of private capital's power and capital's alliance with conservative political forces meant, however, that few new steps could be taken.

If the unions saw the 1951 *Montanmitbestimmung* law as having limited impact for their long-term objectives, yet as containing a significance in the political/legislative area, there seems little question for the unions that the *Betriebsverfassungsgesetz* (Works Constitution Act) of 1952 represented a serious setback in both areas.[12] Briefly this law severely restricted the unions' scope of action within the plant and made the works councils the only legal representative of the workers on the shopfloor. At the same time, this law also limited significantly the *Betriebsräte*'s (works councils) range of activities in the plant. For example, works councils could not participate in the mobilization of strikes, were prohibited from divulging company secrets, including to the unions, and were asked to help maintain a harmonious relationship between employer and employees. Their tasks, according to this law, remained largely confined to the supervision of grievance procedures and certain forms of workplace security.[13] Thus, the unions' original model of an ideal-type *Betriebsrat* – an activist on the shopfloor involved in economic, political and social matters – became merely a mediator of personnel problems.

Another significant defeat for the unions occurred as they tried and failed to extend the provisions of full-parity codetermination – as defined in the *Montanmitbestimmung* law of 1951 – to the rest of the German economy. The unions had to settle for a significantly reduced form of *Mitbestimmung*, a scheme which came to be known as *Drittelparität Mitbestimmung* (one-third parity codetermination) and which was yet another restricting aspect of the Works Constitution Law of 1952. This formula allowed only one-third of the members of the board of directors to be employee representatives. Furthermore, it had the effect of limiting the unions' official role on these boards of directors to only the largest firms in the Federal Republic, since only those were allowed to have outside representatives (that is, union members) on the labor side of the boards. As a result, by 1952, labor in general and the unions in particular were relegated to the position of a minority in most companies within West Germany. Their postwar hopes and objectives for engendering worker participation in economic decisions had been stymied.

ROLLBACK

These major defeats, which the unions saw as a rollback for them and as gains for 'restorative' and 'reactionary' forces, were part of a general process of retrenchment which began in the late 1940s and culminated in the establishment of Germany's liberal postwar settlement in the early 1950s.

First, the unions found themselves denied the right to contribute directly to the reconstruction effort by operating factories that had been occupied by the workers at the end of the war. Having played a major role in the resumption of production and in preventing the dismemberment of firms by the Allies, the unions found themselves hindered from reaping any benefits from their activities. Rather, it was the newly legitimized industrialists who obtained the rewards. A second step in the rollback on union power was the currency reform of 1948. The monetary transition from the old reichsmark to the new deutschemark entailed a considerable disadvantage to the holders of the old currency and especially to small savers and those on fixed salaries and wages. Their purchasing power was cut by the devaluation accompanying the currency switch (one new deutschemark equaled ten old reichsmarks). German consumers still depended extensively on imports, even for the most basic goods; therefore, a devalued German currency meant a much higher relative price for these necessities. The following quotation illustrates the predicament of the German worker during these years: 'If the worker could not buy anything in the three years following the War because there was nothing to buy, then the situation is now one of abundance, however considerably out of reach to the majority of workers since prices have completely outstripped wages.'[14]

A third step in the rollback was the Marshall Plan and its economic implications for the general tenor of postwar German macropolitical developments. While much-welcomed by the German population in general and the German unions in particular,[15] the larger long-term implication of the Marshall Plan was the solidification of a capitalist reconstruction which did not make the unions entirely comfortable. For instance, the unions favored the Marshall Plan's initial goals and humanitarian concerns but, beginning with the first CDU government, they opposed the concept of *soziale Marktwirtschaft* (social market economy) which conflicted with their efforts to reshape West German macroeconomic institutions.

Thus, it was not by chance that Ludwig Erhard, the CDU Economics Minister, became the German politician most heavily criticized by the unions. His persona became synonymous with the evils of the social market economy. What the unions criticized most severely were the economic model's explicit reliance on investments at the cost of domestic consumption, an export-led economic reconstruction at the expense of both production for the domestic economy and the import of essential goods, and the absence of public spending and state-directed economic planning.[16] This economic policy stood in stark contrast to the unions' conception of appropriate economic measures for the reconstruction of West Germany. In addition to the all-encompassing tenets of the Munich Program, the unions also articulated more medium-range policies for the economy. Central to these were the concept of growing wages as the prime mover of domestic consumption, the priority of domestic consumption over extensive investment, a different balance and moderation between exports and imports – thus, the German unions never objected to exports *per se*, only to an excessive concentration on them which resulted in domestic shortages and inflation as well as other problems – and the need for more active state participation in both economic planning and in more traditional monetary and fiscal policy.[17]

In general, then, the social market economy, which formed the basis for the developmental model for the German economy in the 1950s, differed significantly from the unions' original goals as articulated in the Munich Program as well as their more medium-term economic policy preferences.

THE UNIONS' WEAKNESS EXPLAINED

How can this general shortfall be explained? In the first place, the entire domestic rollback has to be seen in the all-important context of the rapidly accelerating Cold War. Nowhere else in Europe did the Cold War affect so many aspects of political life as in the two Germanies, in many ways the staging-places of this confrontation between the superpowers. The effect on German industrial relations and the unions was profound. In addition to a noticeable change of tone in official union discourse, numerous tangible events revealed the distance the unions had come from the substantial radical traditions which had still existed in the immediate postwar period. Thus, for example, by the early to mid-1950s communists became *personae non gratae* among some German unions to the extent that entire locals dominated by communist trade union officials were administratively abolished.[18] Even the more progressive members of the DGB federation, such as IG Metall (the metalworkers' union), denounced communist influence among its membership (without, however, demanding that the KPD (Communist Party of Germany) be declared unconstitutional, as indeed it was by an act of the Federal Constitutional Court in 1956).

This internal hostility toward communists and communism was accompanied by an equivalent aversion to the German Democratic Republic (DDR) in general, and its unions in particular. Hence, for example, as early as September 1950, at the founding Congress of IG Metall, members of an East German delegation were denied participation at the Congress on the ground that 'this [East German] delegation does not belong to our International but to another world union organization whose meetings it should attend instead'.[19] No protocol of a union congress in the 1950s failed to denounce communism, the DDR and communist activities in the West German union movement. Indeed, this castigation of communists often went hand-in-hand with a denunciation both of National Socialism and of various Christian tendencies threatening to split the unitary trade movement. In a sense one can interpret these views as a quintessential confirmation of two important tenets of the postwar German union movement to this day: the rejection of all radicalisms by equating left with right, and the defense of the unitary trade union movement at all costs.

Stronger union response to the rollback of the early 1950s was, moreover, impeded by a disadvantageous situation in the labor market which was very much a legacy of National Socialism and an outcome of the Cold War. Not only were there millions of unemployed West German workers during this period, but the unions also felt responsible for the large numbers of refugees from both East Germany and the former territories of the German Reich now part of Poland and the Soviet Union.[20] The overabundance of labor resulting from this situation was important in keeping wages at a low level.[21] Moreover, the geographic origin of many new workers in West Germany and their concomitant anti-communist convictions contributed to an atmosphere of political demobilization.

A third important reason for the unions' weak response to the rollback lay in their virtual exclusion from positions of power because the CDU controlled the government. Despite the CDU's Ahlener Program, and the unions' nominal abstention from party politics, the unions maintained a constant macropolitical involvement in German affairs ('we are politically independent but not neutral'), remaining especially close to the Social Democratic Party (SPD). The SPD and the labor unions, traditional pillars of the German labor movement since the late nineteenth century, thus continued their *de facto* alliance in the period after 1945.

A fourth factor hindering stronger union response to the rollback followed from the longstanding German tradition of the juridification (*Verrechtlichung*) of all aspects of industrial relations. Examples of this juridification from the postwar settlement years were maintenance of labor peace throughout the duration of a contract, the illegality of non-union-sanctioned strikes, the provision that public employees were not allowed to strike, the lack of union representational rights on the shopfloor and the concomitant preeminence of the work councils.[22] The establishment of the Bundesarbeitsgericht (Federal Labor Court, or BAG) in 1954 further solidified these highly juridified relationships. Although the BAG did not create more laws, it did help in displacing industrial conflict onto a juridical plane. Thus, for example, the issue of lockouts (*Aussperrung*), so much at the center of German industrial relations in the 1970s, became the subject of an ongoing legal battle between unions and employers, beginning in 1955. There were many other such legal conflicts in these years, in most of which the courts decided against the unions as a collectivity, although often not against workers as individuals (that is, grievance procedure). The very existence of the Federal Labor Court (and its predecessors, the *Land* Labor Courts) lent an additional institutional presence to hamper and confuse union actions in the market arena.

A final reason for the union defeats of the early 1950s can be found in the death, on 14 February 1951, of Hans Böckler, the first chairman and 'father' of the DGB. The idea of a new social order based on 'economic democracy' and 'codetermination' lay at the center of Böckler's hopes for postwar West Germany. The realization of *Montanmitbestimmung* was in no small measure due to Böckler's personal influence with Chancellor Adenauer. If Böckler had lived longer, perhaps more could have been obtained in this direction.

As a result of the above-mentioned weaknesses, however, the union plans for the new Federal Republic had been largely thwarted by the end of 1952. The goals of the DGB's 1949 Munich Program had become unattainable for the immediate future, and so new goals had to be found along with a new strategy for reaching them. The process of reorientation was a difficult one, and it was to occupy the unions for the next several years. The chief factor which they had failed to reckon with in 1949 was the miraculous recovery of the West German economy in the 1950s, the so-called *Wirtschaftswunder*.

The *Wirtschaftswunder*: West German Economic Policy, 1948–66

Between the currency reform of 1948 and the 1966–7 recession the West German economy attained consistently high levels of growth accompanied by low levels of inflation and (after about 1956) full employment. This economic context must be the starting-point for any analysis of union behavior during this period. Furthermore, this success occurred thanks to (or perhaps in spite of) a set of economic policies which stood in sharp contrast to the 'Keynesian orthodoxy' being practiced in other countries at the same time. It is important to understand the particular brand of neo-liberalism practiced by Erhard during 1948–66, for the programmatic revisions undertaken by the unions in the late 1950s and early 1960s can be seen as attempts to formulate credible economic alternatives to Erhard's policies.

THE ECONOMY

Although the term 'economic miracle' is usually applied indiscriminately to the years 1948–66, conditions during this time were far from uniform. The economy passed through four complete business cycles (1948–54, 1954–8, 1958–63 and 1963–7), each with its own special character.[23] In addition, there were marked differences between the period prior to 1958, when German growth rates were inordinately high, inflation negligible and unemployment still an issue, and the period after that date, when inflation, labor shortages, budget deficits and external disequilibrium first became a problem. Before the deutschemark attained full convertibility in 1958, the German economy was protected from many harmful developments emanating from abroad. Once West Germany was again fully integrated into the world economic system, a situation was created which posed many new problems for both capital and labor.

The currency reform in June 1948[24] ushered in an unprecedented boom within the Western zone of occupation (later to become the Federal Republic), with industrial production rising 46 percent by the end of that year. Price controls were also lifted at this time, and the cost of living had increased by 14 percent by December 1948, leading the Bank deutscher Länder, or BdL (the forerunner of the Bundesbank), to take restrictive measures.[25] The tight money policy did its job, as prices fell by 10 percent in 1949 and a further 6·2 percent in 1950, but industrial growth also slowed to +21 percent in 1949.

Unemployment, fueled by a constant stream of refugees from the East, stood at about 2 million, or 10 percent, at the start of 1950. Unemployment began to fall, however, with the start of the 'Korea boom' in the summer of 1950. Foreign demand caused by the war meant both strong growth (real

GNP = 10·4 percent) and accelerating inflation (7·7 percent) for West Germany in 1951. Again the BdL reacted to rising prices with credit restrictions, and again this approach was successful. Inflation fell to 2·1 percent in 1952, −1·8 percent in 1953 and +0·2 percent in 1954.[26] Despite a lull after the 'Korea boom', growth remained very strong in 1952 and 1953 (+8·9 and +8·2 percent). The trough of this first business cycle was reached at the start of 1954, but GNP still rose in that year by 7·4 percent. Exports were the main motor behind the extraordinary growth levels of the early 1950s. Exports doubled in 1950–2, and almost tripled (compared with 1950) by 1954. In addition, capital investment was very strong in 1953 and 1954, rising respectively by 17 and 12·6 percent.

Real wages in West Germany increased substantially during this time as well, but productivity rose almost as fast; and as a result, higher wages had little inflationary effect. Real gross wages advanced by 26·5 percent in 1951–4, while productivity (measured as real GNP per employed person) increased by 25·2 percent. The general level of German wages had been below the OECD (Organization for Economic Cooperation and Development) average in the late 1940s, and it remained low in the early 1950s despite hefty increases. Indeed, one of the main reasons for the phenomenal German export success at this time was that both costs and wages in the Federal Republic were substantially below those of its other industrial competitors.[27]

After the 'slowdown' in 1954, boom conditions returned in 1955 and 1956 (GNP +12 and +7·3 percent), with growth again driven on by increased exports (+16·7 and +15·2 percent) and capital investment (+20·8 and +8·6 percent). Exports had become equal to 21 percent of GNP by 1957 (11 percent in 1950), a figure which has remained more or less unchanged ever since. The rise in exports was not matched by a similar rise in imports, however, and the resulting trade surpluses brought with them ever-larger balance of payments surpluses, which were the main cause of West German inflation in 1955–8 (prices rose by 1·6, 2·5, 2 and 2·2 percent during those years). In an effort to increase imports the FRG substantially lowered tariff barriers in 1956 and 1957. A further stimulus to trade liberalization was provided by the formation of the Common Market (EEC) in 1958, of which the Federal Republic was a charter-member. Also in 1958 free convertibility of the mark was restored, in essence freeing capital movements into and out of West Germany.

At the height of the 1955–6 upswing the BdL moved to restrict credit (prime rate raised to 5·5 percent in May 1956), and the result was an actual decline in domestic capital investment (−0·1 percent) in 1957. A real growth rate of 5·7 percent could still be reached, however, due to strong exports (+16 percent) and private consumption (+6·2 percent). By the fall of 1956 the labor market in West Germany had for the first time become very tight, even though unemployment for the year still stood at 4 percent. This figure does not reflect the true labor market situation because it includes newly arrived refugees and refugees temporarily resettled in structurally weak areas, as well as the large numbers of construction workers idle in the winter months because of the absence of winter building technology in Germany at that time. A more accurate reflection of the true state of affairs is the fact that the first office for foreign-worker recruitment was opened in Italy in 1956.

After 1955, there was a marked slowdown in the growth of total employment in the Federal Republic as manpower reserves were used up and the demographic effects of the war (low birthrate after 1939) began to be felt. This meant that economic expansion came to depend ever-more-heavily on productivity growth. The latter accounted for three-fifths of total GNP increase in 1955 and all of it in 1957.[28] Rises in productivity (measured as output per employed person) were, however, limited by the reduction in worktime which began in 1956 (working week reduced from 48 to 45 hours in many industries). In general West German productivity was below the OECD average in the mid-1950s, mainly as a result of the large supply of (relatively) cheap labor available up to that time.[29]

The tighter labor market also contributed to a steady rise in real gross wages which, however, still remained more or less in line with productivity. Real gross wages per employed person increased by 6·2, 5·4, 3·1 and 4·4 percent in 1955–8 against productivity growth of 8, 4·4, 3·4 and 3·2 percent. Wages per hour rose faster during this time because of the worktime reduction after 1956. Most economists expected rising wages to translate into decidedly stronger consumer demand in the late 1950s, but this did not happen, mainly because West German workers and pensioners (who received a sizeable pension increase in 1957) chose instead to save their higher earnings. Savings as a percentage of disposable income jumped from 5·8 percent (1956) to 8·7 percent (1958), which helped to limit inflation.[30] This rise in savings is characteristic of the general insecurity in the Federal Republic in the 1950s about whether prosperity would continue. Conditioned by historical experience many Germans were convinced that a new crash was inevitable.

After the decline in 1957, capital investment picked up again in 1958, encouraged by a decline in the prime rate to 3 percent. A recession in the USA caused a decline in exports for the first half of that year, and the trough of the second postwar business cycle was reached at that time (GNP rose 3·7 percent for 1958 as a whole). Domestic growth factors (especially construction) remained strong throughout the year, and when foreign demand picked up near the end of 1958, another boom period began. Exports shot up 11·4 and 16·3 percent, and capital investment 11·8 and 10·2 percent in 1959 and 1960, leading to real growth of 7·3 and 9 percent during those years. Inflation remained practically non-existent (1959: +1 percent, 1960: +1·4 percent).

In the wake of this strong upturn the Bundesbank [31] attempted to apply the brakes by raising the prime rate to 5 percent in October 1959. The monetary authorities soon discovered, though, that under conditions of free capital movement (established with the return to convertibility in 1958) monetary policy could no longer shoulder the entire burden of stabilization. As interest rates rose short- and long-term capital flooded into the FRG, swelling a balance of payments surplus which was already very large due to West Germany's favorable trade balance. International economic experts urged a revaluation of the mark, which stood at 4·20 to the dollar in 1960, but the government hesitated because the German business community was firmly opposed to any revaluation. In an attempt to ward off the inevitable the Bundesbank lowered the prime rate to 3 percent by March 1961 despite the continuing boom, and the Federal Government tried to boost imports by further trade liberalization. Although these measures were somewhat successful, they were not enough, and the mark was finally revalued by 5 percent (to $1 = DM4) in March 1961. The revaluation was indeed effective: outflows of speculative capital, combined with slower growth of German exports (1961: +3·6 percent, 1962: +3·2 percent) and rising remittances by foreign workers, reduced the current accounts surplus by one-fourth in 1961, and led in 1962 to the first deficit since 1950 (DM–1,480 million).

Perhaps the most important result of the revaluation was the psychological impact it had on business. Since a stronger mark meant higher prices for German products abroad, business was faced with the prospect of limited export expansion at precisely the time when large capacity had been built up in the wake of the 1959–60 investment boom. It reacted on the one hand by taking a more aggressive stance toward labor (see below), and on the other by greatly reducing the level of new investment (+4·6 percent in 1962 and +1·2 percent in 1963 compared to +10·2 percent in 1960). This slowdown in capital spending and exports was at the root of the lower rates of GNP growth in 1961–3 (1961: +4·9 percent, 1962: +4·4 percent, 1963: +3 percent).

The downturn in domestic investment had a variety of other causes in addition to lowered export expectations. The tight labor market of the late 1950s resulted in acute labor shortages at the height of the 1959–60 boom. Unemployment fell below 1 percent in August 1959, and dropped from a yearly average of 2·6 percent in 1959 to 1·3 percent in 1960 and 0·8 percent in 1961, where it was to stay until 1967; 200,000 foreign workers arrived in the Federal Republic in 1960. Full employment invariably brought with it large real wage increases, which outstripped productivity in 1960, 1961 and 1962, sharply reducing profit margins. Real gross wages per employee rose at annual rates of 4·5, 7·9, 7·7 and 5·8 percent in 1959–62, against productivity gains of 6·4, 7·1, 4·2 and 3·3 percent. The result was the appearance of cost-push inflation for the first time in 1961 and 1962, when prices rose by 2·3 and 3 percent.

The low point in the third postwar business cycle had been passed by mid-1963, as the low wage settlements of that year (+3 percent on average, which was equal to the increase in productivity) boosted profits and export demand picked up. A new, albeit weaker upturn was underway in 1964 (GNP +6·6 percent, exports +11·3 percent), and it continued into 1965 (GNP +5·5, exports +10·5 percent). But storm clouds were gathering on the horizon. A number of serious policy errors in 1965 were to lead to West Germany's first major recession during 1966–7, normally considered the end of the *Wirtschaftswunder*. Developments during 1964–5 will be touched on more fully later while discussing the 1966–7 downturn and its aftermath.

By the early 1960s most of the special conditions which were at the root of West Germany's exceptional economic performance in the 1950s had disappeared, and growth rates fell into line with those prevailing in other industrial countries. Thus, while real GNP in the Federal Republic expanded at an average annual rate of 7·6 percent in 1952–8 (US: 2·2, France: 4, Italy: 5·1 percent), growth fell to 5·5 percent in 1959–66 (US: 5 percent, France: 5·5 percent, Italy: 5·9 percent).[32] West Germany's three major advantages in the 1950s – an abundant labor supply, a low cost level and an undervalued currency – had all been reversed by 1962, but a low comparative inflation rate provided a 'trump' which helped keep German products competitive throughout the 1960s.

THE PATTERN OF ECONOMIC POLICY, 1949–66

For seventeen years, 1949–66, West German economic policy was dominated by the neo-liberal ideology of the 'social market economy' (*soziale Marktwirtschaft*) espoused by the Christian Democratic Economics Minister (and after 1963 Chancellor), Ludwig Erhard. This concept, developed by Erhard's chief advisor, Alfred Müller-Armack, was derived from the writings of the 'Freiburg school' of economics founded by Walther Eucken and Franz Böhm in the 1930s. Before detailing actual government policies in the 1950s and 1960s, it will be helpful first to summarize the main ideas of the Freiburg school.[33]

All members of the Freiburg school were staunch anti-Nazis, and many took refuge in Switzerland during the war. National Socialism, with its extensive state interference in the economy, strengthened Eucken's and Böhm's belief that democracy and economic liberalism were intrinsically connected. Their brand of economic liberalism was not of the nineteenth-century *laissez-faire* variety, however. They saw an important role for the state in creating and maintaining the correct framework (or 'order' in their terminology) which would ensure problem-free economic expansion. Once this order had been established, the state was to withdraw and leave medium- and short-term developments to the interplay of market forces.

By far the most important condition of 'order' which the state was to safeguard, according to the Freiburg school, was monetary stability. The success of the entire social market economy depended on the absence of inflationary tendencies, which would distort the indicative function of prices. Eucken and Böhm believed that if price stability could be maintained, the pronounced conjunctural swings of the traditional business cycle would disappear, thus eliminating the need for any kind of fiscal management policies.

In addition to stopping inflation, the state was to discourage concentration and replace monopolies (including state monopolies) with competitive arrangements whenever possible. Most German neo-liberals were not averse to state control of certain basic services and the creation of an adequate public system of social security (thus, the term 'social' market economy). As regards labor relations, the Freiburgers wanted the state to ensure that unions, as well as employers' associations, would be purely voluntary organizations run on a democratic basis. It is, therefore, significant that the closed shop is expressly forbidden by the West German constitution. Actual collective bargaining was to be carried out without any state interference, thus allowing wages to be determined entirely by market forces.

When Ludwig Erhard became Economics Minister of the new Federal Republic in 1949, the Freiburg neo-liberals were given the opportunity to put theory into practice.[34] Fortunately or unfortunately, however, the Americans had seen to it that the power of the federal government in general, and the Minister of Economics in particular, would be limited in the new West German state – precisely to prevent the kind of interventionism opposed by the Freiburgers.

The intentionally decentralized nature of the new country effectively restricted the fiscal weight of the federal government. The Bund (central authorities) was only given two sources of revenue: the turnover tax and personal and corporate income taxes, and the latter had to be shared with the Länder (states). The Bund normally ended up with only about 33 percent of total tax receipts, and federal spending represented only 13·5 percent of GNP in 1960, as against a norm of over 20 percent in other European countries.[35] The central government also had little control over the states' spending policies, and it had to receive their approval to alter corporate or personal income tax rates. A further hindrance to fiscal flexibility was a clause in the West German constitution expressly forbidding federal budget deficits for non-investment spending, except under special circumstances. In addition to these restrictions on fiscal policy, monetary policy was totally removed from the government's control and vested in the hands of a strong, independent central bank modeled on the Federal Reserve.

Thus, the means placed at Erhard's disposal for constructing the new social market economy were modest. He made a virtue of necessity, though, and vigorously applied the two main fiscal tools available to him: tax discimination (the right to grant special personal or corporate tax reductions and exemptions), and the American European Recovery Program (ERP) funds, administered by the Minister of Economics through the Kreditanstalt für Wiederaufbau (Credit Agency for Reconstruction). Erhard employed both these resources to encourage economic activities which he favored (capital formation, exports and investment) and discourage those he thought potentially harmful (excessive domestic consumption and credit financing).

Tax discrimination was an effective instrument of policy because the Federal Republic had very high marginal tax rates on personal and corporate income in the late 1940s and 1950s.[36] These had originally been imposed by the Americans before the currency reform in an effort to cut down the amount of money in circulation. After 1949, the Finance Minister, Fritz Schaeffer, supported the maintenance of high taxes (which, due to weak progression, fell heavily on the middle and working classes) because of an inordinate fear of budget deficits. With rates high, tax reductions or exemptions for various activities were a powerful incentive.

In the early reconstruction period (1948–52) Erhard targeted six areas for encouragement: construction, basic industries (steel, coal and utilities), exports, personal savings, shipbuilding and business self-financing. Many of the special tax privileges granted were set down in section 7 of the

Income Tax Law of 1949, which remained in effect until 1955. In addition to favoring the above-mentioned sectors and activities, the tax law provided for accelerated depreciation on all industrial equipment.[37] Even though indirect state intervention through tax discrimination was originally intended only as an extraordinary measure designed to meet the exceptional circumstances of postwar reconstruction, the pattern of policy remained the same long after West German recovery was complete. Thus, Shonfield could write in 1965:

> In its fiscal practice Germany is much closer to France than to Britain. Subsidies, cheap loans provided by the state, and above all, discriminating tax allowances which support favoured activities, are used with an abandon that could only be acceptable in a society where the average citizen expects the state to choose its favourites and to intervene on their behalf.[38]

Although tax discrimination and subsidies were very successful in promoting investment and capital formation, they led to a highly unequal distribution of assets as well. Thus, in 1966 15,404 persons owned 42·1 percent of all taxable assets.[39] Erhard's response to this state of affairs was his concept of 'people's capitalism' (*Volkskapitalismus*), whereby the purchase of shares by individuals of modest income would be encouraged. The government hoped to point the way by selling a large number of Volkswagen shares to small holders when the company was denationalized in 1961, but the scheme as a whole had little more than symbolic impact. The public perception that the *Wirtschaftswunder* had resulted in a greater concentration of wealth was at the root of repeated union demands starting in the mid-1950s for some form of asset and/or profit-sharing (*Vermögensbildung*).[40]

Another by-product of Erhard's promotion of capital formation was an ever-increasing concentration of industrial power in the hands of a few firms, especially in key sectors of the economy like automobile production, steel, chemicals and energy.[41] This development was anathema to many members of the Freiburg school, who perceived monopolization as a serious threat to the dynamism of the social market economy. Indeed, Erhard tried for nearly five years to push a strong anti-trust law through the Bundestag, but in this effort he was vehemently opposed by the interests of big business, which had the support of Chancellor Adenauer. In the end Erhard had to admit defeat, and the anti-cartel law passed in 1957 bore little resemblance to his original draft, which had foreseen strict government control of mergers and pricing arrangements.

In contrast to the innovative microeconomic policies pursued by Erhard through tax discrimination and subsidies, the macroeconomic policies implemented (until 1957) by the Finance Minister, Fritz Schaeffer, were firmly rooted in the pre-Keynesian world of the 1920s and 1930s. Schaeffer was not so much a neo-liberal as an old-fashioned 'good housekeeper', whose one and only goal was to balance the budget (or better yet, run surpluses) year in, year out. The concept of the budget as an instrument of demand management was totally unknown to him. This pre-Keynesian fiscal conservatism dovetailed well with the views of Freiburgers like Erhard, who were afraid that budget deficits would cause inflation, which for them presented the greatest threat to the social market economy. After it was decided in the early 1950s that West Germany would eventually rearm, Schaeffer began generating substantial budget surpluses in order to 'save up' for the future Bundeswehr. (These accumulated savings, which eventually amounted to about DM20 billion, were called the 'Julius Tower' after the site of the former Prussian war treasury.) Ironically, this bizarre budget practice actually had a positive macroeconomic effect, because it served to counteract the inflationary impact of large German balance of payments surpluses.

Schaeffer's policies proved too extreme even for the budget conscious Federal Republic, and after the 1957 elections he was replaced by another CDU minister, Franz Etzel. Etzel set out to dismantle the 'Julius Tower', and he put through an important personal tax cut in 1958, but pre-Keynesian fiscal conservatism, albeit of a less fanatical variety than Schaeffer's, remained the basis for budget planning right up until 1967. Thus, the OECD could write in its 1966 report on West Germany:

During the post-war period, the primary aim of fiscal policy has not been to adjust total demand in the economy to prevailing supply potentialities. The role that the budget should play as a contra-cyclical instrument does not seem to have entered importantly into consideration . . . One preoccupation of the authorities has been to balance the budget . . . There have been virtually no budget changes deliberately geared to requirements of short term demand management, and the timing of measures taken on other grounds has often been unfortunate from a contra-cyclical point of view . . . The failure of fiscal policy has not been disastrous partly because of the efficiency of built-in stabilizers.[42]

But the OECD had spoken too soon. Even the built-in stabilizers were not able to save the economy from the effects of the misguided budget decisions of 1965, as we shall see later.

Since fiscal policy was making little contribution to countercyclical stabilization throughout the 1950s, except by chance, this task fell entirely to monetary policy. The Bank deutscher Länder was able to do a credible job until 1958 by raising the prime rate during boom periods and lowering it during slowdowns but, as has already been noted, this practice became ineffective after 1958 due to the freeing of capital flows into West Germany. Thus, the Federal Republic was left without any form of short-term economic management after 1958, just when the need for such management had become acute. With the arrival of full employment (and even labor shortages), real wages began to rise rapidly, putting pressure on costs. This internal source of inflation was matched by 'imported' inflation brought by the rush of short- and medium-term funds into Germany. The revaluation of the mark in 1961 hurt the competitiveness of German products and threatened to push the balance of payments into deficit.

It is hardly surprising that in the face of these new economic problems, and the evident inability of the government to deal with them, there was a growing consensus in the early 1960s that a change of economic policy was needed. It was generally agreed that 'modern' methods of economic management (that is, Keynesianism), as well as an incomes policy should be given a try. The result was a series of government calls for wage restraint starting in 1960 (see below), and the creation of the Council of Economic Experts (Sachverständigenrat, or SVR) in 1963. The SVR, most of whose views were close to those of the SPD up until 1967, became one of Erhard's most outspoken critics. It strongly urged a thoroughgoing reform of fiscal practice (a national accounts rather than administrative budget, control of Länder spending, medium-term budget plans, and so on) as a prerequisite to the introduction of Keynesianism. In addition, constant consultation and discussion between employers, unions and the government (the 'concerted action') would provide the basis for a cooperative incomes policy.[43]

Although a series of interministerial studies were carried out in 1962–6 investigating ways to improve macroeconomic policy, and Erhard even introduced a reform Bill in 1966 incorporating many of the changes demanded by the SVR and the SPD (later to become the Stability and Growth Law of 1967), no major changes in policy practice occurred before the change of government in December 1966. West Germany's first postwar recession was finally to give Keynesianism its chance.

The German Unions during the *Wirtschaftswunder*, 1952–66

By 1952 the framework for the new West German society had been largely established, and the unions had to adjust to this new situation. They had lost the battle to shape the Federal Republic in their own image, and would have to develop a new set of goals and methods adapted to their minority position within a country dominated by a successful free market economy and a victorious Christian Democratic party. Union activities during this time can be divided into two distinct categories. On the one hand, there was the continuous struggle within the DGB among various groups with markedly different attitudes toward the new West German political and economic order and the role that organized labor should play within it. This is the history of DGB congresses and programmatic changes. On the other hand, union strategies and accomplishments within the sphere of collective bargaining were determined primarily by intraorganizational concerns, and often had little connection to controversies going on within the labor confederation as a whole. We have, thus, thought it most fruitful to treat the transformation of the DGB and collective bargaining separately within this section.

THE DGB IN THE POST-RECONSTRUCTION ERA

The defeat over the Works Constitution Act (BVG) in 1952 plunged the West German labor movement into an acute crisis. A new order in the economy and society now seemed unattainable and the DGB had, for the moment, no short-term goals to put in its place. To complicate matters the SPD had not adjusted to the idea of a unitary trade union confederation, free from overt political ties. The Social Democrats were angered by DGB support for European integration, and felt that the DGB leadership was all too accepting of the Federal Republic in general, and the CDU-led government in particular. The party was convinced that with open DGB support, the SPD could possibly win the approaching 1953 Bundestag elections.

In order to gain union endorsement in the electoral campaign the SPD first thought it necessary to remove the DGB's 'conciliatory' chairman, Christian Fette. By placing the blame for the BVG defeat on Fette unionists close to the party were able to do this at the DGB's 2nd Congress in October 1952, and replace him with the head of the powerful metalworkers' union (IG Metall), Walter Freitag.[44] Aside from his undying loyalty to the SPD, however, Freitag had few qualities to recommend him for the task of reorienting the West German unions. He certainly had no particular ideas for a new strategy which could pull the labor movement out of the listless state it found itself in during 1952–3.

The confused atmosphere within the unions at that time was not simply due to weak leadership. At the root of the problem was the deeply ambivalent attitude within the working class in general, and organized labor in particular, toward the Federal Republic and its foreign and domestic policies.[45] Labor enjoyed more democratic rights and legal protection in the new state than ever before in Germany, and it was very afraid of antagonizing the government for fear of jeopardizing these freedoms. The traumas of Nazism, as well as for many the experience of the East Zone, still loomed large. But workers also realized that only in a reunified Germany would labor be able to play a dominant role in the near future, because many of the most important working-class strongholds were now located in the East. The uncertainty and potential disruption of the democratic order which any move toward reunification would entail was a frightening prospect for a people who, above all, sought security and calm after decades of turmoil.

The same mixed feelings characterized union positions on foreign policy. Although the American presence was seen as a major impediment to a united Germany, it was also viewed as the best possible guarantor of democracy. The main reason that labor was so opposed to West German rearmament was the belief that a new German army would pose a significant threat to the liberal Federal Republic. The unions had still not recovered from the attempted Kapp Putsch in 1920. In the end many unionists only reconciled themselves to the formation of the Bundeswehr because they thought it a necessary step to retain American support for the FRG. Based on Otto Kirchheimer's study one must conclude that a deep feeling of insecurity and fear of imminent disaster, whether economic or political, pervaded the West German unions in the first half of the 1950s. Continuous economic success, however, served to reconcile more and more of the union movement to the postwar status quo as the decade went on, and this changing attitude was to have repercussions on intra-DGB politics, as we shall see.

Walter Freitag fulfilled the expectations of the SPD by releasing an electoral manifesto in July 1953 which sharply criticized the CDU-led government's record on social policy and urged the population to 'Vote for a better Bundestag' in the words of a DGB slogan. This was generally interpreted as a call to vote for the SPD, and the union stand provoked angry attacks from Chancellor Adenauer and CDU unionists, who saw it as a violation of the DGB's independent status. An open split between Christian and socialist labor leaders was only narrowly avoided. More importantly, the electoral manifesto did little to help the SPD, which was soundly defeated for the second time in four years. The Social Democrats' hope of any government participation in the near future was definitely put to rest, at least for the time being, and this realization provided further impetus to both the party and the unions to reevaluate their futures.

Freitag's embarrassment over the 1953 elections was the signal that a group of young, reform-minded unionists had been waiting for in order to challenge the authority of the DGB's old guard and their ineffective policies. This group, known as the 'Circle of Ten' (*Zehnerkreis*), was led by the young head of IG Metall, Otto Brenner, who had succeeded Freitag at the helm of Germany's largest union. The goal of the Circle was a reorientation of labor activity away from politics and toward collective bargaining, with a concomitant strengthening of the member-unions *vis-à-vis* the DGB.[46] This idea was particularly appealing to Brenner, who foresaw for IG Metall the role of trendsetter for weaker unions in the bargaining process.

The reformers were provided with a theoretical justification for their position by an article by Victor Agartz, the Marxist chief of the union economic research institute (the WWI), entitled, 'Expansive wage policy', which appeared in the December 1953 issue of *WWI Mitteilungen*. Agartz argued that within a competitive capitalist system, labor must act like all other producers and demand the highest price it can obtain for its services. Unions are not bound, he claimed, any more than capitalists to take some abstract 'general good' into consideration when putting forth their claims. They should exploit their own strengths and get all the market can bear, while remaining confident that the economy would adjust by increasing rationalization and productivity, thus creating the opportunity for more wage rises and expanded production. As a concrete example of this 'virtuous cycle' resulting from an aggressive wage stance, Agartz cited the American experience. His so-called 'expansive wage theory', which portrayed labor as just another competitor within a market economy, had the advantage of fitting in well in an ideological climate dominated by neo-liberalism.

The reformers' concrete strategy was to convince the 3rd DGB Congress, to be held in October 1954, to agree to the drafting of a 'plan of action' (*Aktionsprogramm*), which would set down a list of goals which could all be reached in the medium term exclusively through collective bargaining. The member-unions would then be bound to devote all their energies toward fulfilling these goals. With the help of a brilliant speech by Agartz, the reformers won the majority of congress delegates over to their side, and a commission including both Brenner and Agartz was set up to formulate the *Aktionsprogramm*. Their work was completed by the spring of 1955, and 15 million copies of the final text were distributed throughout the Federal Republic on 1 May. The main demands included in the *Aktionsprogramm* were:

- the introduction of the 40-hour working week;
- sick pay for workers equal to that of white-collar employees;
- equal pay for men and women;
- additional vacation pay and Christmas bonuses;
- extension of codetermination;
- improved standard of living for all through higher wages.[47]

The reformers' victory in 1954 and the adoption of the *Aktionsprogramm* marked the beginning of Otto Brenner's dominance within the West German trade union movement. His position was to be strengthened in the coming years by a number of impressive IG Metall breakthroughs in the bargaining arena (see next section, below). In the period up until 1959 Brenner was able to influence substantially DGB positions on a wide range of social and political matters. With the reorientation of the labor movement toward bargaining, the confederation became little more than a spokesman for the member-unions on leading issues of the day. Brenner saw to it that the DGB played no role in the wage negotiations of individual unions.

The history of the DGB in the late 1950s is a chronicle of the organization's unsuccessful attempts to influence government actions in a number of areas, principally social welfare and defense policy. The CDU's inadequate attention to social welfare was a constant theme of union rhetoric, and this new interest in social policy was symbolized by the election of Willi Richter, an expert on this subject, to the increasingly powerless post of DGB chairman upon the retirement of Freitag in 1956. On military issues the unions strongly opposed the decisions to rearm (1954–5) and to seek atomic weapons for the new Bundeswehr (1957–8). This stand was forcefully advocated by Brenner, whose political views were close to those of the left wing of the SPD, which was very anti-military and anti-Nato throughout the 1950s. On all these questions, however, the unions refused (again led by Brenner) to take any action which could have been construed as pressuring the Bundestag, such as calling protest strikes, and so their opposition remained largely symbolic.

Even as the unions, led by IG Metall, were scoring numerous victories through collective bargaining in the late 1950s, resentment was growing toward the metalworkers and their flamboyant chief. The opposition to Brenner within the DGB was initially headed by Heinrich Gutermuth, general secretary of the miners' union, IG Bergbau.[48] Many of the less powerful unions began to resent constantly playing second-fiddle to IG Metall, and Brenner's accomplishments put other leaders under great pressure to produce results lest they lose the confidence of their members. More importantly, many unionists fundamentally disagreed with Brenner's approach to industrial relations. Brenner's speeches were filled with confrontational rhetoric couched in Marxist phraseology, and he was reluctant to meet management representatives to discuss differences in a friendly manner. Also his attitude toward the Federal Republic and its social market economy seemed ambivalent. Lastly, Brenner retained a strong verbal commitment to the aims of the 1949 *Grundsatzprogramm*, especially nationalization. All these characteristics were disturbing to union heads close to the reformist wing of the SPD, who were enthusiastic supporters of the West German state (though not the CDU-led government) and the Western alliance, and who favored a cooperative approach to relations with the employers' associations. The unions, unhappy with Brenner's dominant position, began, after about 1958, to call for a strengthening of the DGB in order to curb the autonomy of member-unions (that is, IG Metall), and a revision of the 1949 program which would tone down many of its more radical aspects.

The mounting opposition to Brenner and the so-called 'activist' unions allied with him (chemical workers, printers, wood workers and leather workers) was more than just an expression of interorganizational rivalry. It was symptomatic of a larger conflict over goals and strategy which had been present within the German union movement since at least 1918. During the Weimar Republic there were two distinct camps within the socialist union confederation (the Allgemeiner Deutscher Gewerkschaftsbund –ADGB), the 'council democrats' and the 'social partners'.[49] The former, mainly represented by IG Metall's predecessor, the DMV (Deutscher Metallarbeiter Verband), favored total worker control of the economy through a series of workers' councils on the plant, firm and regional levels which would regulate both investment and production. Many unionists in the metal industry set up such councils during the revolution of 1918. The 'social partners', on the other hand, were advocates of a form of corporatist cooperation between unions, employers and the state represented by the creation of the Central Labor Community (Zentrale Arbeitsgemeinschaft) in 1918. Both unions and employers' associations would recognize each other as 'agents of order' (*Ordnungsfaktoren*) within their respective areas, and compromises would be reached aimed at the well-being of a given industrial sector as a whole. Harmful and divisive competition and conflict would, thus, be eliminated and both labor and capital would share in the benefits. The same type of arrangements could also be worked out between peak labor and management associations and the state. The 'social partners' generally saw the kind of class struggle propagated by the 'council democrats', who thought that capital had to be subdued and controlled, as outmoded and counterproductive. They strongly desired the recognition by bourgeois society of organized labor as a legitimate interlocutor and partner.

'Social partnership' was the dominant ideology within a number of German unions, notably the miners (IGBE), construction workers (IG Bau), textile workers (GTB), postal workers (DPG) and railway workers (GdED).[50] The reasons for this are complex, but in the case of the first three they are mainly related to various structural peculiarities of the industries concerned which made a more militant strategy à-la-Brenner less attractive and feasible. The membership of these unions has also generally been more conservative, and in the early 1960s attacks on the 'activists' came to center increasingly on their perceived lack of patriotism toward the FRG. A famous slogan of the labor right from this period was 'This state is *our* state'.[51] In addition, the 'rightists' were enthusiastic supporters of the reform within the SPD which culminated in the Bad Godesberg Program of 1959, whereas the 'activists' continued for many years thereafter to have misgivings about this transformation.

The 'social partners' were not the only group clamoring for a change of orientation within the DGB. They found a numerically small but important ally in a number of union intellectuals who were seeking an overt DGB endorsement for the introduction of Keynesian economic policies in West Germany. The object of their criticism was not so much the 'activists' themselves as the 1949 Munich Program, with its commitment to nationalizations and planning. The Keynesians, led by the head of the DGB's economics section, Ludwig Rosenberg, supported the social market economy in the Federal Republic, but found the government's macroeconomic policies outmoded and harmful. The Keynesians had actually established a foothold in the unions as early as 1951 through the DGB's then chief economist Dr Rolf Wagenführ, who had been greatly influenced by the positions of Beveridge and the British Labour Party. This was also the source of Rosenberg's views, for he had spent the war in exile in England. Over the course of the 1950s the power of the Keynesians continued to grow both within the DGB and the SPD. Rosenberg had a close relationship with both Heinrich Deist and Karl Schiller, the leaders of this group within the SPD. The victory of the Keynesians at the 1958 Stuttgart Congress of the SPD, which resulted in the endorsement of demand management in the Bad Godesberg Program a year later, encouraged Rosenberg to seek similar changes within the DGB at the next union Congress in September 1959.

The triumph of the reformers within the SPD and the impending Bad Godesberg Congress, set for October 1959, overshadowed the DGB Congress in September 1959. The revision of the 1949 Munich Program quickly developed into the meeting's major issue. Brenner, and most other 'activists' as well, saw the Munich Program as an important source of ideological legitimacy and continuity which supported their aggressive, confrontational bargaining style. The 'social partners' had always regarded the program, and especially its calls for nationalizations, as a major stumbling-block in acquiring the confidence and trust of management. The employers wanted from labor a clear affirmation of the social market economy, a renunciation of nationalizations and a recognition of the existing political and social order of the Federal Republic as legitimate. The most conservative of all German unions, the construction workers' union (IG Bau), did not even wait for DGB action and eliminated a nationalization clause from its by-laws already in 1957.

In addition to the presence of the SPD reformers working behind the scenes for change, two other events seriously weakened the 'activists' at the 1959 Congress. The first was the crushing blow administered to Brenner by the Federal Labor Court (BAG) at the end of 1958 when it ruled that IG Metall's Schleswig-Holstein strike of 1956–7 was illegal, and ordered the metalworkers to pay DM100 million damages to the employers (see details in following section). Since many both inside and outside the unions blamed this decision on a tactical error by Brenner during the strike, his reputation was seriously tarnished and his influence hence diminished.[52] The second event was the emergence during the 1959 Congress of Georg Leber, the young head of the construction workers, as the new leader of the 'rightist' unions. Unlike his predecessor as leader of the 'social partners', Heinrich Gutermuth, Leber was a charismatic figure and a dynamic speaker capable of going head-to-head with Brenner. He also had developed many new innovations in collective bargaining which could be presented as successful alternatives to Brenner's 'confrontationalism' (see below).

Given all these disadvantages, it was not surprising that the 'activists' were defeated at the 1959 Congress. It was decided to replace the Munich Program and commissions were set up to present concrete proposals to the next DGB Congress, to be held in 1962. Thus, the real battle over the exact content of the new basic program was put off for three years, time enough for compromises to be worked out. Compromises certainly would be necessary since, despite their victory in 1959, the reformers were far from controlling the union movement. IG Metall was still the largest and most powerful member-union and nothing could be passed within the DGB without its approval.

At the regular DGB Congress in 1962 and a special congress held in Düsseldorf in 1963 to announce the new program, a formula was found which met with Brenner's acceptance. Nationalization would still be retained in the new program, although its importance would be greatly reduced. More importantly, codetermination would be emphasized and the DGB would begin a big campaign to reactivate the codetermination issue, which had lain dormant since the mid-1950s. Lastly, the DGB would not attempt to limit the autonomy of the member-unions, as many on the right had been demanding. In exchange the legitimacy of the West German *Rechtsstaat* would be recognized and Keynesianism would provide the basis for the program's economic section. A comparison of the Munich and Düsseldorf documents will illustrate just how these compromises were concretized within the new basic program.

The economic views of the Düsseldorf Program divide into three headings: basic foundations of economic organization; aims of economic policy; and means of implementation.[53] Concerning the *foundations* of economic policy, the new program, as did the old, centered its attention on economic codetermination by workers as the basis of a free and humane social order. In contrast to Munich, however, the Düsseldorf Program linked this to the existence of a 'democratic and social state based on the rule of law [*Rechtsstaat*]'. By choosing this formulation the authors of the Düsseldorf Program implied that their goals could be fulfilled through the present institutions of the Federal Republic which was, in the unions' view, 'a democratic and social state based on the rule of law [*Rechtsstaat*]'.

In the 1949 Munich Program, alongside *Mitbestimmung*, the DGB listed the 'socialization of key industries' as one of the founding-principles of economic organization. The Düsseldorf Program, on the other hand, relegated this goal from that of a founding-principle to the last item in a long list of policy means. Moreover, replacing 'socialization of key industries' as a founding-principle was a list of vaguely specified items which looked more like aims than fundamental principles:

- To give each individual the highest amount of freedom and responsibility, to let him participate in the formation of the economy on equal terms.
- To guarantee him permanent employment suitable to his personal needs.
- To achieve a just distribution of income and wealth.
- To facilitate an optimal growth of the economy.
- To impede the abuse of economic power.
- To use planning and competition to arrive at macroeconomic goals.
- To make possible the understanding of economic dependencies by publishing appropriate information.

Regarding the *aims* of economic policy, the Düsseldorf Program seemed to depart little from its Munich predecessor. It highlighted the importance of full employment and related this goal to steady economic growth, a just distribution of income and wealth and monetary stability. It also addressed key issues such as the responsibility of the democratic state to halt the abuse of economic power. It pointed to the necessity of price stability without which proper economic planning would be impossible. Price increases, the document argues, primarily affected workers, retired people and others on fixed incomes, and affected them unjustly. Given the transformation of the international system and Germany's increasing integration therein, the Düsseldorf Program emphasized the necessity of international economic cooperation and delineated the positive role the unions might play in this regard within the EEC and *vis-à-vis* the Third World. The Munich Program, understandably, contained very little on these matters. Lastly, it addressed the area of technological innovation and automation, both of which it regarded as beneficial to the improvement of living standards and to the humanization of work. It warned, however, that rationalization and automation ought always to be monitored closely lest they endanger jobs.

As to the *means* with which the unions wished to implement their economic policy, the 1963 program involved in many ways a moderation of the tone and substance of its predecessor from 1949. To begin with, the Düsseldorf Program's position on the issue of economic planning was considerably more moderate than was Munich. The 1949 program associated economic competition with a 'chaotic market economy' which could only have adverse effects for the German worker. The 1963 program insisted on the need for what it called a 'macroeconomic planning framework'. In a modern, dynamic economy developments could not be left to themselves. The securing of full employment, steady economic growth and monetary stability presumed sophisticated economic coordination. To that effect it was incumbent to create a macroeconomic national accounting system which would delineate the past, present and future developments of the economy over a certain period of time. The unions would have to participate in this process. Guidelines on the national budget should become compulsory parameters for the state's economic policies. Planning, however, was envisioned by the 1963 program only as part of a package of 'planning and competition'. Where the 1949 program spoke of planning alone as an essential vehicle for the democratization of the economy, the 1963 document mentioned planning as only a small part of an overall framework for an otherwise competitive market economy.

As far as the role of the state in macroeconomic policy was concerned, the Düsseldorf Program also assumed a moderate position. The 1963 document asked for a system of 'investment guidance' (*Investitions-lenkung*). The unions' position on this issue clearly showed their awareness that the scope and quality of investments represented a key ingredient for the success or failure of a modern economy. It also conveyed their perception that the private and public sector existed as legitimate separate entities. Policies in one inevitably affected the other and, thus, required careful coordination. The unions claimed that the basis for investment guidance should be continuous estimates concerning the needs and demands of individual industries, which should then be published. It was in this way that private investment activities would be influenced via the macroeconomic planning framework without, however, depriving the individual firm of its final decision as to the quality and scope of its investments. This investment guidance, however, was to involve considerably less rigorous controls than was the 'regulation of capital formation' envisioned in the Munich Program of 1949.

The Düsseldorf Program was not a complete retreat, however. It did speak of a number of measures for the democratic control of economic power. For the most part these demands were formulated in rather moderate language. According to the DGB, public investment was to be expanded, the scope for the creation and operation of public corporations (*Gemeinwirtschaft*) was to be broadened.[54] The budget was to be used as a means of securing full employment and the tax system was to be reformed to emphasize direct rather than indirect taxes, with the aim of establishing a system based on the motto of regularity, justice and simplicity. On the subject of *Mitbestimmung*, however, the unions retained the Munich Program's firm position: the existing system of *Montanmitbestimmung* was to be expanded to produce full parity on the boards of all major firms regardless of their legal status and area of economic activity.

Finally, the new program was decidedly less hostile to rationalization than its predecessor of 1949. Whereas the 1949 program argued that the effects of rationalization in a capitalist economy were inevitably negative and could be countered only by a direct planning mechanism, the Düsseldorf Program of 1963 emphasized the benefits of rationalization and merely warned of the potential threat to jobs.

As can be seen from the economic section, many of the formulations in the Düsseldorf Program were left purposely vague so that they would have a more radical ring to them than was actually intended. This was especially true of the two terms 'planning' and 'investment guidance'. All that Rosenberg and the other Keynesians meant by the first was the kind of medium- and long-term budget planning later introduced by Schiller through the Stability and Growth Law in 1967 (see below). This had nothing to do with the kind of socialist 'central planning' through nationalized industries envisaged in the Munich Program of 1949. As for 'investment guidance', this was a codeword for Erhard's method of investment stimulation through tax discrimination and subsidies (which would later appear in the 1970s under the name *Strukturpolitik*). The Keynesians generally supported this practice, but felt that it should be linked to an overall plan for encouraging specific industries ('guidance') in whose elaboration the unions would participate. In general most of the unions' economic demands read like an outline for the reforms Schiller was to introduce four years later. Unlike the views of Schiller or the SVR, however, there was no mention of incomes policy as a means of dealing with inflation. The unions' economic thinkers seemed to believe that inflation could be stopped by demand management means plus moral pressure exercised by the government on business.

By the early 1960s most of the labor movement had, thus, come to accept the social market economy of the Federal Republic. The major union criticism of developments in the 1950s was that too much emphasis had been placed on investment and exports and not enough on the cultivation of internal consumption. This one-sided growth was, in the union view, responsible for the numerous imbalances and problems which began to plague the German economy in the early 1960s. A good summary of this basic union perspective, which was to be reiterated after the 1974 crisis, can be found in an IG Metall document from 1957:

> The West German economy would not have become so dependent upon the demand of investment goods and exports if the Federal Government would not have repeatedly – under strong political influence of the employers – countered the growth of private demand in such a stubborn way . . . The relative retardation of private demand is a characteristic for the general post-war development of the West German economy.[55]

Aside from the new basic program, the other issue which dominated the unions in the first half of the 1960s was the question of the Emergency Laws (*Notstandsgesetze*). Many people within both the Free Democratic and Christian Democratic parties felt that the constitution did not provide adequate emergency powers to the federal government in the event of severe internal unrest. They demanded the passage of a constitutional amendment which would expand those powers. Drafts of the amendment were introduced into the Bundestag in both 1960 and 1962. Reformers within the SPD quickly realized that this provided a good opportunity to secure the party's legitimacy by supporting the amendment, while at the same time eliminating some of its harsher provisions. The SPD, thus, more or less approved of the emergency law concept, as did the 'conservative' unions close to the party reformers.

Brenner and the 'activists', however, were totally opposed to any emergency laws, which they saw as a threat to both democracy in general and the unions in particular, since a *de facto* suspension of the right to strike in the event of a national emergency was included in the laws. The issue of the *Notstandsgesetze* dragged on until 1968 and was the occasion for numerous clashes between Brenner and Leber.[56] At both the 1962 and 1966 DGB Congresses Brenner was able to secure majorities for a rejection of any emergency legislation. In the middle of this controversy stood the new DGB chief, Ludwig Rosenberg, whose elevation to that post in 1962 was symbolic of the reformers' victory. Rosenberg personally was for emergency laws, but he was forced by the DGB Congress decisions to publicly oppose them, which he did, not surprisingly, only half-heartedly. Rosenberg's main function over the next seven years was to work out compromises between the DGB's two warring wings, a task which he had proved he could do during the Düsseldorf Program debates.

By the mid-1960s most of the West German labor movement had followed the path the SPD had taken and gone from an opponent to a critical supporter of the existing social and economic order in the Federal Republic. An important group of unions, however, led by IG Metall, accepted this change only grudgingly. They continued to demand fundamental reforms, such as the extension of *Mitbestimmung*, and they tried, at least rhetorically, to keep alive a connection to a more radical past. This repressed radicalism, which remained anchored in the rank-and-file of the 'activist' unions, was to burst out with a vengeance in the late 1960s.

THE UNIONS AND COLLECTIVE BARGAINING

The founding of the Federal Republic meant the creation of a new collective bargaining system as well. Although a certain continuity with pre-1939 Germany was retained through many aspects of labor law and tradition, there was much that could only be worked out in practice. After a period in the first half of the 1950s when bargaining was decentralized and relatively uncoordinated, many aspects of today's highly organized and routinized system began to appear in the latter part of the decade. The trend toward greater predictability continued throughout most of the 1960s, and certainly was an important factor in West Germany's abiding economic success. The forces encouraging the Federal Republic's extraordinary stability in industrial relations are found both in the country's legal system and the labor movement's organization into industrial unions.

The legal system, with its heavy emphasis on juridification (*Verrechtlichung*) of labor activities, has played a key role in shaping union bargaining behavior in the postwar era.[57] Many of the precedents established in Weimar and before were restored in West Germany, including the legal recognition of unions as quasi-official representatives of workers and salaried employees. This brought with it a wide-ranging protection of the unions' status, but also subjected them to pervasive judicial (though not government) regulation. The two main principles of labor law were the concept of *Tarifautonomie* (autonomy of collective bargaining), whereby no outside forces were to interfere in labor negotiations, and the idea of unions as purely voluntary organizations, which made any form of closed shop illegal. In addition, strikes were defined only as an *ultima ratio*, or last resort, and their use strictly circumscribed. Only unions (as opposed to individual groups of workers) were permitted to call strikes, and this only after the expiration of a contract, since contracts between unions and employers' associations were considered legally binding and imposed a 'peace obligation' (*Friedenspflicht*) for their duration. Unions were made liable to considerable damages for any violation of these statutes. Their effect has been to curtail significantly work stoppages, especially in comparison to the experience in Anglo-Saxon and Southern European countries, where juridification is far less advanced.

In addition to the legal framework, industry-wide bargaining is the second key element in West German labor relations. The sixteen industrial unions were initially divided into nine to twelve bargaining regions, and negotiations normally take place either on that level or nationally with a peak employers' association. There are two basic kinds of contracts which are signed. The first are *Lohn- und Gehaltstarifverträge*, which cover wages and salaries and typically run for one to two years. The second are *Manteltarifverträge*, which are general framework contracts dealing with working conditions and non-wage issues like worktime and vacations. They are valid for up to five years. Because even regional bargaining often covers a very large number of workers in several related industries, both these types of contracts can only establish broad guidelines in their respective areas. Concretization must occur at the plant level, and this task falls, thanks to the BVG of 1952, to the works councils.

Although the unions set basic pay rates through collective bargaining, works councils are often able to secure many 'extras', such as bonuses and social benefits, through direct negotiations with the plant management. The result is a 'wage drift' between the wage rises obtained by the unions and the earnings increase which a worker actually receives. This wage drift, which first appeared in the late 1950s, has tended to weaken the unions and reinforce the 'dual' character (works councils vs unions) of West German labor relations.

Juridification, industrial unionism and dualism represent the constants in the Federal Republic's bargaining system which have remained unaltered since the early 1950s. The character of actual wage negotiations has, however, changed greatly since that time. One can identify four distinct phases in the period up to the 1966–7 recession based on the wage policy of IG Metall and its relation to other unions.[58] In the years up to about 1956 IG Metall's 'leading role' was not yet clearly established and bargaining rounds were fairly disorganized. During 1956–8 the union's primacy was uncontested, and it achieved some of its greatest victories. Negotiations became highly centralized. In 1959–63 IG Metall came under pressure from other unions, employers, the federal government, academia and the media to 'moderate' its demands and adopt a more cooperative stance. This is precisely what it tried to do from 1964 onward, partly out of necessity and partly in an attempt to gain recognition and acceptance from society as a whole – a project which paralleled similar efforts by the SPD which began in the late 1950s. This strategy was opposed by the union's rank-and-file and had to be abandoned after 1969, as we shall see in a later section.

As we have illustrated in the economics section, the first half of the 1950s was a unique period for the Federal Republic in many respects. Both output and productivity were rising rapidly, but unemployment was high. Inflation was almost non-existent after 1951, and prices actually fell in 1953. Under these circumstances, employers were loath to grant any wage increases at all, especially since government policy was to encourage investment and exports at the expense of consumption. The unions were forced to call numerous small-scale strikes during this time in order to have the principle of annual wage rises recognized, a goal which had been achieved by 1956.

Union bargaining was far from a model of coherence, however. The leadership of the various member-unions exercised little control over the regional negotiating units, and this led to a plethora of varying demands and results even within the same organization. More importantly, contracts were signed for different lengths of time so that they came up for renewal throughout the year, making a concerted 'wage push' by one or several unions difficult. In addition, medium- or long-term goals for collective bargaining and well-thought-out strategies to implement them were noticeably lacking until the *Aktionsprogramm* of 1955, and consequently much was done on an *ad hoc* basis. Lastly, the unions had not organized strikes since Weimar and they were to discover that many of the old practices were not suited to the new conditions in the Federal Republic.

The first real 'wage round' to occur in the Federal Republic began in late 1952 as a response to the defeat over the Works Constitution Act. A number of unions tried to win wage increases but met with stiff resistance on the part of employers. This situation led to a strike in the printing industry in December 1952, which collapsed after a week, and a six-week strike in the Bremen shipyards in the spring of 1953, which was only settled after intervention by the state government. During the period November 1952 to May 1953, when most of the bargaining took place, the unions were able to push up contractual wage rates by 3·4 percent.[59] In the following twelve months, however, almost no new wage agreements were signed, mainly as a result of the downturn in the economy which took place during that time. Unemployment had risen due to an influx of refugees from the East Zone, and the union bargaining position was weakened by a fear of layoffs. As a result, wage rates only increased by 1·6 percent from August 1953 through August 1954.[60]

After mid-1954, when the economy picked up, numerous unions tried to cash in. The ÖTV (Public Employees and Transport Union) challenged the federal government's determination to deny salary increases to public employees through a week-long strike in Hamburg in August 1954 which won for them a pay rise of 4·5 percent.[61] IG Metall also carried out a strike in Bavaria later that month which was plagued by many of the problems which characterized the bargaining system during this period. The strike was called by the regional leadership without adequate preparation after agreement had already been reached in an adjacent bargaining area. A total strike throughout the region was attempted, even though organizational levels were low in many areas. As a result, the strike front soon crumbled and the union received no more than had been achieved in other regions through negotiations.[62]

The disaster in Bavaria brought home two lessons to the IG Metall leadership. The first was that a coherent bargaining strategy had to be developed before each wage round and then imposed from the center on the various regional union organizations. The second was that an alternative to the 'total' strike had to be devised. IG Metall (and the other unions as well) would have occasion to implement successfully these lessons beginning in 1956, when the push to realize the *Aktionsprogramm* really began. Although the latter had already been announced before the 1955 wage round started in the summer of 1955, it seems to have had little effect on the negotiations of that year. This was due to the fact that many of IG Metall's general framework contracts, which dealt with worktime, were not up for renewal until 1956. Also it had been agreed that the DGB would first attempt to win the 45-hour working week through direct consultation with the BDA, the peak employer's association, and it was engaged in this task well into 1956. As a result, bargaining in 1955 retained much of the chaotic character of previous years, although the unions met less resistance from capital to wage increases, thanks to buoyant conditions in the economy. From August 1955 until August 1956 standard rates rose 7·5 percent.[63] IG Metall had set the pace for other unions by gaining a 7·4 percent increase in Baden-Württemberg at the beginning of the round.

By the summer of 1956 the DGB–BDA talks had broken down and IG Metall began its *Aktionsprogramm* offensive. Direct negotiations between Brenner and the leaders of Gesamtmetall (the metalworking industry's employers' association) superseded regional bargaining and on 25 July 1956 the so-called Bremen Accord was reached, whereby the 45-hour working week would be introduced in October 1956 and a pay rise of 1·3 percent granted.[64] This was equivalent to a total hourly wage increase of 8 percent. Other unions followed IG Metall's lead and, by January 1957, the working week had been reduced for 6·8 million workers.[65] The employers' flexibility on this issue was undoubtedly related to the first appearance of tight labor market conditions during the 1956–7 boom, which made them reluctant to lose workdays through strikes. Brenner added to his 1956 victory at the end of 1957, when another central agreement known as the Bad Soden Accord was signed. It foresaw a 6 percent wage increase in 1958 and a further worktime reduction to 44 hours in 1959. Once again, this deal was imposed from above on the union's regional bargaining authorities. It set the tone for the negotiations in other sectors throughout 1958.

At the same time as the talks which led to the Bremen Accord were taking place IG Metall had opened its *Aktionsprogramm* offensive on another front as well. It had been decided that regional bargaining would take place in a specially chosen region parallel to the IG Metall–Gesamtmetall negotiations with the aim of achieving a breakthrough on other *Aktionsprogramm* demands. The Schleswig-Holstein region had been designated the 'breakthrough point', mainly because it was both small (meaning that a strike would be less costly) and well organized (high unionization levels in shipbuilding). The union asked for paid sick leave for workers, longer vacations and extra vacation pay. The bargaining process broke down and in October 1956 a four-month strike, the longest in the history of the Federal Republic, ensued.[66] In the end most of IG

Metall's demands were satisfied and the union had won another stunning victory, while at the same time establishing its reputation as radical and intransigent.

The Schleswig-Holstein strike was to cost Otto Brenner and his men dearly, however. The union had committed a legal error by calling a strike vote before negotiations had officially been declared over. The Federal Labor Court interpreted this in October 1958 as a violation of the bargaining partners' peace obligation (*Friedenspflicht*). The court sentenced IG Metall to pay the Schleswig-Holstein branch of Gesamtmetall DM100 million (then about $23 million) in damages. This decision was a severe blow to Brenner's reputation, and it had noticeable repercussions on the 1959 wage round, when for the first time in years IG Metall gave up its trendsetter role. The level of wage rate increases in the metal industry was only about 4·6 percent, 2 percent lower than the average during this round.[67] The union rehabilitated itself in July 1960 when it signed the Bad Homburg Accord, which called for the introduction of the 40-hour working week, the key demand of the *Aktionsprogramm*, by mid-1965. In addition, a wage rise of 8·5 percent for 1960 and 5 percent for 1961 was agreed upon. Once again, IG Metall had paved the way for the rest of the DGB.

Yet the Bad Homburg success could not restore IG Metall to its previous position as unquestioned leader in the collective bargaining arena. The union's methods were to be called increasingly into question in the early 1960s by the 'social-partnership' wing of the DGB, led by IG Bau and the flamboyant Georg Leber. Leber developed a number of innovative bargaining strategies during this time designed to serve as an alternative to the hardline tactics of Brenner.[68] His main idea was to improve union–employer understanding through coadministration of various social welfare funds for workers to which each side contributed. Leber shunned all radical posturing, and, as has been mentioned, unilaterally removed a call for nationalizations from his union's by-laws. This reciprocal wooing by IG Bau and the employers culminated in 1961 with the Augsburg Accord in which the latter officially recognized the union as an *Ordnungsfaktor* ('agent of order') within the construction industry. Leber's other principal innovation was his repeated attempts to discriminate against non-union workers when negotiating wage increases in an effort to boost IG Bau's low membership. This type of behavior ran counter to the entire tradition of the German labor movement, which always claimed to speak for all workers, whether unionists or not.

Although Leber was a big hit with the media, his impact on the DGB and on IG Metall was limited by the relative weakness of his own union. A more serious threat to Brenner's radicalism was posed by the federal government's growing interference in collective bargaining after 1960. In the wake of the inflationary pressures generated by full employment, and the threat to German competitiveness presented by the 1961 revaluation, influential circles in the FRG began to call for state control of the unions if they failed to adopt a more 'reasonable' attitude. Erhard refused to go along with this extreme view, but he did use the specter of a German Taft–Hartley Act to try and pressure IG Metall. Keynesians meanwhile urged

Erhard to devise some kind of incomes policy as a way of controlling inflation, and his first hesitant step in this direction came in 1960 with the so-called 'Blessing Memorandum'.

The head of the Bundesbank, Karl Blessing, had been asked in 1959 to study the whole question of wages and recommend a 'scientific' guideline for responsible wage increases. In January 1960 he presented the government with the 'Blessing Memorandum', which stated that in order to preserve price stability, wages should not rise more than productivity.[69] He counted on a productivity gain of 3–4 percent for 1960 and urged that nominal wages be increased by only that amount. Productivity growth, in fact, turned out to be over 7 percent and so Blessing's credibility was lost. In 1961 and 1962 Erhard returned to his old approach of moral suasion, calling on the unions to moderate their demands (in spite of full employment) for the good of the country. The appeal fell on deaf ears, as industrial wage rates rose at a record pace of 8 percent in 1961 and 10·4 percent in 1962, due as much to labor market pressures as to union militancy.[70]

The growing inflationary problem, and the government's seeming inability to deal with it, led Gesamtmetall, the nation's most important employer's association, to the conclusion that a hardline strategy of its own was necessary to break what it saw as a wage–price spiral. The organization's tough new head, Herbert van Hüllen, decided to take IG Metall on in the 1962 bargaining round.[71] For the first time ever the employers reopened all their contracts with IG Metall, and the union countered with a demand for a 10 percent wage rise and increased vacation time to go with the working time reduction of one and a half hours per week already scheduled for 1962 (equivalent to an hourly pay rise of 3·5 percent). Gesamtmetall offered 3 percent, and a strike vote was taken in the key bargaining region of Nord Württemberg/Nord Baden (NW/NB), which IG Metall had chosen as a 'breakthrough' district. A confrontation seemed inevitable, but at the last minute Gesamtmetall backed down and granted an increase of 6 percent plus longer vacations.

The scenario was to be repeated almost exactly in 1963, except this time neither side could afford to give in. The economy was in a downturn, but inflation was still growing, and the federal government as well as the media urged moderate wage settlements if a recession was to be avoided and inflation stopped. Adopting Blessing's old formula Erhard recommended wage rises of 3–3·5 percent, which was equal to the anticipated productivity growth for 1963. Leber had done his part by signing a two-year wage contract, in February 1963, and now all eyes turned to IG Metall. The union asked for 8 percent and the employers initially offered nothing at all. This was subsequently changed to 3·5 percent, but both sides remained far apart. IG Metall again called a strike vote in NW/NB, but this time no eleventh-hour compromise was forthcoming: the strike began on 29 April 1963.[72] IG Metall opted for a 'point strike' (*Schwerpunktstreik*), a tactic first tried in Schleswig-Holstein in 1956–7, where only the largest, most important and best-unionized plants were struck. The employers answered with an area-wide lockout, the first in the FRG's history, which affected about 300,000 workers. When IG Metall decided to call a strike in Nordrhein-Westfalen (NRW), the country's most important industrial area, the government became worried that things were getting out of hand and both sides were invited to Bonn for consultations. Erhard was finally able to work out a deal on 6 May, just before the strike in NRW was scheduled to begin. The result was a 5 percent wage increase for 1963 followed by a 2 percent rise for the first half of 1964. Brenner saw this as a victory because Erhard's 'productivity formula' had been exceeded.

IG Metall's tough stance in 1962 and 1963, during a time of growing economic uncertainty, had done much to damage the union's reputation with the public. West Germany's conservative press constantly depicted Brenner as a socialist fanatic who had little concern for the well-being of the country's capitalist economy. Even the SPD had urged Brenner to avoid a strike in 1963 because it would threaten the party's new moderate image. The strike had been unpopular with the public at large and Brenner saw himself increasingly isolated. He decided that the union had to cultivate a more moderate, responsible image. Gesamtmetall gave him the opportunity in early 1964 when it offered to forget about the DM38 million which IG Metall still owed in damages as a result of the Schleswig-Holstein strike if Brenner would sign a new arbitration agreement which would make strikes more difficult to call. Brenner gave in.

During the 1964–5 and 1966 wage rounds IG Metall's new moderation was much in evidence. At the end of 1964 the union approved a one-year delay in the introduction of the 40-hour week (scheduled for July 1965) in order not to exacerbate an already extremely tight labor market. In return a 7·3 percent wage rise for 1965 and increased vacation time were granted. This result, known as the 1st Erbach Accord, met with universal praise in political circles. Whether intentionally or not, it remained within the guidelines for 1965 set down by the Council of Economic Experts (SVR) in its first report, which had characterized wage increases of between 7 and 8 percent as acceptable.[73] In February 1965, following a deadlock in negotiations in the steel industry, an independent arbiter (H. Meinhold) justified a wage rise of 7·5 percent with the argument that wages should increase at a rate equal to the growth in productivity plus inflation. This became known as the 'Meinhold formula', and was tacitly accepted by both unions and employers as the basis for a cooperative wage policy in the future.

The SVR gave its approval to the Meinhold compromise in its 1965 report[74] and suggested in the same spirit a wage rise of 6 percent for 1966. IG Metall opened the new round at the beginning of the year and the employers again requested that the 40-hour week be put off in view of the labor situation. The new, conciliatory Brenner agreed, and in return won a wage increase of 6 percent for IG Metall just as the SVR had recommended. The definitive arrival of the 40-hour week was set for July 1967, and it was to be accompanied by a wage increase of 1·9 percent for the first six months of that year. Twelve years after its formulation, the major goal of the 1955 *Aktionsprogramm* was finally to become reality.

By the mid-1960s most aspects of the current West German bargaining routine were firmly in place. Wage policy in all unions was highly centralized, with a negotiating strategy worked out by the leadership heavily influencing regional bargaining. A new wage round was usually opened by a major IG Metall settlement, which set the tone for other union accords. The macroeconomic situation, as evaluated by such expert bodies as the SVR, was the key factor in determining union demands. Although this pattern was to be disrupted somewhat by rank-and-file militancy in the late 1960s and early 1970s, it reappeared after the 1974 crisis and remains in force today.

The Unions between Grand Coalition and SPD Reforms, 1966–73

Like no other period before or since in West Germany, the time between December 1966 (Grand Coalition formed) and the oil crisis at the end of 1973 witnessed a close interaction between government economic policy, union wage bargaining and the actual performance of the economy. This is not surprising since it was during these years that Keynesian demand management and a cooperative incomes policy were given their chance in the Federal Republic. The events of this period, therefore, require a slightly different presentation than those of either the *Wirtschaftswunder* or post-1974 years. In the first section, below, both economic policy and results will be discussed together and related to each other, while in the following section union attitudes toward the government and their consequent wage behavior will be elucidated against the background of the economic situation outlined earlier.

Crisis and Recovery: Economic Policy and Development, 1966–73

Although the recession which hit the West German economy in 1966–7 looks mild by current standards, its psychological impact was enormous. It burst the bubble of the *Wirtschaftswunder*, provoked the fall of Erhard and his CDU–FDP (Freie Demokratische Partei – Free Democratic Party) coalition and ushered in a CDU–SPD government committed to a modernization of economic policy along Keynesian lines. The 1966–7 crisis marked the end of Freiburg neo-liberalism as the dominant economic philosophy in the Federal Republic.

The immediate causes of the 1966–7 recession are to be found in the economic policies applied in 1965 and early 1966.[75] After the downturn of 1963, a new boom ensued which reached its peak in 1964 (real GNP +6·6 percent). At the height of this boom, in the summer of 1964, the Bundesbank initiated a restrictive monetary policy to counter accelerating inflation and a deteriorating balance of payments. The federal government's fiscal policy, however, paid no heed to the Bundesbank's concerns: 1965 was an election year, and Erhard intended to pump up the economy to ensure CDU success in September. In January 1965 a large income tax cut covering 1965–6 was introduced and a number of special spending programs were passed just prior to the election. The Bundesbank reacted by tightening credit, and an open conflict between monetary and fiscal policy was the result.

The effects of this conflict did not manifest themselves immediately, though. Growth in 1965 remained strong (+5·5 percent), but the labor market was extremely tight (unemployment 0·7 percent) and inflation rising (+3·3 percent). The government's free spending, and above all strong consumer demand (+6·9 percent) due to the tax cuts, fueled the expansion. Increased private consumption led to a massive rise in imports (+15·5 percent), while exports were growing only moderately (+6·5 percent). West Germany's trade surplus shrank, and the country's hitherto largest current accounts deficit was the result (–DM6·2 billion).

By the spring of 1966 federal budget deficits were climbing due to the tax cuts and electoral spending of 1965 and inflation was accelerating, forcing the Bundesbank to tighten credit still further. Public pressure also forced the government to cut the budget to reduce the shortfall. These restrictive measures were ill-timed, however. Even as they were being implemented the recession was already beginning, led by a precipitous fall in capital investment as well as destocking. The Bundesbank's tight money policy of 1964–6 had done the trick but this had been as much a matter of chance as design. As has been mentioned earlier, all previous Bundesbank attempts to tighten liquidity had since 1958 been met by an inflow of capital which more or less compensated for the liquidity the Bundesbank had removed from the economy, thus rendering the policy ineffectual. In 1965, however, West Germany was running a massive current accounts deficit, which meant that instead of money being added to the banking system from abroad, it was in fact leaving the system, thus sharpening the Bundesbank's already-restrictive credit policy. The head-on clash between extremely low liquidity and very high credit demand (due to the fiscal stimulus) sent interest rates soaring, as they reached their highest level ever in postwar Germany in mid-1966. Under these conditions a large-scale recession was inevitable, and it was to strike with full force in the last quarter of 1966. Growth during the first half of the year still allowed for a rise in GNP of 2·4 percent for 1966 as a whole, but a drop in the expansion of capital investment of 1·2 percent (investment in machinery actually fell by 1·2 percent) was a sure sign of the trouble to come.

Growing budget deficits caused by the developing recession were the immediate reason behind a Cabinet crisis in October 1966, which lead to the formation of the Grand Coalition (CDU/SPD) in December. In the new government Dr Karl Schiller, the SPD's top economist and West Germany's most famous Keynesian, was appointed Economics Minister, while the CSU's Franz Josef Strauss of the Christian Social Union (Christliche Soziale Union – CSU), an old-style fiscal conservative, was Minister of Finance. The immediate tasks of this heterogeneous economic team seemed contradictory. On the one hand, it was necessary, for political and ideological reasons, to reduce significantly the large budget deficit which had brought down the previous coalition. On the other hand, expansionary measures were needed to pull the country out of the mounting recession.

Schiller and Strauss were able to achieve these two disparate goals through some imaginative accounting. First, Strauss cut DM2·6 billion from the basic 1967 budget. Then, in January, Schiller announced a special 'investment budget' of DM2·5 billion to be financed by credit from the Bundesbank, as well as the introduction of accelerated depreciation for all new investment undertaken before 1 October 1967. As it turned out this first 'investment budget' proved too small to counteract the restrictive effects of the budget cuts, and so Schiller inaugurated a second, larger (DM5·3 billion) program in September 1967. In addition to these fiscal measures, Schiller hoped to restore company profits by securing union agreement to wage restraint until a recovery was in sight. In February 1967 he realized the SVR's recommendation for a 'concerted action' by bringing together union and business leaders to discuss the necessity for wage restraint during the crisis.

These short-term steps were only stage one in Schiller's grand reform plans. Stage two involved creating the legal basis for Keynesian demand management in macroeconomic policy. Schiller accomplished this in the Stability and Growth Law (StWG), passed by the Bundestag in June 1967. The law's main points included the introduction of medium- and long-term budget planning, a greater coordination of federal, state and local spending, and the release of yearly economic reports providing 'orientation data' on future 'conjunctural' developments. In addition, and perhaps most importantly, the federal government was given wide latitude to raise and lower taxes, alter depreciation schedules and block expenditures, all on short notice and without parliamentary approval. Only with the use of such tools could Schiller hope to 'fine-tune' the economy.

By the spring of 1967 the peak of the recession had passed and a modest recovery was to ensue in the second half of the year. Since the downturn had begun at the end of 1966, the fall in GNP for 1967 as a whole was only 0·1 percent and at its highest point, in February, unemployment only reached 674,000, or about 3 percent. If one remembers, however, that unemployment had still been 0·7 percent in 1966, the full shock of the recession can be understood. The main source of the fall in output can be found in capital investment, which declined by 6·8 percent in 1967. Luckily for the Federal Republic, export demand remained strong throughout the year (+7·3 percent) and this, combined with a rise in government spending thanks to the various 'investment budgets', prevented a far worse crisis from occurring. One positive result of the recession was a cooling off of inflation, which fell from 3·5 percent in 1966 to 1·7 percent in 1967.

Public opinion generally credited Schiller's recovery program with pulling the country out of the recession by the end of 1967, but it is doubtful whether this was actually true. It was mainly a big upsurge in export demand toward the end of 1967, encouraged by West Germany's lower export costs thanks to union wage restraint and slowing inflation, which put the economy back on the growth path. Exports shot up by 13·3 percent in 1968 and were mainly responsible for the rise in GNP of 6·5 percent which was achieved in that year, despite the fact that capital investment only increased by a modest 4 percent.

As West Germany's trade surpluses mounted throughout 1968 Schiller became increasingly worried by the threat of renewed pressure on the mark, and he urged the unions to negotiate respectable wage rises in order to stimulate consumption and cool the export boom.[76] But the unions were still in a weak position following the recession, and the level of wage increases remained below that recommended by Schiller in both 1968 and most of 1969. As a result, exports continued to soar throughout 1969 and the government came under mounting pressure from its trade partners to revalue the mark. Schiller and the Bundesbank came to favor this course, but industrial interests in the CDU were firmly opposed to it, and during 1969 the battle over revaluation raged within the Grand Coalition.[77] Schiller's main concern was that the new boom was getting out of hand and would lead, after a certain lag, to a price explosion. The economy was expanding at a rate of 7·9 percent in 1969, as exports rose by 10·9 percent and capital investment by 10·5 percent. Schiller cut DM5·4 billion from the budget in the spring of 1969 as a countercyclical measure but this had little noticeable effect. Revaluation seemed the only answer, and Schiller was finally able to carry it out after the victory of the SPD in the September 1969 elections. On 24 October the mark was revalued by 9·7 percent, with the new exchange rate fixed at 3·66 marks to the dollar.

Schiller's fears of inflation were heightened by the wave of large wage increases which occurred at the end of 1969 and the beginning of 1970 in the wake of the wildcat strikes which broke out in September 1969 as a reaction to the policy of restraint practiced by the unions since the 1967 recession. In 1970 the average nominal wages rose by 14·7 percent, the largest increase since 1951. Schiller was convinced that pre-emptive fiscal restrictions were needed more urgently than ever and proposed a package of tax increases and budget cuts to the Cabinet in February 1970. These measures were rejected for the time being, since Chancellor Brandt did not want to raise taxes before a series of important state elections to be held in the spring of 1970. Only in July was Schiller able to levy a refundable surcharge on income taxes and temporarily suspend accelerated depreciation in an effort to slow capital investment which was expanding at a rate of 10·8 percent through 1970.

Despite a rate of investment growth higher than that in 1969, the boom which had begun in 1968 was over by the first half of 1970 as the West German economy started to feel the combined effects of revaluation, large wage increases and budget cuts. GNP rose by 5·9 percent in 1970, but after mid-year the economy fell into a state of 'stagflation' in which it was to stay until mid-1972. Growth was sluggish and inflation accelerating so that Schiller was forced to fight a battle on two fronts. His problems were complicated by the almost continuous crisis of the world monetary system which was occuring at that time.

At the root of this crisis were mounting American balance of payments deficits and a resulting strong downward pressure on the dollar. Everyone saw a devaluation of the US currency as inevitable and, thus, short-term capital flooded into the Federal Republic to take advantage of the imminent revaluation of the mark *vis-à-vis* the dollar. The rush of dollars into West Germany reached alarming proportions by the spring of 1971 and was bringing with it imported inflation. In May Schiller had no choice but to cut the exchange rate of the mark loose from the dollar. The regime of fixed exchange rates was not reestablished until December 1971, when the Smithsonian Accord was reached. The mark was revalued by 13·6 percent against the dollar and the new rate of exchange set at $1 = DM3.22.

The monetary crisis, as has been mentioned, only served to increase the inflationary pressures already present within the German economy. Schiller knew no solution to this problem other than the old policy of fiscal restriction (which had already been tried to little avail in 1969 and 1970), combined with appeals to the unions for wage restraint. In May 1971, at the same time that the mark was floated, a 'stability program' was passed which included DM1·8 billion in budget cuts and DM1·7 billion in tax increases. The measures succeeded in slowing growth (to 3·3 percent in 1971), but did nothing to stop inflation, which rose to 5·2 percent, the highest level in West Germany since 1951. In addition, labor market reserves had totally disappeared and the bargaining position of the unions remained strong, which made the prospect of voluntary wage moderation unlikely. Public opinion was also becoming increasingly alarmed about the large budget deficits which the government was running, despite Schiller's efforts to impose fiscal restrictions. The cost of many expensive social–liberal reform programs could simply not be brought under control at an acceptable political price.

In the face of these worrisome problems besetting the West German economy, and the government's perceived inability to deal with them adequately, voices began to be heard which demanded a radical change in economic policy. The number-one issue in German business and academic circles was inflation, and the consensus was growing that Schiller's Keynesianism plus concerted action had done nothing to halt it. The SVR, in its 1972 report, claimed that Keynesianism had failed, and that monetarism, by which it meant the direct regulation of the money supply by the Bundesbank, was the only way to control inflation.[78] Since this approach could not work under a regime of fixed exchange rates, the authorities were urged to allow the mark to float permanently. An incomes policy would also no longer be important, since 'the market' – that is, unemployment – would take care of the unions.

By mid-1972 this line of thinking was shared not only by the SVR, but also by many people within the Bundesbank and even the SPD, such as the then Finance Minister, Helmut Schmidt. In order to abandon Keynesianism, however, Schiller had to be removed first. This was accomplished in July 1972, when another monetary crisis was underway, caused by a renewed flood of dollars into the FRG. Schmidt argued that the entry of dollars had to be restricted by administrative means, a solution which Schiller vehemently opposed. Schmidt had the Cabinet on his side and Schiller was forced to resign.

The new monetarist strategy, with unemployment as its inevitable by-product, could not be implemented until 1973, since a federal election was scheduled for the fall of 1972. Meanwhile the economic situation had hardly improved. Growth had picked up in the second half of 1972, although the yearly average was still a disappointing 3·6 percent, and inflation had risen to 5·6 percent, and was actually climbing at a much faster rate in the last months of 1972. Unemployment was also higher, albeit still only 1·1 percent. With falling confidence in the economic situation, growth in capital investment was a modest 3·5 percent and government spending and exports were the major sources of expansion.

In February 1973 Helmut Schmidt and the Bundesbank moved to introduce the new monetarist policy. The Bundesbank began direct regulation of the money supply and immediately reduced liquidity sharply. On 11 March, the exchange rate of the mark was freed, this time for good. Schmidt supported the Bundesbank's credit squeeze by putting through an array of budget cuts and tax increases in February and May. Although the authorities felt that these stringent measures were necessary to combat the high rate of inflation, their effect on output and employment, which was first felt in the second half of 1973, was very serious. The 1972–3 upturn had been weak to begin with, and the boom was already over by March 1973, before these policies had taken hold. Growth for 1973 was a respectable 4·9 percent, but by the end of the year capital investment was falling and showed an annual increase of only 0·2 percent. Exports were again the main source of expansion (+11·5 percent) and state spending remained heavy due to decisions made in 1972. The new monetarism could do little about inflation in 1973, when it hit the almost unprecedented level of 7 percent.

Thus, even before the oil crisis occurred in November 1973, the West German economy had started into a nosedive, mainly as a result of extreme government policies designed to put a halt to the galloping inflation which many saw as the legacy of six years of Keynesianism. Orthodox demand management had been given its chance in the Federal Republic and it had failed not because of insufficient growth rates, but because of its inability to come to grips with the number-one West German concern, inflation. Monetarism was to fare much better in that area but at a cost of hundreds of thousands (and later millions) of unemployed. The unions were to suffer heavily, under the effects of these new policies.

Cooperation and Mobilization: The Unions, 1966–73

The SPD's decision to form a government with the CDU in December 1966 met with a mixed reaction from the unions. Predictably the DGB's right wing, which was closer to the SPD party line, strongly supported the move. The union left was skeptical, and IG Metall disapproved. However, since the move came at a time of perceived national emergency (the 1966–7 recession), the entire labor movement, including Brenner's metalworkers, decided to cooperate with the new government's program to revitalize the economy. The DGB and its member-unions agreed to participate in the first meeting of the new 'concerted action', to be held in February 1967.

The news that Brenner would take part in the 'concerted action' came as a surprise to many in West Germany. Yet this fitted in well with the new 'moderate' image that the IG Metall chief had been trying to cultivate since 1964. In the face of the most serious economic crisis faced by the Federal Republic since the war, and with many members of his own union threatened with unemployment, Brenner could hardly turn down Schiller's request to work together with him to put the nation back on the path to prosperity. He did take pains to emphasize, though, that the 'concerted action' was just a forum for discussion and in no way limited his union's collective bargaining freedom.[79] What actually happened is much more ambiguous, as we shall see.

Although in general the Grand Coalition served to unite the labor movement in a time of crisis, one issue on its agenda quickly reopened the old divisions: the question of the Emergency Laws (*Notstandsgesetze*). As part of the coalition agreement, the SPD promised to vote for the laws in the Bundestag, thus making a constitutional amendment possible. Despite the SPD's presence in the government, Brenner continued his campaign against any form of emergency laws. The DGB organized a large anti-emergency laws conference in Dortmund in May 1968 but refused to consider any strike action to block the laws. At the end of May they were duly passed by the Bundestag, thus finally laying to rest an issue which had done more to divide the labor movement in the previous eight years than any other.

With SPD participation in government finally a reality, the unions could resuscitate some of their projects which required legislative approval. Chief among them was the demand for more *Mitbestimmung*, which had been largely forgotten in the late 1950s and early 1960s. In March 1968 the DGB held a *Mitbestimmung* conference and called for the extension of codetermination, operative in the country's coal and steel industries, to the largest West German corporations.[80] Chancellor Kurt Georg Kiesinger responded by setting up a commission of experts, led by Kurt Biedenkopf, to study the problem in detail and make recommendations for future legislation. The Biedenkopf Report was not completed until early 1970 and, by that time, the SPD had entered the 'small coalition' with the FDP. One stipulation of their coalition accord was that the question of *Mitbestimmung* (which the FDP opposed) would not be touched until after the next federal elections scheduled for 1973.[81] In the end the unions had to wait until 1976 for a new codetermination law (see below).

Despite these disappointments, the DGB unions, led by IG Metall, did their utmost to support the government's economic policies on the labor market front from 1967 through late 1969. This was more a result of a serious weakening in the unions' position due to layoffs and widespread anxiety about the future (engendered by the 1966–7 recession) than of any particular altruism. As the recession deepened employers had begun to eliminate many of the non-contractual 'extras' which workers received on top of the standard wage rate. This phenomenon is illustrated by the fact that wage rates rose faster than actual earnings in 1967.[82] The unions could hardly push wage demands at a time when take-home pay was being cut. It is not surprising, then, that in the second half of 1967 many contracts which could have been reopened were allowed to run on. Instead unions tried to reach informal agreements with employers to stop earnings cuts in exchange for a postponement of new wage bargaining until 1968. An accord signed between IG Metall and Gesamtmetall in October 1967 which put off negotiations until March of 1968 was symptomatic of this trend.[83] As a result of this union weakness, nominal earnings per employed person rose by only 3·2 percent in 1967, the lowest amount ever in the Federal Republic's history.

As the economy picked up in early 1968 both Schiller and the SVR recommended wage increases of 5·5–6·5 percent in order to boost consumer spending and speed the recovery.[84] The unions, however, were still demoralized by the recession and were fearful of doing anything that might endanger the upturn. As a result, labor's wage settlements in 1968 were moderate, with the tone set by IG Metall's contract in the metal industry which was to run for eighteen months and called for a 4 percent wage rise for 1968. IG Metall justified its modest demands by claiming they were necessary to obtain employer approval for the *Rationalisierungs-schutzabkommen* (Rationalization Protection Agreement), which was also signed in 1968. This accord provided protection for older workers against layoffs caused by technological change and represented a growing interest in 'qualitative' issues by IG Metall in the wake of the 1967 crisis.

By the start of 1969 the economy was booming and criticisms of 1968's low wage increases began to mount both within union and government circles.[85] IG Metall reacted by convincing Gesamtmetall to reopen their contract two months early, and a new wage package was negotiated in August 1969 providing for an 8 percent pay rise as well as for stepped-up legal protection for union shop stewards (*Vertrauensleute*). This increase lay noticeably above the 5·5–6·5 percent which the government had again recommended for 1969. Trouble arose in early September, however, when the steel industry employers refused to go along with Gesamtmetall and renegotiate IG Metall's steel industry contracts. As a result, a marked gap arose between metal industry wages (DM4·42 per hour) and those in the steel industry (DM3·99 per hour) after the August rises went into effect. In view of the massive profits of many steel firms works councillors tried to arrange pay increases on an individual-company basis, but in all cases their requests were refused. On 2 September, wildcat strikes broke out at the Hoesch works in Dortmund and, in the following two weeks, were to spread to other steelplants as well as coalmines in the Saar region. In nearly all cases management acceded to the demands of their workforce and granted rises, which were formalized when IG Metall signed a new contract with the steel employers on 12 September which included an 11 percent wage increase and an extension of vacation time.

The so-called 'September strikes' served both to put employers on the defensive and to force the unions to take a more militant stance in order to stave off revolt from within their own ranks. The 1970 wage round brought the second highest nominal (14·7 percent) and the highest real wage increases (10·6 percent) in the Federal Republic's history, with only minimal owner resistance. During the next three years average nominal wages were to continue to rise at a rapid pace (1971: +11·9 percent, 1972: +9·4 percent, 1973: +11·9 percent), despite repeated government calls for wage restraint.[86] A very tight labor market and rank-and-file militancy made it impossible for the unions to heed these calls. The strikes of September 1969, therefore, began a five-year mobilization period during which the German labor movement won substantial wage increases through collective bargaining, additional monetary benefits through wage drift and new gains in the area of 'quality of work-life'. This period of hope and optimistic struggle lasted only until the onset of the recession/crisis in

1973–4, when conditions in the labor market and in the political arena changed.

There were three central reasons for the unions' new strategy in the labor market in the late 1960s and early 1970s. The first was the booming economy and the concomitant desire on the part of the unions to share in industry's profits, especially given the existence of almost full employment. Next the unions acted out their traditional belief that wages were one of the major components of economic growth. Finally, the unions faced an organizational imperative to respond to a restive rank-and-file by pursuing a more activist bargaining strategy. Many wage rounds in the early 1970s were accompanied by union-led strikes. (For example, 1971 remains to this day the most strike-ridden year in the history of the Federal Republic.) Unlike the 1969 strikes, which occurred in structurally weak industries and were rank-and-file-led, the 1971 work stoppages evolved throughout most branches of the German economy under the aegis of the unions.

The two most notable strikes of this year occurred in the chemical and metal industries. Both focussed on wages. The strike in the chemical industry was the first official work stoppage in more than fifty years in this sector of the German economy. Strikes in the chemical industry had traditionally been difficult to mount, due to the high percentage of white-collar and professional employees, the technical difficulties of implementing a work stoppage and the consistently high profits of the industry.[87] Whereas the chemical industry remained completely immune to the strike waves of 1969, by 1971 conditions had forced IG Chemie to assume a more militant posture on wages. The 1971 metal industry strike had additional long-term implications. Following the extraordinarily successful wage bargaining round in the German metal industry in 1970, IG Metall could counter industry's attempts at a rollback in the subsequent year only by calling a strike in the negotiating region of Nord Württemberg–Nord Baden, an industrial area surrounding Stuttgart and comprising such key sectors as automobiles (Daimler Benz), electronics (Bosch und Sel, the German subsidiary of ITT) and data-processing (IBM).[88] The importance of the strikes was underlined by industry's use of massive lockouts. Moreover, it established this area as IG Metall's – and by extension the entire German labor movement's – 'showcase' for the implementation of innovative labor market strategies and bargaining policies for subsequent years.[89]

The year 1973 was another notable period of worker militance on wage issues. Concentrated largely in the metal industry, the strikes of that summer introduced a new dimension of industrial conflict in West Germany. As in 1969, some of these strikes – most notably at the Hella factories in Lipstadt, at Pierburg in Neuss, at Ford-Cologne and Opel-Bochum – were not union-sanctioned during their initial phases. More importantly, however, and unlike 1969, these spontaneous strikes were conducted by the 'marginal' segments of the 'German' working class, namely, foreign (and often female) employees.[90]

A further dimension of the unions' new labor market approach was their growing concern for the 'quality of work-life'. The term 'quality' itself, in addition to its specific use as 'quality of work-life' (*Qualität des*

Arbeitslebens) and 'humanization of work' (*Humanisierung der Arbeit* – HdA) was not only mentioned more frequently in union publications at this time, but it was manifested in concrete bargaining and more general union strategies.[91] IG Metall, as has often been the case, provided the lead in this development with its much-celebrated *Rationalisierungsschutzabkommen* of 1968. This issue of 'quality' of working conditions received added attention in a large conference on the subject organized by IG Metall in April 1972. The proceedings of this conference had a profound effect on union thinking about technological developments and rationalization and should be seen as the precursor of the DGB's programmatic document on these issues at its own conference in 1974.[92]

Finally, concern for these qualitative issues culminated in the famous 1973 strike by the metalworkers of Nord Württemberg–Nord Baden in which IG Metall's demands concentrated solely on these questions.[93] Unlike its 1968 predecessor, the subsequent agreement reached by the union addressed fundamental issues of workplace control in addition to those of a more humane work experience and job safety by winning union influence over work breaks and the speed of the conveyor-belt. It may be a tribute to the scope of this collective agreement known as *Lohnrahmentarifvertrag II* (General Framework Contract II) that it remained confined to the small area of Nord Württemberg–Nord Baden. The hardening of German industry's opposition to any similar union demands in other regions attested not only to the far-reaching nature of the Nord Württemberg–Nord Baden contract, but also to the unions' weaker position generally in the face of the recession/crisis which developed one year later.

The unions' approach to collective bargaining during this period found concrete expression in the DGB's new *Aktionsprogramm* published in 1972. Similar to its predecessor of 1955, this program – unlike the more encompassing *Grundsatzprogramms* (basic programs) of 1949 and 1963 – addressed short-term issues and immediate union concerns.[94] Among these were demands for shorter worktime, limiting all weekly work including shiftwork to a maximum of 40 hours; six-week vacations, a demand which was to become a central bargaining point later in the 1970s; higher wages and salaries, especially for lower paid female workers; more equitable distribution of wealth through a reform of the state's fiscal and social policy, restructuring of tax laws; greater job security; increased workplace safety; better vocational education and improved on-the-job training; demands for the protection of the environment; and lastly, the traditional DGB emphasis on *Mitbestimmung* at all levels. Here, for the first time, was found the mention of economic and social councils (with full union participation) which were to oversee economic planning on the federal and *Länder* levels.

The 1972 *Aktionsprogramm* contained two additional components which had been absent from the earlier *Aktionsprogramm*: a focus on the general improvement of living and working conditions, and demands for what the unions called 'structural' changes to be implemented by the state. Moreover, one could discern a distinct change in language and presentation. Compared to its two predecessors, the 1972 *Aktions-*

programm was more assertive and insistent in tone. This change in tone, we believe, was more than a stylistic matter; it denoted a marked shift in political orientation.[95] More generally, new union aggressiveness in the labor market involved more than a tactic for gaining control of an unruly rank-and-file and improving wage levels. Expanding the share of wages in the economy fitted, in fact, into one of the DGB's most cherished and long-held economic tenets, namely, its contention that wages and popular consumption were the prime engines of economic growth and prosperity.

Wage gains and labor market activity were not, of course, the sole elements of the unions' strategy in this period. Unions saw state economic policy as essential, too. With the SPD as a junior partner in the Grand Coalition and Economics Minister Schiller pursuing vigorous demand management policies under the Stability Law, the unions were already pleased in 1968–9 with the contribution of the state to economic policy. The unions' hopes of realizing their economic goals received added emphasis and optimism when the SPD became the dominant government coalition partner in 1969. The two most notable legislative gains of this period were the *Arbeitsförderungsgesetz* (Work Promotion Law) of 1969 and the *Betriebsverfassungsgesetz* (Works Constitution Law) of 1972. The former reflected the unions' desire, since the onset of the recession of 1966–7, for an active labor market policy on the part of the government.[96] Consisting of a series of preventive measures to anticipate potential unemployment the law offered generous reeducation schemes, on-the-job training programs and other possibilities to overcome the structural imbalances between supply and demand in the labor market of a quickly changing economy. The Work Promotion Law empowered a semi-autonomous, quasi-state agency, the Bundesanstalt für Arbeit (Federal Labor Institute) and its 146 local employment agencies to become important procurers of qualified jobs and to function as clearinghouses for the regulation of supply and demand of employment.

The Works Constitution Law of 1972 represented a substantial union victory compared to the earlier 1952 law. However, it still fell short of the unions' desires concerning their aim for participating in economic matters. Explicit criteria delineating union input into the organization of the work process were absent, and middle management (*Leitende Angestellte*) was excluded from the law's jurisdiction. The 1972 Works Constitution Law, nevertheless, contained important benefits.[97] Among these were the legal recognition of the unions on the shopfloor, improved channels of communication between unions and the works councils, new legal rights for unions and works councils to force the employers to implement the law's stipulations and a substantial increase in the works councils' influence on most matters on the shopfloor. The law was important well beyond its legal dimensions. In particular, it had crucial implications for the unions' collective bargaining and organizational strategies. The law indirectly augmented the unions' power to control the implementation of collective bargaining agreements on the shopfloor.[98] In organizational terms the law prodded the unions to improve their shop steward system in order to add to direct union influence on the shopfloor and provide a structural counterbalance to the dominant role of the works councils in the workplace. Thus, despite some partially restrictive measures, the law capped twenty years of union struggle for improved conditions and greater union power in the workplace.

In sum, the period of 1968 to 1973–4 saw the unions mobilize their strength both through the labor market and in political areas. Although they failed to achieve all of their aims, they none the less were able to secure substantial benefits in both arenas. Despite the generally favorable developments of this period, however, the DGB was not without certain worries concerning the course of economic developments. This period witnessed increasing union concern with tendencies toward monopolization both in West Germany and the world.[99] In rather radical language the unions warned of the dangers of excessive concentrations of economic strength for democracy in general and of the adverse effects which could result from the unfettered pricing power which these large firms possessed. This general concern with intensifying concentration also pushed unions toward increasing attacks on the existence and activities of multinational corporations.

Coinciding with their concern regarding monopolies the unions also became worried about certain structural and employment-related problems which seemed beyond the remedies of traditional cyclical responses.[100] Specifically the unions addressed the difficulties in such industries as shipbuilding, steel, watchmaking and textiles which were not benefiting from the overall boom of the German economy. The unions' fear of employment difficulties in these structurally disadvantaged sectors led them to an increased criticism of the capacities of the market alone to solve industrial problems. While they realized the benefits of the SPD's cyclical measures and selective manpower policies, the unions expressed a renewed preference for a more extensive use of economic planning, both on the federal and the regional/sectoral level.

It was in this context that the unions, again led by IG Metall, entered into an intensified debate regarding the implementation of additional measures to counter the structural imbalances in the market. The most important of these measures focussed on the mechanism of *Investitionslenkung* (investment guidance). Although this demand was already mentioned in the Düsseldorf Basic Program of 1963, it was not until the early 1970s that its concretization was extensively debated within the unions as well as parts of the SPD. The unions saw new possibilities of linking the questions of unemployment, structural policy (*Strukturpolitik*) and investment guidance into a coordinated package thereby supplementing their longheld demand-based economic strategies. As to the package's precise implementation, the unions remained vague. Although mentioning the importance of so-called *Investitionsmeldestellen* (investment registries) and the participatory role of the above-mentioned economic and social councils, the unions continued to believe generally that the structure of *Mitbestimmung* would provide the best tools for influencing structural policy and investment.[101]

Although some of these reforms remained merely at the level of discussion, the atmosphere of public discourse was such that the unions remained optimistic about future state action. Contributing to the spirit of general mobilization and high hopes for reforms through the political arena were other significant developments. The SPD's accession under Willy Brandt to the position of major government coalition partner brought dramatic reforms in many areas of public life. Even more important, perhaps, these concrete measures bestowed an optimistic spirit upon the political climate of the Federal Republic. In addition to substantial domestic reforms in such areas as education, health, housing and transportation, the SPD government completely reoriented German foreign policy, culminating in the major breakthrough of *Ostpolitik*. These new directions, internally and in the larger world, created a new temper of the times. By muting the spirit of the Cold War, which until then had permeated most aspects of German public life, the SPD policies not only contributed to a gradual legitimation of the geopolitical status quo in Europe, but also fostered the increasing acceptance of the German Democratic Republic by West Germans. In addition, the SPD induced an atmosphere of dissent and radical critique within the Federal Republic itself. On the one hand the SPD's governmental presence enhanced social reforms, yet on the other this very process stimulated forces which wished to go well beyond them. Thus, the SPD inadvertently lent legitimacy to its own left critics, by providing them with institutional access to German politics through the SPD and the unions.

Most important among these critics of the SPD was that amorphous student-centered movement called the New Left. Largely spearheaded by the Sozialistische Deutsche Studentenbund (SDS) – originally the student youth organization of the SPD which was expelled from the party following the SDS's refusal to adhere to the post-Godesberg non-Marxist line – the German New Left, like its counterparts elsewhere, succeeded in politicizing previously taboo areas of public discourse. The New Left's lasting contribution to German politics lay not so much in its immediate existence, but rather in its organizational, intellectual and sociological legacies. Thus, for example, the unions and the SPD, both major targets of the New Left's criticism, became important recipients of the ripple-effects initiated by the New Left's activism. It was in this context, for example, that one had to view the wide-ranging debates over investment guidance (*Investitionslenkung*) among the Young Socialists (Jusos) and union economists in the early 1970s, since both groups included influential members of the 1960s student movement. Other issues which represented common demands of the unions and the New Left included their opposition to German rearmament (nuclear weapons in general), to the domination of the German print media by the Springer group and to the passage of the *Notstandsgesetze* (emergency laws) in 1968.

These developments also had profound effects on the way the unions viewed the world and their role therein. Enthusiastic supporters of the SPD's *Ostpolitik* (in support of which the unions threatened a general strike in April 1972 when the CDU/CSU called for a vote of no confidence in the government) union publications began referring to the DDR by its proper name, rather than as the 'Eastern Zone' or the so-called German Democratic Republic.[102] Despite the unequivocal rejection of the Soviet-led invasion of Czechoslovakia, the unions began to intensify their contacts with their counterparts in Eastern Europe, including those in the DDR.

In summary, the unions found themselves in a difficult position during 1969–73. Government policy and public opinion were mainly concerned about rising prices, and union cooperation in the anti-inflation battle was expected. Yet mounting rank-and-file militancy and tight labor market conditions made such cooperation very difficult to put into practice. Even when the unions consciously tried to exercise restraint, as in 1973, wages spurted ahead anyway. An alternative might have been for the government to exchange pro-labor legislation (on such issues as *Mitbestimmung* or *Investitionslenkung*) for an open commitment to an incomes policy, but the presence of the conservative FDP as a coalition partner made this impossible during this period. The end-result was that Schiller's attempts to reconcile price stability and full employment failed, ushering in the monetarist policies which were to use unemployment to combat inflation. The unions were to be the first to suffer under this new regime.

Part 4

Slow Growth and Emergent Dilemmas

The German economy was relatively well placed to withstand the shocks of the mid-1970s. It possessed solid positions of comparative advantage in international trade, particularly in the more promising sectors of advanced technology. German capital seemed sensitive also to the dynamic of change and able to project intelligent strategies toward the future. Beyond this, the German economy benefited from a remarkable social consensus on the need to maintain economic competitiveness in a rapidly changing environment. Still, West Germany was far from immune to the economic problems resulting from the oil crisis and its aftermath. If the Federal Republic occupied a strong position in the international market, world trade generally declined and became more competitive in conditions of widespread economic downturn. If German inflation levels were lower than those in most other advanced capitalist societies, inflation still posed a serious problem.[103] Growth levels, moreover, declined substantially in comparison with earlier periods. Certain sectors of the German economy were less well placed to face the changing structures of world markets and they confronted serious problems, even if Germany's international position was strong. With slower growth, serious threats in certain sectors, the need for domestic demand restraint to control inflation and attempts on the part of private capital to restructure in order to maintain a competitive edge, unemployment began to rise. If 'crisis' seemed a strong word for Germany's position after 1973–4, at least in a comparative perspective, changed economic circumstances were threatening enough to undermine earlier optimism about continuing German economic success.

German unions were bound, therefore, to face a newly challenging situation as a result of all this. With the SPD in power and with economic optimism still intact in the early 1970s, the DGB and its constituents had looked forward to an era in which German governments would pursue demand-stimulation policies to expand domestic consumption in impressive new ways. In addition, German unions hoped that friendly governments would move to reinforce the power of workers in the labor market and in economic decision-making processes through new *Mitbestimmung* legislation. Events were to take a different turn, however. Unemployment, low growth and the threat of inflation posed new problems. The SPD, faced with changing economic realities, drew back from implementing the programs which the unions desired to see, turning instead to relatively restrictive demand-management policies. German employers, adapting to new circumstances, began to act in ways which the unions considered to be inimical to them by further restructuring industry to threaten employment security, attempting to limit trade union power at firm and shopfloor levels and developing new patterns of intracapital coordination in capital–labor relations. German unions, therefore, confronted a dramatically changed situation the full implications of which they only came to realize toward the end of the 1970s. From a view that the economic difficulties of the mid-1970s were the hallmarks of a normal recession, the unions' understanding of Germany's economic situation evolved into one which characterized the period as one of persistent crisis. Similarly, response evolved from one which emphasized wage policy in the years immediately following the oil crisis to one which began to grope for more structural solutions to their predicament as the decade came to a close. In sum, these developments posed a number of problems for the unions. First, their hopes for, and ties to, the SPD placed them in a new role, that of hostage to a friendly government. If SPD governments decided to exploit the unions' preference for the SPD in power over the CDU/CSU to pursue policies with which the unions did not agree, what then could labor do? Secondly, the unions fell under direct attack from capital itself. How should they react to such attacks? Thirdly, and perhaps most serious, the unions' frustrated expectations concerning government policy and the new challenges from the employers created a strategic dilemma for West German labor. And as these conditions continued, they intensified the unions' imperatives for reevaluation of their situation. Were the unions' problems the result of the inability to implement fully the particulars of an otherwise sound program of analysis of the political economy, namely, the one which they had pursued since the late 1960s? Or were they the result of the fundamental inadequacy of this traditional model of union analysis? The unions continued to grapple with this dilemma into the 1980s.

Economic Trends and Policy, 1974–81

THE GERMAN ECONOMY SINCE THE OIL CRISIS – DATA REVIEW

To speak of the German economy in the years after the oil shock as being in a more generalized economic crisis is somewhat overdrawn. In fact, the performance of the German economy since 1974 has been much more nuanced and differentiated than the more all-encompassing term 'crisis' would seem to suggest. Perhaps the period could be characterized more accurately as one of slow and uneven growth which has consisted of several discrete phases. The first phase comprised the years 1974–5 when GDP dropped to 0·4 and −1·8 percent, respectively, after having attained growth of 4·9 percent in 1973. The second phase saw some recovery, but on much more modest lines, lasting from 1976 until the end of 1979. During this period growth ranged from 5·3 percent in 1976, 2·8 percent in 1977, 3·7 percent in 1978 and 4·5 percent in 1979. The last phase has been 1980–1, when much stronger recessionary tendencies were in evidence and growth declined to 1·8 and near 0 percent, respectively.

Although GDP did recover from the harshest effects of the oil price-induced shock (at least until 1981), unemployment did not. Having been accustomed to nearly full employment since the late 1960s (the highest unemployment figure for the first few years of the 1970s was 1·3 percent in 1973) the German unions became increasingly apprehensive when unemployment climbed from 2·6 percent in 1974, and ranged from 4·3 to 4·7 percent during the next four years. Although there was a modest decline to 3·8 percent in both 1979 and 1980, unemployment jumped over the 5 percent level in 1981. Since the performance of unemployment mirrored much less the ebb-and-flow of GDP, and with unemployment a much more significant benchmark for workers as to the economy's overall success, the German unions were much quicker to characterize the period in their literature as one of crisis and much less likely to see the period in differentiated phases than were other economic observers.

Another important indicator as to the performance of the German economy during this period was inflation. Very much related to the policy choices made by economic and political leaders inflation was especially feared as a force which had to be brought under control during the early and mid-1970s. From a level of 1·9 percent in 1969, inflation grew continuously during the next three years (3·3, 5·2 and 5·6 percent) and in both 1973 and 1974 reached a decade-high figure of 7·0 percent. In fact, even before the oil shock in late 1973, many anti-inflationary measures were undertaken by policy-makers which, in turn, became targets of union criticism. Yet despite these restrictive economic measures, inflation did not drop quickly, even during the recession years, 1974–5. By 1975 inflation had only dropped to 6·0 percent, a surprisingly high figure given the recessionary tendencies which had been underway since late 1973. The years 1976–9 saw improved results on the inflation front (4·3, 3·7, 2·7 and 4·1 percent, respectively) yet by 1980–1 it had begun to increase once again to over 5·5 percent.

Not unrelated to the above-mentioned changes in GDP, unemployment and inflation were the changes in the share of labor's compensation of total GDP.[104] Averaging 70·5 percent in 1962–9 labor saw its share of total GDP rise to 72 percent during the 1970–3 period and increase still further to 74 percent during 1974–5 after aggressive wage bargaining, particularly in 1974. However, in 1976–7, labor's share of GDP fell back to 72 percent and in 1978 dropped further to 70 percent. The figure remained at 70–72 percent through 1980. These aggregate figures were also reflected more specifically in the key manufacturing industries. After witnessing steady growth in these industries since the early 1960s (1962–5: 5·1 percent, 1965–9: 5·9 percent, 1969–73: 7·5 percent), German labor's average wage increase reached only 4·8 percent during the 1973–8 period and hovered near the 5 percent level through 1980. German unions were especially critical of this development because productivity in these manufacturing industries grew from a level of 4·8 percent average increase during the 1969–73 period to an average 5·1 percent increase in 1973–8. German unions felt that rather than being penalized with lower levels of wage increases, they should share in some of the fruits of the increased productivity. German industry stood in opposition to this view and claimed that slower wage growth in these industries was crucial if the necessary productivity improvements were to be effected for overall economic growth. High productivity increases continued in 1979 at the 5 percent level, but with the ripple-effects of the oil price increase and the general economic slowdown in 1980, the increase in productivity only approached the 1 percent mark.

A final contributor to the West German economy's performance both during the 1976–9 period of moderate growth and during the recessionary phase which began in 1980 was the Federal Republic's record on current accounts. In 1974–8 West Germany ran surpluses of $3·4–$9·8 billion, remarkable figures when compared to other advanced capitalist nations. Part of the reason for the improved economic results which began in 1976 were due to OPEC oil's denomination in US dollars and not in deutschemarks. Coupled with the restrictive fiscal and monetary policies of the Federal Republic during the mid-1970s, the mark appreciated considerably vs the US dollar. In addition, German industry proved quite successful in maintaining its export markets during the last half of the decade since its products maintained their reputation for quality in spite of their price rises which accompanied the mark's appreciation. However, at the time of the second round of oil price increases in 1979–80 the German economy was no longer in such an advantageous position. The deutschemark was no longer appreciating against the dollar, German industry was unable to pass on the higher oil prices in the form of higher prices and German exports met with comparatively reduced success due both to the general contraction of world economic conditions and to the increased competition of Third World and Japanese producers which threatened German manufacturers in some product lines. As early as 1979 these changed circumstances turned a German surplus into a deficit of $5·2 billion. The deficits continued in 1980–1, soaring to $10–$15 billion during each year.[105]

Thus, the data for the 1974–81 period has shown that the German economy was able to bounce back in 1976–9 from the recession years of 1974–5 with improved growth and a current balance surplus. And, although unemployment remained high (by German standards), and wage increases did not keep pace with those of the early 1970s (much to the consternation of the unions), inflation began to moderate and productivity began to rebound. In fact, by 1978–9 the German economic performance began to look so good in international comparison that the Federal Republic was asked to be the 'locomotive' for the more stagnant capitalist economies. Moreover, during these years West Germany was being pointed to as a nation which had been able to achieve stable growth, prudent fiscal and monetary management and still provide a comparatively generous welfare state.[106] Yet by the early 1980s this rosy scenario had to be tempered considerably as the Federal Republic began to suffer many, if not all, of the maladies which were besetting other industrialized nations. Inflation and unemployment continued to creep upward, deficits proved increasingly intractable, economic growth began to stagnate again as it did in the mid-1970s and retrenchment in some welfare measures was implemented. Thus, similar to the events of 1974–5 increasing criticism of economic, monetary and fiscal policy was voiced, particularly by the unions.

THE POLICY SCENARIO RELATED TO THE ECONOMIC TRENDS

Despite the ebb-and-flow of economic events in the years after 1974, in the main the West German economy found itself in a much less favorable position than it did in the years prior to that date. Consequently, West German economic policy became more generally austere. In direct contrast to the 1967–73 period, the government responded to these changes with a series of restrictive policies (which essentially continued throughout the decade and into the 1980s). The government concurred with the Bundesbank's tight monetary policy which had been in place since early 1973 via high interest rates and strict control of the growth of the money supply. The government wished to use monetary policy to break the expectations which were perceived by policy-makers as inflationary. Fiscal policy also became much more restrictive as the government deemphasized its explicit 'global guidance' (or cyclical policies) in favor of tighter budgetary measures. In addition to the abolition of many social reform measures, the state also tightened its labor market policy, in effect accepting a *de facto* tolerance of unemployment, a considerable departure from SPD–FDP policy since 1969. These measures provoked widespread criticism from the unions.

The first of the restrictive policy tools to be employed during this period was in the area of monetary policy. As indicated above, inflation had begun to inch up during the first four years of the 1970s, growing from 3·3 to 7·0 percent in 1970–3, and had become of growing concern to policy-makers. By early 1973 when inflationary tendencies were perceived as approaching dangerous territory, the Bundesbank sharply contracted the expansion of the money supply with the growth rate dropping from 13·7 percent in 1972 to 5·3 percent in 1973 and 5·9 percent in 1974.[107] Shortly after this action the mark began to appreciate rapidly. Yet despite these restrictive measures, the countervailing pressure of the ripple-effects of the oil-price increases contributed to the maintenance of high inflation (7·0 percent) throughout 1974. Consequently, policy-makers feared that the expectation of continued inflation would become imbedded in public perception and would result in an upward spiral of high wage and price increases. For their part the unions were quite sensitive to the question of wages falling to keep pace with inflation and they made a strenuous effort in 1974 to ensure that their wage gains would at least keep pace with the anticipated 1974 price increases. However, these policies found themselves on a collision-course with the restrictive measures of the government and Bundesbank.[108]

The 1974 wage negotiations began in January as the public sector workers' union. ÖTV, was chosen to set the pace for the other unions in the annual wage bargaining round. ÖTV began with wage demands of 15–20 percent, claiming that it had lost ground to inflation during 1973. Furthermore, the union argued that since the projected rate of inflation for 1974 (as estimated in January of that year) appeared to be headed for double digits, such high wage demands were justified. The union eventually settled for wage increases of 12–15 percent after tenacious negotiations which included brief strikes in such visible areas as public transportation and sanitation. With the public sector unions in the lead, other unions also came forward with high demands and the result was a substantial increase in wages throughout the economy.

The government and the Bundesbank were then confronted with a delicate decision. Were they to change overall monetary policy and allow the money supply to expand to accommodate these high wage settlements and, thus, ensure a double-digit inflation rate for 1974? Or were they to hold fast to the monetary policy established in 1973 which would, in effect, prevent employers from adapting to the higher wage settlements by raising prices? The latter course would force employers to begin layoffs since these cost increases were not able to be compensated by higher prices. The choice was made in March as the government and the Bundesbank decided that the situation compelled them to keep the annual inflation rate under 10 percent which, in turn, mandated them to keep the brakes on the money supply. This decision set in place a trajectory which has continued to characterize the monetary policy of the West German government and Bundesbank throughout most of the subsequent period. In essence, monetary policy was afforded a preeminence in the mix of available options, since it seemed to the government and to the Bundesbank to afford a more effective method of controlling the economy's direction than did the more even mix of fiscal and monetary policy during the 1967–73 period. In fact, the Bundesbank took this opportunity to establish a tradition in which it has published each year a target of the country's money-supply growth for the succeeding twelve-month period. The Bundesbank thought that by giving a clear indication of the anticipated growth of the money supply for the coming year that the various economic actors would be able to anticipate and plan better their pricing and wage bargaining strategies. During the 1975–8 period the Bundesbank was quite successful in being able to approximate the targets which it had set each year as Table 2·1 indicates. Thus, with the exception of 1978 when more expansionary policies were pursued, monetary policy remained firm and was largely responsible, in the minds of many economic leaders, for the Federal Republic's recovery from the 1974–5 recession and the subsequent moderate growth which continued for most of the remainder of the decade.

Table 2.1   *Monetary Growth, 1975–8*

Year	Targeted Monetary Growth (%)	Real Monetary Growth (%)
1975	7	8·2
1976	8	9·2
1977	8	9·0
1978	8	11·0

Source: Adapted from Koten, Kletterer and Volmer, 1980, p. 64.

If this restrictive policy was responsible for an appreciating deutschemark and reduced rates of inflation, it also was responsible for another economic development, namely, increased unemployment. Following the successful wage bargaining round of 1974 in which labor saw its share of GDP rise from 72 to 74 percent,[109] the initial union successes were more than offset by the losses in terms of increased unemployment, since the restrictive monetary policy inhibited the employers' ability to raise prices in response to higher wage costs. The unions saw that if they were to continue to demand and receive double-digit wage packages in the face of single-digit money supply growth, then the increased remuneration would come at the expense of large-scale layoffs. Thus, although unemployment did increase during the 1975–8 period to approximately 4 percent, policy-makers argued that this figure would have risen still higher had the unions not moderated their wage demands. In essence, putting the brakes on the money supply from 1974–8 allowed the syndrome of inflationary expectations to be broken because a clear barrier was established to prevent a leapfrogging wage–price spiral.

With the preeminence of monetary policy, came the reduced role of fiscal policy. Not that fiscal policy was to be abandoned, rather it also took a more restrictive cast. The Council of Economic Experts in its annual report of 1974–5 argued that fiscal policy should be relieved of its counter-cyclical responsibilities, since these measures were not performing as well as they had prior to 1973. Consequently, the government became much more insensitive toward traditional stimulative macroeconomic policy objectives. Although willing to engage in a few short-term countercyclical programs and to make token gestures in the direction of demand stimulation, it basically held out for a more deflationary economic strategy. The major reason for this undoubtedly was the government's heightened sensitivity to the German economy's international position. Were the economy to be heated up through extensive demand stimulation, inflation would almost certainly have risen in consequence. The result of this would not have been greater job creation – except in the very short run – but greater problems for the German economy in international trade and payments. German industry still possessed a comparative advantage in important areas even in a more circumspect economic climate. The government, however, apparently read the post–1974 period as a zero-sum economic game. This economic advantage would either increase or decrease depending, to an important degree, on what policy choices the government made. Increasing comparative advantage, or simply maintaining the economy's existing advantage, involved giving German capital maximum leeway. Excessive demand stimulation fueling preexisting inflationary tendencies, plus manpower and employment policies with sufficient clout to restrict capital's freedom to rationalize, all might have worked to increase Germany's vulnerability to an increasingly exacerbated and volatile world economy.

The major legislative vehicle for the more restrictive fiscal stance and tightening of labor market policy was the *Haushaltsstrukturgesetz* (HSG) or Budget Structure Law of 1975. In addition to calling for the reduction of public debt and the scope of the government's unemployment package, it also provided the first concrete steps toward austerity measures in the labor market. Its major concern was to institute cutbacks in many of the social and educational reforms provided by the *Arbeitsförderungsgesetz* (AFG) or Work Promotion Law of 1969. In essence the Budget Structure Law introduced criteria which aimed at severely confining the possibilities of obtaining unemployment compensation, through an explicit tightening of para. 103 of the AFG, which specified which jobs were 'expected' to be taken by whom, when and how. The Budget Structure Law set out to apply more stringent and rigorous definitions to this concept of *zumutbare Beschäftigung* (expected employment).[110] Consequently, the Budget Structure Law became the mainstay of the government's restrictive economic measures. These rollbacks were particularly significant in undercutting the selective manpower policies favored by the unions and established by the Work Promotion Law of 1969.

Thus, in terms of recovering from the low point of the 1974–5 recession, restrictive German monetary and fiscal policies proved successful in strengthening the deutschemark, reducing inflation, providing a modicum of economic growth and fostering increased productivity. Yet these measures also ushered in an era of high unemployment. Although the roughly 4 percent level of unemployment was low by international comparison, it did signify three to four times the amount of unemployment which the Federal Republic was used to during the 1967–73 period. In effect a conscious decision was made in 1974–5 to tolerate sharply higher unemployment in the interest of providing economic growth and stability. The result during this period was slow and modest growth accompanied by continuous union criticism that the unions were being asked to bear the major responsibility in the course of the West German recovery. By late 1977 and early 1978 the partial limits of this strategy were apparent and more stimulative policies were pursued due both to the continued union pressure and to the demands of other advanced capitalist nations that Germany act as a 'locomotive' for the world economy.

The primary effort at a more cautious expansion was the passage of a more stimulative fiscal package, in March 1977, the major effects of which were not felt until 1978. At that time the SPD–FDP coalition realized the necessity of producing programs to stimulate the economy and improve conditions in the labor market. This major package was called the 'Preventive investment program for the future of growth and ecology' better known as the Future Investment Program (*Zukunftsinvestitions- programm*, or ZIP).[111] Helmut Schmidt delineated ZIP's major aims in the following words:

> Economic growth and structural change over the next years necessitate special efforts to modernize public infrastructure and ecological conditions in general. We will thus inaugurate a multi-year public investment program in 1977 for the purpose of steady growth which will, if necessary, contribute to a sufficient development of internal demand thereby alleviating unemployment. This program in which the federal, state and local governments will participate, should entail a number of pathbreaking investments in the expansion of ecologically sound infra- structure, the improvement of public transportation and the proper maintenance of natural living conditions.[112]

The initial proposal envisioned a DM8–10 billion program for the legislative period 1976–80. However, following the unions' enthusiastic support for the government's initiative and their massive lobbying efforts for an increase to DM20 billion, the program went into effect with a DM16 billion budget. Spending was directed toward improving public transportation, energy savings, waterways, construction and vocational education.

These measures were responsible for fostering increased economic growth in the succeeding years. From a figure of 2·8 percent in 1977, GDP growth increased in the two succeeding years to 3·7 and 4·5 percent respectively. Enhancing this growth, too, was the slightly more expansionary monetary policy beginning in 1978 (partially to accommodate the more stimulative fiscal policies) as the money-supply growth exceeded its target in 1978 by 3 percent, whereas in each of the three preceeding years the actual money-supply growth attained levels near 1 percent of the original targets. Not to be discounted as an additional influence on the more expansionary West German economic policies were the efforts made by political and economic leaders of other industrialized countries for Germany to aid the world economy via these more stimulative policies. Policy-makers in other countries, who pointed to the comparatively low inflation figure in West Germany during 1978 (2·7 percent), argued that Germany could afford to stimulate its economy much more in order to help the other major industrialized states overcome the effects of the pervasive stagflation which had beset these other nations, since 1975, much more severely than it had the Federal Republic.

The initial advantages achieved in terms of improved growth due to these stimulative measures proved short-lived when the Federal Republic was confronted with the effects of the second oil price rise during 1979.[113] The situation in West Germany differed substantially from the first oil price rise in 1973. At that time the OPEC countries increased their imports from the developed world in their efforts to develop their economies as quickly as possible. In the late 1970s, however, the OPEC countries took a more restrained position, since they felt that the value of their vast supplies of oil would be enhanced if they developed their resources more slowly and kept prices high. In addition, the generally stagnating condition of the world economy inhibited the purchase of such key German exports as consumer goods and machinery. A second factor which dampened German economic performance after 1979 was the lower interest rate in the Federal Republic as compared with other industrialized countries – ironically brought about, in part, by the strong deutschemark. The cash-rich OPEC countries tended to invest their funds in countries with higher interest rates (such as the USA) where they could receive comparatively higher returns on their investments. Lastly, the strong deutschemark also made foreign travel more attractive for Germans after 1979 and the outflow of currency in the hands of tourists also contributed to the soaring deficits.

The policy response to these events during 1980–1 was one of restraint, both in monetary and in fiscal fields, notwithstanding the pressures of the Bundestag elections which were held in October 1980.[114] And despite the siren-calls for more stimulative measures in advance of the elections, the need to overcome the effects of the higher oil costs was viewed as a higher priority. Of at least equal importance was the need to keep interest rates high in order to attract the flow of investment funds into the Federal Republic, a result enhanced by the tight money policies. As for fiscal policy, the expiration of the 1977 Future Investment Program, or ZIP, was not followed by new similar stimulative programs in 1980–1. Yet as these restrictive measures continued in 1981, with the general approval of the business and banking communities, more strident criticism emerged, too. It came from such expected sources as labor, the left and, in general, the beneficiaries of the Federal Republic's welfare state. But it also came from certain industrial sectors which feared that some of these measures would actually further impede investment. In particular, criticism was raised by some bankers that reduction of funds in some company pension reserves would both threaten the viability of some plans and also industry's cash flow. Other sectors such as electronics, high technology and those industries most dependent on microprocessors feared that cuts by the Federal Ministry for Research and Technology (BMFT) would impede Germany's efforts to remain competitive with countries such as Japan and the USA.[115]

In essence, then, the policy scenario from the onset of the first oil crisis in 1973–4 until the early 1980s can be seen in a much different light than that of 1967–73. The early years of the period (1974–5) were accompanied by restrictive fiscal and monetary policies both to overcome the effects of inflation and to reduce labor's wage share. The middle years of this period (1976–9) saw a slight easing of these measures as the depths of the recession had been overcome and as various forces, both domestic and international, pushed for more expansionary programs. Yet as the effects of the second oil crisis worked themselves through the German and world economies (1980–1) they were accompanied by a return to a more restrictive fiscal and monetary stance.

Union Responses

The response of the German trade unions to the events of the post-1974 period should not be seen one-dimensionally. Nor should it be seen as either an abrupt departure from earlier tactics or a frantic casting about for the appropriate countermeasures. Rather, union response during these years should be seen as one of gradual evolution with two distinct stages. The first was the mid-1970s initial response of wage restraint, the call for the resumption of an expansionary economic policy similar to the recovery during the 1966–7 recession and, in general, that of a better version of the 1960s formula of German Keynesianism. The second was the much less certain and more cautious reevaluation of these traditional methods after 1977 when the unions grew uncertain as to whether their predicament was due to the failure to implement properly these earlier measures, or whether the situation in the later 1970s and early 1980s called for innovative departures in union policies. In the second stage the unions began to explore new analyses and prescriptions as well as to modify their strategies in both the labor market and the political arena, yet by the early

1980s no clear remedies to alleviate their deteriorating position had evolved.

INITIAL RESPONSES

Following the dramatic wage gains by German unions in the 1974 wage bargaining round, the results of the next three years stood in marked contrast. The 1975 wage increases attained levels only half as high as those of 1974. More seriously, with GNP in 1975 declining by 1·8 percent, the increased real wages were countered with increased layoffs by employers, since the restrictive monetary policy impeded the latter's ability to offset real wage increases with higher prices.[116] In 1976 the unions also continued to accept a policy of wage restraint without striving for the dramatic gains of 1974. Wages rose only 5·4 percent that year, but with inflation growing only at a 4·3 percent rate, the unions still received a modest 1·1 percent real wage increase. However, when combined with the increase in productivity during the 1974–8 period of 5·1 percent, the slight gain in real wages still represented a decrease in labor's wage share (from 74 to 72 percent just in 1975–6). And 1977 saw the continuation of this general pattern of wage restraint as labor's share of GNP remained at 1976 levels of 72 percent.[117]

Yet, in characterizing one of the unions' major initial responses to this period as one of wage restraint, it was still wage restraint with a particular purpose. The primary union goal during the first three years of the post-oil-crisis recession was at least to try to maintain real wages, since the era of high wage growth had ended. But by so doing, the unions did not take into consideration the effects that their policies, when combined with restrictive monetary measures, would have on unemployment. Even in early 1977 the unions did not seem to stress the connection between unemployment and real wage growth, despite their wage restraint. In fact, in the union research institute's journal there was a disavowal that the unions' attempts to maintain real wages were associated with the unemployment questions.[118] This was due in part to the unions' actions during the first three years of the recession which saw the problems in the German economy as cyclical and not structural. Via their traditional 'wage-consumption theory' the unions thought that the 'temporary' problem of unemployment would be overcome as soon as they could generate enough demand (via at least maintaining real wage share) to pull the economy out of recession. It was the realization that the German economy's problems were structural and not merely cyclical that delineated the unions' initial responses from the period of reevaluation which began during the latter part of 1977.

A second component of the unions' initial response also derived from their view of the economic problems as cyclical and not structural, namely, the call for an expansionary economic policy in the mid-1970s similar to the one which proved so successful in overcoming the effects of the 1966–7 recession. The unions thought that a similar application of Keynesian demand management on a large scale would help the German economy 'export its way out of the recession' as these measures did ten years earlier. Until 1977 the unions perceived the economic situation as merely a nasty manifestation of a downturn in the business cycle. Seldom using the word 'crisis' to describe their situation until late 1976 and early 1977 they preferred to use the more conventional word 'recession' instead. In addition to this verbal distinction, the unions were very tardy in developing specific strategies to counter the unemployment problem and, in effect, not publishing a major document on unemployment until 1977. Part of this Keynesian demand-management package included the previously mentioned 'wage consumption theory', which had for the unions more than just labor market impact. They argued that by pursuing higher wages workers – who form the majority of the German population – would both receive more income and, in the macroeconomy, stimulate lagging demand and lead the German economy out of its difficulties. The major premiss of the theory rested with the view that the largest impediment to renewed growth was due to insufficient demand. Therefore, any and all measures to stimulate demand continued to be advocated by the unions.

In essence, the unions' initial responses called for a replay of the 1960s formula of German Keynesianism (that is, adequate growth, price stability, full employment and export balance), but in a way which had better and more long-lasting results. They did accept a degree of wage restraint but not so severe as to lose real wage share as they did in the 1966–8 period. In return for these more moderate wage bargaining strategies (often coordinated through Concerted Action), the unions expected a broad and consistent package of stimulative measures which would overcome what was still, for them, a cyclical problem. But when wage share continued to erode, falling to 70 percent of GNP in 1978,[119] and when stimulative measures were resisted rather than implemented by the SPD–FDP coalition, the unions realized that their initial responses had not worked. As a result, in 1977 the unions began a more tentative process of reevaluation which continued into the 1980s.

REEVALUATION OF THE ECONOMIC SITUATION: DIAGNOSES AND PRESCRIPTIONS

Analysis of Unemployment
The factor which proved most dominant in the unions' reassessment of their initial responses was unemployment. In less than ten years the West German labor market was transformed from one which simultaneously had less than 1 percent unemployment *and* millions of *Gastarbeiter* into one in which unemployment stagnated near 4 percent for most of the last half of the 1970s and was to double that figure by the early 1980s. The persistence of this condition accompanied by the shortcomings of the unions' initial responses during the first few years of the post-1973 recession forced the unions by 1977 to intensify their analysis of the source of this new and pressing problem. In essence they characterized unemployment as taking three forms. The first was 'cyclical', a phenomenon which resulted from sluggish demand and deficient growth and which, although not a new form, had clearly intensified since 1974. The second was 'structural', a condition in certain sectors of malfunctioning coordination

between the demanded job/skill qualifications and the existent supply in the labor market, which Germany had hitherto largely avoided. The third (and newest) form was 'technological', which derived from fundamental changes in the workplace and affected previously highly employable groups such as white-collar employees and university-trained personnel as well as highly skilled workers.[120]

Deficient Demand and Cyclical Unemployment.   The first cause of the increased unemployment derived both from the unions' traditional postwar macroeconomic viewpoint and from the general strategies which they pursued throughout the postwar period and continued to pursue in the post-1973 period. They felt that there had been neither enough fiscal stimulus nor a sufficiently aggressive labor market wage-bargaining strategy since the high wage settlements of 1974. Thus, although it is clear that the unions were forced after 1977 to look at structural and technological explanations of unemployment, cyclical explanations continued to be the mainstay of their analysis. The unions reasoned that if renewed economic growth and decreased unemployment had not resulted since the onset of the recession, it was at least partially due to the fact that there had not been sufficient demand during the first few years of the recession. Consequently, this failure to stimulate the economy, which they argued until 1977 was responsible for the failure to increase real wages, after 1977 became an explanation for the continued high unemployment as well.[121]

Structural Problems.   A second major source of unemployment which the unions identified in the late 1970s went beyond ebbs-and-flows of the business cycle and seemed more related to the change in the international structure of production. With the growth of the newly industrializing countries (NICs) and their ability to succeed in the production of those goods which formerly were the mainstay of advanced capitalist countries such as the Federal Republic, certain sectors in the advanced countries experienced increased competitive pressure. Among the most seriously such affected industries in West Germany were textiles, shipbuilding and steel. The unions' chief complaint concerning this phenomenon centered on the quasi-permanent nature of the unemployment which this process produced. Namely, the unions maintained that a portion of the increased unemployment which had developed since 1974 was due to the structural changes in certain industries which saw, in effect, jobs being transferred from the Federal Republic to the NICs.

The unions argued that this process had two aspects. The first consisted of the failure of goods produced by certain German sectors to be as competitive on world markets as those of the NICs. Whereas German industrial leaders blamed higher German wages for the failure to maintain international competitiveness with their products, the unions asserted that the fault lay more with management failure to adapt in certain sectors, particularly steel and shipbuilding. None the less, both management and the unions did agree that, whatever the precise cause, the change in the international structure of production had cost the Federal Republic jobs.

However, the second aspect of this process, capital export, proved a much more contentious issue for both labor and capital as an explanation for structural unemployment. It had already become an important concern to some weaker German unions since 1974.[122] But with investment abroad by German industry having increased each year throughout the late 1970s (seemingly showing a change in emphasis by German industry from the more traditional strategy of solely relying on the export of goods), even the stronger unions voiced their reservations about the potentially adverse effects of such developments if continued into the 1980s.[123] For example, whereas there were only 455,000 people employed in plants abroad which were owned by German firms in 1966, there were more than 1·5 million in 1975. For every 100 domestic jobs in processing industries, there were five in German-owned firms abroad in 1966; yet there were twenty by 1975.[124] Although more concerned with the question of capital export than with structural deficiencies in some sectors *per se*, the unions did see the two as part of the same process. They felt that the very forces which were responsible for such changes in the world economy as continued sluggish growth and stagnating unemployment levels in the advanced capitalist countries, and the rapid growth of such NICs as Brazil, Argentina, Taiwan and South Korea, encouraged the continued export of capital from the developed world to the NICs. Based on OECD reports the unions feared that continued developments along such a trajectory would dramatically increase the number of structurally unemployed.[125]

Technological Change.   The third, and to the unions the most serious, source of the persistently high unemployment lay in the loss of jobs directly attributable to the introduction of such new technologies as micro-processors and other forms of computerization. Whereas German unions had traditionally emphasized their generally positive attitudes concerning technological change and innovation by repeatedly stressing that they were not 'machine-stormers', they became increasingly frightened in the late 1970s by the substantial loss of jobs which this development seemed to engender:

> In the past, the DGB has welcomed the results of rationalization and technical change insofar as it was ensured that, by raising work productivity, it was possible to improve workers' social conditions and no negative effects occurred at their expense ... Should those with ... responsibility fail to do away with mass unemployment, the trade union position on rationalization and technical change must be critically rethought.[126]

Despite their profession of approval for socially responsible techno-logical change, German unions had begun to experience considerable anxiety about rationalization and, more specifically, the likely manifestations of the 'Third Industrial Revolution', involving the introduction of electronic microprocessing into all areas of productive life. Indeed, hardly any union publication during these years failed to mention the adverse effects of the uncontrolled introduction of those versatile computer chips which the unions tellingly labeled 'job-killers'.[127] The coming of intensified rationalization as a consequence of the increasing presence of microprocessors in the German economy introduced, in the unions' view, the most threatening form of unemployment, namely, technological. The unions felt that technological unemployment was far more serious than other forms of unemployment because at least cyclical unemployment could theoretically be overcome by enough demand stimulus and structural unemployment could theoretically be overcome by the proper structural policy. Technological unemployment's major dangers were that workers in all sectors were potentially vulnerable to sudden job loss and that the unions had no immediately viable option to counter this serious development.

Prescriptions to Overcome Unemployment

If the unions' reassessment of the economic situation in the late 1970s caused them to identify unemployment as their most serious concern and to differentiate its causes among cyclical, structural and technological reasons, what prescriptions did they offer as part of their reevaluation process? In essence all the actions which they called upon both the government and their own membership to implement could be found in the general approaches which they elaborated in the pre-1974 period. If one cause of unemployment was due to insufficient demand, then more demand was in order. If another was due to structural problems in certain sectors, then it fell to the unions to press upon the state for the appropriate structural adjustments. And if another was due to the introduction of new production processes, then the unions should use the methods available to them by law, collective bargaining, *Mitbestimmung* and their access to the *Betriebsräte*, to shape the pace and condition of such introduction. Thus, although considerable reevaluation was underway, the legacy of their earlier patterns of responses were very much still in evidence.

More demand.   The two primary vehicles which the unions prescribed to enhance demand and, thus, help alleviate the stagnating unemployment were the ones which they had traditionally used, namely, more stimulative government budgetary policy and a more aggressive union wage policy. Although the unions were pleased at the government's passage of the Future Investment Program (ZIP) in 1977, their ideal–typical vision of the appropriate government stimulus measures was drawn from the expansive 1969–73 'reform euphoria' period and not the more limited landscape of the late 1970s. The unions argued that the state should live up to the mandate of the *Stabilitätsgesetz*, which called for the government to keep all four dimensions of the Keynesian quadrant (that is, adequate growth, price stability, full employment and export balance) in a proportionate and socially equitable equilibrium.[128] According to the unions, the state – especially via the Bundesbank which even more than the US Federal Reserve is structurally independent of the government – had paid too much attention to the inflation dimension at the direct cost of unemployment. Furthermore, the unions opposed any measures to cut the federal budget deficit (which, by 1980, had approached DM30 billion) as long demanded by the conservative opposition as well as the liberal junior partner in the government coalition, and occasionally even proposed by some SPD members during the months preceeding the 1980 election. Although there were some disagreements within the unions as to the potential limits of the public debt, they lent very little credence to the conservative arguments that deficits crowded out private capital from money markets, raised interest levels, or mortgaged the future of subsequent generations.[129] The unions argued that deficit spending was unquestionably the lesser of two evils and that the public debt would undoubtedly be reduced with a full-employment economy working at near-full capacity by a drastic reduction of unemployment payments and a concomitant increase in the taxes of the newly employed workers.[130] Although not against tax cuts in principle, the unions preferred a 'direct fiscal policy' of state investments and expenditures. Tax cuts could potentially both stimulate growth and alleviate unemployment, but the unions argued that by-products such as capital export and speculation might defeat the whole purpose of the exercise. The unions saw direct state intervention as a socially much more equitable measure than any other fiscal alternative.

With respect to union wage policy in the late 1970s, the unions continued to rely on the 'wage–consumption theory' which they had used as a theoretical underpinning both before and after the first oil crisis in 1973. However, since they noted that demand continued to be insufficient in the late 1970s, especially with respect to unemployment, they tried to sketch out more clearly the relationship between the two. The unions' formulation of the 'theory' in the late 1970s linked wage increases, economic growth and, ultimately, a general redistribution of resources and social equalization. In short, the unions favored an economic policy based on high wages → more consumption → more demand → more growth → low or no unemployment. Thus, from a policy which was originally formulated to be part of a more general demand stimulus package, the wage–consumption theory evolved into a policy which was to be used as a major analytical tool in the unions' push for both increased growth and reduced unemployment due to the stubbornness of the business cycle.

Structural Adjustment. With respect to the structural causes of unemployment, the unions argued that state intervention should 'go beyond Keynes'.[131] More specifically the unions distinguished between traditional Keynesianism and more targeted approaches which emphasized sectorally and/or regionally selective aid via direct state action or supervision. In order to overcome the effects of structural unemployment in certain sectors the unions called for change in the hitherto 'global' approach to this challenge and the replacement of the 'sprinkler' policy of blanket programs which would benefit all sectors whether they needed them or not with a 'targeted' *Strukturpolitik* wherein needy regions and/or sectors received large and well-planned investments. *Strukturpolitik*, then, implied a recognition that mere Keynesian macrolevel demand management remained insufficient by itself to alleviate particular structural problems. By way of further targeted stimulus the unions also called for state investments in urban renewal, low-income housing, improvements in the health sector, various social services, ecological investments, new job creations around environmental issues, and reeducation and retraining both on the job and in newly created educational programs.

Given the context of the capital export debate, another potential tool of structural policy surfaced in union prescriptions, namely, the concept of *Investitionslenkung* (investment guidance). Although it had its origins and heyday in the more supportive 1969–73 period and was soon downplayed, it surfaced again during the late 1970s as the unions suggested two different applications of this concept. The first believed that the unions should have a direct say as to the amount, location and form of all private and public investments over a certain amount. Juxtaposed to this rather radical proposal was a more moderate one which merely called for union suggestions and consultations without, however, possessing any binding force or sanctions. Moreover, this view believed that the institution of *Mitbestimmung* should be involved in investment decisions, as it had when IG Metall agreed to let VW invest in the USA in return for certain job-guaranteeing concessions in West German factories. These proposals provoked considerable debate among the various DGB unions, with IG Metall looking more favorably on these schemes than the more conservative IG Bau-Steine-Erden, for example. In a related development IG Chemie had already developed a certain form of investment guidance scheme via its *Branchenausschüsse* (branch committees) whereby the union participated actively in investment decisions of individual sectors, though not necessarily individual firms.[132] The investment guidance/ control issue was introduced again at the 1981 DGB Congress, but the more moderate forces prevailed. The furthest the DGB would go on this question was to call for *Investitionsmeldestellen* (investment registries), which would be tripartite agencies to which all investments over a certain amount were to be reported. However, these bodies would have no means of sanction other than the moral force of persuasion. Thus, union prescriptions on this issue concluded with the all-important qualifications that, in the end, investments should remain in the realm of private decision-making and thus *de facto* continue as a prerogative of the employers.[133]

Although the unions' prescriptions for structural adjustment did go beyond Keynes in terms of a targeted labor market policy and attempts to influence investment, they stopped well short of direct control measures and, consequently, could not be called 'microintervention' such as the schemes proposed by unions in Sweden and Italy .[134] As a result, they remained very much part of the unions' previous prescriptive pattern.

Management or Technological Change.   Technological causes of unemployment proved a much more formidable challenge to the unions than did either of the other two sources. Consequently, union prescriptions – although theoretically innovative on this issue – remained rather tentative and defensive in terms of proposed implementation into the early 1980s. Whereas the unions mounted strenuous opposition to any and all forms of 'replacement rationalization', which had as its primary goal the shrinking of the workforce, they gave their guarded approval to 'expansive rationalization', or that which did not directly threaten jobs. They did so in a fashion which they hoped would afford them as much influence as possible in the shaping of the technological change which was taking place. The primary vehicle which they prescribed for this process was the Humanization of Work (Humanisierung der Arbeit – HdA) Program.[135] First established in 1974 (as a result of union initiatives) the program concerned itself with projecting the implication of technological change on the shape of work. The unions paid great attention to the evolution of this program because they saw in it, by the late 1970s, a mechanism to influence the future course of industrial rationalization.[136] Enhanced job control obtained through the program, the unions argued, might give them greater control over the work process emerging from rationalization. Thereby they felt that better, and not worse, jobs would come out of future change and in the process help alleviate both technological and structural unemployment.[137]

Another dimension of the Humanization of Work Program, as prescribed by the unions, was the attempts at the reduction of the working week. While at first glance this aspect might be considered a tangent of the unions' 'wage–consumption theory', the unions argued that shortening of working hours (without a reduction in wages) went beyond its obvious function as an agent of macroeconomic stimulation. They claimed that such a measure was an essential component of a more humane workplace which, they felt, it was vital to ensure in the face of rapid technological change which produced job loss, dequalification, increasing job stress, and the replacement of skilled workers with new and less qualified ones. In essence, the unions had begun to formulate 'qualitative' prescriptions in addition to the more 'quantitative' ones of the past.[138]

However, in proposing the implementation of these 'qualitative' prescriptions the unions proved much less innovative. Like their approach to investment control, the measures which they outlined to respond to technological change fell within the pattern of their response to more 'quantitative' issues. The unions' proposals on these issues were raised through the state (via union pressure on the SPD–FDP government to expand the Humanization of Work Program), through the institutions of worker participation (*Mitbestimmung* and *Betriebsräte*) and via collective bargaining. Yet in addressing the effects of technological change in these three arenas the unions were unable to develop prescriptions which would overcome the limitations which each of the three posed to their implementation. If the state proved unresponsive in expanding 'humanization' programs due to the pressures of coalition politics, if the avenue of *Mitbestimmung* promised difficulties due to industry's attempts to circumvent some of the law's provisions, or if the employers dug in their heels on the collective bargaining front in the face of the unions' qualitative prescriptions, the unions were stymied. They were stymied because, unlike their general proposals to address the issue of technological change, the unions did not propose methods for these vehicles to go beyond the above-outlined limitations.

Yet despite offering prescriptions for more demand via government budgetary policy and union wage policy, structural adjustment via a more innovative labor market policy and raising the issue of investment control, and management of technological change by proposing a union voice in the pace and condition (that is, worktime reduction) of these changes through traditional union vehicles, the unions still retained the essence of the approaches which were elaborated in the pre-1974 period.

STRATEGIES FOR IMPLEMENTATION

The Political Arena

The unions' hopes for the implementation of their strategies in the political arena continued to be dashed by the government's restrictive measures throughout the late 1970s and early 1980s. As outlined above, the state responded to the economic downturn with restrictive austerity measures; it concurred with the Bundesbank's tight monetary policy via high interest rates and a strict control of the money supply (after a brief loosening in 1978–9); it deemphasized its explicit Keynesian cyclical policies in favor of tight fiscal and budgetary policies; and many social reform programs were abolished or curtailed and large stimulus packages replaced in favor of specific goal-oriented subsidies of particular export-oriented sectors, often in areas of high technology.[139] Yet the SPD government had a convenient, and often justified excuse for not following the unions' suggestions. However willing the SPD might have been to promote greater Keynesianism, its FDP allies were not. In order to stay in power the SPD had to compromise with the FDP.[140] The alternative to compromise was, of course, a return of the CDU to power. Whatever course the CDU in power might have chosen to deal with the new economic setting – and German unionists had few illusions what it might have been – it would certainly have been less willing to listen to union ideas than the SPD–FDP coalition. German unions were, thus, caught in the classic 'hostage to a friendly government' dilemma. One way out of this dilemma might have been for German unions to rethink their picture of the German economy from top to bottom, but as of the early 1980s, they had not done so.

One factor which prevented the unions from fundamentally altering their viewpoint of the economy was that, despite the limitations in the late 1970s, some benefits did accrue to the unions from the state. For example, the unions were generally pleased with the workings of ZIP since it did help to ease unemployment in some areas.[141] However, the dominant feeling maintained that ZIP had been much too little and much too late. It had been skewed to favor the construction industry, for example, in classic public works, anti-cyclical fashion. Bureaucratic snags and abuses were also common. The real issue about ZIP to the unions was that it was 'patching'. It was designed to alleviate cyclical and growth-related unemployment. While the unions felt that such policies were both necessary and useful – in fact, they demanded more of them – they also concluded that countercyclical 'patching' did little to address the additional problem of structural unemployment. Since the unions had already concluded that the situation by the late 1970s was more than a simple recession, but rather signaled the emergence of a longer-term structural unemployment problem due to rationalization and the inability of the German economy to create enough new jobs, programs like ZIP could be little more than temporary remedies. In particular, the unions criticized ZIP's failure to reach the 'problem groups' of structural unemployment such as women, the elderly, young entrants into the labor-force, the unskilled and workers in depressed sectors and areas. ZIP was not enough, then. More and different state intervention in the economy was necessary.

The unions also welcomed certain selective manpower and structural policies to revitalize the Rhine–Ruhr area which were directed to alleviating longstanding unemployment that involved an expenditure of DM5 billion over a ten-year period for job retraining, modernizing the coal industry, industrial diversification and ecological reform.[142] However, the unions also felt that these government policies were too little and too late. They argued that for a DM5 billion program to be expected to fulfill all of these goals and to be stretched over the course of a decade was also a palliative at best. They argued that this region of the country had the most severe structural unemployment and was also subject to considerable capital flight as industry was less enthusiastic about directing new invest-ment into an area which was considered structurally disadvantaged. However, any union attempts to increase the demands for more structural policy to the Rhine–Ruhr were met with frustration due to the FDP's unwillingness to embark on large-scale stimulative measures.

The unions' strategies in the political arena were also hampered by the continued restrictive monetary policies of the Bundesbank. After a loosening of the money supply in 1978 in the context of both ZIP and the request by Western nations that Germany act as the 'locomotive' for the world economy, the Bundesbank put the brakes on again in 1979. Partially due to the Bundesbank's exceeding its money supply target by a 3 percent margin in 1978, and partially to fears that the second oil crisis would hit the German economy harder than the first one, these restrictive measures greatly frustrated the union efforts to obtain greater stimulative measures from the SPD–FDP government. The government continued to maintain that the Bundesbank was independent and would set the monetary course which it felt could best ensure stable recovery and non-inflationary growth. However, many unionists felt that the excuse of the Bundesbank's intransigence allowed some government officials to, in effect, 'get off the hook'. This feeling was especially evident in 1981 as high US interest rates forced German rates to rise as well. This problem was compounded for the unions because the government continued to refrain from either expansive monetary or fiscal policies as German unemployment approached 5·5 percent, the largest since the 1950s.[143]

The unions were exceptionally critical of the more restrictive labor market policy as exemplified by the revisions of the Budget Structure Law. The law remained in force after its 1975 inception and the government-promoted reduction in benefits was taken even further later in the debates and administrative steps surrounding the fifth legislative amendment to the 1969 Work Promotion Law. Thus, an administrative decree was issued in August 1978 by the semi-autonomous, quasi-governmental Federal Labor Institute in which the criteria for 'expected' employment were once again tightened and the sanctions for failing to comply were made more severe. This decree 'expected' individuals to accept jobs below their qualifications if they had tried unsuccessfully over a period of six months to find work in their own job category. As to 'special mobility', the other major area of the administrative decree, the new rule would 'expect' prospective job-holders to move to another part of the country, become weekend commuters and/or increase their daily commuting time between their home and workplace.[144] Although the decree's full severity was not incorporated into the fifth amendment of the 1979 Work Promotion Law, the law did reflect the decree in general intentions, albeit sometimes in muted form. This defeat, of course, ran directly counter to the unions' crisis strategies. The unions posited that increasing rationalization caused by changing economic circumstances had already led industry toward a process of deskilling involving downward economic mobility for a growing number of workers. The government's policies, rather than counteracting this process, actually pushed it further. In contrast the unions had hoped to prod the state in different directions, away from interventions working to the detriment of the unemployed. As things turned out, it fell solely to the unemployed to find another job in an uncompromising labor market. Moreover, there were no 'expectations' stipulated by the state for employers concerning the number of jobs which they offered, their quality, regional distribution and security.[145]

If the government was unwilling to implement the macroeconomic package desired by the unions, the unions felt that it would at least help them gain the extension of *Mitbestimmung* which the unions had long coveted in order to obtain employment gains through an enhancement of union participation and control. Here, again, union hopes were dashed.[146] The unions had never given up their hopes of attaining full-parity codetermination throughout the entire German economy, even following their defeat in the 1952 Works Constitution Act. However, it was not until 1 July 1976, after much arguing among the SPD, the FDP, the employers and the unions throughout the years of the supposedly favorable social-liberal coalition, that the law was finally passed.

The FDP's objections revolved around the contention that an extension of the *Montanmitbestimmung* model to the entire German economy would be unconstitutional and incompatible with the 'free, basic democratic order' of the Federal Republic due to the prospective law's violation of the sanctity of property rights. The essence of the FDP proposals, in clear opposition to those of the SPD and DGB, aimed at assuring an employer majority on the supervisory board at all times. Moreover, the FDP attempted to enhance the representations of all company employees as individuals at the expense of the unions as organizations. Lastly, the FDP only wanted the new law applied to publicly held companies exceeding 2,000 employees.

The SPD's position throughout this period was ambivalent. On the one hand the party still maintained its wish to implement a full-parity *Mitbestimmung* law, and on the other it accepted in the end most of the

FDP's reservations while citing the 'exigencies of the coalition'. It was this factor which also caused severe intra-DGB disagreements, thereby preventing potential large-scale, rank-and-file mobilizations around the issue. Some DGB unions assumed an uncompromising position and maintained their original commitment to full-parity *Mitbestimmung*. Others, however, argued that a watered-down *Mitbestimmung* law was still better than none and that the retention of the SPD–FDP coalition was of paramount importance for lack of any alternatives.[147]

The *Mitbestimmung* law finally passed in 1976 displeased the unions for a number of different reasons. Although there were to be formally an equal number of employer and employee representatives on every supervisory board, the employees' side was to include a representative of the *leitende Angestellte* (salaried middle management). The unions concluded that since this representative was almost certain to side with the employers, the new law gave unequal representation to capital.[148] Next the board chairman was to be nominated by employer representatives alone and, furthermore, invested with the power of a second vote in the case of deadlock on the board. Further, the labor director who, in the 1951 law, was to be nominated by the labor members of the board was, in the 1976 law, to be designated by the full board, giving yet another advantage to capital. In addition, outside union representatives, who formed a majority of the labor side according to the 1951 law, were to be statutorily a minority in the 1976 version. Moreover, unlike the provisions of the 1951 law where the union representatives were delegated by union headquarters from outside the company, the 1976 law stipulated their election by all workers within the firm. Finally, the complex electoral procedures in the 1976 law favored individual and small unaffiliated-group candidacies to the labor side, to the detriment of DGB unions.

Although far from providing parity, and therefore from challenging fundamentally the prerogatives of the employers in any way, the 1976 law none the less met with considerable and unified hostility on the part of the German business community. Numerous firms attempted to circumvent the law by such tactics as diversifying their operations into several subsidiaries with fewer than 2,000 employees, placing their headquarters outside of the Federal Republic, and altering their legal status from publicly held corporations to limited liability companies. Most notably, however, the employers (through twenty-nine employers' associations and nine individual firms) brought a lawsuit in 1977 challenging the constitutionality of the 1976 *Mitbestimmung* law.[149] (This, in turn, led to the unions' abandoning of Concerted Action, the existence of which has not been restored to this day.) The unions interpreted this lawsuit as an open attack.[150] They assumed, correctly, that the court action was much less an attempt to get the Federal Constitutional Court to strike down the 1976 law than a device to set legal limits on any union attempts to promote more far-reaching *Mitbestimmung* in the future.

When the court eventually ruled, in 1979, it rejected the employers' suit.[151] Because the 1976 law fell short of full parity, the court decided that the law did not threaten the legal prerogatives of employers. The unions reacted to the court's decision with considerable satisfaction. Yet the decision was not without ambiguities, as the fact that *all* protagonists in the dispute reacted with satisfaction indicated.[152] Union joy was based on the general conclusion that the court's ruling did not preclude more extensive *Mitbestimmung* in the future, while also concluding that the Basic Law – the Federal Republic's constitution – was neutral on questions of property rights. The political parties who had voted for the 1976 law (all *three* major parties had done so) felt vindicated as well, since the court adjudged the law to be constitutional. The employers, while disappointed by what they considered to be a setback, were also able to find comfort in the decision, however. The court had been silent concerning the constitutionality of any further expansion of *Mitbestimmung*. In contrast to the unions, who understood this silence as an invitation to push for full parity in the future, the employers interpreted it as an indication that the court felt that *only* the 1976 law was constitutional and that, therefore, further developments toward full parity would be ruled out.[153]

Controversy about the meaning of litigation around the 1976 *Mitbestimmung* law could not obscure the realities of the situation from German unions, however. The unions had been unable to prod the SPD–FDP government toward the expansionary Keynesian macroeconomic policies which they felt were needed to better the difficult position of German workers in crisis. Simultaneously, the unions had also hoped that a reinforcement of their labor market power, through the institutionalization of full-parity *Mitbestimmung*, might give them added leverage, through labor market action, to achieve domestic demand stimulation. The 1976 law, although not a negligible reform, fell far short of achieving this goal. Moreover, widespread polemicizing about the law had increased anti-union fervor among German employers. Without favorable state action, and without full-parity *Mitbestimmung*, the unions were reduced to marshaling other resources which they possessed in the labor market to achieve their objectives. As it turned out, this increased 'reliance on their own strength' proved to be a difficult task as well.

At a moment when reliance on the political arena was proving increasingly difficult important threats to the unions' position in the market arena emerged through the legal system. Three decisions taken by the Federal Labor Court in 1977–9 came to be regarded by the unions as part of an 'Industrial Relations Act on the installment plan'.[154] The common denominator in all three decisions was in the explicit individualization of the worker on the shopfloor at the direct expense of the organizational presence of the unions. Taken separately each of these decisions was hard for the unions to accept. Taken together they made it hard for the unions to avoid the conclusion that they had become the object of a concerted attack by employers, through the courts, to limit the unions' shopfloor capacities to resist the degradation of workers' conditions in crisis. Worse still, these discrete decisions came in a context in which the employers had developed a pronounced new fondness for the lockout.

Just as the strike was not mentioned in the Basic Law, neither were lockouts. Lockouts, the unions argued, were a complete legal contrivance resulting from a series of Federal Labor Court decisions, which assumed quasi-constitutional status with the passage of time. Despite the union protests, however, the legalization of lockouts provided the basis for their widespread use by German industry during the late 1970s. The unions' primary response to this offensive was through labor market action. In order to undercut the legal justification of locking out, however, the unions had to turn to the state. Here, again, they met with frustration, despite the SPD's prominent position in government. Anti-lockout legislation, the most desirable way of eliminating the lockout from the union point of view, was rendered impossible by the FDP's position as a coalition partner of the SPD. The FDP, decidedly anti-union and even more strongly in favor of protecting property rights, would not allow any such legislation to pass. Even had the FDP been more flexible, important union leaders feared that the use of the parliamentary route to stop lockouts would inevitably result in an industrial relations act (*Verbändegesetz*) which would curtail the right to strike as well.[155] Thus, the unions were forced to litigate in the courts against the lockout.

As a result of the extensive lockouts which took place in printing, metals and the steel industry during 1978, the DGB and the two respective unions – IG Metall and IG Druck und Papier – initiated mass lawsuits. At least as important as the court actions themselves was the fact that these unions asked every single locked-out worker to sue his/her respective employer for lost wages incurred as a consequence of the lockout. The Federal Labor Court reached its verdict regarding these suits on 11 June 1980. The decision was greeted by the unions 'halfheartedly and with ambivalence'.

While not outlawing lockouts, which was the union's hope, the court did introduce certain measures which were welcomed by the unions. Thus, for example, lockouts were not judged to be capital's legal equivalent to labor's strike. The strike was recognized by the court as an integral part of the unions' *raison d'être* and, therefore, profoundly different from lockouts due to capital's controlling position over the means of production which makes it inherently stronger in industrial conflicts. Moreover, the court held that lockouts could not be aimed solely at union members. In addition, the court agreed with the union position that one of the major aims of lockouts consisted in the substantial financial weakening of union funds. The court, thus, ruled that industry could not henceforth initiate a lockout, thereby relegating it from its previously attacking posture to one of pure defense. Lastly, and perhaps most importantly, the court ruled that lockouts had to occur in a proportional scope to the ongoing strike. In concretizing this last point the court found the printing industry guilty for having abused the lockout in a disproportionate manner by locking out many more people than were on strike. Despite these favorable details, the unions were unsuccessful in completely abolishing lockouts as a matter of law.[156]

The unions originally faced the crisis in 1974–5 with a strategic perspective which faced in two directions simultaneously. Because of the SPD's presence in government, union hopes were great that the state would prove receptive to the implementation of union economic objectives. The unions hoped for success in the labor market as well. Their labor market aspirations were, of course, also connected with their political goals. Through the institutionalization of full-parity *Mitbestimmung* union power in the labor market would be greatly strengthened. In essence union experience in the first few years of crisis demonstrated that the political dimension of union strategy was unworkable. The SPD–FDP government refused to buy the unions' vigorous Keynesian approach to macro-economic policy and insisted instead on a much more cautious and relatively restrictive approach to economic management. Likewise, the same government refused to legislate full-parity *Mitbestimmung*. The unions were, thus, left to their own resorts in the labor market to achieve whatever part of their strategic package was achievable. In general, then, German unions were forced, much against their desires, to alter the relative weight which they placed on political vs labor market actions as the economic problems which they faced worsened. Moreover, as they shifted strategic arenas, they also found themselves confronted with German employers who were prepared to go to great lengths, both through the manipulation of German labor law and through strong resistance to union mobilization, to limit union success in the labor market itself.

The Market Arena

The combination of adverse economic circumstances and growing employer hostility made union action in the market arena difficult for the unions. For a number of reasons as well – the demands of coalition and the economic policy goals of the SPD–FDP government – the unions could no longer count on state aid in the form of protective measures which had been forthcoming prior to the onset of this period. In fact, the weakened position of unions in the labor market began progressively to strip labor of gains in the wage share which it had attained earlier in the 1970s.[157] As a result, the unions faced an evolution in their bargaining strategy given the resumption of wage restraint during 1980–1 in the face of Bundesbank non-accommodation and persistent unemployment. In essence, the unions in their strategies in the market arena carried through on their analysis and prescriptions which they had developed since 1977, namely, their bargaining strategies reflected the switch in union emphasis from wages to jobs. Furthermore, with the emphasis on job issues in collective bargaining, it was the 'qualitative' issues of defense against technological change and rationalization as well as the demand for worktime reduction which found their way into union collective bargaining strategies. Yet the unions' emphasis on 'relying on their own strength' in the labor market achieved for them only limited gains, frustrated expectations from the experience, stiffer resistance from the employers (punctuated with strikes) and, in general, new challenges to face.

Aside from the brief wage push during the negotiations in steel and in metalworking (in addition to the strident debates on the qualitative issues which resulted in strikes in these sectors) in 1978, union wage policy since 1977 was one of general restraint. The wage flurry was partly the result of the more expansive fiscal and monetary policies which resulted from the Federal Republic's short-lived 'locomotive' period, and partly due to the loss of real wages which the unions had experienced in 1975–7. However, with the second oil crisis, the return to more restrictive economic policies, the aggressive stance of the employers and the technological nature of the growth in unemployment, the unions resumed a more restrained wage bargaining policy into the 1980s.

In the important metalworking sector IG Metall had obtained an average annual wage increase of 9·0 percent during the 1970–4 period, but during the years 1975–9 the wage settlements only averaged 5·7 percent. Still more telling was that this figure declined from 6·8 percent in 1975 to 5·4 percent in 1976, increased slightly to 5·9 percent in 1977, but resumed declining to 5·0 percent in 1978 and 4·3 percent in 1979. The significance of these figures showed that the union was able to keep pace with both productivity and cost of living gains during the first half of the decade, yet by the end of the decade it was no longer able to do so.[158] And in the early 1980s it began to receive pressure even to keep its wage demands under the level of a resurgent inflation.[159] Given IG Metall's traditional role during the 1970s of *Lohnführerschaft* (wage leadership), it was not surprising that all German unions moderated their wage demands during the last half of the decade. Thus, with the inability of the unions to obtain the wage settlements which they had in the first half of the 1970s, and the rapid increase in unemployment since 1974, it was also not surprising to find the issue of jobs gaining in importance in relation to the previously sacrosanct issue of wages.

With the unions' primary concerns shifting from wages to jobs, this issue began to surface in the unions' bargaining strategies, beginning in 1978. Thus, it was qualitative issues such as structural and technological unemployment, a reduced working week and attempts to shape aspects of the increasing technological change which the unions began to emphasize. Both because of rank-and-file prodding and because of the unions' own realizations that simple wages-and-hours unionism provided an inadequate response to rationalization, new issues about the shape and quality of the work process came to the fore. Rationalization involved two things: rising unemployment, and the redesign of work. 'Qualitative' issues, as they arose in the 1978 strikes, demonstrated new trade union desires to limit, and if possible control, capital's power to promote both aspects. At the same time, however, the strikes demonstrated how difficult it was for unions, on the defensive, to pursue their labor market goals, quantitative or qualitative.

The first cluster of issues involved the introduction of new technologies (in this case in the printing industry) which were producing loss of jobs, increased job stress and the replacement of skilled workers with unskilled ones. This strike took place in the printing industry. Unlike some unions in the printing industry (for example, in Great Britain), which might oppose the introduction of any and all technology because it might change the job function of a few employees, IG Druck und Papier did not act in a Luddite way.[160] Its chief concern was to participate in the structuring of technological modernization in order to benefit those workers (notably the compositors) who were the most threatened group in the modernization process. Contrary to its pre-1974 emphasis on wage bargaining, union negotiations here were concerned with qualitative stipulations regarding the interaction of the threatened workers with the new technology. The strike proved successful because what the printers achieved was to intervene in the process of job restructuring to oblige industry to redesign work not only to protect employment, but also to ensure that the new jobs emerging from the application of this new electronic technology in printing would be dignified and humane.

A second cluster of 'qualitative' issues which produced a strike was those of deskilling and dequalification of workers, two prime causes of both structural and technological unemployment, which came to the fore in the Nord Württemberg–North Baden metal industry also in 1978. The introduction of new technologies in metal processing, especially after 1973, had rapidly dequalified large groups of workers into lower wage and job categories, and increased layoffs.[161] Hardest hit was electronics which employed a large female laborforce, a particularly vulnerable and disadvantaged group. IG Metall planned well for the strike. The region which was struck was both a critical industrial area and the place in which the union's own most strike-experienced troops and organizations existed. Thus, although the results of the conflict fell short of the unions' original demands, the gains which were codified in the new contract were significant. Important concessions were won toward the union's goal of compressing wage and salary differentials between job categories. And the union did succeed in placing important limitations on the employers' freedom of action in job reclassification and dequalification – possible dequalification was restricted to a limited number of job categories and important safeguards against employer moves were established. In addition, IG Metall gained access to new areas of information previously in the employers' domain concerning job reclassification. Regularized consultation between management and works councils about all new developments affecting the production process was institutionalized, which proved especially significant for the union due to the difficulty in passing full-parity *Mitbestimmung*. Finally, in cases where dequalification eventually did occur, the workers concerned were to maintain their pre-reclassification rate of pay for eighteen months.[162]

The third cluster of 'qualitative' issues centered around working time reduction and took place in the steel industry in 1978–9.[163] IG Metall argued that its major aim in the strike was to negotiate a reduction in the working week in iron and steel. The unions believed that steel was in a far more serious crisis than any other major industry, having experienced a loss of over 120,000 jobs since 1960 with further job loss clearly on the horizon – and that work in iron and steel was unhealthy and dangerous. These two facts formed the backbone of the union's case for the 35-hour week. The employment issue was central in IG Metall's initial proposition of the 35-hour week demand. IG Metall felt that its policy represented a conscious choice in favor of employment for all instead of only higher wages for some. Yet, in the first few days of the strike, IG Metall rapidly backpedaled on the 35-hour week demand. From initial rhetoric about the benefits of 35 hours for employment in steel and its likely impact on employer prerogatives in the rationalization process, the union began to retreat toward more modest claims that 35 hours would mainly contribute to workplace safety and 'humanization'. Then, at mid-point in the strike, the 35-hour demand was refined to mean *Einstieg in* (the approach toward) 35 hours, rather than 35 hours immediately. Despite open rank-and-file criticism of this retreat, IG Metall's leadership continued toward compromise. Confronted with a more unified stance of the employers on this issue and their own indecision on what was to be the major issue in the strike, the union's initial bold proposal foundered and it settled for a modest wage gain and increased vacation time.

The failure of IG Metall to effect the outcome which it originally claimed it wanted pointed up another phenomenon which the union observed in the latter part of the 1970s, namely, the employers' resort to increasingly harsher methods in dealing with unions in the industrial arena.[164] The unions felt that industry's need to effect technological change (and the resulting technological unemployment) was responsible for this development but they also felt that the unions were being asked to bear the brunt of this restructuring effort. As such industry measures emerged more clearly, union publications and high-ranking officials repeatedly began to refer to industry's more combative position and tone, as a 'class war from above'.[165] To the unions the employers' actions looked to be part of a well-coordinated ideological offensive at all levels, aimed at 'total confrontation' between the unions and the employers in the labor market. This multipronged offensive assumed many forms. The unions, however, saw all such forms as part of the general deterioration of German industrial relations which seemed to be in evidence in the late 1970s and early 1980s. Among the more obvious manifestations of this 'offensive' in the eyes of the unions were the employers' claiming that the unions wanted to institute a *Gewerkschaftsstaat* (trade union state), their attacks on the institution of *Mitbestimmung*, the previously mentioned lockouts which took place during the 1978 strikes and the discovery of the existence of a *Tabu Katalog*, which pledged each member of the BDA not to exceed certain guidelines in its negotiations with labor. Among the most serious prohibitions were that no firm could reduce weekly working time below 40 hours, and that no firm could offer a vacation package of more than six weeks' duration.[166]

Thus, while the unions initially looked with great favor on the labor market as the dominant arena in which to pursue their strategies, their experiences during the late 1970s and early 1980s were clearly a mixed blessing. Some gains were achieved, especially in those areas where they had implemented some of their conceptual reevaluations, namely, in some qualitative issues and their attempts to come to grips with the effects of both structural and technological unemployment. However, these gains were offset by the inability to effect a substantial number of qualitative changes. In addition, they faced increasingly sharp conflicts with employers in this important arena and unemployment was projected to increase substantially during the 1980s. Clearly, putting all of their eggs in the basket of market activity would not be sufficient to alleviate the formidable problems which the unions faced at the beginning of the 1980s.

Toward Strategic Reevaluation?

By the early 1980s it had become increasingly clear to the unions that their approach to the recession/crisis had not proved sufficient. They had encountered substantial obstacles to the implementation of their prescriptions for remedies of the economic situation in both the political and market arenas. Consequently, they had reached a point by the early 1980s in which their present difficulties had intensified the imperative for a reevaluation of the strategies which had carried them through the late 1970s and into the 1980s. However, the unions had not yet, at that time, departed significantly from the analyses, prescriptions and strategies which were the foundations of their actions throughout this period. The unions were, thus, faced with a crucial dilemma. Were their failures to achieve their desired successes in either the political or market arena due to an inability to properly carry out a worthwhile, strategic complex of prescriptions? Or, more fundamentally, were their failures due to the inappropriateness of the overall utility of their model of analysis? These remained very much unanswered questions in the early 1980s, but the significant factor in terms of the German unions was that the second question was receiving so much attention given the hitherto almost undisputed belief that the unions' traditional analyses and prescriptions were sound.

In the late 1970s and the early 1980s this second question began to be addressed more extensively in circles both within and without the unions. It primarily took the form of a critical reexamination of the analyses and prescriptions which the unions had developed since the mid-1970s. The first serious criticism of the DGB's policies came with the publication of the 1979 Memorandum, an annual economic report edited by left-leaning academics. The memoranda had been published since 1976 but, until 1979, they had been largely ignored. The 1979 Memorandum was received differently and became the source of much controversy and debate between the DGB and the Memorandum's authors and within the DGB itself.[167] The 1979 Memorandum acknowledged that the West German economy was in crisis and advanced a series of policy suggestions, going far beyond those officially held by the DGB, for unions and other progressive forces to pursue a favorable resolution of the crisis situation. It called for a consistent increase in consumption via an active and aggressive wage policy, a strongly progressive and strictly implemented tax policy geared to redistribute the 'excessive profits of the monopolies', and the increase of state expenditures. It also called for a gradual shortening of the working week to 35 hours along with other worktime reduction measures and demand-stimulus policies. Lastly, the Memorandum envisioned institutions such as *Mitbestimmung*, regional-planning agencies and investment-guidance devices (some still non-existent) as guaranteeing full participation on the part of the unions in the realization of these policies.

While none of these prescriptions were that far removed from the unions' own official pronouncements, all of the prescriptions seemed to be slightly more comprehensive than the unions'. Also they were no longer enough to the left of the unions that union officials felt they could safely ignore them as they had in previous years. And given the difficulties which the unions were facing, union leaders felt that the Memorandum was a serious enough document that it had to be addressed. What had changed the unions' attitude toward the Memorandum? First of all, the wide and vigorous debates around the 1979 Memorandum had opened up new discussion among the principals about Germany's economic situation. In the process the unions began to demonstrate openness to new economic ideas. Secondly, the unions were becoming ever-more aware that a shift to the right was occurring in the politics of the Federal Republic in ways which have been already outlined.[168] Thus, the publication of Memorandum 80 began to be seen as a document around which a new union response to increasingly threatening conditions might be developed. While no new departures had been forthcoming, there was growing skepticism that full-blown Keynesianism supplemented with extensive manpower policies any longer provided the appropriate solutions.

But with unemployment continuing to grow and with the unions beginning to criticize German industry more stridently for its contributions to structural and cyclical unemployment via capital export, automation, rationalization and the introduction of microprocessors in almost all sectors, what did the unions propose? 'Keynes-plus' was the answer toward which the DGB and its constituents began to move.[169] Their Keynesianism was not to be abandoned, but supplemented with new approaches. Thus, the DGB continued to insist that the government and the Bundesbank should shift to vigorous demand-management policies to stimulate the domestic economy. Falling well within the framework of the unions' traditional lexicon were such demands as stimulating consumption, reduced interest rates, substantial public-works jobs, increased deficit spending, and vast new manpower training and relocation programs to fight structural unemployment. However, it was the 'plus' in the unions' 'Keynes-plus' posture which the unions felt would become their major response to the threat of rationalization which had become their central focus since the mid-1970s. Although the unions regarded German industry's high-technology, capital-intensive trajectory as inevitable, they began to see the need to promote active union inputs over the shape of industrial restructuring and technological innovation rather than allowing such rationalization to occur and then trying to mitigate its effects *post hoc*. Two new approaches were developed. The first, macroeconomic in nature, sought to limit the effects of unemployment by spreading the available work among a greater number of workers. To achieve this the unions proposed a number of measures for shortening worktime, in particular, via a reduction of the working week to 35 hours as IG Metall demanded in the steel strike in 1978–9. The second involved what the unions came to call the 'humanization of work'.

The 'humanization of work' approach sketched out by the DGB and its constituents was multifaceted and attempted to maximize a number of not necessarily compatible objectives. In the first place, the unions desired to set limits on the number of jobs that could be eliminated by managerial rationalization. As outlined in the 1981 DGB *Grundsatzprogramm*, through collective bargaining, the unions were to involve themselves in the process of introducing new machines and techniques such that (1) workers remaining on the job dealing with these new technologies did not undergo dequalification in work and/or wage losses, and (2) that those jobs that did remain would be designed with the human needs of workers in mind, as defined by the unions.[170]

The plus in 'Keynes-plus' had another side to it. If the Keynes part of the formula remained largely dependent upon the goodwill of the state and the SPD government, the work reduction/work humanization side of the new DGB strategy relied much more on the organizational resources of the unions themselves. In essence, recent theoretical and strategic changes in the DGB continued trends made necessary from the mid-1970s onwards by the growing unresponsiveness of the SPD–FDP government to union demands. The 1981 *Grundsatzprogramm* and other union documents in the early 1980s, then, concentrated to an unprecedented extent on the mechanics and tactics of day-to-day union action in the industrial arena. Stress was placed on developing new techniques of response to lockouts, to facilitating cooperation between unions and works councils in implementing contracts, and upon improving the 'maneuverability' of unions in the labor market by shortening mediation periods and developing new hit-and-run strike tactics.

Thus, the unions' development of 'Keynes-plus' marked a potentially important watershed for them. While they had come to question seriously some of the major theoretical underpinnings of their *Weltanschauung*, they were not yet prepared to abandon the strategy and tactics which they had employed essentially since the early 1950s. For example, the development of worktime reduction and 'humanization of work' could be seen, on one hand, as important departures in union strategies. Yet, on the other, worktime reduction had the traditional Keynesian economic effect of demand stimulation, and 'humanization of work' could be viewed as an extension of worker participation. These programs, thus, were less significant departures from past union prescriptions than progressive refinements of the unions' earlier positions. Consequently, by the early 1980s the unions found themselves with a foot in each camp on the question of strategic reevaluation, increasingly dissatisfied with past approaches but not yet able to conceptualize the lines of a major new departure.

Part 5

Conclusions

German unions were not, therefore, completely unmoved by the economic downturns which began in the mid-1970s. They faced the early years of this period as convinced Keynesians and fought against the 1974–5 recession by proposing full-blown Keynesian policies. This fight failed, by and large, even if it did not destroy the faith of the German unions that, were their program carried out, their difficulties might be overcome. However, despite continuing faith in Keynesian remedies, German unions had, by the early 1980s, also begun reflecting in new ways on their economic setting, prompted by ever-deepening problems of structural and technological unemployment. Keynes-plus was their answer, involving continuing advocacy of Keynesian approaches in the sphere of public policy, plus new departures in the labor market to alleviate unemployment by reducing the length of the working week and by controlling the shape and extent of technological change. It was not hard to see, in these new departures, older DGB propensities, however. German labor's fundamental design, from the postwar period onwards, involved industrial democracy to be worked through capital–labor codetermination in the economy itself. What looked to be innovations in German union thought and prescriptions in the early 1980s could easily be interpreted as an extension of the *Mitbestimmung* objective to the crucial issue of unemployment under crisis conditions. As the decade turned, then, Keynes-plus and refocussed *Mitbestimmung* seemed to be the unions' prescriptions for changed economic circumstances. It was an uneasy answer, however. The Keynesian side of the package depended for its implementation on political cooperation from a supposedly pro-union government which demonstrably refused to cooperate very much. Because of this, German unions moved toward more 'reliance on their own strength' in the labor market. Yet as their position worsened, as it seemed to do in the early 1980s, and as the labor market situation faced by the unions became ever more difficult, 'relying on their own strength' became an ever-more perilous venture. German unions were, therefore, ripe for a much more profound change in outlook and approach by the early 1980s than they had been willing to contemplate in the 1970s.

Statistical Tables

Table 2·1   *Economic Overview*

	GNP (nominal)	GNP (real)	Industrial production (nominal)	Unemployment (%)	Cost of living (%age change)	Current account (million DM)
1951	+22·3	+10·4	+17·4	7·5	+7·7	+2,301
1952	+14·2	+8·9	+6·7	7·1	+2·1	+2,478
1953	+7·8	+8·2	+8·6	6·4	−1·8	+3,873
1954	+7·4	+7·4	+11·6	6·0	+0·2	+3,669
1955	+14·4	+12	+15·8	5·1	+1·6	+2,235
1956	+10·5	+7·3	+8·5	4·0	+2·5	+4,459
1957	+9	+5·7	+5·4	3·7	+2·0	+5,901
1958	+7·2	+3·7	+2·9	3·7	+2·2	+5,998
1959	+8·8	+7·3	+7·4	2·6	+1·0	+4,152
1960	+11·7	+9	+11·4	1·3	+1·4	+4,783
1961	+9·4	+4·9	+6·4	0·8	+2·3	+3,193
1962	+8·8	+4·4	+4·3	0·7	+3·0	−1,580
1963	+6	+3	+3·5	0·8	+2·9	+991
1964	+9·8	+6·6	+7·9	0·8	+2·3	+524
1965	+9·2	+5·5	+5·1	0·7	+3·3	−6,223
1966	+6·4	+2·5	+1·3	0·7	+3·5	+488
1967	+1·3	−0·1	−2·8	2·1	+1·7	+10,006
1968	+8·4	+6·5	+9·3	1·5	+1·7	+11,856
1969	+11·7	+7·9	+12·8	0·9	+1·9	+7,498
1970	+13·6	+5·9	+6	0·7	+3·3	+3,183
1971	+11·3	+3·3	+1·5	0·9	+5·2	+2,770
1972	+9·4	+3·6	+4·6	1·1	+5·6	+2,731
1973	+11·2	+4·9	+6·2	1·3	+7·0	+12,354
1974	+7·3	+0·4	−2	2·6	+7·0	+26,581
1975	+4·9	−1·8	−6·2	4·7	+6·0	+9,932
1976	+8·7	+5·3	+6·9	4·6	+4·3	+9,915
1977	+6·7	+2·8	+2·7	4·5	+3·7	+9,498
1978	+7·8	+3·7	+2·6	4·3	+2·7	+18,419
1979	+8·5	+4·5	+5·4	3·8	+4·1	−9,644
1980	+6·9	+1·8	−0·2	3·8	+5·5	−29,052

Source: Dresdner Bank, Statistical Survey (supplement to *Economic Quarterly*), July 1981.

Table 2·2   *Capital Formation, Consumption and Exports*

	Fixed capital formation (%age change)	*Government consumption (%age change)*	*Private consumption (%age change)*	*Exports (%age change)*
1951	+5·3	+9·7	+7·9	+35·7
1952	+8·7	+9·7	+9·2	+12·8
1953	+17·0	+0·3	+11·0	+16·1
1954	+12·6	+2·6	+6·1	+24·0
1955	+20·8	+4·6	+10·4	+16·7
1956	+8·6	+0·6	+8·8	+15·2
1957	−0·1	+4·8	+6·2	+16·0
1958	+4·2	+8·3	+5·1	+4·8
1959	+11·8	+9·0	+5·7	+12·6
1960	+10·2	+6·0	+8·0	+13·0
1961	+7·1	+6·5	+6·0	+3·6
1962	+4·6	+10·4	+5·4	+3·2
1963	+1·2	+6·7	+2·9	+7·6
1964	+11·3	+1·1	+5·0	+8·1
1965	+4·8	+5·1	+6·9	+6·5
1966	+1·2	+2·4	+2·9	+10·3
1967	−6·8	+3·6	+1·0	+7·3
1968	+4·0	+0·1	+4·5	+13·3
1969	+10·5	+5·1	+7·9	+10·9
1970	+10·8	+4·6	+7·3	+7·2
1971	+6·4	+6·3	+5·2	+6·1
1972	+3·5	+4·6	+4·0	+6·4
1973	+0·2	+5·5	+2·5	+11·5
1974	−9·9	+4·3	+0·3	+11·8
1975	−4·2	+4·5	+2·5	−6·0
1976	+5·0	+2·4	+3·6	+11·2
1977	+4·1	+1·0	+2·9	+3·9
1978	+6·3	+3·9	+3·4	+4·4
1979	+8·5	+2·8	+2·8	+5·0

Source: Elmar Altvater, Jürgen Hoffmann and Willi Semmler, *Vom Wirtschaftswunder zur Wirtschaftskrise*, Berlin, Olle & Wolter, 1980, p. 210.

Table 2·3   *Wages and Productivity per Person*

| | Gross wages per employed person | | Productivity (real) |
| | (nominal) | (real) | (GDP per employed person) |
	(%age change)		(%age change)
1951	+16·3	+8·0	+7·7
1952	+7·9	+5·7	+6·9
1953	+5·9	+7·8	+5·7
1954	+5·2	+5·0	+4·9
1955	+7·9	+6·2	+8·0
1956	+8·0	+5·4	+4·4
1957	+5·2	+3·1	+3·4
1958	+6·7	+4·4	+3·2
1959	+5·5	+4·5	+6·4
1960	+9·4	+7·9	+7·1
1961	+10·2	+7·7	+4·2
1962	+9·0	+5·8	+3·3
1963	+6·1	+3·0	+3·0
1964	+8·9	+6·5	+6·3
1965	+9·0	+5·4	+4·9
1966	+7·2	+3·6	+3·1
1967	+3·2	+1·8	+2·9
1968	+6·1	+4·5	+6·9
1969	+9·2	+6·2	+6·2
1970	+14·7	+10·6	+4·4
1971	+11·9	+6·2	+2·7
1972	+9·4	+3·4	+3·8
1973	+11·9	+5·0	+5·0
1974	+11·0	+3·7	+2·8
1975	+7·1	+1·0	+1·9
1976	+7·7	+3·1	+7·0
1977	+7·0	+3·5	+3·2
1978	+5·3	+3·2	+2·7
1979	+5·9	+1·8	+3·2

Source: Bergmann, *et al.*, *Gewerkschaften*, 1976, pp. 450, 455; and SVR, *Herausforderung von Aussen*, Stuttgart, Kohlhammer, 1979, p. 80.

Table 2·4 Statistical Comparison

Year	1969	1970	1971	1972	1973	1974	1975	1976	1977	1978	1979
Growth of Real Gross Domestic Product at Market Prices (%age change from previous year)											
France	7·0	5·7	5·4	5·9	5·4	3·2	0·2	4·9	2·8	3·3	3·4
Germany	7·8	6·0	3·2	3·7	5·9	0·5	-2·1	5·6	2·8	3·2	4·4
UK	1·5	2·3	2·8	2·4	8·0	-1·5	-1·0	3·7	1·3	3·4	0·8
Italy	5·7	5·0	1·6	3·1	6·9	4·2	-3·5	5·7	1·7	2·4	3·8
Sweden	4·8	5·3	-0·2	1·6	3·4	4·2	0·8	1·3	-2·7		
Consumer Prices (%age change from previous year)											
France	6·4	4·8	5·5	6·2	7·3	13·7	11·8	9·6	9·4	9·3	10·7
Germany	1·9	3·4	5·3	5·5	6·9	7·0	6·0	4·5	3·9	2·7	4·1
UK	5·4	6·4	9·4	7·1	9·2	16·0	24·2	16·5	15·9	8·3	13·4
Italy	2·6	5·0	4·8	5·7	10·8	19·1	17·0	16·8	17·0		
Sweden	2·7	7·0	7·4	6·0	6·7	9·9	9·8	10·3	11·4	10·1	7·2
Current Balances (millions of dollars)											
France	-1,475	68	525	284	-675	-5,980	-66	-6,097	-3,328	+3,735	+1,456
Germany	1,913	870	830	795	4,604	9,852	3,463	3,433	4,234	+8,762	-5,247
UK	1,112	1,754	2,653	338	-2,592	-8,575	-4,106	-1,511	511	1,400	-5,000
Italy	2,340	1,133	1,902	2,043	-2,662	-8,017	-751	-2,816	2,465		
Sweden	-196	-264	210	264	1,221	-950	-1,614	-2,089	-2,782	-2,500	
Unemployment (as %age of total laborforce)											
France	1·6	1·7	2·1	2·3	2·0	2·3	4·0	4·4	4·9	5·2	5·9
Germany	0·7	0·6	0·7	0·9	1·0	2·2	4·1	4·1	4·0	3·8	3·2
UK	2·0	2·2	2·9	3·2	2·3	2·1	3·4	5·1	5·5	5·5	5·3
Italy	3·4	3·1	3·1	3·6	3·4	2·9	3·3	6·6	7·1	7·2	
Sweden	1·9	1·5	2·5	2·7	2·5	2·0	1·6	1·6	1·8	2·2	2·1

Sources: OECD, *Labor Force Statistics*, 1969–72, May 1975, 1973–5, May 1976, 1976–8, November 1979; OECD, *Economic Outlook*, December 1979; and OECD, *Economic Surveys: Germany*, May 1980, *United Kingdom*, February 1980, *France*, May 1980, and *Sweden*, April 1980.

Table 2·5   *Membership of DGB Unions (31 December 1980)*

Union	Total	Manual workers (blue-collar workers)	Employees (white-collar workers)	Civil servants
1 Metalworkers' Union (IG Metall)	2,622,267	2,234,361	387,906	—
2 Public Service and Transport Workers' Union (ÖTV)	1,149,689	568,250	488,883	92,556
3 Chemical, Paper and Ceramic Workers' Union (IG Chemie)	660,973	540,774	120,199	—
4 Construction Workers' Union (IG Bau, Steine, Erden)	533,054	487,218	45,836	—
5 Postal Workers' Union (DPG)	450,201	136,232	37,777	276,192
6 Railroad Workers' Union (GdED)	406,588	205,795	9,867	190,926
7 Mineworkers' Union (IG Bergbau)	367,718	320,041	47,504	173
8 Commerce, Banking and Insurance Workers' Union (HBV)	351,328	50,851	300,477	—
9 Textile-Clothing Workers' Union (GTB)	293,766	266,531	27,235	—
10 Food-Processing Workers' Union (NGG)	253,001	204,669	48,332	—
11 Education and Science Union (GEW)	183,793	—	42,732	141,061
12 Police Union (GdP)	165,900	8,133	13,480	144,287
13 Wood and Plastic Workers' Union (Gewerkschaft Holz)	157,142	146,428	10,714	—
14 Printing and Paper Workers' Union (IG Druck)	143,970	118,824	25,546	—
15 Leather Workers' Union (Gewerkschaft Leder)	55,689	52,153	3,536	—
16 Artists and Musicians' Union (Gewerkschaft Kunst)	45,252	—	45,252	—
17 Horticulture, Agriculture and Forestry Workers' Union (GGLF)	42,196	36,594	2,845	2,757
DGB totals	7,882,527	5,376,454	1,658,121	847,952

Source: DGB, *Geschäftsbericht*, 1978–81, p. 468.

Notes

The authors would like to express their gratitude to Thomas C. Ertman for his invaluable help in the closing stages of this project.

1 Dieter Schuster, *Die deutsche Gewerkschaftsbewegung* (Düsseldorf: DGB Verlag, 1974), p. 77; and Helga Grebing, *Geschichte der deutschen Arbeiterbewegung* (Munich: Deutscher Taschenbuchverlag, 1966), pp. 279–80.

2 Eberhard Schmidt, *Die verhinderte Neuordnung* (Frankfurt: Europäische Verlagsanstalt, 1970), pp. 74–87; and Theo Pirker, *Die blinde Macht*, 2 vols (Berlin: Olle & Wolter, 1979), Vol. I, pp. 160–3.

3 Gerhard Leminsky and Bernd Otto, *Politik und Programmatik des deutschen Gewerkschaftsbundes* (Cologne: Bund-Verlag, 1974), p. 32; Dieter Schuster, *Die deutsche Gewerkschaftsbewegung* (Düsseldorf: DGB Verlag, 1974), p. 76; and Hans Limmer, *Die deutsche Gewerkschaftsbewegung* (Munich: Günter Olzog Verlag, 1970), pp. 84 ff. See also the collection: Heinrich August Winkler (ed.), *Politische Weichenstellung in Nachkriegsdeutschland*, Sonderheft No. 5 of the periodical *Geschichte und Gesellschaft* (Göttingen: Vandenhoeck & Ruprecht, 1979); and Eberhard Schmidt, *Ordnungsfaktor oder Gegenmacht? Die politische Rolle der Gewerkschaften* (Frankfurt: Suhrkamp, 1975), pp. 12–13.

4 On the organization of the DGB, see Schuster, *Die deutsche Gewerkschaftsbewegung*, op. cit., pp. 79–84; Leminsky and Otto, *Politik*, op. cit., pp. 461–75. On membership figures, see Leminsky and Otto, *Politik*, op. cit., pp. 455–60.

5 It was above all the far right which tried to form a rival trade union confederation. To this end it established the Christliche Gewerkschaftsbewegung Deutschlands (Christian Union Movement of Germany – CGB). This union has, however, remained completely insignificant in German industrial relations; see Grebing, *Geschichte*, op. cit., pp. 262–3.

6 Leminsky and Otto, *Politik*, op. cit., p. 248.

7 Der deutsche Gewerkschaftsbund, *Protokoll des Gründungskongresses des deutschen Gewerkschaftsbundes* (Cologne: Bund-verlag, 1950). This translation, like all others in this chapter, is provided by the authors.

8 Fritz Naphtali, *Wirtschaftsdemokratie, Ihr Wesen, Weg, und Ziel* (Frankfurt: Europäische Verlagsanstalt, 1966).

9 DGB, *Geschäftsbericht 1950–51*, pp. 182–96; and Leminsky and Otto, *Politik*, op. cit., pp. 33–4.

10 IG Metall, *Geschäftsbericht des Vorstandes der IG Metall 1952–53* (n.d.), pp. 403–4; Eberhard Schmidt, *Die verhinderte Neuordnung*, op. cit., pp. 74–87; see also Eugen Loderer, 'Die Montanmitbestimmung–Faustpfand der Wirtschaftsdemokratie', copy of a speech presented at the IG Metall Iron and Steel Conference, Dortmund, 3 July 1980, pp. 7–8; and Schuster, *Die deutsche Gewerkschaftsbewegung*, op. cit., p. 78.

11 DGB, *Protokoll des ausserordentlichen Bundeskongresses des deutschen Gewerkschaftsbundes* (Cologne: Bund-Verlag, 1951), p. 100. For a good account of the fight for *Montanmitbestimmung* 1945–51, see 'Der Kampf um die Mitbestimmung', in IG Metall, *Protokoll des 7. ordentlichen Gewerkschaftstages der IG Metall* (n.d., 1962), pp. 241–2; see also Eugen Loderer's speech, 'Montanmitbestimmung–Faustpfand der Wirtschaftsdemokraties'; Herbert Wehner has called the Montanmitbestimmung 'one of the pillars of our social system in the Federal Republic': interview in the *Frankfurter Rundschau*, 18 July 1980.

12 IG Metall, *Geschäftsbericht 1952–53*, p. 7; IG Metall, *Geschäftsbericht 1954–55*, p. 9; and Schmidt, *Die verhinderte Neuordnung*, op. cit., pp. 193–225.

13 See the text of the Betriebsverfassungsgesetz of 1952: *Betriebsverfassungsgesetz und Wahlordnung* (Munich: Beck, 1978).

14 DGB, *Protokoll des Gründungskongresses*, op. cit., p. 186.

15 Hans Böckler at the founding congress of the DGB: 'The unions salute . . . the help which the American people has granted through the Marshall Plan', ibid., p. 325.

16 DGB, *Geschäftsbericht 1950–51*, pp. 229–30, 244–5; DGB, *Geschäftsbericht 1952–53*,

pp. 363–5; IG Metall, *Geschäftsbericht 1950–52*, pp. 35–6, 39; IG Metall, *Geschäftsbericht 1952–53*, pp. 22–3; and IG Metall, *Geschäftsbericht 1954–55*, pp. 31, 36, 38–9.

17   IG Metall, *Geschäftsbericht 1954–55*, pp. 36, 38–9.

18   Doris Nolle, 'IG Bau-Steine-Erden 1949–1957-Die Entwicklung zu einer kooperativen Gewerkschaft', in Claudio Pozzoli (ed.), *Jahrbuch Arbeiterbewegung 6- Grenzen gewerkschaftlicher Politik* (Frankfurt: Fischer Taschenbuch Verlag, 1979); and Karl Anders, *Stein für Stein* (Hannover: Verlag für Literatur und Zeitgeschichte, 1969), pp. 257–8.

19   IG Metall, *Niederschrift der Verhandlungen des 2. ordentlichen Gewerkschaftstages der Industriegewerkschaft Metall für die Bundesrepublik Deutschland in Stuttgart*, vol. 15, no. 20 (September 1952), p. 73.

20   The expellees from former German territories east of the Oder–Neisse rivers who came to West Germany is put by Kindleberger at 9 million. In addition, 3 million refugees from the DDR entered West Germany before the construction of the Berlin Wall in 1961. See Charles Kindleberger, *Europe's Postwar Growth* (Cambridge, Mass.: Harvard University Press, 1967), pp. 30–1. For union sympathy toward refugees, see DGB, *Protokoll des Gründungskongresses*, op. cit., pp. 190, 195.

21   Kindleberger, *Europe's Postwar Growth*, op. cit., pp. 28–30. For example, wages accounted for only 54·7 percent of total income in Germany in 1953, as compared to 65·5 percent in England and 66·2 percent in the USA. Indeed, Germany's wage level was even lower than those of France, Belgium and Austria. On the low level of wages in Germany both absolutely and in comparison to other industrial countries, see IG Metall, *Geschäftsbericht 1952–53*, pp. 18–19, 30.

22   On *Verrechtlichung*, see Rainer Erd, *Verrechtlichung industrieller Konflikte* (Frankfurt: Campus, 1978); Ulrich Zachert, Maria Metzke and Wolfgang Hamer, *Die Aussperrung* (Cologne: Bund-Verlag, 1978); Rainer Kalbitz, *Aussperrungen in der Bundesrepublik* (Frankfurt: Europäische Verlagsanstalt, 1979); and Michael Kittner and Hans-Hermann Wohlgemuth, *Die Aussperrung*, Schriftenreihe der IG Metall, No. 90 (September 1981).

23   This portrait of the West German economy during 1948–66 is based on: Henry C. Wallich, *Mainsprings of the German Revival* (New Haven, Conn.: Yale University Press, 1955); Karl Hardach, *The Political Economy of Germany in the Twentieth Century* (Berkeley, Calif.: University of California Press, 1980); and Karl Neumann, *Konjunktur und Konjunkturpolitik* (Frankfurt: Europäische Verlagsanstalt, 1972); and on the annual economic surveys of the OEEC (later OECD), entitled, *Economic Conditions in the Federal Republic of Germany*; after 1961, *Economic Surveys of the OECD: Federal Republic of Germany*.

24   The currency reform (*Währungsreform*) of 1948 involved the conversion of the old reichsmarks into deutschmarks (DM) at a rate of exchange which hurt savers and favored property-owners.

25   Policy description and figures through 1951 are from Wallich, op. cit., esp. pp. 74–5, 80–1, 88–9.

26   All statistics from the years 1952–80 which appear in the text are derived, unless otherwise noted, from the statistical appendix, where their sources are given.

27   See the British government publication *Overseas Economic Surveys: The Federal Republic of Germany* (London: HMSO, 1955), p. 205.

28   OEEC, *Economic Conditions*, 1956, para. 6; 1958, para. 6, p. 9.

29   OEEC, *Economic Conditions*, 1956, para. 27.

30   OEEC, *Economic Conditions*, 1960, p. 12.

31   The Bundesbank superseded the Bank deutscher Länder in 1957.

32   Hardach, *The Political Economy*, op. cit., pp. 186, 192.

33   Our characterization of West German neo-liberalism and the Freiburg school is based on Geoffrey Denton, Murray Forsyth and Malcolm Maclennan, *Economic Planning and Policies in Britain, France and Germany* (London: Allen & Unwin, 1968), pp. 34–50; and Elmar Altvater, Jürgen Hoffman and Willi Semmler, *Vom Wirtschaftswunder zur Wirtschaftskrise* (Berlin: Olle & Wolter, 1980), pp. 277–82.

34   Our discussion of economic policy until 1966 is based on Denton, *et al.*, op. cit.; Altvater, *et al.*, op. cit.; and Andrew Shonfield, *Modern Capitalism* (London: Oxford University Press, 1965).

35 Shonfield, op. cit., p. 268; OECD, *Economic Surveys*, 1963, p. 19.
36 Shonfield, op. cit., p. 265.
37 For a detailed discussion of tax discrimination and para. 7, see Shonfield, op. cit., pp. 282–6; and Altvater, *et al.*, op. cit., pp. 289–300.
38 Shonfield, op. cit., p. 296.
39 Jörg Huffschmid, *Die Politik des Kapitals. Konzentration und Wirtschaftspolitik in der Bundesrepublik* (Frankfurt: Suhrkamp Verlag, 1969), p. 31.
40 *Vermögensbildung*, which literally means 'asset creation', is a general term for a wide range of policies designed to increase the savings, property and/or asset ownership of German workers. They all aim to encourage investment, rather than consumptive spending, of that portion of wages and salaries not needed for basic necessities.
41 See Huffschmid, *Die Politik*, op. cit., pp. 36–63, esp. tables on pp. 47–8.
42 OECD, *Economic Surveys*, 1966, pp. 25–7.
43 See the SVR's 1965–6 report, *Stabilisierung ohne Stagnation* (Stuttgart: W. Kohlhammer, 1965), paras 187–92.
44 Our account of internal DGB politics during the 1950s is based on Pirker, *Die blinde Macht*, Vol. II, as well as the other sources cited specifically below.
45 Otto Kirchheimer provided a fascinating portrait of union attitudes in the mid-1950s in the unpublished study which he carried out for the Rand Corporation, entitled, 'West German unions: their domestic and foreign policies', Rand Memorandum RM-1673-RC. Our characterization of union views is derived from this study and internal union documents.
46 On the 'Circle of Ten', see William Graf, *The German Left since 1945* (New York: Oleander, 1976), pp. 123–4.
47 A discussion of the *Aktionsprogramm*, including a list of its demands, can be found in Joachim Bergmann, Otto Jacobi and Walther Müller-Jentsch, *Gewerkschaften in der Bundesrepublik. Vol. I, Gewerkschaftliche Lohnpolitik zwischen Mitgliederinteressen und ökonomischen Systemzwängen* (Frankfurt am Main: Aspekte, 1976), pp. 165–7.
48 On growing opposition within the DGB to Brenner, see the articles in *Der Spiegel*, 'Bremse für Brenner', 15 January 1958, and 'Otto der Gusseiserne', 4 November 1959.
49 On divisions within the ADGB after 1918, see Limmer, *Die deutsche Gewerkschaftsbewegung*, op. cit., pp. 50–4. On the ADGB in general, see Gerard Braunthal, *Socialist Labor and Politics in Weimar Germany* (Hamden, Conn.: Archon, 1978).
50 On the different factions within the DGB and their political attitudes, see the chapter 'Ideologische Richtungen im DGB', in Frank Deppe (ed.), *Kritik der Mitbestimmung* (Frankfurt: Suhrkamp Verlag, 1973).
51 See the speech by Hans Katzor of the GdED, quoted in Deppe, op. cit., pp. 223–4; emphasis in original.
52 See the article in *Der Spiegel*, 'Otto der Gusseiserne', 4 November 1959.
53 For the entire preceding presentation of the unions' 1963 Düsseldorf Program, see DGB Bundesvorstand, *Grundsatzprogramm des deutschen Gewerkschaftsbundes* (n.d., 1963); for the above-listed comparisons between the 1963 and 1949 DGB programs, see ibid., and DGB, *Protokoll des Gründungskongresses*, op. cit., pp. 318–26.
54 The German term *Gemeinwirtschaft* defies an exact English translation. Indeed, the *Gemeinwirtschaft* division of the Bank für Gemeinwirtschaft, the union-owned bank in Germany, has published a mimeographed manuscript on precisely this difficult problem, entitled, 'The term "Gemeinwirtschaft" and its renditions in English and French translations': Karl Kühne, *Der Begriff 'Gemeinwirtschaft' und seine Wiedergabe bei der Ubersetzung in das Französische und Englische* (Frankfurt: Bank für Gemeinwirtschaft, 1970). Suffice it to say that it is not exactly synonymous with 'state-run economy' nor with 'planned economy'. Three characteristics connote a *Gemeinwirtschaft*: (1) the enterprise is commonly owned by some non-profit organization – such as a political party, trade union, or church – but operates in a market economy; (2) although publicly owned, the enterprise or corporation is legally and structurally separate from the state; and (3) the profit mechanism is maintained as are other microeconomic features of a 'regular' corporate entity.

The general German term *Gemeinwirtschaft* is further complicated by its specific use on the part of the German unions, who call all the companies which they own by the generic name *gemeinwirtschaftliche Unternehmungen*. After lengthy pondering of the proper English translation, we have decided that the term 'community-run public corporations' best conveys the term *Gemeinwirtschaft* as it is used in this particular case by the German unions in their 1963 Düsseldorf Program. For an excellent analysis of this problem as a whole and in connections with the union-owned companies in particular, see Achim von Loesch, *Die Gemeinwirtschaftliche Unternehmung* (Cologne: Bund Verlag, 1977). See also Kurt Hirche, *Die Wirtschaftsunternehmen der Gewerkschaften* (Düsseldorf, Wien: Econ-Verlag, 1966).

55 IG Metall, *Gechäftsbericht 1956–57* (n.d.), p. 21.

56 On the internal DGB clashes over the *Notstandsgesetze*, see the *Spiegel* articles: 'Gewisse Unruhe', 16 May 1966, and 'Rohe Eier', 13 March 1967. For an overview of the *Notstandsgesetze* discussions, see Schmidt, *Ordnungsfaktor*, op. cit., pp. 64–9.

57 On the main elements of labor law and *Verrechtlichung*, summarized below, see the references in n. 22, above.

58 Our periodization of bargaining trends in 1952–66 is loosely based on Otto Jacobi's study of IG Metall's *Tarifpolitik*, which appears in Bergmann, *et al.*, op. cit., pp. 231–56. The other main source on collective bargaining in the 1950s to which we are indebted is the chapter on West Germany in William Fellner, *The Problem of Rising Prices* (Paris: OECD, 1961). Pirker, *Die blinde Macht*, op. cit., Vol. II, also discusses several important wage rounds.

59 This is the figure for contractual wage rates (*Tariflöhne*) of male industrial workers cited by Fellner, op. cit., p. 327.

60 ibid.

61 The only account of the ÖTV strike appears in Pirker, *Die blinde Macht*, op. cit., Vol. II, pp. 105 ff.

62 For a detailed account of the Bayern strike, see Pirker, op. cit., Vol. II, pp. 107–23; also Bergmann, *et al.*, op. cit., pp. 269–77.

63 Fellner, op. cit., p. 327.

64 For the details of IG Metall's wage bargaining in 1951–74, see Bergmann, *et al.*, op. cit., pp. 231–56.

65 Fellner, op. cit., p. 343.

66 On the Schleswig-Holstein strike, see Bergmann, *et al.*, op. cit., pp. 277–84; Pirker, op. cit., Vol. II, pp. 212–22; and the articles which appeared in issues 3, 4, 6 and 7 of *Der Spiegel* in 1957.

67 Fellner, op. cit., pp. 348–50.

68 See the article by W. Müller-Jentsch, 'IG Bau-Steine-Erden: Juniorpartner der Bauindustrie', in Otto Jacobi, Walther Müller-Jentsch and Eberhard Schmidt (eds), *Kritisches Jahrbuch 1973* (Frankfurt: S. Fischer, 1973), as well as the article on Leber, entitled, 'Die Leber-Party', *Der Spiegel*, no. 13, 1963.

69 The Blessing Memorandum is discussed in Robert Flanagan and Lloyd Ulman, *Wage Restraint: A Study of Incomes Policy in Western Europe* (Berkeley, Calif.: University of California Press, 1971), p. 185.

70 See Table 2·1 on wage rate and earnings increases in the Statistical Tables.

71 For details of Gesamtmetall's new 'confrontationalist' strategy, see Dietrich Hoss, *Die Krise des 'Institutionalisierten Klassenkampfes'* (Frankfurt: Europäische Verlags-anstalt), pp. 83–99.

72 On the 1963 strike, see Hoss, op. cit.; and Claus Noé, *Gebändigter Klassenkampf. Tarifautonomie in der Bundesrepublik Deutschland* (Berlin: Ducker & Humblot, 1970).

73 Sachverständigenrat, *Stabilisierung*, paras 98–100; SVR, *Jahresgutachten 1964*, Bundesdrucksache IV/2890, para. 235.

74 SVR, *Stabilisierung*, para. 98.

75 Our description of economic conditions and policy in 1966–73 is based on OECD, *Economic Surveys*; SVR, *Jahresgutachten*; Altvater, *et al.*, op. cit.; and Jürgen Krack and Karl Neumann, *Konjunktur, Krise, Wirtschaftspolitik* (Frankfurt: Europäische Verlagsanstalt, 1978).

76 See *Der Spiegel* articles: 'Vorschuss auf den Mai, no. 49, 1967, and 'Mut zur Pflicht', nos 1–2, 1969.

77 On the 1969 revaluation, see SVR, *Im Sog des Booms* (Stuttgart: W. Kohlhammer, 1969), paras 101–7.

78 Altvater, *et al.*, op. cit., p. 330.

79 See the interviews with Brenner that appeared in *Der Spiegel*, no. 14, 1967, and no. 21,

1969, as well as in Leo Brawand (ed.), *Wohin steuert die deutsche Wirtschaft* (Munich: Verlag Karl Desch, 1971), pp. 158–80.

80 See *Der Spiegel* articles: 'Stärker als Banken', no. 12, 1968, and 'Tür zur Macht', no. 44, 1968.

81 'Die Zeit läuft', *Der Spiegel*, no. 24, 1973.

82 See the table on wage drift in Helmut Arndt (ed.), *Lohnpolitik und Einkommensverteilung* (Berlin: Duncker & Humblot, 1969), p. 487.

83 'Wer mault, muss gehen', *Der Spiegel*, no. 24, 1967; and 'Rosen um Mitternacht', *Der Spiegel*, no. 45, 1967.

84 See n. 76, above; also SVR, *Im Sog*, op. cit., pp. 25–7.

85 On the 1969 round, see SVR, *Konjunktur im Umbruch* (Stuttgart: W. Kohlhammer, 1970), pp. 17–19. On the *Septemberstreiks*, see Schmidt, *Ordnungsfaktor*, op. cit.; also Studienreihe des soziologischen Forschungsinstituts Göttingen (SOFI), *Am Beispiel des Septemberstreiks-Anfang der Rekonstruktionsperiode der Arbeiterklasse?* (Frankfurt: Europäische Verlagsanstalt, 1971).

86 See Statistical Tables. On the 1970–3 wage rounds, see the yearly *Jahresgutachten* of the SVR for 1970–1 to 1973–4.

87 On the 1971 strikes in the chemical industry, see Kurt Steinhaus, *Streiks in der Bundesrepublik* (Frankfurt am Main: Verlag Marxistische Blätter, 1975), pp. 83–93; and Willi Dzielak, Wolfgang Hindrichs, Helmut Martens, Verena Stanislawski and Wolfram Wassermann, *Belegschaften und Gewerkschaften im Streik: Am Beispiel der chemischen Industrie* (Frankfurt: Campus, 1978).

88 On the 1971 IG Metall strike, see Regine Meyer, *Streik und Aussperrung in der Metallindustrie* (Marburg: Verlag Arbeiterbewegung und Gesellschaftswissenschaft, 1977).

89 Numerous reasons have been mentioned by German trade union officials and knowledgeable scholars of the German labor movement for Nord Württemberg–Nord Baden's 'vanguard' role in IG Metall's collective bargaining strategy. Among these are the area's high concentration of famous and economically crucial firms such as Daimler-Benz, Robert Bosch and IBM; the concentration of advanced production in the electronics and automobile industries; the geographic smallness of the area, which not only has made strikes financially manageable for IG Metall, but also has limited the scope of industry's most potent weapon, the lockout, which according to German labor law can only be employed in that particular negotiating district which is being struck by the union. This last point concerning the importance of the negotiating district's size is absolutely central for a proper understanding of why, for example, IG Metall has conducted very few strikes in Nordrhein–Westfalen, which comprises the highly industrialized Rhine–Ruhr area. Any strikes in that negotiating area could potentially be countered by a district-wide lockout by industry which, given the size of Nordrhein–Westfalen and the German unions' tradition of supporting locked-out workers with the same compensations as their striking colleagues, would lead to a severe financial drain on the unions' coffers.

An interesting, and perhaps quite relevant point for the preeminence of Nord Württemberg–Nord Baden as IG Metall's 'showcase' district, especially in comparison with Nordrhein–Westfalen, was mentioned by a few experts interviewed in the course of our research. This reason concerned both intraunion organizational dimensions and macropolitical ones. Thus, the argument holds, whereas IG Metall was endowed with a superb organizational leadership in Nord Württemberg–Nord Baden, it lacks its equivalent in Nordrhein–Westfalen. Of equal significance, the argument continues, could be the fact that IG Metall's membership in Nord Württemberg–Nord Baden, albeit loyal and conscientious unionists, might be to a disproportionate degree politically conservative, since the state of Baden–Württemberg and the city of Stuttgart, the major urban center in the Nord Württemberg–Nord Baden bargaining district, have consistently elected CDU governments. This is in marked contrast to Nordrhein–Westfalen, and especially the Rhine–Ruhr region, where IG Metall members appear not only to be solidly social democratic, but where a certain radical tradition, dating back to the interwar and pre World War I days, has maintained a respectable presence among the bargaining area's working class.

90 On the 1973 strikes, see Eberhardt Schmidt, 'Spontane Streiks 1972/73', in Jacobi, *et al.*, *Kritisches Jahrbuch 1973*, op. cit.; also Walther Müller-Jentsch, 'Die spontane

Streikbewegung 1973', in Otto Jacobi, Walther Müller-Jentsch, Eberhardt Schmidt (eds), *Kritisches Jahrbuch 1974* (Frankfurt: Fischer, 1974).

91   IG Metall, *Geschäftsbericht 1971–73*, esp. p. 18.

92   Heinz O. Vetter (ed.), *Humanisierung der Arbeit als gesellschaftliche und gewerkschaftliche Aufgabe* (Frankfurt: Europäische Verlagsanstalt, 1974).

93   For an excellent and extensive study of this important collective bargaining achievement, see *Werktage werden besser* (Frankfurt, Cologne: Europäische Verlagsanstalt, 1977); and IG Metall, *Geschäftsbericht 1971–73*, pp. 14, 146–8.

94   The *Aktionsprogramm* of 1972 as quoted in Leminsky and Otto, op. cit., pp. 63–77.

95   For an excellent point-by-point comparison of all DGB *Aktionsprogramme*, see Gerhard Leminsky, 'Zum neuen Aktionsprogramm des DGB', in *Gewerkschaftliche Monatshefte*, December 1979.

96   See, for example, DGB, *Geschäftsbericht 1965–68*, pp. 203–7, 240. For the text of the *Arbeitsförderungsgesetz*, see *Arbeitsförderungsgesetz* (Neuwied, Darmstadt: Luchterhand, 1978), pp. 151–284.

97   For the text of the *Betriebsverfassungsgesetz*, see Gerd Siebert and Barbara Degen, *Betriebsverfassungsgesetz 1972* (Frankfurt: Nachrichten-Verlags-Gesselschaft, 1972). On the *Betriebsverfassungsgesetz*, see Schuster, *Die deutsche Gewerkschaftsbewegung*, p. 124; and IG Metall, *Geschäftsbericht 1971–73*, pp. 16, 18.

98   Thus, it is not by coincidence that the above-mentioned qualitative gains in the form of the pathbreaking Lohnrahmentarifvertrag II occurred the year after the new Works Constitution Law took effect. IG Metall, thus, had the legal wherewithal to implement the complicated terms of its contract on the shopfloor.

99   IG Metall, *Geschäftsbericht 1971–73*, pp. 54, 56, 64; and DGB, *Geschäftsbericht 1969–71*, pp. 176–7.

100 IG Metall, *Geschäftsbericht 1968–70*, p. 50, and *Geschäftsbericht 1971–73*, p. 64.

101 On *Investitionsmeldestellen* and *Wirtschafts- und Sozialräte*, see IG Metall, *Geschäftsbericht 1974–76*, pp. 109–11.

102 Compare, for example, IG Metall's anti-DDR attitude in the early 1960s (for example, *Protokoll 1962*, op. cit., pp. 78–9) to its acceptance of *Ostpolitik* in the 1970s: *Geschäftsbericht 1971–73*, pp. 15–16; *Geschäftsbericht 1974–76*, p. 15; and *Geschäftsbericht 1977–79*, pp. 17–20. On *Ostpolitik*, see also DGB, *Geschäftsbericht 1969–71*, introduction, and *Geschäftsbericht 1972–74*, pp. 4–6.

103 Growth in 1973 was 4·9 percent, while inflation was 7·0 percent: Dresdner Bank, *Statistical Survey*, July 1981.

104 Jeffrey Sachs, 'Wage, profits, and macroeconomic adjustment in the 1970s: a comparative study', paper presented at Conference of the Brookings Panel on Economic Activity, Massachusetts Institute of Technology, Cambridge, Mass., USA, October 1979, p. 17 ff.

105 See *German Tribune*, 5 April 1981, p. 6.

106 See Douglas D. Anderson, *Germany B: The Uncertain Stride of a Reluctant Giant* (Cambridge, Mass.: Harvard Business School, 1980); and Morton Kondrake, 'The German challenge to American conservatives', *New Republic*, 29 September 1979.

107 See Sachs, op. cit., p. 33.

108 Norbert Kloten, Karl-Heinz Ketterer and Rainer Vollmer, 'The political and social factors of Germany's stabilization performance', paper prepared for Brookings Project on the Politics and Sociology of Global Inflation, 1980, pp. 49–64.

109 Sachs, op. cit., p. 17.

110 'Massmahmen zur Verbesserung der Haushaltsstruktur', *Bulletin* (Bonn: Presse- und Informationsamt der Bundesregierung, September 1975), pp. 1097–8.

111 Hartmut Tofaute, *Das Programm für Zukunftsinvestitionen der Bundesregierung vom Frühjahr 1977* (DGB-Bundesvorstand, 1978), p. 11.

112 ibid.

113 See Rudolf Herlt, 'Raw material and travel costs push trading balance into deficit', *German Tribune*, 16 March 1980, p. 7.

114 John Tagliabue, 'Germany battles its recession', *New York Times*, 28 August 1980, p. D-1.

115 John Tagliabue, 'Bonn budget cuts questioned', *New York Times*, 17 September 1981, p. D-17.

116 See Kloten, *et al.*, op. cit., pp. 69–70.

117 See Sachs, op. cit., pp. 18 ff.
118 See 'Umverteilungsprogramm statt Beschäftigungsprogramm – zum Jahresgutachten des Sachverständigenrats', *WSI-Mitteilungen*, vol. 30, no. 1 (1977), p. 1.
119 Sachs, op. cit., pp. 18 ff.
120 Gerhard Brandt, Bernard Kündig, Zissis Papadimitriou and Jutta Thomae, *Computer und Arbeitsprozess* (Frankfurt: Campus, 1978); Günter Friedrichs, 'Mikroelektronik – eine neue Dimension von technischem Wandel und Automation', *Gewerkschaftliche Monatshefte*, vol. 31, no. 4 (1980), pp. 277–89; and IG Metall, *Geschäftsbericht 1977–79*, pp. 417–26.
121 Andrei S. Markovits and Christopher S. Allen, 'Trade union responses to the contemporary economic problems in Western Europe: the context of current debates and policies in the Federal Republic of Germany', *Economic and Industrial Democracy*, vol. 2, no. 1 (1981), p. 61.
122 Karl Buschmann, 'Probleme der internationalen Arbeitsteilung in der Textil und Bekleidungsindustrie', *Gewerkschaftliche Monatshefte*, vol. 29, no. 6 (June 1978), pp. 355–67.
123 Günter Pehl, 'Eine neue internationale Arbeitsteilung setzt sich durch', *Die Quelle*, vol. 29, no. 5 (May 1978), pp. 275–7. For an excellent analysis of the Federal Republic's switch from being a major goods exporter to becoming an important capital exporter as a consequence of its growing role in the global economy, see Klaus Busch, 'Führt Kapitalexport zu Arbeitsplatzexport?', *WSI-Mitteilungen*, vol. 32, no. 9 (September 1979), pp. 493–501; and Folker Fröbel, Jürgen Heinrichs and Otto Kreye, *Die neue internationale Arbeitsteilung* (Reinbeck bei Hamburg: Rowohlt, 1977).
124 Pehl, op. cit., pp. 276–7.
125 OECD, *Investing in Developing Countries* (4th rev. edn, 1979).
126 *DGB Report*, No. 13/3, 1978, pp. 5–6.
127 On the future dimensions of the development of microprocessors and computer chips, see 'The fight over computer chips', *New York Times*, 16 September 1980. On the term 'job-killers', and a representative discussion of this syndrome since the crisis, see Peter Kalmbach, 'Rationalisierung, neue Technologien, und Beschäftigung', in *Gewerkschaftliche Monatshefte*, vol. 29, no. 8 (August 1978), pp. 455–67.
128 See Anderson, op. cit., p. 7.
129 See 'Memorandum '80: "Gegen konservativ Formierung – Alternativen der Wirtschaftspolitik" ', *Blätter für deutsche und internationale Politik*, vol. 25, no. 5 (May 1980), pp. 608–29; and DGB, 'Öffentliche Haushalte im Zeichen des Steuerpakets', *Abteilung Wirtschaftspolitik*, 3 November 1978.
130 See Wilfried Höhnen, 'Ursachen der Wachstumsschwache', unpublished ms., 10 January 1979; and 'Staatsverschuldung im Meinungstreit', *Gewerkschaftliche Monatshefte*, vol. 31, no. 2 (February 1980), pp. 103–8.
131 Indeed, it is interesting to note that the German translation of the inter-European union paper *Keynes Plus* is entitled *Uber Keynes hinaus*. See Clas-Erik Odhner, *Participatory Economics of Keynes Plus* (Stockholm: n.d., 1978); and Europäisches Gewerkschaftsinstitut, *'Uber Keynes hinaus Gestaltung der Wirtschaftspolitik durch Alternativen'* (Brussels: n.d., 1978).
132 See Markovits and Allen, 'The West German trade unions' role in democratization and participation: social partnership or class conflict?', paper presented at 11th World Congress of the International Political Science Association, Moscow, 12–18 August 1979; and Manfred Krüper, 'Muster für einen Branchenfond', *Gewerkschaftliche Umschau*, no. 6 (November–December 1978), pp. 6–7.
133 'Dokumentation: Das Grundsatzprogramm des DGB von 1968 und der Entwurf von 1979 im Vergleich', *Gewerkschaftliche Monatshefte*, vol. 31, no. 1 (January 1980), p. 50.
134 Andrew Martin and George Ross, 'European trade unions and the economic crisis: perceptions and strategies', *West European Politics*, vol. 3, no. 1 (January 1980), pp. 33–67.
135 See the following articles on technology which appeared in *Gewerkschaftliche Monatshefte*, in April 1980: Hans Janssen, 'Technischer Wandel und Rationalisierung aus tarifpolitischer Sicht'; Karl-Heinz Janzen, 'Technologiepolitik und Gewerkschaften'; Erwin Ferlemann, 'Rationalisierung und Humanisierung: Unauflösbarer Widerspruch oder gewerkschaftliche Aufgabe?'; and Günther Friedrichs, 'Mikro-

elektronik – eine neue Dimension von technischem Wandel und Automation', and 'Stellungnahme des DGB zur staatlichen Förderung neuer Technologien und zur Humanisierung des Arbeitslebens'.

136   ibid.; see also Frieder Naschold, 'Humanisierung der Arbeit zwischen Staat und Gewerkschaften', *Gewerkschaftliche Monatshefte*, vol. 31, no. 4 (April 1980), pp. 221–30.

137   As to the unions' recent interest regarding this matter, see Gerhard Leminsky, 'Humanisierung der Arbeit aus eigener Kraft'; Frieder Naschold, 'Humanisierung der Arbeit zwischen Staat und Gewerkschaften'; and Willi Pöhler, 'Staatliche Förderung für die Verbesserung der Arbeits und Lebensqualität', in *Gewerkschaftliche Monatshefte*, vol. 31, no. 4 (April 1980), pp. 213–20, 221–30, 230–42.

138   IG Metall, *Geschäftsbericht 1977–79*, p. 93, and *Geschäftsbericht 1974–76*, p. 125. The term 'qualitative' merits a brief explanation. The German unions use this term to describe most bargaining aims and actions which are not specifically and directly wage-related. Thus, this concept usually includes such issues as protection from rationalization, workplace safety, humanization of the work process and all attempts at worktime reduction, despite the latter's 'quantitative' implications as well.

139   On this new type of *Strukturpolitik*, see Volker Hauff and Fritz Scharpf, *Modernisierung der Volkswirtschaft – Technologiepolitik als Strukturpolitik* (Frankfurt Cologne: Europäische Verlagsanstalt, 1975); and J. Esser, W. Fach and G. Simonis, 'Grenzprobleme des "Modells Deutschland" ', and 'Modell Deutschland – Anatomie und Alternativen', (editorial), in *Prokla 40*, vol. 10, no. 3 (1980), pp. 40–63, 1–13.

140   Although the FDP has without any doubt altered numerous pieces of legislation in directions which were certainly not welcomed by the SPD, there seems little doubt that to the SPD government and the bulk of its parliamentary section, the FDP served as a convenient alibi *vis-à-vis* SPD radicals such as the Young Socialists.

141   Tofaute, op. cit., pp. 14–15; and 'Zwischenbalanz des DGB zum 16-Milliarden DM Programm', *Die Quelle*, vol. 29, no. 9 (September 1978), pp. 48–56.

142   'Hilfe für Regionen mit mehr als sechs Prozent Arbeitslosen', *Frankfurter Rundschau*, 17 June 1979; 'Bonner Arbeitsmarktprogramm kommt an', *Süddeutsche Zeitung*, 8 August 1979; IG Metall, *Geschäftsbericht 1977–79*, pp. 71, 77–9; Der Bundesminister für Arbeit und Sozialordnung, *Arbeitsmarktpolitisches Programm der Bundesregierung für Regionen mit besonderen Beschäftigungsproblemen* (Bonn: Bundesministerium für Arbeit und Sozialordnung, 1979); 'Problemgebiete des Arbeitsmarktes holen auf', *Frankfurter Rundschau*, 22 April 1980; and Franz Heinrichs, 'Neues Leben auf den Halden?', *Metall*, 30 May 1979.

143   Carola Böse-Fischer, 'Bonn digs in heels as calls for booster program become louder', *German Tribune*, 5 April 1981, p. 6.

144   *Dienstblatt der Bundesanstalt für Arbeit*, Runderlass 230/78.

145   See the articles: 'Welche Arbeit zumutbar ist, soll im Einzelfall geprüft werden', *Frankfurter Rundschau*, 17 May 1979; 'Einigung der Koalitionspartner', *Handelsblatt*, 17 May 1979; Norbert Möller-Lückling, 'AFG-Regierungsentwurf wird den Aufgaben nicht gerecht', *Die Quelle*, vol. 30, no. 2 (February 1979), pp. 112–13; and Gerd Muhr, 'Was bringt die 5. Novelle zum Arbeitsförderungsgesetz', *Die Quelle*, vol. 30, no. 7–8, pp. 424–5.

146   IG Metall, *Geschäftsbericht 1974–76*, pp. 429–33; and *Geschäftsbericht 1977–79*, p. 26; see also the speeches of Eugen Loderer, 'Montanmitbestimmung – Faustpfand der Wirtschaftsdemokratie', and Rudolf Judith, 'Montanmitbestimmung in Gefahr!', presented at the IG Metall Iron and Steel Conference, Dortmund, 3 July 1980.

147   ibid.

148   Federal Ministry of Labour and Social Affairs, *Co-determination* (Bonn: Bundesministerium für Arbeit und Sozialordnung, 1976), pp. 7–45; see also the German edition, *Mitbestimmung* (Bonn: Bundesministerium für Arbeit und Sozialordnung, 1978), pp. 29–48; and IG Metall, *Geschäftsbericht 1974–76*, p. 432.

149   'Das Mitbestimmungesgesetz ist verfassungsgemäss', *Frankfurter Allgemeine Zeitung*, 2 March 1979; see also DGB, *Geschäftsbericht 1975–77*, pp. 29–33; and IG Metall, *Geschäftsbericht 1977–79*, p. 31.

150   IG Metall, *Geschäftsbericht 1977–79*, p. 31; DGB, *Geschäftsbericht 1975–77*, pp. 29–33; and Kittner, 'Zur verfassungsrechtlichen Zukunft', op. cit., p. 324.

151   IG Metall, *Geschäftsbericht 1977–79*, pp. 31–3; and 'Das Mitbestimmungesgesetz ist verfassungsgemäss', *FAZ*, 2 March 1979.

152 'Worum es in Karlsruhe ging', *Frankfurter Rundschau*, 2 March 1979, p. 2; and 'Für alle etwas', *Frankfurter Allgemeine Zeitung*, 2 March 1979, p. 1.

153 *Blick durch die Wirtschaft*, 5 March 1979, and *Im Namen des Volkes; DGB Nachrichten-Dienst*, 7 March 1979.

154 Ulrich Zachert, 'Aussperrung und Gewerkschaften', in *Gewerkschaftliche Monatshefte*, vol. 29, no. 5 (May 1978), pp. 280–9; Zachert, *et al., Die Aussperrung*, op. cit.; and Kittner, 'Verbot der Aussperrung', op. cit.

155 See Eugen Loderer's statements in: 'Aussperrung verbieten!', *Metall*, 19 April 1979, p. 17.

156 Hans Hermann Wohlgemuth, 'Zur Auseinandersetzung um die Aussperrung', in *Gewerkschaftliche Monatshefte*, vol. 30, no. 3 (March 1979), pp. 145–52. See also the various accounts of the court's decision in many German newspapers on 12 and 13 June 1980: 'Kampf gegen Aussperrung geht bis zum Verbot weiter', in *Welt der Arbeit*, 12 June 1980; 'Gemeinsame Erklärung des DGB, der IG Metall, under der IG Druck', *Die Neue*, 13 June 1980; and 'Jeder Ausgesperrte ist ein Ausgesperrter zuviel', *Frankfurter Allgemeine Zeitung*, 12 June 1980.

157 Real wages rose only 1·5 percent in 1975 and 1977 and actually declined by 0·5 percent in 1976, compared to increases of 5·5, 8·5 and 4·5 percent in 1969, 1970 and 1971, respectively. See OECD, *Economic Surveys: Germany*, June 1979, pp. 17–19; and *WSI-Mitteilungen*, vol. 32, no. 3 (March 1979), pp. 121–6.

158 Rudi Schmiede, 'Entwicklungstendenzen der Tarifpolitik der IG Metall in den siebziger Jahren – eine Übersicht', unpublished manuscript, July 1980; and IG Metall *Geschäftsbericht, 1977–79*.

159 Wolfgang Gehrmann, 'Situation allows little scope for higher incomes', *German Tribune*, 9 November 1980, p. 6.

160 On the 1978 Druck und Papier strike, see Klaus Pickshaus and Witich Rossmann, *Streik und Aussperrung, '78. Hafen-Druck-Metall*, Series Soziale Bewegungen – Analyse und Dokumentation des IMSF, Nachrichten-reihe 13 (Frankfurt: Nachrichten-Verlag, 1978), pp. 19–47; Otto Jacobi, Eberhard Schmidt and Walther Müller-Jentsch (eds), *Arbeiterinteressen gegen Sozialpartnerschaft: Kritisches Gewerkschaftsjahrbuch 1978/79* (Berlin: Rotbuch Verlag, 1979), pp. 10–46; and Projektgruppe Gewerkschaftsforschung, *Tarifpolitik 1978: Lohnpolitische Kooperation und Absicherungskämpfe* (Frankfurt: Campus, 1979), pp. 187–276.

161 See Gerlach, 'Tarifbewegungen'; Pickshaus and Rossmann, op. cit., pp. 48–68; Projektgruppe Gewerkschaftsforschung, *Tarifpolitik 1978*, pp. 23–146; Eckart Hildebrandt, 'Der Tarifkampf in der metallverarbeitenden Industrie 1978', in Jacobi, *et al., Arbeiterinteressen*, op. cit.; and Eugen Loderer, 'Erfolgreicher Kampf um soziale Besitzstandsicherung', *Gewerkschaftliche Monatshefte*, vol. 29, no. 5 (May 1978), pp. 257–61.

162 On the contract agreements, see Hans Janssen, 'Sozialen Rückschritt verhindert', *Der Gewerkschafter*, vol. 26, no. 5 (May 1978), p. 18; Pickshaus and Rossmann, op cit., pp. 64–6; Hildebrandt, op. cit.; and IG Metall, *Geschäftsbericht 1977–79*, pp. 522–3.

163 On the 1978–9 steel strike, see Wolfgang Gehrcke (ed.), *Die Schlacht um 35 Stunden* (Dortmund: Weltkreis-Verlag, 1979); IG Metall, *Der Arbeitskampf in der Eisen- und Stahlindustrie* (n.d.); Otto Jacobi, Eberhard Schmidt and Walther Müller-Jentsch (eds), *Arbeitskampf und Arbeitszeit: Kritisches Gewerkschaftsjahrbuch 1979/80* (Berlin: Rotbuch Verlag, 1979), pp. 9–58; and Gert Hautsch and Bernd Semmler, *Stahlstreik und Tarifrunde 78/79*. Series Soziale Bewegungen – Analyse und Dokumentation des IMSF, No. 7 (Frankfurt: Institut für marxistische Studien und Forschungen, 1979), pp. 25–43.

164 IG Metall, *Geschäftsbericht 1974–76*, p. 125, and *Geschäftsbericht 1977–79*, pp. 13, 35–9.

165 Günter Pehl, 'Arbeitgeber gefährden den sozialen Frieden', *Die Quelle*, vol. 29, no. 12 (December 1978), pp. 659–60; 'Vetter befürchtet die totale Konfrontation', *Frankfurter Rundschau*, 22 January 1979; and 'Rohde: Tabu-Katalog ist Klassenkampf von oben', *Frankfurter Rundschau*, 17 January 1979.

166 For the text of the *Tabu-Katalog*, see *Frankfurter Rundschau*, 26 January 1979; and *Die Zeit*, 26 January 1979.

167 *Memorandum 1979*: 'Vorrang für Vollbeschäftigung – Alternativen der Wirtschaftspolitik', *Blätter für deutsche und internationale Politik*, vol. 24, no. 5 (May 1979), pp. 614–33.

168   See *Suddeutsche Zeitung*, 29 June 1979, p. 4; and 'Der Kandidat des grossen Geldes', *Metall*, 18 July 1979.
169   Gernot Müller, 'Die Rolle der staatlichen Konjunkturpolitik bei Entstehung und Verlauf der Krise seit 1973', *WSI-Mitteilungen*, vol. 33, no. 4 (April 1980), pp. 174–86. See also Europäisches Gewerkschaftinstitut, *Uber Keynes hinaus: Gestaltung der Wirtschaftspolitik durch Alternativen*, the principles of which the DGB is increasingly espousing. Finally, see the entire issue of *Gewerkschaftliche Monatshefte* of February 1980.
170   See DGB, *Aktionsprogramm '79* (n.d., 1979), for an initial formulation of some of these themes, and in their later manifestation, see DGB, 'Grundsatzprogramm 1981', *Die Quelle*, vol. 32, no. 4 (April 1981), pp. 211–38.

3 Trade Unions in Sweden: Strategic Responses to Change and Crisis

Andrew Martin

Part 1

Introduction

The main thrust of the economic strategy with which Swedish unions sought to cope with the problems posed by the mid-1970s international economic crisis was toward increased influence by both the state and unions on microeconomic decisions, particularly concerning investment, which had earlier been left almost entirely to management. This, however, is not so much a new position adopted in response to the crisis as a further elaboration of one that the unions had already been developing in the preceding years.

The lead in formulating this position has been taken by the Swedish Confederation of Labor, or LO (*Landsorganisationen i Sverige*), the larger of the two principal confederations in which Swedish unions are organized. Embracing nearly half the laborforce, its affiliates consist almost entirely of blue-collar workers. From their origins the LO unions have been intimately linked to the Social Democratic Labor Party, or SAP (*Socialdemokratiska Arbetareparti*). Although they have no constitutional role analogous to that of unions in the British Labour Party, union branches affiliated to the party comprise the core of its local organization, and between three-fifths and three-quarters of LO members vote for the party. Collectively affiliated union members account for the bulk of the party's membership, the unions provide much of the party's funds, almost all union officials consider themselves Social Democrats and there is considerable overlapping membership between party and union bodies.[1] Within both LO and the party, they are each strongly identified as parts of a single labor movement.

The other main confederation, consisting of white-collar unions and accounting for somewhat over a fifth of the laborforce, is the Central Organization of Salaried Employees, or TCO (*Tjänstemannens Central-organisationen*). Unlike LO, TCO has no links with the SAP or, for that matter, any other party. Although as much as two-fifths of TCO members' votes go to the SAP, the rest is spread across the entire party spectrum. This includes not only the small communist party on the left and the Center Party on the right, both of which get some LO member-support, but also the other so-called 'bourgeois' parties, the liberals and conservatives, for which hardly any LO members vote. The widely divergent political orientations of TCO members, and officials, make the confederation the target of partisan competition and also subject it to considerable internal strain on issues over which there is clear partisan conflict. This tends to make it difficult for TCO to adopt positions similar to LO's to the extent that they are identified as distinctively Social Democratic positions.[2] Nevertheless TCO has come to largely share LO's prescription for Sweden's economic problems, even if TCO's position differs in some respects, particularly in its unwillingness to go as far as LO in encroaching on the property basis of managerial authority. Thus, there is a large, and perhaps growing, area of agreement between the two confederations concerning the need for a greater state and union role in industrial decision-making.

This position implies a substantial departure from the division of roles among the state, labor and capital, referred to as the 'Swedish model', around which a large degree of consensus prevailed during much of the four and a half decades of virtually continuous Social Democratic control of the state, alone or in coalition, since 1932. The essentials of the Swedish model can be initially summed up briefly. The state's role is confined primarily to stabilizing the overall level of demand and determining its division between private and public consumption, principally through fiscal policy, while the bulk of production for the market continues to be conducted by capitalist firms. The unions' role is confined to regulating industrial relations jointly with the management of those firms, maintaining 'industrial peace' and determining wages through collective bargaining, while the management continues to decide not only what is to be produced, but how it is to be done. In short, the environment in which production decisions are made is conditioned by state and union action, but the decisions themselves are left to the management of the predominantly capitalist firms.

Couched in these broad terms the relationship among the main actors in the Swedish political economy is obviously quite similar to that in most of the industrial societies with plural-party politics and capitalist economies, despite the exceptional amount of power Swedish labor has apparently had in both the market and state arenas. The difference which that may nevertheless have made perhaps lies in the dynamics of the way the relationship has evolved. Established along these lines earlier than in the other countries with which we are concerned, in the 1930s rather than after World War II, the erosion of the relationship since the late 1960s has taken place under conditions of sufficient union power to define the range of possible policy responses to the economic crisis precipitated in the mid-1970s in what would appear to be a quite distinctive way. Thus, union power attaches particular significance to union prescriptions in Sweden. Yet political division confronts the unions with difficult strategic dilemmas in translating that power into policy.

Our discussion proceeds as follows. We begin with a description of the Swedish model as it was established and conceived in the context of mass unemployment in the 1930s. Next we examine its modification in the context of sustained growth and inflationary pressures in the earlier postwar period. We then turn to the growing union disenchantment with various features of the Swedish model in the later 1960s and the resulting developments in union strategy that defined the perspective within which their response to the 1970s crisis was framed. We analyze that perspective and response in some detail, concluding with a discussion of the significance of union ideas for Swedish politics.

Part 2

The Shaping of the Swedish Model

Establishment of the Swedish Model

The relationships among the state, labor and capital that prevailed throughout most of the postwar period in Sweden were established after the SAP converted their gains in the 1932 election into what came to be recognized as sustainable control of the state. Both unions and employers adapted their strategies to this shift in the distribution of power in the state arena in the light of the implications they believed it had for their respective interests. The result was a kind of settlement or, as the Swedish sociologist Walter Korpi puts it, an 'historical compromise'[3] between the Social Democratic labor movement and Swedish capital, the terms of which comprise the Swedish model. As World War II drew to a close, the movement adopted a program committing it to more interventionist policies than those pursued in the interwar period, much like the programs for postwar reconstruction put forth by the left in other countries. As was largely the case in the other countries, however, the Swedish labor movement was compelled to abandon its postwar program. To implement it would have required a shift in the distribution of power beyond that in the 1930s. This proved impossible, and the terms of the interwar settlement were reaffirmed, not to be significantly challenged by the Social Democratic labor movement until the late 1960s.

RESPONSE TO THE DEPRESSION: POLICY INNOVATION AND POLITICAL POWER

A major innovation in economic policy was a central ingredient in both the redistribution of political power on which the settlement was based and in the redefinition of the respective roles of the state, labor and capital embodied in the settlement. In response to the Great Depression, the Social Democrats broke with the orthodox liberal view of economic policy they had essentially accepted during the 1920s. At the initiative of Ernst Wigforss, the Social Democrats' only significant theorist and subsequent Finance Minister, they called for a loan-financed expansion of public works in which workers would be paid at normal union rates, claiming that this would set in motion a cumulative process of increasing demand and reducing unemployment. In other words, they proposed to cope with the problem of unemployment by the kind of expansionary budget policy for which Keynes provided the theoretical rationale a few years later, but which he and others were already advocating.[4] Bidding for support primarily on the basis of this program, the SAP made substantial gains in the 1932 election. It nevertheless failed to win a parliamentary majority, leaving it in need of some other party's support if it was to carry out its recovery program. This posed an obstacle that had previously proven insuperable.

Growing rapidly since its founding in 1889, the SAP already became the largest in the directly elected Second Chamber by 1915, overtaking the liberal party with which it was allied in a prolonged campaign for universal suffrage and parliamentary supremacy. Three years later that campaign came to a successful conclusion, when the proto-revolutionary atmosphere fed by the fall of dynasties abroad induced leading industrialists to limit the risks by breaking down conservative resistance to the requisite constitutional changes. At the same time, this removed the basis for the SAP's alliance with the liberals. This was not expected to matter, for the Social Democrats believed that political democratization would enable them to win majorities, making it possible to go on to the process of 'economic democratization'.

Although Social Democratic ideology looked to parliamentary power as the means for achieving socialism, that goal had long been relegated to some indefinite future as it had in the other reformist labor movement parties of Europe. However, party control of the state was expected to make it possible to achieve more immediate goals of the kind that market action could not, particularly the reduction of unemployment, as well as reforms of the kind identified with the welfare state. In the process it was also expected that union power in the market arena would be strengthened. However, universal suffrage did not have its anticipated consequences, neither in the first election under the new rules in 1921 nor in the following elections. Without a majority of its own, the SAP continued to depend on parliamentary support by another party in order to govern, but the liberals were no longer willing to provide it.

Once economic issues replaced constitutional issues as the main line of cleavage in Swedish politics, the liberals realigned with the conservatives and the recently formed Farmers' Party to form a 'bourgeois' majority that blocked the Social Democrats' modest reform initiatives. Concerning the distribution but not the production process, they were aimed at making taxes more redistributive and strengthening unions' ability to win wage increases, or resist cuts, if only by keeping the unemployment benefits system from being used as a strike-breaking instrument. One minority SAP government was brought down on the tax issue and two on the strike issue. With no potential alliance partners and unable to win a majority of its own, the party was effectively neutralized. Even if the growth in its working-class support had continued at its earlier pace, the size of the working class was still too small for that to suffice; but it actually stagnated. The party did not, in fact, offer those it claimed as its distinct constituency any solution to the main economic problem affecting them, unemployment, severe in the early 1920s and chronic for the rest of the decade. Apart from blaming it on capitalism, the Social Democrats went through most of the decade without any alternative to the dominant liberal economic doctrine that prescribed balanced budgets and free trade.[5]

The Social Democrats' break with this doctrine also opened up the possibility of overcoming the obstacle posed by its continued inability to win a parliamentary majority. They managed to hold onto office and implement their recovery program by getting the support of the Farmers' Party in exchange for agreeing to agricultural tariffs (already enacted) and the introduction of additional supports for farm income. Having abandoned liberal orthodoxy in the interest of their own working-class constituency, the Social Democrats were ready to do so in the interests of the farmers as well. While this meant an increase in workers' living costs, it was deemed a price worth paying to be able to launch a reflationary program that promised more jobs and real income gains for workers as well as farmers. The bargain was accordingly struck and the Farmers' Party, after replacing a leader who would not go along, gave the SAP the parliamentary support it needed. Having succeeded in staying in power and implementing their policy in this way, the Social Democrats could plausibly claim credit for the recovery that followed, and reaped the reward of increased support in the 1936 election.[6]

In fact, the claim was not entirely justified, because the economic effects of the Social Democrats' program were limited. The stimulus it provided was small and its impact delayed by a major construction-industry strike. A recovery of exports, aided by the previous government's devaluation, gave Sweden's recovery its initial impetus. The budget stimulus to domestic demand helped sustain the recovery but was cut back prematurely, suggesting that the Social Democrats did not quite have the courage of their Keynesian convictions. Thus, the political significance of their policy innovation was more far-reaching than its economic consequences.

This emerges the more sharply when we compare the way labor movement parties in Britain and Germany responded to the Depression. At the time the Swedish Social Democrats were proposing what came to be known as Keynesian policy, their counterparts in the other two countries were rejecting union pleas to do likewise, insisting that, short of replacing capitalism with socialism (which they neither could nor intended to do), there was no alternative to balancing budgets and letting the business cycle inherent in capitalism run its inevitable course as rapidly as possible. The political implications of the contrasting budget-policy positions must be stressed particularly because deficits permitted the formation of coalitions that efforts to balance budgets, however futile, ruled out. The Swedish Social Democrats could accordingly reconcile increased spending on public works with the agricultural subsidies. This enabled them to forge the coalition needed to stay in office without trying to offset these expenditures with politically as well as economically counterproductive tax increases. In contrast, their counterparts in Britain and Germany rendered incompatible the interests of their own constituencies and those of equally indispensable potential coalition partners.[7]

REORIENTATION OF UNION STRATEGY

The establishment of Social Democratic control of the state on a basis clearly more durable than in the past prompted a significant reorientation of the unions' strategy in the market arena. Throughout its history LO's strategic outlook has been decisively conditioned by its ties to the SAP, the results it expected from the party's political strength and the experiences that largely confirmed those expectations. The awareness that its organizational resources have been crucial to the party's strength not only in mobilizing electoral support, but also in underpinning the effectiveness of its economic policy when in office, has been an important factor shaping the way LO has tried to use those resources in the market arena. Still, LO has been careful to retain the autonomy needed to meet the distinctive requirements of its own strength in the market arena, itself a prerequisite of the support it can bring to the party. Thus, LO, along with the party, has been continuously confronted with the sometimes difficult problems of reconciling the imperatives of market and state arena strategies that typically besets such union–party movements.

The links between the SAP and the blue-collar unions are rooted in the latter's origins. When the party was founded, Sweden's industrialization was still in its 'take-off' phase, not only later than Britain but also France and Germany, whose Social Democratic movement served as a model for Swedish socialists, so that Swedish labor as well as capital may have gained some of the advantages of 'backwardness'. Viewing unionization as the key to political mobilization of the working class the party's initial priority was placed on organizing unions, for which it performed the functions of a central organization for over a decade. While the party's role gave unionization a powerful impetus, it also proved an obstacle to recruiting workers resistant to simultaneous membership in the party. This was a factor in the establishment of LO as a separate central body in 1898. Nevertheless, the unions and party continued to be linked, in the many ways noted earlier, and to view themselves as interdependent components of a common movement. Thus, while continuing their organizing drive, the unions threw their weight behind the campaign for universal suffrage, the movement's primary political goal, by mounting a three-day general strike protesting suffrage restrictions in 1902.[8]

The importance attached to politics by the unions was reinforced by their direct confrontation with employers in the market arena. The Swedish Employers' Confederation, or SAF (*Svenska Arbetsgivareföre-ningen*), was founded in 1902 in an effort to achieve unified action among employers in the face of the rapidly growing working-class challenge demonstrated most dramatically by the general strike earlier that year. Although employers also joined with the conservatives to form a national party at the beginning of the century, they achieved more success in the market than state arena in the pre World War I period. SAF's policy, as opposed to employers who vainly tried to break the unions, was to recognize their right to organize but to insist on management's 'right to manage', requiring its own affiliates to include a clause affirming managerial prerogatives in all collective agreements. A reciprocal recognition of these rights was embodied in the so-called December Compromise of 1906 between SAF and LO. A long period of strikes and lockouts was thereby ended only to be followed by a renewed escalation of conflict over those rights, culminating in a general strike and lockout in 1909.

The outcome was a major defeat for the unions, which temporarily lost half their members. However, SAF failed in its effort to consolidate its victory by incorporating its interpretation of the disputed rights, among other things, into law. Legislation to that effect introduced by the conservatives was blocked by the liberals in the interest of preserving their alliance for suffrage reform with the SAP. Thus, the party's position in the state arena, modest as it still was, proved crucial in protecting the unions against the employers' effort to use the state to reinforce their power in the market arena.[9]

However, the failure of universal suffrage to produce parliamentary majorities for the party revealed the limits of its power in the state arena. Given the frustration of Social Democratic policy initiatives by the unified bourgeois bloc in the 1920s, the unions were thrown back upon their resources in the market arena. Strengthened by recovery from the 1909 general strike and by renewed growth the unions resorted to strikes at a rate that was among the highest in all the industrialized capitalist economies during the 1920s.[10] This, of course, is what made the strike issue the fateful one for the minority Social Democratic governments in 1923 and 1926. It also led SAF to revive its post-general strike demands for legislative restrictions on strikes. With the liberals now joining the other two bourgeois parties, legislation meeting those demands part-way could be enacted in 1928. It made strikes over issues covered in collective agreements illegal while the agreements were in force, and set up a special labor court to adjudicate disputes over such issues. Mass demonstrations against the legislation by the unions and SAP were futile, but the new restrictions also had little effect on industrial conflict, intensified by employer efforts to cut wages after the onset of the Depression.[11]

The same economic conditions leading employers to press for wage cuts naturally undermined the unions' capacity to resist them, and the unions suffered a series of major defeats in the increased industrial conflict that ensued. However, the SAP's success in establishing a more secure basis for controlling the state than they had been able to provided the unions with a 'political alternative' to market action, as Korpi puts it, making possible a restoration of employment and with it the revival of the unions' market bargaining power. In this new context the unions reevaluated the role of strikes, apparently accepting greater restraint in their use as essential to the effectiveness and even continued availability of this political alternative. As the decade progressed there was, in fact, a sharp decline in strike activity to the very low levels that brought Sweden its reputation for industrial peace. This was coupled with an institutionalization of industrial relations through the conclusion of the so-called *Saltsjöbaden* Basic Agreement between LO and SAF in 1938 and a concentration of control over the unions' use of the strike weapon in LO, culminating in a major revision of its constitution in 1941.[12]

The process began with an intervention by LO in the 1933–4 construction-industry strike that delayed implementation of the recovery program. The members of one of the unions involved rejected a settlement (providing for wage cuts) proposed by mediators and accepted by all the other unions. Faced with the threat of a lockout against all the construction unions by SAF and even the hint of emergency legislation to end the strike, all the LO unions except the hold-out combined to force the latter to override its members and accept the settlement. Nothing in LO's rules authorized the decision by its representative council to intervene in an affiliate's internal affairs in this way, but it reflected the strong consensus that the strike weapon had to be more effectively controlled in what was collectively believed to be the interest of the labor movement as a whole, for which LO had to serve as the instrument.[13]

This consensus may well account for the change that occurred in the unions' attitude to the labor laws enacted in 1928. Having protested them at the time, LO no longer called for their repeal in the 1930s. One reason was that they turned out to give union members some protection against victimization, to which unemployment made them especially vulnerable. Since the effect of limiting strikes to conflicts over new contracts was to strengthen leadership control over strikes, though, this was undoubtedly another reason for leaving well enough alone. At the same time LO was concerned with avoiding any further legislation limiting the right to strike, for which there was still pressure from the employers, the bourgeois parties and, in response to the construction strike, even the Social Democrats to some extent. LO could presumably expect more favorable legislation from a Social Democratic government. Indeed, it pressed for a law guaranteeing trade union rights to organize, aimed primarily at overcoming employer obstruction of white-collar unionization, which was enacted over SAF's objections in 1936.[14] Nevertheless, LO viewed legislative intervention in industrial relations as risky, since hostile parties could always return to power and union bargaining power in negotiations for new contracts could be severely impaired if they did not retain the option to strike without legal limitations. What was important was where the power to exercise that option was lodged. A way of concentrating that power more securely in LO, while avoiding legal limits on its use, was to agree on a set of rules for the private government of industrial relations with the already highly centralized employers organization.

This approach was proposed to LO in 1935 by SAF's director, who had persuaded his own organization to abandon its earlier pursuit of further legislative restrictions on strikes on the ground that, in view of the Social Democrats' evident political strength, there was little prospect of favorable legislation – a judgement confirmed by the enactment of the 1936 law. Each of the two peak organizations accordingly had its own reasons for entering into the negotiations that resulted in the 1938 agreement. Among other things the organizations undertook to refrain from strikes and lockouts that endangered essential social functions and from using tactics aimed at 'third' parties, two kinds of danger for which legal remedies had been urged. In addition, the Agreement set out detailed procedures for contractual negotiations and for settling disputes over contract provisions, capped by a joint committee which could to some extent function as a substitute for the labor court.[15]

While SAF already had the authority over its own members to interpret and enforce the commitments made in the Agreement, LO did not. The deficiency was largely made up by a revision of LO's constitution at its 1941 Congress. The key change provided that, to all intents and purposes, affiliated unions may not resort to a strike without approval of LO's secretariat (executive body), subject to appeal to its representative assembly (with delegates from all the unions). Unions that strike despite LO's disapproval can be denied the financial support LO is otherwise obliged to give, and may ultimately be expelled. Representatives of LO's secretariat may sit in on negotiations by affiliates and propose settlements. Unions rejecting the proposals may then be denied financial support in any conflicts involved. In turn, model rules made obligatory for all affiliates confined the right to approve or reject a settlement, or to propose a strike, to the individual unions' executive bodies, ruling out binding votes by the membership such as the one that blocked settlement of the 1934 construction strike.[16]

In themselves the formal sanctions given to LO are not as important as what they signaled. Most of the strike funds remained at the disposal of the individual unions and expulsion could only be an exceptional, last-resort measure, fraught with risks. What the rules changes did was to legitimize LO's role as a means of exerting pressure on individual unions, or groups within them, that refused to go along with a market strategy agreed on by the rest of the unions. Broadly, as we have seen, the strategy adopted in the 1930s was to make the strike weapon an instrument of the labor movement as a whole, subordinating its use to the supposed requirements of the party's economic policy when it was in office, while holding the weapon in reserve against the time when this political alternative might not be available. Joint regulation of industrial relations with the unions' even more centralized employer counterpart was viewed as serving that strategy, and centralization of control over the strike weapon within LO and to that end within its component unions, was essential to implementing it.

The terms on which that joint regulation was to be carried out according to the Basic Agreement were essentially those arrived at in the December Compromise three decades earlier. The difference, besides the removal of much of the ambiguity on issues over which conflict had soon reopened, was that the terms were more likely to be observed because the mutually recognized distribution of power in both the state and market arenas left little room for change. Although SAF failed to incorporate its conception of managerial prerogatives explicitly into the Agreement itself, the restrictions on those prerogatives won by LO were very limited, leaving them largely intact.

SWEDEN'S 'HISTORICAL COMPROMISE' AND ITS POSTWAR
CONFIRMATION

In combination, the pattern of economic policy introduced by the Social Democratic government in the 1930s and the Basic Agreement defined the main features of the relationship among the state, labor and capital characterizing the Swedish model. Even if the effects of the economic policy were modest in practice, in principle it established the basic lines along which the Social Democrats were to try to manage Sweden's capitalist economy throughout most of the subsequent decades in which they remained in power. That was to use the state budget to shape the environment in which production decisions are made, while leaving the decisions themselves to managers whose authority and criteria for decision-making continued to be those derived from capitalist institutions. Similarly, the Basic Agreement defined the unions' role in shaping the environment in which production decisions are made, while the decisions themselves are left to the managers of the capitalist firms.

In referring to the crystallization of this relationship between labor and capital in the Swedish political economy as an 'historical compromise', Korpi emphasizes its character as an accommodation to the redistribution of power that had occurred. Wigforss had described it as a shift of 'political power' in favor of labor, while 'economic power' remained in the hands of capital. His view of the consequences of that shift are summarized by Korpi as follows:

> The need for co-operation arose from the fact that economic and political power had now become dissociated, and that within the foreseeable future neither the labor movement nor private capital could realistically hope to resolve the inherent conflict of interests between them through the surrender of the other party.[17]

Although it was not paralleled by a comparable agreement between the Social Democratic government and private business, despite initiatives Wigforss took toward one, the Basic Agreement between the peak organizations in the labor market reflected the wider recognition of the mutual veto power of labor and capital, and a belief that there was a common interest in managing conflict between them in such a way as to maximize the material outcome for both by facilitating economic recovery and growth – in other words, as Korpi puts it, to turn the conflict into a 'positive-sum game'. The scope for such an outcome made available by unutilized capacity and unemployed labor undoubtedly underpinned the adoption of this strategy of cooperation by making it easy to subordinate the issue of how the results of production would be distributed. Implicitly this is just what the Basic Agreement did, for it was designed only to assure industrial peace in the process through which distributive conflict continued, without addressing the distributive issue itself.

The limits of the shift in power toward the Social Democratic labor movement were forcefully demonstrated in the immediate postwar period. Even during the 1930s and especially toward the end of World War II, it was not expected either in the party or the unions that the simple form of Keynesian macroeconomic policy the party had introduced would suffice to eliminate unemployment, not to speak of achieving the wider social goals to which the movement had declared its commitment. Wigforss himself viewed the policy as only 'a step toward the citizens' control over their work'. The fact that unemployment had only been reduced by about half by the time the war broke out was understood as showing that more had to be done even on that score; the experience of controls used to run the wartime 'siege economy' was interpreted as demonstrating that more could indeed be done. To avoid a recurrence of unemployment and reduce it more than it had been, as well as to go on with the distributive and allocative reforms that had been postponed, it was concluded that the lessons of wartime planning had to be built on to meet peacetime needs. How that was to be done was sketched out in a *Postwar Program of Swedish Labor*, prepared by a joint party–LO committee in 1944.[18]

The Postwar Program had much in common with the programs for postwar planning and reforms worked out in many of the other countries that had actually been involved in the war. The state was assigned a 'leading part' in 'coordinating' the economy so as to assure full and efficient use of resources, primarily by the planning of investment, private as well as public. A 'national body representing public, private, and cooperative enterprise and the trade unions as well as Parliament and Government' was to guide the 'overall development of investment'. Within that framework its regional and sectoral development would be guided by similarly representative bodies. To make the planning effective the state's control over the supply of capital was to be extended by using the central bank, establishing a 'network of commercial banks under government control' and nationalization of the insurance industry. The composition and direction of foreign trade was to be subjected to extensive state supervision both through an export credit system and state trading in some commodities. Monopoly in production for domestic consumption was to be curbed by setting up competing state or non-profit firms where possible and by nationalization otherwise. The subordination of the economy to democratic control in these and other ways was to be extended to the 'internal sphere of workplaces' by enabling workers and their representatives 'to influence the technical and economic administration' of enterprise as well as 'general plans for any branch of industry, or for agriculture, trade and industry as a whole'.

The program clearly foreshadowed the turn that Social Democratic labor movement policy began to take in the late 1960s. In the immediate postwar years, however, the movement was forced to abandon its effort to extend the scope of not only state but also trade union action into the sphere of production decision-making that had been reserved to management under the terms of the interwar settlement. Initial steps taken toward implementing the program, through the establishment of government commissions to map out specific plans, assured the bourgeois parties' withdrawal from the four-party coalition that had governed during the war. It was organized business that took the lead in opposing the program, however, mounting an intense campaign against it in which it was attacked as leading to a centrally planned economy that would destroy freedom. The impact of this campaign was heightened by the onset of the Cold War, and particularly the communist coup in Czechoslovakia. At the same time inflation rather than the expected return of unemployment proved to be the most pressing economic policy problem. The liberal and conservative parties took up the 'anti-planning campaign' and inflicted substantial losses on the Social Democrats in the 1948 election.[19] In the preceding election the latter had already lost the absolute majority they had won for the first time in 1940. After the further setback in 1948, the Social Democrats felt compelled to reconstitute their alliance with the Farmers' Party, which came back into a second 'Red–Green' coalition government in

1951. It was only the continuation of this coalition that enabled the Social Democrats to stay in office despite yet more losses in 1952. Thus, the Social Democrats were driven back to dependence on the Farmers' Party for control of the state and a pattern of economic policy that excluded any state intervention in the microeconomic decision-making of Swedish capital. In other words, the terms of the 'historic compromise' were reaffirmed, reflecting the limits of the redistribution of power that had occurred in the 1930s.

It was within those limits that the Social Democratic labor movement was nevertheless faced with the necessity of adapting the pattern of policy developed in response to mass unemployment to the problems posed by the inflation that accompanied low unemployment. While the initiative for developing that pattern in the 1930s came from the SAP, the initiative for modifying it to cope with the problems of inflation came from LO. We turn to this in the next section.

Adaptation to Inflationary Growth

Although the *Postwar Program* assumed that 'widespread unemployment' would be 'the most serious problem confronting the postwar world', it anticipated the possibility of inflation at least in the years immediately after the war's end. 'Repeated economic crises resulting in unemployment and loss of output' were inherent in 'our present economic system', which is why it was necessary for 'society . . . to be reorganized' in a 'socialistic direction', along the lines laid out in the Program. However, there was also a danger of 'speculative inflationary price increases similar to those which occurred in 1919–20' which would 'increase the risk of a subsequent slump as was the case after the first World War'. To meet this danger the techniques for managing the siege economy had to be kept intact. In addition to price controls, these included a form of voluntary wage restraint based on annual agreements between LO and SAF.[20]

The wartime negotiation of wage rates by the peak organizations was viewed as an exceptional emergency measure, with wage bargaining returned to the national union level when the war ended. LO's representative council nevertheless continued to make recommendations concerning the desirable pattern of wage settlements in view of national economic conditions. By 1947 it was clear that inflationary pressures were increasing rather than subsiding, to which the government – again run by the Social Democrats alone – responded by trying to get producer groups to agree to stabilize prices and incomes as they had during the war. Initially LO only went so far as to recommend restraint to its affiliates, but accelerating prices accompanied by an 8 percent rise in manufacturing wages was viewed as requiring more effective measures. In 1948 LO responded to renewed government appeals by getting its affiliates to agree to freezing wage rates by prolonging existing contracts for another year (namely, 1949), on the condition 'that employers be forced by price control to meet cost increases out of current profit margins'.[21] This was repeated in 1949 for the next year, after the government increased subsidies in an effort to dampen the price effects of the large devaluation of the Swedish crown following that of the British pound. A further extension was rendered impossible by the worldwide inflationary surge unleashed by the Korean War, resulting in a wage explosion that just kept pace with prices. Accepting this as an inevitable 'one-time' adjustment to a higher price level, the government ventured to reestablish price stability by calling for renewed restraint, though not a freeze, in 1952. This time, however, LO was reluctant to go along.

It became evident that LO was now being called upon to restrain wages not as an exceptional measure to deal with inflationary pressures stemming from wartime shortages or the strains of transition to peacetime, but as a regular way of coping with inflationary pressures associated with more persistent full employment than had been expected. In other words, Sweden's Social Democratic government was trying to curb those inflationary pressures by the incomes policy approach that has been so widely resorted to in the postwar period. By this time, however, LO had come to regard the approach as a dangerous one for unions, and it urged the government to adopt an alternative it set forth in *Trade Unions and Full Employment*, a policy statement adopted at its 1951 Congress.

THE LO ALTERNATIVE TO WAGE RESTRAINT: THE STRUCTURAL CHANGE STRATEGY

The LO's alternative, referred to as the 'Rehn model', after one of the staff economists responsible for its formulation,[22] embodied a significant modification of the economic policy conception introduced by the Social Democrats in the 1930s. The basic issue it addressed was the one that dominated OECD area economic policy discussion throughout most of the postwar period: how to reconcile full employment with price stability. The prevailing, but not unanimous, view has of course been that the management of aggregate demand is not enough. Even if it sufficed to achieve full employment, contrary to the doubts expressed in the *Postwar Program*, the required level of demand was expected to bring inflation with it. Tight labor markets would generate a wage–price spiral sustained by the possibility of passing wage increases on in higher prices as long as the required level of demand was maintained. The only remedy offered by demand management alone was a reduction in demand that would increase unemployment. Hence, the notion of a 'tradeoff' between inflation and unemployment, analyzed in terms of the 'Phillips curve' for some years following Phillips's famous article in 1958. To improve the tradeoff demand management accordingly had to be supplemented by something else. The supplementary device most widely looked to was, of course, restraint – voluntary if possible or imposed if necessary – on the part of those in a position to raise their prices, particularly the unions whose bargaining power was strengthened by sustained full employment. LO agreed that something else was necessary but rejected wage restraint, at least as the principle way of trying to reconcile full employment and price stability. Its grounds for doing so point to important limits on the extent to which LO was willing to tailor its strategy in the market arena to the party's conception of economic policy.

Essentially two related objections to relying on wage restraint to avoid inflation are laid down: it is bound to fail and, in the process, undermine the trade union movement. No matter how much restraint the unions exercise in negotiating wage contracts, wages will not be kept from rising because wage drift cannot be prevented. As long as there is sufficient demand, employers will compete for labor by bidding up wages. The amount of drift is likely to be all the greater the more that wage claims are held back. At the same time the incidence of wage drift is bound to be uneven, precipitating efforts to restore relative earnings. This will demonstrate to their members that the unions have been turned into 'bodies for ... adapting wages policy to the general economic policy' instead of performing their 'main task of getting increased wages for their members'. The threat this poses to the unions' survival is aggravated by the 'distrust' that 'arises between groups enjoying wage-drifting' and those who do not, creating as well the 'risk of discord between the different unions'. This 'will inevitably prove disastrous, in the long run, to trade union solidarity'.

> Finally, the authority of the Confederation of Trade Unions is reduced both vis-à-vis the national unions and ... the community, as it has shown itself incapable of 'managing' its wages policy. In the long run, the strain may become overwhelming and undermine the position of the trade union movement. Bearing this in mind, the trade union movement should make it perfectly clear that it cannot and should not accept any such unconditional responsibility for the preservation of national economic stability.[23]

This warning against the danger to organizational cohesion, and even survival, if unions should take on the role of 'adapting wages policy' to 'general economic policy' marks a clear shift of emphasis compared with the way the relationship between strategies in market and state arenas was viewed in the 1930s. Then greater trade union solidarity was called for to avoid undermining economic policy; now the modification of economic policy was being called for to avoid undermining trade union solidarity. This, as we shall see, is an emphasis that persists, conditioning union responses to more recent economic problems as well as those of the early postwar period. The possibility that the unions could accept some responsibility for stability if it is not 'unconditional' is, nevertheless, left open in the 1951 statement. The main task to which it is addressed is spelling out what an acceptable division of responsibilities might be.

LO's alternative to the government's call for restraint was based on an analysis focussing on differences in profitability among firms and sectors and fragmentation of the labor market into partially separate submarkets. From this, the conclusion is drawn that the full-employment goal has to be disaggregated, relying on 'general' fiscal policy to maintain full employment in most of the economy and 'selective' manpower policy in the remainder. While these two kinds of policy are carried out by the government, wage bargaining should be coordinated by LO in accordance with a 'solidaristic' wage policy, understood as equal pay for equal work regardless of a firm's profitability, or ability to pay. The interaction of government and union policies is expected to make non-inflationary full employment possible in the following way.

First, fiscal policy would be more restrictive than in the early postwar years, keeping demand high enough to assure full employment in most of the economy but not in the least profitable activities. Part of the increased restrictiveness would be achieved through the introduction of indirect, that is, sales, taxation. This is expected to diminish the scope for price increases to compensate for increased wage costs, shifting the burden of restraining wages back to employers. The combined effect of such fiscal policy and continued wage pressure would be a squeeze on profits. Because wage pressures would be shaped on the basis of a solidaristic wage policy, however, the profits squeeze would have a differential effect on firms, hitting them harder the less profitable they are. The least profitable would consequently be forced to become more efficient or shut down, while the most profitable ones would be encouraged to expand.

Workers in the least-profitable firms would consequently be threatened with unemployment. However, instead of meeting that threat by raising demand generally – thereby relieving inefficient firms of the need to modernize or shut down while increasing inflationary pressures where labor markets were already tight – it was to be done primarily by selective measures directed specifically to the workers involved. These would be designed principally to enable them to transfer to new jobs in the expanding firms, through the provision of retraining, information and financial support during the transition process. Under circumstances where this does not suffice to provide protection against unemployment, temporary subsidies would be necessary to prolong existing employment until alternatives become available as well as to create new jobs in the public sector. In this way a process of structural change in industry would be facilitated, increasing the proportion of efficient, low-cost activities capable of paying standard rates without putting increased pressure on prices. At the same time manpower policy would assure that the costs of structural change would be shifted from the workers involved to the society as a whole. Thus, non-inflationary full employment would be accomplished primarily through a profits squeeze that accelerated structural change rather than an attempt, inevitably futile, to repress inflation by direct restraint of wages and prices.

In addition, the whole approach required the coordination of wage bargaining on the basis of solidaristic wage policy by LO. LO could do so only in so far as the government implemented the prescribed fiscal and manpower policies. Assuming those conditions are met, solidaristic wage policy would perform two functions. One has already been indicated. That is to bring about the differential profit squeeze designed to accelerate structural change by compelling firms to pay standard rates regardless of their capacity to do so. The other embodies an additional contribution unions can make to maintaining non-inflationary full employment once it is achieved by the other measures. That is to prevent the kind of interunion wage rivalry that can act as an autonomous source of inflationary pressure, generating a wage–wage spiral that would disturb the non-inflationary full employment. Under the specified conditions, then, unions would be able to accept a significant but circumscribed responsibility for seeing that their 'wages policy is coordinated with the general economic policy'.[24]

What is not clear from this formulation is the extent to which the union responsibility involves wage restraint in the sense of forgoing increases that could otherwise be got. This would seem to depend on the levels at which the standard rates for equivalent jobs are set, and hence the degree to which profits are squeezed on average. The ambiguity of the Rehn model in this connection bears on an issue that is fundamental in principle and has proven to be crucial in practice. The issue is whether profits would be squeezed so hard that they would be too low to elicit the level of investment required to maintain full employment over the long run.

In itself, solidaristic wage policy need not necessarily result in insufficient profits from that point of view. While it implies that profits are squeezed most in the least profitable firms, it also implies that profits are squeezed least in the most profitable firms. Standard rates could conceivably be set at levels that would leave the more profitable firms with all the profits needed to induce and finance enough investment to make up for the decline of the less-profitable firms. There are repeated references to the necessity of a 'wage increase which agrees, in the long run, with the increase in productivity', and the like.[25] But this is part of the argument for the whole combination of policies designed to make a 'stable wage trend' possible rather than for wage restraint as such. Moreover, the main thrust of the argument suggests that the basis for setting the standard rates is not the average level of profits needed to elicit the investment needed in an economy undergoing the accelerated structural change on which the whole approach is predicated. Instead, the basis seems to be the average level of wages needed to keep wage drift low enough for LO to retain its affiliates' support for its coordination of wage bargaining.

LO's centralization following the Basic Agreement did not go so far as to enable it to impose a wage policy on its affiliates, so their agreement is essential to the coordination by which interunion wage rivalry is to be avoided. Thus, the possibility of a 'stable wage trend' is viewed as contingent on the unions' ability 'to agree on a joint policy'. The joint policy on which they are expected to be able to agree, solidaristic wage policy, does imply at least some restraint in so far as the resulting contracts prevent workers in the most profitable firms from getting more than the standard rates, even though the firms can pay more. However, those workers might get it anyway through wage drift, the firms paying what they can to get and keep the workers they need. This is precisely what supposedly undermines support for the unions both by workers who benefit from drift and by those who do not, making it dangerous for unions to agree to solidaristic wage policy if standard rates are set so low that a lot of drift occurs. Accordingly, 'the profits made by firms' must not 'allow for much wage-drifting'.[26] This seems to imply that in order for LO to retain its affiliates' support for coordinated wage bargaining profits have to be squeezed hard enough to keep drift so low that there is not much need for restraint, even in the most profitable firms. If so, the average level of profits may indeed be too low for sufficient growth of expanding firms to offset the contraction of declining firms.

While this issue was not addressed in the 1951 LO statement, Rehn himself brought it up in an earlier article. He anticipated that the squeeze on profits integral to the structural change approach would result in a decline in business savings. As he saw it, the problem was one of compensating for this decline in savings. 'Profits, the source of desperately needed investment', could not be lowered 'without securing another source of capital accumulation'.[27] The solution he offered was an increase in public sector savings. In principle the means for accomplishing this was already built into the model by the restrictive fiscal policy needed to press profits down against wages. While profits were being squeezed, budget surpluses would be generated, resulting in a shift of savings from business to the public sector. To assure a sufficient growth of public sector savings, however, he thought it advisable to insulate it from short-term budgetary policy by specific institutional arrangements. Building the accumulation of a surplus into the reform of the national pension system already being discussed in the early postwar period seemed to him a good way to do it.[28] This, as we shall see, is precisely what happened.

Rehn summed up his argument as follows:

Full employment implies a redistribution of economic power in favor of the working classes, in particular trade union members. They must profit from this increased power but at the same time labor must assume the responsibility for both stability and progress by allowing the State to tax away that part of the wage increments which were previously the basis of saving and investment by the private owners of industry.

The members of trade unions cannot be expected to accept private capitalists as the owners of all the new capital. Thus, if we wish to avoid inflationary wage increases, the increase of the national wealth must be to a rather large extent the result of collective saving done by the masses on the basis of high wages and high taxes.[29]

This solution to the problem of investment has been understood as an integral part of the Rehn model and was reflected in subsequent LO discussion explicitly concerned with the problem. What remains unexamined in the Rehn model, as originally formulated, is the issue of whether the compensatory increase in collective savings can be effectively channeled into investment. The problem of investment is evidently conceived as one arising at the savings end of the savings–investment process, so that it is essentially a matter of the aggregate supply of capital. The important thing from this macroeconomic, and quintessentially Keynesian, perspective is that a sufficient supply of savings is assured. If that is done, and the demand for output is sufficient, investment would take care of itself: the composition of investment would be guided by the differential profitability that solidaristic wage policy would preserve, although at a lower level of average profitability. This assumes not only that sufficient collective savings can be accumulated to maintain or, if necessary, increase the aggregate supply of savings, but also that it will be available in forms that capitalist firms will regard as appropriate for financing investment, and that the firms will go on investing at the required rate despite the curtailed profits on which the need for collective savings is predicated.

That the validity of these assumptions is by no means self-evident was already pointed out in the initial discussion of the Rehn model.[30] Even if investment was 'desperately needed' in principle, however, meeting the need no longer seemed to pose any problem in practice in the later 1950s and early 1960s, for a vigorous boom in industrial investment took place in those years. It was only in the latter half of the 1960s, as we shall see, that investment came to be seen as problematical again, precipitating efforts to deal more explicitly with the issue raised by the squeeze on profits prescribed by the Rehn model.

THE REHN MODEL AND KEYNESIAN POLICY

Looking back recently at the policy adopted by LO in 1951 Rehn recalls it as a 'conscious break with the oversimplified form of Keynesianism' that relied solely on managing aggregate demand. Acknowledging its effectiveness when it is a matter of reducing mass unemployment, he sees demand management alone as counterproductive when it is a matter of going the rest of the way to 'real full employment' and maintaining it. The closer to full employment an economy gets, the more necessary it is to turn to methods of reducing the residual unemployment that do not have demand-stimulating multiplier-effects – that is, which increase employment selectively while the growth of aggregate demand is restricted.[31] While such a combination of demand management with selective manpower policy certainly goes beyond the form of Keynesian policy introduced in the 1930s, it does not mark a break with Keynesian policy more broadly conceived.

As abundantly indicated by the extensive discussion in which the 'economics of Keynes' has been distinguished from the kind of 'Keynesian economics' identified simply with Keynes's prescription for the specific problems of the Depression, the latter is indeed an oversimplified form of Keynesianism or, as Joan Robinson put it, 'bastard Keynesianism'.[32] The Depression prescription evidently flows from a more general judgement that, left to itself, capitalism cannot be expected to provide full employment. This, as the various 'post-Keynesians' emphasize, is central to Keynes's own break with what he referred to as the 'classical position'. It is in order to counteract capitalism's tendency to produce unemployment that the state's intervention is necessary. That the state should have to intervene in different ways not only during different phases of the business cycle, but also at different stages in the development of capitalist economies, is to be expected from this point of view.

Thus, to insist that maintaining full employment calls for a policy mix different from, and more complex than, that required to overcome mass unemployment, as LO's economists did, seems quite consistent with a legitimate Keynesianism. The Rehn model mix of demand management and manpower policy may, thus, be viewed as a second type or phase of Keynesian policy, reflecting the implications of Keynes's basic position under postwar conditions very different from the interwar situation in which Keynesian policy was initially developed. While Keynes was primarily concerned with spelling out the implications of his position for the immediate problems of the 1930s, he evidently saw that they went considerably further under the quite different conditions of more or less continuous full employment. If those conditions persisted over the long run, he anticipated that 'a somewhat comprehensive socialization of investment will prove the only means of securing an approximation of full employment'.[33] This may be viewed as yet a third type or phase in the development of Keynesian policy. Thus, the collectivization of savings regarded as eventually necessary according to the Rehn model would seem to take it beyond the second and toward this third phase.

The limits to the scope of state action called for by the Rehn model are also those characterizing Keynesian policy. For Keynes, the 'traditional functions of government' had to be extended only to bring aggregate investment to the level required for full employment but not to determine the composition of investment. Even when he spoke of the socialization of investment, it was the supply of capital not its allocation to which he was referring. He saw 'no reasons to suppose that the existing system seriously misemploys the factors of production which are in use ... It is in determining the volume, not the direction, of actual employment that the existing system has broken down'.

> If our central controls succeed in establishing an aggregate volume of production corresponding to full employment ... the classical theory comes into its own again ... then there is no objection to be raised against the classical analysis of the manner in which private self-interest will determine what in particular will be produced, in what proportions the factors of production will be combined to produce it, and how the value of the final product will be distributed between them.

In short, it is only necessary to establish 'the environment which the free play of economic forces requires if it is to realize the full potentialities of production'.[34]

As we have seen, this was essentially the division of functions embodied in the interwar settlement between Swedish labor and capital that was reaffirmed in the early postwar years. By and large the Rehn model did not violate the terms of that settlement. Unlike the Postwar Program, it did not involve any intervention in the microeconomic decisionmaking of capitalist firms nor any effort to influence them in accordance with any planning for sectoral development or the like. On the contrary, the structural change on which it relied was one shaped by entirely autonomous managerial responses to market forces – or whatever else enters into their decisions. It is those decisions that alter the composition of demand for labor, with manpower policy simply easing the adaptation of the labor supply to those changes in demand, increasing both the efficiency and acceptability of structural change. While manpower policy accordingly modifies the preceding pattern of policy by adding an important element of disaggregation or selectivity to the management of aggregate demand, this selectivity is applied to the labor market but not the capital market.

To be sure, the whole policy mix is designed to exert considerable influence on the market forces to which the firms respond. The squeeze on profits and its particular distribution among firms depend on using both fiscal and wage policy in specific ways, each of which involves some modification of the interwar pattern. A substantial increase in the public sector share of GNP is implied by the expansion of both manpower policy and conventional welfare state expenditures while simultaneously achieving budget surpluses that restrict aggregate demand growth and offset the decline in business saving. The latter, in turn, implies at least a partial shift of the savings end of the savings–investment process from capitalist firms to the state, thereby attenuating a central element of the way in which the process is organized by capitalist institutions. This may well be an aspect of the Rehn model that should be regarded as transcending the limits embodied in the settlement. Still, the extension of the state's role on the supply side of the capital market is not conceived as carrying with it any intervention in the allocation of capital within the private industrial sector. Within the latter the investment end of the process is left to capitalist firms as before. Thus, despite the modifications it made in the pattern of policy on which the interwar settlement was built, the Rehn model leaves undisturbed the boundaries of state, and also union, action that are fundamental to that settlement: state and union action are confined to the environment within which managerial decisions are made – neither encroaches on managerial prerogatives at any level of the firm, from overall business strategy to the operation of individual workplaces.

If that is the case, could the political basis for implementing the initial form of Keynesian policy in the 1930s, reinstated with the formation of the second Social Democratic–Farmers coalition in 1951, suffice for implementing the modified form of Keynesian policy proposed as well? As to be expected in a union policy document of this sort, *Trade Unions and Full Employment* does not address this question of political strategy. That a Social Democratic government is a necessary condition for carrying out the proposed policy is apparently taken for granted. A brief comment implies that a different policy would be likely if 'a bourgeois government comes to power', making it necessary for the unions to pursue a different market strategy to defend the 'interests of the working class'.[35]

While a Social Democratic government might indeed be a necessary condition, it was evidently not a sufficient one. In the early 1950s the party leadership, particularly Per Edvin Sköld, who succeeded Wigforss as Finance Minister, did not accept LO's position.[36] Even if it had, however, it could not have implemented it at the time, for the Farmers' Party on which it was dependent opposed some of the budgetary policies essential to LO's approach. For that approach to be implemented, then, the SAP's leadership had to be won over to it, and the SAP's control of the state had to be established on a political basis different from the one it had relied on for much of the time since 1932. In addition to these conditions for performing the tasks assigned to the state by the Rehn model, the conditions for performing the task assigned to the unions had to be met as well. At the time of the 1951 Congress it was by no means clear how solidaristic wage policy could be translated into a negotiating strategy on the basis of which LO could actually coordinate its affiliates' wage bargaining. By the end of the decade, however, these conditions for implementing the prescription for non-inflationary full employment to which LO was committed, at least formally, had been largely met. How this happened and LO's often decisive role in making it happen is reviewed in the next section.

CONDITIONS FOR IMPLEMENTATION: THE MARKET ARENA

The ambiguity in LO's 1951 policy statement concerning the extent to which unions can take on responsibility for wage restraint was paralleled by the apparent inconsistency of LO's responses to the government's recurrent pleas for restraint in the following years. When the government called for a 3 percent limit to contractual increases in 1952 as part of an effort to restore price stability following the 'one-time' adjustment to the Korean War inflation, LO's representative council declared such a low increase 'out of the question' in view of the high levels of prices, profits and demand for labor that prevailed. Still, it did urge the member-unions to exercise as much restraint as possible, providing they got a price-index clause to protect real wages if inflation rose more than anticipated.[37] This demand precipitated a turn of events that had important long-range consequences for Sweden's wage-determination system, including LO's capacity to coordinate its affiliates' wage bargaining.

The employers' confederation rejected any price indexing of wages, unless it was part of an overall agreement made with LO rather than separate agreements negotiated with the individual unions, on the ground that the unions' efforts to keep abreast of one another were likely to push wages up. SAF's power over its own affiliates was sufficient to make it difficult if not impossible for the unions to win the index clauses in individual negotiations. Thus, it was SAF that compelled the unions, or most of them, to agree to central negotiations by LO in order to get the real wage protection they wanted.[38] The resulting agreement was not itself a binding wage contract, as defined by Swedish labor law, but a 'frame agreement', setting forth the general pattern of wage changes. It was still up to the individual unions to accept it and then negotiate the actual wage contracts with their employer counterparts. As it turned out, these features of the first peacetime wage agreement between LO and SAF defined the basic form of centralized wage bargaining that became a regular part of Sweden's wage-determination system. At the time, however, the central agreement was viewed as an exceptional occurrence, and the procedure was not used again until 1956. In the interim LO wage policy went through further fluctuations.

At the beginning of the 1953 wage round LO conceded that there was very little scope for a general wage increase and recommended that its affiliates, negotiating separately again, should concentrate on getting improvements for relatively disadvantaged workers. This recommendation was made in the context of a downturn that reduced market pressures on wages, and of a growing squeeze on the profits of firms exposed to international competition that increased their resistance to wage increases. Under these conditions, of course, it did not take much restraint by the unions to keep wage increases low. In contrast LO took no position whatever on the wage policy its affiliates should follow during the recovery in 1954.[39] By 1955 inflationary pressures had reappeared, to which the Finance Minister reacted by once more calling for restraint. This was categorically rejected by Axel Strand, LO's chairman, in a parliamentary speech sharply attacking the government for carrying out an excessively expansive economic policy and then trying to shift the burden of coping with its consequences onto the unions, thereby arguing much along the lines of the 1951 statement.[40] This proved to be something of a turning-point.

Viewing the new flare-up of conflict between party and unions over such an important issue as extremely dangerous from a political standpoint, Tage Erlander, the Prime Minister and party leader, called a conference to iron out the differences between them. Erlander took the occasion to declare his own conversion to the LO position, particularly the selective manpower policy which he understood to be the heart of it. While Sköld, the Finance Minister, remained unconvinced, his retirement soon after led to his replacement by Gunnar Sträng who, whether because he had been a union official or whatever, was more open to the LO argument. Yet while acknowledging the government's primary responsibility for economic stability, he too was to repeatedly emphasize the importance of restraint by the unions in order to avoid disrupting stability and, particularly, to meet what he regarded as an increasing need for investment to maintain international competitiveness.[41] That the SAP leadership was ever completely won over to the Rehn model is doubtful.

The extent to which the LO leadership believed in the organization's own declared position is also a bit doubtful. By the beginning of the 1956 wage round the leadership had already accepted anew the necessity of restraint on the ground of Swedish industry's ostensibly worsened cost position relative to its international competitors. At the same time, restraint was regarded as impossible unless interunion wage rivalry could be avoided through the device of central negotiations. Accordingly, and at LO's initiative this time, a central agreement was again negotiated in 1956.

SAF certainly regarded the central negotiations as desirable, although it resisted the extra increases for lower-paid workers that LO demanded. Then and subsequently, however, LO had to press for a wage package including relatively greater increases for lower-paid workers in order to retain support for its conduct of central negotiations among unions with a large proportion of such workers. Devising a combination of wage demands on which all its affiliates could agree, and which could be satisfied sufficiently to preserve the credibility of its wage policy, proved to be a persistent problem for LO. Devising a wage package on which TCO as well as LO unions could agree to bargain jointly posed an even more difficult, and for a long time insuperable, problem. Yet if the central negotiations were to serve as a mechanism for inhibiting wage rivalry between white-collar and blue-collar unions, as well as among the latter, the negotiations had to include the white-collar unions too. An attempt to do so was made in 1956. TCO participated in the negotiations, but this was the last as well as the first time it did so. Although TCO did not accept LO's low-wage formula, its affiliates were still dissatisfied with the way it handled the negotiations and resolved to proceed on their own in the future. As their rapid growth continued wage competition between them and LO became an increasingly important limitation on the effectiveness of the central negotiations as a mechanism for avoiding interunion wage competition.[42]

There was considerable dissatisfaction with the 1956 agreement among LO unions as well, leading to a decision to go into the 1957 round separately. But now SAF again succeeded in forcing them into central negotiations, which culminated in a two-year agreement. The LO unions did not even attempt to bargain separately in 1959, and in 1960 it was taken for granted that the wage round should begin with central negotiations.[43] Thus, the central negotiations had by then become an established part of the wage-determination system, the 1956 agreement turning out to be the first of a series unbroken down to the present.

It must be stressed that the central negotiations are only part of the system. Individual unions and their employer counterparts continue to negotiate the actual wage contracts, even though their parameters are set in the central agreements. In addition, local bargaining, collective and also individual, continues to play an important part in the system, contributing to the wage draft that has on average accounted for about half of the total annual increase in earnings. Thus, the system is not as centralized as the central negotiations – and the attention typically concentrated on them – might suggest.[44] This means that the limitations on the extent to which the unions, and particularly the central confederation, can exercise restraint without endangering their organizational cohesion, so strongly emphasized in LO's 1951 statement, have remained as compelling since the introduction of central negotiations as before. This will be apparent in connection with more recent developments.

CONDITIONS FOR IMPLEMENTATION: THE STATE ARENA

Whatever uncertainty there may be about how much the LO leadership actually believed in the pattern of policy set forth in the 1951 statement, there was still no way it could be implemented until the SAP was not only willing, but also able, to implement it. In order for it to do so it had to strengthen its parliamentary position sufficiently to govern alone again. What made this possible was not a new initiative in economic policy as in the 1930s, but a major extension of the welfare state, the introduction of a new pension scheme. At the same time, the scheme was in fact designed to serve as an instrument for the public sector savings which was called for by the Rehn model. And in both the formulation of the scheme and the political struggle to enact it LO was the major driving-force.

As enacted in 1959, the pension reform superimposed a universal, compulsory, inflation-indexed, earnings-related supplementary pension, financed by employer contributions – that is, a payroll tax – on a system of universal, flat-rate pensions, financed out of general taxation, that had been established in 1947. In combination with the flat-rate pension the supplementary pension was designed to provide retirement income equivalent to two-thirds of an individual's highest fifteen-year average income from earnings. A national pension fund referred to as the AP fund (*Almänna Pensionsfonden*) was set up to administer the new system, accumulating a large surplus during a twenty-year transition period while the system was going into effect, and investing that surplus in the bond market. It was this last feature that was most opposed by business and financial interests, which attacked it as an attempt to take over control of the capital market.[45]

The pension reform concluded a campaign of more than two decades by LO, spearheaded as in so many other instances by the metalworkers' union. Civil servants, private sector executives and growing numbers of white-collar workers already had considerable income security in old age, while most blue-collar workers had little or none at all beyond the flat-rate state pension. Within LO pressure built up to eliminate this inequality, either by collective bargaining or legislation, but with increasing conviction that it had to be the latter. Legislation came to be seen as the only way to provide pensions on the same terms for all workers at the same time, not just those with sufficiently strong bargaining power and financially solid employers. In addition, it came to be viewed as the only way to provide them consistently with other objectives that assumed increasing importance: inflation-proofing, labor mobility and the accumulation of a large surplus.[46]

Opting for the legislative route was characteristic of the LO's strategic outlook. To the extent that the collective bargaining route made pension provision contingent on differentiated market positions it was potentially divisive, fostering particularistic rather than solidaristic orientations, undermining the credibility of LO's claim to represent the working class as a whole and threatening its organizational cohesion. The decisive advantage of legislation was its potential for working in the opposite direction in all these respects.

In this instance as in any other, however, the availability of the political alternative to market action was contingent on whether the SAP was able and willing to provide it. Precisely because its control of the state had become precarious, the party was hesitant to do so. A commitment to pension reform along the lines LO proposed was certain to make the Farmers' Party withdraw from the coalition on which the SAP had come to depend again, for the Farmers' Party opposed any kind of compulsory scheme. The other two bourgeois parties were not only opposed to LO's approach, but also expected its adoption by the SAP to give them just the issue they needed to finally drive it out of office. This expectation rested on the conviction that LO's proposal would be seen as a threat to the pension rights many white-collar workers already had, so that the pension issue would draw them into a majority that would bring a bourgeois government into office.[47]

On the other hand, white-collar workers without pension rights any better than those of blue-collar workers stood to gain from the LO proposal. If adoption of the proposal enabled the SAP to mobilize those white-collar workers' support, while the others who already had adequate pensions could be assured they had nothing to lose, the SAP might be able to win a sufficient share of the white-collar vote to dispense with Farmers' Party parliamentary support and govern alone. This would not only make it possible to resolve the immediate pension issue to LO's satisfaction. In addition, it promised to contribute toward solving the long-term political problem confronting the party as a result of the changes in social structure, typical of advanced industrial societies, that were simultaneously eroding the social base of the Farmers' Party and increasing the proportion of white-collar workers in the population relative to the blue-collar workers comprising the SAP's core constituency. The resulting decline in the Farmers' Party's strength made its support a waning asset anyway. In the absence of any alternative coalition partner the SAP could retain control of the state only on the basis of increased electoral support, for which a larger margin of white-collar support was essential.

The party leadership actually had little confidence that this would, in fact, happen if it adopted LO's pension-reform approach. Still, it felt compelled to go ahead with it. The pressure from LO was becoming intense and a failure to push for the kind of reform that LO demanded would severely strain the relationship between it and the party. Moreover, the days of the Red–Green coalition were plainly numbered. Both partners concluded from their losses in the 1956 election that they suffered from their association with each other. And within the Farmers' Party there was a strong current bent on assuring its survival by establishing a new political profile, distinguishing it more clearly from the Social Democrats, as well as the other bourgeois parties, in order to expand its appeal beyond its traditional constituency. To this end withdrawal from the coalition was deemed necessary. While the Social Democrats' decision on the pension issue provided the occasion, another would presumably have been found in its absence. At the same time, this end would not be served by joining with the other two bourgeois parties, either in a common position on the pension issue or in forming a government. Thus, the SAP was spared a unification of the opposition which, for the moment, it could not have withstood. Once out of the coalition, the Farmers' Party changed its name to Center Party and began moving toward what proved to be a highly successful survival strategy of articulating the growing protest against environmental destruction, nuclear energy and the concomitants of industrial growth generally.[48]

Under the circumstances the distribution of white-collar workers' attitudes to pension reform assumed pivotal importance for the course of Swedish politics. This, in turn, rendered crucial the position on the issue taken by TCO, the confederation of white-collar unions. Still only a quarter the size of LO at the time, TCO was growing rapidly, nearly doubling its membership in the dozen years since the merger that brought it into being in 1944. The Social Democratic labor movement played an important part in launching white-collar unionization, especially in the private sector, opening the way for it with the 1936 legislation and providing organizational aid in the early stages. Nevertheless, as pointed out at the outset, TCO is not part of the Social Democratic labor movement. Non-partisanship was regarded as essential to recruitment of white-collar workers, for many of whom the distinctions between themselves and blue-collar workers, in terms of political identification along with income and status, remained important. Accordingly linked to none of the parties, TCO has been the target of intense activity by all of them, subjecting the organization to severe internal conflict among supporters of the different parties whenever its position on highly partisan issues was at stake. In such situations the only way to keep the organization from being torn apart was to take no position at all, which was what happened on the pension issue.[49]

During the course of its preparation the Social Democrats' pension Bill underwent changes aimed at winning TCO support. Besides offering supplementary pensions to TCO members who did not have them, the relationship of benefits to earnings was designed to be attractive to members who did have them, even on highly generous terms. A temporary 'opting-out' period was also offered for those who still believed they would lose by inclusion in the new state scheme. LO consented to such tactical concessions as long as the basic principles of its approach were retained. A proposal embodying this combination of principles and concessions was reported out of a commission consisting of party and interest-group representatives according to standard Swedish procedure. Although the TCO representative joined with the LO and SAP representatives in supporting it, while all the others opposed it, TCO itself did not endorse it. All that the Social Democrats and LO succeeded in getting was TCO's neutrality instead of opposition, for which some TCO union leaders close to the liberal and conservative parties had strenuously pressed.[50] This may nevertheless have been enough to tip the scales against the liberal and conservative parties' hopes of riding back into power on a wave of white-collar opposition to the Social Democratic pension scheme.

The electoral impact of the pension issue was tested on several occasions. A 1957 referendum yielded ambiguous results. However, a special election held in 1958, when the then minority Social Democratic government dissolved the Second Chamber after its pension Bill was defeated, resulted in a reversal of the SAP's steady decline since its 1940 peak. While this indicated that the pension issue was helping the Social Democrats, it did not resolve the issue. The net result of a Social Democratic gain of five seats while the communists lost one was a majority of one over the three bourgeois parties, but this left the two blocs in a deadlock because the Social Democratic speaker could not vote. It was broken, permitting the pension Bill to pass, only because a liberal MP who belonged to LO decided to abstain.[51] Enacted under these circumstances, the pension reform continued to be opposed by the bourgeois parties which called for its repeal or modification during the 1960 election campaign. The Social Democrats fought the campaign by subsuming the pension issue, along with the reintroduction of a sales tax, within the larger one of expanding or contracting the welfare state, or 'strong society', which the conservatives conveniently said they would roll back. Clearly ratifying the narrow parliamentary decision, the election resulted in a one-seat SAP majority over the bourgeois parties' combined total and, together with the communists, an overall socialist majority.[52]

Thus, the pension issue enabled the SAP to shift the basis of its control of the state from a parliamentary coalition to an electoral constituency large enough for it to govern alone. However, the initial Social Democratic labor movement attempt to forge a 'wage-earners (*löntagare*) front' cutting across the division between blue-collar workers (*arbetare*) and white-collar workers (*tjänstemän*), institutionalized by their organization in separate union confederations, was only marginally successful. The SAP's electoral gains were due as much to increased mobilization of its own blue-collar core constituency as to the addition of white-collar workers to its constituency. To be sure, there was a significant growth in the Social Democratic share of white-collar votes from 32 to 39 percent between the 1956 and 1960 elections, exceeding the increase in the share of the blue-collar vote from 73 to 78 percent. But the increase in the proportion of blue-collar support came out of a substantially larger increase in blue-collar turnout, which rose from 80 to 87 percent over the two elections, while white-collar turnout rose only from 86 to 88 percent.[53] This growth in blue-collar support was apparently due, above all, to the massive extent to which the LO unions threw their organizational resources behind pension reform. In Erlander's judgement the bourgeois strategists' biggest mistake was their failure to anticipate how the pension struggle 'would weld together the trade union and political labor movement as never before'. To him, it was 'an incredible experience to witness all over the country the enthusiasm and will to win that suffused the trade union people's efforts. The pension struggle was their struggle'.[54]

While the Social Democrats succeeded in defining the issues involved in the political battles over the pension scheme and reintroduction of indirect taxation in terms of expanding the welfare state, both measures established instruments of the kind needed to carry out the economic strategy embodied in LO's 1951 policy statement. While those battles were going on, yet another of the needed instruments, manpower policy, was also put into operation, although with much less controversy.

The mechanism for manpower policy was already in existence in the form of a Labor Market Board, or AMS (*Arbetsmarknadsstyrelsen*), set up in 1948. A comprehensive reorganization and expansion of manpower policy was begun in 1957, however. A new director, thoroughly committed to LO's conception of its function, was appointed to AMS. The funds at its disposal were vastly increased, nearly quadrupling in real terms during the four years 1957–60, after increasing only two and a half times over the preceding eighteen years. Although most of the accelerated expansion of its funds took place after the Farmers' Party withdrew from the coalition government in 1957, the process began while the coalition was still in office. What made the expansion uncontroversial, for some time after the break-up of the coalition as well as before, was that a recession was underway, so that expansion of AMS expenditures resembled its traditional function of alleviating cyclical unemployment. This pre-supposed a reduction in expenditures when the recession was over. Some reduction did occur in 1961 but only to a level still more than twice as high as prior to the recession, and this evoked considerable opposition from the bourgeois parties.[55] By this time, however, the Social Democratic government had the political power to proceed despite the opposition. What it did do is set up a commission of inquiry on manpower policy, which it used to turn much of the opposition into support.[56] It is tempting to view this as testimony to the consistency of at least this component of the Rehn model with the terms of the historical compromise. In contrast, the pension fund's rapid growth became the target for renewed conservative attack in the 1960s, pointing again to the more ambiguous role of collective savings in Sweden's political economy.

Together with the conventional apparatus of fiscal policy, the institutional changes made in the later 1950s substantially increased the capacity of both state and unions to perform the functions assigned to them by the Rehn model. This, of course, did not necessarily mean that the available instruments would be used to perform those functions or, if the attempt were made, it would prove effective. During the early 1960s, however, both the government and LO unions pursued policies that seemed to approximate the Rehn model increasingly, and the results seemed to confirm its efficacy. Thus, the shifts in fiscal policy from demand stimulus to restriction, followed by renewed stimulus as recessionary tendencies reappeared in the years around the turn of the decade, were viewed by economists as notably well timed.[57] Manpower policy, as we have seen, underwent a major expansion, continuing after a brief slowdown. There was as yet no indication that LO's efforts to implement its solidaristic wage policy were reducing the gap between low- and high-wage workers, but the possibility that it kept the gap from growing was acknowledged. The consensus at LO's 1961 Congress was that it was necessary to try harder, without any serious doubt as to coordinated bargaining itself.[58]

In general, the discussion at the Congress displayed a considerable sense of accomplishment by both the Social Democratic government and the unions. Nevertheless, a report to the Congress on *Coordinated Industrial Policy* warned of increasing difficulty in matching that accomplishment in the future.[59] This report was not a policy statement formally adopted by LO. On the other hand, it sets forth the rationale for LO's exceptional willingness to accept structural change more comprehensively and systematically than any other confederation document, including the 1951 policy statement that made structural change the key to non-inflationary full employment. At the same time, the 1961 report foreshadows some of LO's responses to the difficulties it later encountered, and which the report anticipated with considerable accuracy. Accordingly, a brief review of the report's main themes can serve to sum up the perspective on the economy that prevailed within LO during much of the earlier postwar period as well as to provide a look ahead toward the kind of modifications made in the effort to adapt that view to changing conditions.

Part 3

The Erosion of the Swedish Model

Prospective Problems and Potential Solutions

Sweden's dependence on its position in the international economy was generally taken for granted as much in union as other discussion of economic policy, but *Coordinated Industrial Policy* makes it more explicit and central than ever, for it proceeds on the premiss that the requirements of adaptation to the international economy will become more pressing than in the past. In his address to the 1961 Congress Rudolf Meidner, chairman of the committee that prepared the report, warned that the 'very favorable external conditions for the Swedish economy prevailing in the preceding postwar period' can no longer be counted on: 'For a little country like Sweden with its limited domestic market and significant export dependence to maintain its rate of progress, it will in all certainty require greater exertion, more intensive investment activity, and a more rational utilization of our resources.'[60]

Several sources of increasing international competition are cited. One is economic integration within the two European trading blocs: EFTA, of which Sweden was a member at the time, and the EEC, with which Sweden was expected to have some form of association short of membership. Another is competition in and from the newly industrializing 'poor countries'. While the latter promise growing markets, stiff competition in those markets can be expected not only from Western countries, but also the Soviet Union and other 'Eastern bloc' countries. 'Grants and credits by both power blocs will hasten the industrialization of the poor countries.' This will make them 'steadily more important as purchasers of capital goods', which Sweden has to sell, but the trade liberalization making such exports possible will also make it harder 'to insulate ourselves from the under-developed countries and prevent the import of their cheap goods to the Swedish market'.

> This applies not only to raw material producers or manufacturers of cheap mass-produced semi- and finished products such as textiles . . . traditionally . . . the main export articles of the poorer countries . . . they may at a later stage constitute a serious threat to quality production as well. This is already the case with Japanese exports.[61]

The pressures on Sweden due to increased international economic integration are expected to be great not only because it has so small and open an economy, but also because it is a 'welfare society' compelled to compete with 'other social systems that sacrifice some of our values: either full employment (as in the shocking examples of the USA and Canada) or the individual right to choose one's workplace (which does not exist in countries with fully extended planned economies)'.[62]

The report's central thesis is that the only way to assure continued fulfillment of these and other 'generally accepted values of the working class movement', given the intensification of international competition, is to maximize the 'adaptability' of the economy. Accordingly, 'mobility of the factors of production' is the 'core of our program'.[63] In its details the program is an elaboration of the structural approach embodied in the Rehn model. The mobility of capital is to be assured by rigorously subjecting firms to the forces of competition, and ways of removing obstacles to those forces in various areas of policy are pointed out. Tariffs and import controls that remain despite Sweden's predominantly free-trade tradition should be successively removed, particularly where they discriminate in favor of particular products. The 'subsidy elements in our existing system of company taxation should be eliminated'. The capital market should be made more competitive, both by reducing the extent to which companies can avoid the discipline of the market through self-financing and by increasing competitiveness on the supply side of the capital market, particularly by eliminating the restriction of pension fund placements to loan capital. Further action against monopolistic and restrictive practices should also be taken. To sum up, increased mobility of capital is to be achieved primarily by such 'general' measures, avoiding efforts to steer investment in specific directions, with the principal exception of assuring credit for priority sectors such as housing.[64]

Increased mobility of labor, on the other hand, is absolutely contingent on 'selective' manpower, or labor market, policy. The more effective trade, credit and tax policy is in promoting structural change, the larger in size and more effective in implementation manpower policy has to be in order for 'society' to fulfill its 'responsibility for the costs of adjustment'. Thus, manpower policy has the 'key role', so that the resources with which it has to work determines the 'force with which general, structure-improving policy can be driven'.[65] In addition to full employment, the precondition for permitting the accelerated structural change viewed as necessary, then, is a commensurate expansion of manpower policy.

Taken separately, however, this array of general and selective measures is not regarded as sufficient. In addition, the report argues, their use has to be coordinated, and for that purpose new institutional arrangements have to be set up. First of all, short-term 'stabilization policy measures must be fitted into the general perspective of structural policy in quite a different way from past practice', so that 'stabilization and structural weapons . . . supplement and support, instead of conflicting with, one another'. Such coordination requires planning, not aimed at directing investment according to 'any detailed blue-prints of the economy of the future', which are precluded 'precisely because of the emphasis on adaptability', but designed to provide both the government and other actors with an overall view within which to understand the relationships between particular measures and developments and the pattern of long-term structural change. A new department of industry and employment should be created to conduct such planning. In addition, it should be responsible for organizing the rationalization of branches whose structure is no longer viable, including the assurance of finance needed to carry out whatever reorganization is necessary, while avoiding the 'long-term subsidizing of unprofitable economic activity'. Finally, the new department should oversee the more active use of state enterprise, expanded where needed and brought together under a new state holding company, as an instrument for structural change. To aid the department in performing its functions an 'investment council', with representatives of industry, labor and credit market institutions, including the central bank and pension fund, should be attached to it.[66]

In advocating such an 'active', though limited, industrial policy role for the state, the 1961 report goes beyond LO's 1951 policy statement, reviving some of the themes of the Postwar Program, although very tentatively and in what would seem to be a more liberal, market-oriented spirit. Indeed, the report's outlook seems quite similar to the 'liberal corporatist' initiatives toward 'indicative planning' being taken in Britain at about the same time.[67] The report also struck a different note, however, venturing a suggestion for new institutional arrangements for financing as well as planning investment at the industry level to be set up by collective bargaining between unions and management. Agreements would be negotiated to establish and allocate money to 'branch-rationalization funds', jointly administered by unions and management, with possible government representation as well. In the light of agreed requirements for rationalization the funds could use the money for 'the financing of expanding firms, temporary support to firms . . . considered to have good long-term prospects, or the liquidation of unprofitable enterprises'. The argument offered for branch funds was twofold. First, rationalization could be readily and effectively carried out, through cooperation between management and labor, at the branch level where it had to occur as much as at the national level. Secondly, the capital formation required for structural change could be provided 'in a form that does not involve a continuous increase in the concentration of property among the owners of capital'.[68]

The second argument concerns the relationship between solidaristic wage policy and the finance of investment. In the Rehn model, it will be recalled, it was apparently assumed that in order to minimize wage drift and the threat it posed to coordinated wage bargaining, standard rates would be set so high as to not only drive out the least efficient firms, but also leave the more efficient firms without enough internal savings to finance their expansion. The solution was to finance the investment externally out of increased public savings. As indicated by its call for expanding the pension fund's role in financing industry, the 1961 report clearly looked to such a solution as well. However, at the time the report was written, the problem of insufficient internal savings had evidently not arisen. On the contrary, the report condemns the prevailing level of self-financing as excessive. Two objections to it are advanced. One is that it has a conservative effect on industrial structure, enabling firms that should be weeded out to prolong their existence. The other is that it has an unacceptable effect on income distribution both within labor and between labor and capital. Profits high enough to permit so much self-financing frustrate solidaristic wage policy because they also permit so much wage drift as to nullify any reductions in differentials unions might succeed in negotiating. If the unions would be able to make those reductions stick despite the tendency of 'market forces' to reestablish them, then 'the most serious objections to excessive self-financing' would arise, 'namely that the growth in national wealth largely accrues to the owners of business enterprises'.[69]

This discussion suggests that the unions had not pressed profits very aggressively over the preceding decade. Intermittent compliance with the government's repeated appeals for restraint may have been part of the reason, along with lingering fears of the employment effects in low-profit firms. In that connection the report observes that unions cannot do much to improve the relative position of low-wage workers 'without the support of a much better and more efficient labor market policy than that which has been applied hitherto'.[70] The further expansion of manpower policy urged by the report would presumably ease union inhibitions against enforcing standard rates in the low-profit sectors. It would not meet the distributive objections to doing so in the high-profit sectors, however. This is where branch rationalization funds would come in. In so far as the increased cash flow that standard rates made possible in high profit firms was channeled into the funds rather than accumulated by the firms themselves, that flow could be used to finance investment without leading to a 'growth in the assets of the owners of capital'.[71]

The branch funds are seen as a new kind of financial 'institutes without owners' in which an increasing share in ownership of productive enterprise would accumulate, assuming that what they would provide is a form of equity financing. Over the long run, as the report points out, this would have fairly far-reaching implications:

> Since we do not believe that either general socialization or sharply increased taxation should form the main lines of advance for attaining our general economic policy objectives, we are prepared to accept the consequences for the structure of ownership, namely the growth of a new sector to which in the long run our proposals must lead, which we term *social enterprises without owners*.[72]

The idea of social enterprise without owners had already been broached some years earlier by Wigforss, who saw it as an alternative to nationalization for gradually replacing private by social ownership, which of course implied an end to the historical compromise.[73] The LO report revives the idea in very cautious, low-key terms. Yet, in turning to it as a way of avoiding the unacceptable distributive consequences that would flow from an effectively implemented solidaristic wage policy as long as firms are organized on a capitalist basis, the report acknowledges a dilemma that has since loomed increasingly large.

At the time, however, the idea aroused little interest, as did the more conventional institutional innovations proposed by the report. All of them, branch funds included, were addressed to problems which, by the report's own account, lay in the future. These problems were deprived of any immediate urgency by the performance of the economy in the first half of the 1960s. During that period unemployment hovered around 1·5 percent, inflation rates fluctuated around 3 percent and GNP growth averaged over 4 percent in constant prices.[74] In addition, the savings–investment mechanism seemed to be working roughly as it was supposed to. Although there was 'an apparent fall in profits and self-financing', the decline in business savings was being amply offset by a rapid accumulation in the new national pension fund and an unanticipated maintenance of household savings. The 1965 *Long-Term Survey*, the government's normally quinquennial projection of economic trends and prospective policy problems, reported that 'the growth rate of capital equipment was greatly accelerated between the Fifties and the first half of the Sixties'.[75] Structural change was evidently not being hampered by any shortage of capital. The adequacy of the Social Democratic labor movement's economic strategy, and the effectiveness with which it was being implemented, accordingly seemed to be confirmed. The confidence this engendered was particularly strong within the party leadership, as reflected in the self-congratulatory report, *Results and Reforms*, presented to the party's 1964 Congress.[76]

This confidence, bordering on complacency, did not survive very far into the second half of the 1960s. From the middle of the decade on there was substantially more economic instability and a growing tendency toward balance of payment deficits at high levels of activity. As predicted by LO's 1961 report, changes in the international environment were creating problems that were proving intractable to the economic strategy as far as it was being carried out. But other problems, not anticipated by the report, emerged as well, calling into question some of the essential features of the strategy. What made it urgent for LO and the party to seek ways of coping with this combination of problems was the political consequences it had, posing direct threats to the Social Democratic labor movement's power in both the state and market arenas. A sharp setback to the Social Democrats in the 1966 local government elections and a wave of wildcat strikes that broke out in late 1969 were only the most dramatic demonstrations of these threats. Other indications of the movement's renewed vulnerability accumulated as well. In response LO and the party adopted a succession of new policy positions over the decade stretching from the mid-1960s to the mid-1970s that added up to a substantial reorientation of the movement's economic strategy, even while preserving and extending some of its earlier characteristics. We turn now to a description of the way this reorientation took place.

Vulnerability in the State Arena: The Industrial Policy Response

The Social Democrats' share of the vote in the 1966 local government elections fell to 42·2 percent, the lowest since 1934. In the process they lost control of Sweden's two largest cities. If it had been a parliamentary election, they would have lost control of the government. Indeed, the bourgeois parties interpreted the outcome as a harbinger of victory in the parliamentary election just two years away. The Social Democrats suffered defections to the left as well as right, with the Communists' share of 6·4 percent the highest since their previous peak of 11·2 percent in 1946, marking a substantial recovery from the plateau of around 4 percent on which they stayed for much of the intervening period. The distribution of gains among the bourgeois parties is complicated by the presence of *ad hoc* electoral alliances among various combinations of the three parties in some areas. What is most noteworthy is that the Center Party's 13·7 percent was its highest since 1934, marking the continuation of its recovery from its nadir of 9·4 percent in 1956 (the earlier figures refer to the party in its previous incarnation as the Farmers' Party).[77] The communist and Center Party gains reflected their particular success in pressing a variety of issues on which the Social Democrats were vulnerable, and which cast doubt on their claims to managing the economy effectively.

One of these issues was inflation. The 6·2 percent increase in consumer prices during 1965, while low by current standards, was close to twice as high as the average increase over the preceding five years.[78] Prices rose less rapidly in 1966, but the means by which the government dampened the inflationary pressure aggravated other issues. Among them was a shortage of housing. Despite a rate of housing construction that had been increasing toward the highest in the world over the preceding years, it still fell behind rising demand. This was due partly to rent control but even more to the rapid movement of population from areas of declining industry to the main urban conurbations in which industrial expansion was increasingly concentrated. Thus, the level and distribution of housing needs was a corollary of the structural change on which Social Democratic economic policy relied, so when the government resorted to a temporary slowdown of housing construction to cope with short-term stabilization problems, it exacerbated the housing shortage generated by its long-term growth strategy.[79]

The discontents aroused by the housing situation came on top of others in both the expanding and declining regions. In the former new migrants experienced the stresses of adjustment to new social environments, including isolation and lagging provision of communal infrastructures, while old inhabitants reacted against the crowding and, particularly in Stockholm, rather drastic physical reconstruction associated with the rapid urban growth. And in the declining regions those who stayed behind suffered the consequences of broken social networks and the eroding economic base for collective services.[80] There is hardly anything surprising or distinctive about these phenomena, but the Social Democrats had evidently failed to anticipate the reactions against them. Even in terms of jobs, on which policy had been focussed, the consequences of structural change were not being compensated for some despite low overall levels of unemployment and the large increase in manpower-policy expenditures. The government's effort to curb the inflationary surge aggravated this problem as well. Thus, the rate at which plants closed down or reduced operations jumped following the government's restrictive measures, with twice as many workers being notified of layoffs on these grounds in 1966 as in 1965.[81]

While inflation offered ammunition for all the Social Democrats' opponents, the other issues fitted the needs of the Center and Communist parties particularly well. Both were in the process of defining new political profiles. As noted earlier, the Center Party that was created out of the old Farmers' Party sought to enlarge its constituency by becoming a party of protest against the centralization, regional decline and environmental destruction that seemed to be the concomitants of the expansion of large-scale, export-oriented industry promoted by Social Democratic policy. Beginning somewhat later the Communist Party was also in the process of transformation.[82] A new leadership sought to revive its fortunes by adopting what has come to be called a Eurocommunist position and capitalizing on the emergent 'New Left'. The latter mounted a critique of Social Democratic policy as subservient to the needs of capital which was considerably more sophisticated, and hence more potentially effective, than the repeated slogans of the old left.[83]

The precise extent to which these issues account for the Social Democrats' losses is not the important point for us. What is important is that they were perceived by the Social Democrats as calling into question not only the effectiveness with which their economic strategy was being implemented, but also the adequacy of the strategy itself. This opened up scope for currents of opinion that had already been critical of Social Democratic economic policy, within LO as well as the party, prior to the 1966 electoral débâcle.

ECONOMIC INSTABILITY AND THE COSTS OF STRUCTURAL CHANGE

LO's economists had been increasingly critical of the government's implementation of even the most conventional ingredient of its economic strategy, short-term demand management. At least since its 1951 policy statement, LO's spokesmen continuously stressed that the primary responsibility for non-inflationary full employment rested on the government, and that a sufficiently restrictive fiscal policy was crucial to meeting that responsibility. If full employment was to be maintained in the face of fluctuations in economic activity, however, it was still clearly necessary for the degree of restrictiveness to vary. The timing of short-run changes in the demand effects of fiscal policy was accordingly as important as their average magnitude over the course of the business cycle. In the LO economists' judgement the government was not timing fiscal policy changes as well as it should even in the early 1960s when, as noted earlier, other economists commended it for being especially successful in this respect.

At best, according to the fall 1962 issue of LO's semi-annual *Economic Outlook*, what can be accomplished by domestic economic policy is limited by what is going on in the international economy. Given 'foreign demand's decisive role' for economic fluctuations in Sweden, it argued, domestic economic policy can only be a 'modifying factor', counteracting fluctuations in external demand by measures aimed at achieving changes in domestic demand in the opposite direction: 'If economic policy's main function is to "bridge over" a recession and keep employment up until better times come, it is all the more essential that the measures are taken at the right point in time.'[84] The difficulty of forecasting and the institutional framework of budget decision-making were recognized as posing serious obstacles to getting the timing of fiscal policy right. But this only underlined the importance of putting the process of fiscal policy change into motion at the first signs that a change was likely to be necessary. This, an LO review of fiscal policy in the preceding decade concludes, the government typically failed to do,[85] and successive issues of *Economic Outlook* criticized the government for again failing to do so in the early 1960s.

Thus, the measures taken to stimulate demand in the summer of 1962 'should have already been taken in fall 1961 when export growth fell off'.[86] Less stimulus would then have been necessary, there might have been less of a decline, and the effect of the stimulus could have been ended at an earlier stage in the recovery of export demand, making it easier to respond to it without having to compete as much for resources with domestic demand. The 1961–2 recession was still a very mild one, however, and the LO economists were primarily wary of the danger of shifting to more restrictive fiscal policy too late in the upswing. This is just what they held was happening by the fall of 1963, when it became apparent that there would be a substantial state budget deficit in the following year instead of the surplus they regarded as necessary. If the government failed to fulfill its responsibility by making fiscal policy restrictive enough soon enough, there was a risk that it would try to shift the burden of coping with the resulting inflation and deterioration in the balance of payments onto monetary or wage policy, neither of which can bear the burden effectively or without serious negative side-effects. Excessive reliance on monetary policy slows down the very investment needed to make the most of rising export demand and, as LO had long insisted, the unions cannot 'alone bear the responsibility for national economic balance'.[87] These apprehensions were confirmed by the course of events.

The economy's expansion in 1964 substantially exceeded the government's forecasts, with GNP growth reaching a postwar high of 7·5 percent. With no more than a slight slowdown in expenditure growth, however, fiscal policy remained strongly expansive throughout that year and well into the next. The major restrictive fiscal measure, a sales-tax increase which LO had urged the government to introduce in January 1965, did not take effect until a half-year later. This was too late to prevent the acceleration of price increases referred to earlier or to keep the balance of payments from going into a larger deficit, relative to GNP, than any since 1952. Although these disturbances were minor when viewed from our present perspective, they marked a clear break with the preceding years' stability. As the evidence of overheating built up during 1965 the government did turn to monetary policy, as the LO economists anticipated, tightening it successively over the year.[88] By that point, though, there was nothing more to be gained by pushing the unions for wage restraint, for the government and employers had already succeeded in getting the unions to accept relatively low contractual increases in a two-year agreement covering 1964–5. The extent to which those increases fell short of what employers could pay was demonstrated by a level of wage drift about twice as high over the two years, compared with the long-term tendency of wage drift to roughly equal contractual increases.[89] Wage restraint consequently succeeded only in subjecting the unions to considerable internal strain, to which we shall return, without keeping actual earnings down, just as LO typically argued.

At least in retrospect, the LO economists' view that fiscal restraint came much too late in the mid-1960s upswing was generally shared by other economists. In a comparative analysis of fiscal policy by the OECD it was observed that, 'Against the background of the previous achievements in the art of demand management', the Swedish government's 'performances around 1964 and 1965 are incomprehensible'.[90]

While it was accordingly clear that the government's implementation of the economic strategy to which the Social Democratic labor movement was ostensibly committed was flawed, there were also growing doubts about the adequacy of the strategy itself, no matter how effectively it was implemented. LO's 1961 report, *Coordinated Industrial Policy*, was an early expression of such doubts. As we have seen, it viewed the combination of general demand management and selective manpower policy as insufficient to make the structural-change approach work, even if it did not question the soundness of the approach as such. Its focus was on the overall economic process, however, while in the subsequent years, LO began to give increasing attention to the actual effects of the process on workers. Evidence was accumulating that the costs of structural change were by no means being fully shifted from the affected workers to the society as a whole, despite the expansion of manpower policy. Moreover, there was a growing awareness that the costs had to be understood much more broadly than in terms simply of income gains or losses – although net losses in these terms were also being recognized – and that various costs were being borne by workers subject to change in the production process even if they did not lose their jobs. Some of the evidence percolated up through the union organization, some was provided by new work by social scientists and some was gathered by surveys that LO conducted among its members for the first time. Much of this evidence was brought together in a report on *Trade Unions and Technological Change*, for which Meidner was also responsible, prepared for LO's 1966 Congress.[91]

The report acknowledges more explicitly than any previous LO document that 'the objectives of increased economic efficiency' can come into conflict with 'those of adequate job security, job satisfaction, and work adjustment for the individual worker'.[92] The committee which prepared the report was originally set up in 1962 to explore the potential dangers of automation being emphasized in the USA. Ultimately, however, the committee concluded that it was not automation as such but the whole process of rationalization that was creating a wide range of problems both for those who became unemployed as a result and those who did not.

In particular, the report observes that 'the costs associated with the fraction of labor turnover that was not "voluntary" on the part of the individual worker' includes

not only the actual costs of removal but also the losses sustained in the process of disposing of old and acquiring new housing, the interruptions in the children's school attendance, foregone non-wage benefits, reductions in income or additional periods of training. To these must be added the social and psychological sacrifices often involved in a change of environment and adjustment to a new social setting. At the same time, there are costs incurred by society, both by the depopulated local authorities in the form of lost economic and population bases for their social services, and for the recipient local authorities which ... must create new services.[93]

Moreover, the individual costs tend to be concentrated in various categories of workers, especially older workers and women, for whom it is most difficult to find any new jobs, not to speak of the better jobs at higher pay which mobility from less to more efficient firms was supposed to make possible. The proportion of such workers is likely to be highest in firms being forced out of business by technological change, precisely because they are the firms that have not been expanding and, therefore, have an older workforce. Among other things, a study was cited showing that two years after a plant shutdown nearly a quarter of the affected workers had not found new jobs, as well as studies showing that many such workers dropped out of the labor force. Thus,

the favorable overall figures for employment and unemployment tend to disguise significant problems of adaptation for workers made redundant by plant shutdowns. To a surprising extent, these individuals tend to leave the labor force. We consider this rejection of workers desiring jobs in the midst of a so-called full employment economy to be a seriously disturbing development.

Still, the report rejects the conclusion that

the structural transformation of industry should be halted or slowed down. We urge instead that our national manpower policy program, which is at present ineffective in dealing with this problem, be expanded to the point where it can have a significant impact.[94]

For our present purpose it is not necessary to describe the specific ways in which manpower policy was to be expanded, which were spelled out in a ten-point program adopted by the Congress.[95] It is probably fair to say that they add up to an extension of the accepted strategy rather than any significant modification of it. On the other hand, there are respects in which the report suggests that manpower policy could not cope adequately with the consequences no matter how ambitiously developed. One is at the level of industrial structure. The report recalls the need for an 'active industrial policy' that had already been stressed in the 1961 report. This theme was pressed at the 1966 Congress by motions calling for the 'coordination of industrial policy' in a new department and the use of collective savings as an instrument of industrial policy, particularly by changing the rules governing the national pension fund so as to enable it to invest in equity capital at least to the same extent as private insurance companies. The huge amount of money at the national pension fund's disposal, projected to match the combined lending capacity of all the commercial banks and private insurance companies in the near future, prompted a cautious response to the relevant motions by LO's secretariat. As pointed out by the chairman of the Metalworkers' union, from which the motions had come, using the national pension fund as an instrument of a 'conscious industrial policy' presupposed the existence of such a policy, establishing the 'general guidelines for an industrial policy consistent with international competitiveness . . . technological possibilities . . . and our total resources of capital and labor'. But he saw this as making it just that much more important to develop such a policy, as more and more countries in Europe were already doing.[96]

A second respect in which the reports point toward a need to go beyond the prevailing approach in order to cope with the problems generated by technological and structural change is at the enterprise level. The importance of union participation in the planning of change within the enterprise is stressed, at a stage early enough to affect the design of change, as a means of minimizing the burdens it imposes on the affected workers. A revised agreement on joint consultation reached earlier in the year by LO, TCO and SAF is commended for enlarging the possibility for union participation.[97] However, the possibility is seen as significantly limited by the prevailing conception of managerial prerogatives:

> Any consultation on an even footing can hardly take place as long as the clause concerning management's exclusive right to manage and allocate labor as well as freely hire and dismiss workers remains in the collective agreement.[98]

The clause referred to was one which SAF's affiliates were bound by its constitution to include in all collective agreements with unions. The unions were beginning to put increasing pressure on SAF to eliminate that requirement, embodied in para. 32 of its constitution, but SAF had so far agreed only to limited restrictions on managerial prerogatives, such as advance notice of layoffs and adjudication of disputes over layoffs and dismissals by the joint machinery set up under the Basic Agreement. As we shall see, the pressure mounted in subsequent years, ultimately by-passing SAF resistance by turning to the 'political alternative'; but for the time being the issue was sidestepped. Although the reference to the clause in *Trade Unions and Technological Change* was part of the summary on which LO's ten-point manpower policy program was apparently based, the language of the program itself omitted this challenge to managerial prerogatives. Nor did it come up in the brief Congress discussion of 'industrial democracy', even though dissatisfaction with the new joint consultation agreement was already voiced. With respect to union power at the workplace – which is what the 'industrial democracy' issue was really all about – as well as industrial policy, the caution with which the leadership of both unions and party greeted the modest proposals being made in the early and mid-1960s was only overcome by later events which precipitated initiatives that went considerably further in some dimensions.

THE TURN TO INDUSTRIAL POLICY

The current of opinion in favor of more interventionist industrial policy that was building up in LO was paralleled by a similar one within the Social Democratic Party. Its leading exponent within the party leadership was an economist, Krister Wickman. These two currents merged in a joint LO-party committee on industrial policy, chaired by LO's research director Clas-Erik Odhner. Set up in 1965, in accordance with a resolution passed at the party's 1964 Congress, the committee's mandate was to prepare an industrial policy program for the party's next regularly scheduled Congress in 1968.[99] However, it took the 1966 election setback to galvanize the committee into action. One of the principal conclusions drawn from the party's election postmortem was that its neglect of the 'negative effects of structural rationalization' was a major reason for the outcome.[100] To avert the almost certain defeat in the forthcoming parliamentary election to which that outcome pointed, the party leadership deemed it ugently necessary to demonstrate the party's capacity to deal with those effects. To that end it scheduled an extra party Congress for October 1967 and called upon the joint LO-party committee to draw up 'the guidelines for the party's and trade union movement's common industrial policy program' for presentation to that Congress.[101]

As it turned out, the committee's preliminary report for the 1967 Congress and the final report for the party's regular 1968 Congress, just a few months before the election, served largely to provide a rationale for measures the government had already taken. This, together with the intensive promotion of internal party discussion of industrial policy, suggests that the committee's task was at least as much a part of the party's effort to mobilize its rank-and-file as a part of the policy-formation process. In any case the government did not wait for the results of the process.

Already in January 1967 it announced its intention to establish a new institution to channel collective savings into industry. Initially described as a 'fund for rationalization and structural change' the proposal was concretized in the form of a new State Investment Bank, scheduled to go into operation in July of that year. It was designed to provide long-term capital for investment projections, especially in areas of advanced technology. The Bank's lending was to be financed by borrowing up to five times its capital, provided from the state budget in gradually increasing amounts. In this way the Bank was expected to tap the rapidly growing savings being accumulated in the pension fund, channeling those savings more actively and selectively into industrial investment than they had been in the past. The fact that the Bank was rushed into operation less than half a year after the government's vague indication of its intention to do something of the sort was further testimony to the need felt by the Social Democratic leadership for some concrete demonstration of its new policy initiative. At the same time, the rapidity with which it was set up, shortcircuiting the traditional procedure of a lengthy government inquiry and consultation with interested organizations, intensified the hostility with which the bank was greeted by the business community, especially the private commercial banks. But these attacks undoubtedly served only to reinforce the mobilizing effect of the new industrial policy.[102]

In addition to the bank, a series of other institutional changes were made to implement the policy, most of which were surrounded by less controversy. A new division responsible for industrial policy was set up within the Finance Ministry in March 1967. Headed by Wickman, it was transformed into a separate Ministry of Industry in 1968. In that year governmental support for technological research and development was consolidated in a new Board for Technical Development. A state-owned development company to exploit technological innovations and a special committee to work out ways of using the rest of the state enterprise sector as an instrument of industrial policy were also set up. The outcome of the latter was the establishment of a state enterprise holding company in 1970 to take over responsibility for a number of state companies scattered among various ministries.[103]

The argument for this series of measures presented in the joint LO–SAP committee's reports was essentially the same, though cast in broader ideological terms and with greater urgency, as that set forth in LO's *Coordinated Industrial Policy*.[104] The end of the postwar era of 'very favorable conditions', anticipated at the beginning of the decade, is now at hand. Full employment, higher living standards and greater social justice has to be won in the face of stiffer international competition, driven by fundamental, accelerating technological and economic change. Now as before, there is no way to achieve these goals except through continual adaptation of industry to the forces of change. Insulating industry against them can only bring illusory security, merely making the adaptation harder when it can no longer be postponed. Even if industry continues to be exposed to these international forces, however, its response cannot be expected to be adequate nor consistent with equality, security and, ultimately, democracy if 'economic forces are given free play'.

While this has been the case all along, increasing concentration of power in industry is making it all the more so. In response to harder competition abroad, competition at home is being replaced by cooperation and coordination among firms concentrated increasingly within a few large financial groups, especially those dominated by the three major private commercial banks. This made possible economies of scale and long-term planning that improved the firms' viability in the tougher international environment. But the resulting power to shape the economy's development is both too great to be left beyond democratic control and too narrow to achieve the required changes in industrial structure, since they often cut across the financial groups' boundaries. Therefore, the process of structural change has to be stimulated, supported and steered in accordance with a 'conscious and active industrial policy'. In the broadest terms, the Social Democratic labor movement must 'continue to extend political democracy toward economic democracy'.

This was not translated into any systematic conception of what a demo-cratically controlled economic development scenario would look like. The industrial policy program was simply spelled out in terms of a variety of measures grouped under several broad problem areas. Among these measures were many but not all of the ones that LO had proposed in the pre-ceding years. The measures indicated were confined largely to those the government had already introduced or was contemplating. The reports were careful to omit mention of some LO proposals on which the government had not yet decided, including those it eventually did adopt. Thus, LO's views about what had to be done to implement the structural change strategy under more difficult conditions than those under which it was originally conceived were partially but not entirely incorporated into party policy.

Many of the measures enumerated are addressed to problems associated with the mobility of labor and capital on which the structural change strategy was conceived as depending. With respect to labor, the problem is not so much one of increasing mobility as one of assuring that it takes place on acceptable terms. This is said to require still more expansion of manpower policy in its by now traditional forms. But increased emphasis is placed on newer forms aimed at easing the impact of change. These include requirements for longer advance notification of plant closures or reorganization in order to allow enough time to prepare and implement 'social plans' to deal with the employment effects, and for changes in job design, recruitment policy and location practices to make it easier for workers whose jobs disappear to find new ones. 'Industrial democracy' is mentioned as a means of influencing the impact of technological change, but there is no reference to the obstacle posed by managerial prerogatives pointed out in LO's 1966 report.

As far as capital is concerned, the emphasis is reversed: the problem is insufficient mobility rather than the social terms on which it takes places. Lack of competition in the capital market is seen as the major obstacle. This is attributed to the concentrated ownership and control of the commercial banks, ties between them and individual firms, and the exclusion of other types of banks from industrial financing. Planning within their own spheres of control, the powerful banking-industrial groups cannot bring about needed reorganization that cuts across those spheres of control. Part of the remedy is to expand alternative sources of capital. In addition to establishing the new State Investment Bank, this is to be done by activating and coordinating the existing State Commercial Bank and Postal Savings Bank, authorizing all banks to engage in all types of business, and tapping the growing accumulation of savings in the national pension fund for industrial investment more effectively. While the State Investment Bank is cited as a means for doing so, there is no mention of LO's proposal that the pension fund be authorized to invest in equity capital instead of only loan capital – a measure implying some alteration of the social terms on which capital mobility occurs.

The reports do not assume that mere removal of obstacles to capital mobility will assure sufficient investment in expanding production to make up for declining production. What is also required is planning that cuts across existing structures of ownership and control, embracing the economy as a whole as well as being democratically accountable. Such planning can only be carried out by the government, which therefore has to be equipped to do so. The new Ministry of Industry is described as providing the means for meeting that need through 'rolling plans' to guide the use of various industrial policy instruments. The existing long-term (five-year) macroeconomic projections are to be expanded and supplemented by detailed analyses of the composition of activity, laying the basis for programs of structural change in specific industries. These plans and programs are to be worked out with the assistance of consultative councils representing firms, unions, public and private financial institutions, and other interests relevant to an orderly shift of labor and capital from weak to strong activities, while minimizing the social costs of the transition.

Although the term is not used, the kind of planning envisioned can be characterized as 'indicative'. No direct control over investment decisions of private firms is contemplated. The planning process is to be a 'cooperative' one between government and industry. However, fuller disclosure of firms' condition and plans is declared to be necessary to provide the information needed for planning. Moreover, some instruments for influencing private investment are cited. One is the long-established investment-reserve system. It provides tax exemption for a portion of profits that firms may set aside in special accounts if they are subsequently invested under conditions specified by the government. Originally set up to smooth out business fluctuations by inducing firms to shift investment from booms to slumps, the system began to be used as a means of influencing the type and location as well as timing of investment. This system is viewed as an instrument which can be put to further use for industrial policy purposes. The corporate taxation system's conservative effects on industrial structure pointed out by the earlier LO analysis is not mentioned, however.

The state enterprise sector is seen as offering another means of influencing investment and, indeed, for achieving a variety of goals concerning the social terms on which structural change takes place, as well as its economic effectiveness. To realize the potential of the state sector, a miscellaneous assortment of firms accounting for a smaller portion of the economy than in most other European countries, the need for some new governmental institution with responsibility for the sector is stressed. Although LO's proposal that it take the form of a state enterprise holding company was ultimately implemented, the reports make no mention of it.

Yet another instrument with underutilized potential pointed to is state support for technological research and development. The importance of R&D to maintain competitiveness in the face of accelerating technological change abroad is stressed. To expand the technical resources for developing new products and increasing productivity, assure their effective utilization and enable society to capture the financial as well as technical benefits of its investment in those resources, the existing state institutions have to be 'concentrated and strengthened'. Establishment of the new agency for supporting technological R&D and the new state development company for exploiting new products and processes, together with the

State Investment Bank, are cited as the means for accomplishing these ends.

Among the additional measures set forth are a number aimed at controlling technological and structural change in the interest of regional, environmental and consumer concerns. These, along with the others included in the reports, seem calculated to demonstrate the Social Democratic Party's responsiveness to the wide range of issues it had appeared to neglect, and on which it was politically vulnerable. At the same time, as we noted, the industrial policy program presented to the 1968 Congress avoided committing the party to any measures the government had not already decided to introduce.

Bold in its declaration that the structural-change process could not be left to take care of itself, the program was notably cautious in the forms of state intervention which it prescribed. It can perhaps be characterized as a modest revival of the approach taken in the Postwar Program, thereby marking a departure from the terms of the settlement between the Social Democratic labor movement and Swedish capital that was reaffirmed when the Postwar Program was abandoned. In contrast with the situation two decades earlier, the new industrial program was actually being implemented, modest as it was. The fact that the government had been so poorly equipped to do anything of the kind made it difficult to achieve the program's aims. There was a good deal of error in the trial-and-error process of learning to do what governments in some other countries had been doing a lot longer. A considerable amount of dissatisfaction with these initial efforts was voiced within LO and the party, along with criticism from business and other quarters, in subsequent years. This was manifested in a revised industrial policy program adopted by the party's 1972 Congress.[105] But this, in turn, reflected much else that had happened by then, building pressures for more radical departures from the terms of the settlement that we shall describe in detail.

The program's main immediate effect seems to have been political rather than economic. If the main function of the program was to mobilize the Social Democratic labor movement in the face of the looming threat of electoral defeat, it was apparently a success. In the 1968 election the Social Democrats won an absolute majority in the Second Chamber, the only time they did so other than in 1940. To be sure, other factors contributed. Although the government's belated response to the 1965–6 boom coincided with a slowdown in some of Sweden's major foreign markets to produce the highest unemployment for a decade in the winter of 1967–8, its political effect was blunted by an expansion of manpower policy programs to the highest level yet, coupled with a substantial increase in public sector employment.[106] The Soviet invasion of Czechoslovakia also helped the Social Democrats, who turned the election campaign into a kind of national protest against the Soviet action, damaging not only the communists, but also the bourgeois parties, whose uncertain capacity to govern became a liability at a time of international crisis.[107] At the same time, however, the controversy over the interventionist turn taken by Social Democratic economic policy, especially business reaction to the State Investment Bank's rapid establishment, helped the party to revive the ideological distinction between it and the opposition parties, and restore its identity as a party of social change. In so far as this rekindled the party activists' enthusiasm it was undoubtedly an important factor.

In the short run, then, the threat to the Social Democratic labor movement in the electoral arena was met. To the extent that this was accomplished largely by an exercise in symbolic politics the ingredients of success were ephemeral. Moreover, the result was also short-lived because a new single-chamber Parliament was scheduled to replace the bicameral Parliament in 1971, requiring a new election in 1970. This left the Social Democrats with just two years in which to enjoy their majority instead of the four they would have had in the past. Without the buffer of staggered, indirect elections to the First Chamber, Social Democratic control of the state would be much more sensitive to voter reaction to its policy performance. Therefore, the extent to which the measures comprising its industrial policy actually improved its ability to manage the economy in the face of growing difficulties was soon likely to have a direct bearing on the party's power. Before the next election took place, however, the Social Democratic labor movement's vulnerability in the market arena had also been dramatically revealed, adding new impetus to the modification of its overall strategy.

Vulnerability in the Market Arena: The Industrial Democracy Response

Beginning in the mid-1960s LO ran into increasing difficulties in performing the task assigned to it by the Rehn model. That task, it will be recalled, is to 'coordinate' union wage bargaining on the basis of a standard-rate, or 'solidaristic', wage policy. This is designed to encourage the structural change by which non-inflationary full employment is to be maintained, while also inhibiting the interunion wage rivalry that could otherwise undermine the stabilization effects of the structural-change strategy. For this task to be peformed, solidaristic wage policy has to be translated into a specific package of demands on the basis of which the unions can agree to LO's coordination of their wage bargaining.

There are two features of the wage-determination system that make this difficult. One is that union members' wage increases cannot be completely determined by negotiated agreements, so that some get additional increases of varying amounts in the form of wage drift. The other is that white-collar unions are organized in separate unions outside LO, with distinctive economic and organizational interests, making them reluctant to coordinate their wage bargaining with LO on any basis on which agreement within LO can be reached. The problems LO encountered as a result of these features from the mid-1960s on were not new, but they were intensified, ultimately calling into question the feasibility of the structural-change strategy.

As we have seen, solidaristic wage policy was understood in the Rehn model's original formulation as equal pay for equal work, regardless of employers' varying profitability, or ability to pay. In the absence of any system for determining what constituted equal work the policy came to mean the improvement of lower-paid workers' relative position. While remaining a standard-rate policy, then, solidaristic wage policy became increasingly egalitarian, aimed at diminishing differentials among different groups. While an element of egalitarianism had always been present to some degree, it was undoubtedly strengthened by the resurgent salience of equality in Swedish politics since the mid-1960s, spurred by such factors as the New Left's emergence as well as studies showing the persistence of inequality. This development was clearly manifested within the Social Democratic Party, and was reflected in a sharper emphasis on equality in its program by the end of the decade.[108] In any case the evolution of solidaristic wage policy in an egalitarian direction was evident in the succession of packages of demands on which it proved possible for the LO unions to agree.[109]

In principle such agreement among its affiliates is a prerequisite to LO's coordination of their wage bargaining through central negotiations with its employer counterparts. Never having been given permanent authority to pursue those negotiations, LO has to be authorized to do so anew at the start of each wage round. In practice the LO unions have no realistic alternative to central negotiations as long as SAF retains the capacity to coordinate the employers' wage bargaining regardless of what the unions do, and as long as SAF continues to favor such negotiations. While there may not be much choice as far as this is concerned, LO's affiliates, whose members have differing ranges of pay and possibilities of benefiting from wage drift, depending on differences in pay systems as well as employers' profitability, nevertheless have to agree on the specific set of demands to be pursued.

In order for the agreed package of wage demands to serve as a basis for the unions' continued support of LO's conduct of central negotiations on their behalf it has to have some discernible effect on the actual course of wages. The effect may obviously be limited by employer resistance. But even if LO largely succeeds in incorporating the demands into the central agreement, the level and distribution of wage increases may still diverge from the intended pattern as a result of wage drift. Some drift is unavoidable, given the decentralization that remains in the wage-determination system despite the system of central negotiations. It also provides an essential element of flexibility without which the difficulties of reaching agreement over the intended distribution of increases might be insurmountable. On the other hand, as the level of drift increases, so do the risks of tensions within and among the unions, as stressed in LO's 1951 statement and repeatedly in subsequent documents. The more drift there is, the greater the demonstrable gap between what the unions settled for and what they could have won, and the larger the disparity between the intended and actual distribution of wage increases. This makes unions more vulnerable to the charge of failing to defend their members' economic interests, and solidaristic wage policy less credible as a basis for legitimating and securing agreement to coordinated bargaining.

This, then, is why LO has to aim at standard rates high enough to limit the scope for drift. On the other hand, the structural-change strategy presupposes sufficient expansion of firms profitable enough to pay the standard rates to offset the contraction or elimination of firms not profit-able enough to do so. If standard rates are set so high as to assure very little drift, the rate of expansion might well fall considerably short of the rate of contraction, defeating the strategy's ultimate purpose of maintaining full employment as well as avoiding inflation. This, as we suggested earlier, confronts LO with a fundamental dilemma. While its 1951 statement did not address the dilemma, LO has in fact been continuously wrestling with it, trying to strike a balance between standard rates high enough to prevent excessive drift and low enough to permit sufficient employment growth in expansive firms to replace declining employment in contracting firms. As we shall see, the balance has been an elusive one.

WAGE BARGAINING IN THE MID-1960s

One source of the difficulty LO has experienced is that the scope for drift is not a function of wage rates alone, but of their level relative to the level of demand. To the extent that demand is subject to control at all it is by the government's macroeconomic policy. This underscores the dependence of LO's ability to perform the wage-policy task assigned to it on the effective-ness with which the government performs the macroeconomic-policy task assigned to it. This, it will be recalled, is understood as keeping fiscal policy sufficiently restrictive, exerting pressure on profits from above, so to speak, while standard-rate wage policy exerts pressure on profits from below, jointly producing the differential profit squeeze that forces structural change. In operating in this way fiscal policy is also expected to limit the scope for drift sufficiently to permit LO to perform its wage-policy task. The consequences that the government's failure to perform its macro-economic policy task effectively have for LO's wage policy are strikingly illustrated by what happened during the two-year central agreement for 1964–5.

Over the two years, as noted earlier, drift substantially exceeded contractual increases. The latter amounted to 2·1 percent in 1964 and 4·1 percent in 1965. Drift was 5 percent the first year, more than twice as high as contractual increases. Although the contractual increases were much higher in the second year than in the first, drift was still higher – at 5·8 percent it was the highest level since 1951. Totaling 10·8 percent over the contract period as a whole, drift was 75 percent greater than contractual increases, totaling 6·2 percent, a difference greater than any since the early 1950s. During the most recent preceding contract period in which drift exceeded contractual increases (1959–60) drift was just 16 percent greater.[110]

LO had clearly captured a much lower portion of what it proved possible for employers to pay than in any agreement since the unbroken series of central negotiations began. Part of the explanation is that the 1964–5 agreement was reached at an early stage in the recovery from the moderate economic slowdown in 1962–3. The government called for restraint to avoid impairing the recovery, and the employers offered stiff resistance to increases beyond what they deemed compatible with the rate of economic growth forecast by the government. The forecast turned out to substantially underestimate the strength of the recovery. But even when this became evident, as we have seen, the government failed to make its fiscal policy restrictive enough soon enough to keep the upswing from developing into an inflationary boom, accompanied by an extremely tight labor market. This was reflected in unemployment of just three-quarters of a percent in the third quarter of 1965.[111]

While LO had performed the task assigned to it by the Rehn model, then, the government had not, opening up the scope for a sharp increase in wage drift, generating the kind of strains within the unions so often anticipated. Recognized as too low as soon as the agreement was reached, it met a great deal of rank-and-file hostility. As far as lower-paid workers were concerned LO had managed to extract much less of a relative improvement than it had sought, and even this was further diminished by exceptionally high drift for other workers. LO was, consequently, under great pressure to make sure that negotiated increases in the next agreement would leave much less room for drift. This pressure was reinforced by the decision of two unions to pull out of the central negotiations and go it alone.[112]

LO also decided to set its sights high in the next round of negotiations in an effort to come to grips with the problem posed for it by the white-collar unions' separate wage bargaining. Since LO's coordination of wage bargaining was confined to its own affiliates, its capacity to perform the function of inhibiting interunion wage rivalry required by the structural-change strategy was impaired, as was its capacity to perform the function of keeping wage growth in line with economic stability, which it tended to accept as its responsibility in practice.

This limitation mattered less when the white-collar unions accounted for a relatively small proportion of union membership, as was the case when the Rehn model was originally formulated. However, the membership of those unions rose rapidly during the subsequent decades, growing by 250 percent during 1950–70, while LO membership went up only 14 percent. Over the same period the white-collar unions' share of total membership rose from just under a fifth to just under a third.[113]

Most of this was in unions affiliated to TCO, which accounted for 27 percent of total union membership in 1970. The remainder, just under 5 percent, was in unions belonging to the Central Organization of Professional Employees, or SACO (*Sveriges Akademikers Central Organisation*). To all intents and purposes the distinguishing criterion of SACO union membership is the possession of a university degree. Much smaller than either of the other two confederations but growing much faster, SACO has spearheaded resistance to the egalitarian thrust of LO's wage policy. A separate organization of state employees, or SR (*Statstjänstemännens Riksforbund*), with under 1 percent of union membership in 1970, subsequently merged with SACO to form the organization now referred to as SACO-SR.[114]

As indicated earlier, TCO does not negotiate wages on behalf of its affiliates as LO does, the 1956 negotiations being the only exception. In the private sector the industrial white-collar unions have negotiated separately or jointly, in varying combinations culminating with the formation in 1973 of a negotiating organization or 'cartel' of the major unions, the PTK

(*Privattjänstemannans kartellen*). In the public sector separate cartels of TCO unions organizing local and central government employees respectively do the negotiating, along with SACO and SR in the central government sector.[115] Although there were, and continue to be, important differences and tensions between them, their wage policies during much of the postwar period had in common the objective of maintaining differentials relative to the LO unions. For a long time they largely succeeded in doing so by holding off on any negotiations until LO had settled. They could do this because employers in the public as well as private sectors accepted both the practice and its objectives.[116]

However, those objectives came increasingly into conflict with LO's solidaristic wage policy as it was given a more egalitarian cast. As long as the white-collar unions persisted in their wage policy, the most LO could accomplish was the reduction of differentials within the confederation. What was worse from LO's point of view was that the white-collar unions demanded 'compensation' for any changes in blue-collar workers' living standards that could be interpreted as reducing inequalities between them and the white-collar workers. Some of these were changes that affected industrial workers' average wages, such as shifts from lower- to higher-paying jobs inherent in the process of structural change, or premium pay for night and holiday work which accompanied the shift toward continuous operations and also reflected increased efficiency. Others were changes that reduced differentials in non-wage working conditions, such as the length of the working week, notice of layoff, or dismissal and severance pay. In a famous statement in 1964 Arne Geijer, LO's chairman, condemned compensation for such changes as utterly indefensible, since the inequalities they remedied were unjustifiable in the first place. Moreover, by insisting on such compensation as well as the same percentage increases in wages, Geijer contended, the white-collar unions were refusing to bear their part of the burden of an economically responsible wage policy, thrusting it entirely on LO. At the beginning of the next round of negotiations LO observed that 'there is nothing to indicate that greater restraint by the LO groups in the current tight labor market will induce corresponding restraint by other groups'. On this ground it decided to demand a large general increase as well as a greater relative improvement for lower-paid workers.[117]

While LO was determined to make up for settling for too little in 1964 and to win increases too high for the white-collar unions to match in 1966, the end of the boom and anticipated decline made SAF as determined to resist. The negotiations were unusually tough, marked by two breakdowns, notice of a general overtime ban by LO and a notice of a general lockout by SAF in response.[118] A three-year agreement which a mediation commission finally got them to accept yielded contractual increases in the successive years of 4·3, 3·5 and 2·9 percent in industrial workers' average hourly wages, totaling 10·7 percent over the agreement period as a whole. This proved to be just about enough to keep abreast of wage drift, which was very slightly higher, totaling 11·2 percent over the same period.[119]

However, the distribution of contractual increases had a stronger low-wage profile than ever before. For the first time the increases were specified entirely in absolute rather than percentage terms (which SAF preferred to doing so partly in absolute and partly in percentage terms as LO had proposed). These increases were supplemented with extra increases for the low-paid workers. In addition, earnings guarantees were introduced in a form designed to close a large part of the gap in average earnings between unions with low and high wage drift.[120] This was an important stage in the evolution of the complicated formula into which solidaristic wage policy was translated.

On the other hand, the white-collar unions were not brought any closer to coordinated wage bargaining with LO. In fact, wage rivalry between the two groups of workers was sharply intensified by what happened in the rest of the 1966 negotiating round. Once the LO–SAF agreement was concluded private sector and state white-collar workers, other than teachers, soon reached agreements providing for between 18 and 20 percent over the same three-year period. Although this was nearly twice as high as the contractual increases won by LO, it was a little less than the average total increase in earnings, including drift, experienced by LO members.[121]

Somewhat later, however, the teachers won increases that were much higher. These were the fruits of aggressive bargaining by SACO that culminated in an unprecedented strike by the secondary and university teachers in SACO.[122] In going on strike they were exercising a right that had just been granted by legislation enacted in 1965. It authorized state employees to engage in collective bargaining on the same basis as other workers, and established a new, formally autonomous agency, the Swedish Government Employee Negotiating Board, SAV (*Statens Avtalsverk*) to act as their employer counterpart. SACO started with a 'point strike' at selected schools, which SAV countered by locking out all SACO teachers, though not TCO teachers in the same schools, to which SACO in turn responded with a three-day sympathy strike by higher civil servants.

Teacher dissatisfaction had been running high because increases had been delayed pending revision of their pay structure. Moreover, SACO had developed an extensive rationale for large wage increases. It took the position that its members were entitled to compensation for earnings forgone while they acquired their higher education, using 'lifetime earnings' as a basis for comparison, and also for the effects of income taxation. These effects were greater for its members, it argued, because their higher nominal incomes were subjected to higher marginal tax rates, further diminishing the real effects of nominal increases already eroded by inflation.

Eventually, as we shall see both LO and TCO felt compelled to bring the effects of income taxes on real wages to bear on discussions of wage policy, although their views on the appropriate distributive profile of the tradeoff between wages and taxes was different from SACO's. In the mid-1960s, however, neither LO nor TCO accepted SACO's position. TCO did agree that marginal tax rates should be reduced but rejected the notion that tax increases should be fully compensated by wage increases on the ground that the social services paid for by the taxes were part of the increase in living standards workers enjoyed. LO still rejected any consideration of the effects of income taxes on purchasing power, condemning SACO's 'real-wage' doctrine as entirely out of place in collective bargaining, declaring that the after-tax distribution of income was a political matter to be decided democratically by Parliament. The bitterness of LO's objections was only intensified when SACO teachers ended up with an increase of 35 percent over a three-year period. The TCO teachers, who had not struck, got even more because their increases were retroactive – strikers not being entitled to retroactivity according to Swedish rules. LO's reaction to all this was that it would do its utmost to see to it that there was 'never another 1966'.[123] What it could do was not clear. In a much-cited speech at the 1967 SAP Congress Geijer suggested that achievement of greater equality in Sweden might not be possible without sacrificing the tradition of collective bargaining without state intervention, implying that it would require a state-led incomes policy.[124] This was a warning rather than a proposal – though it was, indeed, difficult to see how the state could avoid involvement once the interrelations between wages, including those of the state's own employees, and the system of taxes and transfers were explicitly brought into the picture, as they were by SACO.

WAGE POLICY AND THE EFO MODEL

Concern about the effects of escalating interunion wage rivalry on wage levels led SAF and the two main union confederations to explore the possibilities for achieving a greater degree of coordination in wage bargaining. The effort did not achieve that aim, but it did yield a systematic framework for analyzing the relationships between wage changes and the economy that was widely accepted until recently. It is referred to as the EFO model after the names of the research directors of TCO, SAF and LO – Gösta Edgren, Karl-Olof Faxén and Clas-Erik Odhner – who were the joint authors of the report in which it was presented.[125]

SAF took the initiative in 1967 by proposing that it and the two confederations agree to a new, highly structured procedure for simultaneously negotiating wages of both LO and TCO union members.[126] It comprised a five-stage sequence following a fixed schedule, based on an estimation of the scope for increases made by experts appointed by the organizations, according to a method to be specified in the agreement.

In stage one the experts calculate for the economy as a whole how much hourly labor costs can increase, given the projected growth in labor productivity, subject to the rate of investment needed to achieve the GNP and foreign-trade growth targets set in the government's quinquennial long-term survey and annual national economic budgets. The scope for labor-cost increases is limited by the level of profits required to achieve the needed investment, given the price level required to maintain international competitiveness and balance of payments equilibrium. If the experts fail to agree by a certain date in the year prior to which contracts expire (redrawn to expire simultaneously), a board of arbitration consisting of an impartial chairman and two members appointed by the employers and two by the unions decides on an estimate binding on all parties. In stage two the scope for contractual increases is calculated by deducting projected wage drift, increases in labor costs mandated by legislation or collective agreements from the scope for increases in labor costs. In the remaining three stages the scope for contractual increases is allocated between the LO and TCO sectors of the labor market, distributed within each and translated into wage contracts by industrial-level negotiations. The prohibition of strikes and lockouts for the duration of collective agreements would extend to issues settled at each successive stage.

SAF's scheme would have turned the central negotiations system into a kind of private incomes policy designed, it would seem, to assure the profits estimated to be necessary to bring about the investment required for economic growth and external equilibrium. The scheme rests very heavily on the assumption that these magnitudes are technical matters that can be determined by experts. In all, it is a remarkably explicit and systematic employers' wish-list. Not surprisingly, neither LO nor TCO accepted the proposal.[127]

The arguments against it were set forth most fully in a memorandum by Odhner, LO's research director.[128] In it the 'ideas of economic relationships on which the proposal is built, and particularly [those concerning] the relationship between prices, wages, and productivity' are rejected as 'too greatly simplified, not to say false'. But the 'most important objection' is to the idea of taking 'the central problem of income distribution – the distribution between wages and profits – from negotiations' and leaving it up to the 'experts'. To assume the possibility of determining the distribution between wages and profits 'objectively', the memorandum implies, is to assume away the real conflict of interests that exists between employers and employees, and between the different groups of employees not only in LO and TCO, but also SACO, creating a situation in which the employers can 'divide and rule'. The 'main task of the organizations is, after all, to look after the interests of their members'. Adoption of SAF's proposed scheme would deprive the 'trade union movement, and for that matter SAF', of 'much of their *raison d'être*', replacing them with 'a government office for the determination of wages', which is something the unions 'naturally cannot accept'.

Nevertheless, the memorandum states, LO agrees that changes in the way negotiations are conducted are needed to make their outcomes 'more satisfactory from the point of view of the whole economy'. Such changes would have to proceed from 'more realistic . . . starting points', however. The 'most important' is that the unions must be able to perform their task of seeking 'the greatest possible share of the real gross national product'. To make sure that this is still 'kept within the bounds of available resources' two additional requirements have to be met. One is a 'more realistic conception of the way the economy functions'. The other is 'that the negotiations take place simultaneously for the whole labor market, so that one can guarantee a certain reasonable relation between wage agreements for different sectors and groups'. 'If it is possible to agree on such a common conception and on the wage negotiations taking place simultaneously for all groups, an important step towards an improvement would have been taken.' Agreement on the former proved easier than the latter.

According to Odhner, the 'basic long-term model of the economy' needed for a more realistic conception of how it functions 'is not yet worked out for Swedish conditions'. He suggests, however, that it should be possible to build one along the lines of a two-sector model of inflation in a small, open economy presented in the 1966 report of a Norwegian government commission on incomes policy headed by the economist, Odd Aukrust.[129] The idea of such a model had also been adumbrated in the 1961 report of a Swedish government commission on stabilization policy of which Odhner had been secretary.[130] It was precisely a model of that kind that was worked out after SAF's proposal was rejected and the three organizations authorized their research directors to make a new effort to arrive at a 'common conception' of the relationships between wage formation and the economy.

The two sectors into which the economy is divided in the model are referred to as the competitive, or C, sector, whose output is largely exported or competes with imports, and the sheltered, or S, sector, whose output is neither exported nor subject to competition from imports.[131] For purposes of the model the principal differences between them lie in price formation and productivity growth. In the C sector prices are set on the world market. In the S sector, mark-up pricing is normal. Exchange rates are assumed to be fixed, so that international price movements are imported into the economy. In the C sector productivity growth is higher than in the S sector. Productivity growth is assumed to follow a trend set by factors independent of wages, such as world technological development, with sectoral differences accounted for by factors like market size, industrial structure and type of production.

Wage growth is the same in both sectors, however. The C sector acts as the wage leader, with wage increases in that sector being transmitted to the S sector through solidaristic wage policy and the demand for labor in the latter. Since productivity growth in the S sector is lower, profit margins can only be maintained in that sector by raising prices more than in the C sector. In so far as this happens the domestic inflation rate – the weighted average of price increases in the two sectors – is higher than the rate of price increases on the world market. This, however, is regarded as acceptable. What is important for Sweden's small, open economy with its heavy dependence on foreign trade is not price stability, but the continued competitiveness of the C sector over the long run. The crucial requirement for wage behavior is that it be consistent with this imperative.

A sufficient level of investment to keep abreast of world technological development is identified as the essential condition for the C sector's continued competitiveness – 'we are not free to choose our own rate of technological development'. In turn, the level of investment is a function of its expected profitability. Accordingly, the extent to which wage behavior is consistent with the imperative of long-term competitiveness depends on its effect on profits and, through that, on investment.

The relationships among wages, profits and investment are analyzed in terms of the 'margin' or 'room' for increases in income – that is, wages and profits – from the growth in the C-sector product. This margin corresponds to the sum of the increase in world market prices and increase in C-sector productivity. The disposition of the margin is determined by collective bargaining. The result may be division of the margin between wages and profits, absorption of the entire margin by wages, or an increase in wages that exceeds the margin. At any given time the economic implications of any of these outcomes depends on whether investment is at the level required for long-run competitiveness at the time. Three situations can be distinguished to illustrate the argument.

First, if investment is at the required level, it can be expected to continue at that level if the profit share remains unchanged, assuming that the profit share has a constant relationship to the profitability on which investment depends. Under these conditions an increase in wages that absorbs the entire margin will be consistent with long-run competitiveness, since it permits the relative shares of wages and profits to stay the same.

If, on the other hand, the level of investment is too low and the assumed relationship between the profit share and profitability prevails, raising the level of investment requires an increase in the profit share. Under these conditions a wage increase that absorbs the entire margin will not be consistent with long-run competitiveness. To permit the profit share to rise the wage increase has to be confined to less than the entire margin.

A situation in which the profit share is higher than it has to be is apparently contemplated as well, although the report is not consistent in this connection. Such a situation could arise, for example, if the relationship between the profit share and the profitability required for a given level of investment changes, which could be the result of changes in the capital–output ratio, the structure of financial capital, the level of risk premiums, and the like. If the profit share can consequently be lowered without bringing investment below the required level, then a wage increase that exceeds the margin will still be consistent with long-run competitiveness.

All the preceding cases are constructed on the assumption that macroeconomic equilibrium prevails – in the sense that there is no 'general demand surplus or demand deficit'. Wage negotiations will ordinarily be affected by various short-term factors, including deviations from macroeconomic equilibrium in either an inflationary or deflationary direction. Over an extended period, however, the division between wages and profits cannot deviate very far from that required to maintain long-run competitiveness without generating counteracting tendencies. Thus, if negotiated increases take up so little of the margin that profits rise 'abnormally', both wage drift and negotiated increases will rise to take up the slack. Similarly, 'wages . . . could not in the long run rise so much . . . beyond the limits formed by productivity and price developments that . . . profitability and competitiveness . . . became insufficient', for then the effect of falling 'exports, investment and employment' on 'the situation in the labor market' would reduce the rate of wage increases.

Accordingly, a kind of 'dynamic equilibrium' tends to operate over the long run, making the division between wages and profits in the sector product follow a 'main course'. The margin created by productivity growth and international price increases indicates the central tendency of the main course. However, the EFO Report stresses that the main course is indeterminate over a significant range of variation, so that it is to be understood as a 'corridor' rather than a precise path. This is explained on the ground that the relationship between profits and investment is a complex and uncertain one, into which a number of factors enter that are subject to change, both deliberate and unintentional. Among these factors are some that can be influenced by policy, such as the availability and conditions of external financing, which affects the need for profits as a source of internal financing. Consequently, a given level of investment may be consistent with considerable variation in the division between wages and profits, depending partly on the policies carried out at the time.

Both directly and in combination with alternative patterns of policy such variation in the division between wages and profits has significant implications for the social distribution of income and power. On this issue the organizations engaged in wage bargaining have fundamentally conflicting interests and values. Although they have a common interest in and acknowledged responsibility for assuring the C-sector's long-run competitiveness, then, they are bound to differ over the division between wages and profits through which it is to be accomplished. There is no way to resolve this difference except through the collective bargaining process and, implicitly, the political process that determines the policies through which investment may be affected. The report disavows any intent to 'paper over these fundamental differences' between the negotiating organizations. Its declared purpose is rather to provide them with a valid basis for analyzing the economic implications of wage changes, recognizing that they will necessarily evaluate those implications differently.

Although the EFO model bears a stronger resemblance to Odhner's critique of the 1967 SAF proposal than to the proposal itself, it can plausibly be viewed as staking out neutral ground on which both employers and unions can stand, particularly when it is also compared with the Rehn model. The latter, as we have seen, calls for contractual increases that squeeze profits sufficiently to minimize the drift that threatens the unions' internal cohesion. Implicitly, it makes profits a residual in the sense that they are what is left after the contractual increases required to satisfy the requirements of organizational cohesion. SAF's proposal, on the other hand, seems to take the opposite position. To all intents and purposes it makes contractual increases a residual in the sense that they can consist of whatever is left after the profits deemed necessary to satisfy the requirements for investment, plus the increments to labor costs that are not controlled by negotiated agreements, such as legislated social charges and wage drift.

The EFO-model main course would seem to mark the path of compromise between these two positions. The corridor it runs through lies between contractual increases that leave too much room for drift and too little room for investment. It thereby defines a region within which contractual rates can vary while still maintaining the relationship between expanding and contracting activities in the C sector required for the long-run viability of Sweden's position in the international economy. As long as contractual increases remain within these boundaries the level at which they are set as a result of the relative bargaining power of labor and capital does not matter, provided that there are corresponding adjustments in the factors entering into the relationship between profits and investment. Thus, while identifying the availability and conditions of external equity financing as a factor affecting the level of profits needed to maintain the required level of investment, the EFO model cites both collective and private savings as equally acceptable sources of equity capital. In this way the EFO model is able to accommodate widely divergent outcomes of distributive conflict between labor and capital.

Reflecting on the EFO model a decade after it was formulated SAF's contributor to it pointed out that it was precisely the model's neutrality with respect to alternative sources of equity capital that was most objectionable from the employers' point of view, for outcomes that made it necessary to provide equity capital out of collective savings to solve the problem of investment were fundamentally unacceptable.[132] But by this time, as we shall see, the problem of investment had become acute and the issue of whether to provide the equity capital needed to solve it out of collective or private savings had become a central one in Swedish politics.

This issue was much less salient at the time the EFO model was formulated, however. Neither its neutrality with respect to that issue nor the fact that it undermined the employers' characteristic argument against wage increases that exceeded economy-wide productivity growth were sufficient for SAF to disown it. Since both LO and TCO participated in developing it, it offered some prospect of dampening the interconfederal wage rivalry regarded as a dangerous source of wage pressure, especially by the export industries that dominated SAF at the time. On the other hand, SAF never formally adopted the EFO model as a basis for its wage-policy positions nor did LO. Only TCO explicitly rested its wage-policy statements on it, though the significance of this was diminished by the fact that TCO was not a negotiating body.[133] Some of its affiliates did use it to back up their wage demands. In the most important case, as we shall see, its use was part of a strategy for avoiding simultaneous negotiations. Thus, it did not provide a basis on which wage bargaining could be coordinated across the whole labor market. On the other hand, it did provide a conceptual framework which was for some time generally accepted as the basis for evaluating the implications of wage changes for the economy.

Following their rejection of SAF's 1967 proposal and pending completion of the EFO study, LO and TCO undertook a separate effort to work out a basis for coordinated bargaining in the forthcoming negotiations for an agreement to follow the one for 1966–8. Whatever obstacles there may have been to reaching agreement between LO and TCO, the continued resistance to any negotiating role for TCO by its own affiliates rendered it impossible. Some other efforts by SAF and the government to get the various negotiating parties together also proved abortive.[134]

As the 1966–8 agreement approached its termination LO announced its determination to achieve a much greater relative improvement for low-wage workers and in the next agreement make it stick across the whole labor market. In the absence of any agreement to engage in joint or simultaneous bargaining LO decided on a strategy of refusing to settle in advance of the white-collar unions, as it had always done in the past. In this way it hoped to make it impossible for the white-collar unions to maintain differentials by relating their demands to a settlement already made by LO. It also expected all negotiations to be deadlocked, so that the establishment of a single mediation commission to overcome the deadlocks in all the negotiations would provide the mechanism for bringing about similar settlements in all the negotiations.[135]

What LO did not anticipate was that a white-collar union could frustrate this strategy by settling before instead of after LO. That, in fact, is what was done by SIF (*Svenska Industritjänstemannaförbundet*), the union of white-collar workers in the private sector. SIF had long been among the TCO unions most opposed to any coordination of wage bargaining by TCO, not to speak of LO. It viewed its autonomy as essential to preserving its own wage policy, designed to leave maximum room for individual wage-setting, which largely precluded much impact on the relative position of low-paid workers. While SAF was interested in wider coordination in order to dampen wage rivalry, it did not want it to be brought about by a single mediation commission as LO anticipated, because it saw this as opening the way for intervention in wage bargaining by the Social Democratic government. So SAF was willing to go along with SIF, provided the overall increase was kept low, which SIF felt compelled to accept as the price for evading LO's coordination effort. [136]

The resulting one-year agreement was viewed by SIF as a holding operation, giving it time to develop a more comprehensive, long-term wage strategy together with the two unions organizing most of the rest of the white-collar workers in industry, SALF (*Sveriges Arbetsledareförbund*), the foremen's union, and CF (*Civilingenjörsförbund*), the engineers' union. In addition to strengthening their bargaining power in relation to the employers and their autonomy relative to LO, this effort was part of a struggle for power within TCO, between private and public sector unions and between the central organization and its affiliates. The EFO model proved useful to SIF in this connection, for it provided a basis for formulating wage demands without any explicit reference to what the LO unions had got, even if relativities remained an important concern. The initial result was a five-year agreement, covering 1970–4, signed between the three unions and SAF at the end of 1969. This was followed by a similar agreement, though for three years, between HTF, the union of white-collar workers in commerce and SAF.[137] For the time being, at least, this put the white-collar unions in industry beyond the reach of any LO effort to incorporate them in simultaneous negotiations. The basis was also thereby laid for the consolidation of the private sector white-collar unions' coordination of their own wage bargaining by the formation of their new negotiating body, PTK, in 1973. This has taken us ahead of our story, however, so we must return to what happened in the rest of the labor market after the one-year settlement between SIF and SAF for 1969–70.

Essentially LO succeeded in implementing its strategy of forcing similar settlements as far as the public sector white-collar unions were concerned. The negotiations were deadlocked and a mediation commission charged with working out settlements in all the negotiations was appointed, and it became convinced that an all-round settlement pretty much on LO's terms was the only way in which they could accomplish their mission. LO held out for such a settlement, making the negotiations drag on until just before the summer vacation, when most of the parties finally accepted the commission's final proposal, embodying most of what LO wanted. Except for the private sector white-collar workers, two-year agreements were made providing for increases in the private and public sectors as similar as possible, given the widely different pay systems. The increases were in absolute terms so that the lower the starting position, the higher the percentage increase. The LO–SAF agreement also stipulated that workers whose hourly earnings were less than a low-income norm set at 96 percent of the industry average were entitled to additional increases, to be distributed by local negotiations from a pool equivalent to half the difference between their earnings and the low-income norm. This, in virtually unchanged form, was the low-wage formula on which LO's affiliates had agreed.[138]

In all, the result was apparently a triumph for LO. It had succeeded in implementing its solidaristic wage policy more effectively than ever before not only within the LO–SAF area, but also over much of the rest of the labor market as well. But its wage-policy troubles were not over. On the contrary, it was soon confronted by renewed challenges, not from the white-collar unions as in 1966, but from within its own ranks.

THE ERUPTION OF RANK-AND-FILE DISCONTENT

During the winter of 1969–70 a wave of wildcat strikes of unprecedented magnitude swept over Swedish industry. It began in December 1969, with an unofficial stoppage at LKAB, the state-owned ironmines above the Arctic Circle, which lasted almost three months. Shorter strikes broke out at many of the large industrial firms in the rest of Sweden. A total of 216 were reported in the official statistics, resulting in 155,600 lost working days compared with 465 in 1968 and a mere 35 in 1967.[139] To be sure, the official statistics substantially underestimate the volume of wildcat strikes, partly because many are very short or go unreported to avoid the issue of legality. Just a little over a quarter of such strikes in the metal industries had been reported in 1955–67.[140] Even if the proportion was larger in 1969–70, the level of unofficial strike action was far beyond anything experienced in Sweden before. The surge of rank-and-file militancy elsewhere in Europe, from the events of May–June 1968 in France to the more recent, and more nearly analogous wildcat strikes in Germany and Italy, which received extensive media coverage in Sweden, undoubtedly encouraged Swedish workers to take similar action. However, the Swedish unions' hold on their members' loyalty was being directly strained by factors broadly similar to those operating in Germany and Italy.

To a large extent the wildcat strikes in Sweden can be viewed as a dramatic confirmation of the proposition, embodied in LO's 1951 wage policy statement and reiterated since, that the unions expose their organizational cohesion to serious danger if they settle for wage increases that capture too little of the scope for increases created by the course of the economy. How much too little they settled for in the 1969–70 agreement is indicated by the wage-drift figures. During 1970, the second year of the two-year agreement, drift was 7·2 percent, the highest yet and more than twice as high as the contractual increases of 3·4 percent.[141] This reflected not only the fruits, formally illicit, of the wildcat strikes, but also increases granted to head off stoppages as well as to keep labor from being bid away. Just as in the mid-1960s, a boom that was only getting underway at the time a new central agreement was negotiated proved much stronger than anticipated. And just as before, the government's failure to tighten fiscal policy in time was seen as a major contributing factor.[142]

The fiscal stimulus in response to the recession that hit its trough in 1967 had also been delayed. Initially the government relied primarily on selective manpower policy which, as we have noted, underwent its greatest expansion up to that point.[143] While this policy mix could be seen as complying especially faithfully to the Rehn model prescription, it could also be seen as a further instance of mistimed fiscal-policy change. In any case the delay in shifting to a more restrictive fiscal policy once the recovery was clearly in progress certainly violated the prescription. Thus, at the end of the decade as in the middle of it, the loss of support to which the unions are prone if they perform the task assigned to them by the Rehn model while the government fails to do its part was forcefully demonstrated.

This time, however, rank-and-file disaffection took the much more serious form of widespread action in defiance of the 'web of rules' to which the unions were committed. The unions' ability to secure compliance with the rules and retain their members' support was thereby revealed to be much weaker than virtually everybody apparently assumed. LO and its affiliates were accordingly confronted with a crisis of authority, presenting a very real threat to their organizational cohesion.

To restore their authority it was necessary for them to reestablish the credibility of their claims to the support of their members. In so far as these rested on the unions' ability to protect their members' immediate interest in the greatest possible wage growth, it was essential to demonstrate this by securing contractual increases in the next wage round high enough to absorb so large a portion of any scope for increases the economy was likely to provide as to sharply limit the possibilities for wage drift. This, as we shall see, is what LO strenuously tried and largely succeeded in doing in the three-year central agreement negotiated for 1970–3.

A policy aimed at contractual increases that pre-empted most of the scope for increases did not necessarily promise a sufficient solution, however. For one thing it was difficult to forecast the required level of increases, especially in a world of increasing economic instability. In fact, the decline in economic activity in the early 1970s exceeded expectations just as the expansion during the life of the 1969–70 agreement did, amplifying the effect of the contractual increases on the level of drift, in opposite directions, in each case. In addition to making it difficult to be sure that contractual increases are set high enough to limit drift, such instability also increases the risk that they will be set so high as to dampen investment to an extent that union members' long-term interest in employment is jeopardized. Thus, as we shall also see, although an intensified squeeze on profits could render the problem of organizational cohesion more tractable, it could also aggravate the problem of investment, thereby sharpening LO's basic wage-policy dilemma.

At the same time, since such a pre-emptive wage policy had to be carried out at the confederal and national levels of union organization, it offered no remedy for an entirely different source of weakness in the unions' claim to their members' support. That was the substantial limits on what they could do for their members through their normal mode of operation, collective bargaining, at the local level, to which most members' direct experience of unions was largely confined. These limits were inherent in the structure of industrial relations through which LO sought to implement its strategy as it evolved ever since the 1930s, and of which the more recently developed system of centralized wage negotiations was a part. On the one hand, what local unions could do to press wage claims was limited by the concentration of authority over wage issues at the national and confederal levels. On the other hand, what they could do to advance their members' interests with respect to non-wage workplace issues was limited by the employers' success in keeping such issues within what they marked out as the exclusive domain of managerial prerogatives beyond the reach of collective bargaining. In so far as support for unions depends on their ability to protect their members' interests at the workplace, with respect to both wage and non-wage issues, these limits evidently left unions at the local level without a great deal that they could do to engage the interest and commitment of ordinary rank-and-file members.

It is true, as emphasized repeatedly, that the centralized wage negotiating system does leave room for local negotiations. The contracts into which central agreements are translated have to be implemented, in turn, at individual firms. This requires negotiations to determine how norms for the distribution of wage increases defined in terms of averages or otherwise are to be applied, and the like, Where piecerates or other performance-based pay systems are in use, such negotiations are both continuous and complicated. By and large, however, local unions enter into those negotiations with serious disadvantages that stem from overall union strategy and structure. Most importantly, they are deprived of the strike weapon both because union rules have concentrated authority over its use at the confederal and national level, and because the legally prescribed 'peace obligation' is in force once national contracts are signed. To be sure, employers are also deprived of the lockout weapon, but this leaves intact the power advantage inherent in their position, and against which strikes are the only real counterweight. This is essentially available at the local level only in unofficial, illegal form. It is also true that the extent of the employers' advantage varies with the state of the labor market. In so far as the unions' centralization contributes to full employment by enabling the Social Democratic Party to control the government this may be regarded as a price worth paying for the limits on local unions' bargaining power, more than offsetting their disadvantages. But in so far as tight labor markets enhance workers' opportunities for 'exit' rather than the unions' capacity for 'voice' as the route to higher pay the unions' claims to their members' support is not very effectively strengthened.[144]

As far as non-wage issues are concerned, the sweeping definition of managerial prerogatives which the employers were still able to enforce at the time of the 1969–70 wave of wildcat strikes severely limited what unions at all levels could do through collective bargaining. This definition was enshrined in the SAF constitution's para. 32, referred to earlier, which required the association's members to include in all contracts with unions a stipulation reserving 'the right of the employer to engage and dismiss workers at his own discretion; to direct and allot work; and to avail himself of workers belonging to any organization whatsoever, or to none'.[145] Some modifications in management's exclusive rights to determine these matters had been effected by the end of the 1960s. These concerned primarily layoffs and dismissals. The Basic Agreement already required a week's notice and discussion – but not negotiation – with union representatives in case of disputes, which could be referred to the LO–SAF joint committee for mediation, plus layoffs in order of seniority among otherwise equally qualified workers when business conditions dictate reductions in force.

In the 1964 central agreement, advance notice to the unions was extended to two weeks and binding arbitration of disputes by the joint committee, with financial penalties for unjustified dismissals or layoffs, was introduced. These modifications obviously did not go very far, however, applying only to the right to fire. Even that was not much diminished: the notification requirement was brief, selection of who gets laid-off was not effectively regulated, decisions were subject only to consultation and arbitration but not negotiation, sanctions did not extend to restoring the jobs of workers who were wrongly terminated and it remained impossible to contest personnel policy as opposed to individual cases.[146]

Meager as these constraints over the right to fire were, none whatever had been imposed on the vast range of decisions concerning who does what, with what equipment, in what kind of work environment, subject to what kind of discipline and everything else affecting workers other than the terms of employment – wages, hours and fringe benefits. All that the unions were able to accomplish in the broad area of workplace issues, apart from dismissals and layoffs, was a series of agreements providing for works councils. These were bodies in which management and union representatives could discuss and exchange information but not negotiate about production problems and changes, personnel policy, health and safety, and other workplace matters. The advances LO and TCO won in the 1966 agreement were that job satisfaction got equal status with productivity as goals of the councils; that employers were obliged to provide information concerning changes in production technology, organization, and the like, before making decisions about them; and that additional subcommittees could be attached to the councils. There was great variation in the extent to which practice conformed to these principles. In some enterprises there was apparently a degree of sustained collaboration between management and unions that far exceeded what the works councils were mandated to do and, for that matter, what para. 32 permitted. But these were exceptions. An LO survey showed that information was provided in advance of decisions concerning plant operations in a little over a quarter of the cases studied, and that experience fell far short of expectations in many other respects.[147] Even if all the expectations had been fulfilled, however, the managerial prerogatives asserted by the employers would have remained essentially undisturbed.

Although wage and non-wage issues may be analytically distinguished as in the preceding discussion, this is not to imply that they are always clearly separable in concrete situations. The capacity of local unions to negotiate wages, limited as it was anyway, could be further impaired as long as they were barred from negotiating at all on non-wage issues. Thus, employers could frustrate negotiations over wage disputes by the simple expedient of turning the disputes into non-negotiable matters of job reassignment or respecification, at least when the disputes involved one or a few workers. By the same token unions might give voice to non-negotiable workplace grievances by turning them into wage disputes. Of course, the symmetry is flawed, since unions could not legally resort to action in the form of strikes even in wage disputes, while there was no comparable legal barrier to the employers' use of their right to 'direct and allot work' as a tactic in such disputes. The interpretation of wildcat strikes as a protest against authority relations and workplace conditions – even when explicitly declared to be – has been dismissed on the ground that they are really aimed at wage increases. In so far as wage and non-wage issues can spill over into or serve as surrogates for each other the reverse might as well be true.[148]

Wage issues undoubtedly dominated the 1969–70 strike wave, but non-wage issues certainly added fuel to it, as illustrated by the LKAB strike.[149] It broke out at one unit over a long-simmering dispute over wage rates, brought to a head by the local application of the recently negotiated national wage contract. The latter, as we have seen, reflected the increasing egalitarian thrust of LO wage policy more strongly than any of the preceding central agreements. The miners could plausibly see themselves as losing the most from this development. Although male mineworkers were still among the most highly paid workers in industry, their relative position had declined during the 1960s. Their average hourly earnings rose less than those of male blue-collar workers in any other industry, so that over the decade they fell from 26 to 13 percent over the industry average.[150] Over the same period LKAB's demand for labor was eased by a 160 percent increase in productivity, measured in terms of tons per worker.[151] This happened at a time when the supply of labor in northern Sweden was fed by the continuing decline of agriculture, making it the region with the greatest decline in employment. How much the decline in the miners' relative wage position was due to the resulting state of the regional labor market and how much to solidaristic wage policy has apparently not been ascertained. At any rate the 1969 boom in the economy reversed the trend in demand for labor at LKAB. As alternative jobs become more plentiful workers left at an increasing rate – at least partly reflecting dissatisfaction with working conditions. LKAB consequently experienced labor shortages and recruiting difficulties for the first time in a decade. At the same time, it enjoyed high profits.[152] The situation clearly lent itself to an effort by the miners to reverse or, at least, stem the decline in their relative wage position.

The work stoppage that started it all was not simply about the level of pay, however. It also gave vent to resentment over the arbitrary and unilateral manner in which management repeatedly changed wage rates and the basis for computing them. As the strike spread to other units at LKAB dissatisfaction with wages was combined with an accumulation of grievances against managerial practices and attitudes built up over an extended period. Many of them were concerned at the way in which management carried out the intensive rationalization that underlay the rapid productivity growth. Workers' views on the rationalization process as well as other matters were supposed to be taken into account through a system of works councils and associated subcommittees which had been in existence at LKAB for a long time. Proving to be little more than a channel for transmitting information about decisions already taken, however, the system gradually lost whatever support among workers it ever had. Their experience of management was dominated instead by an elaborate system of controls built up over what had been highly autonomous work groups, applying an authoritarian approach to management derived from General Motors and codified in the so-called '31 Theses on Leadership'.[153] When this document was brought to light, it intensified resentment already running high over such issues as arbitrary piecerate changes, job reassignments and disciplinary actions, as well as subordination of health and safety concerns.[154]

In part, this pattern of managerial dominance reflected the ineffectiveness of the union, both locally and nationally, and it was as much against it as the management that much of the strikers' hostility was directed. The capacity of the miners' union local branches to constrain the management was undermined by a see-saw struggle for control between Social Democrats and communists – stronger in the north than anywhere else in the country – with each side tending to exploit every issue as a political weapon. Links between the members and the national union, highly centralized and headquartered in the distant capital, were further weakened by this political conflict, to which the national leadership responded by shutting the LKAB locals out of virtually any representation at the national level.[155] To the Social Democrats' left critics the situation was a prime exhibit of elite domination and deals made at the expense of the rank-and-file.

The strikers built up their own organization for formulating and pressing their demands. With the help of much media coverage, they won nation-wide support and concrete help in the form of contributions to a strike fund. Sanctions for the illegal action were clearly out of the question. In the settlement finally reached through LO mediation the strikers won many of their demands. Most significant was replacement of the piecerate system by monthly wages. That was accompanied by some wage increases, plus redress of various other grievances. Other demands, like replacement of the management and institutionalization of the local bargaining system that emerged during the strike, were lost. Given the miners' experience of what could be done, however, any restoration of prestrike managerial practice was improbable. Another by-product of the strike was a new chairman of the national union and increased representation of the northern miners in the union's national bodies.[156]

In the absence of information on the other strikes comparable in detail to that available on the LKAB strike we cannot say whether issues of workplace power and conditions were combined with wage issues to the same extent in the others. The LKAB strike may well have been something of a special case, for the degree of both managerial authoritarianism and union ineffectiveness there may have been exceptional. Yet this may be more a matter of degree than kind. As we have seen, the limited ability of unions on the local level to contest managerial power was built into the industrial-relations structure throughout Swedish industry. To the extent that this did, indeed, weaken the unions' claim to their members' support, as we suggested, it was undoubtedly an important factor in the loss of authority brought into sharp relief by the 1969–70 surge of unofficial strikes.

INDUSTRIAL DEMOCRACY: THE ATTACK ON MANAGERIAL PREROGATIVES

To restore their authority, then, it was essential for the unions' power at the workplace to be enlarged. The problem from LO's perspective was how this could be done without weakening the LO unions' capacity for concerted action on which their overall strategy depended not only in the market arena, but the state arena as well. Given this imperative, it could not be done by enlarging the unions' power to press wage claims at the local level, especially if it meant returning to them some of the control over the strike weapon that had been concentrated at the national and confederal levels. Occasional motions calling for the restoration of a 'local strike right' at union and LO congresses were consistently rejected on the ground that it would make solidaristic wage policy impossible.[157]

Alternatively, of course, it could be done by enlarging the unions' power to press non-wage workplace issues at the local level. To accomplish this, however, it was necessary to overcome the employers' insistence on their exclusive jurisdiction over such issues, as epitomized by para. 32. LO's acquiescence to para. 32 had been an integral part of the historical compromise on which the Swedish model was based. According to its terms, it will be recalled, production decisions are left in the hands of management (in state as well as private firms, as illustrated by the LKAB case), while the Social Democratic labor movement endeavors to use its control of the state to shape the macroeconomic environment in which those decisions are made. Within the framework established by management's production decisions and the state's macroeconomic policy, wages are jointly determined by management and unions through collective bargaining.

To extend union power into the domain from which it was excluded by para. 32 would accordingly mean altering one of the main elements in the historical compromise. Nevertheless, this was the course LO evidently felt compelled to pursue. With the adoption of a new program on 'Industrial Democracy' at its 1971 Congress,[158] LO launched a drive to eliminate the barrier to local union power posed by para. 32, by negotiation if possible and by legislation if necessary. That it would be necessary to turn to the political alternative was generally expected, and that is how it turned out. A stream of legislation was enacted in the early 1970s on employment security, occupational health and safety, shop stewards rights and, finally, a Law on Joint Determination in Work, in which SAF's para. 32 was rendered null and void.

LO's reliance on the power of the state to bring about the change in industrial-relations structure as well as the nature of the change itself marked a major shift of policy. The logic of this shift was not spelled out explicitly by LO in the terms in which we have presented it. We have instead inferred it from the situation in which LO was placed by the wildcat strike wave and the rapidity with which LO responded in its aftermath, which was reminiscent of the rapidity with which the Social Democratic government responded to its 1966 election setback by launching its industrial-policy program. As in the case of industrial policy, however, developments prior to the precipitating event pointed in the direction of the industrial democracy initiative.

Social Democratic ideology had, of course, included the idea of industrial democracy all along. A major effort to concretize it and move it to the top of the agenda was made by Wigforss in the 1920s but it proved abortive, overshadowed by the Social Democrats' political setbacks and the economic problems of the Great Depression. Moreover, it failed to strike a responsive chord in the unions, where worker participation in production decisions was viewed with familiar misgivings. If it took place through the unions, they would have to share responsibility for the consequences, compromising the independence needed to defend their members' interests. If it took place through new institutions separate from the unions, it could create a rival organization, competing with the unions for the workers' loyalty. Confining worker participation to discussion within some mechanism for joint consultation therefore seemed prefer- able, avoiding the risk of 'dual loyalty' while keeping it under union control.[159] Industrial democracy was thereby reduced to the system of consultative works councils built up under agreements between LO, TCO and SAF in 1946, 1958 and 1966.[160] This approach seemed satisfactory as long as union leaders could retain the belief that the combination of general and selective policies carried out by Social Democratic governments would suffice to protect workers from the burdens of technological and structural change, while union wage policies would assure them a fair share of its benefits.

This belief was gradually eroded during the 1960s, however, as we have noted earlier. There was a growing conviction that the rationalization of production by technological and structural change was imposing greater costs on workers than had been anticipated or than could be compensated by manpower policy, no matter how 'active'. By intensifying the pace of work, creating new and often unperceived physical dangers, increasing stress and social isolation, and in other ways, the rationalization process was now seen as hurting workers who retained their jobs in firms keeping up with technological change as well as workers who lost jobs in firms that failed to keep up. Increasing labor turnover, absenteeism and recruitment difficulties were interpreted as reactions to the process, while complaints filtering up through the unions, and repeatedly expressed in motions at union congresses, pinpointed many specific sources of dissatisfaction. In addition, surveys by LO and some national unions recorded its content and widespread prevalence.[161]

At the same time, if workers displaced by change were older or otherwise disadvantaged in their ability to meet the physical, psychological, or educational demands of the jobs becoming available, they were having increasing difficulty in finding alternative jobs. For growing numbers of them, reentry into industry was becoming impossible despite the generous retraining and relocation assistance being provided and the comparatively low overall unemployment. And for growing numbers of those who kept their jobs, insecurity about how long they could continue to do so in the face of further change added to the stresses resulting from the changes that had already occurred.[162]

All this combined to cast increasing doubt on the assumption that production decisions could be left to management. To do so meant that management was free to make such decisions without taking into account workers' needs, leaving them with no choice but to adapt or leave. If there was to be any adaptation of technology to workers, instead of a situation in which workers simply had to adapt to the technology chosen by management, they had to have the power to make their needs a constraint in decisions about technology. Since union organization was the only even potentially effective means for exercising such power, unions had to gain a voice in the decisions about technology and the related questions of how and by whom it was to be utilized. What stood in the way was the prevailing regime of managerial prerogatives.

It will be recalled that such arguments, including the conclusion that para. 32 blocked any effective solution, found expression in LO's 1966 document on *Trade Unions and Technological Change*. Yet, at that point, LO was not prepared to grasp the nettle of managerial prerogatives. While looking mainly to further elaboration and expansion of manpower policy to remedy the consequences of change, it preferred to stick to the joint-consultation approach to influencing change. However, that approach was becoming increasingly untenable in the face of its patent ineffectiveness in dealing with the sources of dissatisfaction.

It is admittedly difficult to know how much the dissatisfaction stemmed from decreasing tolerance for conditions that may have been no worse – or perhaps even better – than in the past. Particularly among new entrants to the labor force who had spent more years in less rigid schools than their predecessors, and who had not experienced the unemployment that had made previous generations more concerned with just having a job than the kind of work it involved, there may have been much less willingness to tolerate dangerous or boring jobs. This evidently extended to authority relations as well as physical conditions. Declining tolerance of hierarchical organization may well have been reinforced by the resurgence of critical ideological currents. Their expression in the renewed emphasis on equality in the Social Democratic Party included the demand for a 'democratization of working life'. Several motions at the party's 1969 Congress called for the elimination of para. 32 as an essential step in that direction.[163] The

New Left's challenge of all established authority, bureaucratic as well as capitalist, also contributed to an atmosphere in which the legitimacy of managerial prerogatives was being progressively eroded.[164] In that atmosphere the unions could no longer afford to avoid the issue of power at the workplace.

Management's own response to the situation put additional pressure on the unions. Production and profits obviously stood to suffer from the reactions to the process of rationalization cited earlier. Moreover, the attenuation of rank-and-file loyalty to unions, which had in the past been able to ensure industrial peace, posed dangers for management as well as unions. But it was also necessary from the employers' standpoint to contain and channel the union response lest it undermine management's ability to manage. The employers' approach was to promote experimentation with new forms of work organization, partly within the framework of the 1966 revision of the works councils agreement, but also partly on its own. SAF's technical department was given the task of stimulating and disseminating the results of such experiments, of which those at the Volvo and Saab auto plants were the most widely publicized. In all of these work reorganization projects local union involvement was accepted as indispensable. None the less, management at both the association and plant level was evidently determined to retain the initiative and ultimate power to decide what could and could not be done.[165]

This put the unions in a difficult position. On the one hand, the proliferation of work reorganization projects could make it seem that management was more responsive to worker discontent than the unions. On the other hand, to the extent that union involvement in projects or in other ways was confined within the limits of joint consultation, it was difficult for the unions to demonstrate any capacity of their own to respond.

All these factors evidently combined to convince LO's leadership that the time had come to go beyond joint consultation. In June 1969 it was decided to set up a committee to formulate a new program on industrial democracy. Headed by the vice-chairman and subsequent chairman of the Metalworkers' union, which had been especially active in pressing for change in this area, and including leaders from several other unions, the committee was to prepare concrete proposals for presentation to LO's 1971 Congress.[166] Thus, LO was already moving rapidly toward a frontal assault on managerial prerogatives before the 1969–70 wildcat strikes. What the strikes did was impart greater urgency to the movement and overwhelm any lingering doubts that the assault was imperative.

The general thrust of the program prepared by the committee and adopted by the Congress is to bring the whole range of managerial decisions, at all levels of the enterprise, within the scope of collective bargaining.[167] In this way unions at the local level could become the channel for workers' participation in decisions affecting their worklife, while the independence required to preserve the unions' capacity to protect their members' interests would be preserved. Since para. 32, and the Labor Court's interpretation of it as part of valid contracts, was an obstacle to extending the scope of collective bargaining to those decisions, it would have to be eliminated. And since the employers were clearly unwilling to eliminate it by agreement with the unions, it would have to be done by legislation. Such legislation would be part of a comprehensive reform of labor law, putting unions on an entirely new legal footing. On this basis they would proceed to negotiate the details of joint regulation of workplace issues, backed by any further legislation that might prove to be necessary. Rather than summarizing the program in detail, we shall describe the legislation passed over the following five years, for it embodied a very large part of what LO called for in the program and at various subsequent occasions. Before proceeding to that, however, it is important to note that TCO adopted a position very similar to LO's.

The two organizations worked together extensively in formulating proposals and participating in various committees set up by the government to make recommendations for legislation. Just a few months after LO decided to set up its committee on industrial democracy, TCO set up a counterpart. Its reports, to TCO's 1970 and 1973 congresses, presented arguments closely paralleling LO's.[168] The constellation of factors moving TCO in this direction was only partly the same, however. Although we cannot discuss these factors in detail, some indication of what they probably were is necessary. The radicalization of the ideological climate certainly affected TCO as it did LO, laying down a challenge from without and finding expression within. Although TCO is formally non-partisan, there is a strong left current in it, illustrated by the fact that 46 percent of its members voted for the Social Democrats in 1968.[169] In addition, the example of rank-and-file militancy abroad followed by the wildcat strikes at home pointed to the vulnerability of TCO as well as LO unions. On the other hand, the wildcat strikes were largely confined to LO unions. Moreover, TCO's capacity to coordinate wage bargaining was not at stake, since it had none to begin with. The separate bargaining arrangements that the different groupings of TCO unions were developing could be jeopardized by an erosion of member-support, but support was not being strained by anything like the tension between solidaristic wage policy and wage drift within LO.

The very fact that TCO was not a wage-negotiating body and that its affiliates were forming separate bargaining organizations gave TCO a particular incentive to pursue the industrial democracy issue quite different from LO's. To justify its existence and keep the different groupings of white-collar unions within its fold it was essential for TCO to have an alternative function to perform. Typically it has been to draw together and articulate the white-collar unions' positions on the wide range of public policy issues of common interest to them. Of course, many such issues, particularly general economic policy and tax policy, are difficult to separate sharply from wage policy. Indeed, TCO engaged in repeated exercises in the formulation of wage policy, if not negotiation. The distribution of functions between TCO and its affiliates has been a recurrent source of tension within the organization.

Differing political affinities within TCO also made the formulation of positions on public policy problematical, given the support such positions implied for different political parties – the disabling intensity of conflict within TCO on the national pension reform in the 1950s is a case in point. On the whole the public sector TCO unions have been closer to the Social Democrats and the private sector unions closer to the bourgeois parties. Political differences reinforced different wage-policy stakes to produce different orientations to LO. This cluster of factors entered into the struggles for leadership within TCO and, linked to the outcome, over the relative responsibilities of TCO and its affiliates.[170]

Against this background industrial democracy was apparently an issue that offered TCO an opportunity to bolster its status as the white-collar unions' umbrella organization. Understood as an issue of union power at the workplace, industrial democracy was patently a trade union issue. In pressing it, TCO would accordingly be functioning as a voice of the unions rather than as an interest group more loosely identified with white-collar workers. At the same time, in so far as SAF barred negotiations over workplace issues, and legislation was the only way of overcoming that barrier, TCO would be performing its accepted function of pursuing union interests in the political arena without encroaching on the functions its affiliates were reserving for themselves or the bargaining organizations they were developing. Moreover, on what was clearly a matter of trade union rights, TCO could not only adopt a position similar to LO's, but also join forces with it to realize their joint goal without being vulnerable to the charge of violating its non-partisanship. We do not have the evidence to demonstrate that this is how the TCO leadership saw the organizational implications of a campaign to enlarge the scope of collective bargaining, but it is clear that TCO had strong incentives to take up the issue. In any case it played an active role in shaping and securing the laws bolstering union power at the workplace during the first half of the 1970s.

Among the most important consequences of TCO's involvement was the additional stake it gave the SAP to take up the cause of industrial democracy. As pointed out earlier, the party's control of the government came to depend entirely on its own electoral strength once the Farmers'/Center Party ceased to be a potential source of parliamentary support and as long as neither of the other two bourgeois parties was a realistic alternative. The SAP's electoral strength, in turn, depended on attracting a substantial margin of support among white-collar workers in addition to its core constituency of blue-collar workers – the SAP got its largest share of the TCO-member vote when it won its majority in 1968. TCO's position on policy issues could make a difference to the size of that margin, putting a premium on policies that TCO could support even if it could not support the SAP explicitly. Such policies were not easy to find, because the more clearly a policy was identified as Social Democratic, the more likely political divisions within TCO would make it difficult for it to take a stand, as in the case of the 1950s pension-reform battle. Industrial democracy, as both TCO and LO defined it, did not suffer from that drawback, however, perhaps because it was so clearly a trade union issue. At the same time, the fact that the two confederations were developing a common set of demands which they jointly pressed was evidently marking out an area of interests common to the members of both federations. By championing these common interests and translating them into the government's legislative program the Social Democrats could strengthen their claim to being the party of all wage-earners, including white-collar workers in TCO as well as its traditional constituency of blue-collar workers in LO.

Besides offering a way of dealing with the problems of electoral strategy defined by the organizational context in which the changes in occupational structure were occurring, industrial democracy also seemed to fill the more immediate need for a new theme around which to mobilize the party's militants. Industrial policy lost its efficacy for that purpose as the measures involved failed to fulfill the ambitious expectations attached to them and economic policy proved no more effective in coping with instability after the measures than before. Industrial democracy and the working environment seemed to be the best available alternative.[171]

The Social Democrats did, in fact, introduce these themes in the 1970 election campaign, though as yet on a minor scale. As it turned out, they lost the majority they had won in 1968 in the 1970 election. The need for an effective mobilizing issue was consequently even greater in the next election, and the Social Democrats gave the 'democratization' and 'renewal of working life' much greater prominence in the 1973 campaign, but with no better results.[172] On the contrary, their parliamentary position declined further, and they managed to stay in office only because the communists won enough seats to produce an exact tie between the socialist and bourgeois blocs.

Without analyzing the Social Democrats' decline in any detail, two reasons why the industrial-democracy issue failed to avert it may be suggested. One is that it was overshadowed by the government's faltering economic policy. This was marked by a level of unemployment in 1972 considerably higher than the preceding peak in 1968, undermining what was still the Social Democrats' principal claim to support to a much greater extent than in the late 1960s. The other is that the industrial-democracy issue did not produce the kind of political polarization that drew sharp ideological lines between the two blocs. Both the liberals and Center Party adopted the issue as their own and went on to concentrate their campaign on the economy, where the Social Democrats were most vulnerable.[173] Paradoxically, although the absence of clear partisan division on the 'democratization and renewal of working life' made it easy for TCO to take a position on the issue similar to LO's, it also deprived the Social Democrats of any distinctive claim to represent an interest thereby defined as common to all wage-earners.

While industrial democracy failed to meet the SAP's needs in the electoral arena, its promotion of the specific measures corresponding to the rhetoric, plus the support which the liberals and Center Party were more or less committed to give them in the evenly tied 1973–6 session of Parliament, assured passage of legislation that largely fulfilled the LO–TCO objectives. A brief survey of the legislation's content concludes this section.

The first in the series of laws enacted since 1971 that introduced major innovations was a 1973 revision of the 1949 Work Safety Law. It expands the scope of health and safety regulations, extends their application to virtually all employment and substantially strengthens the position of union safety stewards. Among other things it gives the safety steward the right to halt any process he or she regards as imminently and seriously dangerous, pending a judgement from a state safety inspector. It also guarantees the safety stewards' job security and right to do what they regard as necessary to perform their duties, as well as training and time to perform them without loss of pay. Safety stewards who dispute any change in their job status, including reassignment or dismissal, are entitled to retain their job, pay and working conditions unless and until the employer can get a judgement to the contrary from the Labor Court.

This law thereby introduces the principle that the union's view of a disputed matter should prevail while it is being adjudicated, transferring what is referred to as the 'interpretation prerogative' from the employer to the union. In doing so it shifts the burden of initiating a legal challenge and of proof from the union, on which it had lain in the past, to the employer. The safety steward's right to stop imminently hazardous processes rather than having to first summon a safety inspector, leaving workers subjected to the hazard in the meantime, can be seen as a special instance of the principle, which was given progressively wider application in subsequent legislation.

Another innovation made in the Work Safety Law revision that has more far-reaching implications is that the authority of safety stewards and union members of obligatory safety committees is extended beyond existing conditions to the planning of changes. Employers must provide them with information about anticipated changes in plant layout, equipment, new construction, and so on, in advance of the changes, which can be held up by the union representatives on grounds of health and safety. Finally, the concept of health and safety is widened to embrace the work environment in broad terms, including its impact on workers' psychological as well as physical well-being.[174]

Several of the laws impose restrictions on management's authority to hire and fire, with particular emphasis on protecting those vulnerable to job insecurity because of age or union activity. Two laws in 1971 made modest beginnings in this direction, followed by three in 1974 that went much further. One was the Security of Employment Act. It requires employers to give notice of termination ranging from one to six months in advance, depending on length of service and age. It makes all unreasonable dismissals illegal, the conception of 'unreasonable' being framed in such a way as to especially protect older workers and union officials. In cases where a union disputes the reasonableness of a decision to terminate someone's employment the interpretation prerogative is assigned to the union as in the Work Safety Law, so the affected person is entitled to retain his or her job at full pay pending adjudication of the employer's claim – if he chooses to press it – by the Labor Court.

Another, the Law on Employment-Promoting Measures, was designed primarily to increase employment opportunities for older and otherwise disadvantaged workers. Employers must notify both the local union and local employment office of impending layoffs up to six months in advance, depending on the number of workers involved. Tripartite committees –

including employer, union and employment office representatives – are thereupon supposed to be set up to seek ways to assure continued employment, such as postponing layoffs, temporary subsidization, or intrafirm transfers. In addition, tripartite 'adjustment groups' are supposed to be set up to modify personnel policy and redesign jobs so as to adapt local demand for labor to the locally available labor supply. Local employment offices are not only authorized to require employers to supply information on these matters, but also to change their practices and even hire only persons referred to them by the offices if this should be judged necessary.

The third law in this group, the Law on Union Officials' Status at the Workplace, essentially extends to all union officials the protection provided to safety stewards. It lays down various rights of officials, including rights to information, and time and training for union work at the employer's expense, as well as further guarantees against discrimination in earnings and job assignments. Again, in any disputes over these rights, the union's view prevails unless and until the Labor Court upholds the employer's contrary view.[175]

Another group of laws provides for employee representation on boards of directors. The first is a 1972 law giving unions the right to select two representatives to serve as regular members of the boards of most private industrial corporations and cooperatives with 100 employees or more. This was put into effect for an experimental period of three years. In 1976 it was replaced by a permanent statute, extending employee board representation to all industrial firms with twenty-five employees or more and strengthening employee representatives' rights in some respects. Simultaneously, legislation was enacted establishing the same employee membership on bank and insurance company boards. Also, a modified form of employee representation on the decision-making bodies of central and local government agencies was provided for.

What must be stressed in this connection is that the small size of employee board representation – not even approaching parity – is not conceived as a first, timid step toward German-style *Mitbestimmung*. On the contrary, it reflects the Swedish unions' basic decision against following the West German unions' route to participation in decision-making through board membership. Instead board membership is looked upon mainly as a way of increasing the unions' access to information needed to put them in a better position to influence decision-making at all levels, from the enterprise as a whole down to the shopfloor, through the alternative route of collective bargaining.[176]

The main effort down this route so far is embodied in the Law on Joint Determination in Work referred to as MBL (*Medbestämmandelagen*) enacted in June 1976. It replaces the three laws that established the basic legal framework of industrial relations in the 1920s and 1930s, retaining most of the essential features of that framework but strengthening the union's position within the enterprise in crucial respects. Most importantly, it specifies that unions can negotiate agreements providing for joint-determination rights in all matters concerning hiring and firing, work organization and management of the enterprise generally. To emphasize the nullification of SAF's para. 32 that this entails, the declaration that collective bargaining applies to all these matters is made in para. 32 of the new law. The 1976 law also gives unions a so-called 'residual right to strike' if settlements on joint determination are not reached, even though there may be an agreement in force on other issues and strikes over such issues remain illegal during the life of the agreement.

Whatever additional rights might be won in joint-determination agreements, certain minimum standards are set by the law. One is that management is required to initiate negotiations in advance of important changes in operations, such as expansion, contraction and reorganization, as well as in an individual's tasks and working conditions. With respect to all other changes, management is obliged to negotiate if called upon to do so by the union. In the latter case, as well, management has to postpone implementation of any decision until negotiations are completed, except under exceptional circumstances like emergencies. Management is also required to supply information from company accounts and other data concerning company operations and plans to unions, and to conduct whatever studies may be needed to supply any additional information unions request, subject to the obligation to observe management's designation of any information as a business secret.

The presumption in favor of the union's view of a disputed question introduced in the earlier safety and job security legislation is extended by the 1976 law to all disputes involving joint determination agreements, as well as work assignments and discipline. In disputes over wage issues the employer retains the interpretation prerogative subject to a time limit within which he is obliged to enter into negotiations over the issue and, if not settled, submit it to the Labor Court. Otherwise the union's view is to prevail. Unions are also given a veto right over work given to outside contractors if they regard this as circumventing collective agreements or the law.[177]

The principle of joint determination through collective bargaining is applied to the public as well as private sector. The 1965 law giving public sector employees collective bargaining rights contained a counterpart to SAF's para. 32 that limited the scope of collective bargaining even further. This limitation was excluded in a new Law on Public Employment, enacted along with the general Joint Determination in Work Law. On the other hand, a partial equivalent remains, as indicated in an agreement between the public sector negotiating bodies and the affected unions. That agreement acknowledges that collective bargaining cannot 'infringe on political democracy'. Thus, the 'purposes, character, extent, and quality' of public administration that are decided by elected bodies are placed beyond the scope of collective bargaining. Where the line is to be drawn is to be determined on a case-to-case basis by a committee on which the unions have minority representation.[178]

Olof Palme, the Social Democratic Prime Minister and party leader, hailed the series of labor-law reforms enacted during 1971–6 as the 'greatest diffusion of power and influence since the introduction of universal suffrage'.[179] So extravagant a claim testifies more to the weight attached to the 'democratization of working life' in the effort to revitalize the party's ideology than to what had actually been achieved. Still, the legislation certainly opened up the possibility for a significant redistribution of workplace power. The extent to which it would occur depended on how actively and effectively the unions and their members realized this possibility – realizing the democratic potential of universal suffrage has, of course, also been a prolonged, and incomplete, process. To the extent that the legislation does make it possible for unions at the local level to reengage the interest and commitment of their members by providing them with ways of affecting their daily work experience to a much greater extent than they could in the past, it undoubtedly can contribute toward solving a problem that posed a serious threat to the LO unions' capacity to mobilize support not only in the market arena, but in the state arena as well. And in so far as it substantially enlarges the power of unions at the workplace without significantly redistributing power within unions from national to local levels, it preserves their capacity to combine their resources in the service of a coherent strategy in both arenas. To reinforce its organizational capacity in this way, however, LO had been compelled to reject one of the essential terms of the settlement between labor and capital that had been in effect since the 1930s. To resolve the wage policy dilemma that nevertheless remained, as we shall see in the next section, LO felt compelled to make another, more fundamental, break with the terms of the settlement.

Wages, Profits and Investment: Toward Collective Capital Formation

As the time to negotiate a new central agreement to replace the one for 1969–70 approached LO had to wrestle anew with the two problems besetting its efforts to implement its solidaristic wage policy throughout the labor market: the one posed by drift and the one posed by the white-collar unions' separate negotiations. The first had been rendered acute by the wildcat strikes, making it imperative for LO to secure contractual increases high enough to minimize the scope for drift. As for the second, since the private sector white-collar unions' long-term agreements had put themselves beyond the reach of LO's efforts for the time being, the possibilities were limited to the public sector.

The two problems were intertwined. While the exceptionally high drift during the 1969–70 agreement period frustrated the agreement's intended distributive effects within LO, it enabled LO union members' average hourly earnings to increase a good deal faster than those of white-collar union members, thereby accomplishing a more effective reduction of differentials than LO was able to attain through negotiations. LO was determined to prevent the white-collar unions from undoing these distributive effects of the high drift. Accordingly, when the public sector white-collar unions demanded large increases to make up for the drift their members did not get, LO declared that it would have to demand increases high enough to preserve the reduced differentials between blue-collar and white-collar workers. Conceding that this would far exceed the economic scope for increases, Geijer argued that it was unavoidable as long as there was no coordination of wage bargaining across the labor market as a whole that could keep interunion wage rivalry from pushing wage increases that far.[180] In other words, distributive conflict among different groups of workers, within and between union confederations, intensified distributive conflict between workers and employers. In so far as profits were consequently squeezed to such an extent that there was insufficient investment in expanding production to offset contracting production, the structural change strategy was thwarted, and the long-term interests of all workers, blue collar and white collar, in employment were threatened. By the time LO's 1971 Congress met the threat was perceived as a real one.

THE 1970–3 CENTRAL AGREEMENT

In the absence of agreement by LO and the other unions to coordinate their wage bargaining, LO again sought to force simultaneous settlements as in the preceding central negotiations. In LO's negotiations with SAF its distributive demands were aimed at further diminishing fringe-benefit differences between LO and TCO union members, as well as continuing to improve the relative position of lower-paid workers. In particular, it demanded pension and sick-pay benefits, supplementing state benefits, which white-collar workers had and blue-collar workers did not, and also a gradual elimination of the differences between them in retirement ages, which were two years higher for blue-collar workers in the private sector (and even higher in the public sector).[181] Thus, the emphasis on reducing inequalities between members of LO and other unions was more pronounced than in the previous negotiations. At the same time, the low-wage provision it sought, although similar in construction to the one in the expiring agreement, was aimed at a somewhat smaller improvement in the relative position of lower-paid workers.[182] The design of these demands clearly suggests that LO unions were shifting the egalitarian thrust of their wage policy away from differences between LO members to differences between members of LO and other unions.

Events did not follow LO's projected scenario this time either, however, and it was again because other negotiators frustrated LO's efforts to achieve simultaneous and similar settlements by laying the basis for a settlement – though not actually reaching it in this instance – long before LO and SAF were anywhere near that stage. This time it was the state negotiating agency, SAV, and the state sector unions, including the LO union of state employees, SF (*Statsanställdas förbund*), as well as the cartel of TCO unions in the state sector, TCO-S, that seized the initiative.

With the SF taking the lead, the state sector unions demanded a substantially greater relative improvement for lower-paid workers than LO was demanding in the private sector. To their surprise, as well as everyone else's, SAV not only agreed but did so at a very early stage, in December 1970, before any of the negotiations had really got under way. This apparently did not reflect an effort by the Social Democratic government, imbued with renewed egalitarian fervor, to reinforce LO's solidaristic wage policy. It is explained instead as a way of meeting intense dissatisfaction, on the verge of breaking out in wildcat strikes, by members of TCO police unions. Since concessions for this group alone were ruled out, the response had to take the form of terms applicable to all state employees at the same wage level. This, in turn, established a pattern that had to be followed in the much larger local government sector, and that was bound to exert heavy pressure on the private sector as well.[183]

Before these consequences of SAV's low-wage bid could work their way through the system, however, another more dramatic event intervened, a strike by SACO and SR. It started at the beginning of February 1971, when SACO union members in selected local governments walked out, followed by SACO members in the central government and SR members in the state railways. SAV responded by lockouts which ultimately extended to the military officers – perhaps the only instance of a state taking such action against its own armed forces. Having reached this point the work stoppage was finally ended after six weeks by special emergency legislation requiring cessation of the strikes and lockouts for a period of six weeks. This broke the strike, which was not resumed after the legislation expired.[184]

By the time the strike was ended nearly four times as many working days were lost as in the wildcat strike wave in late 1969 and early 1970.[185] The stoppage's magnitude was, of course, due to the lockout, which plays a part in Swedish industrial conflict approximated in no other country with free trade unions with the possible exception of West Germany. SACO, which took the lead, had evidently not expected SAV to take a leaf out of the private employers' book and make such full use of the weapon, particularly since it had not done so in response to SACO's first and relatively successful strike in 1966. SACO summoned much the same arguments as before, having issued another report on lifetime earnings in the interim, except that now it claimed not only that the differences between its members and those represented by other unions had been further diminished, but that its members had also suffered an actual decline in real post-tax income.[186]

SACO's data were disputed, but its main problem was its inability to evoke much public sympathy. It was seen as trying to maintain a privileged position originating in a bygone era when educated labor was scarce and the premium it commanded was accepted as fair. Olof Palme pinpointed the vulnerability of SACO's position, and of white-collar workers generally, in saying that 'the whole development of wages has to be different when 85 percent instead of 3 percent has education at the gymnasium level', making it 'entirely unreasonable to retain the wage gaps of the past'.[187] Perception of the SACO strike as an effort to protect a position of unfair privilege clearly contributed to Social Democratic support for the emergency legislation to stop it. Nevertheless, the state's resort to its coercive authority in a labor dispute was, in varying degrees, viewed as an unwelcome precedent by unions and employers.

Events in the public sector continued to dominate the course of the wage round. In May a commission set up to mediate the state sector dispute prior to the strike submitted a final proposal for a three-year settlement incorporating the low-wage provision SAV had offered. Negotiations in that sector dragged on another month, but shortly after the proposal was made public, a settlement that followed it very closely was reached in the local government sector in which no mediation commission had been appointed.[188] Although the state sector still had to settle, the pattern of increases throughout the public sector, including both the overall level and its heavy loading in favor of lower-paid workers, was pretty clear.

A separate commission set up to mediate the LO–SAF negotiations proceeded on the premiss that there could be no agreement that did not give LO members roughly what the public sector workers were getting, even if precise comparisons were rendered difficult by the differences in pay systems. The proposal it accordingly made on this basis was rejected by SAF as much too costly in view of the downturn that was already underway, while also objecting to the particular form of the low-wage provision LO demanded. LO thereupon began turning on the pressure by giving notice of an overtime ban and then a strike of 10 percent of its members in SAF companies.

Instead of countering with lockout threats according to the usual saber-rattling scenario, SAF mounted an advertising campaign stressing the economic danger of a settlement along lines demanded by LO and closely approximated by the mediation commission's proposal. There was a good deal of support within SAF for going to the brink or even beyond. However, the prevailing view was that there was a real risk that the government would block any new breakout of open conflict by again resorting to emergency legislation. In this case the legislation would most likely turn the mediation commission's proposal into a binding settlement. Such an outcome seemed all the more plausible when the Finance Minister said he did not believe there could be a settlement that differed much from the commission's proposal. The pressure this put on SAF, combined with some modifications in the proposal that LO did accept along with promises by the government to relax the price controls it had imposed in 1970, led to the conclusion of an agreement on the eve of the summer vacation in late June.[189]

Thus, the 1970–3 agreement resulted from a sequence of events very different from the one LO had envisioned. It was also different from the one assumed by the EFO model, and normally followed in practice, in which the industries exposed to international competition, the C sector, which are almost entirely in the private sector, act as the wage leader. This is how it would have been, said Geijer in the aftermath, 'if we had had our way'.[190] Instead SAV's initiative, with the government's apparent concurrence, made the public sector the wage leader. Paradoxically the state sector unions' ambitious low-wage demands, which SAV accepted so early and fully, were pressed most aggressively by LO's state sector union, pointing up the limits of LO's ability to coordinate its own affiliates' bargaining. Once SAV made its offer a pattern was established that may well have resulted in contractual increases in the C sector significantly higher than they would have been if LO had achieved the aims it declared at the beginning of the negotiations, even though these aims included an overall increase high enough to pre-empt much of the scope for drift.

As it turned out, contractual increases in industrial workers' average hourly earnings, totaling 18·2 percent over the 1970–3 agreement period, were more than one and a half times as high as drift, amounting to 11·7 percent over the same three-year period.[191] The excess of contractual increases over drift during this period was greater than in any preceding agreement period. The exceptionally low level of drift reflected the inter-action of high contractual increases with a sharp contraction of demand.

This fall in demand was due to the government's shift to a restrictive fiscal policy after a downturn had already occurred, reinforcing the effects of a contraction in demand in some of Sweden's trading partners. The perverse timing pattern of fiscal policy changes displayed in the 1964–8 boom to recession cycle was, thus, being repeated in the 1969–72 cycle. The strength of the policy-augmented recession is indicated by the fact that unemployment was even higher in 1972 than in 1968, 2·7 as against 2·2 percent, which was indeed higher than in any postwar year except 1958. 1972 was also the year in which contractual increases most exceeded drift, 7·4 percent compared with 3·3 percent, or well over twice as high. In the same year the share of profits in C-sector value added fell to 20·7 percent, compared with 22 percent in 1967, when it was at its lowest level during the preceding recession, and lower than in any other postwar year.[192]

By this reckoning C-sector profits were squeezed particularly hard between LO's pre-emptive wage policy and the government's very restrictive fiscal policy. In the process the threat to organizational cohesion posed by wage drift was largely eliminated, at least for the time being. But if the successively lower profit shares at their low points in the two recessions reflected a trend, and its consequence was declining investment, as the EFO model suggested it might be, the drift may have been reduced to tolerable levels at the cost of future as well as current employment. That there was, indeed, a declining share of profits and that it was already resulting in insufficient investment during the second half of the 1960s was the conclusion drawn by the government's 1970 *Long-Term Survey*.

SOLIDARISTIC WAGE POLICY AND THE PROBLEM OF INVESTMENT: THE MEIDNER PLAN

According to the *Survey*, deficits in the balance of current payments in the boom years of 1965 and 1969–70 that were considerably higher than in the preceding period pointed to a structural deterioration in Sweden's position in the international economy. Restoration of the economy's long-run external equilibrium was accordingly identified as the central problem of economic policy. To solve the problem during the coming five-year period the *Survey* estimated that industrial investment would have to grow by a 6·5 percent annual rate, more than twice as fast as in the preceding quinquennium and faster than at any time since the investment boom of 1958–62.[193]

A decline in profit margins averaging 1·2 percent per year during the 1960s was cited by the *Survey* as the principal obstacle to the needed acceleration of investment. The fall in profits had reduced business savings to such an extent that a declining portion of investment was self-financed even though the rate of investment itself had gone down. Because a large part of the required increase in external financing took the form of borrowing, the debt–equity ratio increased. Assuming no further decline in profits, nor any increase either, the *Survey* pointed out that a marked further decline in self-financing would have to occur if the required investment was to take place. If financed by a corresponding increase in borrowing, the result would be an additional increase in the debt–equity ratio. Firms whose financial vulnerability was thereby increased would be expected to be less willing to undertake the more risky new investments, making it likely that the total increase in investment would fall short of what was needed. If so, the *Survey* concluded, 'economic policy would be faced with the task of promoting the supply of risk-bearing capital, besides taking varied measures to stimulate investment propensity in private business'.[194]

If the 1970 *Long-Term Survey*'s perception and diagnosis of an emerging problem of investment was correct, the issue left unresolved by the Rehn model now had to be faced. That issue, it will be recalled, is whether the increase in collective savings designed to offset the decline in business savings can be effectively channeled into investment, so that investment will remain at the required level despite the profits squeeze resulting in the decline of business savings. Collective savings did increase more than enough to offset the decline of business savings to which the *Survey* pointed. Virtually all of this increase was accounted for by the accumulation of a large surplus in the AP fund established at the beginning of the decade.[195] However, in so far as it was channeled into industry, it was in the form of loan capital. Yet, according to the *Survey*, the need was for an increased supply of equity capital. The question for LO, then, was how collective savings could be tapped to meet this need.

There were two lines along which LO sought to provide an answer. One was to turn the institution for collective savings at the national level that was already in existence, the AP fund, into a source of equity capital by authorizing it to purchase shares as well as bonds. The other was to turn some of the equity capital generated at the level of the firm into collective savings by transferring a portion of profits in the form of new shares to a new institution set up and administered by the unions. Both were developments of ideas broached earlier, but the issue to which they were addressed was confronted with much greater urgency at LO's 1971 Congress.

A motion by the Metalworkers' union stated that the central issue was 'how increased resources can be provided for investment without having negative effects on the distribution of wealth'. It cited the 1970 *Survey*'s analysis stressing the need for increased investment and for increased equity capital to finance it. But it declared that capital formation could no longer be carried out as in the past, when financing investments largely by profits increased the concentration of wealth and power among the few 'who dominate ownership in banks and industry'. Other motions and a wage policy report called for alternative mechanisms for capital formation on the related ground that the existing mechanism tended to undermine solidaristic wage policy.[196] The adoption of these motions marked the beginning of intensified efforts to promulgate solutions to the problem of investment consistent with the basic organizational and ideological premises underlying LO's structural change strategy.

Since the AP fund was in place, transforming it into a source of equity as well as loan capital was a relatively straightforward matter. The argument for doing so had already been put forward a decade earlier in the report on *Coordinated Industrial Policy*. While that did not have the status of an official policy position, the 1966 LO Congress formally called upon the government to authorize the AP fund to purchase shares.[197] The rights thereby acquired were also viewed as an instrument of an industrial policy needed to guide structural change, though, as indicated earlier, the nature of the policy was still quite vague at that point. The government's only response was to include the question among those to be considered by a Capital Market Commission set up in 1968 to conduct a comprehensive review of the AP fund's role in the capital market. By the time LO's 1971 Congress met the Commission had done nothing on the question, and the Congress decided to put renewed pressure on the government for action. This took the form of a long memorandum submitted to the government shortly thereafter, stating the case for equity-financing by the AP fund and demanding the introduction of legislation to that end in the following session of Parliament.[198]

Invoking the 1970 *Survey*'s argument as evidence of the need for increased industrial investment, and for risk capital to finance it, this memorandum stresses the importance of how the investment is brought about. First, there is the matter of allocation. The assurance that investment would go where needed to preserve industry's international competitiveness could be provided only with the aid of planning over a longer time perspective than market signals could provide. While large corporations understood this, the planning could not be left to them; the whole society's future was at stake, so the society ought to have a much more effective role in the planning process. More had to be done than industrial policy had accomplished thus far.

Secondly, there is the matter of financing. The memorandum builds on the 1970 *Survey*'s argument that the main need is for more equity capital. The choice is whether to meet the need from private or collective savings. The private options are rejected on the ground that they are inadequate and have unacceptable consequences from both the allocative and distributive points of view.

Internally generated private savings are inadequate because profits are too low to permit investment to be financed internally to such a large extent as in the past. However, that was an excessive level of self-financing, so letting profits return to levels high enough to provide the needed capital is no solution. Such a high degree of self-financing renders firms insensitive to stabilization policy and exerts a conservative effect on industrial structure. (This has also been LO's critique of the corporate tax system's bias in favor of further growth by firms that have been able to generate profits in the past.) It also tends to increase the already-high concentration of wealth and power. This runs counter to the trade union movement's demands both for a reduction of inequality and a 'real influence not only on the volume [of investment] but also on how and where it is carried out'. Financing investment out of external private savings is rejected for similar reasons. The supply of such external savings is found to be inadequate on the ground that industry only financed 4 percent of its investment during

1965–9 by raising equity capital on the stock market. To increase the supply would again presuppose further increasing inequality of both wealth and power.

This leaves collective savings as the only adequate and acceptable source of increased equity-financing. Since collective savings are already available in one form – the AP fund – it should be put to use without waiting until other forms, such as LO was considering, were designed. Various technical arrangements for doing so are reviewed without insisting on any of them. The main thing is to go ahead. In addition, LO calls for the merger of the three separate funds into which the AP fund was divided and for a trade union majority on the new single board.

This time LO got results, though they took two years to materialize and were not all that LO wanted. The government passed LO's memorandum to the Capital Market Committee with specific instructions to come up with a recommendation. The outcome was legislation establishing a new unit in the AP system authorized to purchase shares. Designated as the Fourth Fund, to distinguish it from the three existing units which were kept separate, the new unit went into operation with its own board and administration in January 1974. Initially it was authorized to purchase shares up to a limit equal to only a little more than 5 percent of the fees paid into the system in that year alone. This was nevertheless almost as much as the average net amount of equity capital raised during the 1960s on Sweden's relatively small stock market, from which international transactions are virtually excluded. The Fourth Fund limit was doubled in 1976, by which time it had shares in twenty-six companies. On the basis of substantial holdings in six of them, including Volvo, the Fourth Fund gained representatives on their boards. While no limit was originally placed on the size of its holdings in any one company, a 10 percent limit was imposed in 1979. At the same time, the amount it was authorized to draw from the rest of the AP system for investment in shares was increased. It adopted the practice of voting 40 percent of its shares directly and assigning the other 60 percent to the local unions in the companies.[199]

The second line along which LO sought a way to provide equity capital in the form of collective savings was a variant of the idea underlying the 'branch funds' also referred to in the 1961 report on *Coordinated Industrial Policy*. As we have seen, the funds were suggested as a way of coping with the problems posed by the untapped potential for wage increases that solidaristic wage policy tends to leave in high-profit firms, at least in so far as the policy works as it is supposed to. Depending on how that potential is utilized, it will be recalled, it has various distributive consequences that are unacceptable from LO's point of view. If it remains in the form of profits, it adds to shareholders' wealth, regardless of whether they are plowed back or distributed, running counter to the labor movement's declared intention of reducing inequality between labor and capital. And if it is used to pay wages in excess of standard rates, in the form of wage drift, it frustrates the intended distributive effects of solidaristic wage policy and erodes it as a basis for the LO unions' agreement on coordinated wage bargaining.

What this implies, although it was not put precisely in these terms, is that it is difficult if not impossible to sustain solidaristic wage policy unless it is accompanied by some mechanism that shortcircuits the links between the additional cash flow that standard rates permit in high-profit firms and the incomes of both shareholders and workers. Branch-rationalization funds, to which the cash flow could be diverted, could be understood as a mechanism of that kind. Although their expected effect on private share-holders was left vague, the suggestion that the funds would transform firms into 'social enterprises without owners' implies that the funds would provide a collective alternative to private shareholders as a source of equity capital, progressively diminishing the latter's proportion of equity capital.

Nothing came of the idea at the time, as we have seen, nor in 1966 when it was brought up again. At mid-decade solidaristic wage policy was only beginning to be effectively implemented. But by the 1971 Congress, as indicated earlier, LO was increasingly successful in making the relative improvement of lower-paid workers stick, particularly through the device of earnings guarantees. In this way drift made possible by the potential for increases left untapped by standard rates in high-profit firms is partially transmitted to other firms. This amounts to an *ex post* correction of standard rates, raising their average level to more closely match the scope for drift in the high-profit firms, thereby intensifying the profit squeeze in the other firms.

In effect, the Rehn model prescription of setting standard rates sufficiently high to keep drift within limits consistent with organizational cohesion was being applied more forcefully than it apparently had been a decade earlier. The potential for creating a problem of investment inherent in this approach had also materialized, compounding the problems posed for solidaristic wage policy by uneven profits and drift. To cope with those problems now it had become essential to resolve the larger dilemma of reconciling solidaristic wage policy with the level of investment needed to make the structural-change strategy work in the more unfavorable international environment in which Sweden found itself. Hence, as urged in several of the motions passed by the 1971 Congress, the time had come to devise a mechanism for collective capital formation in the form of branch funds or whatever, through which solidaristic wage policy could be reconciled with the need for increased investment without leading to increased concentration of wealth and power.

The task of preparing a proposal for some such mechanism for presentation to the 1976 Congress fell to a committee headed by Rudolf Meidner, who had been responsible for the 1961 and 1966 reports as well as a participant in formulating the Rehn model. A preliminary version of the proposal was issued in 1975 and made the subject of an intensive internal publicity campaign, including study circles in which some 18,000 members answered a questionnaire concerning various issues involved.[200] A revised version was submitted to the 1976 Congress, which adopted its main principles, though not the details which were designed primarily to illustrate possible arrangements. Known as the Meidner Plan, after its principal author, the proposal can be summarized as follows.

A certain percentage of pretax profits, on the order of 20 percent, earned by all private firms above some specified size, say, fifty employees, would be transferred in the form of new, directed issues of shares to a new institution, called 'wage-earner funds', set up for the purpose and administered entirely or primarily by the unions. The portion of profits allocated to the funds would constitute new equity capital, remaining at the disposal of the firms in which profits are generated, and would be exempted from corporate taxation in the same way as profits set aside for future investment according to the so-called investment reserve-fund system. Instead of accruing to private shareholders, however, the claims to the new wealth created by investing the allocated profits would accrue to the funds.

Neither the new shares nor the dividend income would be distributed to workers individually. Instead the shares would be held permanently by the funds and the dividend income would be used for purchase of additional shares and a variety of services for all workers. These would include education and the technical support needed to make effective the increased voice in workplace and enterprise decisions gained as a result of the 1970s legislation, referred to earlier. The voting rights as well as claims to wealth that go with share ownership would also accrue to the funds. This would give unions additional leverage on enterprise decision-making. Eventually the funds would gain controlling shares in the firms.

In sketching the possible organization of the proposed system different functions are assigned to different bodies. The firms that generate the profits allocated to the funds retain the use of the funds for investment. What the allocation does is transform the increment to equity capital resulting from the profits from internal to external capital. The shares corresponding to the new equity capital are held by a central 'equalization fund', directed by a board selected by all unions in all confederations. The fund also receives all the dividend income, but most of it is redistributed among a set of branch or industry funds, directed by boards selected partly by the unions in the respective branches and partly by other unions, and possibly by the government and other interest groups. Voting rights for selecting board members of companies whose shares are held are distributed between the local unions in the companies and the branch funds, with local unions voting all the shares up to 20 percent of the total and half of the shares beyond that.

The rationale for the proposal presented in the Meidner committee report and the LO executive's motion recommending its adoption is framed in terms of three objectives which are derived from the motions passed at the 1971 Congress which gave the committee its mandate, and at the 1973 Metalworkers' Congress as well. The three objectives which the proposed system of collective capital formation is claimed to meet are summarized approximately as follows:

(1) to provide solidaristic wage policy with the mechanism it needs to operate without redistributing income from labor to capital in high-profit firms;
(2) to counteract the concentration of wealth and power associated with the self-financing of investment;
(3) to reinforce the rights to influence industrial development which

workers have on the basis of their work, as affirmed in the labor-law reforms.

The common thread running through these objectives is described as the reduction of inequality of income, wealth and power between labor and capital.

The point is made that an increase in capital formation is not one of the objectives which the system is designed to meet. Instead the system must only be 'neutral from the point of view of capital formation'. This is characterized as one of the requirements or conditions imposed on the design by other trade union objectives. Of these, full employment is cited as by far the most important. Since 'high capital formation' is essential to meet that objective, the system must be so designed that it does not make it more difficult to attain the required level of capital formation. In addition, it must be 'cost-, wage- and price-neutral', having no inflationary effect, while leaving the division between wages and profits to be determined by collective bargaining. Finally, it must not obstruct solidaristic wage policy's main objective of 'equalizing income among different groups of workers'.

Given these objectives and constraints, certain features are designated as essential to the fund system. Allocations to the funds must be a function of profits if the system is to provide solidaristic wage policy with the support it needs. The workers' share of the profits must nevertheless remain in the firms in which they are generated in the form of increments to equity capital, so as to leave the firms' capacity, and incentive, to invest unimpaired. At the same time, the funds that hold the capital must not be tied to individual firms. Moreover, the workers' capital must be permanently held by the funds, without ever being distributed to individual workers. These features are essential to maintain the basic principle of solidaristic wage policy that workers' income should not depend on the profitability of the firms in which they are employed, nor on sources other than wages, such as proceeds from the sale of shares, and also to preserve the power to influence enterprise decision-making that workers collectively gain from the accumulation of shares. Although the funds should not be tied to individual firms, their shares in each firm must be used to strengthen the influence of the firms' employees.[201]

It is evident that this rationale puts less emphasis than we have on the role which wage-earner funds could play in solving the problem of investment inherent in the Rehn model. Since there has been much discussion, and confusion, about changing conceptions of the functions to be served by wage-earner funds, the difference in emphasis pointed out here calls for further comment. While playing down the role of the funds in increasing capital formation, the Meidner committee report acknowledges that

insofar as most of the capital comes from company profits . . . [it] would be easier to accept on distributive grounds if part of the increase in assets generated via self-financing were to accrue to employees as a group than if, as in the past, this simply brought about a further increase in the existing shareholders' wealth. In that sense, and only in that sense, can the wage earner fund system be said to promote increased capital formation.[202]

Yet that is a very important sense, indeed, to the extent that 'negative effects on the distribution of wealth' built into the existing mechanism for private capital formation is the major obstacle to providing 'increased resources . . . for investment', in the language of the 1971 Metalworkers' motion. How much of an obstacle it is depends on the extent to which the unions are compelled by organizational and ideological imperatives to counteract the 'negative effects' by pursuing wage policies that squeeze profits, as prescribed by the Rehn model, and how successful they are in doing so. The experience of the second half of the 1960s, as described by the 1970 *Survey*, suggests that they were increasingly successful in doing so.

Given the distribution of power and dynamics of wage determination in the labor market, then, the increased capital formation required to solve the problem of investment that emerged could not take place unless there was a change in the mechanism of capital formation that eliminated or at least diminished the distributive effects inherent in the mechanism as it exists. To the extent that the change accomplished this, it would presumably permit unions to pursue wage policies that did not squeeze profits as hard. A system of collective capital formation meeting the distributive objectives specified in the Meidner committee report would accordingly be a prerequisite for a solution to the problem of investment. In that case the increase in capital formation that the system would make possible, as compared to the level possible in the absence of the system, would not simply be a peripheral by-product of its introduction but one of its central functions.

In the Meidner committee report the link between the distributive terms on which capital formation takes place and the level at which it takes place seems to be viewed as much looser. The required level of capital formation is not treated as if it depends on the introduction of a system of capital formation capable of meeting the specified distributive objectives. It seems to be assumed that capital formation will take place at the required level anyway, but that it will do so on unacceptable terms unless wage-earner funds are introduced. It is the distributive objectives themselves that a system of collective capital formation is primarily designed to achieve; a sufficient level of capital formation is simply a constraint imposed on the way in which the system has to be designed.

This shift of emphasis can probably be at least partly understood in the light of economic developments between the 1971 and 1976 congresses. There was a surge of profits and investments during 1973–4 that deprived the problem of capital formation of most of the urgency it had at the beginning of the decade. This was during the years in which much of the work in formulating the wage-earner fund proposal was being done. Under the circumstances the need to assure a sufficient level of capital formation could not provide a very compelling case for changing the institutional mechanism through which it was organized. On the other hand, the distributive terms on which it was taking place were no less unacceptable from LO's perspective. If anything, they were even more unacceptable, and the wage policy that the unions pursued had proved to be no obstacle.[203] Hence, there was still a need for a system of collective capital formation.

Yet, as we shall see when we review the course of economic developments in the 1970s in more detail, the high profits and investment in 1973 and 1974 turned out to be a temporary deviation from a pattern that resembles much more closely the Rehn model long-run profits squeeze. Indeed, the problem of investment reemerged with much greater urgency than it had at the beginning of the decade. And, in response, capital formation was introduced as a new, fourth objective into successive revisions of the wage-earner funds idea worked out jointly by LO and the SAP.[204] From the long-term perspective in which we view the wage-earner funds proposal, however, capital formation was not a new objective at all, but one that had been integrally linked all along to the three distributive objectives by the logic underlying the whole evolution of LO policy that began with the Rehn model. When viewed from that perspective, then, wage-earner funds as well as the Fourth Fund can be seen as a response to the dilemma of reconciling solidaristic wage policy with the need for investment that was left unresolved in the Rehn model's original formulation.

While both the Fourth Fund and wage-earner funds are aimed at resolving the dilemma by channeling collective savings into investment in the form of equity capital, there are significant differences in the ways in which they do so. In principle, setting up the Fourth Fund does not alter the degree to which business savings may be reduced by the long-term trend in the squeeze on profits. What it does is simply change the form in which some of the offsetting increase in collective savings is made available for investment – that is, from loan to equity capital. This might well result in increased investment because more of it can be financed by risk-bearing capital, and possibly because the cost of capital may be reduced by the increase in its supply. What remains unaffected is the level of profits the wage-determination system permits, given the need to minimize the threat to solidaristic wage policy, arising not only from the overall level of drift, but also the unevenness of its distribution associated with the variation in profits. Wage policies aimed at averting this threat might still squeeze profits too much for investment to stay at the required level. This could be the consequence of setting rates high enough to keep drift at the most profitable firms within tolerable limits, which would intensify the squeeze on less profitable firms, as implied in the Rehn model's original formulation; or of compensating for drift generated at the most profitable firms by making less profitable firms pay additional increases, as required by the earnings guarantees that LO succeeded in winning since the mid-1960s; or of a combination of both, as seemed to happen in each central agreement following one in which standard rates had not been set high enough to keep drift within tolerable limits.

In contrast with the Fourth Fund, wage-earner funds open up the possibility of relaxing the squeeze on profits, thereby diminishing the degree to which business savings are reduced, without a corresponding increase in the threat to solidaristic wage policy. Wage-earner funds could have this result since, in principle at least, their effect would be to weaken the link between profits and shareholder income in much the same way as solidaristic wage policy is designed to weaken the link between profits and workers' income. In so far as they do the former, they would make it easier to do the latter.

Other things being equal, any increase in profits plowed back into investment would be accompanied by a smaller increase in private shareholders' wealth with the funds than without, the difference varying with the portion of profits allocated to the funds plus the effect of corporate taxes on the portion of profits not allocated. Other things are not likely to be equal, of course, given all the factors that might affect the relative growth of the funds' and shareholders' wealth. At the least, wage settlements permitting an increase in retained profits would not imply a corresponding transfer to private shareholders of wealth that unions do not 'take out' for their members in the form of wages. To that extent, such wage settlements would not have the 'negative effects on the distribution of wealth' which LO sought to avoid.

At the same time, the designation of some cash flow as subject to allocation to the funds – in other words, for investment – could diminish the scope for wage drift as well as distribution in the form of dividends. The combined effect should be to make it easier to reconcile solidaristic wage policy with an increase in investment induced and partially financed by an increase in profits. The legitimacy and viability of wage settlements that permitted this would presumably be further bolstered by the element of control over investments gained by workers through the 1970s labor legislation and such reinforcement of that control as may be provided by the ownership vested in the wage-earner funds. In short, while the Fourth Fund provides equity capital by drawing on the collective savings that replaces business savings reduced by high standard rates, wage-earner funds offer the possibility of lower standard rates that permit a higher level of business savings, corresponding roughly to the portion of those savings collectivized in the form of equity capital held by the funds.

Both the Fourth Fund and wage-earner funds have important implications for the distribution of power as well as wealth, since the ownership rights that accompany the provision of equity capital include claims to control as well as income. In this respect the implications of wage-earner funds would seem to be considerably more far-reaching than those of the Fourth Fund, although the extent to which this may be so depends on a great many variables. Among these are the limits placed on Fourth Fund share purchases, the rules governing allocations to wage-earner funds and profit rates.

The amounts the Fourth Fund is authorized to draw from the rest of the AP system were indicated earlier.[205] A more important limitation is the fact that the growth in the AP-system surplus reached its peak in the early 1970s and began to decline. It is likely to continue as the number of persons entitled to full-pension payments increases, depending on how much the AP system earns from its investments and whether the rate of payroll-tax payments into the system is raised.[206] Accordingly, the long-run effectiveness of the AP system as a mechanism for collective savings, and therefore a source of equity capital, is limited, and with that its potential as a means of establishing collective control over Swedish industry.

Wage-earner funds would seem to have a much greater potential for that, at least as proposed in the Meidner Plan. There would be an automatic increment to the funds' holdings in all the companies covered by the scheme in every year in which they made any profits. The growth in holdings would admittedly be slow. For example, it would take about thirty-six years to accumulate a majority holding in a company, assuming an allocation of 20 percent of a pretax rate of return on equity averaging 10 percent.[207] Gradually but inexorably, however, the role of private-property institutions as the basis for financing and controlling firms would be diminished. Throughout the industrial core of the Swedish economy, private property would be progressively displaced not by state ownership, but by an alternative form of social ownership, transforming firms into something along the lines of the 'social enterprises without owners' envisioned by Wigforss.

Long before that stage was reached, though still only gradually, the ownership transferred to the funds would give unions in individual firms additional leverage with which to gain access to and influence the enterprise decision-making process. The Fourth Fund also contributes to the union voice in enterprise decisions, since unions have been given the right to vote 60 percent of the Fund's shares in the few firms in which the Fund has representatives on the boards.[208] However, the prospect of increasing union participation this way is much less than that offered by wage-earner funds, given the limits on the growth of the Fund's holdings mentioned earlier.

KEYNES AND BEYOND: THE EVOLUTION OF LO POLICY

The two forms of collective capital formation pressed by LO in the 1970s can be viewed as steps in the evolution of Social Democratic Labor movement policy along several dimensions. One is the development of Keynesian policy for full employment in a succession of changing situations. Inherent in the logic of the Rehn model, as we suggested in our initial discussion of it, was a development toward something like the socialization of investment which Keynes believed essential if full employment was to be maintained over the long run.[209] We characterized the socialization of investment as the distinguishing feature of a third type or phase of Keynesian policy. The combination of macroeconomic policy and manpower policy prescribed by the Rehn model was identified as a variant of the second type. In contrast with the initial type, which relies on expansive macroeconomic policy to move from mass unemployment toward full employment, the second rests on the premiss that once the transition to full employment is made, the inflationary pressures associated with it make it unsustainable through macroeconomic policy alone. The latter must be supplemented by other policies, with reliance on incomes policies characterizing the principal variant and reliance on structural change, as in the Rehn model, characterizing the main alternative.

The Rehn model can be viewed as a second type of Keynesian policy only from a short-term stabilization policy point of view, however. Since the element of wage restraint in it is limited, aimed at producing the kind of profits squeeze that stimulates structural change rather than at preventing wages from squeezing profits, it creates the need for a collective substitute for business savings. In this way the Rehn model leads to a situation in which it is not possible to go on sustaining full employment without a socialization of investment, although the process leading to the situation is somewhat different from that through which Keynes believed it would come about. The collectivization of savings through the national pension system, as recommended by Rehn, marked a first step toward third-phase Keynesian policy. By making collective savings available for investment in the form of equity as well as loan capital the Fourth Fund and wage-earner funds mark further steps in the same direction.

However, both of the latter may also be viewed as steps in the evolution of LO policy along another dimension that lies outside the boundaries of Keynesian policy. These, as noted earlier, confine policy to the aggregate magnitudes of economic activity. Designed to assure a macroeconomic environment in which microeconomic decisions will result in full employment, Keynesian policy leaves the decisions themselves to actors responding to the 'free play of economic forces'. By and large this division between public policy and private decisions corresponds to the division of functions between the Social Democratic labor movement and Swedish capital embodied in the Swedish model. In particular, this leaves decisions about what, how and where to produce to the managements of the capitalist firms in which most industrial production takes place in Sweden.

As we have seen, Social Democratic labor movement policy remained within the boundaries it had in common with Keynesian policy over most of the long era of Social Democratic rule. Since the mid-1960s, however, the thrust of the movement's policy has been to extend the reach of state and union power to the production decisions themselves. Each of the two main LO initiatives we described earlier, on industrial policy and union workplace power, and their translation into governmental policy, have been in this direction. This is true of the two approaches to collective capital formation proposed by LO as well. Although they are designed to perform the Keynesian function of assuring an aggregate level of savings, in appropriate forms, commensurate with the level of investment required for full employment, they are also intended to reinforce the capacity of both state and unions to influence decisions at the enterprise and workplace levels. This, it will be recalled, was put clearly in LO's memorandum on AP-fund share purchases: 'The trade union movement strives for a real influence not only on the volume of investment but also how, where, and when investments are carried out.'

There is an important respect in which the changes embodied in the Fourth Fund and wage-earner funds lie outside the boundaries of this second dimension along which LO policy has evolved as well. In both their design and implementation the introduction of industrial policy and extension of union workplace power did not encroach on the private property institutions on which the appropriation of profits and selection of management in capitalist firms are based. On the other hand, because of the claims to wealth and control that accompany equity capital, collective alternatives to mechanisms for providing equity capital based on private property institutions encroach directly on the institutional basis of capitalist firms. Thus, LO's proposals for collective capital formation transcend the limits within which Social Democratic labor movement policy hitherto remained, marking a more fundamental departure from the terms of the historical compromise than either of the other two initiatives we have described.

Together, then, the three major initiatives LO took between the mid-1960s and mid-1970s comprise a significant modification in LO's overall economic strategy. This did not entail an abandonment of the structural change strategy in general. It concerned instead the institutional conditions believed necessary in order to make it work, given the organizational and ideological imperatives underlying the strategy to begin with.

Thus, the fundamental premisses on which the strategy rests remain essentially unchanged. The 'development model' Sweden must follow is still derived from its position as a small, open economy whose standard of living is highly dependent on participation in the international economy, so that continuous adaptation of production to changes in its international economic environment is imperative. The main institutional features of the political economy are also conceived in much the same way as before. Most of the production on which the country's participation in the international economy depends is organized by firms expected to remain capitalist, at least for a long time to come, so that private property institutions continue to be a fundamental source of power. That power still has to be counterbalanced by the Social Democratic labor movement's power in the state arena and labor market. The production decisions made by the firms will have acceptable social outcomes – in terms of employment, economic security, distributive justice, and so on – only if they are made within a context shaped by the state and unions. The state must, therefore, continue to be controlled by the Social Democratic Party, so that the cohesion of the LO unions on which its power depends has to be maintained. Hence, coordination of their action in the market arena remains essential, so that solidaristic wage policy and centralized control over the strike weapon must be maintained. The structural change strategy is still the economic strategy the Social Democratic labor movement must pursue within the framework of the existing political economy to assure that Swedish economic development continues on acceptable terms.

What is changed is the conception of how the state and unions must shape the context of production decisions. In the Rehn model, as originally formulated, state and union action was designed primarily to keep up the pressure for adaptation to change without attempting to influence the way in which the adaptation takes place and the consequences it has for workers. State policy in general, and manpower policy in particular, is relied on to protect workers from bearing the costs of adaptation and shifting them to the society as a whole. In the modified version of the strategy, on the other hand, state and union action is designed to influence the process of adaptation itself, with respect to the pattern of change in the composition of industrial production as well as the way it affects workers and their communities. Much of the modification can be conceived as a shift from actions aimed at shaping the factors taken into account in the decisions to actions that enter directly into the process of decision-making by which the factors are taken into account. These actions range from drawing management into essentially voluntary discussions and analyses of the kinds of reorganization that may be needed, through negotiations on which financial concessions are contingent and compulsory negotiations over changes in enterprise or workplace organization to binding restrictions or procedures concerning personnel and the disposition of profits.

While structural change was by no means accepted unconditionally in the original version, it was primarily the state that had to meet the conditions while very little in the way of conditions was imposed on management. Now the conditions are not only imposed on management as well; they are also more exacting. Thus, it had been accepted that the burden of adapting to production decisions supposedly dictated by economic and technological imperatives fell entirely on workers – to move where the jobs are and adapt to the technology chosen – even if the costs were supposedly shifted to society through manpower and other policies. Now manpower policy is no longer believed capable of absorbing all the costs, no matter how generous. Instead the demand is for management to bear more of the burden of adaptation – by bringing jobs and adapting technology to workers.

More generally, the conditions for pursuing a wage policy that permits sufficient growth of expanding activities to offset the decline of contracting activities have been made more stringent. Since the differential squeeze on profits exerted by solidaristic wage policy was conceived as an essential element in the structural change strategy, its distributive effects were accepted as an unavoidable corollary that only structural change itself could remedy. Now tolerance for the distributive effects as well as confidence in that remedy have diminished. Profits have instead become acceptable only in so far as their distributive effects are blunted, and their allocation to investment assured, through institutional arrangements giving unions some of the control over the disposition of profits previously reserved to those whose authority is derived from private property institutions. In short, the acceptance of structural change has been made contingent on extending the reach of state and union power to decisions previously made on the basis of authority and criteria derived exclusively from private property institutions.

Although we have traced the modification of LO strategy to mid-1976, when the LO Congress met and the law on Joint Determination at Work had been enacted, it was not significantly affected by the severe economic crisis through which most of the other OECD countries had been suffering since the OPEC oil embargo and initial fourfold price rise. As noted earlier, the impact of that crisis was not really felt in Sweden until 1977. Thus, the three main elements in the modification we described were responses to problems which were perceived to be increasingly pressing since the mid-1960s but before the Swedish economy was engulfed by the international economic crisis. Once it did hit Sweden, however, LO did not feel compelled to alter its basic position. On the contrary, it argued that implementation of its strategy, as it had developed by the mid-1970s, had been made more urgent than ever by the onset of the crisis in Sweden, and that it provided the only effective way of coping with it. By then this view was widely shared within TCO as well, except that divisions within it over wage-earner funds prevented it from taking an explicit stand in favor of them, even though its documents elaborated essentially the same argument for them as LO did.[210] Accordingly, the position taken by LO was not confined to it, but was to a very large extent a broad trade union position. By that time, however, the political conditions for putting this trade union strategy into effect had been eliminated by the Social Democrats' defeat in the 1976 election. For the first time in forty-four years Sweden was governed by the bourgeois parties, precluding the implementation of the trade union prescription for coping with the crisis.

THE SOCIAL DEMOCRATIC RESPONSE: TACTICAL DILEMMAS AND ELECTORAL DEFEAT

To be sure, even if the Social Democrats had remained in office, it would not necessarily have meant that the trade union prescription would have been applied. Although LO's industrial policy and industrial democracy initiatives had been incorporated in Social Democratic policy, the wage-earner funds proposal had not been. Indeed, the party leadership was clearly not ready to accept the proposal, at least not in the particular form it took. Having been adopted by LO only a few months before the election, it was evidently viewed by the party leadership as an electoral liability.

It was certainly the target of sharp, ideologically charged attack by business and the bourgeois parties. The reactions ran the gamut from strident condemnation of the idea as 'the biggest confiscation ever seen in the Western world' to the solidly reasonable and highly technical critique and counterproposal issued by a joint committee set up by SAF and the Federation of Swedish Industries, IF (*Industriförbundet*). The gist of the counterproposal is a scheme to give individual workers ordinary shares that would become negotiable after some waiting period.[211] This, of course, is the kind of individual profit-sharing approach adopted by business in many countries. Variously heralded as 'people's capitalism', 'property-owning democracy', and the like, such schemes are presumably designed to bolster the legitimacy of the property institutions on which capitalism is based without in any way altering them. Quite expectedly, the bourgeois parties advocate roughly comparable approaches, stressing the income and participation benefits they would supposedly bring to individuals, in contrast with the concentration of power in union bureaucracies that would allegedly result from collective profit-sharing along the lines urged by LO. Once the 1976 election campaign began in earnest the opposition parties intensified their attack, warning that if the Social Democrats remained in power, they would proceed to impose 'collectivistic socialism'. This, the Center Party leader insinuated, meant socialism of the 'East European' variety, while the liberal leader predicted that LO's funds system would lead to 'an increased concentration of power' that would be 'a threat to freedom'.[212]

The intensity of this opposition is hardly surprising, given both the substantive and tactical circumstances. Since the Meidner Plan would set in motion a process that steadily eroded the private property institutions underpinning capitalist firms, it put socialism back on the political agenda more clearly than any Social Democratic intiatives since the Postwar Program or perhaps the party's wealth-tax proposal in 1928.[213] On both of those previous occasions the party suffered major electoral setbacks, and the leadership obviously feared a similar result this time. The bourgeois parties were bound to make the most of the issue, for the Social Democrats' uninterrupted electoral decline since 1968 made the prospect of finally ousting them from office very real. The wage-earner funds issue seemed to offer a way of assuring that it happened.

Yet the intensity of the opposition to the proposal did not necessarily make it an electoral liability. It could instead make it the kind of ideologically polarizing issue around which the SAP could reestablish its commitment to social change, rekindle its activists' enthusiasm and harness it to a remobilization of the party's constituency that could turn the tide. Pension reform and industrial policy had provided such issues, and wage-earner funds could conceivably do the same. Using the idea of wage-earner funds in this way would certainly have been consistent with the ideological thrust of the new program the party adopted at its 1975 Congress. Considerably more radical than the previous program, dating from 1960, the new program declares that the movement is embarking on a third stage in its struggle to develop a democratic-socialist alternative to both capitalism and communism. The 'democratization of political life' is specified as the achievement of the first of the two preceding stages, while establishment of the welfare state was the outcome of the second. Now, in the third stage, the task is the 'democratization of economic life'. Expansion of 'collective influence and ownership' through the workers' 'right to codetermination' and 'participation in the firm's capital formation' is cited among the means for achieving economic democracy.[214] Although the Meidner Plan resulted from an exclusively LO effort, carried out without any consultation with the party, it could easily be viewed as spelling out concretely elements of the 'economic democracy' to which the party was ostensibly committed.

Moreover, the wage-earner funds issue offered a possibility of attracting some support among TCO members. At the time, TCO had not adopted a position on wage-earners' funds parallel to that taken by LO, as it had with respect to the issue of union workplace power. In fact, the 1976 TCO Congress accepted the recommendation of a report on the subject that it take no position on it, but give it further consideration. Although the report is noncommittal, its analysis of the main aspects of the question is nevertheless very similar to LO's, pointing toward similar conclusions. What is particularly significant is that it virtually rules out the individual profit-sharing approach advocated by organized business and the bourgeois parties. Such an approach has little to commend it to the more than 60 percent of TCO members in the public sector. For them, LO's approach would presumably be more attractive. For one thing, whatever services the funds would finance out of their income would be available to all workers regardless of where they work. For another, the public sector members' position would be improved relative to private sector employees who are the main beneficiaries of wage drift, in so far as the funds system would siphon off some of the more profitable firms' ability to finance wage drift. To a lesser extent this also is true of TCO private sector members who are typically on fixed weekly or monthly salaries. But it is apparent that many of the latter take an opposing view concerning the individual shares approach.[215] Such conflicts within TCO would undoubtedly make it difficult for it to settle on a definite policy. But this obviously need not prevent the Social Democrats from bidding for the support of those TCO members whose interests are consistent with the kind of scheme put forth by LO. A reasonable measure of success in doing so is all the Social Democrats would need.

Such considerations evidently could not overcome the party leadership's reluctance to translate the rhetoric of economic democracy into anything as explicit as the Meidner Plan. While the leadership may have regarded ideological radicalization as necessary or irresistible within the party, it evidently viewed such radicalization as fraught with risks in the electoral arena. The emphasis in its 1976 campaign was not on new initiatives to achieve economic democracy, but on preserving what had been accomplished, including the very substantial feat of lowering unemployment in the face of a severe world recession. Ideas about the collectivization of profits obviously did not fit in with such cautious campaign tactics.[216]

Quite apart from considerations of electoral tactics, there were genuine doubts and differences within the party concerning the substance of LO's proposal. Many aspects of it were unclear or undeveloped and there were many uncertainties about the economic effects that funds were likely to have not only in the long run, but in the short run as well. As far as their cumulative impact on the structure of the economy is concerned, one of the most important questions concerned the amount of power the funds would give unions over firms and how that power might affect the implementation of national economic policy decided in the political process. That there remained many serious unresolved questions like these that require much further discussion was widely recognized, within LO as well as the party, regardless of how radical the perspective in which the funds were viewed.[217] This by itself, though, did not necessarily mean that the party could not seize the ideological offensive and mount a campaign for the 'democratization of economic life', in which collective profit-sharing would play a part at least in principle.

However, there seems to have been another tactical consideration that probably contributed to the party leadership's reluctance to embrace wage-earner funds even in principle. The likelihood of reversing the decline in the 1976 election was judged to be uncertain at best, even without a confrontation over socialism. In the face of the real possibility that the Social Democrats, even together with the communists, would not win a parliamentary majority in 1976, the leadership seemed to be trying to lay the basis for staying in power with the support of the liberals, either in a formal or informal coalition. There were many indications that the Social Democrats were, at the very least, concerned with leaving that option open. Among these signs were the so-called Haga Agreements over tax policy negotiated in 1974 and 1975 between the Social Democrats and liberals (and the Center Party as well in 1975), and which the LO and TCO said they would 'take into account' in the forthcoming wage-bargaining rounds.[218] There was also the care which Olof Palme took to exempt the liberals from some of his attacks on the bourgeois parties. He especially singled the liberals out for praise for being 'constructive' in connection with the industrial democracy issue.[219] But it was a lot easier for the Social Democrats to respond favorably to LO's demands and still find common ground with the liberals with respect to industrial democracy than on collective profit-sharing, given the fundamentally different systemic implications of LO's positions on the two issues. Accordingly, the Social Democratic leadership was bound to view a commitment to collective profit-sharing along the lines advocated by LO as a serious liability in the parliamentary as well as the electoral arena.

At the same time, there could not be any outright disavowal of a policy officially adopted by an LO Congress. To do so would severely strain the party's links with the unions. Unlike the British Labour Party, which has repeatedly displayed a willingness to subject its relationship with the unions to such strains, this is something the Swedish Social Democratic Party has consistently tried to avoid. The priority it has placed on working out policies compatible with LO's perceived interests – which, of course, include the cohesion of the labor movement as well – has undoubtedly been crucial to the party's success in staying in power so much longer than its British counterpart.[220] Whatever risks the party leadership may have seen in going along with LO's position on wage-earners' funds, it undoubtedly considered the risks involved in an open breach with the unions as far greater. Of course, repudiation of the idea of wage-earners' funds would also inevitably arouse intense opposition within the party itself, given the symbolic importance that had come to be attached to them as a token of the party program's radicalization.

Unable to take a stand either for or against the LO proposal, the party leadership seemed to fall back on trying to avoid taking any stand on it at all. It was rather clear that it would have preferred not having the idea of wage-earners' funds come up, or at least delaying it from coming up until after the 1976 election. However, once the 1971 LO Congress had decided that a proposal on the question should be prepared for consideration at the next Congress, scheduled for just a few months prior to the 1976 election, nothing could have headed off the proposal that was ultimately accepted except strong pressure against it from powerful elements in the union leadership. There was no such pressure, presumably because most union leaders perceived the problem pretty much as it was described in the report to the Congress. It was apparent that it was proceeding according to its preordained timetable long before the preliminary version was issued in August 1975. Knowing that it would inevitably be confronted with the issue, the party took the opportunity to give it a plausible basis for postponing the time when it had to take a definite stand on it. In January 1975 Sträng, the Finance Minister, set up an official commission of inquiry to study the matter of wage-earners' funds, in accordance with the standard Swedish procedure. The establishment of such an inquiry had, in fact, been part of a 1974 agreement with the liberals. The commission was not to begin working seriously until after LO came up with a specific proposal, and the commission was not expected to report its findings until 1978 or 1979.[221] Consequently, when Palme was repeatedly pressed for his view of LO's proposal, he was in a position to say that it was too soon to make any decision, pointing out that a commission had been appointed to consider the matter and that in the normal course of events it could not be expected to provide the basis for a government decision until after the 1979 election. This, in turn, meant that there was really no possibility of introducing wage-earner funds, even if it were decided to do so, until the 1980s.

It was quite true that the procedure could not be expected to run any faster than that, especially in so complex and far-reaching a matter. The labor-law commission set up some months after LO adopted its industrial-democracy program in mid-1971 did not report until four years later. On the other hand, the party leadership did not wait until the labor-law commission had reported to declare its commitment to abolishing para. 32. And when a government wants to act quickly, it can entirely short-circuit the standard commission procedure, as the Social Democratic government did when it reached and implemented its decision to establish the State Investment Bank in a matter of months. So the fact that there was a commission looking into the question of wage-earner funds was not a very convincing argument that they ought not to be an issue in the 1976 election. Under the circumstances the party's unwillingness to take a clear stand on the issue had the appearance of evasiveness, which could hardly help dispel whatever fears the bourgeois parties' scare-tactics might have aroused.

By taking such an ambiguous position on the Meidner Plan, the party may have made itself all the more vulnerable to the attack mounted against it. In any case the issue certainly contributed to its defeat, though not very much. The available evidence indicates that it lost more votes on other issues. Among them were some 'affairs' or scandals in which some prominent Social Democrats were accused, in some cases legitimately and in others not, of taking advantage of tax breaks by real-estate speculation. Trivial in themselves, these affairs tapped feelings in the electorate of disillusion and distrust of a Social Democratic elite that had been in power too long.[222] The most important issue on which the party lost votes, however, was its stand in favor of nuclear energy. The Center Party leader, Thorbjörn Fälldin, seized the initiative and mounted an intensive campaign against the official Social Democratic position on this issue in the final weeks prior to the election, during which it became the dominant and ultimately decisive issue. The support the Social Democrats lost on that issue was considerably greater than the tiny margin by which their share of the vote declined from their share in 1973. It seems pretty clear that the effect of Fälldin's anti-nuclear offensive was to reverse both the serious decline in support for the Center Party since 1973 and also the recovery of support for the Social Democrats registered in the preceding months of 1976. That recovery was apparently a response to the substantially improved economic situation, compared with what it was in 1973, on which the Social Democrats relied as their main bid for support.[223]

At any rate, the Social Democrats' defeat cannot be attributed primarily to the Meidner Plan. While they did lose some votes on the issue, it was not nearly as salient among voters as the bourgeois parties tried to make it.[224] Moreover, the SAP may have lost more by allowing itself to be put on the defensive on the issue than it would have gained if it had gone on the ideological offensive, as it had on the pension and industrial policy issues. They might still have been defeated on the nuclear issue, but it would not have taken much to win.

Whatever difference the Meidner Plan made, or would have made if the party had handled it differently, the issue it addressed was not one that would go away. Built into the fundamental dilemma confronted by LO in its effort to implement its structural change policy, it was one on which LO and the party would have to hammer out some agreement. This they proceeded to do in the years that followed, but those were years in which it was not the Social Democrats, but the bourgeois parties, that had to cope with the serious crisis into which the Swedish economy was finally plunged. The dimensions of that crisis, the policies with which the several bourgeois governments in office since 1976 tried to manage it and the unions' response are described in the next part.

Part 4

The End of the Swedish Model?

The International Economic Crisis and its Impact on Sweden

The growing instability in the international economy prior to the fourfold OPEC oil price rise had already been making the management of the Swedish economy increasingly difficult. By the early 1970s many of the assumptions incorporated in the original formulation of the EFO model had already become obsolete, including relatively low growth rates of world market prices and the fixed exchange rates of the Bretton-Woods system. While these and other factors did not deprive the basic idea of the EFO model of its validity, they complicated its application and made it essential to modify the assumptions on which it had to proceed. To the extent that this was not done and the impact of short-run fluctuations increased it was more difficult to estimate where the longer-run 'main course' lay.

A major aim of Swedish economic policy under the Social Democrats had been to offset fluctuations in the international economy. This was difficult under the best of circumstances, as LO's *Economic Outlook* observed in the early 1960s; it was all the more so a decade later. The consequences of mistimed shifts in macroeconomic policy were potentially more serious as well. Such mistiming had already aggravated fluctuations under the less unstable conditions of the 1960s. Under the increasingly unstable conditions of the 1970s these effects were bound to be greater. What seemed like a serious mistiming of macroeconomic shifts in the early 1970s did look for a while like a major success when the international crisis following the oil price rise broke out. As it turned out, however, the impact of the international crisis on Sweden was not averted, but only delayed and even aggravated.

That the task of coping with the crisis fell to the first Swedish government run by the bourgeois parties in over four decades did not mean a drastic reversal of the whole pattern of past policy. But it did mean that the political as well as economic conditions under which unions had to operate were very different from those under which the Swedish model had evolved. Already eroded by LO's responses to the difficulties with which its economic strategy had to cope in the preceding years, the survival of the Swedish model under these new conditions was in doubt.

INTERNATIONAL INSTABILITY AND SOCIAL DEMOCRATIC POLICY

While the 1970 *Long-Term Survey* anticipated that it would take five years to restore balance of payments equilibrium, and then only if there was a substantial increase in industrial investment, the payments deficit was already replaced by a surplus in 1971, followed by surpluses in 1972 and 1973 as well. This was not due to an even faster growth of industrial investment, however. Instead it was the consequence of a sharp decline in domestic demand, which made imports fall behind exports, and a domestic recovery that lagged behind the early 1970s boom in the international economy.[225]

Having failed to shift toward a restrictive fiscal policy in time to dampen the inflationary boom in the Swedish economy in 1969–70, the government reacted strongly to the balance of payments deficit that accompanied it by adopting a fiscal policy that reinforced a downturn already under way. The result, as indicated earlier, was a deeper domestic recession than any since the late 1950s. Although the government again relied primarily on selective manpower policy measures – increasing expenditures on them to an even higher proportion of GNP than in the late 1960s recession – these did not suffice to keep open unemployment from rising to the highest level since 1958. Casting doubt on the Social Democratic government's continued commitment to full employment, its policy evoked strenuous protests from the unions and apparently contributed to a loss of electoral support that just missed putting the party out of office in the 1973 election. The socialist and bourgeois blocs emerged from the election with exactly the same number of seats in Parliament, making it necessary to repeatedly break tie-votes by drawing lots when it proved impossible to negotiate compromise positions between the Social Democrats and one of the bourgeois parties.[226]

Meanwhile, the highly synchronized booms in most of the other OECD countries were fueling the sharpest rise in world market prices since the Korean War period, enabling Swedish industry to enjoy rapid growth in both export sales and prices. The result was a powerful surge in profits, especially in the resource-based sectors that benefited from the very high commodity prices characterizing the international inflation that preceded – and contributed to – the initial OPEC oil price rise. A decline in Swedish unit costs relative to those in the advanced OECD countries, especially West Germany, contributed to the sharp rise in profits. While productivity rose with the recovery of capacity utilization, the relative growth of hourly wages was slower in Sweden.[227] A one-year wage agreement for 1974 was particularly important in this connection.

The 1974 agreement resulted in a contractual increase in industrial workers' hourly wages of 5 percent, up somewhat from the 4·1 percent in 1973, the last of the three years covered by the preceding agreement. However, the 1973 increase was the lowest in the three-year period. Even so, it slightly exceeded drift, which rose to 4·0 percent in 1973 after having been less than half the level of contractual increases in the preceding year of peak unemployment. In 1974, however, the rise in drift accelerated sharply to 6·8 percent, demonstrating that the scope for increases had been greatly underestimated in negotiating the agreement for that year.[228]

The oil crisis certainly had a good deal to do with the moderation of the 1974 agreement, which had been concluded with exceptional dispatch in January of that year in order to avoid exacerbating the impact of the crisis. On the other hand, the contractual increases it provided for were probably not markedly lower than might have been expected under more normal circumstances. Since contractual increases had exceeded drift, profits had been particularly low, and unemployment unusually high during the period covered by the previous agreement, there was no question of having underestimated the scope for increases in that agreement. If anything, the scope might have been exceeded, redistributing income from capital to labor more than was consistent with the required growth of the C sector. In addition, a considerable amount of equalization of wages since 1970, at least within LO, suggested that solidaristic wage policy had been achieving its intended effects. At the same time, earnings exceeded consumer price increases enough to yield pretax growth in real wages of 2–3 percent annually.[229]

Finally, the unions and government entered into the first of a series of deals in which the unions agreed to limit their demands in return for a reduction in workers' tax burdens. As mentioned earlier, TCO and LO became increasingly concerned about the effects that high marginal tax rates combined with inflation had on their members' disposable income as rising nominal wages pushed them into higher tax brackets. Although TCO had already called attention to the problem in 1964, it gave it renewed emphasis in 1971. And in 1973 LO offered to limit its wage demands if its members could achieve an equivalent increase in purchasing power through a reduction in income taxes, to be financed by an increase in the general payroll tax paid by employers, thereby keeping a smaller increase in wages from being translated into correspondingly lower labor costs and higher profits. After discussions with LO, TCO and SACO, the government agreed to a variant of the deal, replacing the basic pension contribution paid by employees by a new social charge paid by employers as of 1974. Both TCO and LO continued to distinguish their position from SACO's by calling for preservation of the redistributive pattern of income taxes while rates were lowered.[230]

All things considered, then, neither what rank-and-file union members were experiencing nor what union leaders knew about the relevant variables at the time were likely to result in demands much higher than those actually won at the beginning of 1974. It was probably in leading to such an early settlement that the oil crisis had its main effect on the level of the increases; if the negotiations had taken longer, the profits boom would have become clearer and wage demands revised upwards.

As it was, the extremely favorable cost and price position of Swedish industry during 1974, particularly in the C sector, produced a veritable profits explosion. After having fallen to a postwar low of 20·7 percent in 1972, the share of profits in C-sector value-added jumped to 26·1 percent in 1973 and 33·7 percent in 1974, the highest level since the Korean War boom. This was accompanied by a rise in the growth rate of industrial investment to 9·6 percent in 1973 and 10·8 percent in 1974, the highest level since 1961 and well above the rate estimated as necessary by the 1970 *Survey*. Since industrial investment had stagnated during the preceding recession, averaging 3 percent in the first three years of the decade, the five-year average of 5·9 percent still fell under the *Survey*'s target, but not by much.[231] Viewed just in terms of these figures the problem of investment that had seemed so urgent at the beginning of the decade had all but disappeared.

The boom subsided in the face of the sharp decline of demand in most of Sweden's trading partners, as most of the OECD area governments responded to the oil price rises by restrictive policies that aggravated the deflationary effect of the transfer of income to OPEC, accelerating the downturn that was already under way. Sweden's Social Democratic government was one of the few that responded instead with an expansionary policy, stimulating domestic demand to offset the decline in external demand. In this way it sought to 'bridge over' the OECD area recession, as it had typically tried to counteract declines in external demand in the past. The Swedish economy was believed to be in an especially good initial position for such a maneuver, given the current balance surpluses during 1971–3 and Swedish industry's favorable relative costs. Although the current balance became negative again in 1974, this was believed to be a price that Sweden could and should pay to absorb its share of the OECD deficit against OPEC, and to maintain full employment pending the recovery in the rest of the OECD area.[232] As it turned out the recession was much deeper and longer than anticipated; and by the time the recovery came Sweden's economy proved to be in a very poor position to take advantage of it. Thus, while the impact of the international economic crisis on Sweden was delayed, it was not averted. On the contrary its impact was amplified, plunging Sweden into a crisis in some respects even more severe than that from which the other OECD countries were emerging.

A major ingredient in the crisis was a wage explosion during 1975–6. Precipitated by the profits explosion of 1973–4, it displayed the same pattern in the operation of the wage-determination system observed in the mid-1960s and at the turn of the decade. As we have seen, the central agreement for 1974 provided for contractual increases that fell far short of the scope for increases. That the settlement was much too low was recognized by employers as well as unions almost immediately. The subsequent industry-level bargaining was viewed as a second round of the 1974 negotiations, in which higher increases were conceded. Even so, industry and local bargaining was accompanied by a wave of wildcat strikes that resulted in more working days lost than during the winter of 1969–70, although there was no single strike as large as the one at LKAB.[233] Neither the upward adjustment of contractual increases nor the high drift could keep earnings from falling behind the C-sector profits that were being pulled up by international prices. Moreover, the drift was very unevenly distributed because of the wide dispersion of profits. Together, the wildcat strikes and high, uneven drift were clear signs that the 1974 agreement had subjected the LO unions' organizational cohesion to severe strain.

For LO, the conclusion was inescapable: the level and distribution of wage increases in the next agreement would have to repair the damage. Its opening statement in the next round of negotiation described the situation as follows:

The strong and very uneven international price rise . . . brought about a

very strong profit increase in various branches . . . The substantial wage
drift that the good profitability has given rise to is therefore unevenly
distributed . . . Much of the equalization achieved by the emphasis on
low wages in the year's [agreement] has therefore been lost.

Accordingly, 'the wage earners as a group must take out their share of
productivity growth and win back some of the [lost] share of wages in the
value of output', and 'the emphasis on low wages must be intensified'.[234]

In the months preceding the new negotiations the government made
several moves to moderate the wage pressures that were building up.
Among them was a repetition of the tax–wage deal made the previous year.
This time, in view of the changed parliamentary situation, the government
brought the liberal party into the discussions with TCO and LO in May
1974, culminating in the first of the Haga Agreements, so designated
because of the place where the discussions were held. The Social
Democrats and liberals agreed to enact an income-tax cut for 1975 to be
offset by a further increase in employers' social charges, which the union
confederations agreed to 'take into account' in formulating their wage
demands. A second Haga Agreement, providing for a similar tax package
for 1976, was reached between the government and two middle parties in
March 1975, while the negotiations for the new central agreements were
still deadlocked.[235]

It should be emphasized that these steps toward a tax-based incomes
policy or 'social contract' were very limited. In agreeing simply to take the
tax changes into account, the union confederations made no commitments
about how much their wage claims might be affected, nor could TCO do so
anyway since it is not a negotiating body. Moreover, the employers were
not a party to the agreement at all. If they had participated in the
discussions, they would certainly have resisted the increase in social
charges to offset the income-tax cuts that were an integral part of the
package. Hourly labor costs would be somewhat lower if wages were
reduced by the whole amount by which social charges were increased,
since social charges are added to any increment in wages but, of course, not
to an increment in social charges themselves.

The government also responded to union pressures to do something
about 'excess profits' directly with two measures requiring firms with
profits exceeding specified levels to allocate a portion of the profits to
blocked accounts, from which they could later be withdrawn for investments of designated kinds, such as improvements in the work
environment, subject to approval by the unions in the firms concerned.
Proclaimed as assuring that the excess profits would be invested rather than
distributed to shareholders, both measures exempted the profits invested
under the specified conditions from corporate taxes. This was no more
than an extension of the existing investment reserve-fund system, giving
firms the option of sheltering up to 40 percent of profits in essentially the
same way, except that only government and not union approval is required
to invest the profits involved. These measures did not satisfy the unions,
which understood that the ultimate distributive effects were left essentially
unchanged.[236]

On the other hand, the government did not do what many economists were urging it to do, which was to revalue the crown. Instead of such a revaluation during the 1973–4 profits boom, when it might have reduced profits and wage pressures, there was a small devaluation of the crown against the stronger OECD currencies early in 1973. This was followed shortly thereafter by Sweden's entry into the European monetary 'snake', but the effect that eventually had in pulling the crown up with the German mark came too late to blunt the export profits boom. Instead it came after hourly labor costs in Sweden jumped relative to those in West Germany and even more relative to trading partners outside the 'snake'.[237]

Besides pursuing this 'perverse' exchange-rate policy, the government added to the pressures for high nominal wage increases in other ways. Its effort to bridge over the slump in external demand did so not only through its effect in maintaining a tight labor market, but also through the optimistic expectations concerning the OECD area recovery on which the effort was predicated, and which entered into the other actors' calculations. By the time the government issued its revised budget in April 1975 it recognized that the expectations were overoptimistic. It characterized the 'present international recession as the deepest since the 1930s', making the task of bridging it over more difficult than anticipated.[238] But by April it was too late for this more realistic assessment to affect the course of the central negotiations, which the government had already decisively influenced in its capacity as an employer.

Again, as in 1971, the public sector negotiating bodies deviated from the practice of letting the private sector act as wage leader by settling before a private sector agreement was reached. The private sector negotiations were long and tense, but not primarily because of employer resistance to the high overall level of the wage demands. SAF recognized that a high settlement was unavoidable in view of the profits boom that had occurred. Emphasizing the uncertainty in the economic outlook, however, it wanted a one-year agreement as a hedge against wrong predictions instead of the two-year agreement called for by the unions. It also opposed the LO unions' demand for a particularly large increase for low-wage workers and especially the white-collar unions' demand for a provision that would completely maintain their members' earnings position relative to that of blue-collar workers benefiting from drift.

Since the Finance Minister agreed on the desirability of a one-year agreement, SAF looked to the public sector for support on this issue. In late March, however, the local government negotiating body offered a two-year agreement, with essentially the low-wage profile the unions wanted. The state sector followed suit and agreements along these lines were concluded throughout the public sector in mid-April. Once the public sector employers had conceded these key union demands, it became virtually impossible for SAF to go on resisting them, so two weeks later it signed a similar agreement with LO. SAF did go on resisting PTK's demand for a 100 percent earnings guarantee, but finally conceded most of what PTK demanded after it demonstrated its readiness to strike.[239]

The LO agreement resulted in contractual increases of 11 and 7·8 percent in 1975 and 1976, respectively. Wage drift in the first year was 8·6 percent, lower than contractual increases, but still the highest ever recorded, reflecting the continued tight labor market and high profits in 1975. Drift in the second year was much lower, 3·6 percent, or less than half of contractual increases, reflecting the sharply deteriorating situation in industry. The total increase in adult industrial workers' average hourly earnings over the two years was 31 per cent. Including payroll taxes and social charges, hourly labor costs rose by 39·2 percent. This was the largest two-year rise since the Korean War period.[240]

At the same time, wage growth was slowed by the deep recession in most of the rest of the OECD area, opening up a large gap in unit labor costs between Sweden and its trading partners. This cost gap was aggravated by the untimely appreciation of the Swedish crown. Consequently, the recovery of Swedish exports lagged behind even the belated and limited OECD area recovery to a substantially greater extent than could be explained just by the large proportion of investment goods in Swedish exports, and Swedish producers lost market shares at home as well as abroad.[241]

This 'cost crisis' laid bare and made more intractable a 'structural crisis'. The competitiveness of several sectors that had contributed a large part of Sweden's exports had been steadily eroded by changes in the international pattern of comparative advantage. This was particularly the case in forestry and iron-mining and industries built on them, including steel and shipbuilding. The extent of these sectors' vulnerability to foreign competitors, whose lower costs they could not approach even if Swedish costs generally had not been out of line, had been obscured by the early 1970s boom. When the boom collapsed, the cost gap hit these sectors especially hard, especially steel and shipbuilding, both of which suffered the additional penalties of heavy concentration on the tanker market that was destroyed by the oil price rises. But while large portions of these sectors were evidently no longer viable, the collapse of profits even in those sectors that would be competitive in the absence of the cost gap kept them from expanding sufficiently to take up the slack.[242]

The effects of all these factors did not really make themselves felt until 1977. In that year, however, exports, production, profits and investment in Swedish industry as a whole fell even further than they had in the OECD area generally during the exceptionally deep recession of 1975. The only respect in which the Swedish economy was less hard-hit was the rate of open unemployment. This was still kept remarkably low by dint of massive expenditures on manpower policy, employment subsidies and rescue operations on failing companies, ranging from loans and grants to outright nationalization. In combination, however, all these factors contributed to large deficits in the central government budget and current balance of payments.[243] When the international economic crisis finally made its impact on Sweden, it accordingly confronted Swedish economic policy with problems more serious than any since the Great Depression.

By the time this became apparent, however, responsibility for economic policy had changed hands for the first time in forty-four years. The end of Social Democratic rule had obviously not been brought about by the economic crisis, since the policy of bridging over the recession had delayed its impact until after the election. On the other hand, the fact that the Social Democrats had spared Sweden the high unemployment that continued to afflict most other OECD countries even as they were climbing out of the trough of the recession did not help the Social Democrats either. As we have seen, they were unable to turn their apparently successful economic policy into an election asset, being narrowly defeated on other issues, of which nuclear energy was the most important. Although the liberals and conservatives were opposed to the Center Party on the nuclear issues, they joined in a coalition government headed by Fälldin, the Center Party leader.

The unions were consequently faced with a situation unlike anything that most of their members and leaders had ever experienced during their working life: the most serious economic crisis since the Great Depression and a government controlled by the bourgeois parties for the first time since then. How that government responded to the crisis could be expected to have profound implications for them.

ECONOMIC CRISIS AND THE BOURGEOIS GOVERNMENT

The dimensions of the economic crisis into which Sweden was slipping were only gradually becoming evident by the time the new government came into office. It must be pointed out that the statistics becoming available at the time exaggerated the magnitude of the problems, particularly the balance of payments deficit. It was subsequently discovered that there was a systematic negative bias in the balance of payments statistics, making the deficits appear larger than they actually were. This, of course, meant that the export industries' earnings, profits and therefore national income were understated. Consequently, a major revision of the national income accounts had to be undertaken. At the time of writing this had been done only for the 1970s, so that data for preceding years is not strictly comparable. More serious for our purpose is that some particularly important measures of industry's international competitiveness have only been recalculated for the second half of the decade, so that postcrisis developments cannot be compared with precrisis developments in this connection.[244] The government was, in fact, accused of using measures of Swedish industry's international position it knew to be wrong to justify excessively contractive policies aimed at dampening wage increases.[245] For that matter, the preceding Social Democratic governments were attacked for overreacting to payments deficits and being overzealous in pursuing contractive policies, even if the flaws in the payments data had not yet been recognized. While the crisis was not quite as severe as it seemed for a time, however, it was still more so than any with which Swedish economic policy had to cope since the 1930s, as in the rest of the OECD area.

In any case the emergent cost gap was defined by the new government as the most serious economic problem as soon as it came into office. Its response took shape more slowly not only because the deterioration still had some way to go and because it took some time to recognize its full extent, but also because the government's options were narrow. Many looked to it to restore the 'effectiveness of markets' which the Social Democrats had allegedly impaired, particularly by their increasingly interventionistic policies over the preceding decade.[246] However, the new government could not embark on a drastic reversal of past policy like that carried out by the Thatcher and Reagan governments in Britain and the United States. The political constraints against such a course were compelling. Unlike Thatcher and Reagan, the Fälldin government had to reckon with a strong and cohesive opposition that continued to offer a credible alternative government. Under the circumstances, the first bourgeois government in nearly half a century could not afford the political risks of appearing less concerned about full employment or the economic security of pensioners and others than the Social Democrats.

In addition, the divergence of views within the coalition was sufficiently wide to preclude any such drastic action. The principle institutional base of support for the bourgeois coalition is, of course, the private business community. The conservative party has the closest ties with business. Even so, there are no formal links between the conservatives or either of the two other parties and the national organizations of business, except for a strong residual association between the Center Party and the farm proprietors' organization. The liberal party is the least well endowed with an extraparty organizational base. At the same time, the electoral constituencies of both middle parties inevitably include union members, and this makes it necessary for them to maintain a political profile that distinguishes them from the conservatives as well as the Social Democrats. For example, it would be difficult for them to participate in a coalition government headed by a conservative Prime Minister, which ruled out such a government even though the conservatives became the largest of the three parties in the 1979 election.[247]

Given the political conditions narrowing the first Fälldin government's options on the one hand, and the increasing severity of the economic crisis on the other, the main thrust of the government's effort to cope with the crisis was to improve Sweden's relative cost position without allowing open unemployment to increase. The principal ingredient of the government's response was devaluation, coupled with measures to make it work and supplement its effects. Whether it worked depended on how much of its export price effects were offset, first, by price increases by firms trying to restore their margins and, secondly, by wage increases stemming from union efforts to preserve real wages in the face of the domestic inflationary effects. Given the conventional wisdom that Swedish firms are price-takers on the international market, plus the expectation that they would try to take advantage of devaluation to recapture lost market shares, the first contingency was not considered a problem. How the wage-determination system operated was, therefore, seen as the crucial factor.

The government rejected the idea of a 'social contract' approach that some prominent economists urged on it, but which had in any case been ruled out by both sides of the labor market. Instead the government counted on a combination of economic policies to diminish both the capacity and desire of the unions to press for compensatory increases, and on stiffened employer resistance to such increases.[248]

The devaluation was carried out in three installments. A small initial devaluation in October 1976 was not combined with any major policy changes, and even the January 1977 budget was essentially an expansionary one. However, devaluations in April and August (which were accompanied by withdrawal from the 'snake') were parts of packages marking a major shift in economic policy and its reinforcement, respectively. These two devaluations added up to 15 percent relative to the currencies of Sweden's main trading partners. The brakes were put on domestic consumption by increasing the value-added tax (VAT) from nearly 18 to 21 percent. Prices were temporarily frozen, after which they were subjected to advance-notification requirements. The scope for lower export prices created by devaluation combined with reduced domestic demand were expected to improve export performance, while the price restrictions limited the devaluation's inflationary effects and, hence, the pressure for compensatory wage increases. In addition, the government sought to reduce labor-cost pressures on both export and domestic prices directly by eliminating the general payroll tax (not the AP contributions and other social charges). It announced its intention to do so in August 1977, scheduling a cut from 4 to 2 percent to go into effect in January 1978. In the following April the government introduced legislation eliminating the tax entirely as of July 1978.[249]

At the same time, the government had to blunt the employment effects of its restrictive policy lest it leave itself open to attack. Therefore, as noted earlier, it continued, expanded and added to the whole array of programs that had been introduced by its predecessors. This included the long-established retraining and temporary employment activities run by the manpower-policy agency, as well as the investment-reserve system. Also included were more recent measures encouraging 'labor hoarding', such as wage subsidies for firms that kept on workers, who would otherwise be laid off, to produce for inventories and undergo training, and the employment-security legislation that delayed and made more difficult layoffs and dismissals. On top of this the new government vastly increased expenditures to keep companies in trouble from going out of business. In addition to providing loans, loan guarantees and grants, it bought up a number of the companies, especially in steel and shipbuilding, introducing a degree of 'ashcan' or 'lemon socialism' without precedent in the decades of Social Democratic rule.[250]

In these ways the level of open unemployment was kept remarkably low, rising from a low of 1·6 percent in 1975 to 1·7 percent in 1977, and a peak of 2·2 percent in 1978, before slipping back to 2·1 percent in 1979. However, depending on how it is calculated, the addition of 'hidden' unemployment in the form of workers in manpower programs, those whose wages were subsidized and those who dropped out of the labor market, could bring total 'real' unemployment in 1977 to between 7 and 10 percent, or even higher if one counts the workers who would have been unemployed if not for the steel and shipbuilding rescue operations.[251]

Wage Bargaining and the Economy in the New Political Context

The unions' militancy and bargaining power may not have been dampened as much as they might have been if there had been a marked rise in open unemployment. Nevertheless, the redistribution of income from labor to capital implied by an effective devaluation was accommodated in the next two central agreements, to a small extent in one for 1977, and to a greater extent in another effectively covering 1978–9, although it formally covered only the first ten months of 1979 in order to keep the agreement in force until just after the next election. It would, therefore, seem that the government's strategy for dealing with the cost dimension of the crisis achieved its intended effects, at least in the short run. To see how this happened we turn to a brief review of the two rounds of central negotiations.

MANAGING THE COST CRISIS: THE 1977 AND 1978–9 CENTRAL AGREEMENTS

The political and economic conditions under which negotiations for a new agreement to replace the expiring one for 1975–6 took place were unprecedented. Never before had central negotiations been conducted when the government was controlled by the bourgeois parties. At the outset no one, including the government, knew how it would try to cope with the economic crisis, the dimensions of which were still only emerging, and how it would affect the relative bargaining power of the organizations in the labor market. To determine this, and what they could get as a result, the latter engaged in a tense, protracted process of stalling, maneuvering and threatening. It only culminated in an agreement after LO gave notice of a general stoppage if SAF, and PTK as well, did not accept the 'final proposal' of a mediation commission which LO considered satisfactory.[252]

There were two distinct conflicts to be settled. The larger one was between SAF and the two union organizations. The other was between SAF and PTK. SAF went on the offensive in the larger conflict by issuing its own set of demands in November 1976, instead of waiting for the unions to make the usual opening bid. These demands were for a three-year agreement providing for no wage increases whatsoever except in so far as the scope for them was created by changes designated as necessary to increase productivity. Most of the changes would diminish recent legislative and contractual gains made by the unions with respect to hours, holidays, sick leave, severance pay, job security, local union officials' rights to paid time for union work, and so on. It was to be expected that SAF would take a hard line. It could reasonably assume at least benevolent neutrality from the new government, depriving the unions of a political alternative to collective bargaining. In particular, this put SAF in a position to dig in its heels and resist the demands that LO and PTK jointly formulated for a new basic agreement to apply the law on joint determination, or MBL. Quite apart from that, the fact that profits had collapsed while open unemployment seemed low made the employers perceive the economic situation as serious considerably before workers generally did.

The substance of SAF's opening gambit plus the style in which its new, aggressive chairman, Curt Nicolin, presented it had the effect, perhaps intended, of getting PTK to finally agree to bargain jointly with LO on wages as well as on MBL. However, the two union organizations still did not adopt a common position on the extent to which white-collar workers should be guaranteed compensation for blue-collar workers' wage drift. The issue is complicated by differences in payment systems that make it difficult to compare earnings. Although LO also has many members that do not benefit from drift, it had accepted an 80 percent earnings guarantee for them. PTK, on the other hand, wanted a repetition of the 100 percent guarantee it had won in 1975 and made a separate demand to SAF to that effect which the latter absolutely refused. While LO did not favor PTK's position in this second dispute, it was difficult for it to openly oppose it without jeopardizing their joint bargaining.

SAF's hard line in the first conflict and the complications introduced by the second contributed to the prolongation of both. Up to a point both employers and unions had a common interest in such prolongation. The employers had a stake in putting off a settlement as long as possible, for as long as there was no new agreement they could go on paying wages at the existing rates, with at least the possibility that the new rates would not be retroactive. Moreover, the longer the negotiations dragged on, the easier it would be for the unions to agree to a low settlement.

The unions themselves needed time for this very reason, for the leadership did view the economic situation as more serious than it appeared to the rank-and-file, even if it did not accept SAF's diagnosis or prescription. And as noted earlier, the unions also needed time to find out what the government's economic strategy was going to be. However, when the second devaluation and accompanying measures were announced in early April 1977, it became clear that the government was going to use devaluation to counteract the effects of nominal wage increases, future perhaps as well as past, on Sweden's relative labor costs. It was also apparent that this could mean a cut in real wages. Minimizing that cut as much as possible now became the unions' principal goal. The way they hoped to achieve it was by incorporating into the new agreement a clause providing for an additional increase if the consumer price index exceeded a specified level at a designated time during the year. They concluded that they would have to settle for a low agreement but would do so only if it included such a clause.

The addition of such a clause was one of the changes LO and PTK called for in a proposal offered by the mediation commission. The commission had been set up the previous month when the unions declared the negotiations deadlocked in response to SAF's proposal to table further discussion of wage issues until September and concentrate on productivity issues. This had made it clear that the employers were interested in protracting the negotiations as long as possible, as did their refusal to accept the commission's initial proposal as a basis for resuming negotiations.

To put pressure on SAF to enter into serious bargaining the unions turned to industrial action, despite the risks to which they would be exposed if open conflict broke out under the unfavorable economic and political conditions. They began the standard escalation of measures:

termination of the contracts that had been extended beyond their expiration, followed by bans on overtime, new hiring, and job-related travel outside working time, and then notice of partial strikes. SAF replied to the latter with lockout notices. The climax came when LO countered with an ultimatum threatening a general work stoppage if SAF did not accept the mediation commission's 'final proposal'.

The proposal offered the unions much of what they had jointly demanded – a one-year agreement, a formula for proportionally greater increases for low-paid workers and a price-index clause, without any of the changes SAF had demanded in the name of productivity – in exchange for a very modest overall increase that was not retroactive. On the earnings guarantee issue, the proposal offered the 80 percent rule that SAF and LO had agreed on, rather than the 100 percent rule on which PTK was still insisting. LO evidently concluded that the proposal embodied the most the unions could expect overall, and that PTK as well as SAF could be compelled to accept it if they were confronted by the prospect of bringing the whole economy to a halt. This is as it turned out, with SAF signing agreements with LO and PTK, respectively, in May. Negotiations for an MBL agreement got shunted aside in the course of the wage negotiations, and the 1977 agreement said no more about it than that the parties would continue negotiating on the question. In other words, SAF succeeded in disengaging MBL negotiations from wage negotiations, preventing the latter from serving as leverage for the former, and in putting off any agreement on it until 1982.

The economic result of the 1977 agreement was a contractual increase in industrial workers' average hourly wages of 5·4 percent, including the increases triggered because the consumer price index exceeded the designated threshold. Wage drift added another 3·3 percent, bringing the total to 8·7 percent. This fell far short of what was needed to protect industrial workers' real wages in the face of a 12·8 percent increase in consumer prices, to which the devaluation and VAT increase contributed between three and four percentage points.[253]

In other words, the price clause was not so constructed as to block the kind of cut in real wages that had to occur if the domestic price effects of the devaluation were not to be offset by wage increases that wiped out its external price effects. But the agreement went only part of the way toward closing the cost gap. Adding social charges to the wage increases, total hourly labor costs in industry went up by 10·5 percent. The estimated result was only a very slight decline in relative hourly labor costs. This was more than offset by the decline in productivity flowing from the sharp drop in capacity utilization.[254] After these wage and productivity changes are taken into account, the net result of the devaluation was a small decline in Sweden's relative unit labor costs. Estimated at about eighteen index points in 1976, with 1973 as the base-year, the cost gap relative to the OECD area came down roughly one point, plus or minus about a half-point depending on the weighting system used.[255]

Since the largest devaluation, in August, was carried out after the 1977 central agreement was concluded, it could be viewed as an intrument by which the government 'corrected' the outcome of wage negotiations it regarded as too high. This is apparently how it was, in fact, viewed by both the government and LO.[256] What remained to be seen was how much of the resulting real wage cuts the unions would try to recoup in the next round. The government might then try to correct the result with yet another devaluation, but it would then seem to be drawn into a vicious cycle of repeated devaluations from which it would be difficult to get out. Thus, it was still not demonstrated that the government's strategy for coping with the cost dimension of the crisis was working.

By the time negotiations for the new central agreement got under way the ambiguities of power and policy surrounding the beginning of the previous round had been largely removed. The basic thrust of the government's policy was reconfirmed by its January 1978 budget. A great deal of evidence concerning the extent of Sweden's economic difficulties had accumulated, which LO noted in its opening statement. Moreover, the unions' members could plainly see that there was very little hiring going on and that the number of companies in trouble was growing. Under the circumstances LO gave top priority to defending its members' purchasing power, making an 'effective guarantee against unanticipated price increases' an indispensable element of any agreement. PTK, which now recognized it had to settle for an 80 percent earnings guarantee, or less than 100 percent in any case, again joined forces with LO, with essentially the same goal. In addition to insisting on a price clause, they agreed to demand proportionally higher rises for lower-paid workers, while setting their sights on a very moderate overall increase over a contract period limited to one year.

Even this was regarded as too much for employers who were experiencing very low profits in 1977, even though the wage contracts for that year resulted in real wage cuts. SAF signaled its determination to get as low an increase as possible and again called for a long-term contract, while pressing most heavily for changes in the low-pay formula that would give employers more leeway. This proved to be the most difficult issue, leading to a resort to a mediation commission, which proposed minor changes in the low-pay formula only for the first year of an agreement that was to run for twenty-two months – until after the next election – at the end of which all wage contracts would expire simultaneously. A price clause was designed in the form of a reopener rather than a fixed increase tied to the price level at designated dates. It gave the unions the right to new wage negotiations after any month in which the CPI rose by more than 7·25 points from January 1978, and any month during 1979 in which it rose by 5 percent from December 1978. A settlement was reached along these lines in March 1978.[257]

Since the first-year price threshold was just barely crossed at the end of 1978, the unions did not invoke their right to new negotiations for that year. Contractual increases in average hourly wages of industrial workers came to 2·7 percent, while drift was at 3·0 percent, making the total 5·7 percent. In 1979, however, the price threshold was crossed in August, triggering tough, prolonged negotiations. The complicated package of increases that resulted makes it difficult to specify the increases for the second year of the agreement on a basis comparable with the data for previous years. The most nearly comparable estimate is a contractual increase of 3·9 percent which together with drift of 3·5 percent adds up to 7·4 percent. Allocating the results of the reopened negotiations differently, the total is estimated at 7·8 percent.[258]

The price reopener enabled the unions to protect purchasing power somewhat better than the price clause in the 1977 agreement, but industrial workers still took a further cut in real wages. The price rise of 7·5 percent in 1978 was much lower than in the preceding year but still exceeded average wage increases enough to produce a 1·8 percent decline in pretax real hourly earnings. The inflation rate accelerated again in 1979, reaching 9·7 percent for the year as a whole and resulting in an additional decline of 1·9 percent if we take the higher estimate of nominal increases. The decline of average real hourly earnings was, therefore, 3·7 percent over both years, bringing the total in 1977–9 to 7·8 percent. This offset a little over two-thirds of the 11·5 percent jump in real wages that accompanied the 1975–6 wage explosion, reducing the average annual growth of real wages over the five years to just under three-quarters of 1 percent.[259]

Since nominal wage increases were lower than they would have had to be to compensate for the devaluation's domestic price effects, much if not all of those effects were apparently absorbed by the cut in real wages. Over the three years during which this cut occurred, capital's share in C-sector value-added rose from its postwar low of 15·6 percent in 1977 to 26·1 percent in 1979.[260] This suggests that the redistribution of income from labor to capital implied by an effective devaluation was accommodated by the wage-determination system.

With the help of what the Budget Minister called 'the responsible agreement reached in the private labor market in 1978',[261] the government had apparently managed to bring off one of the few effective devaluations among the many that have been attempted. As noted earlier, however, the government's strategy for reducing the cost gap was not confined to devaluation. It also included elimination of the 4 percent general payroll tax. Since the government announced the second of the two stages in which the elimination of the tax occurred six weeks after the private sector settlement in 1978, LO complained that the government had altered the conditions under which the agreement had been made. LO argued that the scope for increases had been calculated after deducting the payroll tax the employers had to pay – that is, what was left of it after half of it had been cut in January. Now, by eliminating the other half, the government was providing the employers with a 'double deduction', which amounted to 'giving the workers' money to the employers'. Such 'correction' of wage settlements after they were made, as in the case of the August 1977 devaluation, 'means that in future negotiations the workers cannot rely on the government's declared economic policy'.[262] In fact, as we have seen, the government had declared its intention to eliminate the payroll tax, although it did not say when it would complete the task, so the measure could hardly have been a surprise. Nevertheless, LO probably had to make some sort of public protest, having entered into a settlement that rendered it vulnerable to rank-and-file discontent. Quite apart from that, LO was opposed to elimination of the payroll tax on wider grounds that applied to the rest of the bourgeois government's tax policies, to which we shall return.

By facilitating some reduction in relative prices and recapture of market shares, the effects of devaluation and elimination of the payroll tax on Sweden's relative unit labor costs contributed to a recovery of industrial production and, therefore, of productivity growth as capacity utilization increased. Productivity growth, which was 4·6 and 6·9 percent in the C sector in 1978 and 1979, respectively, in turn reinforced the effects of the other factors in reducing relative labor costs. By 1979 all or most of the cost gap that had opened up between Sweden and trade-weighted OECD averages since 1973 had been eliminated, the estimates varying with differences in weighting systems. Some of the improvement in costs was used to achieve reductions in relative export prices and some to restore margins. It is not possible to estimate how much of the rise in Sweden's relative export prices and loss of market shares since the wage explosion were reversed since the relevant revised data for the period prior to it is not yet available. The new data show some recapture of shares, especially since 1978, and a new small loss in 1979, when Sweden's relative export prices increased by 3·5 percent after declining by 6 and 5·5 percent, respectively, in the two preceding years.[263]

These indicators suggest that the government's approach to coping with the cost dimension of Sweden's economic crisis was working, at least thus far. What remained uncertain, however, is whether it could continue to work long enough to provide the conditions under which the structural dimension of the crisis could be eased, and whether the government was pursuing other policies that could contribute to a solution of this more fundamental, long-term problem.

STRUCTURAL CRISIS: ALTERNATIVE STRATEGY OR PRESCRIPTION FOR STALEMATE?

Ultimately the solution to Sweden's basic economic problem depended on the adaptation of Sweden's industrial structure to irreversible changes that had been taking place in the international pattern of comparative advantage. In other words, there would have to be new investment in existing and new sectors and products which had potential for expansion to replace the sectors and products that cannot compete with new producers on the world market whose costs, for other inputs as well as labor, are far lower than any that can be realistically expected in Sweden. As yet, the required recovery of industrial investment had not materialized. On the contrary, a 17 percent decline in industrial investment in 1977, the biggest drop in the postwar period, was followed by an even greater decline, of 22 percent, in 1978. There was a 4 percent rise in 1979, but that is ascribed entirely to public sector firms, and it was hardly the government's intention to rely solely on public enterprise for the renewal of Swedish industry.[264] If private industrial investment was to recover, however, it would obviously do so only under conditions of both demand and costs that would make the investment sufficiently profitable.

What the government could do about demand was severely limited by the fact that it was demand in the world market that industry depended on for upwards of half its output.[265] There was nevertheless scope for government action to assure as much of a contribution to capacity utilization from domestic demand as possible. Yet the strategy that had been adopted to make the devaluation work relied heavily on restricting domestic demand, contributing to extremely low-capacity utilization and deepening the collapse of investment. Under conditions of such low demand, with such a high level of 'hidden' unemployment lurking in the background, plus the exceptionally low profits that prevailed, it is not very surprising that the 1977 and 1978–9 wage settlements were low enough to make the devaluation work. An indication of the weakness of pressure on wages by demand and profits at the time is the fact that wage drift was lower than contractual increases in the first and third years covered by the two agreements, exceeding contractual increases only very slightly in the second year and averaging 32 percent less than contractual increases over the period as a whole.[266]

But what would happen if demand and profits were restored sufficiently for industrial investment to reach and remain at levels required to solve the structural problem? If the operation of the wage-determination system in the past was any indication, the answer had to be that wage drift would increase, precipitating demands for even higher contractual increases. As a result, the cost gap would probably be reopened and the squeeze on profits renewed, so that the recovery of industrial investment would be cut short before there has been enough of it to solve the structural problem. In other words, the problem of investment to which LO's proposal for collective capital formation was addressed would reappear. That this could happen was pointed out with increasing frequency in 1979, as the recovery that began in 1978 gathered strength.

Already at the beginning of the year Gunnar Nilsson, LO's chairman, warned in a speech in Parliament that the 'high but unevenly distributed profit increases that can be expected this year' could lead to a repetition of the situation in 1974, which would 'mean great problems' in the wage negotiations to be started in the fall. 'If no special measures' are taken to deal with those profits, 'we will get a new illustration of why wage earner funds are necessary'.[267] While he did not specify the measures, he certainly did not expect it to be possible for a system of wage-earner funds to be introduced in time, even if the Social Democrats won the election to take place in September.

Others who saw essentially the same danger, such as the head of the Metalworkers' union, suggested the establishment of some sort of provisional wage-earner funds. Yet others, such as a Social Democratic economist, proposed something like the allocation of 'excess profits' to special funds like the work-environment funds of 1974.[268] The research directors of LO and the Metalworkers urged a revaluation of the crown. LO's spring 1979 *Economic Outlook* characterized the failure to do so in the first half of 1973 as the 'biggest single mistake in Swedish economic policy over the past ten years'. In addition, it urged that the payroll tax be restored and its proceeds funneled into a 'structure fund' proposed by the

Social Democrats, which would supply capital for investment in expanding industry instead of relying on higher profits across the board to provide it.[269]

While it might, indeed, be the case that the problem of investment could not be solved on the basis of private savings as long as the wage-determination system continued to operate as it had in the past, it might not be if the operation of the system could be changed. Conceivably it could be changed if the political conditions under which it operated were changed, as they indeed had been. As we have seen, the Swedish model of industrial relations evolved under conditions of virtually continuous Social Democratic control of the government. Now that Social Democratic control had ended, at least for the time being, the distribution of power and dynamics of interaction among the actors in the labor market might be modified. The extent of this possibility had not really been tested during the three years in which the bourgeois parties had been in office so far.

For one thing, the economic conditions that prevailed throughout most of this period were not those under which the wage-determination system was likely to pose the problem of investment. Thus, it was only toward the end of this period that such economic conditions were perceived to be returning. For another, the effects of the change in political conditions could not be expected to materialize immediately, particularly in view of the caution with which the first bourgeois governments after such a long period of Social Democratic rule had to proceed. Failure to do so could make the bourgeois governments a temporary aberration. On the other hand, if the bourgeois parties returned to office after another election, the change in political conditions would be more strongly confirmed. It could then have more palpable consequences for the operation of the wage-determination system.

An intriguing suggestion of what those consequences might be, and how they might increase the possibility of solving the problem of investment on the basis of private savings, is provided by arguments for changes in the wage-determination system that SAF advanced in 1979. In particular, SAF argued that there should be a reallocation of functions between central and local negotiations, and that there should be a redefinition of the norm by which the economic implications of wage increases should be assessed.

The first argument was made in a new statement on wage policy issued in the spring of 1979. In it SAF proposes that central agreements be limited to assuring 'labor peace in industry' and establishing 'a frame for total labor costs', while the rest of the wage-determination process takes place in as 'decentralized forms as possible'.[270] That is, the central agreements' task is to remove the threat of strikes and lockouts from local negotiations and establish the overall scope for increases whose distribution among workers is left to local negotiations.

The second argument was made in a symposium on the EFO model in October 1979 by Faxén, the SAF economist who was one of its authors. He argues that the EFO model should be abandoned as the basis for setting the scope for increases. In part, this is on the ground that the assumptions and conditions on which its validity depends no longer hold.[271] More significantly, however, the profitability norm to which wage growth should conform over the long run is rejected as inadequately formulated. As interpreted from SAF's point of view, the main course does aim at assuring the required growth of investment and this, in turn, is understood to mean sufficient profitability for the investment to be financed without unacceptable debt–equity ratios. However, the EFO model is faulted for failing to distinguish between the profitability levels needed to assure sufficient external equity capital from private savings on the one hand, and collective savings on the other. Depending on tax and inflation rates the levels may differ. Under the rates that have prevailed profitability has been too low to maintain a sufficient flow of equity capital from households, leaving collective funds as the only source. In view of this outcome SAF finds it 'difficult to accept' the EFO-model's postulated 'neutrality with respect to whether external financing comes from the household sector or collective funds'.[272] Thus, it is precisely because SAF is on the other side of the basic systemic issue of how capital formation is organized from LO that leads SAF to call for change in the way wages are determined.

The norm to which SAF would have wage growth conform in place of the EFO-model main course is price stability. This is understood to mean that average productivity growth, throughout the private sector rather than only the C sector, defines the scope for increases. No automatic linkage of wages to prices should be allowed to breach it, although this evidently does not rule out price thresholds if they make the government hold inflation down.[273] By setting overall wage growth on this basis central negotiations are evidently expected to assure sufficient profitability for investment to be financed by private savings. Distribution of the increases within those limits by local negotiations is apparently aimed at making it possible to gear them to firms' ability to pay.

Although this is not stated explicitly, it is clearly implied by the function assigned to local negotiations. They are to calibrate wage differences to all the variations in circumstances on which they should be based, including 'market and production conditions, and individual values, qualifications and performance'.[274] To facilitate recruitment and encourage efficiency, differentials must be sufficiently large and flexible; the task of manpower policy is then to facilitate the mobility of labor in response to those differentials. In short, wage determination must be decentralized as much as possible to restore the allocative effectiveness of wages in both the labor market and the firm. To that end provisions aimed at controlling the distribution of wage increases at the local level must be excluded from the central agreements.

This obviously rules out the type of provisions analyzed earlier through which solidaristic wage policy has been incorporated into the central agreements. In so far as such provisions translate wage drift into general increases, as we suggested earlier, their elimination might well lower the overall growth of wages, in addition to restoring the effectiveness of wages as a management tool and market signal. On the other hand, if such provisions are necessary in order for the LO unions to agree on the coordination of wage bargaining through central negotiations, their elimination could well make the continuation of central negotiations impossible. Deprived of their function in controlling the distribution of increases, they might also be no longer available for the functions SAF would still have them serve. For SAF, this might nevertheless be a price worth paying. While grounds for this supposition are largely speculative, they suggest the far-reaching implications SAF's wage-policy proposal could have.

SAF's stake in central negotiations might be expected to depend on how much weight it attaches to averting the risk of open conflict over wages. One of the EFO-model's main aims, according to Faxén, was to lower the risk of such open conflict by providing employers and unions with a common basis for expectations about what they could win. This would consequently not diverge by much, so that the cost of compromise would be perceived as less than that of conflict. The price-stability norm in the new wage policy was presented as a comparable basis for reducing the diversity of expectations that makes open conflict likely.[275] This looks very much like a return to SAF's 1967 proposal, to which LO could be expected to object on the same grounds as it did then. Indeed, while agreeing on the EFO-model's role in peaceful conflict resolution, Odhner, the LO economist who was also one of its coauthors, replied that the price-stability alternative was 'hardly something that creates agreement and tends to keep peace'.[276]

Thus, in so far as the price-stability norm is designed to assure the profitability on which private equity financing is contingent more unambiguously than the EFO model does, the unions would presumably reject it as the basis for estimating the scope for increases. The fundamental conflict over the financing of investment out of private or collective savings could accordingly lead to divergent assessments of open conflict. The relative costs of compromise and the risks of open conflict would then be increased if the employers insisted on limiting wage growth on the basis of the price-stability norm, and increased even more if they also barred any central distribution of the wage growth. But if open conflict is what it took to achieve these two aims of the new wage policy, it might be worth the cost from SAF's viewpoint. If the conflict is not resolved peacefully, the likelihood of state intervention becomes greater. But the state may be expected to intervene differently, with different consequences for the outcome, depending on what Faxén referred to as the 'political factors' – that is, which parties are in power. Each side's assessment of the risks attached to open conflict may be expected to differ accordingly. Thus, a wage policy that 'regularly presupposes open conflict as a normal part of the conflict resolution process itself' is conceivable.[277]

It will be recalled that open conflict was very much a part of the industrial-relations system before the Social Democrats achieved sustainable control of the state in the 1930s. It was soon after Social Democratic rule was perceived to be durable that SAF and LO agreed to the set of arrangements for peaceful resolution of industrial conflict characterizing the Swedish model which laid the basis for the system of central negotiations established in the postwar period. Once the Social Democrats ceased to control the state, and their prospects for regaining durable control became dimmer, open conflict might again become a normal part of the 'manner by which the conflicting claims of labor and capital are resolved' in Sweden.

Central negotiations might then have to be eliminated. For one thing, if open conflict became a normal stage in central bargaining, the whole economy would quickly be brought to a standstill every time, which the state would probably be compelled to prevent. A more decentralized system might render open conflict more tolerable by making it possible to limit its scope at any one time. For another the unions might be unwilling and, indeed, unable to enter into central negotiations if SAF succeeded in redefining and restricting the functions of the negotiations in accordance with its new wage policy. While this would obviously mean that the negotiations could not perform functions assigned to them, SAF might still judge that the benefits outweigh the costs. In addition to achieving the intended effect of making wages more responsive to market forces and managerial control, the shift to a decentralized wage-determination system might also achieve significant political effects.

If, as we suggested, solidaristic wage policy is a necessary condition for the LO unions' organizational cohesion and this, in turn, is essential to their ability to mobilize electoral support for the SAP, the impossibility of implementing solidaristic wage policy in the absence of central negotiations would seriously impair the effectiveness of the SAP's most important electoral resource. Given the small electoral margins on which the SAP's control of the state has depended, that could mean that the party, at least on its own, might never regain control of the state.

The political conditions for a wage-determination system whose operation permitted higher industrial investment to be financed out of private savings might then be firmly established. Under those conditions the whole pattern of economic policy could contribute to making wage growth consistent with private capital formation. Union bargaining power would not be reinforced directly by the state's action as an employer nor indirectly by 'ultra-Keynesian' policies guaranteeing full employment regardless of wage levels.[278] Tax policies would underpin the effectiveness of both labor and capital markets. In addition to income-tax indexation, already introduced, marginal rates would be further reduced to increase the effect of wage differentials, for which scope would be enlarged by cutting non-wage labor costs in the form of social charges. Lower marginal rates, more favorable treatment of capital gains and elimination of 'double taxation' of profit income, together with lower inflation due to lower wage growth, would shift the flow of household savings to equity capital. To bring expenditures down in step with the decreased revenues the public sector's size would be reduced and its financing altered. Transfers and free services would be concentrated on those with greatest 'need', fees introduced for services to others as much as possible, and private provision of income security and services encouraged, particularly through collective bargaining so as to coordinate fringe benefits with differentials. Thus, deuniversalization of the welfare state would also improve the efficiency of labor and capital markets. Overall, as expressed by the well-known conservative economic historian, Erik Dahmén, the mixture in the 'mixed economy' would be 'changed in a direction opposite to the one heretofore ... strengthening the private capitalist elements which have for long been driven to retreat'.[279]

This vision of a future political economy that extends back not merely to the early 1960s and late 1950s, but in some respects even to the 1920s, has been drawn not only from the SAF discussion, but also from the diagnoses and prescriptions with the same general thrust that have proliferated since the bourgeois parties came into office in 1976.[280] Consistent with much of their announced goals and even some of the measures already taken, SAF's new wage policy might be all the more attractive to them in so far as it promised to create a durable basis for their control of the state by eroding the LO unions' organizational cohesion.

Yet this vision would seem to be unambiguously inviting only to the conservative party. The middle parties undoubtedly have a stake in the particularistic orientation among unions that a more decentralized bargaining system would tend to generate, since it would presumably enlarge the possibilities of mobilizing support in LO as well as TCO unions. On the other hand, the strategy for restoring the efficiency of labor and capital markets along the lines sketched above runs counter to the whole aim of subordinating market forces to control that pervades the trade union movement. As expressed in terms of solidaristic wage policy and, more recently, 'industrial democracy', this aim appears to be no less characteristic of TCO than LO unions, facilitating their increasing collaboration in the state as well as market arenas, even if partisan identification is still ruled out for the TCO unions. The opportunities which that non-partisanship leaves open for the middle parties could well be jeopardized if they became clearly committed to the restoration of an unfettered capitalist market economy.

Thus, the political conditions for such a reversal in the trend of development of Sweden's 'mixed economy' would by no means be assured if Sweden continued to be governed by bourgeois-party coalitions. It is also not at all clear how much of a stake SAF has in the kind of scenario extrapolated from its wage-policy discussion. The employers may not have much to lose by way of tactical coordination if they drive the decentralization of wage determination so far that central negotiations become impossible, for SAF's capability for coordination might remain largely intact. However, the costs of the open conflict it would probably take to drive decentralization that far, and of decentralized bargaining without the protection against strikes afforded by central agreements, might well be regarded as prohibitive. Swedish unions' very high degree of organization gives them the capacity for massive resistance, and the escalation of conflict from particular industries to the economy as a whole would not necessarily be averted by the absence of centralized negotiations. Fragmented and uncoordinated industrial conflict could be even more costly, as the experience of Britain's highly decentralized bargaining system suggests. By contrast, 'labor peace' undoubtedly offers the competitive advantages claimed for it, from enabling delivery dates to be met and securing acceptance of technological and structural change.

It was therefore not clear what SAF may have hoped to accomplish under changed political conditions and whether those conditions would be sufficient to accomplish that. It would presumably become clearer if the bourgeois parties succeeded in retaining control of the government in the 1979 election. They did so, and a half year later open conflict broke out in the labor market on a scale unmatched since the four-month engineering industry strike in 1945. Beginning in the public sector on 25 April and extending to the private sector on 2 May, strikes and lockouts lasting until 11 May directly involved a quarter of the labor force and brought the whole economy to a standstill. Many aspects of the process leading to this massive breakdown of Sweden's vaunted industrial peace suggest that SAF's strategy had, in fact, undergone a fundamental shift and that, in its view, the bourgeois parties' return to office had created the conditions under which it could bring about changes in the wage-determination system that made it possible to solve the problem of investment on the basis of private savings. In other words, it would be possible to reverse the basic direction in which Sweden's political economy had been developing. The outcome of the conflict suggests, in turn, that if SAF had indeed tried to implement such a strategy, it failed, and that it did so because the political conditions for its success had not actually been met.

Yet the course of events culminating in this outcome involved so many factors, interacting in such a complicated way, that this interpretation is by no means indisputable. The question of its validity cannot be settled within the limits of the information, and space, available, but the episode is of sufficient importance to warrant an extended discussion. We begin with the sources of ambiguity in the political and economic conditions under which negotiations for a new wage agreement took place in 1980, and then turn to an account of the conflict.

THE 1980 STRIKE AND LOCKOUT

The 1979 election took place at a point in the course of economic developments that was about as favorable for the bourgeois parties as it possibly could be. The upswing in the economy was probably the bourgeois parties' most important electoral asset. The credibility of their capacity to govern, always subject to doubt because of their policy differences and conflicting tactical interests, had been damaged by the break-up of the three-party government headed by Fälldin in October 1978. The division between the Center Party and the other two over the nuclear-energy issue was brought to a head by the need for decisions on reactor programs, precipitating a Cabinet crisis. It was resolved with the establishment of a minority liberal government, made possible because the Social Democrats, along with the Center Party, agreed not to vote against it in Parliament. The conservatives – who had sought a liberal–conservative minority coalition government, which would evidently have been damaging to the liberals – were thereby isolated.[281] When the Three Mile Island accident led to an agreement to hold a referendum on nuclear energy in the spring of 1980 that issue, which divided the Social Democrats as well as the bourgeois parties, was taken out of the election campaign. Relegation of the wage-earner fund question to an official commission of inquiry largely blunted it as an election issue.

For the Social Democrats, the most troublesome issue proved to be the tax advantages enjoyed by homeowners relative to tenants.

Unemployment was the issue on which the bourgeois parties would have been most vulnerable but, as we have seen, they made sure that their opponents would be deprived of that advantage. They not only devoted large sums to keeping open unemployment down, but pursued a highly expansionary fiscal policy that reinforced the effect of the European recovery. This fueled a preelection boom that brought open unemployment down to 1·8 percent in the last quarter of the year when the election was held.[282] It also contributed to a resurgence of inflation.

For the year as a whole, as noted earlier, the rate was 9·7 percent as compared with 7·8 percent in 1978, but this obscures the rapid acceleration of inflation toward the end of 1979. While the threshold of 5 percent inflation since December 1978 specified in the reopener clause in the current wage agreement was passed in August, this was not yet enough to make inflation a major election issue. By December 1979 and January 1980, however, the monthly rate had climbed to its highest level since the Korean War. Although the new round of oil price rises in 1979 received a lot of attention, it accounted for less than a fifth of the increase in the consumer price index.[283]

At the same time, GDP grew by 4·3 percent in 1979, the fastest rate since 1973. Fiscal policy provided a powerful impetus to this growth, its stimulative effect being estimated at 3·8 percent of GDP, higher than in any of the preceding five years. The other side of this fiscal stimulus was a central government budget deficit that rose from 8·5 percent of GDP in 1978 to 10·5 percent in 1979, precisely in a phase of the business cycle when a decline in the deficit might have been expected. Finally, there was a sharp deterioration in the balance of current payments from virtual equilibrium in 1978 to a deficit of 2·2 percent of GDP in 1979[284]

Whether the government lost control of the upswing or was engineering a political business cycle, the timing of economic developments did lend credibility to the bourgeois parties' claim to have brought about an economic recovery. This undoubtedly helped them return to office, though they just barely managed to do so. Their election margin over the socialist bloc dropped from nearly four percentage points in the 1976 election to a mere two-tenths of a point in the 1979 election, and their parliamentary majority fell from eleven seats to just one.[285] Thin as their margin was the bourgeois parties nevertheless still controlled Parliament. Since the forthcoming referendum obviated the necessity of agreeing on nuclear-energy policy, a new three-party coalition government was formed, again headed by Fälldin.

To resume the task of rectifying the structural disequilibrium in Sweden's external economic position pursued by the two preceding governments, some way to sustain the recovery of industrial investment that had just barely begun in the latter part of 1979 would have to be found. This would have to be done in the face of the international downturn following the second OPEC oil price shock on the one hand, and the wage pressures being built up by accelerating inflation and rising profits on the other. Thus, the second Fälldin government faced the prospect that both demand and cost – including non-labor as well as labor inputs – factors were likely to dampen the industrial investment on which the needed structural change depended. It would be a formidable challenge for any government, of whatever composition, to devise a policy mix capable of minimizing the demand and cost constraints that loomed ahead. It proved a challenge that the Fälldin government could not meet.

The most dramatic demonstration of the government's failure to meet the challenge was the massive 1980 work stoppage.[286] To cite this as evidence of the government's failure is to imply that it could have avoided it by acting differently. The consensus among participants and observers seems to be that it could, indeed, have done so. However, the things that many of them would have had the government do would have run in very different directions, with widely divergent implications for the ways in which the conflicts that erupted in the stoppage would be resolved.

At the same time, the government's capacity to act, to meet any of these expectations in a consistent way, or work out a more comprehensive solution of its own, was significantly impaired. As we have noted, it was in office by virtue of a mere one-seat majority. Moreover, the three-party coalition was strained not only by the nuclear energy issue, but many others as well. Although the coming referendum made it possible to circumvent the issue in forming the government, the parties entering it and especially the Prime Minister himself were preoccupied with advancing their opposing positions in the referendum campaign. The outcome would have a bearing not only on the substantive resolution of the issue, but also the composition of the government. There was a real possibility that the coalition would not survive the results of the referendum, inhibiting coordination and cohesion within the government and creating uncertainty among the other actors.

The new central agreement to be negotiated was for the period beginning in November 1979, since the preceding agreement ran out at the end of October. However, the negotiations triggered by the price clause in the 1978–9 agreement, which began in early September, dragged on until early December. They ended with SAF's acceptance of a mediation commission proposal only after LO and PTK put an overtime ban into effect.[287] This amounted to a first installment in the negotiations for the next agreement, in which the December increases would have to be counted according to SAF.

Before the outcome was known, LO issued its opening statement for the next round of negotiations, setting forth its basic position without presenting any specific wage demands, which it in fact did not do until early March. Its point of departure was the deterioration in economic prospects resulting from the weakening of international demand and burdens of the new oil price rises. To maintain employment and defend workers' living standards it was essential that the 'technical and economic competitiveness of exports be so strong that capacity can be utilized better'. This required policies differing from those pursued by the government in many respects, and two in particular. One was a macroeconomic policy that maintained domestic demand to a greater extent than the 'belt-tightening' policy to which the government was committed so as to assure the capacity utilization on which continued investment, productivity growth and competitiveness depended. The second was a policy on taxes and expenditures that assured a more just distribution of income than that resulting from the government's policies.

The second of the policy areas proved to be crucial as far as the wage negotiations were concerned. Alluding to the real wage cuts borne by workers under the two preceding governments, the LO statement declared that:

> The wage earners have heretofore shown social responsibility in the face of worsened economic conditions, at the same time that the bourgeois government has worked to distribute the burden more unjustly. The bourgeois tax proposal implies that the lower paid must get a significantly larger wage increment than the higher paid in order to preserve their purchasing power.[288]

Thus, a high nominal wage increase was declared necessary to counteract the redistribution of purchasing power in favor of higher-income recipients attributed to the income-tax changes already enacted and proposed by the bourgeois governments. These began with the substitution of different 1977 tax-rate changes for those provided for in the third Haga Agreement in 1976, which was just between the former Social Democratic government and the two main union confederations. This was followed by a succession of reductions in marginal tax rates and the introduction of inflation indexation as of 1979.[289] LO charged that these changes resulted in greater increases in disposable income, the higher the level of income, at the same time that the reduction of taxable income through interest deductions is greater, the higher the level of income. Moreover, LO pointed out that the indexation system was so constructed as to build inflation into the economy by adjusting tax scales on the basis of the preceding year's inflation rates. Altogether, LO concluded, these features of the tax changes did not make lower nominal wage claims more acceptable, as the government claimed, but much less so instead.[290]

LO accordingly called for a 'revision of the indexation system' – or alternatively, its elimination – and an agreed 'tax reform on the Haga model concentrated in low and middle incomes', offset by a restoration of the payroll tax. This, it said, is what was required to pave the way for a lower nominal wage increase that would improve the C sector's cost position further and diminish domestic inflationary pressures. According to LO's autumn 1979 *Economic Outlook*, to gain full advantage of such a tax reform, it would have to be combined with other measures. These included intensive efforts by the government to hold down prices, primarily through price surveillance. This was necessary not only to curb domestic inflationary pressures, but also to make sure that export prices are not raised in order to increase profits rather than recapture market shares, as happened over the preceding years (confounding the conventional wisdom that Swedish firms are price-takers on the world market). Moreover, measures to tie the increased profits of firms into investment would be necessary, in the form of allocations to investments according to plans and timing agreed with unions at the firms.[291]

LO representatives reiterated this position, especially the need for the tax changes, in various forums. In the January 1980 general debate on economic policy in Parliament LO's chairman, Niisson, warned that the new central negotiations were starting out under the most difficult conditions he had ever experienced, making it imperative that the Prime Minister 'do something' to avert the 'crash' to which the economy was heading. He indicated what should be done along the lines of the LO position, which had also been spelled out in a motion introduced in Parliament by the Social Democrats.

Nilsson's speech came at a critical point, for on that day SAF informed LO and PTK of its opening position. SAF argued that the burdens to which industry had been subjected over recent years had made it too small to carry the Swedish economy. The second round of oil price rises dashed whatever hopes for improvement there were at the beginning of 1979. Firms have now been saddled with additional costs by the December price-clause agreement, additional wage payments according to the earnings guarantees and increased social charges. These, plus uncontrollable drift in the period ahead, already raise labor costs for 1980 by 6–7 percent. Any additional wage increases would lead to increased inflation, worsened competitiveness and a further decline in industrial employment. These conditions, together with 'the combination of inflation and marginal tax effects', make it impossible to improve the wage-earners' position beyond the 'significant compensation for price increases given to consumers by the tax reform that goes into effect at the beginning of this year'. SAF accordingly proposed the extension of the previous agreement to the end of the year without provision for any increases in contractual wages.

Not surprisingly, the proposal was rejected by both LO and PTK. The latter had an alternative proposal of its own, however. At a press conference the next day PTK's chairman, Ingvar Seregard, declared that the only way to avert an imminent breakdown of negotiations was an agreement to a 'social contract' among the government, the opposition, the unions and employers. This would make it possible to directly couple a decrease in marginal tax rates with a corresponding reduction in wage claims by higher-paid workers, thereby decreasing the differences in nominal wages. Other measures could be included in the agreed package, such as an increase in the general VAT rate while removing it entirely from basic foods. Although such political intervention in collective bargaining was alien to the Swedish model, and Seregard was normally opposed to incomes policies, he argued that the 'equilibrium in Parliament has deprived the country of a purposeful economic policy'. Since the country was in a 'crisis situation', such an 'unconventional alternative' to normal negotiations was necessary.[292]

Among the other unions, only SACO–SR supported this initiative. LO did not go along with PTK, still looking to the government for a prior commitment to tax and economic-policy changes as a condition for wider discussions. The two private sector union organizations had been trying to work out the terms on which to negotiate jointly with SAF, as in the previous two central negotiations. They shared a similar view of the economic situation, the need to maintain industry's international competitiveness and the need for tax changes to make it possible to maintain their members' purchasing power with lower nominal increases than would be required as things stood, as well as for some provision for allocating profits to investment with union participation. At the same time, they were equally opposed to SAF's 'zero-increase' position. Nevertheless, the issue of how much differentials between their members should be reduced, and how they should even be measured, remained an obstacle to agreement between them on a common negotiating position. If that obstacle could have been overcome, perhaps LO would have joined with PTK in calling for some kind of 'unconventional alternative'.

The prospect for that had, in any case, been significantly diminished the day after Seregard suggested it, when the four public sector union groups presented a joint demand for wage increases of 11–13 percent. This was the first round of central negotiations in which all four of the groups, the central and local government LO unions and central and local government TCO cartels, had managed to agree to joint bargaining. Having done so, they introduced a powerful new influence in the process. There had been coordination of LO and TCO unions within each of the separate parts of the public sector before, as we have seen, but the obstacles to joint efforts over the whole public sector had hitherto proved insurmountable. What evidently made it possible to overcome them was the recognition that the public sector was coming increasingly under attack by the bourgeois parties and private industry. The four groups – whose leaders came to be dubbed the 'gang of four' during the conflict – had made their first joint move the previous June when they gave notice of termination of existing contracts and announced their intention to seek an increase in real wages for all public sector employees.

The public sector unions' coordination reinforced the efforts at coordination among public sector employers within the organization that had been set up for the purpose, OASEN (*Offentliga arbetsgivares samarbetsnämnd*). In November 1979 OASEN declared that the public sector employers would negotiate jointly and indicated the common policy they would pursue. In essence they affirmed their commitment to the C sector's role as wage leader, saying that there should therefore be no settlement in the public sector until one was reached in the private sector. In addition, the establishment of uniform standards within the whole public sector was set as an objective.

The public sector unions rejected OASEN's argument as a justification for not settling first. They declared their own acceptance of the EFO-model principle that the scope for increases in the economy as a whole had to be geared to the scope for increase in the C sector. But they insisted that once that had been determined, the distribution among workers had to be settled on the basis of other principles, such as the improvement of low-paid workers' relative position throughout the economy, which did not coincide with divisions between public and private, or industry and service, sectors. As explained by Sigvard Marjasin, chairman of the LO local government union, SKAF (*Svenska Kommunalarbetareförbundet*), which had overtaken the Metalworkers as LO's largest union, they rejected the notion that the 'available room for increases shall first be distributed by the private sector before the public employees can claim their share'.[293] They proceded to advance their claim, based on their own EFO-model calculation, and pressed OASEN to enter into negotiations. The latter responded by restating its earlier position.

By specifying the level of increases they sought, the public sector unions altered the situation on the union side. Until then, the private sector unions had refrained from committing themselves to a number on the chance that the government would enable them to keep it low by making the necessary tax changes. Now they were in a bind. They could readily reject SAF's zero bid as unacceptably low, but it was a different matter to reject the public sector unions' bid as too high. That was the employers' task – in this case, the central government's. It would have made things easier if the government had indicated some limit to the increases it regarded as acceptable at an earlier stage, when it was clear what the public sector unions would do but before they did it. PTK's social-contract gambit was apparently timed as it was in an effort to head off the public sector unions, giving the government an occasion to respond in some way that would make a smaller nominal increase acceptable before the public sector unions' claim.

LO still hoped for an immediate government response, but there was none before events went much further. There was nothing for LO to do under the circumstances but specify its own claim, which it did at an overall level of 11·3 percent – in other words, about the same as the public sector unions' claim. This was followed by a recommendation to LO's affiliates to notify their employer counterparts of termination of contracts, which had been extended beyond their expiration date, thereby clearing the way for industrial action.

SAF's reaction to LO's claim was to send letters to LO and the government elaborating its position that there is no way that an increase in nominal wages could increase real disposable income in the face of inflation and taxes, and proposing its own version of an unconventional alternative to normal negotiations. It identified the continued growth of public expenditures while production stagnated as the key obstacle to recovery. Although taxes to finance the expenditures have been so high as to result in declining real wages after taxes and declining competitiveness, through compensatory wage increases and increased social charges, budget deficits have grown along with the balance of payments deficits resulting from declining competitiveness, so that Sweden has become dependent on foreign borrowing. Given the insufficient production to support the country's consumption and the combined effects of inflation and marginal taxes, there is no way to sustain wage-earners' real income by a negotiated wage increase. Whatever level might be agreed on, a real income cut of some 2–3 percent is likely.

As SAF saw it, there are only three ways to provide the resources that would enable workers to avoid such further cuts: a further reduction of investment, a further increase in foreign borrowing and a limitation of public expenditures. The first is the opposite of what is needed. Investment has to be encouraged by a wage agreement that permits increased competitiveness and by elimination of double taxation of profits in order to channel private savings into equity capital. The second offers no solution because lenders in the international capital market will not continue to accept borrowing for consumption instead of investment. The only way, therefore, is to limit the growth of public expenditures so as to permit tax reductions without budget deficits.

SAF went on to say that the growth of expenditures has been strongest in the local government sector, increasing local taxes as well as central government support, while social-insurance recipients receive compensation for the impact of increased international prices that workers cannot get. 'It is unreasonable' for workers to make such large sacrifices while the public sector is expanding: 'all citizen groups must bear the effects' of such price increases. 'Only those in the worst position can be excepted.' On these grounds SAF called upon the government to set up a 'delegation' or committee to cooperate with the parties on the labor market to work out reductions in public expenditures and the tax changes that would enable the workers to share in the resources thereby made available.[294]

With this presentation of SAF's argument, all the actors in the labor market had taken public positions on what the government had to do to make a wage settlement possible. Common to all of them was some change in taxes, though this was least-stressed by the public sector unions, which also presented the most optimistic view of the overall economic situation. But there was a wide divergence in both the substance of the tax changes called for and the procedures by which they were to be linked to wage claims. The unions generally envisioned a further shift in the tax structure from direct to indirect taxes, altering the palpable effects on disposable income and its distribution without lowering aggregate revenues, since lower revenues would diminish the possibility of maintaining public expenditures without increasing budget deficits.

SAF, on the other hand, pushed for lower taxes all along the line, resisting compensatory increases of social charges on employers and, notably, advocating elimination of double taxation of profits by exempting dividends from income taxation. At the same time, since it rejected further growth in budget deficits on the ground that the resulting borrowing requirements were dangerous, it called for reductions in public expenditures. In so doing it was urging the government to carry tax policy further in the direction in which it had been taken since 1976, and to go much further in the direction of the expenditure restraining policies on which it had embarked. Thus, SAF's position implied a reversal of the long-term growth of the public sector that had taken place under the Social Democrats which would, in turn, imply expanded scope for private enterprise in the service sector.

The public sector unions naturally saw this as a direct threat to them. Marjasin accused SAF of trying to finance its wage settlement at the expense of 'not only public employees, but pensioners, families with children, and the sick'. He also accused SAF of trying to drive a wedge between the private and public sector unions which would, in turn, enable SAF to break up coordinated wage bargaining in the private sector and make solidaristic wage policy impossible.[295] In fact, there was virtually no coordination between the private and public sector unions, and the latters' strategy of seizing the initiative, more effectively than ever, aggravated tensions between unions in the two sectors which had been apparent earlier and which SAF could readily exploit.

In this way, as well, the private sector unions were put in a difficult position. In order to accept a nominal wage increase that was as low as possible they needed the government's help in the form not only of tax changes, but also of explicit resistance to the public sector unions' claim. Neither form of help had as yet been forthcoming. But now SAF had proposed ways in which the government should provide that help that were unacceptable. This was particularly the case as far as LO was concerned, for it shared with the Social Democrats a commitment to a public sector through which there was a large flow of funds to provide jobs, services and transfer payments. From LO's point of view, an acceptable solution could have been achieved if the middle parties had been willing to break with the conservatives and negotiate a package of tax changes with the Social Democrats, which could be enacted with the latter's support. The middle parties did just that in 1981, leading to the break-up of the three-party coalition and establishment of the third Fälldin government, a minority Center–liberal government. However, this could hardly have happened while the nuclear energy issue was still pending, although that is when it would have had to happen in order to avert the 1980 labor market conflict.

SAF's proposal was for something utterly different and LO rejected it. Since SAF's letter did not explicitly reply to LO's wage claim, and the delegation it proposed was viewed as a substitute for negotiations, LO interpreted it as a refusal to negotiate, so LO declared that negotiations had broken down. To pressure the government to appoint a mediation commission, the next step normally required to get negotiations going again, LO announced an overtime ban. This was the first in the escalating series of 'conflict measures' culminating in the open conflict.

Up to this point the government's efforts to head it off consisted of informal and unorganized contacts by the Prime Minister and some other ministers with various principals in the private sector. Fälldin decided, at one point, to handle all the contacts himself in the expectation that he would be put in a position to assert national leadership by the outcome of the referendum. He anticipated that the anti-nuclear option, 'line 3', would win a plurality over the other two, enabling him to reconstruct the Cabinet without the conservatives and settle the wage dispute with the support of LO and the Social Democrats. The best way to do that, he concluded, was by special legislation that would translate a comprehensive package deal into law. He got no such mandate from the 23 March referendum, in which line 2, in favor of putting the existing and planned twelve reactors in operation but eventually eliminating nuclear energy, won the most votes. A package deal was prepared and proposed anyway. It offered to introduce a freeze on prices, rents and public sector fees, a flat reduction of income taxes at low- and middle-income brackets and compulsory allocation of 25 percent of profits to special investment funds, provided that unions and employers reach an 'agreement on largely unchanged conditions'. This meant holding wage rates 'largely' at their existing level. In other words, the bottom line, literally, was essentially SAF's zero-increase position.[296]

LO turned it down as 'too late, insufficient, and tied to unrealistic conditions'. This ruled out any possibility of Social Democratic support for an emergency law to impose a settlement in line with the package, which was opposed by TCO and the liberal party as well. Now it was up to the mediation commissions appointed the day before the package was announced. The prospects for them were clouded by refusal of the most experienced mediators to take on what they viewed as a hopeless task, the government's insistence that the mediation efforts be carried out in close consultation with it, and an announcement by the private sector commission's chairman suggesting that he shared SAF's view that no increase was possible.

The escalation process resumed as LO put its overtime ban into effect, refusing the commission's request to suspend the ban while mediation efforts proceeded. SAF countered with everything it had, giving notice of a one-week general lockout of all LO union members in SAF firms. If it achieved its intended effect, SAF's chairman declared, the lockout would be an 'investment in the future' that was worth the cost.[297] This failed to make LO back off, but SAF acceded to the commission's request to postpone the lockout for a few days beyond the deadline. In the breathing-space provided the commission came up with a proposal that a small amount be made available for individual union negotiations pending a general settlement. SAF accepted, and since this amounted to a modification of its initial position, LO accepted it as well. SAF withdrew its lockout notice and LO ended its overtime ban, although it set a dead-line for notification of new action if no further progress was made by then.

Meanwhile the public sector unions returned to the offensive, giving notice of a ban on overtime and new hires to be followed in a few days by selective strikes. Thus, the public sector unions were the first on the union side to resort to a work stoppage. They were faced with the need to increase the pressure on the public sector employers by the emerging possibility that the private sector would settle first, and for less, in conformity with OASEN's declared strategy. Hence, when the public sector mediators presented them with a preliminary proposal like the one that broke the private sector deadlock, the 'gang of four' rejected it, along with the request to hold off on industrial action. They put their overtime ban into effect and the central and municipal government associations – but not the counties, which run the medical system – gave notice of a partial lockout to begin on the day the strikes were scheduled to start.

The temporary respite in the private sector ended when the commission made its first proposal for an overall settlement. While declaring it unsatisfactory, SAF accepted it as a basis for negotiations. LO did not do so, saying that it offered essentially no improvement over SAF's initial position and the government package. Accordingly, it announced that the mediation effort had broken down, reinstating its overtime ban and giving notice of point strikes involving about 100,000 members to begin on 2

May. SAF responded by declaring a general lockout to coincide with the strikes. The public sector unions rejected a similar proposal, and the strikes and lockouts in that sector began as scheduled.

It was still not certain that the same would happen in the private sector. There were some days still to go, giving the mediators time to present a new proposal which departed further from SAF's position by offering 2·3 percent. This was still a long way from LO's initial claim, so it turned the proposal down. It also turned down the Social Democrats' idea of a no-confidence motion in Parliament on the ground that it would confirm SAF's propaganda to the effect that the strike was political, when it was in fact a trade union struggle over wages. This became the theme of the 1 May rallies around the country. The next day 750,000 LO members were locked out and Swedish industry ground to a halt. That the stoppage would not necessarily be a brief demonstration was indicated a few days later when SAF announced its intention to prolong the lockout for another week in response to LO's refusal to set any time limit on its selective strikes. Further extensions of the lockout could be expected as long as LO did not back down.

What brought the conflict to an end on 11 May was a decision by the government that it could not afford to let it go on indefinitely. To determine what it would take to end it government representatives sounded out the principals. The conclusion was that the unions would accept a settlement that roughly split the difference between their initial positions and the one that SAF and the government had taken, plus implementation of the package the government had offered, except for the price freeze which LO regarded as useless. The mediation commissions were then pressed to work out detailed proposals at the overall levels that would achieve the desired result. They came up with proposals for one-year agreements, providing 7·3 percent in the public sector and 6·8 percent in the private. This was more than the unions in either expected to end up with and they consequently accepted.

The public sector employer negotiating bodies also accepted. In insisting that they would not settle before the private sector, they had been acting according to the government's position. Now that the government had changed it, they had no choice but to go along. SAF, however, rejected the proposal, issuing a ten-point statement reiterating their general view of the situation, criticizing the public sector for acting as wage leader, and saying that the 'proposal and negotiations behind it make it necessary to reconsider the Swedish negotiating model'. LO responded by vowing to continue the struggle as long as SAF did, whereupon the Prime Minister called in the SAF leaders to prevail upon them to accept. They emerged from the meeting announcing that they had very reluctantly agreed. 'We have not achieved our goal', Nicolin declared, so 'now it is up to the government to take responsibility for the country's economy'.[298]

Nicolin seemed to be saying that SAF had taken responsibility for the economy but that the government had failed to do what was necessary for SAF to fulfill it. This brings us back to the question of what SAF's strategy really was and what the government would have had to do to enable it to succeed. This is the question that was raised by the SAF discussion of wage policy prior to the 1980 conflict. The answer, according to some LO leaders, is that SAF's aim was in fact to bring about, or at least set in motion, a basic change in the wage determination system's mode of operation. As they saw it, the 1980 conflict was the result of an unsuccessful attempt by SAF to achieve that aim, an attempt that was made because SAF misjudged the situation in important respects. Most importantly, it misjudged the extent to which the situation had been changed by the bourgeois parties' control of the government.

This view was spelled out in an article by LO's negotiations secretary, Harry Fjällström.[299] For the Swedish model to provide industrial peace, he began, Social Democratic control of the government was necessary. Only then would economic policy be consistent with the 'interests of the majority' and a 'reasonable distribution ... A bourgeois government accordingly implies ... an obvious change in the conditions for the Swedish model', for then 'capital's interests steer both policy and production'. Capital, therefore, saw the change of government in 1976 as an opportunity to reverse the gains made by the labor movement that were against its interests. There are two kinds of gains, in particular, on which the employers' sights were set. One is the 'breakdown of the owner interest's total domination of production' as a result of the labor-law reforms. The other is the effectiveness with which solidaristic wage policy diminished employers' ability to use wages as a management tool. With respect to the first, the employers demanded various amendments in the recently enacted legislation and 'saw to it that' negotiations for an agreement on MBL came to nothing. With respect to the second, SAF sought to drive down the wage increases provided for in central agreements so as to leave as much room for discretionary changes as possible.

It was the pursuit of the second aim that led to open conflict in 1980. SAF's 'zero position' was 'an attack on central negotiations and therewith' on 'LO's solidaristic wage policy'. The success of the attack was contingent on action by the government to 'force wage earners to accept low or no wage increases at all'. Fjällström saw no other way to explain SAF's refusal to negotiate, despite the successive steps taken by LO that would ordinarily have led to negotiations, except that the employers 'counted on government action that would resolve the situation without it being necessary for SAF to really go to the bargaining table'.

This was a 'strategic mistake', however, for SAF overestimated the cohesion of the bourgeois coalition and, hence, of the government's capacity for action. It also misjudged the attitude of LO union members in the face of white-collar-worker gains, inflation and rising profits. Finally, it misjudged the effects of its offensive measures. On the one hand, SAF expected its measures to induce the unions to back down because of their longstanding concern for industrial peace, as if it meant a 'permanent truce, regardless of how [the employers] acted'. On the other hand, SAF 'probably believed' that the government would finally step in and 'forbid the whole conflict'. Since the conflict did not turn out as SAF expected it to, Fjällström concluded, it 'contributed to improving the conditions' for the next round of negotiations: 'The bourgeois government's demonstrated weakness and the labor movement's stability constitute the most significant constraints.'

According to this view, then, the 1980 conflict was indeed a test of the strategy implicit in SAF's new wage policy statement and critique of the EFO model summarized earlier. Yet, other interpretations are possible. It could be argued that SAF had no more intention of resisting further increases in labor costs to the point of precipitating open conflict than on the many previous occasions when its initial position was that there was no room for any increases. Instead the newly formed coalition of public sector unions was the driving-force, as evidenced by the repeated instances in which they seized the initiative and raised the ante. This is most plausibly explained as an effort to force a public sector settlement before there was one in the private sector that could be expected to be lower and which could then not be exceeded. To preserve freedom of action, in the face of joint LO and SAF efforts to tie wage developments throughout the economy to whatever view of the C sector's requirements they could finally agree on, the public sector coalition had to force the pace of escalation. There were precedents for the success of such efforts on previous occasions when the public sector settled first.

On this occasion, however, the government's determination not to let it happen was underestimated. Once the conflict broke out in the public sector, legislation to suspend it was possible. There was a precedent for this as well, in 1971. But two circumstances removed the possibility this time. First, Fälldin's attempt to apply such legislation to the labor market as a whole, before open conflict had broken out in any part of it, wasted that option. Secondly, by the time open conflict did break out in the public sector, the conflict between SAF and LO had reached the point where LO could not back down as long as the public sector unions did not. Once the conflict in the private sector had started, emergency legislation could not easily be confined to the public sector. But legislation encroaching on LO's right to strike could not have got Social Democratic support, and a weak and divided bourgeois coalition could not risk it on its own. That the question of legislation came up at all, however, is to be viewed as a symptom of the government's prior inability to carry out the whole series of subtler moves required to avert the conflict. These included the elaboration of a credible economic policy, spelling out its April package in detail, prompt appointment of mediation commissions, allowing them to function normally, and so on.

The point here is not to decide on the most convincing explanation, but rather to stress the difficulty of doing so. For our purposes, Fjällström's view of what happened is an important indication of how LO leaders perceived what happened, for it is consistent with what was said in private. There can hardly be much doubt that the stakes were high in the conflict between LO and SAF and that a stronger and more cohesive bourgeois government could have provided the political conditions under which SAF might have achieved what Nicolin had in mind as its goal, which was probably at least a somewhat lower settlement in both the private and public sectors. At the same time, the extent of the conflict between the public sector unions and all the other actors, including the private sector unions, should not be underestimated. Differences between the private and public sector unions within LO over the kind of wage policy that was consistent with the economy's needs surfaced in the aftermath of the 1980 conflict. The need to resolve these differences gave rise to an important discussion, particularly between the Metalworkers and SKAF.

Whatever the explanation for the course taken by wage bargaining in 1980, it made the task of coping with the structural dimension of Sweden's economic crisis even more difficult than the new deterioration in the international economic environment would have made it anyway. Looking at the results of the agreement for 1980, it provided for contractual increases in industrial workers' average hourly wages that very substantially exceeded drift. The amounts involved are more than usually uncertain because the available data on drift are tentative and subject to different interpretations, depending on how increases won in the December 1979 price-clause negotiations are estimated and allocated between the two years. Adding a 2·1 percent increase resulting from the December 1979 agreement to a 4·4 percent increase resulting from the May 1980 agreement comes to a 6·5 percent total increase in contractual earnings in 1979–80.[300] This estimate seems to be the one most comparable with the LO data used for preceding years. With wage drift estimated at 3·3 percent, the total increase in adult industrial workers' average hourly earnings in 1979–80 was 9·8 percent.[301]

This outcome is notably consistent with the pattern of alternation between low agreements, in which contractual increases fall short of drift, and high agreements, in which contractual increases exceed drift, observable throughout most of the sequence of central agreements since the early 1960s which we reviewed earlier. Only the two low agreements in a row for 1977 and 1978–9 deviated from this pattern, which was perhaps to be expected after the very high agreement for 1975–6. A further stretch-out of the pattern in 1980 might have been possible, but only under political conditions in which the unions could have got significant concessions on income and power distribution issues or, alternatively, in which they could have been defeated in an open conflict. In other words, under the political conditions prevailing in 1980, it was not possible to alter the wage-determination systems' normal mode of operation as far as its economic effects were concerned. All that the effort to do so accomplished was a costly work stoppage that aggravated the situation.

Continuing Crisis and Alternative Responses

The direct loss of industrial production attributed to the general work stoppage, together with a subsequent strike by a breakaway dockworkers union, is estimated at between 1·5 and 2·0 percent on an annual basis: 'The total loss of exports . . . is estimated at around 2 percent, while the loss in the case of raw materials seems to have been somewhat higher.'[302] The effect on Sweden's relative cost position cannot be stated on the basis of available data. Unit labor costs are estimated to have risen 7·4 percent in 1979–80, compared with increases of 4·0 and 1·5 percent in 1977–8 and in 1978–9, respectively. However, more of the increase in unit labor costs in

1979–80 is accounted for by a drop in productivity growth, from 7·0 to 2·2 percent, than by the increase in hourly labor costs, from 8·6 to 9·8 percent.[303] The decline in productivity growth is attributed primarily to a reduction in the 'productivity reserve' provided by underutilized capacity while there was little investment in new capacity. In the absence of the relevant comparative data we cannot tell whether the increase in unit labor costs has reopened the cost gap. Whatever the case, a lower increase in hourly earnings, permitting a lower increase in unit labor costs, would presumably have permitted the recovery of investment that was finally under way to be sustained a little longer than it was.

STARTING OVER: GOVERNMENT POLICY, 1980–2

If the 1980 agreement worsened Sweden's relative cost position, it probably did so only marginally. Even if, as some argued, it was necessary to do more than restore relative costs to what they were prior to the 1975–6 agreement, the 1980 agreement did not create a cost problem on anything like the scale of that following the mid–1970s wage explosion.[304] On the other hand, several years had gone by without much of the investment in internationally competitive production needed to solve the underlying structural problem. Reflecting its persistence, the balance of payments and central government budget deficits were far larger in 1980 than in 1977. Moreover, the international economic environment was more unfavorable. Although the OECD recovery had slowed down in 1977, area GNP growth that year was more than twice as high as in 1980, 3·7 compared with 1·2 percent.[305] Thus, very little had been accomplished toward extricating Sweden from its economic crisis. Essentially the economy was back where it was in 1977. While the situation was certainly not as difficult in cost terms, it was evidently more so in structural terms. In effect the second Fälldin government had to start again to do what its predecessors had not been able to do.

While broadly similar, the policy scenario has also been not exactly the same. The most important similarity lay in a turn toward a highly restrictive macroeconomic policy at a special session of Parliament in September 1980. Since this occurred just as activity in the OECD area was turning down, the setback to industrial investment and threat of increased open unemployment was bound to increase. There was also another devaluation a year later.[306]

As noted before, the fall in private industrial investment was reversed in the latter half of 1979. 'Improved profitability ... rising production and capacity utilization' gave private industrial investment enough of an impulse to make it 12 percent higher in 1980 as a whole than in the preceding year, but it turned down again in the second half of 1980. Total industrial investment, public and private, is estimated to have fallen 4 percent in 1981, after having risen 17 percent in 1980.[307] The recovery of industrial investment would hardly have been sustainable in the face of the serious new downturn in the OECD area generally, no matter what happened to Sweden's relative cost position, but the recovery might well have been reversed less quickly and less sharply if it had not been for the massive work stoppage and the size of the wage increase that brought it to an end.

Under all the circumstances, including the special ones derived from the experience of 1980 and the determination to avoid a repetition of it, the low agreement for 1981–2 that SAF and LO reached fairly quickly and smoothly in early 1981 was entirely to be expected. A PTK strike, aimed at preserving differentials relative to LO, threatened to precipitate another major work stoppage, but intense pressures, not least from LO, brought it to an end on terms consistent with the SAF–LO agreement while leaving a number of issues unresolved.[308]

By the time the current two-year agreement runs out, however, it is likely that economic policy will once more be confronted by the problem of making the wage-determination system operate in such a way as to permit a recovery of industrial investment to continue. There were already strong signs in late 1981 that the problem would be posed much more clearly in the next wage round than it was in 1980. It appeared that corporate profits would recover to the highest levels since 1974, and wage drift was reported to be rising more than expected.[309] If these trends held, the problem would be inescapable. How it would be met would be largely determined by the outcome of yet another election to take place before the next round of central negotiations.

No matter what the outcome of the election would be, the income-tax structure was not likely to pose the critical problem it did for the 1980 negotiations. As noted earlier, the middle parties broke with their conservative coalition partner to reach an agreement with the opposition Social Democrats on a tax-reform package. Starting with an abandonment of tax changes for 1982 planned by the three-party government, the agreement was to reduce marginal rates to 50 percent up to income levels covering most employees, change the structure of deductions to make them more egalitarian and offset the resulting revenue loss by an increase in payroll taxes. The package was bitterly opposed by the conservatives, leading them to withdraw from the coalition. It was replaced by a third Fälldin government, a middle-party minority coalition. The agreed tax package was enacted with Social Democratic support in April 1982. LO and TCO regarded the legislation as reasonably satisfactory, making the tax structure much more favorable to lower nominal wage increases than it was in 1980.[310]

If our understanding is correct, however, it would be the problem to which wage-earner funds are addressed as much if not more than the income-tax problem that would be crucial to what happens in the next wage round. And in this connection the election outcome would certainly make a difference. The political cleavage over the fundamental issue of how savings were to be accumulated and channeled into equity capital was crystallized during the period 1976–82 while the successive bourgeois governments were in office and the Social Democrats in opposition. The governments pursued a pattern of policy that operated to reinforce the reprivatization of savings, channel it into equity capital and erode political support for the Social Democratic labor movement alternative of providing equity capital out of collective savings. An agreement on the form that alternative should take was worked out by LO and the SAP over the same period. A political battle reminiscent of that over pension reform in the late 1950s was shaping up and, as in the earlier case, the white-collar unions were torn by a struggle over their political souls by the contending forces.

Running through the pattern of policy pursued by the bourgeois governments were two strands. One consisted of doing very little to arrest the decline of the AP system as a mechanism for collective savings. The other involved a series of measures to make private share-ownership more attractive. It was unnecessary to take positive steps to reduce the growth in the AP system's surplus because that was built into it from its inception. Initially, it will be recalled, revenue based on rapidly increasing payroll-tax payments was to substantially exceed payments to a slowly increasing number of people entitled to gradually rising pensions based on years worked. A large surplus, augmented by earnings from investing the surplus, would consequently accumulate during a long transition period. As the pension system came into full operation, however, the growth in its surplus would slow down and the surplus could even decline. This would depend on whether the payroll tax continued to be raised, by periodic parliamentary decisions, and on how the interaction of many factors including economic growth, inflation, interest rates, credit-market regulations and the composition of the system's portfolio affected its earnings from investment.

The rapid growth of the AP fund in its initial years made it the single largest source of lending in the 'organized credit market' – that is, the financial institutions subject to central-bank regulation, which does not extend to transactions by non-financial firms, At its peak in 1970–1 the AP fund accounted for over 40 percent of net lending.[311] Ever since then, its share of lending in the credit market has declined. There is nothing to stop this decline in the absence of a decision to do so by, for example, substantially increasing the payroll-tax rate, its base, or both. It would not be correct to say that the governments in office since 1976 did nothing to stem the decline in the AP fund's position. The payroll-tax rate was increased slightly, from 12 to 12·25 percent, as of 1981. However, the base was reduced by changing the method of calculating it. In addition, a 1979 law requires the Fourth Fund to turn over 80 percent of its earnings to the other three funds, from which its capital is drawn, instead of using the proceeds for reinvestment. This strengthens the system's lending capacity at the expense of its capacity to supply equity capital. On the other hand, the upper limit of the amount the Fourth Fund could draw was raised from 1 to 1·85 billion crowns in two installments, in 1978 and 1980.[312] The second was enacted under the minority liberal government in the face of opposition by organized business, which declared that increasing the AP system's role in supplying equity capital was to 'go the wrong way'. The right way, in its view, was to 'increase profitability so that a sufficient increase in risk capital can be brought about by an increase in retained earnings and in households' interest in participating in new issues'. In response, the government argued, among other things, that the Fourth

Fund's presence supported the stock market, making it easier to market new issues.[313]

The long-run trends in demography and the AP system's financial position were seen as threatening its capacity to meet its pension commitments, precipitating an intensive debate over ways of maintaining its capacity or reducing its commitments. The options depend on underlying economic development and basic policy choices, however. For the time being the AP system's revenues, from payroll fees and earnings from investment, still exceed its payments. What had happened is that the surplus has virtually stopped growing in current terms, which means that it has declined in real terms. It has fallen increasingly short of the rising central government budget deficit so that, given the approximate balance of local government budgets as a result of central government support, the consolidated public sector deficit has increased.[314] In other words, the public sector has ceased to perform the collective savings function assigned to it by the Rehn model, while the share of private savings in total savings has been rising steadily.

An increase in the portion of private savings going into equity capital has been the objective of the second strand in the pattern of policy pursued by the bourgeois governments in this area. It consists of a series of changes in the tax treatment of income from shares. One provided some additional partial relief from double taxation of profits (by corporate and personal income tax) as a step toward its full elimination. Another provided a tax credit on income invested in 'share savings funds' – equivalent to mutual funds – plus complete tax exemption on all dividends and capital gains derived from that investment. The tax credit, amounting to 30 percent, is available on such investments up to a limit of 4,800 crowns per year, roughly equivalent to industrial workers' average monthly earnings, provided that the shares are held for five years. The establishment of special 'fund companies' to purchase and vote shares of listed companies with the money invested in share savings funds was authorized, subject to rules limiting holdings in any one company to 10 percent of the fund's assets and 5 percent of the voting rights in any company.[315]

The most recent of the measures extended these tax advantages to employee purchases of shares in the companies for which they work. The companies are authorized to set up their own counterparts to the general share savings funds, differing in that they only purchase the companies' own shares, so that the risk-spreading rule is removed from them. Several large companies already had employee share-ownership schemes, to which the tax breaks could not be applied, while many others set up such schemes after the measure went into effect at the beginning of 1981. They were so eager to start that they offered their employees interest-free short-term loans to enroll in the schemes. Largely on the basis of such loans there was a rapid growth in participation in the schemes. Early in the first year of operation, the Federation of Industry estimated that more than 1 billion crowns of new equity capital would be generated over the year as a whole. This would come close to the increase in household share purchases that the 1980 *Long-Term Survey* said would be necessary for industry to raise enough equity capital for the required rate of investment. The response to the new measure also triggered a marked rise in prices on the Swedish stock exchange.[316]

These prospects for the employee share-ownership schemes' economic success were evidently not all that accounted for the companies' eagerness to get them going. When the idea was first broached by the conservative Minister of Economic Affairs in 1977, it was recognized as an alternative to LO's proposal for collective share ownership and even referred to as a 'bourgeois Meidner fund'.[317] And as the measure went through Parliament it was attacked by the Social Democrats and LO as simply a political tactic designed to undercut support for wage-earner funds, while leaving the fundamental inequality in the distribution of wealth and power essentially unchanged. Although such tactical aims were disavowed in public, they were acknowledged in private, and it was obvious that the companies involved had joined the government in an effort to erode support for wage-earners funds.

Indeed, as the election approached, the continued growth of share purchases and prices in 1982 was invoked as demonstrating that there was no need for wage-earner funds in order to provide equity capital. At the same time, the funds were denounced as a grave threat to Swedish democracy as well as the economy by the bourgeois parties and organized business. They mounted a campaign against the funds more intense than any since the idea was launched. An amount of money unprecedented in Swedish politics was poured into an apparent effort to make the election turn on the issue, which was defined as a matter of saving Sweden from being transformed into an East European dictatorship.

The threat apparently did not seem very credible to an electorate which could look back to decades of Social Democratic capacity to govern at no particular cost to Swedish democracy. At any rate wage-earner funds ranked low among the issues that concerned the voters. The massive campaign against the funds did not prevent the Social Democrats from returning to office, with three more seats than the bourgeois parties' combined total, and an overall socialist-bloc majority of twenty-three.[318]

THE SOCIAL DEMOCRATIC LABOR MOVEMENT CONSENSUS ON WAGE-EARNER FUNDS

The Social Democrats did not win their 1982 election victory by evading the issue of wage-earner funds as they did when they lost in 1976, although the issue was no more decisive in the recent election than the earlier one. The party went into the election committed in principle to a form of wage-earner funds on which they had reached agreement with LO. Thus, the anti-funds campaign was against a position the Social Democrats had definitely taken, although the way the position was described in the campaign often bore little relation to it. It will be recalled that the leadership was extremely reluctant to embrace the Meidner Plan LO adopted shortly prior to the 1976 election. In the years since then, the leadership evidently became convinced that there can be no solution to the problem of investment without at least some kind of fund system. Moreover, there was a good deal of enthusiasm for the idea among party as well as union activists, and failure to incorporate it into the party program could be dangerously divisive. There was also a good deal of controversy over alternative forms, modes of operation and long-run implications of wage-earner funds, giving rise to a lively and fascinating debate within the Social Democratic labor movement.[319] What was clear was that the party had to come to terms with the idea. The pace at which it did so was set by the schedule of party and LO Congresses, the party alone in 1978 and both in 1981, and the fact that the government commission appointed by the Social Democrats was expected to complete its work before the 1982 election. If the party was not compelled to take a clear stand in the 1979 election, it could not avoid doing so in 1982.

As indicated earlier, joint LO–SAP committees were established to hammer out a mutually acceptable form that might be both technically feasible and tactically viable. One version was prepared for the 1978 Congress, which adopted it as a basis for further work, and another for the Congresses in 1981. A fundamental part of the committees' task was to reconcile the somewhat different approaches to collective capital formation taken by the party and LO.

Essentially the approach on which the party leadership relied involved the accumulation of collective savings in the public sector through taxes which were then channeled back out to industry through a variety of public or semi-public lending bodies. This approach was typified by the AP system in its original form together with the Investment Bank and similar credit-market institutions.[320] The essence of the LO approach was a partial collectivization of ownership rights, to both income and control, as exemplified by allocating a portion of profits in the form of shares to institutions wholly or partly controlled by unions as in the Meidner Plan. Introduction of the Fourth Fund into the AP system modified the party's approach in the direction of LO's to some extent, although the element of union participation in it has been marginal. It seems fair to say that the version of wage-earner funds adopted by both the party and LO in 1981 amounts to a further modification of the party's approach in the direction of LO's, providing for a considerably greater element of union participation in the administration of ownership rights accumulated by the new institutions, but a good deal less collective profit-sharing than in the Meidner Plan.

Both the 1978 and 1981 versions are quite complicated. The earlier one was an intermediate product, so we shall confine our account to the later one.[321] It preserves the Meidner Plan's basic principle of collective rather than individual share ownership, with trade union participation in administering new institutions set up to hold the shares. Unlike the Meidner Plan, however, both the financing of investment by the institutions and income from the investments are tied to the AP system.

Instead of being financed by the compulsory allocation of a fixed percentage of all profits, the principal source of money for the present version of the funds would be an increase of 1 percent in the payroll tax paid into the AP system. The latter would turn the proceeds over to the funds, of which there would be one in each of the twenty-four counties into which Sweden is divided. The funds would invest the proceeds in shares, purchased in the stock market or directly from firms. Although regionally based, the funds would invest in companies all over the country, seeking a 'good return' on their capital like ordinary investment companies. An additional source of financing would be a kind of excess profits tax, based on 20 percent of 'surplus profits' – exceeding a specified 'normal' rate of return on equity – paid in cash to the AP system and similarly turned over for investment by the funds. Thus, the partial collectivization of profits on which financing of the funds was entirely based in the Meidner Plan has been relegated to what seems to be a marginal role in the present version. Just how marginal it would be depends on the level of profits specified as normal.

The payroll-tax increase would shift a portion of the labor share in value added to capital across the board, but the associated increment to wealth would accrue to the funds instead of private shareholders in the form of equities purchased from the proceeds of the payroll-tax increase. The extent to which unions would correspond to the proceeds would depend on the extent to which unions accepted the reduction in the labor share instead of trying to compensate for it by increased wages – in other words, the extent to which the scheme makes a corresponding degree of wage restraint possible. The excess-profits tax – the 'profit sharing' component of the scheme – would supposedly make such restraint less vulnerable to disruption by high profits and associated wage drift. In other words, it would be expected to underpin solidaristic wage policy as a basis for coordinated wage bargaining, and hence whatever degree of wage restraint it permits.

The earnings from the investments would be a source of revenues for the AP system, the funds having an obligation to provide a specified rate of return on the capital, which is conceived as having been made available to them by the AP system. Thus, both the financing and revenues of the wage-earner funds would operate to strengthen the effectiveness of the AP system as a mechanism for collective savings, counteracting the tendency toward the reprivatization of savings referred to earlier. Tying the funds to the AP system also defines pension payments as the stake individuals have in the funds. While providing an individual stake, it is one that differs in crucial respects from that involved in the individual share-ownership schemes favored by business and fostered by the bourgeois governments. Unlike the latter, it is universal among all wage-earners, guaranteed to all of them on the same terms, and dissociated from the differential profit-ability of the specific firms in which workers are employed or hold shares. What makes the present form of wage-earner funds something more than a larger, more elaborate Fourth Fund is the element of union participation in determining the investment policy of the funds and exercising the claims to control in the individual firms whose shares are held. The exercise of those rights is divided between the local unions in the firms and the funds in about the same way as in the Meidner Plan.

It is not necessary to review the argument made for the present version since it is essentially the same as that made for the one LO adopted in 1976. In our view, as indicated earlier, this is the case notwithstanding the official contention that capital formation is a new, 'fourth' objective added to the three earlier ones set for wage-earner funds. The joint LO–SAP committee report does make some points about the systemic implications of the funds that are worth noting, however.[322] It cites two 'totally contradictory' criticisms of the funds frequently made in the public debate over them. One is that the funds would mean that 'the market economy will gradually be replaced by a planned economy in which firms will be unable to make their own production decisions', leading eventually to a 'centrally directed bureaucratic society' which would 'threaten democracy'. The 'directly opposite' view is that wage-earner funds 'serve the aim of strengthening the existing system', the drive for 'profits and competition', so that 'workers and their organizations are tied to the capital owner role and tamed into cooperating without protest'. The LO–SAP report characterizes both criticisms as wrong.

Against the first it argues that 'the market economy is not threatened by the funds but is on the contrary a precondition for them'. The proposal leaves to firms the responsibility for managing their resources in such a way as to survive, subject to the constraints that markets and existing laws impose on them. Without this autonomy, as in centrally planned economies, there is no scope for workers directly affected by the production process to influence it. In other words, industrial democracy is only possible in a market economy with decentralized production decisions.

It is precisely by increasing the possibility of realizing the potential for industrial democracy in such a system that wage-earner funds bring about a change from the existing capitalist system. They introduce 'a new category of owners' for whom profits are more a 'means than a goal'. While workers have an interest in profits because they are needed for the firm 'to survive, develop, and provide secure jobs', and for the funds to provide a 'reasonable return on their capital', the maximization of profits ceases to be the goal. As long as there are sufficient profits to satisfy these other requirements the workers' interest is in using the 'margin' for maneuver beyond that to change the production process, to 'democratize working life, to see that technical development takes place in the workers' interests, and to build scope for personal development into the job'.[323]

The two contradictory attacks against which these defenses are presented are obviously from the right and the left respectively. The attacks from the left are not what posed the difficult political problem for the Social Democrats, however. It was the massive campaign against wage-earner funds from the right that made them a potential electoral liability, and the affirmation of the funds' consistency with a market economy was clearly addressed to a central theme in that campaign. Tactical considerations may also have contributed to two of the main departures from the Meidner Plan pointed out earlier – the shift from profit-sharing to a payroll tax and the identification of an individual stake in the form of pension benefits.

Ultimately these as well as other tactical considerations were governed by the fundamental strategic problem with which the SAP had to cope once it decided to incorporate wage-earner funds into its program, however much its form differed from that given them by the Meidner Plan. In taking this position the SAP ruled out any possibility of controlling the government with the parliamentary support of one of the middle parties, as it did when it had the support of the Farmers' Party. That there was a real possibility of a parliamentary coalition with one or both of the middle parties is strongly suggested by the agreement the SAP struck with them on taxation. On the more fundamental issue of wage-earner funds, however, there was no possibility of compromise, although there were minorities in both middle parties willing to contemplate some kind of scheme that combined collective and individual share-ownership. For LO, however, an element of individual share-ownership would defeat the whole purpose of the funds, while for the dominant factions within the middle parties, the objections to collective profit-sharing were insurmountable.

The SAP was, thus, faced with a clear choice. It could seek to return to office with the support of one of the middle parties, but it could do so only if it refused to adopt a policy LO had come to regard as essential. This would subject its relations with LO to severe strain, diminishing the level of electoral mobilization it could expect from LO, and jeopardizing the prospects of cooperation over economic policy if it nevertheless got into office. The alternative was to adopt LO's position on the funds and rely on mobilizing the electoral support of its LO core constituency and enough additional support among TCO union members to win control of Parliament on its own. In other words, the SAP was still faced with the same basic problem of political strategy with which it had to cope ever since it could no longer count on Farmers' Party support to remain in office.

This focusses attention once more on the importance of the positions taken by the TCO unions. While the wage-earner funds issue was the one on which the distribution of attitudes within TCO unions was most critical for the Social Democrats and at the same time most dispersed, these attitudes did not exist in isolation. The impact of divisions within TCO over wage-earner funds may well have been blunted by considerable convergence not only within TCO, but also between TCO and LO on issues of economic policy generally. We conclude this part of our discussion with a brief comparison of recent trends in TCO and LO positions.

UNIONS AND THE ECONOMIC CRISIS: STRATEGIC CONVERGENCE AND ITS LIMITS

On the whole there has been a growing convergence between LO and TCO union perspectives on overall economic strategy. At the same time, the convergence has been limited by the differences in their location in both the market and state arenas. These differences cut across each other to some extent, however. Thus, as we have seen, location in the labor market defines three main organizational clusters in wage negotiations: the LO private sector unions that negotiate with SAF, the private sector white-collar unions in PTK that also negotiate with SAF and the public sector unions in both LO and TCO that have formed a coalition to negotiate with the public sector employers combined in OASEN. The positions taken by these three union groups during the successive wage rounds since the onset of the crisis provides some insight into how they perceived it. Of course, these positions reflect their estimates of their bargaining power and the tactics they should consequently pursue not only with respect to the employers' organizations, but also to each other. Since economic conditions decisively affect bargaining power, perception of the former undoubtedly enters into estimation of the latter.

As noted earlier, it took some time for all the actors in the Swedish political economy to recognize the severity of the crisis into which the economy was slipping. Even as it became apparent, however, the unions attached less weight to the 1975–6 wage explosion as a factor in creating a cost gap than academic economists or business did. While a loss of market shares was already observed in the wage-policy report to LO's 1976 Congress, the report attributed it primarily to the differences between Swedish and foreign demand levels and the 'disadvantageous' composition of Swedish exports rather than wage-cost divergence.[324] LO's expectations were more optimistic than SAF's as they headed into the 1977 negotiations and it was only as they proceeded that LO's view was altered. By the time negotiations for the next agreement began toward the end of 1977 LO shared the serious view of Sweden's economic situation held by most other actors and observers, and acknowledged the divergence between real-wage growth in Sweden and its trading partners as an important factor. It ascribed the real-wage cuts borne by workers during the year to the government's economic policy but implicitly accepted them as necessary to reduce the gap.[325]

On the other hand, TCO's research department rejected the prevailing view, expressing skepticism about the size of the cost gap embodied in it and arguing that Sweden's relative-wage costs were still on their long-term trend.[326] However, the point of view taken by the private sector TCO unions engaged in wage bargaining – that is, PTK – was essentially the same as LO's.[327] In fact, a committee of LO, PTK and SAF economists had begun to work out an agreed picture of the economy on a recurrent basis, even if the union and employer organizations continued to draw different conclusions from that picture.

A common recognition that changes in the economic and political conditions had weakened their bargaining position relative to the employers is what brought LO and PTK into joint negotiations with SAF in 1977, despite the persistence of disagreements over differentials that had previously blocked joint negotiations. These considerations held even more strongly in the negotiations for the 1978–9 agreement during which LO and PTK both emphasized the importance of restoring Swedish industry's competitiveness. As the situation appeared to ease in 1979, the differences between LO and PTK evidently outweighed the risks of bargaining separately once more, and joint negotiations were abandoned. When PTK's independent initiative for a social contract failed, it sat out the conflict that ensued, subsequently negotiating an agreement comparable to the one that settled the conflict. Even when the economy was thrown back to a position much like that in 1977, LO and PTK could not overcome their differences again. Local tensions over differential rates of increase between LO and PTK union members flared up.[328] These were reflected in the negotiation of the 1981–2 agreement in which LO and SAF settled first and PTK's effort to hold out for better protection of differentials by striking was frustrated by the combined opposition of LO and SAF, plus the weight of 'public opinion'.

Thus, the interests of the segments of the labor force represented by LO and PTK continue to prevent the two organizations from arriving at a common wage policy. Yet a number of developments have been diminishing the differences in the wage policies of LO and some private sector TCO unions, which may ease the way toward a resumption of joint bargaining in the future. In particular, SIF adopted a new wage-policy program at its 1978 Congress that comes considerably closer to LO's policy.[329] The general union of white-collar workers in private industry, SIF is the largest union in TCO and dominates PTK. While the new SIF program retains the principle of individual wage-setting, solidaristic wage policy is declared to be the basis from which the criteria should be derived. The generation of a 'fair' wage structure on that basis is affirmed as the union's wage-policy goal. Solidaristic wage policy is defined in the same way as by LO: equal pay for equal work, regardless of an employer's ability to pay. The equivalence of work is understood primarily in terms of 'level of difficulty', with skill and experience given subordinate roles while merit-rating and performance-based payment systems are rejected entirely. Pending the development of a job-classification system based on level of difficulty, the spread between lowest and highest wages within SIF is to be reduced. To that end a standard 'lowest wage' – or minimum wage – should be established for all SIF members and, ultimately, across the whole labor market.

All of this is highly congruent with LO thinking. The convergence is not only by SIF toward LO, however. LO took a step toward SIF's position when it adopted the standard minimum wage concept for the first time in 1980.[330] LO made another modification in its wage policy that brought it closer to PTK's. That was the adoption of PTK's practice of excluding certain kinds of wage increments from the calculation of earnings growth, including wage drift. Such so-called 'non-level-influencing increments', based on age, length of service and skill upgrading, enable individuals' earnings to increase more than the calculated averages.[331] The fact that this had applied to white-collar and not blue-collar workers was a source of distortion in comparisons of earnings growth between them, making the relative growth of blue-collar earnings seem greater than it was and enabling white-collar workers to use their earnings guarantee clauses to get further increases.

While these trends toward convergence in wage policy can ease the way toward joint negotiations, the absences of a common 'difficulty'-based job classification system and consistent wage statistics open to all organizations continue to present obstacles, which are not likely to be removed before conflicting views over differentials are diminished. While the changes in the nature of work resulting from changing technology, further blurring the blue-collar–white-collar distinction, could contribute to this, it could also increase the respective organizations' stake in pressing their conflicting views to justify their separate existence.

As long as this basic distributional conflict between the union organizations persists, it might be expected to inhibit convergence on other issues. Yet, in at least some major areas, this does not seem to have happened. A decision by LO and PTK to engage in joint negotiations for a general MBL agreement helped pave the way for joint wage negotiations. When the latter broke down, joint efforts over MBL issues nevertheless continued. They reached an agreement concerning collaboration on those issues between their local unions and continued efforts to reach national-level agreements with employers' organizations. Negotiations with SAF collapsed in early 1979. Shortly thereafter, however, LO and PTK reached an agreement with the state enterprise negotiating body, SFO (*Statsföretagens förhandlingsorganisation*) and with the cooperative movement's counterpart, KFO. Off-and-on negotiations with SAF finally culminated in a national frame agreement on the application of MBL within the private sector in 1982.[332]

Convergent positions and joint action on the non-wage workplace issues has, of course, been easier than on wage issues. A strong basis had been laid by cooperation between TCO and LO in the push for legislation to expand union workplace power. Conflicts have arisen between TCO and LO unions over policies to pursue in specific situations, such as between journalists and printers over the consequences of the technological trans-formation of newspaper production. But the new workplace rights have also been used by both TCO and LO unions in specific production units which joined forces against their counterparts in other production units in conflicts over which should be shut down in the course of reconstructing an industry, as in the case of steel.[333] In all, extension of union participation in workplace and enterprise decision-making has enlarged the scope of common policy and action between white-collar and blue-collar unions at local and national levels.

Convergence is also evident with respect to national policy concerning the process of industrial restructuring. TCO and its affiliates did not focus much attention on industrial policy until after the impact of the international crisis hit Sweden – in other words, much later than LO. The impact on the economy as a whole and the crisis that engulfed whole sectors and firms, while technologies emerged that affected white-collar jobs to a degree that only blue-collar jobs had been affected earlier, gave industrial policy new urgency to the TCO unions. These concerns were articulated in a report on *An Offensive Industrial Policy*, prepared by TCO for a conference it organized on 'Industry in the 1980s' in late 1978.[334] At its 1978 Congress shortly thereafter SIF mandated the preparation of an industry-policy program for its 1981 Congress. The ideas developed in SIF, in turn, fed into the preparation of a TCO industrial-policy report for its 1982 Congress.

We cannot compare the conceptions of industrial policy developed in TCO and LO in detail, so we shall merely stress certain points. The very fact that TCO and its affiliates have expanded the scope of their activity to the broad area of industrial policy with which LO had long been concerned is important in itself. In addition, the role of industrial policy in the economic system is conceived in similar ways.[335] Essentially it is not to supplant the market mechanism, but to supplement and correct it where it cannot bring about structural change in ways that are socially optimal and acceptable from a trade union point of view. The point of departure is the same as the premiss underlying the original formulation of LO's structural-change strategy: production unable to pay high wages has to be replaced by production that can, and it is only the latter that can assure employment over the long run, given the dependence of Sweden's small open economy on its international viability. But as LO concluded in the mid-1960s, it is emphasized that the process of change can only be reconciled with trade union demands for job security, a 'good working environment', and satisfying work if its pace and direction is shaped by continual efforts by the state, unions and industry to anticipate and control it. These efforts must, in turn, be coordinated within the framework of an overall economic policy that makes the required investment possible. And as LO has stressed in industrial-policy discussions since the mid-1970s, and especially in the 1981 Congress report on the subject, the implementation of such policy has become all the more difficult as a consequence of changes in the operation of the market mechanism resulting from the power of trans-national enterprise.[336]

By and large TCO's specific industrial-policy proposals move in the same direction as LO's as well. That the former are at an earlier stage of development is suggested by the tendency to think in terms of industrial 'branches' or sectors, as if the standard statistical classifications provide relevant units of analysis and even of policy. Thus, it is proposed that planning and coordination of measures be organized on the basis of a system of branch commissions or 'boards',[337] This is consistent with the way in which structural change was conceived in the past, as illustrated by LO's old idea of 'branch funds'. But in rejecting that idea, and in its recent industrial-policy discussion, LO displayed an awareness of the importance of variations in performance within branches and of processes that cut across branches, linking suppliers of inputs, manufacturers and users in development chains or 'blocks', which were often the real contexts of growth.[338] These differences in approach do not seem to reflect barriers to convergence that are durably based on the organizations' situations in the market or political arenas.

Not surprisingly, such obstacles to convergence have had the greatest impact on the organizations' positions on collective capital formation. As mentioned earlier, TCO took up the question in a series of documents debated at successive Congresses. These documents took a consistently favorable view of wage-earner funds, beginning as early as 1972 in a brief report on *Corporate Taxation and Wage-Earner Funds*. Neither this report nor a fuller one presented to the 1976 Congress recommended that TCO back the establishment of such funds. However, the logic of such funds as a solution to the fundamental dilemma of wage policy to which LO's proposal was addressed was presented with remarkable clarity, making the conclusion seem inescapable. TCO's 1976 Congress was only called upon to authorize the preparation of a proposal to be acted on at its

1979 Congress. The report, circulated for discussion in 1978, proposed that in principle a 'system of wage-bill based wage-earner funds be established'. It added that 'for wage policy reasons a system for the sharing of profits over a certain level ['excess profits-sharing'] was also necessary', but that its form required further study.[339] This will be recognized as more like the scheme on which LO and SAP subsequently agreed than the Meidner Plan.

Since a decision by TCO for or against wage-earner funds could readily tip the political balance one way or the other, the stakes were high. Organized business and the press sympathetic to it concentrated intensive efforts on mobilizing opposition to the leadership's favorable stance among TCO's affiliates and their members. And since TCO's position ultimately hinged on the position SIF took, it became the focus of those efforts. SIF was to decide at its 1978 Congress the stand it would take at the following year's TCO Congress. To that end it sounded out its membership through questionnaires circulated at study groups. There was a majority in favor among those participating, but since they accounted for just 2 percent of the membership, the Congress called for the circulation of a draft motion to the TCO Congress prior to a decision on it.[340] The draft motion approving the TCO proposal in principle, sent out with a brief statement in favor of it, elicited a stronger but negative response from locals representing 40 percent of the membership. SIF's motion was accordingly changed to recommend postponement of a decision until TCO's 1982 Congress, after a better basis for a decision had been laid, and that is what happened.[341]

In the interim the conflict within TCO, and particularly SIF, was intensified. The leadership of both organizations evidently remained convinced. While the industrial-policy report prepared for SIF's 1981 Congress acknowledged that the issue was to be dealt with separately, it expressed the view that

> It is indispensable that some form of fund for collective capital formation under wage-earners' influence be created, if capital formation on the necessary scale is to be brought about in forms acceptable to unions . . . The scope for large wage gains will be limited in the forthcoming years because they would lead to excessive consumption and insufficient savings, and since the competitiveness of industry exposed to international competition cannot be weakened. We cannot however accept abstention from wage gains in the interest of capital formation unless we as wage-earners have a share in the returns on the capital that is created through our abstention, and [unless] guarantees are established that the investments really come into being. This can be achieved by construction of some form of funds for collective capital formation.[342]

The position could hardly be put more clearly.

Yet when a detailed statement proposing that SIF adopt such a position was circulated, it evoked an even stronger negative response than the earlier draft motion. As a result, SIF's leadership felt compelled to recommend to the 1981 Congress that 'SIF should not work for the establishment of wage-earner funds' as a means for increasing the savings and investment needed to 'create the conditions for secure employment'. This was presumably passed, defining SIF's stand at TCO's 1982 Congress. The latter, according to the only information available at the time of writing, specified 'four trade union requirements' concerning capital formation without taking a stand for or against wage-earner funds.[343]

Thus, on an issue that became highly politicized, as in the pension-reform conflict, TCO could not take the same position as LO, despite the considerable efforts of its leadership to convince lower-level leaders and members that it was the right one simply from a trade union point of view. The wide spectrum of partisan orientations within its affiliates provided a receptive target for the concentrated campaign to mobilize opinion against the position that a large part of the leadership in TCO and some of its affiliates, including SIF, apparently held. On the other hand, the campaign succeeded only in neutralizing TCO but not shifting it into explicit opposition to the Social Democratic labor movement.

Perhaps this was enough to reduce the electoral risks of wage-earner funds to a tolerable level for the SAP, given the weight it could give other issues. Moreover, since the version with which it went into the election was very similar to the one for which an extended case had been made within TCO, the party could reasonably count on sufficient support for that version, or at least indifference to it, to attract the margin of TCO votes needed to win the election. This is apparently how it turned out, putting the party in a position to implement an economic strategy which, with the exception of its collective capital-formation component, had wide support in both LO and TCO unions. Even with respect to that component, as we have noted, the convergence between the two confederations, or at least its major public sector and most important private sector affiliates, had come a long way. Accordingly, establishment of some form of wage-earner funds might well establish the conditions under which union wage policy would permit a shift from consumption to investment of sufficient magnitude to enable industrial investment to remain at the level required to adapt the structure of Swedish industry to the international economic environment of the 1980s. Whether the new Social Democratic government will introduce the funds, and whether industry will accept them as part of a new 'historical compromise', remains to be seen.

Part 5

Epilogue: The Logic of Union Economic Strategy in Sweden

Our discussion has concentrated on LO and the evolution of its overall economic strategy, with particular emphasis on the relationship between union wage policy and the state's economic policy. Historically LO has been the dominant organization in the Swedish trade union movement. Its links to the Social Democratic Party have been decisive in shaping the structure of Swedish politics, providing the principal resources for the party's exceptionally strong position in the state arena. In turn, the interaction of the politically powerful Social Democratic labor movement and Sweden's highly organized and internationally oriented capitalist class has been crucial in shaping the development of the country's political economy. The stakes that both LO and the party have had in maintaining the movement's capacity to act as a counterpart and counterforce to Swedish capital have given them strong incentives to work out a common economic strategy capable of reconciling the tactical imperatives imposed by their respective positions as organizations in the market and state arenas.

LO's stake in Social Democratic control of the government is obvious and essentially the same as that which any trade union movement has in control of the government by a political party that may be expected to provide a more favorable environment for union action in the labor market, as well as the achievement of other goals, than other parties. At the same time, this stake puts LO in a position of dependence on the Social Democrats similar to the relationship between unions and associated parties in other countries with similar political economies, like those considered in the rest of this study. This, as shown in the other chapters, renders the unions vulnerable to becoming hostage to the parties. Thus, they may be compelled to acquiesce in and even cooperate with policies they find unsatisfactory because failure to do so may result only in the associated parties' replacement in office by others likely to pursue policies that are considerably more unsatisfactory. Yet it would seem that LO has not been held hostage by the Social Democrats in this way, at least if we can judge by the extent to which LO's policy initiatives have been incorporated into the party's policy. If this has, in fact, been the case, how is it to be explained? We cannot pretend to have an adequate answer to this question, but we can suggest where at least part of the explanation may lie.

Despite LO's stake in Social Democratic control of the government, the support it has provided has not been unconditional. The main condition on which it has insisted is that the policies pursued by Social Democratic governments be consistent with the LO unions' ability to perform the functions in the labor market on which their claims to membership support rest. Throughout most of the period we have studied this has been confined to the unions' wage-bargaining function. To be sure, LO and its affiliates have been willing to curtail, but not eliminate, that function at the local level in the interest of controlling strike action and coordinating wage bargaining. However, they have insisted both on non-intervention by the state in that bargaining and the limits to which it can contribute to the effectiveness of the state's economic policy by restraining wage growth.

At the same time, LO's stake in maintaining Social Democratic control of the government has given it a strong incentive to devise an economic strategy through which Social Democratic governments can manage the economy effectively without the degree of wage restraint that would undermine the unions' claims to membership support. This is the essential point of LO's structural change strategy, as originally formulated in the Rehn model and elaborated since. Although the SAP has repeatedly hesitated to adopt the successive steps in the evolution of the strategy, from its inception down to the Meidner Plan, it has sooner or later incorporated those steps in its policy in at least some form. And when the LO unions concluded that their claims to membership support could no longer rest primarily on the performance of their wage-bargaining function and had to be extended to bargaining over the whole range of non-wage workplace issues, the Social Democrats readily used their political power to make it possible. The variation in the SAP's readiness to incorporate LO's initiatives into its policy has certainly been, in part, a function of its estimation of the electoral opportunities and risks attached to doing so. Yet the party has done so even when the electoral risks seemed significant, whether they, in fact, were or not. The burden of the explanation is, thus, shifted to the party's behavior.

The party's stake in making the most of the organizational resources that LO provides, despite the electoral risks that might be attached to the policies it had to pursue in order to do so, is surely a part of the explanation. The organizational resources of LO and its affiliates enable them to provide two forms of support that are very important for the party. The first is the contribution they can make to the effectiveness with which the SAP can mobilize electoral support. The party cannot win an election solely with the support of LO union members, even if their support is completely mobilized, but it does not take very much beyond that to win.

The second is the contribution the LO unions can make to the effectiveness with which the party can manage the economy. Again, a Social Democratic government cannot rely on coordinated wage bargaining to prevent the transmission of inflationary pressures it fails to avert by its policies – fiscal, monetary, exchange rate, and so on. But to the extent that it does succeed in averting such pressures it can count on coordinated wage bargaining to contribute to the maintenance of stability by inhibiting interunion wage rivalry and industrial action. Moreover, it has been able to count on a degree of acceptance of structural and technological change that is probably unparalleled by any other trade union movement, even though that acceptance has been contingent on increasingly stringent conditions.

Finally, LO's strategy for reconciling economic stability and growth with the unions' essential functions as labor market organizations seems to have been a reasonably effective one. Whether it really has been is, of course, subject to dispute. The satisfactory performance of Sweden's economy until the mid-1960s, judged by the conventional criteria, may have been more a matter of luck than policy. The same might be said of the economy's deteriorating performance since then. The critics of the LO economic strategy tend to argue that the earlier performance was as good as it was because the strategy had not yet evolved to the point where it began to do serious damage, and that it has been doing so increasingly since the mid-1960s. Alternatively it might be argued that the performance might have been better all along, since the mid-1960s as well as before, if the LO strategy had been more effectively and consistently implemented, and that it now offers the only way of avoiding the downward spiral of stalemate, stagnation and decline displayed so clearly in Britain. In any case the Social Democratic leadership seems to have by and large regarded the LO strategy as economically effective as well as politically necessary. This suggests that LO economic ideas – most notably those of Rehn, Meidner and Odhner – have been an important factor in the political power of the Social Democratic movement, for those ideas have provided an economic strategy on which a remarkably durable union–party alliance has been maintained.

At the same time, as has been emphasized, the Social Democratic labor movement is not the whole Swedish labor movement. Indeed, as the occupational structure continues to change, the white-collar unions outside the Social Democratic labor movement are approaching the LO unions in their importance. The TCO unions clearly have a stake in preserving their separate organizational existence, and the positions of their members in the market and state arenas compel those unions to maintain their distinct wage policies and formal non-partisanship. Yet, as we have seen, their economic-policy positions seem to have come increasingly close to those of LO, even with respect to such an ideologically charged issue as wage-earner funds. We cannot offer an adequate explanation of this either, but here, too, we can suggest where part of the explanation may lie.

To begin with, the TCO unions share with the LO unions the same fundamental organizational imperatives. They have to be able to perform the functions in the labor market on which unions' claims to membership support depend. In general the TCO unions can only welcome an economic strategy consistent with preserving that ability. To be sure, there are elements in LO's design of such a strategy that threaten their ability to pursue an autonomous wage policy. They nevertheless accept the general logic of the LO strategy, including the desirability of minimizing interunion wage rivalry. They even accept the necessity of loosening the link between profits and both wage and property income in order to solve the problem of investment, at least at the leadership if not the rank-and-file level.

In addition, the TCO unions have a stake in Social Democratic control of the government in so far as it offers better prospects for maintaining full employment, and the reinforcement of bargaining power that comes with it. They have no incentive to oppose Social Democratic labor movement policies that have that result, even if their members' interests may conflict to some extent with the distributive consequences of those policies as well as their systemic implications. Finally, there is again the importance of LO's economic ideas. They have provided the language with which economic developments have been analyzed from a trade union perspective, offering the principal alternative to the increasingly conservative thrust of the academic economics that lends itself more readily to the articulation of business interests. Thus, the dominating position LO occupies in Sweden's political economy would seem to rest in significant measure on the power of its economic ideas, which may indeed have been essential to the effective utilization of the power it derives from its numbers and organizational structure.

Statistical Tables

Table 3.1   *Employment and Unemployment in Sweden, 1950, 1960 and 1963–81 Percent*

| | Employment Change from prior year | | | Share of total | | Unemployment Share of laborforce | | |
Year	Total	Mining and manu- facturing	Govern- ment	Mining and manu- facturing	Govern- ment*	Open†	Labor Market Board‡	Total§
1950	n.a.	n.a.	n.a.	32·0 ‖	9·0‖	1·6¶	n.a.	n.a.
1960	n.a.	n.a.	n.a.	35·0 ‖	13·0‖	1·6¶	0·5	2·1
1963	n.a.	n.a.	n.a.	34·5	14·3	1·7	0·8	2·5
1964	1·4	0·1	5·4	34·3	14·9	1·6	0·8	2·4
1965	0·7	0·0	3·7	34·1	15·3	1·2	0·9	2·1
1966	0·1	−1·5	4·8	33·5	16·0	1·6	1·0	2·6
1967	−1·1	−3·5	6·4	32·7	17·2	2·1	1·3	3·4
1968	1·0	−2·4	7·6	31·6	18·4	2·2	1·7	3·9
1969	1·9	1·0	7·3	31·4	19·3	1·9	1·7	3·6
1970	2·0	1·5	8·4	31·2	20·6	1·5	1·8	3·3
1971	−0·2	−3·5	6·7	30·2	22·0	2·5	2·1	4·6
1972	0·3	−1·7	5·2	29·6	23·1	2·7	2·6	5·3
1973	0·4	1·3	3·6	29·9	23·8	2·5	2·8	5·3
1974	2·0	1·9	6·1	29·9	24·7	2·0	2·5	4·5
1975	2·0	1·4	5·1	29·7	25·5	1·6	2·2¶	3·8
1976	3·7	−0·4	4·8	29·5	26·6	1·6	2·6	4·2
1977	1·9	−3·7	4·1	28·4	27·7	1·8	2·9	4·7
1978	0·4	−3·9	5·1	27·2	29·0	2·2	3·4	5·6
1979	1·5	−0·4	5·1	26·7	30·0	2·1	3·6	5·7
1980	1·1	1·4**	3·3	26·8*†	30·7	1·9	2·9	4·8
1981	−0·2	−3·2**	2·5	26·1*†	31·5	2·5 ،	2·7	5·2

* Central and local government employees.
† Unemployment based on labor force surveys.
‡ All persons participating in training, relief works, sheltered employment and other programs administered by the Labor Market Board.
§ Sum of open unemployment and persons in Labor Market Board programs.
‖ Based on Census data; not fully comparable with laborforce survey data for later years.
¶ Insured unemployment adjusted by linking to labor force survey series average of unemployment 1961–7.
**Data for 1975–81 not strictly comparable with data for earlier years.
*†Estimated by linking data from *The Swedish Economy* with Central Statistical Bureau series for earlier years at 1979.

Sources: Employment, 1950 and 1960, from Erik Westerlind and Rune Beckman, *Sweden's Economy. Structure and Trends*, 5th edn (Stockholm: Prisma, 1964), pp. 24–5; 1963–9, from Statistiska centralbyrån, *Statistiska meddelanden*, N 1976:7.4, appendix 5, pp. 36–7, 41, 43; 1970–9, from *Statistiska meddelanden*, N 1980:4.4, appendix 5, pp. 38–40; 1980, from *The Swedish Economy*, 1981: 1, p. 90 and 1981: 2, p. 96; 1981, from *Konjunkturläget*, 1983: 2, p. 75. Unemployment, 1950 and 1960, from Assar Lindbeck, *Svensk ekonomisk politik* (Stockholm: Bokförlaget Aldus/Bonniers, 1968), p. 206; 1960–9, from *Arbetsmarknads-politik i förändring*, SOU 1978: 60, p. 97; 1970–81, from *The Swedish Economy*, 1979: 3, p. 83 and 1982: 3, p. 73. Persons in Labor Market Board programs, 1960–74, from *Arbetsmarknadspolitik i förändring*, op. cit., p. 113; 1975–81, from *The Swedish Economy*, 1982: 3, p. 74.

Table 3.2   *Annual Rate of Change in Industrial Workers' Hourly Wages and Consumer Prices in Sweden, 1948–80. Percent.*

Year	Contractual*	Change from preceding year			Real earnings‡
		Wage drift*	Total earnings*	Consumer prices†	
1948	3·5	3·3	6·8	4·3	2·5
1949	0·0	3·1	3·1	2·0	1·1
1950	0·0	5·0	5·0	1·0	4·0
1951	16·0	6·3	23·3	15·8	7·5
1952]§	10·6	3·7	14·8	7·7	7·1
1953	0·5	2·4	2·8	1·6	1·2
1954	1·3	3·4	4·8	0·8	4·0
1955	5·1	3·6	8·7	3·1	5·6
1956]	4·3	3·8	8·1	4·5	3·6
1957 ⎤	2·6	2·9	5·5	4·3	1·2
1958 ⎦	2·6	2·1	4·7	4·8	−0·1
1959]	2·0	2·6	4·6	0·7	3·9
1960 ⎤	3·9	4·5	8·4	3·9	4·5
1961 ⎦	3·6	4·2	7·8	2·5	5·3
1962 ⎤	4·6	3·7	8·3	4·3	4·0
1963 ⎦	2·9	4·2	7·1	2·9	4·2
1964 ⎤	2·1	5·0	7·1	3·5	3·6
1965 ⎦	4·1	5·8	9·9	6·4	3·5
1966 ⎤	4·3	4·4	8·7	4·7	4·0
1967	3·5	3·2	6·7	3·1	3·6
1968 ⎦	2·9	3·6	6·5	2·0	4·5
1969 ⎤	5·8	5·5	11·3	4·8	6·5
1970 ⎦	3·4	7·2	10·6	8·7	1·9
1971 ⎤	6·5	4·2	10·7	7·1	3·6
1972	7·4	3·3	10·7	5·7	3·0
1973 ⎦	4·3	4·2	8·5	7·6	0·9
1974]	5·1	8·1	13·2	10·5	2·7
1975 ⎤	11·0	8·6	19·6	10·1	9·5
1976 ⎦	7·8	3·6	11·4	9·4	2·0
1977]	5·4	3·3	8·7	12·8	−4·1
1978 ⎤	2·7	3·0	5·7	7·5	−1·8
1979 ⎦	3·9	3·5	7·4	9·7	−2·3
1980]	6·0	3·5	9·5	13·7	−4·2

   * All wage changes are from November to November. Data from 1955 on not strictly comparable with data for earlier years. Data from 1979 and 1980 not necessarily comparable with data for earlier years.

   † Change in annual averages of consumer price index in 1948–63; change from December to December in long-term consumer price index in 1963–80.

   ‡ Real earnings computed by subtracting change in consumer prices from change in total earnings.

   § Braces indicate years covered by central agreements.

Sources: Hourly wages of adult industrial workers, 1948–54, from Rudolf Meidner, 'Samordning och solidarisk lönepolitik under tre decennier', in *Tvärsnitt* (Stockholm: LO; 1973), p. 48; 1955–80, supplied by Ingvar Ohlsson, LO Research Department. Consumer prices, 1948–63, from Assar Lindbeck, *Svensk ekonomisk politik* (Stockholm: Bokförlaget Aldus/Bonniers, 1968), p. 200; 1964–80, supplied by Edward Palmer, Konjunkturinstitutet.

Table 3.3　*Union Membership in Sweden, 1950–80*

	1950	1960	1970	1980	1950	1960	1970	1980
		(thousands)				*(percent of labor force)**		
All confederations†	1,594	1,970	2,557	3,413	51·3	60·7	65·3	*80·6*
LO:　Total	1,278	1,486	1,680	2,127	41·2	45·8	42·9	50·2
Largest union‡	220	286	370	515	7·1	8·8	9·5	12·2
TCO: Total	272	394	719	1,043	8·8	12·1	18·4	24·6
Largest union§	60	107	208	296	1·9	3·3	5·3	6·9
SACO–SR‖	44	73	115	225	1·4	2·3	2·9	5·3
SAC¶	n.a.	18	23	18	n.a.	0·6	0·6	0·4

* Percentages for 1950 and 1960 are based on Census labor force data and are therefore not strictly comparable with percentages for later years which are based on labor force survey data.
† See text for full names and descriptions.
‡ Largest LO union is the Metalworkers' union, except in 1980 when it is the local government workers' union, or SKAF (*Svenska Kommunalarbetareförbundet*).
§ Largest TCO union is the Union of Clerical and Technical Employees in Industry, or SIF (*Svenska Industritjänstemannaförbundet*).
‖ SACO and SR were separate organizations until their merger in 1974.
¶ SAC is a small syndicalist organization, *Sveriges arbetares centralorganisation*, which stands for Central Organization of Swedish Workers.

Sources: Union membership, from *Statistiska årsbok* (Stockholm: Statistiska centralbyrån, various years). Percentage of labor force, computed on basis of labor force data in Table 3.1.

Table 3.4   *Work Stoppages in Sweden, 1945–81*

Year	Strikes	Lockouts	Employees involved	Total	Working days lost Type of stoppage Legal	Illegal	Lockouts*
					(thousands)		
1945	163	—	133·2	11,321			
1946	136	1	1·3	27			
1947	81	—	56·9	125			
1948	47	—	6·1	151			
1949	31	—	1·0	21			
1950	21	1	2·4	41			
1951	27	1	15·1	531			
1952	31	1	2·1	79			
1953	17	3	26·2	582			
1954	44	1	7·7	24			
1955	18	—	3·9	159	n.a.	n.a.	n.a.
1956	12	—	1·6	4			
1957	19	1	1·6	53			
1958	9	1	0·1	15			
1959	16	1	1·2	24			
1960	29	2	1·5	18			
1961	12	—	0·1	2			
1962	10	—	3·5	5			
1963	23	1	2·8	25			
1964	14	—	1·9	34			
1965	8	—	0·2	4			
1966	25	1	29·4	352			
1967	7	—	0·1	†	0·4	‡	—
1968	7	—	0·4	1	0·7	0·4	—
1969	40	1	9·0	112	48·5	63.9	n.a.
1970	134	—	26·7	156	0·2	155·6	—
1971	59	1	62·9	839	812·3	26·5	n.a.
1972	44	—	7·1	10	2·2	8·3	—
1973	48	—	4·3	12	0·3	11·5	—
1974	237	—	27·0	57	34·8	22·2	—
1975	289	1	37·5	358	14·8	343·2	0·9
1976	123	—	10·5	26	6·9	18·7	—
1977	105	2	18·4	119	105·0	13·8	49·5
1978	173	2	17·8	42	23·0	19·0	0·1
1979	207	—	35·3	29	0·8	27·8	—
1980	204	4	744·8	4,471	4,432·4	38·4	4,096·4
1981	66	1	99·2	209	202·0	7·2	24·2

* Working days lost as a result of lockouts out of total days lost.
† Total of only 400 days lost.
‡ 35 days lost in wildcat strikes.
Sources: Statistiska årsbok, various years; working days lost in legal and illegal stoppages, 1967–72, from Lennart Brantgärde, Nils Elvander, Folke Schmidt and Anders Victorin, *Konfliktlösning på arbetsmarknaden* (Lund: CWK Gleerup Bokförlag, 1974), p. 192.

Table 3.5   Selected Economic Indicators for Sweden, 1950–81. Percent.

	Averages				1970	1971	1972	1973	1974	1975	1976	1977	1978	1979	1980	1981
	1951–4	1955–9	1960–4	1965–9												
Annual rate of change																
GDP	3·6	3·3	5·2	3·6	5·5	1·0	2·1	3·8	4·1	0·8	1·5	−2·4	1·3	4·3	1·9	−0·9
Industrial production*	1·9	4·1	7·6	5·3	6·1	1·2	2·4	6·9	5·4	−1·7	−0·8	−5·4	−1·7	6·3	0·4	−3·6
Industrial investment†	2·2	5·0	4·8	4·6	3·8	1·1	3·9	9·9	10·7	1·6	0·2	−20·6	−21·7	3·4	19·2	−8·6
Share of GDP																
Foreign trade‡	25·8	25·1	25·1	24·8	27·7	26·9	23·4	26·1	32·7	28·4	28·6	28·4	27·9	31·2	31·0	30·6
Payments balance§	0·3	−0·2	0·2	−0·5	−0·8	1·0	1·3	2·8	−1·0	−0·5	−2·1	−2·6	0·0	−2·2	−3·5	−2·6
Government expenditures||	n.a.	n.a.	32·6	39·5	44·2	46·1	47·2	45·6	48·8	49·7	52·6	58·6	60·3	61·8	62·7	65·9
Government revenues minus expenditures¶	n.a.	n.a.	2·1	3·1	4·1	5·1	5·0	4·1	2·0	2·8	4·6	1·7	−0·4	−2·7	−3·9	−5·4
Capital share, C-sector value added**	33·0	29·0	26·0	23·5	25·5	19·3	17·6	24·5	33·7	26·9	19·3	15·6	17·5	26·1	28·0	27·5

* Index of production in manufacturing and mining, 1968 = 100.
† Investment in plant and equipment in manufacturing and mining, in 1975 prices.
‡ Exports + imports ÷ 2. Data prior to 1970 not strictly comparable to data for later years.
§ Balance on current accounts for goods, services and transfers. Pre- and post-1970 data not strictly comparable.
|| All expenditures of the 'consolidated public sector', including consumption, investment and transfers, by all levels of government, central and local, net of intergovernmental transfers.
¶ Total revenues and expenditures of consolidated public sector.
** All allocations other than for wages and salaries, including depreciation and owner income, in the EFO model C-sector. Data prior to 1970 adjusted by ratios declining from difference between 1970 revised and old national accounts to 0 in 1951.

Sources: GDP, 1950–77, industrial production and investment, 1950–81, from Statistiska centralbyrån, supplied by Edward Palmer, Konjunkturinstitutet; GDP, 1978–81, from *The Swedish Economy*, 1982: 2, p. 12. Foreign trade, 1950–71, from Erik Westerlind and Rune Beckman, *Sveriges ekonomi*, 8th edn (Stockholm: Prisma, 1974), p. 104; 1972, from *The Swedish Economy*, 1981: 2, statistical appendix, table 6; 1973–81, from *The Swedish Economy*, 1982: 3, statistical appendix, table 6. Payments balance, 1951–9, from Erik Westerlind and Rune Beckman, *Sweden's Economy. Structure and Trends*, 5th edn (Stockholm: Prisma, 1964), pp. 12–13; 1960–9, from Erik Westerlind and Rune Beckman, *Sveriges ekonomi*, 8th edn (Stockholm: Prisma, 1974), pp. 16–17; 1970–6, Statistiska centralbyrån, supplied by Edward Palmer, Konjunkturinstitutet; 1977–8, *The Swedish Economy*, 1981: 2, p. 65; 1979–81, *The Swedish Economy*, 1982: 3, p. 44. Government expenditures and government revenues minus expenditures, 1960–9, from *OECD Economic Outlook*, 29 (July 1981), tables H8 and 9; 1970–81, from *The Swedish Economy*, 1983: 2, p. 149. Capital share, C-sector value-added, 1951–69, from Statistiska centralbyrån, supplied by Jan Herin, Institute for International Economic Studies, Stockholm University; 1970–9, from *Lönepolitik för 80-talet* (Stockholm: LO, 1981), p. 39; 1980–1, estimated from operating surplus in manufacturing, *The Swedish Economy*, 1983: 2, p. 127.

Notes

1 Early developments are summarized in Dankwart A. Rustow, *The Politics of Compromise* (Princeton, NJ: Princeton University Press, 1955). For union members' voting behavior, see Sören Holmberg, *Svenska väljare* (Stockholm: Liber Förlag, 1981), p. 339. On organizational, financial and other LO–party relationships, see Sveriges Socialdemokratiska Arbetareparti, *Utveckling av organisation och verksamhet* (Stockholm: Socialdemokraterna, 1975), pp. 28–9; Leif Lewin, *Hur styrs facket? Om demokratin inom fackföreningsrörelsen* (Stockholm: Rabén & Sjögren, 1977), pp. 90–1; Walter Korpi, *The Working Class in Welfare Capitalism* (London: Routledge & Kegan Paul, 1978), pp. 301–5; and *Facklig-politisk verksamhet: Inventera-planera-genomföra* (Stockholm: Socialdemokraterna, 1978); and *Dagens Nyheter*, 16 August 1973.
2 TCO's position in the political arena is analyzed in Christopher Wheeler, *White-Collar Power: Changing Patterns of Interest Group Behavior in Sweden* (Urbana, Ill.: University of Illinois Press, 1975).
3 Korpi, *The Working Class*, op. cit., p. 80.
4 ibid., pp. 80–1. Swedish economic policy during the Great Depression is surveyed in H. W. Arndt, *The Economic Lessons of the Nineteen-Thirties* (London: Oxford University Press, 1944), pp. 207–30; and Erik Lundberg, *Business Cycles and Economic Policy* (Cambridge, Mass.: Harvard University Press, 1957), pp. 54–5. Controversies over the origins and extent of innovation in economic policy by the Social Democrats are reviewed in Bo Gustafsson, 'A perennial of doctrinal history: Keynes and the Stockholm school', *Economy and History*, vol. XVI, no. 1 (1973), pp. 114–28; and Carl G. Uhr, 'The emergence of the "new economics" in Sweden', *History of Political Economy*, vol. 5, no. 1 (Spring 1973), pp. 243–60.
5 Rustow, op. cit., pp. 85–102; Stig Hadenius, Hans Wieslander and Björn Molin, *Sverige efter 1900* (Stockholm: Aldus/Bonniers, 1969), pp. 70–125; and Berndt Öhman, *Svensk arbetsmarknadspolitik 1900–1947* (Stockholm: Prisma, 1970), pp. 68–79, 103–11.
6 Olle Nyman, *Svensk parlamentarism 1932–1936* (Stockholm: Statsvetenskapliga Föreningen, 1947).
7 On the economic effects of Social Democratic policy, see sources cited in n. 4, above. See also Leif Lewin, *Planhushållningsdebatten* (Stockholm: Almqvist & Wiksell), pp. 89–117. For the British case, Alan Bullock, *The Life and Times of Ernest Bevin* (London: Heinemann, 1960), Vol. 1, chs 16–18, is essential. See also Dennis Kavanaugh, 'Crisis management and incremental adaptation in British politics: the 1931 crisis of the British party system', in Gabriel A. Almond, Scott C. Flanagan and Robert J. Mundt (eds), *Crisis, Choice and Change* (Boston, Mass.: Little, Brown, 1973). Especially illuminating on the German case is W. S. Woytinsky, *Stormy Passage* (New York: Vanguard, 1961), pp. 458–72.
8 In addition to works by Hadenius, *et al.*, Korpi and Rustow cited above, see also Donald Blake, 'Swedish trade unions and the Social Democratic Party: the formative years', *Scandinavian Economic History Review*, vol. 8, no. 1 (1960), pp. 19–44; and Yngve Myrman, *Maktkampen på arbetsmarknaden 1905–1907* (Stockholm: Stockholms Universitet, 1973).
9 Bernt Schiller, *Storstrejken 1909* (Gothenburg: Akademiförlaget-Gumperts, 1967), and 'Years of crisis, 1906–1914', in Steven Koblik (ed.), *Sweden's Development from Poverty to Affluence, 1750–1970*, trans. Joanne Johnson (Minneapolis: University of Minnesota Press, 1975), pp. 197–228.
10 Walter Korpi, *Den demokratiska klasskampen* (Stockholm: Tidens Förlag, 1981), pp. 172–3; and Korpi, *The Working Class*, op. cit., pp. 94–6.
11 The standard work on Swedish labor law in English is Folke Schmidt, *The Law of Labour Relations in Sweden* (Cambridge, Mass.: Harvard University Press, 1962). A more critical view from a labor standpoint is presented in Per Eklund, 'Rätten i klasskampen - en studie i rättens funktioner', and Sten Edlund, 'Perspektiv på arbetsdomstolen', in *Tvärsnitt* (Stockholm: Prisma, 1973), pp. 399–453, 457–83.

12 Ragnar Casparsson, *Saltsjöbadsavtalet in historisk belysning* (Stockholm: Tidens Förlag, 1966); and Jörgen Westerståhl, *Svensk Fackföreningsrörelse, Organisationsproblem, Verksamhetsformer* (Stockholm: Tiden, 1945).

13 Axel Hadenius, *Facklig organisationsutveckling: En studie av Landsorganisationen i Sverige* (Stockholm: Rabén & Sjögren, 1976), pp. 46–53.

14 T. L. Johnston, *Collective Bargaining in Sweden* (London: Allen & Unwin, 1960), pp. 125–7.

15 Sven Anders Söderpalm, *Direktörsklubben: Storindustrin i svensk politik under 1930-och 40-talet* (Stockholm: Zenit/Rabén & Sjögren, 1976), pp. 14–15; Johnston, op. cit., pp. 169–90; and Hadenius, *Facklig organisationsutveckling*, op. cit., pp. 48–54.

16 Hadenius, *Facklig organisationsutveckling*, op. cit., pp. 54–8; and Korpi, *The Working Class*, op. cit., pp. 209–236.

17 Korpi, *The Working Class*, op. cit., pp. 84, 80–6.

18 *The Swedish Labour Movement's Postwar Programme* (Stockholm: LO, n.d.), English trans. of *Arbetarrörelsens efterkrigsprogram* (Stockholm: LO, 1944).

19 Söderpalm, op. cit., pp. 114–29, 139–44; and Hadenius, *et al., Sverige efter 1900*, op. cit., pp. 191–210.

20 Johnston, op cit., p. 279.

21 *Trade Unions and Full Employment* (Stockholm: LO, 1953), English trans. of *Fackföreningsrörelsen och den fulla sysselsättningen* (Stockholm: LO, 1951), p. 54. The course of wartime and early postwar wage developments is summarized on pp. 49–72. See also Johnston, op. cit., ch. XV; and Hadenius, *Facklig organisationsutveckling*, op. cit., pp. 72–5.

22 The economist was Gösta Rehn, who points out that his colleague, Rudolf Meidner, played an important part in developing the idea, so that it should be referred to as the 'Rehn–Meidner model'. Although we shall use the briefer reference, Meidner's contribution should be kept in mind.

23 LO, *Trade Unions and Full Employment*, op. cit. (hereafter cited as TUFE), p. 87.

24 ibid., pp. 88–99.

25 ibid., pp. 91, 94, 96, 99.

26 ibid., p. 92.

27 Gösta Rehn, 'The problem of stability: an analysis and some policy proposals', in Ralph Turvey (ed.), *Wages Policy under Full Employment* (London: William Hodge, 1952), p. 53.

28 Tage Erlander, *1949–1954* (Stockholm: Tidens Förlag, 1974), pp. 86–8.

29 Rehn, in Turvey, op. cit., p. 54.

30 Erik Lundberg, 'A critique of Rehn's approach', in ibid., esp. p. 67.

31 Gösta Rehn, *'Finansministrarna, LO-ekonomerna och arbetsmarknads-politiken'*, in Jan Herin och Lars Werin (red.), *Ekonomisk debatt och ekonomisk politik* (Stockholm: P. A. Norstedt Förlag, 1977), p. 213.

32 Joan Robinson, *Economic Heresies: Some Old-Fashioned Questions in Economic Theory* (New York: Basic Books, 1971). See also Hyman P. Minsky, *John Maynard Keynes* (New York: Columbia University Press, 1975); and Axel Leijonhufvud, *On Keynesian Economics and the Economics of Keynes* (London: Oxford University Press, 1968).

33 John Maynard Keynes, *The General Theory of Employment Interest and Money* (London: Macmillan, 1936), pp. 375, 378.

34 ibid., pp. 378–9.

35 TUFE, p. 77.

36 Tage Erlander, *1955–60* (Stockholm: Tidens Förlag, 1976), p. 41; and Rehn, 'Finansminstrarna', op. cit., pp. 214–16.

37 TUFE, p. 67.

38 Hadenius, *Facklig organisationsutveckling*, op. cit., pp. 81–2.

39 ibid., pp. 83–4.

40 ibid., p. 85.

41 Erlander, *1955–60*, op. cit., pp. 37–42; and Hadenius, *Facklig organisationsutveckling*, op. cit., p. 92.

42 ibid., pp. 85–7.

43 ibid., pp. 92–6.

44 There is no comprehensive analysis of the wage-determination system, but aspects of its

multilevel character are treated in Johnston, op. cit., ch. XIV; Gösta Edgren, Karl-Olof Faxén and Clas-Erik Odhner, *Wage Formation and the Economy* (London: Allen & Unwin, 1973), pp. 52–7, 134–42, 144–50; Horst Hart och Casten v. Otter, *Lönebildningen på arbetsplatsen* (Stockholm: Prisma, 1973); and Anders Victorin, 'Lönebildningsprocessen', in Lennart Brantgärde, Nils Elvander, Folke Schmidt and Anders Victorin, *Konfliktlösning på arbetsmarknaden* (Lund: CWK Gleerup Bokförlag, 1974), pp. 170–90.

45 Hugh Heclo, *Modern Social Politics in Britain and Sweden* (New Haven, Conn.: Yale University Press, 1974), pp. 228–53.

46 Heclo, op. cit.; and Björn Molin, *Tjänstepensionsfrågan. En studie i svensk partipolitik* (Gothenburg: Akademiförlaget-Gumperts, 1965).

47 Åke Ortmark, *Maktspelet i Sverige* (Stockholm: Wahlström & Widland, 1968), pp. 160–8, 124–30, 200–7; Heclo, op. cit., pp. 238–9; and Erlander, 1955–60 op. cit., pp. 129–261.

48 David A. Swickard, 'The new opposition in the welfare state: the case of the Swedish Center Party', PhD dissertation, Government Department, Harvard University, 1976.

49 Wheeler, op. cit., ch. 6.

50 ibid.

51 Heclo, op. cit., p. 246–7.

52 Bo Särlvik, 'Party politics and electoral opinion formation: a study of issues in Swedish politics 1956–1960', *Scandinavian Political Studies*, 2 (1967), pp. 167–222.

53 ibid.

54 Erlander, *1955–60*, op. cit., p. 261.

55 Berndt Öhman, 'LO och arbetsmarknadspolitiken efter andra världskriget', in *Tvärsnitt*, op. cit., pp. 138–43; and Rehn, 'Finansministrarna', op. cit., pp. 222–4.

56 *Arbetsmarknadspolitik, Betänkande avgivet av 1960 års arbetsmarknadsutredning*, SOU 1965: 9.

57 Bent Hansen, *Fiscal Policy in Seven Countries 1955–1965* (Paris: OECD, 1968), p. 383; and Assar Lindbeck, *Svensk ekonomisk politik* (Stockholm: Aldus/Bonniers, 1969), p. 83.

58 Hadenius, *Facklig organisationsutveckling*, op. cit., pp. 96–7.

59 *Samordnad näringspolitik* (Stockholm: LO, 1961), trans. into English as *Economic Expansion and Structural Change*, ed. T. L. Johnston (London: Allen & Unwin, 1963), pp. 22–8. All references are to the English edition.

60 *Kongressprotokoll 1961* (Stockholm: LO, 1961), p. 336.

61 *Economic Expansion*, op. cit., p. 27.

62 *Kongressprotokoll 1961*, op. cit., p. 339.

63 ibid., p. 338; and *Economic Expansion*, op. cit., pp. 41–54, 167.

64 *Economic Expansion*, op. cit., pp. 60–91.

65 ibid, pp. 119–34, 168.

66 ibid, pp. 171, 78–9.

67 Jacques Lereuz, *Economic Planning and Politics in Britain* (London: Martin Robertson, 1974).

68 *Economic Expansion*, op. cit., pp. 156–8.

69 ibid., p. 73.

70 ibid., p. 153.

71 ibid., p. 159.

72 ibid., p. 161; italics in original.

73 Ernst Wigforss, 'Samhällsföretag utan ägare', in *Vision och verklighet* (Stockholm: Prisma, 1967), pp. 145–56. The essay was originally published in 1959.

74 See Tables 3.1 and 3.5.

75 *The Swedish Economy 1966–1970* (Stockholm: Ministry of Finance, 1966), p. 14, English trans. of the 1965 *Longtidsutredningen*.

76 *Resultat och reformer, Riktlinjer för socialdemokratisk politik* (Stockholm: Social-demokraterna, 1964).

77 Hadenius, *et al.*, *Sverige efter 1900*, op. cit., p. 286.

78 See Table 3.1.

79 Ortmark, op. cit., pp. 26–7, 42–3.

80 LO, *Trade Unions and Technological Change*, ed. and trans. S. D. Anderman (London: Allen & Unwin, 1967); this is trans. of *Fackföreningsrörelsen och den tekniska utvecklingen*, (Stockholm: LO, 1966), p. 122.

81 Lars Matthiessen, 'Finanspolitiken som stabiliseringspolitisk instrument', in Erik Lundberg, m.fl. *Svensk finanspolitik i teori och praktik* (Stockholm: Aldus/Bonniers, 1971), p. 205; and Öhman, op. cit., pp. 141–2.
82 Åke Sparring, *Från Höglund til Hermansson, Om revisionismen in Sveriges kommunistiska parti* (Stockholm: Bonniers, 1967).
83 Göran Therborn (ed.), *En ny vänster* (Stockholm: Rabén & Sjögren, 1966).
84 *Ekonomiska utsikter*, hösten 1962, p. 34.
85 ibid., hösten 1963, p. 25.
86 ibid., hösten 1962, p. 34.
87 ibid., hösten 1963, p. 28.
88 Matthiessen, op. cit., pp. 203–4.
89 See Table 3.2 and Hadenius, *Facklig organisationsutveckling*, op. cit., pp. 98–9.
90 Hansen, op. cit., p. 383.
91 LO, *Trade Unions and Technological Change*, op. cit.
92 ibid., p. 238.
93 ibid., p. 122.
94 ibid., pp. 134–5.
95 *LO:s Arbetsmarknadspolitiska program* (Stockholm: LO, 1967).
96 LO, *Trade Unions and Technological Change*, op. cit., p. 21; and *Kongressprotokoll 1966*, op. cit., p. 404.
97 LO, *Trade Unions and Technological Change*, op. cit., pp. 222–37.
98 ibid., p. 255.
99 Olle Svenning, *Socialdemokratin och näringslivet* (Stockholm: Tidens Förlag, 1972), p. 81; and Roger Henning, *Staten som företagare. En studie av Statsföretag AB:s mål, organisation och effektivitet* (Stockholm: Rabén & Sjögren, 1974), pp. 20–2, 31–46.
100 Svenning, op, cit., p. 74.
101 *Näringspolitiken. Näringspolitiska kommittens första rapport* (Stockholm: Socialdemokraterna, 1967), p. 3.
102 Svenning, op. cit., pp. 75–80.
103 Henning, op. cit., p. 38.
104 The following is a summary of both reports, the preliminary one cited in n. 101, above, and the final one, *Program för aktiv näringspolitik. Näringspolitiska Kommittens slutrapport* (Stockholm: Socialdemokraterna, 1968).
105 *Näringspolitik, Rapport fran SAP–LO:s näringspolitiska arbetsgrupp* (Stockholm: Socialdemokraterna, 1972); Svenning, op. cit., pp. 114–64; Axel Iveroth, *Industri och samhälle* (Stockholm: Bonniers, 1968); and Erik Lundberg och Anne Wibble, ' "Nymerkantilism" och selektive ekonomisk politik', in Erik Lundberg and Torkel Backelin (eds), *Ekonomisk politik i förvandling* (Stockholm: P. A. Norstedt, 1971), pp. 1–28.
106 See Table 3.1. The proportion of voters who believed the Social Democrats were better at reducing unemployment than the bourgeois parties rose from one-third to two-thirds over the year preceding the election. Letter from Gösta Rehn, 13 March 1982.
107 Bo Särlvik, 'Voting behavior in shifting "election winds": an overview of the Swedish elections 1964–1968', *Scandinavian Political Studies*, 5 (1970), pp. 241–2; and Hadenius, *et al.*, *Sverige efter 1900*, op. cit., pp. 273–9.
108 Hadenius, *Facklig organisationsutveckling*, op. cit., p. 104; Rudolf Meidner, 'Samordning och solidarisk lönepolitik under tre decennier', in *Tvärsnitt*, op. cit., pp. 42–61; Therborn, *En ny vänster*, op. cit., pp. 132–56; *Svenska folkets inkomster*, SOU 1970: 34, Betänkande avgivet av låginkomstutredningen; *Jämlikhet, Första rapport fran SAP–LO:s arbetsgrupp för jämlikhetsfrågor* (Stockholm: Prisma, 1969); and *Protokoll, Sveriges Socialdemokratiska Arbetarepartis 24:e kongress 1969* (Stockholm: Tidens Förlag, 1970), pp. 631–6.
109 Hadenius, *Facklig organisationsutveckling*, op. cit., pp. 102–4, 105–16; and LO, *Lönepolitik, Rapport till LO-kongressen 1971* (Stockholm: Prisma, 1971), pp. 36–48, 93–115.
110 See Table 3.2.
111 Matthiessen, op. cit., p. 204.
112 Hadenius, op. cit., p. 102.
113 See Table 3.3.

114   See ibid.; and Everett M. Kassalow, 'Professional unionism in Sweden', *Industrial Relations*, vol. 8, no. 2 (February 1969), pp. 119–34.
115   Svante Nycander, *Kurs på kollision. Inblick i lönerörelsen 1970–71* (Stockholm: Askild & Kärnekull, 1972), pp. 32–4; and Victorin, op. cit., pp. 170–6.
116   Nycander, op. cit., pp. 10–12.
117   ibid.; and Hadenius, *Facklig organisationsutveckling*, op. cit., p. 102.
118   ibid.
119   See Table 3.2.
120   LO, *De centrala överenskommelserna mellan LO och SAF* (Stockholm: LO, 1979).
121   Mats Fagerström, *Den stora lönematchen. En bok om avtalsförhandlingarna 1969* (Stockholm: Almqvist & Wiksell, 1969), pp. 7–8; and Nycander, op. cit., p. 12.
122   The following account is based on Kasselow, op. cit.
123   Nycander, op. cit., p. 12.
124   *Protokoll. Sveriges Socialdemokratiska Arbetarepartis extra kongress 1967* (Stockholm: SAP, 1968), pp. 362–3.
125   Gösta Edgren, Karl-Olof Faxén, Clas-Erik Odhner, *Lönebildning och samhällsekonomi* (Stockholm: Rabén & Sjögren, 1970), published in English as *Wage Formation and the Economy* (London: Allen & Unwin, 1973).
126   Swedish Employers' Association, 'The 1967 proposal for wage stabilization', in *On Incomes Policy, Papers and Proceedings from a Conference in Honour of Erik Lundberg* (Stockholm: Industrial Council for Social and Economic Studies – SNS, 1969), pp. 223–31.
127   Nycander, op. cit., p. 14.
128   Clas-Erik Odhner, 'The government agency for the determination of wages', in *On Incomes Policy*, op. cit., pp. 233–42.
129   Odd Aukrust, 'Inflation in the open economy: a Norwegian model', in Lawrence B. Krause and Walter S. Salant (eds), *Worldwide Inflation: Theory and Recent Experience* (Washington, DC: Brookings, 1977), pp. 107–66.
130   *Mål och medel i stabiliseringspolitiken. Betänkande avgivet av stabiliseringsutredningen*, SOU 1961:42.
131   The following is a summary of the EFO model as presented in the works cited in n. 125, above. See also Lars Calmfors, 'Inflation in Sweden', in Krause and Salant, op. cit., pp. 493–544.
132   See n. 273, below.
133   TCO, *Tjänstemännens lönepolitik. Rapport från TCO:s lönepolitiska utredning* (Stockholm: Prisma, 1973).
134   Nycander, op. cit., pp. 17–18; and Fagerström, op. cit., pp. 8–9, 18–21.
135   ibid., pp. 13–17, 22–6.
136   ibid., pp. 27–35.
137   Nycander, op. cit., pp. 22–3.
138   Fagerström, op. cit., pp. 36–130.
139   Folke Schmidt, 'Rättsläget vid vilda strejker', in Brantgärde, *et al.*, *Konfliktlösning*, op. cit., p. 192; and Casten v. Otter, 'Sweden: Labor reformism reshapes the system', in Solomon Barkin (ed.), *Worker Militancy and Its Consequences, 1965–75* (New York: Praeger, 1975), pp. 214–15.
140   Walter Korpi, *Varför strejkar arbetarna?* (Stockholm: Tidens Förlag, 1974).
141   See Table 3.2.
142   Matthiessen, op. cit., pp. 208–9.
143   See Table 3.1.
144   On local wage bargaining, see Hart and Otter, op. cit.; and Korpi, *Varför strejkar arbetarna?*, op. cit.
145   SAF rules, quoted in Bernt Schiller, 'LO, paragraf 32 och företagsdemokratin', in *Tvärsnitt*, op. cit., p. 304.
146   ibid., pp. 355–9.
147   Cited in *Protokoll. Svenska Metallindustriarbetareförbundets 28:e kongress 1969*, op. cit., pp. 272–3.
148   See ibid., pp. 285–6; and Korpi, *Varför strejkar arbetarna?*, op. cit., pp. 52–6, for examples.
149   The discussion of the LKAB strike is based mainly on Edmund Dahlström, Kjell Eriksson, Bertil Gardell, Olle Hammarström and Rut Hammarström, *LKAB och*

demokratin. Rapport om en strejk och ett forsknings-projekt (Stockholm: Wahlström & Widstrand, 1971); and Anders Thunberg (red.), *Strejken. Röster, dokument, synpunkter från en storkonflikt* (Stockholm: Rabén & Sjögren, 1970).

150   LO, *Lönepolitik*, op. cit., p. 50.
151   Thunberg, op. cit., p. 221.
152   Dahlström, *et al.*, op. cit., pp. 20–1.
153   Thunberg, op. cit., pp. 207–12.
154   Dahlström, *et al.*, op. cit., pp. 68–89, 129–49.
155   ibid., pp. 26–7.
156   ibid., pp. 150–75.
157   For example, Motions 48, 73 and 74, and the Executive Committee's reply in *Protokoll. Svenska Metallindustriarbetareförbundets kongress 1977*, op. cit., pp. 168, 182–5.
158   LO, *Demokrati i företagen. Rapport till LO-kongressen 1971* (Stockholm: Prisma, 1971).
159   Schiller, 'LO, paragraf 32 och företagsdemokratin', op. cit., pp. 316–32, 352, 387–8.
160   ibid., pp. 344–62; and *1966 års avtal om företagsnämnder m m. Kommentar utgiven av SAF LO TCO* (Stockholm: SAF, LO, TCO, 1967).
161   See no. 80, above; Schiller, 'LO paragraf 32 och företagsdemokratin', op. cit., pp. 363–73; LO, *Demokrati i företagan*, op. cit., pp. 37–48; LO, *Kongressprotokoll 1971*, pp. 431–501, 518–601; Svenska Metallindustriarbetareförbundet, *Kongressprotokoll 1969*, pp. 258–93, and *Kongressprotokoll 1973*, pp. 233–318. An influential survey of research is Edmund Dahlström, Bengt G. Rundblad, Bo Wingårdh and Jan Hallin, *Teknisk förandring och arbetsanpassning* (Stockholm: Prisma, 1966). Bertil Gardell, *Produktionsteknik och arbetsglädje* (Stockholm: Personaladministrativa rådet, 1971), is one of the most substantial pieces of research. Among the studies conducted directly under union auspices is Bo Ohlström, *Kockumsrapporten* (Stockholm: Prisma, 1970), a survey of discontent among shipyard workers.
162   See the study of geographical mobility in *Att utvärdera arbetsmarknadspolitik*, SOU 1974: 29, ch. 7; and LO, *Report on Labour Market Policy* (Stockholm: LO, 1975).
163   *Protokoll, SAP:s kongress 1969*, pp. 43–70.
164   See n. 108, above.
165   Eric Rhenman, *Företagsdemokrati och företagsorganisation* (Stockholm: SAF, 1964) was a path-breaking effort to define the issues confronting employers. The Development Council is discussed in two papers by Karl-Olof Faxén, 'Development of collaboration in firms', (SAF, January 1971), mimeo., and 'Research on self-developing forms of organization', presented to International Economic Association, August 1971. In addition to many reports in Swedish on individual projects, SAF has published a summary analysis in English, *Job Reform in Sweden* (Stockholm: Swedish Employers' Confederation, 1975).
166   Schiller, 'LO, paragraf 32 och företagsdemokratin', op. cit., pp. 375–84.
167   The following summarizes the report cited in n. 158, above.
168   TCO's position is summarized in its comments on the report of the committee on labor law, *Demokrati på arbetsplatsen. Förslag till ny lagstiftning om förhandlingsrätt och kollektivavtal*, SOU 1975:1; and TCO, *TCOs yttrande över Arbetsrättskommittens betänkande* (Stockholm: TCO, 1975). The TCO and LO representatives on the committee issued a minority report going further than the majority in various respects, and their minority report became the basis of the legislation proposed by the Social Democratic government: see SOU 1975: 1, pp. 930–61.
169   Holmberg, op. cit., p. 339.
170   See n. 2, above; also Nycander, op. cit., pp. 23–5.
171   On industrial policy, see Svenning, op. cit., pp. 101–64. Olof Palme, who replaced Tage Erlander as SAP leader and Prime Minister in 1969, made the 'renewal of working life' a major theme. The importance he attached to that theme in relation to the TCO is reflected in his speech to the 1973 TCO Congress, 'Tjänstemännen och arbetslivets förnyelse', reprinted in Olof Palme, *Att vilja gå vidare* (Stockholm: Tidens Förlag, 1974).
172   A poll by SIFO (Swedish Institute of Public Opinion) a few months before the 1973 election showed that only 4 percent of the electorate thought that industrial democracy was one of the three most important issues, whereas 41 percent thought that employment and labor market issues were among the most important: cited in John D.

Stephens, 'The consequences of social structural change for the development of socialism in Sweden', PhD dissertation, Department of Sociology, Yale University, 1976, New Haven, Conn., USA, p. 304.

173   See Table 3.1 and Olof Petersson, 'The 1973 general election in Sweden', *Scandinavian Political Studies*, 9 (1974), 219–28.

174   Arbetarskyddslagen, SFS 1972: 829. Proposals for a new occupational health and safety law were presented in the report of a commission on the work environment, *Arbetsmiljölag*, SOU 1976:1, and enacted in modified form in 1978.

175   The 1971 laws and proposals for subsequent legislation are spelled out in the report of the Commission on Employment Security, *Trygghet i anställningen*, SOU 1973: 7; Lag om anställningsskydd, SFS 1974: 12; Lag om vissa anställningsfrämjande åtgärder, SFS 1974: 13; and Lag om facklig förtroendemans ställning på arbetsplatsen, SFS 1974: 358.

176   Lag om styrelserepresentation för de anställda i aktiebolag och ekononomiska föreningar, SFS 1972: 829, and SFS 1976: 351.

177   Lag om medbestämmande i arbetslivet, SFS 1976: 580.

178   Lag om offentlig anställning, SFA 1976: 600.

179   For speech during parliamentary debate, 2 June 1976, see *Snabbprotokoll från riksdagsdebatterna* No. 151 (1975–6), p. 139. A more modest characterization is presented, retrospectively, by LO's negotiations secretary, Harry Fjällström: 'The labor legislation (carried out in the 1970s) has led to a change in positions: the workers' influence has increased. But the changes are insufficient; the decisive decisions concerning the conditions for production's direction and development continue to be made by the owner interest.' From Anders Broström, *Storkonflikten 1980* (Stockholm: Arbetslivcentrum, 1981), p. 166.

180   Hadenius, *Facklig organisationsutveckling*, op. cit., p. 106; and Nycander, op. cit., pp. 53–4.

181   ibid., pp. 26–30; and LO, *Lönepolitik*, op. cit., pp. 76–81.

182   Hadenius, *Facklig organisationsutveckling*, op. cit., p. 107; and Nycander, op. cit., pp. 166–70.

183   ibid., pp. 40–61.

184   ibid., pp. 70–124, 144–58.

185   See Table 3.4.

186   Bertil Östergren, *Makten och ärligheten. Om likheter och olikheter* (Stockholm: Askild & Kärnekull, 1970), pp. 67–78; and Nycander, op. cit., pp. 76–9.

187   ibid., pp. 31, 78–85.

188   ibid., pp. 130–43, 159–65.

189   ibid., 171–203.

190   ibid., p. 202.

191   See Table 3.2.

192   Matthiessen, op. cit., pp. 212–16; and Tables 3.1 and 3.5.

193   *The Swedish Economy 1971–1975 and the General Outlook up to 1990: The 1970 Long-Term Economic Survey* (Stockholm: Allmänna Förlaget, 1971). This is a translation of SOU 1970: 71. See pp. 98–101, 123–5.

194   ibid., pp. 153–7, 163.

195   Aleksander Markowski and Edward E. Palmer, 'Social insurance in Sweden', in George M. von Furstenberg (ed.), *Social Security versus Saving* (Cambridge, Mass.: Ballinger, 1980); and *Kapitalmarknaden i svensk ekonomi*, SOU 1978: 11, ch. 8.

196   LO, *Kongressprotokoll 1971*, op. cit., pp. 815–18, 843, 859–60.

197   LO, *Kongressprotokoll 1966*, op. cit., pp. 397–406.

198   The relevant portion of the government's original directive to the Capital Market Commission and the text of LO's memorandum to the government are printed in the Commission's special report on equity financing by the AP fund, *Näringslivets försörjning med riskkapital från allmänna pensionsfonden*, SOU 1972: 63, pp. 15–24.

199   SOU 1978: 11, pp. 452–4; *Kapitalmarknaden i svensk ekonomi. Bilaga 4, Industrins tillväxt och långsiktiga finansiering*, SOU 1978: 13, p. 116; and Regeringens proposition 1978/79: 165, pp. 124–30.

200   Rudolf Meidner, Anna Hedborg and Gunnar Fond, *Löntagarfonder* (Stockholm: Tidens Förlag, 1975). The results of the survey are presented in the report containing the revised version of the proposal, *Kollektiv kapitalbildning genom löntagarfonder. Rapport till LO-kongressen 1976* (Stockholm: Prisma, 1976), pp. 165–92.

201 ibid., pp. 9–19. Our summary of the proposal is drawn from pp. 41–132.
202 ibid., pp. 127–8.
203 See below, pp. 286–90
204 See below, pp. 325–9.
205 See above, p. 268.
206 SOU 1978: 11, pp. 455–61.
207 Meidner, *et al.*, op. cit., p. 79.
208 SOU 1978: 11, p. 454.
209 See above, p. 206.
210 See below, pp. 333–5, 280–1.
211 Sveriges Industriförbund och Svenska Arbetsgivareföreningen, *Företagsvinster, kapitalförsörjning, löntagarfonder* (Stockholm: Näringslivets förlagsdistribution, 1976). A summary of various positions from the point of view of organized business available in English is Per-Martin Meyerson, *Company Profits, Sources of Investment Finance, Wage Earners' Investment Funds in Sweden* (Stockholm: Federation of Swedish Industries, 1976). The remark about 'confiscation' is by Hans Werthén, head of Electrolux, quoted in *Fortune*, vol. XCIII, no. 3 (March 1976), p. 156.
212 *Boston Globe*, 20 September 1976; and Steven Kelman, 'Letter from Stockholm', *New Yorker*, 1 November 1976.
213 Hadenius, *et al.*, *Sverige efter 1900*, op. cit., pp. 116–17.
214 Sveriges Socialdemokratiska Arbetareparti, *Reviderat förslag till nytt parti program* (Stockholm: Tiden, 1975), pp. 17, 20–1.
215 TCO, Löntagarkapital (Stockholm: TCO, 1976); and *TCOs Kongress, 1976: Snabb protokoll*, 3, pp. 141–55.
216 On the election campaign, see Kelman, 'Letter from Stockholm', op. cit., and Hendrik Hertzberg, 'Sweden's unassailable socialism', *New Republic*, 9 October 1976.
217 The discussion can be followed in the LO and SAP congresses, *LO-Tidningen*, LO's weekly newspaper; *Tiden*, the party's theoretical journal; and *Sju socialdemokrater om löntagarfonderna* (Stockholm: Tidens Förlag, 1979), a collection of largely critical essays, including some by people who were only marginally Social Democrats and one economist who left the party over the issue.
218 See below, pp. 288–9.
219 Palme refers to the increased 'respect' for the Liberals in a long interview in *Dagens Nyheter*, 19 April 1975. This Stockholm newspaper is the principal national daily which, though 'independent', tends to be sympathetic to the liberals. In the parliamentary debate on the Codetermination in Work Law Palme anticipated that the liberals would join with the Social Democrats rather than the bourgeois parties to achieve future reforms. He observed that 'social liberalism is a tender plant that thrives best in the shelter of a strong social democracy': *Snabbprotokoll från riksdags-debatterna*, 1975/76, No. 151, p. 144.
220 See the section on Britain in this volume; also Andrew Martin, 'Is democratic control of capitalism possible?', in Leon N. Lindberg, Robert Alford, Colin Crouch and Claus Offe (eds), *Stress and Contradiction in Modern Capitalism* (Lexington, Mass.: D. C. Heath, 1975).
221 *Löntagarna och kapitaltillväxten. Slutrapport*, SOU 1981: 44, pp. 11–12, 23, 223.
222 'Det svenska valet 1976', *Indikator. SIFO:s nyhetsbrev*, 1 November 1976, pp. 7, 12–15.
223 Sören Holmberg, Jörgen Westerståhl and Karl Branzen, *Väljarna och kärnkraften* (Stockholm: Liberförlag, 1977), esp. ch. 8; and Olof Petersson, 'Väljarna och valet 1976', *Valundersökningar*, Rapport 2 (Stockholm: Statistiska centralbyrån, 1977), pp. 206–14, 230–1.
224 'Det svenska valet 1976', op. cit., pp. 16–18.
225 *The Swedish Economy*, 1973: 3, pp. 7–10, 68–71.
226 Sven Grassman, *Ekonomins gångjärn* (Stockholm: Almänna Förlaget, 1974); and Petersson, op. cit., pp. 206–8.
227 LO, *Lönepolitik for 80-talet. Rapport till LO-kongressen 1981* (Stockholm: Tidens Förlag, 1981), p. 45.
228 See Table 3.2.
229 ibid.
230 Nils Elvander, 'Staten och organisationerna på arbetsmarknaden i de nordiska

länderna. En komparativ översikt', in Brantgärde, *et al.*, op. cit., p. 116; TCO, *Tjänstemännens lönepolitik*, op. cit., p. 46; TCO, *Skatter och standardutveckling* (Stockholm: TCO, 1971), pp. 14–15, 21–3; LO, *Löner, Priser, Skatter. Rapport till LO-kongressen 1976* (Stockholm: Prisma, 1976), pp. 69–77, 87–103.

231   LO, *Lönepolitik för 80-talet*, op. cit., p. 39; see also Table 3.5.

232   *The Swedish Budget 1974/75* (Stockholm: Ministry of Finance, 1974), p. 27; and ibid., 1975/76 (Stockholm: Ministry of Finance, 1975), pp. 7–11.

233   See Table 3.4; and Bo Ohlström, *Vilda strejkar inom LO-området 1974 och 1975* (Stockholm: LO, 1977).

234   LO, *Verksamhetsberättelse 1974* (Stockholm: LO, 1975), pp. 80–1.

235   The two Haga Agreements are discussed from the Liberal Party's perspective, in 'Frågor och svar om "Haga II" ', Folkpartiets Riksorganisation, 1975.03.04.

236   Svenska Metallindustriarbetareförbundet, *Rapport om industri och sysselsättning*, 1977, pp. 3–4; and *Dagens Nyheter*, 6 and 10 November 1974.

237   Villy Bergström, Sven Grassman, Erik Lundberg and Göran Ohlin, *Politik mot stagflation* (Stockholm: SNS, 1977), pp. 18–19.

238   *The Swedish Economy*, 1975; 2, pp. 8, 40–3.

239   The course of negotiations is briefly summarized in *Svenska Årbetsgivareföreningens verksamhet 1974* (Stockholm: SAF, 1975), pp. 14–23, and ibid., 1975 (Stockholm: SAF, 1976), pp. 17–29; and LO, *Verksamhets berättelse 1974* (Stockholm: LO, 1975), pp. 79–83, and LO, *Verksamhets berättelse 1975* (Stockholm: LO, 1976), pp. 48–68.

240   See Table 3.2.

241   Bergström, op. cit., pp. 54–5. Lars Calmfors, 'Lönebildning, internationell konkurrenskraft och ekonomisk politik', in *Vägar till ökad välfärd*, DS Ju 1979: 1, Bilaga 3, pp. 130–1. It should be noted that a TCO economist contested the cost-crisis thesis when relative unit labor costs are viewed over a longer period. See Hans Engman, 'Svenska löner stiger inte snabbast i världen', *TCO-Tidningen*, 1977, no. 20, pp. 10–11. At an earlier point LO's position was also skeptical. See LO, *Löner, Priser, Skatter*, op. cit., pp. 80–1. More recently, however, LO statements have reflected acceptance of the view that Sweden's relative cost position was worsened in the later 1970s and that rapid rise in hourly wages in 1975–6 was a contributing factor: see speech by Gunnar Nilsson, chairman of LO, in Parliament, 31 January 1979, Riksdagen 1978/79, *Snabbprotokoll*, No. 77, pp. 11–12.

242   Bergström, op. cit., pp. 71–4. It must nevertheless be pointed out that structural problems were coming to a head independently of the post-1975 deterioration in relative costs, so that 'losses in market shares that occurred in many cases probably would have taken place even with a "normal" Swedish cost and price development': ibid., p. 57. This is the conclusion drawn from an interview study of seventeen large industrial firms.

243   The preceding summarizes the accounts in ibid.; and *The Swedish Economy*, 1978: 2.

244   For example, market shares and relative prices for Swedish industrial exports; see *The Swedish Economy*, 1982: 1, pp. 54–7.

245   Sven Grassman, 'Perspektiv på devalvering', and 'Skämt och allvar i ekonomisk-politiska debatten', *Ekonomisk debatt*, 1978: 5 and 8, pp. 302–14 and 607–11.

246   See, for example, *Vägar till ökad välfärd*, esp. pp. 121–58, and Erik Dahmén, 'Does the mixed economy have a future?', in Bengt Rydén and Villy Bergström (eds), *Sweden: Choices for Economic and Social Policy in the 1980s* (London: Allen & Unwin, 1982).

247   For a general account of the political parties, see M. Donald Hancock, *Sweden: The Politics of Postindustrial Change* (Hinsdale, Ill.: Dryden Press, 1972), pp. 108–45.

248   Bergström, op. cit., pp. 80–7; and 'Regeringens ekonomiska åtsträmningspaket', government press release, 4 April 1977.

249   *The Swedish Economy*, 1978: 2, pp. 196–200; and 'Regeringens stabiliseringsprogram, hösten 1977', government press release, 29 August 1977.

250   Bo Carlsson, Frederik Bergholm and Thomas Lindberg, *Industristödpolitiken och dess inverkan på samhällsekonomin* (Stockholm: Industriens Utredningsinstitutet, 1981), pp. 21–38.

251   Bergström, op. cit., pp. 28–37, 64–74; see also Table 3.1.

252   The account of the negotiations is based on Karl-Olof Andersson, *Spelet om lönerna, Ett reportage kring avtalsdramatiken 1977* (Stockholm: Pogo Press, 1977); *Svenska*

Notes 357

Arbetsgivareföreningens verksamhet 1977 (Stockholm: SAF, 1978), pp. 15–21; and LO, *Verksamhetsberättelse 1977* (Stockholm, LO, 1978), pp. 54–65.
253 See Table 3.2 and *The Swedish Economy*, 1978: 2, pp. 109–11.
254 Anders Röttorp, 'Sveriges relativa kostnadsutveckling under 1970-talet', *Industrikonjunkteren*, 1978; cited in Calmfors, op. cit., pp. 130–31.
255 LO, *Lönepolitik för 80-talet*, op. cit., p. 45.
256 LO, *Verksamshetberättelse 1977* (Stockholm: LO, 1978), pp. 66–8; Lars Wohlin, 'Första årets ekonomiska politik', *Ekonomisk debatt*, 1977: 6, pp. 334–45; and 'Åtstråmningspolitiken – ett steg på vägen till balans', *Ekonomisk debatt*, 1978: 7, pp. 507–18.
257 LO, *Verksamhetsberättelse 1978* (Stockholm: LO, 1979), pp. 57–71; and *Svenska Arbetsgivareföreningens verksamhet 1978* (Stockholm: SAF, 1979), pp. 14–18.
258 See Table 3.2; *The Swedish Economy*, 1982: 1, p. 109; and Olle Bolang, *Utslagen, Den svenska modellen efter 1980 års storkonflikt* (Stockholm: SNS, 1980), pp. 17–18.
259 See Table 3.2.
260 LO, *Lönepolitik för 80-talet*, op. cit., p. 39.
261 Regeringens prop. 1978/79: 150, Bilaga 1, 23 April 1979, p. 6.
262 LO, *Verksamhetsberättelse 1978*, op. cit., p. 12.
263 *The Swedish Economy*, 1982: 1, p. 56.
264 *The Swedish Economy*, 1980: 3, p. 106.
265 This refers to the export share of production in the engineering industry. It was around 38 percent for industry as a whole in the late 1970s: *Den internationella backgrunden. Långtidsutredningen 1975, Bilaga 1*, SOU 1976: 27; and *Att välja 80-tal. IUI:s långtidsbedömning 1979* (Stockholm: IUI, 1979), p. 147.
266 See Table 3.2.
267 *Snabbprotokoll från riksdagsdebatterna* 1978/79, No. 77.
268 Bert Lundin, then chairman of the metalworkers' union, cited by Carl Johan Åberg, 'Som man bäddar får man ligga', in Broström, op. cit., p. 159; and Nils Lundgren, 'Årets finansplan', *Ekonomisk debatt*, no. 1 (1979), p. 72.
269 *Ekonomiska utsikter*, våren 1979, p. 28; and Per Olof Edin, *LO-Tidningen*, 1978: 27, p. 7.
270 *Rättvis lön – lönepolitiskt program* (Stockholm: SAF, 1979), mimeo, p. 12.
271 It is argued that international prices can no longer serve as a parameter because they have been made too difficult to estimate by flexible exchange rates, increased variation in national inflation rates and large imbalances in international payments. In addition, the assumed relationships between the C and S sectors no longer hold, with the private component of the S sector unable to maintain margins by markup pricing while local and central governments have diverse effects on wage costs unanticipated in the EFO model: Karl-Olof Faxén, in 'Höstens lönerörelse', *Ekonomisk debatt*, 8: 1979, pp. 578–9.
272 ibid., see also SAF, *Om kapitalmarknaden i svensk ekonomi* (Stockholm: SAF, 1978).
273 'Höstens lönerörelse', op. cit., p. 579; and *Rättvis lön*, op. cit., p. 8.
274 *Rättvis lön*, op. cit., pp. 1–5, 12.
275 'Höstens lönerörelse', op. cit., 579–60.
276 ibid., p. 580.
277 ibid.
278 The Social Democratic government's policies are characterized in this way in Hans Tson Söderström and Staffan Viotti, 'Money wage disturbances and the endogeneity of the public sector in an open economy', in Assar Lindbeck (ed.), *Inflation and Employment in Open Economies*, Studies in International Economics (Amsterdam: North-Holland, 1979), Vol. 5, pp. 71–98.
279 Dahmén 'Does the mixed economy have a future?', op. cit., p. 122.
280 See n. 246, above.
281 Olof Petersson, *Regeringsbildningen 1978* (Stockholm: Rabén & Sjögren, 1979).
282 *The Swedish Economy* 1980: 3, tables and charts section, p. 40.
283 ibid., pp. 94–5, and tables and charts section, p. 42.
284 See Table 3.5; and *The Swedish Economy*, 1980: 2, pp. 148, 162.
285 Holmberg, op. cit., p. 27.
286 Except where otherwise indicated, the following account is drawn from Bolang, op. cit.; Broström, op. cit.; *LO-Tidningen, SAF-Tidningen, PTK-nytt*, various issues.

287   *LO Verksamhetsberättelse 1979*, pp. 56–7.
288   ibid., pp. 59–60.
289   Axel Hadenius, *Spelet om skatter: rationalistisk analys av politiskt beslutsfattande* (Stockholm: Norstedt, 1981).
290   *LO-Tidningen*, 1979, no. 47, pp. 1, 16.
291   LO, *Ekonomiska utsikter, Hösten 1979*, op. cit., p. 23.
292   *PTK-nytt*, 1980, no. 1, pp. 2–3; and Bolang, op. cit., p. 99.
293   Sigvard Marjasin, 'Avtalsrörelsen 1980: ett försök att splittra löntagarna, in Broström, op. cit., p. 59.
294   Text in Bolang, op. cit., pp. 102–4.
295   Marjasin, op. cit., p. 61.
296   Text in Bolang, op. cit., pp. 107–8.
297   ibid., p. 45.
298   Bertil Jacobson, 'Vad hände under 1980 års konflikt?' in Broström, op. cit., p. 43.
299   The following is a summary of Fjällström's argument in his 'Bakgrunden till 1980 års konflikt', in Broström, op. cit., pp. 163–74.
300   See Table 3.2.
301   *The Swedish Economy*, 1981: 2, pp. 99–101.
302   ibid., p. 56.
303   ibid., pp. 138–40.
304   TCO, *Lönepolitikens samhällsekonomiska förutsättningar* (Stockholm: TCO, 1982), p. 57.
305   *The Swedish Economy*, 1981: 2, pp. 27, 65, 143. The comparisons are in terms of proportion of GDP.
306   Regeringens proposition 1980 U:1; 'The economic policy statement', in *The Swedish Budget*, 1980/81, 1981/82, 1982/83; *The Swedish Economy*, 1982: 2, pp. 206–12.
307   *The Swedish Economy* 1981: 1, pp. 119–20.
308   LO, *Verksamhetsberättelse 1981* (Stockholm: LO, 1982), pp. 62–86; *Svenska Arbetsgivareföreningens verksamhet 1981* (Stockholm: SAF, 1981); and *PTK-nytt*, 1981, no. 5, whole issue.
309   *Sweden Business Report*, 6 November 1981, pp. 1–2; and *LO-Tidningen*, 1981, no. 47, p. 16.
310   See no. 289, above.
311   See n. 194, above.
312   Regeringens proposition 1978/89: 165, pp. 108–30.
313   ibid., p. 114.
314   *The Swedish Economy*, 1981: 2, p. 155.
315   Regeringens proposition 1980/81: 45.
316   *Sweden Now*, vol. 15, no. 3, (1981), p. 11.
317   *Dagens Nyheter*, 28 September 1977.
318   *Från Riksdag & Departement*, vol. 7, no. 291 (October 1982), p. 2.
319   See n. 217, above.
320   An illustration of this approach is Krister Wickman, 'Kapitalbildning och investeringsutveckling inför 1980-talet, in Kjell-Olof Feldt m.fl., *Ekonomisk politik inför 1980-talet* (Stockholm: Tidens Förlag, 1977).
321   *Arbetarrörelsen och löntagarfonderna. Rapport från en arbetsgrupp inom LO och socialdemokraterna* (Stockholm: Tidens Förlag, 1981).
322   ibid., pp. 108–13.
323   This idea is elaborated more fully in a book by two LO economists intimately involved in the whole process of working out the proposal: Per-Olof Edin and Anna Hedborg, *Det nya uppdraget* (Stockholm: Tidens Förlag, 1980).
324   LO, *Löner, Priser, Skatter*, op. cit., p. 80.
325   LO, *Verksamhetsberättelse 1977*, op. cit., pp. 43–4.
326   *TCO-Tidningen*, 1977: 20, pp. 10–11.
327   *PTK-nytt*, 1977, no. 1, p. 2.
328   *LO-Tidningen*, 1981: 20, p. 11.
329   *SIFs lönepolitik: Lön 80, Slutrapport från lönepolitiska utredningen* (Stockholm: SIF, 1977).
330   LO, *Lönepolitik för 80-talet*, op. cit., pp. 71–5.
331   ibid., pp. 85–7.

332 Sections on 'Företagsdemokrati', in LO's *Verksamhetsberättelse* for the years 1978–82; and *PTK-nytt*, various issues.
333 Bo Hedborg, *SSAB-Fusionen: Erfarenheter kring förändringsstrategier och löntagarkonsultroll* (Stockholm: Arbetslivcentrum, 1978).
334 TCO, *En offensiv industripolitik* (Stockholm: TCO, 1978).
335 TCO, *Offensiv industripolitik – ett måste för 80-talet* (Stockholm: TCO, 1981); SIF, *Samordna Industripolitiken! Rapport från SIFs industripolitiska utredning* (Stockholm: SIF, 1980); and LO, *Näringspolitik för 80-talet, Rapport till LO-Kongressen 1981* (Stockhom: Tidens Förlag, 1981).
336 ibid., pp. 231–41.
337 TCO, *Offensiv industripolitik*, op. cit., pp. 115–30.
338 LO, *Näringspolitik för 80-talet*, op. cit., pp. 262–3.
339 TCO, *Företagsbeskattning och löntagarfonder* (Stockholm: TCO, 1972); TCO, *Löntagarkapital* (Stockholm: TCO, 1976); TCO, *Löntagarfonder ur TCO-perspektiv – en debattskrift* (Stockholm: TCO, 1978); and TCO, *Löntagarkapital genom fonder – ett principförslag* (Stockholm: TCO, 1978).
340 SIF, *Protokoll från kongressen 1978* (Stockholm: SIF, 1978), pp. 330–65.
341 *TCO Kongress 79, Protokoll* (Stockholm: TCO, 1979), pp. 107–22.
342 SIF, *Samordna industripolitiken!*, op. cit., p. 76.
343 *7 dagar*, vol. 2, no. 27 (July 1982), p. 22.

Conclusion

George Ross and Peter Gourevitch

Economic crises have come in many different forms. Whenever they have come, they have upset existing arrangements of accommodation among different social groups. They have also invariably challenged prevailing conventional wisdom about basic social exchanges. In short, economic crises are moments of great upheaval. They make the world confusing and chaotic for individuals and collectivities who live through them. They can also be moments of great social creativity. Confusion, chaos and questioning lead groups to reflect anew on ways of rearranging their social world, and on what new coalitions might be formed. Economic crises, in other words, tend to be crucibles for substantial social change. Such change is rarely straightforward, however. Almost always it takes a succession of viable new arrangements before it can be consolidated.

By the twentieth century trade unions emerged as central collective actors in capitalist societies. They, too, have been repeatedly challenged in basic ways by the coming of economic crises. Indeed, in one form or another, the transfer of resources from labor to capital has been the classic conservative strategy in times of economic disruption, a transfer which has almost always involved dramatic attacks on unions. In some situations, in fact, more radical movements, such as fascism, have mobilized particularly virulent attacks on labor as part of a broader offensive against democracy. Modern unions have not been simply the objects of crises, however. They have also been, and continue to be, able to alter outcomes. If they have rarely, if ever, been able to attain their own objectives, they have at least been able to render the political system more complicated so as to prevent other actors from realizing their own objectives. Unions have resources, often substantial ones, which allow them to block the strategic goals of others, or to take initiatives of their own. Unions' resources have also been considerable assets to their political allies.

The experience of the 1930s underlines the importance of unions as proposers of ideas, builders of coalitions and/or resisters of attacks on them. In Sweden and the USA the 1930s mark the emergence of social democratic coalitions that replaced classical liberalism's untrammeled market by demand-stimulated full employment, the welfare state, and certain corporatist practices in agriculture and industry. In Sweden the labor movement dominated this political realignment. The Social Democratic Party and the trade union organization (LO) led the way in articulating ideas, working out bargains with other social groups and political parties, and administering the new arrangements through control of the government. In the USA labor's role was less central, but none the less important in the complex maneuvering among different groups of businessmen, farmers and wage-earners which mark the various phases in the evolution of the New Deal. In France the Popular Front was certainly less successful, but the effort to try demand stimulus and welfare arrangements derived much of its impetus from the labor movement and left parties.

In the UK and Germany social democratic arrangements were not tried in the 1930s. In both countries the trade union movement showed some interest in breaking with economic orthodoxy in favor of demand-stimulus ideas, but in both cases the labor-affiliated party did not go along. In Britain the attitudes of MacDonald and Snowden toward Keynes and the Liberals prevented the formation of a coalition government around a new program and led to the split of 1931, which in turn led to the exclusion of the labor movement from political influence until World War II. British labor remains deeply marked by this experience. The German union movement and its political party allies were deeply divided about how to confront the crisis both programmatically and organizationally. While the behavior of labor was not by itself the prime cause of this outcome, and while labor was certainly one of its major victims, such splits were certainly important factors in allowing anti-union and anti-democratic solutions (which were none the less remarkably Keynesian in terms of economic policy) to gestate and prevail.

The general lesson of the different trajectories of the 1930s is that unions were essential bearers of new economic-policy notions that would eventually reshape the political economy of contemporary societies, even if the unions were not the exclusive bearers of such ideas and even if they failed to carry the day during the Depression. Instinctively most unions were 'Keynesian' in a popular sense – in favor of solutions to the crisis which promoted mass consumption and averse to waiting interminably for the supposedly self-correcting mechanisms of the market to play themselves out. Even without the benefit of the Keynesian economic-theoretical corpus (formulated in any case *after* the major policy trajectories had already been chosen), trade unionists found in under-consumption thinking and the organizational defense of wages the stimuli for new thinking about economic policy. What happened in each country depended on the relation of their ideas to other variables: the labor movement's resources, institutional settings and the willingness of other actors to form alliances with labor.

In the great crisis of the interwar period, then, the behavior of the labor movement played a significant role in shaping policy and political outcomes. This is likely to be even more true in today's economic crisis, since the Great Depression and World War II have in the long run enhanced significantly the presence of organized labor in the central processes of contemporary political economy, making it likely that the ideas and strategies of unions would be more important in the chaos and confusion of the contemporary crisis of international capitalism than they were in the 1930s. Such, at least, was the basic premise of our study.

The 'Social Democratic' Cases: Sweden, the UK and West Germany

Volume One of this project, *Unions, Change and Crisis* (Allen and Unwin, London, 1982), concluded with a comparative chapter which analyzed

French and Italian unions using an actor-centric exchange framework. In this perspective unions were seen as autonomous strategic actors, endowed with their own specific sets of ideas, values and perceptions, and their own decision-making procedures. They stood consciously at the center of a series of different, interrelated sets of exchanges. They provided 'payoffs', or incentives (material, ideological, solidaristic), to their members in the workforce in exchange for resources of activism, support and loyalty. To provide such incentives the unions required arrangements both in market and political spheres. In the market they sought material and institutional goods (agreements on wages, hours, working conditions, employment security, and the like, plus the establishment of union and working-class 'rights' and entitlements) in exchange for the delivery of a disciplined and predictable laborforce. In the political sphere they sought favorable state policies in areas such as taxes, welfare and public expenditure in exchange for union-generated political resources (voting, campaign finances, activism). These various 'deals' generate a complex set of relationships between unions and a dense network of other actors (businesses, political parties, government organization, interest groups). In ordinary circumstances unions – like other actors – will tend to settle into stable exchange relationships in terms of both policies and organizational linkages. Change will occur only when the cost of maintaining old patterns becomes too high or the opportunity to obtain new resources becomes inviting – circumstances most likely to be produced by crises, economic or military.

This framework (see Volume One , *Unions, Change and Crisis*, for a more detailed analysis of the differences between it and other models such as the 'liberal optimist' perspective associated with Kerr and Lipset) is useful for comparing trade union movements across countries. It presumes that unions *are*, indeed, actors on their own, with their own particular contexts. Thus, even if unions, when observed from a great enough comparative distance, look the same – that is, are organizations with a social base of a specific kind which bargain in similar ways and intervene politically in certain fashion – they actually *differ* from one another, sometimes substantially, within this general pattern of similarity. Each union, or national union organization, as is the case for our study, will have its own identity, its own specific combination of historically constructed ideas, perceptions, reflexes and organizations, and its own particular system of exchanges with the rank-and-file and other actors. Each union is likely, therefore, to respond to outside stimuli toward change in a different way.

Volume One of our study concentrated on France and Italy because certain initial similarities in the setting and exchange patterns of French and Italian unions brought out sharply the differences which accounted for the divergence in behavior so striking in the late 1970s and first years of the 1980s. France and Italy are the two countries of our five whose union movements had major components linked in the political sphere to communist parties. What, in turn, characterized these communist parties in the period from 1947 to the late 1970s – the years of postwar boom and the coming of crisis – was that they were always in opposition. Although each of the unions associated with these CPs, the French CGT and the

Italian CGIL, developed their own relationships with the state and ruling political parties, the political exchange relationship of greatest significance to them was one which involved union efforts to mobilize support on behalf of parties which never came to power and for policies which were never enacted. For these reasons, among others, the CGT and the CGIL tended, when looked at comparatively, to appear 'ideological' and 'political' in their interactions with their membership-base. Since these unions were unable to provide workers with the material and institutional benefits available to unions with party allies in power or likely to be so (with the sympathy in state agencies which this might have provided), they used ideological benefits as a partial substitute. Political fragmentation of trade union organization was both an historical consequence and a sustaining cause of this kind of ideological unionism. Efforts to mobilize workers were often made around ideological themes which were not broadly shared by the workers, and they repeatedly proved divisive of an ideologically pluralistic workforce. The existence of organizationally polycentric union movements in both countries created, in turn, a competitive market situation among different unions. In both countries, then, union development was deeply marked by the effects of the continuous interunion competition. Periods of interunion cooperation did recur, of course, as common interests overcame the ongoing causes of divisiveness. But such periods themselves often turned into moments of strategic jockeying between different unions and, as a result, tended to be brief.

The actor-centric approach which we used in Volume One allowed us to uncover what we believed to be plausible reasons why the evolution of French and Italian unions, which started out quite similar in the immediate postwar period, had diverged so much by the 1970s that each union movement had a dramatically different understanding of, and approach to, the crisis. Differences in the unfolding structures of political coalitions, plus differences in the sphere of interunion competition, were among the major causes of these divergences. Faced with crisis in the 1970s the major French unions, each in its different way, retained a 'maximalist' perspective on economy and polity: the symptoms of crisis could only be successfully treated by radical political surgery. In Italy, in contrast, a more 'accommodationist' approach had come to exist. Italian unions did not abandon the goals of social change. But they did reformulate these goals away from their own earlier maximalism. Even if the unions had developed no new affection for capitalism, they did not regard the troubles of the Italian economy as the result of capitalism *per se* and, thus, to be resolved by the abolition of the capitalist system. Rather, the problem resided in a specifically Italian 'model of development' which had proved inappropriate for promoting Italian success in the new international environment. Proposals to change this model of development through investment control, in particular, to promote new and more just growth, were the core of the Italian unions' response to crisis.

The union movements of Sweden, the UK and West Germany, examined in this volume, are 'similar cases', collectively different from the 'similar cases' of France and Italy. All three – LO in Sweden, the TUC in

Britain and the DGB in West Germany – have longstanding and well-developed ties to social democratic parties which are the dominant parties on the left. Partly for this reason, all three are the only major blue-collar peak organizations in their societies: ideologically based trade union pluralism, at least among unions representing industrial workers, does not exist. The social democratic parties, to which the unions have forged links, have moreover all been at some time a majority party *in power*, or when out of power, a plausible candidate for returning to power at some proximate future date.

For a union, a governing party is able to promise that certain kinds of policies which the union desires *can be delivered* and, therefore, transformed into payoffs which will be tangible for the union's base. In exchange for these payoffs, or the plausible promise of them in the near future, the union is better able to generate electoral support for the party and accept certain duties of restraint and moderation. Such moderation is vital to the success of the exchange. In office the Social Democratic Party must govern. It must assume managerial responsibility for the success or failure of a sophisticated capitalist economy, over and above, and even at the expense of, the policy payoffs it may owe to its union ally. To the degree that the union derives benefits from having its party ally in power it has a direct interest in having the party succeed at these managerial tasks and will, thus, try to refrain from actions, in either market or political arenas, which might compromise this success.

Over time this exchange between unions and social democratic parties tends to crystallize into definite 'deals' whose terms can be specified and whose evolution can be followed. The union and the party each behaves strategically: the union so as to facilitate the general economic management tasks of the governing party, or the party's bid for an electoral majority; the party so as to provide the union with the programs needed for organizational maintenance. As this exchange develops the union *de facto* (sometimes *de jure* as well, as with statutory societal corporatist arrangements) *comes to share* general managerial responsibility with its party-ally, both in thought and deed. This 'cooperative' approach – as opposed to the 'oppositional' stance characteristic of the French and Italian cases – may very well persist even when the Social Democratic Party is out of power if the union hopes that its moderation may help bring the party back to office.

This 'social democratic' exchange between union and party may not always be as straightforward as we have just described it. As we have explained, unions – even 'cooperative' ones – are at the center of a *number* of exchange relationships – not only the one with its party-ally – whose pull upon the union may be strategically contradictory rather than complementary. A union which desires to be 'cooperative' because of its political relationship with a party-ally may be unable to do so satisfactorily because its rank-and-file (dissatisfied with the payoffs coming its way in the labor market) may not wish to cooperate. Here, of course, organizational variables such as centralization will be important in affecting the leverage of union confederations over their rank-and-file. Beyond this the specific 'deal' struck between union and party-ally may also cut in different directions. The union may hold the party's program 'hostage' for policies more radical than those that the party feels comfortable with. Also likely, however, is the opposite 'hostage' situation in which the party, usually in power, retreats from policy commitments made to the union – usually invoking 'realistic' constraints of economic management – obliging the union to choose between complying or jeopardizing the longevity in power of the party-ally.

The great complexity of unions' positions in the actor-centric approach which we have used can, thus, be considerably simplified for the purposes of reviewing the social democratic cases. The unions, *qua* unions, all stand in similar relationships to their bases. They must act in ways which will generate the payoffs needed to sustain rank-and-file support. To achieve this goal the most important axis of exchange between the unions and other actors has consistently been that with social democratic party-allies. These parties have provided privileged access for unions to influence state economic policies. Historically, however, the evolution of this union–party exchange relationship presents itself as a series of 'deals'. The union and the party each develops sets of expectations about the relationship which each believes to be congruent with its essential goals, in the union's case the goal of maintaining rank-and-file support. Movement from deal to deal has occurred when such expectations have not worked adequately to contain new contradictions. In the union's case this has occurred when policies implemented by the party-ally have not been consistent with satisfactory relationships with the rank-and-file. Thus, the unions evolved from deal to deal in the postwar period toward the positions with which they ultimately confronted economic crisis in the 1970s.

The First Deal: Reform and Postwar Settlement

The immediate postwar years involved the renegotiation of the bases of European political economies. Mobilized by the experiences of the Great Depression and World War II, unions sought extensive change in their societies. They had both 'reformist' and 'radical' goals. The 'reformist' goals included full employment, higher wages, the social services of the welfare state and greater social equality – a package which can be characterized as 'popular Keynesianism'. The 'radical', or 'socialist', goals consisted of extensive structural transformation of the political economy: comprehensive planning, full socialization of investment and worker control. In the early postwar years most unionists believed the two types of change were inseparable: reformism required socialist restructuring. Private capital and bourgeois political forces were seen as too conservative, anti-union and anti-working class to cooperate in creating a better life. To the unions in these countries, then, the 'Socialist' program was largely instrumental, a means of realizing full employment, prosperity and security, rather than an end in itself.

In postwar Western Europe what the unions got was the reformist part of their program. They were by and large blocked in getting the radical parts. Many elements of the modern mixed-economy welfare state derive from this period, but socialist reforms were either not carried out at all or else, where implemented, turned to different purposes from those the unions claimed to desire. In all the countries we studied unions were obliged to analyze the meaning of this complex experience. In some sense they had been 'defeated', but the meaning of the setback in relation to the successes obtained was by no means clear, and led to ongoing debate in each country.

In different ways in different places, but ultimately in all these Northern European countries, the new mixed economy did indeed 'deliver the goods' which trade unionists wanted. Reconstruction, expanded international trade, technological innovation and rationalization, consumerism and judicious state economic management of a Keynesian kind – these all contributed to the celebrated postwar boom. Such unforeseen economic success played on the ambiguity of the unions' postwar 'radical' posture. If the desired goods could be obtained *without* extensive structural reforms, if a state management of demand to promote private sector profitability could also produce full employment and prosperity, then the 'radical' instrumentalities originally proposed were not really necessary. Thus, in each country, union movements and their social democratic party-allies lived through 'revisionist' *crises de conscience* in which 'socialism' old-style was shelved in favor of the more 'modern' and 'realistic' outline of a pluralist mixed economy/welfare state.

This trajectory, however varied it was in our three cases, led to broadly similar union–party 'deals'. Whether because the social democrats were *in* power (Sweden), or because they *had* been in power and no longer were (as in the UK), or because they had not *yet* come to power (as in West Germany), unions decided that the Social Democrats were most likely to pursue aggressive Keynesian demand-stimulating macroeconomic policies once in power. Unions supported the Social Democrats not because they expected major structural reforms, but because they judged these parties to be better providers of minimum union goals. Conservative political forces could not be trusted to refrain from anti-labor policies, liberal or repressive, when in power.

The first postwar formulation of the union–party accord was a relatively simple one. In the political arena the unions offered political support, votes, activism and money in exchange for aggressive demand management on behalf of full employment, social-welfare programs, and some union voice in party and governmental decision-making. In industrial matters the Social Democrats would facilitate the unions' labor-market activities by maintaining a system of industrial relations favorable to union purposes. Conversely, unions would promote a degree of industrial peace to accommodate the efforts of the Social Democrats to mobilize a political majority.

Within this common framework the variation between national cases in the details of this first union–party 'deal' was considerable, however. In Sweden the foundation of the 'postwar settlement' was built, in fact, in the 1930s. LO and the Social Democrats were able to impose an 'historic compromise' on organized business. While the political left lacked the power to deprive private capital of its control over enterprises, Swedish business was none the less obliged to accept as durable the union–party ability to use control of the state as a way of establishing the macro-economic context in which enterprise decisions were made. What might have been a stalemate of the kind many writers have attributed to postwar Britain turned instead into the accommodation first formalized in the 1930s and then developed after the war. There was something of 'structural-reformist' thrust in the late 1940s, beaten back by the Cold War, so it is not incorrect to speak of a Swedish 'postwar settlement'. But once defeated at this point LO returned toward a growth-oriented stance on economic management, conceding to capital autonomy at the firm level and control over profits in exchange for a favorable industrial-relations system, full employment and Europe's most well-developed system of social services.

British unions did less well than their Swedish counterparts. Rather than attaining Keynesianism gradually beginning in the 1930s, they progressed by fits and starts, advance and rollback. Instead of engineering a critical realignment during the Depression leading to labor hegemony over a new coalition, Labour split badly in 1931, opening the way to Conservative dominance for the next fifteen years. It took the war and the 1945 electoral victory to bring about big changes in policy and politics. With Labour in power, unions pushed both for 'socialism' (nationalization, planning and controls) and for moderate reformism. The more sweeping goals were abandoned by 1948, when it became clear that neither the party, nor many unions, were willing to continue with physical planning. The radicals found themselves increasingly isolated and unable to shape policy. The return of the Conservatives in 1951 contributed further to Labour's move toward the center. The Conservatives themselves seemed willing to accept the commitment to full employment, to much of the welfare state and to Keynesianism. More generally the Conservative-run 1950s were by and large prosperous. Neither economic nor political circumstance seemed to justify radical critiques. The stop–go macroeconomic policies of the Conservatives certainly provoked sharp criticism, but to the unions there was not too much wrong that the proper application of Labour Keynesianism couldn't cure.

The German DGB reached similar conclusions more belatedly and via yet another route. Its brand of socialism – forged out of reactions both to the Great Depression and fascism – proposed not only public ownership and planning, but also *Mitbestimmung*, industrial democracy. DGB radicalism was, however, beaten back by the Cold War and the formation of the Federal Republic. In these years the trade union movement did make some gains, compared to the interwar period: control of labor by authoritarian means was at least discredited by fascism, a modern industrial-relations system was being institutionalized, the trade union movement became strong, unified and autonomous, and economic growth got under way. Yet despite the obvious difference from Weimar and from the Nazi period, the path of German development in the 1950s had more in common with that of France and Italy than with the British and Swedish cases. In contrast to both the UK and Sweden, West Germany in the 1950s was not a laboratory for full-employment welfare-state Keynesianism. If Erhard's 'social market economy' was somewhat less liberal than advertised, it was far from what the DGB desired in terms of state economic policy. Moreover, there was considerable unemployment and wages were relatively low throughout the decade. By the early 1960s both the DGB and the SPD had embraced Keynesianism. The DGB's ultimate 'deal' with the SPD aimed, then, not at perpetuating an already-established Keynesianism, but to attain it in the first place.

The Second Deal

The irony was, of course, that this new trade union appreciation of the political and economic world had barely come into being when new problems emerged to call it, and the sociopolitical 'deal' to which it contributed, into question. The very successes of the post World War II mixed-economy, Keynesian welfare state created a number of substantial contradictions. As full employment approached, labor markets tightened, putting unions and workers into a more powerful position to press for wage gains in labor negotiations. Successful Keynesianism, thus, seemed to create inflationary wage pressures.

The simple Keynesian equilibrium of Deal I was also premised on growth to produce full employment and steadily rising real income for both labor and capital. This meant encouraging private sector capital to invest in new activities of higher profitability, while older branches of industrial activity where returns were low would be allowed to decline. Workers in declining branches would, thus, face problems of adjustment and unemployment. Simply allowing the market to function implied that workers themselves would bear the high costs of moving between regions or acquiring for new skills. Even with steady economic progress, such problems tended to elicit industrial protest and required state resolution.

In time the unions were obliged to respond to these new problems. The result – which varied between Sweden, the UK and West Germany – led to a redefined 'Deal II' between unions and Social Democratic party-allies. The situation also led to somewhat modified union economic analyses. The basic exchanges which had constituted the old deal persisted. Unions continued to supply, or to offer, political support of various kinds and industrial good behavior to the party-ally in exchange for policies oriented to full employment, a well-endowed welfare state and favorable labor-market conditions. On top of this, however, new stipulations were developed. The problem of inflationary wage pressure seemed to lead the unions to absorb more of the conventional economic wisdom of their time. Inflation caused difficulties for the party-ally in managing the economy. These might threaten the party's ability to stay in power which, in turn, might jeopardize the supply of Keynesian policies and labor-market tolerance which the unions wanted. Thus, the unions themselves came to take on a greater degree of 'managerial' responsibility alongside their party-allies. Productivity bargaining in the labor market was one manifestation of this new reasonableness, the unions admitting that the growth of technology was an important factor in generating material returns to workers. General labor-market moderation taking macroeconomic goals into consideration – whether voluntary wage restraint or cooperation in more formal union–party arrangements – often became one of the goods which the unions exchanged with their party-allies. Sometimes the unions also asked for manpower policies of one sort or another to cope with growth-connected distortions as part of the exchange for their new reasonableness.

National variations between LO, the TUC and the DGB tended to grow as Deal II developed. Not surprisingly, in the Swedish case, where Social Democratic rule persisted without interruption, the unions developed the most elaborate Deal II and adapted their economic thought in the most sophisticated manner. In Sweden Deal II emerged from party–union tension over policies for curbing inflation. When inflation unexpectedly persisted in the early postwar years, the Social Democratic government responded with something like an incomes policy, relying on price controls and wage restraint to repress inflationary pressures. LO's experience of compliance led it to reject this approach as futile and dangerous. Wage drift could not be prevented no matter how restrained wage claims were, undermining the unions' claim to their members' support. This was a threat to the unions' organizational cohesion, their strength in the labor market and, implicitly, their capacity to mobilize electoral support for the party. LO proposed instead a strategy that relied on structural change to maintain non-inflationary full employment.

This was to be accomplished by a combination of 'general' fiscal and 'selective' manpower policies implemented by the state and a 'solidaristic wage policy' – equal pay for equal work regardless of firms' ability to pay – carried out by the unions. The standard-rate wage policy would hit firms harder the more inefficient they were, forcing them to modernize or close down, provided that fiscal policy did not keep demand high enough to permit inefficient firms to pass their higher costs on in prices. At the same time, firms efficient enough to pay the standard rates would be encouraged to grow and absorb workers who lost their jobs in declining firms. LO viewed the mobility of labor that this scheme required as acceptable on condition that manpower policy (retraining, relocation assistance, financial support) was carried out on a sufficient scale to shift the costs of moving from declining to expanding firms from the workers involved to the society as a whole.

To carry out solidaristic wage policy LO would coordinate union wage bargaining. This would, in turn, keep interunion wage rivalry from being an autonomous source of inflation. Thus, the unions would provide a limited form of wage restraint. Since coordinated wage bargaining presupposes a squeeze on profits sufficient to minimize wage drift, business savings would, however, no longer suffice to finance investment. To maintain investment lower business savings would have to be offset by collective savings – budget surpluses made possible by tighter fiscal policy but ultimately channeled through a new pension scheme – which would also tend to reduce the inequality of wealth.

Like incomes policy, LO's distinctive policy mix went beyond simple Keynesian demand management, but it was designed to do so without the strains that incomes policy tends to put on unions' organizational cohesion. At the same time, LO's strategy pointed toward the 'socialization of investment' which Keynes believed necessary to maintain full employment over the long run. The union–party conflict over the response to inflation was not resolved immediately, but by the end of the 1950s economic policy approximated the LO strategy to an increasing extent.

The TUC's movement toward a Deal II package was much less complete, coherent and sophisticated than LO's. Already in the 1950s the British economy had begun having trouble sustaining growth and full employment. Inflation and chronic balance of payments problems emerged whenever aggressive demand expansion was pursued, leading the government to put on the brakes in order to protect the pound. Occasional bouts of unemployment ensued. Worse still, from the unions' point of view, wage push was held to be a major cause of inflation and the unusually decentralized nature of unions and bargaining was blamed. Very quickly the Tories and Britain's press made 'the unions' a central political issue, partly to try to intimidate them, and partly as a way of indirectly attacking the Labour Party. This complex of events, which stretched into the early 1960s, deepened the TUC's and the unions' mistrust of the Conservatives and raised strong doubts about their commitment to the terms of the postwar settlement, and especially to full employment and free collective bargaining.

By the early 1960s the TUC and most of its constituents were divided on the question of political strategy. The Conservatives' third consecutive electoral victory in 1959 had reinforced the unions' desires to get Labour back into office but it had at the same time suggested to some union leaders that an accommodation with the Conservatives was a strategic necessity that could no longer be postponed. Labour itself, in the tumultuous conflicts of the late 1950s ('Ban the bomb' and 'Clause four', Gaitskell vs Bevan) had lived through its postwar *crise de conscience* and had emerged less 'socialist' and more committed to Keynesian 'realism' than ever before. Moreover, both the unions and the Labour leadership were beginning to be conscious of the deeper structural problems of the British economy. The first movements toward Deal II came from such awareness.

Given Britain's two-party system and the unions' links to Labour, explicit union–party 'deals' often got worked out in the construction of Labour's electoral platforms. Such was the case in the pre-1964 period. At this point the major concern of both unions and party seemed to be the poor performance of the British economy. What emerged was a resurrection of planning taken from the postwar radical package, greatly recast in a Keynesian mold by borrowing 'indicative planning' from the French. The Tories themselves also had, in fact, begun to flirt with this model and had secured rather hesitant TUC participation in a newly created tripartite institution, the National Economic Development Council. Through 'indicative' planning, both on national and branch levels, the state preferably, but not necessarily, under Labour control would selectively encourage new activities, aglow with the 'white heat of technology'. Productivity would improve, allowing better wages and employment, plus an expanded and more deliberately egalitarian welfare state (especially in education). In exchange the unions were willing to consider serious productivity bargaining, plus some moderation on wages.

When Labour took power, this new arrangement was briefly put into effect. The irony here was that the high technology and planning policies which had been part of the preelectoral package were quickly abandoned in the face of ever-more intractable economic difficulties–inflation, imports and balance of payments. Unable to deliver a quick prosperity, the Labour government none the less needed support for day-to-day survival. The TUC and its constituents complied by agreeing to a voluntary incomes policy. The British approach to Deal II illustrates one of the more obvious problems for the unions in the social democratic arrangement. Mistrustful of the Conservatives, the unions had reasons to want Labour to come to power and stay there, almost regardless of what the party did while in office. The party needed what the union had to offer, to be sure, but the union wanted what the party in power had to offer even more. Thus, the party, once it had obtained union support to be elected, could hold the union 'hostage', even to the point of not honoring basic programmatic commitments.

The case of the DGB was different yet again, situated somewhere between the confusion and improvisation of the British situation and the sophisticated order of the Swedish. Deal II in Germany was struck in the brief years of the Grand Coalition, when the SPD first came to power and when Finance Minister Schiller moved toward an explicit Keynesianism. These years, 1966–9 (much later than the Swedish shift and somewhat later than the British), were a moment when the postwar boom was beginning to show signs of severe wear and tear. Growth persisted, indeed, even more strongly than it had in the 1950s, but in the context of increasing international openness and competition, tight labor markets and rising inflation. In 1966–7 the German 'miracle' experienced its first clear interruption in the form of a major recession and soon thereafter there emerged signs of labor difficulties – 'new demands' about working conditions and workplace authority following, in part, from a wave of capital-intensive rationalization in key industrial sectors. These developments prodded the German unions to rethink their simple Keynesian approach.

The DGB and its constituents began to accept their share of macro-economic 'managerial responsibility'. They openly recognized and actively participated in linking their own wage demands and government macroeconomic policy through 'Concerted Action'. Voluntary wage restraint in contractual negotiations was the major union contribution here, following from union acceptance of the government's projections for the economy. The new 'deal' was struck in the recession of 1966–7. In exchange for union acceptance of contractual 'responsibility', the DGB expected clear returns from the government – legislation to put an active manpower policy into place, a more progressive 'works constitution' act, plus in the longer run an improved *Mitbestimmung* scheme.

The Shock of Crisis: Deal III?

Problems with Deal II were encountered everywhere. The implementation of wage restraint proved difficult. Where labor markets were tight and/or where the union peak associations were relatively weak *vis-à-vis* their base, it was very difficult to make the rank-and-file accept restraint. Growing wage militancy was reinforced in the later 1960s by the emergence of 'new demands' about workplace authority and working conditions. Increasingly unions found that when they stuck to their Deal II commitment to promote 'responsible' wage behavior, they faced a rebellious rank-and-file. Moreover, wage drift seemed inevitable. At the same time, unions often found themselves faced with some variety of the 'hostage' dilemma – failure of the governing party to provide all óf the policy returns for which the unions had bargained.

The economic crisis of the 1970s intervened, then, at a moment when, in all three cases, strains on the Deal II package had already provoked reevaluation of existing strategies and arrangements. Unions reacted to the new situation – faster inflation, disinvestment, sharp international competition and shifting relations among factor costs – from within the framework they had constructed to cope with the problems which their late 1960s strategic package had raised. Thus, union responses to crisis in the 1970s were powerfully colored by union thought and strategy developed, not during the crisis, but by prior strategic reflection and reevaluation.

Two tendencies appear in union analysis of the new situation: reassertion of the original postwar compromise, and the development of more radical critiques of capitalism. For some unions, the crisis led to demands that the basic outlines of Deal II be restored or fully respected in ways which they had not been – in essence a response which involved very little new economic and strategic thought. For other unions, however, reevaluation led to criticism of the basic outlines of *all* postwar Keynesian deals, drawing on renewed skepticism about the efficiency and the justice of the market and private sector capital as primary instruments for capital accumulation. After a hiatus of three decades or so, some unions thus returned to anti-capitalist positions. While a number of specific themes from the earlier period reemerged, the new criticisms had certain distinctive features of their own. Whereas the postwar discussion had analyzed change in terms of 'socialism', there now tended to be talk of the need for structural change to create new national economic growth in the context of a complex international market. If private capital and market mechanisms were newly mistrusted, it was less because they had failed to conform to a social vision than that they were not working to 'deliver the goods' of full employment and expansion. The discourse of the 1970s involved technological change, reindustrialization and productivity: the left, or some of it, refused to leave these terms as the monopoly of the right. While the crisis provoked an anti-Keynesian 'return to free market' movement on the right, it moved some unions in new directions as well.

In the Swedish case, the Deal II formula began to break down after the mid-1960s. Stiffer competition and increased instability in the international economy amplified the swings between inflation and recession. This, plus intensified wage rivalry between LO and the rapidly growing TCO white-collar unions, made solidaristic wage policy more difficult to implement, while pressures to do so more effectively were intensified by resurgent egalitarianism. These factors combined to squeeze profits harder, resulting in accelerated rationalization and structural change.

That the burdens of this change could not be shifted entirely from the workers involved by manpower policy, despite its vast expansion, became increasingly apparent. Political resistance to geographical mobility increased in both declining and growing regions. So did discontent about the impact of change on job security and working conditions. Union ineffectiveness in dealing with such non-wage workplace issues combined with dissatisfaction with the effects of union wage policy on wage differentials to precipitate an unprecedented wave of wildcat strikes in 1969–70 that revealed a serious erosion of union authority.

From the mid-1960s to the mid-1970s LO responded to these challenges with a series of initiatives that substantially modified its structural-change strategy without supplanting it. First, it called for direct state support for, and influence on, structural change. This was to be accomplished by more actively channeling collective savings into industry through new state institutions in the capital market and by the development of a kind of indicative planning to anticipate and guide its sectoral and geographical composition. This initiative reinforced a tendency in the same direction in the party, which proceeded to introduce 'new industrial policy' aimed at achieving the desired influence on industrial development. The second was a demand for the abolition of managerial prerogatives which placed workplace issues beyond the scope of collective bargaining. The party responded with a stream of legislation on 'industrial democracy', opening up all issues to collective bargaining and strengthening the unions' position in the workplace.

The third was a proposal to increase the flow of collective savings into equity capital in ways that would gradually shift the wealth and control that goes with equity capital from private shareholders to new institutions for collective capital formation, 'wage-earner funds', controlled wholly or partly by the unions. To this idea, as formulated in LO's 1976 Meidner Plan, the party found it more difficult to respond. While the first two initiatives went beyond the terms of the 'historical compromise' between Swedish labor and capital by imposing some constraints on capital's autonomy with respect to investment and production, they did not encroach on the private property institutions on which that autonomy was based. That, however, is just what wage-earner funds would do, thereby putting socialism back on the political agenda, if not in the traditional form of nationalization, at least in the form of gradually extended 'finance socialism'.

While this seemed fraught with electoral risks to the party, LO viewed it as essential to reconcile the increased investment, required to meet the need for industrial restructuring imposed by stiffer international competition, with the solidaristic wage policy on which its organizational cohesion rested. Thus, in response to difficulties that it encountered in the changing economic environment prior to the mid-1970s crisis, LO was driven by the organizational logic underlying its structural-change strategy to modify it in ways that clearly transcended the limits of Sweden's postwar settlement. LO reached this position shortly before the 1976 election in which the Social Democrats lost control of the government for the first time in forty-four years. Tension between LO and the party over collective capital formation, which contributed marginally to the loss, remained to be resolved while the party was in opposition and a succession of bourgeois-party governments tried to cope with the impact of the international economic crisis which was not felt until after the election.

The British case was infinitely more complex. Deal II broke down very rapidly in the UK after 1964 when Labour returned to power. Earlier hopes that planning for growth might allow full employment and expansion collapsed in the face of inflation and balance of payments difficulties. The TUC and its constituents then found themselves in a classic 'hostage' situation, where they had to consent to an incomes policy simply in order to allow the Labour government to survive. Unfortunately for the TUC, this situation coincided with the height of the British 'shop steward movement' whose impact on rank-and-file militancy aggravated the difficulties already posed by fragmentation for the TUC in sustaining its part of the union–party bargain.

Under the pressure of slow growth and the shop stewards the incomes policy, and with it the British Deal II, broke down. The party was less and less able to deliver what the unions wanted – the growth necessary to sustain full employment. In turn, the unions were less and less able to deliver what the party-ally wanted, wage restraint. In a context in which the unions had, rightly or wrongly, become the major scapegoat for Britain's economic problems the party-ally decided to make its political future easier by attacking the unions. This attack, expressed through the establishment of the Donovan Commission and then *In Place of Strife*, provoked strong opposition by the unions in defense of their organizational autonomy. The subsequent breakdown of union–party relations was severe. In the 1970 election many in the union movement refused to do much to see Labour returned; working-class votes were more important than ever before in the Tory victory. Internal difficulties in the Labour Party coalition also emboldened important factions of the Conservative Party to begin rolling back major provisions of Britain's basic postwar system of social accommodation, rollbacks which were symbolized by the Conservatives' Industrial Relations Act and the new government's liberal economic policies.

Union reevaluation in the early 1970s of Déal II took place, then, in the context of a Labour defeat and feelings of mutual betrayal in both unions and party. To avoid a repetition of this situation in advance of the next election (1974) union and party leaders proposed a new 'Social Contract': the party and the unions should establish an explicit new program of exchanges. The unions promised electoral support, plus vaguely specified wage moderation under a Labour government. In return, the party was to provide a complex package of policies: growth-oriented planning, government intervention in the market to promote specific sectoral industrial restructuring and 'planning agreements' to permit greater union/worker influence in the definition of such programs. Beyond such policy questions the unions thought anew about the specificity of Britain's economic problems – the excessive role of the financial sector, the realities of British industrial weakness and backwardness. Unions became ever-more aware of the constraints imposed on formulating strategies by the structural weaknesses of the economy. While British union thinking showed some parallels with the Swedish innovations on industrial democracy and the collectivization of investment, the British proposals were tamer and the emphasis was in one very important respect quite different. Swedish unions in the 1970s felt organizationally and ideologically secure. British unions, in contrast, had experienced heavy attacks on their traditional legal and customary positions in the market arena itself. Hence, a central feature of the unions' new program was the repeal of the Tory Industrial Relations Act, plus the enactment of additional legislation to increase union rights in the workplace.

The German 'reevaluation' was much less dramatic and forward-looking. In the late 1960s the DGB got caught between a more militant rank-and-file and its own involvement in Concerted Action with its *de facto* wage restraint. The major German unions negotiated new contracts in the midst of the downturn of 1966–7. Once the boom of the late 1960s began, however, these contrasts appeared much too generous to capital in the eyes of the rank-and-file. In the face of serious and unprecedented problems with a rebellious base the unions began to make more aggressive wage demands. At the same time, with a Social Democratic led government pursuing anti-inflationary policies, the unions faced a 'hostage' situation in which they had to gauge the effects of labor-market action on the political viability of the government.

In the face of this complex dilemma the DGB and its major constituents reverted to their earlier Deal II demands. If only the government would consent to more expansionary policies, plus manpower policies and enhanced *Mitbestimmung*, then the various claims on the unions could be reconciled. In short, German unions, facing difficulties within a relatively strong economy, decided that difficulties could be resolved by fuller commitment from its party-ally in government to the Keynesian policies which seemed to have worked so well in the recent past. In comparison with British and Swedish unions, the German movement responded to the economic disruptions of the late 1960s and 1970s by staying closest to the Keynesian system of exchanges worked out earlier.

The Swedish response departed furthest from the terms of the settlement between labor and capital within which Deals I and II had been confined. LO's prescription for coping with the impact of international crisis and change in Sweden accepted the need for a shift of resources from consumption to investment in internationally competitive production to replace production that was no longer viable. It insisted, however, that the shift could occur only if there were institutional changes that broke the link between the provision of equity capital and the concentration of wealth and power in private hands. To this end the accumulation of savings would have to be organized increasingly in collective forms, enabling unions and the state to assure that what was withdrawn from consumption flowed into investment that strengthened the competitiveness of domestic industry, thereby assuring jobs in industry and a public sector that could be expanded on the renewed industrial base.

Deal III embodied this policy formula, but only after the LO-party tension over the most far-reaching component of it, wage-earner funds, was resolved. This occurred in the political context of a six-year succession of governments composed of one, two, or three of the bourgeois parties. They pursued policies aimed at achieving industrial restructuring by holding down wage costs while reviving the mechanisms for channeling private savings into investment that presupposed income inequality and precluded any encroachment on the private-property basis of capitalist firms by the unions or state. Since this meant that the shift would be on terms unacceptable to LO and also some white-collar unions, wage costs could be kept down only at levels of capacity utilization too low for the needed investment to occur.

The difficulty of overcoming this contradiction without implementing LO's alternative approach, together with the interest in preserving their partnership, led the Social Democratic Party and LO to work out a jointly acceptable version of wage-earner funds. This amounted to a modification of the Meidner Plan, but it retained the basic idea of tying a shift from consumption to investment to the establishment of institutions for collective capital formation that give local as well as national unions a voice in investment and production decisions.

The possibility, and the nature, of LO–party agreement on this component of Deal III was conditioned by the stance adopted by TCO unions. Their position had not been a significant factor in formulating the industrial-policy component since they gave attention to it only after the mid-1970s crisis, when they developed positions parallel to the Social Democratic labor movement's. On the other hand, TCO's support for the industrial-democracy component was decisive in the party's acceptance of it, offering the party an opportunity to champion a cause defined as common to both blue- and white-collar workers. When it came to collective capital formation, TCO and its most important private sector affiliate advanced essentially the same general case for it as LO did, but were prevented from taking an explicit position in favor of it by sharp internal divisions over its systemic implications and partisan identification. Intense efforts by business and the bourgeois parties to mobilize opposition to wage-earner funds succeeded in forcing the white-collar organizations into neutrality but not opposition, leaving the Social Democrats with some political room for maneuver on the issue.

Except for the divisions in TCO over wage-earner funds, then, the Deal III policy formula embodied an economic strategy of the trade union movement as a whole and not merely of LO, and the Social Democrats' return to office in 1982 established the political conditions for implementing it. The extent to which the Social Democrats are willing and able to translate it into policy that will prove effective in alleviating Sweden's economic problems in the face of continued international stagnation remains to be seen. In Sweden, too, the unions could become hostage to a party-ally unable to cope with formidable economic problems on acceptable terms.

In Britain the situation was far more strained. The union package to transcend the impasses of 'Deal II' was more complicated, less universally agreed upon by the unions themselves, projected on a more threatening political situation and forced on a less promising economic environment. Labour returned to power on the back of a massive strike wave in 1974, just as the first oil shortage was developing. The Tories had been severely chastised at the polls for having provoked labor strife by violating centrist compromise. Labour's victory stemmed, in part, from the argument that it could better manage relations with the unions. Party and unions alike had an incentive to make good on this hope and, for a year, lived together in a fruitful 'honeymoon' period. The government carried out a number of its promises to the unions, and the unions attempted to keep wage demands within reasonable limits. More aggressive demand stimulation allowed a consumption boom, while the unions were able to make substantial labor market gains. The unions also obtained what they wanted most in their pre-1974 program – repeal of the Tories' Industrial Relations Act, plus new legislation to solidify their position on the shopfloor and in collective bargaining. Conversely, the 'structural-reform' parts of the package (increased state intervention to direct investment and change in British industrial structures, and 'planning agreements' to enhance this process and integrate unions and workers into its formulation 'democratically') were very slow in emerging.

Within a year, however, things turned sour. Soaring inflation and acute balance of payments difficulties sent the government to the IMF for help. Deflation and austerity followed, bringing rising unemployment and cutbacks in welfare-state spending. The schemes for investment control and industrial democracy received little attention in this context. As usual in Britain, the unions were made the public scapegoat for the sudden shift. Having obtained the industrial-relations legislation they desired, they were now faced with a Labour government which not only failed to move toward a new Deal III, but seemed eager to retreat from even earlier formulations of union–party Keynesian deals. The unions were, thus, put in yet another difficult 'hostage' situation as the government established an emergency wage-restraint package which it insisted on extending and strengthening repeatedly. Yet, with the Tories moving strongly to the right toward Thatcherism, the unions had strong reason to avoid having them return to office. The TUC had to resume rescue operations to save a Labour government which was rapidly reneging on many of its postwar commitments and making some of the TUC's own constituents increasingly reluctant to rescue it.

These pressures put severe strains on the internal cohesion of the TUC which, given the autonomy of national and local unions, had never been very great. Understandably certain constituents began to wonder whether the prevailing package of exchanges between union and party was worth preserving. Some unions seemed to prefer something more closely resembling 'business unionism', where the unions took a greater distance from partisan politics and relied on their considerable market power to make things happen. Others, in touch with the left of the Labour Party, began reasserting the pre-1974 'new deal' proposals, with some significant additions, and managed to get these officially adopted by the TUC in 1977–8. Earlier analyses were reiterated which held British capital, and finance capital more specifically, responsible for British economic problems. If capital and the market could not be trusted to generate the growth which was needed for full employment, selective state intervention would be necessary, although there was little union clarity about the specific nature and thrust of such intervention. The 'alternative economic strategy', as it came to be called, also contained a significant dose of protectionism. In official TUC documents such protectionism was always presented as partial, selective and temporary, to be applied only as needed to get a new industrial strategy off the ground. The more 'radical' unions were generally much less cautious on this issue, however, reflecting the substantial wave of protectionist sentiment rising in the British labor movement (and coinciding with strong anti-EEC feelings as well). In addition, the Alternative Economic Strategy advocated a strongly expansionist approach to macroeconomic management to be deployed behind such temporary protection while the new programs for interventionist capital formation were being implemented.

After four years, the Labour government's balancing-act collapsed. The failure of its economic policy and the strike wave in the winter of 1979 fully expressed the deterioration of the union–party exchange relationship in Britain. Three governments in succession, two Labour and one Tory, fell because of industrial conflict. In strong contrast to Sweden and Germany, Britain, so long regarded as the embodiment of moderate politics, moved even further away from its shaky Keynesian consensus. Thatcher's policies demonstrated that the British right and parts of British capital had decided that there was no Keynesian way out of the crisis. Only a rather brutal transfer of resources from labor to profit would work, to be accomplished through a long-term economic 'cure' of recession and high unemployment.

Thatcherism was, to be sure, only *one* outcome of the progressive disintegration of basic postwar social agreements in Britain. The obvious impasse of British Keynesianism had profound implications for the Labour Party as well. Instead of drawing together against the increasingly reactionary Tory foe, Labour split, very badly. A number of Labour leaders and MPs quit to form the Social Democratic Party. Those who remained settled into an extended civil war between the Bennite left and the more moderate center and right. In important ways this disaggregation of Labour was about economic policy. The Social Democrats, who were extraordinarily quiet about program, seemed to advocate a carefully restricted Keynesianism. The Labour Party leaders had similar proclivities, but defined their positions negatively, for the most part, *against* the strident advocacy of the Alternative Economic Strategy coming from the Bennites.

At the time this chapter was being written, then, the political and economic world around British unions was coming apart, making future union responses to persistent crisis extremely difficult to predict. The crisis itself, its effects having been exacerbated by Thatcherism, undercut the movement's strength through massive unemployment. Beyond this all variants on the unions' strategic package depended upon the existence of a party-ally that could make a plausible claim on political power. But the Labour Party was weakened and divided in ways which made its existence problematic. Thus, not only its return to power, but its very existence, the basis of the TUC's longstanding political exchange relationships – which had provided the core of the unions' strategic package – threatened to disappear. The unions are themselves divided over policy and strategy. The opposition of some unions has blocked Benn's effort to take over the party leadership; the support of other unions provides him with an important political base. The situation remains quite fluid. It could well bring profound change to British unions, change of an 'historic switch-point' variety, which might put a closure around everything we have discussed.

In Germany – in contrast to Britain, but parallel with Sweden – the basic strategic exchange between the Social Democratic Party and the trade unions remains intact. The German case differs from both the others, however, in the unions' response to crisis. The DGB and its constituents reconstituted their earlier simple Keynesianism in the mid-1960s, as we have noted, reaching what we have called a 'Deal II' position. With some minor modifications, this remained their posture throughout the 1970s There was little movement in Germany, in other words, toward the selective interventionist/industrial democracy package that was so striking in Sweden and, less coherently, in the UK. Perhaps the major reason for the difference lies with divergent economic and political contexts: the Social Democrats ruled through the decade, putting the unions in the 'hostage dilemma', though in the framework of a relatively robust economy which helped keep the hostages happier than their counterparts elsewhere.

Union–party relations in West Germany were not without tensions, however. When the SPD–Free Democrat coalition moved in 1973 to tighter monetary policies, the 'deal' of the 1960s was stretched thin. Unions cut back their objectives and some important projects, such as the full extension of *Mitbestimmung*, were never implemented. As a consequence the unions withdrew from Concerted Action. The union response, from the oil crisis through 1977, was to demand regeneration of the old expansionist 'deal'. Economic difficulties were seen as transitory, as passing phases of a business cycle to be fought with Keynesian techniques of higher consumption through redistribution of private income. Any squeeze on profits was to be confronted by loosening the Bundesbank's monetary policies to allow increased borrowing by firms. A weakening of international demand for German products would be met by expanded internal demand.

After 1977, as conditions worsened, unions revised their thinking away from these simple consumptionist views but, again, in ways basically continuous with DGB positions in the 1960s. The SPD ministers, invoking the reluctance of their Free Democrat coalition partners, would simply not accede fully to union demands for more expansionist macroeconomic policies. Instead there was more and more talk of the need for adaptation and modernization of German capital in the face of more difficult international circumstances. The unions basically accepted this view of German economic problems. What they demanded was that the government take a more active role in overseeing private sector investment (through *Strukturpolitik* and 'investment guidance') and that the regional and/or employment difficulties caused by rationalization be handled through various manpower-policy programs. The unions also developed new concerns in their labor-market activities and about the introduction of new technologies, the humanization of work and work-sharing through reduction of general worktime.

Overall the DGB's pressures on the SPD were relatively moderate. The comparative weakness of economic crisis in Germany reinforced the unions' desire to maintain their party-ally in power. Indeed, after 1977, in deference to the government's deeper economic problems, the DGB seemed willing to retreat from its earlier demands for aggressive demand stimulation toward more restrictive macroeconomic management in the interests of restructuring German capital in the new international setting. In exchange, the unions asked mainly that their base be protected against the worst consequences of readjustment. The major threats to this relatively conservative union response to crisis were twofold: the crisis could worsen, as it seemed to be doing in the early 1980s, and the Social Democrats' exit from power would most certainly open a new and less favorable situation. Both prospects made it conceivable that new, anti-Keynesian policies might emerge in Germany, as they have in the UK, in ways which might force the unions toward the strategic reevaluation that they had been able to postpone in the 1970s.

Conclusions: Prospects for New Deals

Enough evidence is now in to justify our characterization of recent changed economic circumstances as a *crisis*. When existing systems to produce goods and services cease to perform properly, great uncertainty ensues. Uncertainty in the realm of thought, perceptions and prescriptions is only one dimension of this. Uncertainty about relationships of precedence and power between different social groups is another. The present situation is one of these essential turning-points, a moment when societies review their modes of thought and adjust, perhaps in major ways, basic patterns of accommodation among groups.

We began with a rough-and-ready model for such turning-points, drawn from the Great Depression and its aftermath. European (and North American) trade unions developed new views about the economy, their own positions and strategies, and the ways in which different social groups ought to relate. These views were refined in specific ways from country to country in a decade and a half of complex struggles, from the 1930s through World War II and, finally, into the immediate postwar period. Unions had no difficulty developing 'Popular Keynesian' responses to the Depression – sometimes even before sophisticated economic theorists began to think along similar lines. Amid the Depression a vision that insufficient demand, especially from workers and other less well-off groups, was one underlying cause of difficulty was easy for unions to conceive. What unions were less certain about was the instrumentalities necessary to turn their societies toward more active demand stimulation, even if they were reasonably sure that these instrumentalities would have to be statist. Amid the catastrophe of the Depression it was not surprising that many unions felt that the free market had failed and would have to be superseded in basic, new ways – through planning, public ownership and wealth redistribution – to reach the desired ends of full employment and general prosperity.

In retrospect it is obvious that European societies did eventually adopt much of what the unions advocated, often after struggle in which parts of private capital and the political right were resoundingly defeated in their quest for solutions based on rather brutal transfers of resources from lower social strata to profit. Of course, the full-blown Keynesianism which emerged after 1945 was a product of many things besides union pressure. The Keynesian coalitions which came into being during the postwar boom years included many different groups, while the Keynesianism which was put forward for the postwar mixed economy was very different, in its policy outlines, from the aggressive 'Popular Keynesianism'-cum-market forms of structural changes which were originally advanced by labor. Still, the core of what unions had desired during the turning-point years of the Great Depression, demand stimulation for near-full employment, was eventually enacted. At the same time, however, the 'free market' was preserved in the new setting. Keynesianism was turned toward providing a macroeconomic framework within which the private sector oligopolies that were the dynamic core of European economies might prosper.

For a while this postwar 'compromise' worked, and to those who remembered the 1930s, worked surprisingly well. In recent years, however, compromise has weakened. Increasingly sharp debate has reopened. Europe appears to be at another turning-point. We do not yet know the outcome, but it is possible to outline the shape of the great debate which has emerged about it. The central issue concerns investment: not enough, and/or not the right kind.

The political right and parts of business in most places have proposed a generally familiar recipe – even if it comes in different forms in different places. If investment is the problem, the position goes, then state policies ought to transfer resources from income and social overhead to private sector profit. Once such a transfer took place the free market would take over. Investment would follow the regeneration of private profit, in turn promoting new growth. The social implications of this recipe are clear everywhere. Margins for economic maneuver are very small. Any substantial transfer of this kind would have to upset the existing balance of power and relationships between social groups. Among other things, full employment would fall by the wayside, union power would be dramatically weakened and welfare-state provisions severely cut back.

It was not likely that unions would accept this perspective, for obvious reasons. Still, most unions came themselves to see that there was indeed an investment problem to be resolved. Our research has provided explanations for such union perceptions. From the unions came new views of the economic world, neither from abstract economic reflection nor because of any direct response to the 'independent variable' of crisis. Rather, new union thought and strategy emerged organically in response to contradictions and problems in earlier union positions. The crisis of the 1970s intervened at a moment when, in most places, the unions had already formulated new ideas because of the strains in an earlier Keynesian strategic deal. Union response to crisis flowed from these new ideas, rather than directly from crisis events. In almost all cases, however, these ideas, while not abandoning earlier stress on the centrality of demand, posited that investment was a prior problem to be solved before demand manipulation could assure high levels of employment and prosperity.

The unions knew that stimulating new investment by necessity would involve the task of generating new investment resources. The resource transfer problem, which the right sought to resolve in ways which deeply threatened the unions, was a real one, to which the unions needed solutions which would be less painful than those of the right. In addition, the right's approach – 'transfer to private profit/return to the free market' – was problematic on the issue of the specific direction of new investment. Higher levels of profit in itself provided no guarantee that such profit would be invested productively. Perhaps more important, in the context of a crisis whose most important dimension was probably the construction of a new international division of labor, there could be no guarantee that private sector capital would invest its new-found profits in the national economy where they originated. In this respect not only were the right's proposals a direct threat to unions, they were also profoundly ambiguous. Rather than halting deindustrialization and rising unemployment by regenerating domestic growth, they might well achieve the opposite ends.

For unions to move beyond their boom-year Keynesianism and focus on investment, then, they had to resolve issues about the specific direction of investment. In particular, they had to devise formulae which might insure both that new investment would really follow any transfer of resources and that such investment would occur in ways which would address the central problems of their own society. Moreover, because new investment, even when targeted and implemented properly, could only occur if some prior transfer of resources to capital had been worked, the issue of how such a transfer could be made without social injustice had inevitably to be faced.

New interest in the generation, structures and control of investment has been, in fact, the major theoretical and strategic response of unions to crisis, with the West German unions being the only partial exceptions among the union movements we have reviewed in our volumes. Such new concern is not as substantial a break with the unions' past as it may seem at first sight. The distance is not that great between a situation in which unions pushed for aggressive demand stimulation in a mixed economy whose basic outlines the unions accepted, and a situation in which the unions announce a new mistrust of the market and seek new state activity to promote investment. Unions still, for the most part, seek full employment of their supporters, general growth and prosperity and the maintenance of the welfare state. What moved the unions from the first position to the second was simple: awareness that Keynesianism in the postwar mixed economy would no longer allow the achievement of such goals. Still, the conversion of unions to investment-control postures has involved significant new willingness on their part to interfere with market mechanisms and to do so in new ways.

With renewed distrust of the market and new desires for 'structural reform' have the unions returned to their preboom 'radicalism'? In some cases there may be continuity of a kind, unions casting about in old program files to come up with new ideas. Even where this is true, however, the effects of forty years of boom and Keynesianism have changed the meanings of old proposals. Today economic-policy concerns clearly overshadow moral and political goals – even if these have not entirely disappeared. Regenerating enough new growth to allow full employment and a full range of welfare-state programs is the essential aim. Here most of our unions have become quite sophisticated. They are rapidly shedding illusions that even new, carefully directed, investments in industry alone will create full employment. Their analyses are becoming much more complex. In particular, there is too much evidence about the low level of new job creation which follows from investment, directed or not, in the advanced technological activities which hold the key to future industrial success. Thus, unions are concluding that such investment, even if it brings no resolution in itself to employment problems, is necessary for broader *national* economic success, allowing the generation of new surplus which can, in turn, permit the public and service sector job expansion which will achieve full employment.

The instrumentalities which unions propose for implementing new national investment control vary greatly from case to case, of course, from statist, centralized methods such as nationalizations, central planning and state investment banking to more decentralized mechanisms such as wage-earner funds. And aside from an almost universal fetishization of the *same* 'high-tech' activities (electronics), the unions have few specific 'industrial-policy' goals. Their new aims are more general. They have concluded that the 'free market' is no longer adequate either in its provision of capital or foresight in resource allocation, to take the kinds of future risks needed to ensure *national* economic success. New arrangements are needed, then, to allow the assumption of such risks – arrangements which can facilitate projection into the future to foresee promising new areas of economic activity, which can mobilize the capital necessary to expand in such areas and which can ultimately carry such new projects to fruition. The *national* economic focus of this is primordial. The crisis has drawn most unions closer perhaps than they have ever been to the actual substance of basic national economic policies and decisions. They are no longer content, that is, to delegate such decisions to private sector actors and state officials, as they had been throughout much of the postwar period. In a word, unions are becoming more nationalized – often nationalistic as well – in a crisis one of whose central dimensions is the rampant internationalization of private capital. The unions are themselves quite aware of this. Consciousness is high in many union movements that the unions have become custodians of the national economic interest at a moment when private sector capital has, perhaps definitively, become rootless, cosmopolitan and indifferent to national difficulties.

Union demands for national investment control, however varied in their actual content, are usually tied to new union considerations about the problem of social justice. Such considerations follow almost inevitably from union recognition that new investment will necessitate a transfer of resources from workers to investable surplus. In order to justify such a transfer the unions often propose new 'tradeoffs' – union support for new investment is made conditional upon the establishment of those new investment instrumentalities desired by the unions *plus* 'tradeoffs' for justice. Sometimes these tradeoffs are contained in the proposed new instrumentalities themselves – public ownership and wage-earner funds leading, in time, to decentralized public ownership. Sometimes they involve workers' control/industrial democracy procedures – planning agreements, works councils, and the like. Sometimes the tradeoffs proposed involve both types of change.

Implementing any of these new schemes necessitates much more than union good intentions and assiduous union actions. Unions must also find viable coalition partners of like mind in the political realm. Needless to say, the crisis has had the same challenging and disorienting effects on the political left, the unions' usual source of such coalition partners, as it has had on the unions. In consequence, the viability of certain left parties as allies has become questionable. Likewise there is no guarantee that the theoretical and strategic evolution of left parties in crisis will be parallel to that of unions, thus finding parties of like mind may be problematic as well. As we have noted in our earlier review of national trajectories, in both the British and German cases important questions about party-allies exist, as they did for both the French and Italian unions surveyed in Volume One.

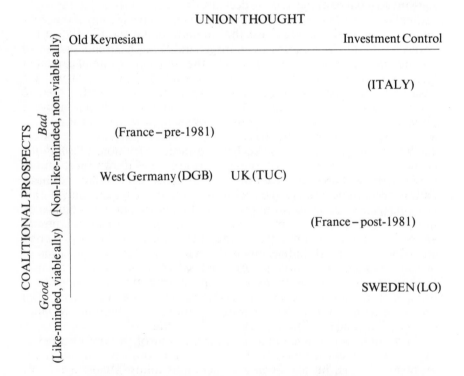

Figure 3.1   *Union thought and party coalitional prospects.*

Much of what we have just said can be represented diagrammatically. Figure 3.1 arranges the union movements we have studied in both volumes on two continua: those of changing thought and strategy in one dimension, and coalitional prospects on the other. By 'coalition' we mean here the ability of the union movement to find an ally in the realm of party politics. It would also be possible, though diagrammatically more complicated, to explore varying possibilities in different countries of unions finding 'social allies' as well – elements of business, professionals, white-collar workers, small owners, agriculture, and service sector and government sector, which might support elements of a labor program either through interest-group accommodation or via party politics. Figure 3.1 looks only at union–party 'coalitions'.

The figure should situate the social democratic unions reviewed in this volume rather well *vis-à-vis* one another. The Swedes, with clear new proposals and with a viable, like-minded Social Democratic coalition partner that has recently returned to power, are in a privileged position, poised to test their new notions in practice. The British unions are somewhat less clearly converted to a much less coherent package of investment control and industrial-democracy measures – that is, its constituents are not uniformly convinced of the programmatic wisdom of the 'alternative economic strategy', while the strategy itself is full of ambiguities. Rather more importantly, British unions have a less and less viable and like-minded coalition partner. The crisis has already caused the Labour Party to split once – creating the SDP – and may well split it again, depending upon the outcome of the struggle between the Labour right and the Bennites. In all this Labour's electoral prospects have suffered greatly. The parallel between the 1930s and the present period comes inevitably to mind. In the 1930s splits in the labor movement allowed the pursuit of liberal economic policies in the Great Depression which were ruinous for the unions. The present situation, in which an uncertain union movement and a split party face the Thatcherite offensive, may not be that different. In West Germany, as we have seen, the DGB has yet to break theoretically and strategically with its boom-period Keynesianism, perhaps because of the relative strength of the German economy and the longevity in power of the SPD. The DGB is, thus, 'behind' other union movements in its evolution. Indeed, there is good reason to predict that German unions will face a difficult situation in the very near future. The German crisis may deepen, and will do so within a changed political context. With the SPD out of power for the first time since the mid-1960s, the German unions are likely to face a government determined to shift economic policies firmly away from the Keynesianism which they desired. In consequence the DGB and its constituents will be forced to reevaluate their situation in ways which circumstances have not yet promoted. They may well then be obliged to move in the theoretical and strategic directions taken already by most of their European colleagues. Whether, in this context, the SPD in opposition will turn out to be a viable and like-minded ally is difficult to ascertain.

We write, of course, in the midst of the turning-point. Outcomes are not yet known, or knowable, even if the basic framework of the great debate of the times is clear. The unions have found their new positions, for the most part, as we have just asserted. Whether they will be able to generate the resources necessary to make these new positions prevail will not be clear for some time.

Index

References in *italics* are to tables